D1871509

The War Within –
Between Good and Evil

The War Within – Between Good and Evil

Reconstructing Morality, Money, and Mortality

Bhimeswara Challa

GYAN

© **Bhimeswara Challa**

All rights reserved. No part of this work may be reproduced, stored, adapted, or transmitted in any form or by any means, electronic, mechanical, photocopying, microfilming, recording or otherwise, or translated in any language, without the prior written permission of the copyright owner and the publisher. The book is sold subject to the condition that it shall not, by way of trade or otherwise, be lent, resold, hired out, or otherwise circulated without the prior publisher's written consent in any form of binding or cover other than that in which it is published.

The views and opinions expressed in this book are the author's own and the facts reported by him have been verified to the extent possible, and the publishers are not in any way liable for the same.

Published, 2020
Published by

Gyan Publishing House
5, Ansari Road
Daryaganj, New Delhi-110002
Phone: 011-47034999, 9811692060
www.gyanbooks.com
E-mail: books@gyanbooks.com

Printed at: G. Print Process, Delhi.

Cataloging in Publication Data--DK

Courtesy: D.K. Agencies (P) Ltd. <docinfo@dkagencies.com>

Challa, Bhimeswara, author.

The war within : between good and evil : reconstructing morality, money, and mortality / Bhimeswara Challa.

pages cm

Includes bibliographical references and index.

ISBN 9788121219792

1. Ethics. 2. Money. 3. Mortality. I. Title.

LCC BJ1012.C43 2020 | DDC 170 23

Dedication to a Daughter

In fond remembrance of my daughter Padma priya Challa, who died, solitary through her life, at the age 54, on 22nd March 2020. She was innately loving and giving, exceptionally endowed-- a rare blend of beauty, brilliance, and above all, as a friend described her, an 'enormous heart' ---- much admired but much misunderstood. She was a bundle of pure joy while growing up, scaled high academic and professional heights, but a slew of fateful setbacks set in and a life of uncommon promise went woefully wrong. She was carefree about her future and whenever I worried she used to reassure me: "don't worry, dad; I will die before you". She is now headed to a far, far better and more caring place, surely to join the many she loved down here who are already up there.

By the way she led her life, she helped me to settle my karmic dues of this life at her own expense and, as per this book, by her very inability to sufficiently 'feed' the 'good wolf' in its fight with the 'bad wolf' in her 'war within' she aided me in waging my own war. After saying thanks to her even if posthumously --- for thanks must be said wherever they are due, as my mother once said --- I will now meander in the remains of my time bearing, in the words of Greek philosopher Aeschylus (Agamemnon, 1602) "even in my sleep pain that cannot forget falls drop by drop upon my heart".

So long, my love; rest in paradisiacal peace; and please, take my hand when I come; God I Implore on bended knees: give her your merciful forgiveness she prayed for; free her from all future pain; and shelter her at your lotus feet.

Contents

Epigraph—*Why me?*

If a writer is different from others because, simply put, he writes, then what does he seek by giving so much of himself with so little certainty of anything in return? The fact is that every book is, *ipso facto*, autofictional, if not a covert confessional, a kind of dancing star borne out of the intense chaos in the writer himself. That is perhaps why it has been said that "there is book inside every person".

Maybe that is what writing eventually crystallizes into—the 'book' inside the writer turns into the *persona* of a poem or prose. Many have spoken about why writers choose to put themselves in the firing line; why, so to speak, they want to choose to stand naked, to be probed and disrobed at a public haunt, why they don't flinch from facing, in Philip Roth's words, daily frustration, not to mention humiliation. There is always something of the siren call of the rolling waves and a Sisyphean struggle in their perseverance and pluck. There have always been much easier ways to earn a living, and, as they say, make both ends meet.

And so very often, every visible sign of success in the literary world turns out to be extraneous to the real value of literature; it has never been more so than now. Not only writing but even reading has taken a beating. That is a huge tragedy, for reading itself is an act of creation—writing can't exist as more than words without a reader, so to speak. In this day and age, few have the urge or élan or leisure to read anything in black and white, either for engagement, for entertainment, much less for enlightenment. The pen might be mightier than the sword elsewhere, but merit is certainly not mightier than money in the province of publishing. Although the intimate conversation between writer and reader—some yet to be born—is almost magical, the rude reality is that once the writing is done with, the writer is rendered marginal to the reading. As a result, as Kurt Vonnegut says, a writer has to be no different from a drug salesman, or maybe a dealer of used cars, to get to see 'what he says' in print.

And yet, there is still hope in humanity because countless people continue to write—and die, unknown and unwept. It is not that they are selfless souls or murdered martyrs. It is like death; every person knows everyone will die, but expects he himself will not. Similarly, everyone who writes hopes that he would somehow prevail, unlike many others, and live to experience the dawn of his dream; to be recognized, rewarded, and respected, to become rich and famous, and autograph copies of his book at a packed bookstore. And then the intoxicating euphoria: the world might come to an end, but the author himself would live on through his work. We can take some consolation from what Jorge Borges puts across: "When writers die they become books, which is, after all, not too bad an incarnation".

The crux of the matter is that the 'why' of writing embraces a rainbow of reasons but, in the end, it remains what George Orwell said: 'a mystery, something which one would never undertake if one were not driven by some demon that one can neither resist nor understand' (*Why I Write*, 1946). That 'mystery' is what underlies all my scribbling, besides giving me a chance, as Byron puts it, "to withdraw myself from myself", and to heal the wounds of a labored life spent in seeking in vain. It brought to my mind the famous poem of Rumi lamenting about the pain and sorrow in his heart: God tells Rumi, "Stay with it; the wound is the place where the Light enters you". For some, as long as the wound stays open, that light becomes life by way of writing.

In the preface of my previous book—*Man's Fate and God's Choice: an Agenda for Human Transformation* (2011)—I wrote, not yet aware of Orwell's words, that that book was a 'mystery to myself'. Fiction, I can somewhat relate with, to give life to what I truly am deep inside, through characters in a story. Even articles in journals can be explained away; they let me have my say on issues of topical relevance. But this sort of scholarly nonfiction on an esoteric subject is positively presumptuous, if not utterly audacious. Nothing of my life in this life had prepared me or deserved it. The mystery has deepened with the present book, to the point that I sometimes felt that I was possessed. Much to my surprise and delight, my first major nonfiction work was widely well-reviewed. I felt good when the ordinary next-door-neighbor kind of people said things like, "do people still write books like this?" And it was never clear to me what people meant when they asked, 'How did you write this book?' And I used to murmur: *I* did not *write* the book; the book *got written* by me. I meant the author is the unknown; I was only a scribe. It was not meant as a sleight of a phrase or a show of cleverness. I always felt I was more a conduit than a creator; more a monkey than the organ grinder. I am the builder, not the architect, in a reversal of what Herman Melville said about himself while writing *Moby Dick* (1851). After getting my first book 'successfully' published, I felt totally drained but relieved.

'That's it!' I told myself; 'I am now immortal; I can live on earth even if I die'. The rest, as Einstein said about the mind of God, are details. It has been said that the story of one's life ends long before one dies. I then thought my story ended the day my preceding book, being done with me, bid farewell to me. That being the premise, there was no need anymore to subject my wearied and worn-out body to the demanding drill of crouching before a computer, half-blind and with a broken back. It was time to move on, to go with the flow, and wait to wither away, and get prepared for, in Churchill's phrase, the 'meeting with my Maker', whether He was prepared or not. But it then seemed that the 'meeting' went into pause mode, either because the Maker was busy, or because He had other plans for me, other ordeals to put me through before I fulfilled my *prarabdha*.

Precisely when and how the idea of writing this book germinated is still a blur. Perhaps it could be the time when I read somewhere that Prophet Muhammad called the internal *jihad*—the fight against one's own self—the 'Greater Jihad'. This grabbed my attention for two reasons. First, post-9/11, the word *jihad* is usually identified with terror and fanaticism; the Prophet's interpretation turns it into a positive tool for human transformation. Second, it seemed to reflect the troubled state of my own consciousness—I too needed to fight my own inner jihad, to exorcize the malice in my mind. It doesn't matter which creed or faith or religion one subscribes to; everyone has to battle his inner demons, and live with the wrenching sense of 'I am complicit no matter what I do'. However distasteful it might be, we must not flinch from facing the ugly truth that man alone is capable of 'motiveless malignancy' and 'vengeful violence'. It became clear to me, as scriptures and sages have so tirelessly told us, that everything *is* contingent in life—on power, on history, and most of all on flawed human nature—and good and evil are both intrinsic in our psyche, and that the way the conflict takes shape, defines our personality. If we can recognize that, we will also realize that those who commit the darkest deeds, and whom we so routinely dismiss as monsters, could be anyone: a sleeping partner, our next door neighbor, or even worse, ourselves, when things get very wrong in the war within. That is why we sometimes feel a sneaking sympathy, if not empathy, to schizophrenic villains. We must face the fundamental fact that while we have, to an alarming extent, succeeded in controlling the elements of nature, we have woefully failed—indeed made no serious attempt either—to control our own selves, the world within. Furthermore, there is no such thing as our 'true self': 'man is not truly one, but truly two'.[1] How can we then take sides in the war within? It all amounts to one jolting insight. While there is much talk of apocalyptic or 'existential threats' like climate change, what is being ignored is that the most important and immediate of them all comes from our own two 'selves', and from the fight between them to control us. In other words, the only way to prevent or abort the much-debated 'end of the world', or a dystopian future is to 'win' the war within.

Once such thoughts caught hold of my mind, I started studiously searching for sources and similar references, in holy books and classical literature, on the innate duality of good and evil. It soon became apparent that the conflict between good and evil is a connecting thread in literature, and is sometimes considered to be an essential template of the human condition. I realized that to understand man in all his dimensions, we must recognize, as Will Craig tells us, that "the life you life is the outward expression of your inner journey" (*Living the Hero's Journey*, 2017). That 'journey' must be at the forefront of human thought and effort, which are now egregiously, almost grotesquely misdirected. But it also struck me that, more fundamentally, our principal problem is that we try to control that which is beyond our control. The ancient Greek Stoic philosopher Epictetus once said, "Some things are up to us and some things are not up to us". What is outside us is not 'up to us'; whereas what is 'within' ought to be 'up to us'. What we do is the reverse; try to control others and everything around us, and ignore what is *in situ* and inside us. And this is the reason why so many of us feel that life is "terrible, hostile, and quick to pounce on you if you gave it a chance", like Virginia Woolf's Mrs Ramsay (*To the Lighthouse*, 1927). So many of us today ask, "How could a man ever be sure of any other man?" to recall the words of Dorothy Hughes (*The Davidian Report*, 1952). Or, for that matter, of his own self.

I found out that although such a train of thought has long been a recurring refrain in the human condition, the scripture that most eloquently exposed this seminal 'inner conflict' was none other than the great Indian epic, the *Mahabharata*, and in particular its centerpiece, the famous *Bhagavad Gita*, which

1. Stevenson, R.L. 1886. The Strange Case of Dr Jekyll and Mr Hyde.

Einstein said was the main source of his inspiration and guide for the purpose of scientific investigation and formation of his theories. In the Mahabharata, every major character was fighting his own 'war within' between two opposing moral imperatives, be it the *Kuru* grandfather *Bhishma*, the virtuous *Yudhishthira*, the star-crossed but noble *Karna*, or even the arch-villain *Duryodhana*. The very first chapter of the Bhagavad Gita is usually rendered as 'Arjuna's sorrow' or 'Arjuna's despondency', which could well be titled *Arjuna's War Within*. When the Pandava prince and mighty warrior Arjuna put aside his celestial bow and refused to fight, Lord Krishna (his *sarathi* or charioteer) instantly realized that to persuade the reluctant master-archer to participate in the horrific but necessary Kurukshetra war, he had to first help Arjuna 'win' his own 'war within'. For Arjuna, it was a profound conflict between his *dharma* (righteous duty) as a *Kshatriya*, the warrior class, and his delusions, dilemmas, and doubts about killing those he venerated. And that too, for something as transient as worldly gain and ephemeral glory. But for Lord Krishna, the agenda was two-pronged, and the audience more than Arjuna alone. One, he had to make Arjuna pick up his bow and fight and kill. But his second, and far more subtle, task was to dispel the delusions and dilemmas of future generations, to help them to fight and win their own wars within. In fact, some even say that the Bhagavad Gita was meant for us mortals, and that Arjuna's so-called sorrow is our predicament, and that Arjuna, himself semi-divine, and Lord Krishna the supreme godhead engaged in the dialogue of the Gita for the sake of humanity.

That is why Krishna's words of guidance to Arjuna remain just as relevant today, eons after the Kurukshetra. Krishna knew that *we*, the people of the most immoral age, the *Kali Yuga*, would face even more daunting dilemmas than Arjuna, and that we would need what Aeschylus called 'the awful grace of God' to make choices, even though we may not know what the consequences of those choices might be. In our own times, as Mahatma Gandhi aptly said, everybody has a Krishna residing in his heart as the Indwelling Self, a guide who could be our own charioteer, to not only steer us but save us as we wander around confused and lost in what Jorge Borges called the 'labyrinths of life'.

While the Bhagavad Gita was upfront among the scriptures relevant to this subject, I also realized that the idea of an eternal inner struggle for control of our consciousness is not confined to any particular religion or ancient culture or native tradition. A bedrock belief in Christianity is that all Christians are engaged in a spiritual battle of some sort on a daily basis. Striking a similar note, Zoroastrianism mentions the two opposing forces, *Ahura Mazda* (Illuminating Wisdom) and *Angra Mainyu* (Destructive Spirit), which are constantly in conflict. But the more I persisted, the more I was astonished that the core thought of a deeper world and of a fierce inner struggle between good and evil—what Carl Jung called *persona* and *shadow*, and William Blake called 'angels' and 'devils'—had crossed the minds of many great sages, thinkers, writers, mystics, and philosophers almost autonomous of each other. Not only that, many famous people have openly talked about their own personal struggles, about their own divided self, their inability to live in sync with any specifically codified life philosophy. Tolstoy, for instance, experienced and indeed spoke freely about, a fierce conflict between his insatiable erotic appetite and a deep yearning for sanctity. Gandhi talked of a streak of cruelty inside him. But the reference each made was as a lament, something they regretted but could not help. Some of these utterances find mention in the body of my book. It is baffling but true that billions of words and thousands of books on an avalanche of subjects have been written by many gifted and great writers, but not one on a subject of such importance as the war within—the war for supremacy of our consciousness. Instead of going *within* to fix what is internally amiss, we have long tried to make sense of what is wrong with us by, as it were, 'passing the buck' to all sorts of ideological 'isms'—capitalism, communism, liberalism, consumerism, materialism, militarism, etc. That is true cause of the climate crisis that now threatens human civilization and our planet. Simply put, without consciousness-change, we cannot combat climate change, and for consciousness-change, we need to wage and win the war within. And we need to cultivate qualities like *prema* (love in Sanskrit), *chesed* (benevolence in Hebrew) and *maitri* (loving-kindness in Pali), and lead a life of 'sharing and caring'.

I realized what a titanic task it would be to write a book on such a mystic subject, as there was nothing in literature for me to use as a launching pad. I wondered: should I abandon this leap in the dark, spare myself all this trouble and turmoil? At that stage, perchance or providential, I stumbled upon a Toni Morrison quote: "If there's a book you really want to read, but it hasn't been written yet, then you must write it". While I was mulling over the timing of this, another piece of sound advice came to my mind: "Don't write the book you *know* you can write. Write the book you know you *can't* write yet". And there is that fountain of wisdom, the Bible, which tells us that "to everything there is a season, and a time to every purpose under the heaven". But why were all these promptings crowding my mind? Was this time the chosen 'season' and the mere *me* the blessed means? Was this the book that I 'knew I can't write yet write I must'? From the solitary stillness of my soul, an inner voice whispered: *Yes, yes!* So I scrambled and started. I was off and running. Yet it wasn't easy to, so to speak, alchemize lightning into light, to transform a stray thought into a scholarly story, and breathe life into humdrum prose.

In the absence of any firm footing, I was forced to fall back on my imagination, which Einstein said 'is everything; a preview of life's coming attractions'. It was daunting and draining, exhausting and exhilarating. Down the road, many a time I felt like crying a halt; and doubted my ability to undertake such a monumental venture, to single-handedly write on something no one ever did. I asked myself: Who do you really think you are? Stick to your strengths, don't await a rude awakening of your limitations! Still, I hung on. Guidance and help came from whom we might call the 'supreme ghost-writer', and sources and supplies came tumbling down like an avalanche. Like in the case of my previous book. In all honesty, I did not write that book too; *the book got written by me*. As it always happens, one source led to another, one search to many others. It also straightaway struck me that although the subject is essentially metaphysical and mystical, this attempt had to be firmly anchored around the ground realties. And whatever I suggested had to be 'doable' sans any special skills. For, human nature being what it is, however critical and crucial it might be, if there is nothing in it for a doer, nothing will get done. This meant that the book had to be, in one go, transcendental and topical, intellectually invigorating and physically practical.

It has sometimes been said that 'there is a time to venture out, and a time to journey within'. Now is the time for both; we have to 'venture out of our cocoons of convenience and comfort', and 'journey within'. While embarking on this journey, we must recognize that it is indispensable but not easy.

And let us be crystal clear: the thrust of consciousness-change is to liberate the consciousness from the near-monopolistic hold of the mind. And that is the only way we can redesign the present paradigm of intelligence, which perhaps is the most pressing need of the hour. We have to, as Joseph Campbell said, learn to 'rely on our intuition, our true being' (*The Power of Myth*, 1988), which means our heart, not our mind. While trying to get a grip on the fundamentals of this war, it became clear that while the war is within, the frontlines are two: the deep recesses of our inner world, and the heuristic normalcy of everyday existence. For one of the lessons of life is that for anything to be permanent it must first become the normal. As Annie Dillard reminds us, "How we spend our days is, of course, how we spend our lives. What we do with this hour, and that one, is what we are doing" (*The Writing Life*, 1989). If we spend it wisely and humanely, then not only will our life be well spent, but also the war within will tilt in favor of righteousness. All that we need to do is to cultivate conscious living and be awake and aware of whatever we do, aware of what we let in through our sense organs, and ensure that they are of the right kind.

What all this brings out is the inherent comic tragedy of the human 'condition', that our salvation lies, of all things, in a venture so odious as war, which has long been denounced as mass murder, ultimate evil, outlet for the worst in us, and so on. But some say that much as we might not like to admit it, warring is very much a part of who we are, perhaps even a part of how we have evolved. That could well be so; for if war is a constant within, how can it not but get reflected outside? The paradox is that it is a war and, at the same time, *not* war in the classical sense. What we have to view as a 'win' here is very different from any other; strange as it may sound, the antihero is also a hero; the evil within is not a villain, no reprobate to be expelled. And, yet, this war embodies our only hope for the future; the hope to set right so much that has gone wrong for so long. And if we, like Arjuna, turn away and say 'we don't want to fight any more wars', much less something that cannot be seen or heard or felt, then nothing will change for the good in our world or in our consciousness. It is only by the active, even aggressive, acceptance of, and engagement in this 'war' that we can put an end to all our ills, biases, and prejudices, and enable each of us to be better than what we have been. And our behavior will become benign, and that will allow us to put an end to what so often we are tempted to do to each other almost reflexively—go for each other's throat in our outer life.

As a writer, I try to step aside and be an observer, to better grasp the focus and thrust of much of what we do, of what consumes our mind, attention, and action, without changing which we cannot change the context and character of human life. From that angle, it didn't take too long to realize that they can only be the interrelated themes of *morality*, *money*, and *mortality*—the 'three Ms'. Nothing of any significance in human life will become any better unless we can find a way to think through and deal with them very differently from their present paradigm. Indeed, that alone will make a decisive difference to the war. Moral is what we want to be, and often fail in practice, and bad thoughts and urges seduce us easily. Modern man lives in what someone described as a state of 'ethical brokenness', having to choose between existential destruction and moral capitulation. Good people always did bad things but not with today's banal ordinariness. We are living in tempestuous times when people are seriously soul-searching and asking such questions as: Are we worthy of survival? Is the human species 'expendable? Is the best we can do now is to stop reproduction? And, *à la* Bill McKibben, has the Human Game begun to play itself out?

We cannot meaningfully address such questions without giving somber thought to two of our basic moral flaws: malice in the mind and what Jews call *Sinat chinam* (baseless hatred). We must work around money in a way that it ceases to be the chief source of human strife and suffering, and gets transformed into a potent source of moral power. With the advent of the digital economy, and in a world that is almost wholly 'financialized', it seems to me that there are new opportunities for money to work differently, both as a token of exchange and a store of value that needs to be flushed out. As for mortality, what has to change is our obsession with physical immortality, without regard to its ethical, social, and intergenerational implications. The real challenge, it seems to me, is to strike a balance between obsessive care of our physical body—which the *Dhyanabindu* Upanishad says is a 'mud vessel'—and the ability to get detached from it, much like a snake treats its skin. I may mention in this context that the idea of focusing my second book around these three subjects, which I call obsessions, arose in my mind even as I was finishing the earlier work, and a mention to that effect was made in my first book. But it was much later that their centrality to the 'war within' crossed my mind.

The bottom line is this. Even if the so-called technological 'singularity' occurs in our natural lifetime, or if there is a breakthrough in radical life-extension and the human morphs into a '*Homo Immortalis Omnipotent*', and even if we do become a multiplanetary species, we cannot evolve in the right direction unless we turn our skills, weapons and wisdom inwards. The war within is a catalyst for internal liberation and renewal. If we want to get off the gravy train and escape getting consumed by the 'merit-based' rat race, the war within is our only glimmer of hope. We make multiple choices every day but not all are of equal moral value, and to do the right thing is an 'inside-job', to win the war within. Whether we like it or not, we are all proxy participants in this war through every minute, awake or asleep. To see that this war results in the right outcome, we don't have to become all-sacrificing altruists or super-heroes. It simply depends on how we routinely act and reflexively react to everyday situations and circumstances. As the philosopher Theodor Adorno famously said, "Es gibt kein richtiges Leben im falschen"—a wrong life cannot be lived rightly. For a righteous life to be still possible and for the good in us to prevail over evil in the war within, we need to change both the content and context of everyday life. Fact is that anything we see, hear, taste, touch, or smell can trigger unintended behaviors and impulses. Depending on what they are, they serve as the 'feed' to one or the other sides in the war within. This is the subtle subtext of human life. Whatever we want to achieve and whatever happens to us, hinges on the myriad choices, chores, and doings of daily life. If we—at least in numbers that amount to a critical mass—can summon the will and wisdom to conduct ourselves in the dharmic or righteous way, we can still avert what David Wallace-Wells, in his book *The Uninhabitable Earth*, calls the Great Dying, and save humanity from the ignominy of being branded by posterity as the "only species to have minutely monitored its own extinction", to quote Sara Parkin.[2]

This book, like its predecessor, is *trans-genre* and not an easy read. But its time has come. I can put my neck out and say what the great Greek historian Thucydides said about his work: "My work is not a piece of writing designed to meet the taste of an immediate public, but was done to last forever". I do dream that this input, however minute it might be, will contribute to bringing about what Thomas Mann called a purer, more honorable way of being human.

Nearly eighty years since, we will do well to re-read what John Steinbeck wrote: "There is a crime here that goes beyond denunciation. There is a sorrow

2. Sara Parkin, green political activist and former member of the UK Green Party.

here that weeping cannot symbolize. There is a failure here that topples all our success" (*The Grapes of Wrath*, 1939). My current offering reminds us that in fact, such a 'crime' and such a 'failure' is 'within', that the present human story is a self-made meltdown. And we will not be the only ones who will face the fallout. It will be hundreds of future generations, an astronomical number of humans like us, or similar to us. If we cannot reverse the present trend in the war within and the forces of evil swamp the forces of good, then it is better that we collectively roll off the cliff. Being humans we don't know for sure but, in all probability, we are not yet quite there and, recalling the last scene in the classic 1959 movie *On the Beach*, we can all still take comfort from the Salvation Army street banner—"*There is still time… Brother.*"

Bhimeswara Challa
Hyderabad, India
September 2019

What I Owe to Whom

We all know that no man is an island, and that nothing in life can be done in anyone's life without the involvement of many others in some way or the other. We cannot live through a single day, even physically, without being obligated to a host of others. We seldom notice it, but in whatever we do, we constantly make each other, and merge the 'I' with the 'We'.

If the purpose of life, as George Eliot once said, was to make life less difficult to those around us, be it one's spouse or a servant or stranger, or even a murderer, then writing too serves a 'purpose'. It is a way to encapsulate countless hours of one person's sustained suffering, introspective reflection and inspired imagination into a few fleeting hours of laid-back reading by the rest of humanity.

What I wrote in the preface to my previous book, I cannot do any better: "If 'no one is a stranger' on the voyage of life, any potential reader would be my soul-mate, those who yearn, as Richard Bach (*Jonathan Livingston Seagull*) said, 'to make life come to life'... we know that a book does not just happen". In that preface, I also said, "Apart from the actual author and publisher, there are always unseen forces and invisible actors who facilitate the process and the product. Being invisible should not deny the right to be remembered; death should not annihilate deserved gratitude". In that context, I expressed my gratitude to my beloved parents and siblings, "who gave me boundless love, without which any urge for creativity would have long been smothered". I shall say the same again, and again. They are all 'up there' somewhere, save a sister, Kamakshi, waiting to envelop me in their embrace. And every day now seems too long; it is now a race between decay, debility, and death. And I hope the last wins.

But, among those who are 'down here', I must mention my family—my wife Nirmala, my son Ram, my daughter-in-law Margie, my grandson Varun, my daughter Padma and her 'son', the 'divine' dog Whiskey, truly the best of us. In particular, my wife's silent and steadfast cooperation greatly helped me to keep writing for so long, through thick and thin, when many other more mundane things got neglected.

Like the earlier one, this book is also entirely the fruit of my own solitary travail and the offspring of the promptings of the unseen author. But among the things that made this practically possible, I must highlight and salute the extraordinary and dedicated contribution of my editorial support, more appropriately my collaborator, Vijay Ramchander. He was a thorough professional as well as a person of the highest integrity, a rare blend these days. Without his painstaking effort, this book, indeed like the previous book, would not have seen the light of the day. There are several other individuals who anonymously assisted me in subtler ways, like the helper at home, the driver on the road or the friend in need.

Indeed for anything to be accomplished, many people contribute, whose very existence we might not be even aware of, bringing to mind the grace that Buddhists offer as a prayer before a meal: "Innumerable beings brought us this food. We should know how it comes to us." A book is no less.

Last and most important, I would be committing one of the *panchamaha-patakams* (most heinous sins) characterized in Hinduism—ingratitude—if I do not place on record my profound gratitude to the divine 'Author' who hand-picked me to be his human scribe in the writing of this book and made sure my life does not end entirely in vain.

The Beginning

The Twin Questions and Twin Inabilities

Why can't I be good? Why do I do bad? Such angst-filled questions and reflective ruminations have, ever since man became self-aware, crossed the minds of many among us, not only saints and rishis, epic heroes, and moral philosophers but even evil geniuses and plain folks. Notable among them is Saint Paul, acclaimed as one of the authors of the *New Testament*,[1] Saint Augustine, the author of *The City of God*,[2] and Sage Veda Vyasa, the author of the great Indian epic *Mahabharata*, which, it is often said, is the last word on the nuances of ethical dilemmas that harass human life.[3] And the Pandava prince Arjuna, a central character in the same epic, asked Lord Krishna, "Why is a person impelled to commit sinful acts, even unwillingly, as if by force?" What is strange is that Arjuna's arch enemy and villain, Duryodhana, also strikes a similar refrain and confesses, "I know what is *dharma*,[4] but am not able to practice it. I know what is not dharma, but I am not able to keep away from it."[5]

In our own times, Gandhi, the ardent advocate of *ahimsa* or non-violence, lamented, "What evil resides in me?" From Arjuna to Saint Paul to Gandhi, no one has been able to come to terms with who they *seemed to be* from the outside, and who they felt they *really were* deep within their own better selves. In the words of Ralph Barton,[6] "the human soul would be a hideous object if it were possible to lay it bare". They (and all of us, too) cannot understand how they could be 'who they did not want to be', and, worse, felt compelled to do what they hated to do. We also don't understand why, when the ideals and imperatives of life are to be cooperative, compassionate, loving, and selfless, we are so competitive, callous, aggressive, and selfish. As Carl Jung noted, "Unfortunately, there can be no doubt that man is, on the whole, less good than he imagines himself or wants to be".[7] Jung aptly sums up the tragedy of the human condition and simplifies the direction of our aspiration and effort—try to do on the whole, more good and less bad in whatever we do routinely and reflexively. The primary reason why even great saints have been frustrated is due to the fact (which this book highlights) that we have not connected it to the war within.

Like it or not, we have a horrifying history of avarice, aggression, hatred, rape, torture, murder and war; a penchant for deeds so shocking and nauseating that the eternal question of 'Why?' seems heartrendingly inexplicable. This, in fact, was what Sage Vyasa was lamenting about: "When all the good things we want (wealth, pleasure, liberation) we can get by being good, why do we humans choose the bad way?" The answer perhaps is because the bad way is the *easier* way, the way of human nature. Some prefer to call human nature the 'human condition', some others call it a malaise or malady, an impediment to overcome to become whole. Statements like 'humanity must free itself from the human condition' are commonplace. The awful awareness that any of us can be wicked without will, that we harbor inside not just little weaknesses and innocuous foibles, but a directly positive demonic dynamism, has been traumatic and deeply unsettling. It is a terrible thing; our soul is in constant flux, we live in fear of what we might do any moment, which temptation might turn out to be too much, and what circumstance might make perfectly 'honorable' people do utterly dishonorable things. And we have no control over own competence, our own creativity can be both awesome and awful. For the first time in human history, we face a wrenching question: what are we all capable of and, even more, what are we capable of being induced or tempted to do? At the heart of our gnawing yearning—and gaping shortcoming—is to bridge the chasm between one man and another. Jean-Jacques Rousseau said, "Identify myself with my fellow, and I feel that I am, so to speak, in him, it is in order not to suffer that I do not want him to suffer. I am more interested in him for love of myself".[8] To a large extent, it all comes down to why we have become, in the words of Jeremy Griffith (*Freedom*, 2017), extremely tortured, disfigured, soul-dead, and furiously angry real human beings.

Ezra Pound once pronounced, "All ages are contemporaneous" (*The Spirit of Romance*, 1910). Similarly, all serious questions are contemporaneous. And today's 'contemporariness' is infinitely more complex than the days of Rousseau or Pound, let alone St. Paul or Sage Vyasa. And that includes a fundamental change in the content and context of 'being human'. Historically, we have not found any 'serious answers' for any serious question, for the robust reason that addressing them requires us to tread the territory of *thought beyond thought*, a kind of candid introspection we have been dreading to do. What is strange and surprising is that, in our implicit acquiescence of evil as a permanent characteristic of our finite existence, we have tended to forget the existence of the world of the 'good within', what Jack Kornfield calls 'secret goodness' (*The Wise Heart*, 2008). Why it is 'secret' is hard to fathom; indeed, one of the most intriguing and unexplainable things about the human hallmark is why it takes such a struggle to show goodness, while it is so common for the human to be gross. So much so, even when we do good, we rarely *feel* that good, as much as we don't feel bad when we do bad. Fact is, we must be mad about doing good to do good, but bad we can do with much ease. Why evil is so shameless and good so shy is hard to understand. It may be because the good we do is subtle, suffused, and silent, while evil action is direct, stinging, and sharp. And we must never forget that, as Daniel Deronda (in George Eliot's 1876 novel by the same name) says, "No evil dooms us hopelessly except the evil we love… and make no effort to escape from". And the evil we denounce in our shambolic world is nothing but our refusal to see it as a reflection of our own self in others. Henry Wood says, "the highest attainment to be sought is the incapacity to see evil".[9] And, evil is always only relative to good; but, paradoxically, if we refuse to perceive and resist it as evil, then it becomes evil absolute and utterly sabotages the very man who wants to live with it. What is missing is that we inexplicably ignore our own ordinary goodness; we fail to see that magnanimity is as natural to us as monstrosity. That is why the lure of evil is so hard to resist. It is also because it is embedded impersonally in the institutions and conditions of our social, industrial, technical, and general life.

And then, we have what Herbert Marcuse (1965) once called 'repressive tolerance' in our civic virtue, a tool for maintaining the *status quo* and the current class power structure. Evil appears anonymously in our corrosive contemporary culture not only as injustice, indifference, and intolerance, but even as obscene affluence in an interpersonal realm; and it appears so insidiously that nobody can be held directly liable or responsible. And that 'anonymity' allows us to do evil while still feeling good about ourselves. Anyone can be a wolf in a sheep's clothing; even more unnerving is how everybody knows that it is a wolf but pretends not to know. Because we fear what we might actually see. One could always become the other; one is forever hounded and haunted. Interpersonal and invisible evil[10] has never been so pervasive and penetrative as it has been over the past century. It is so perilous that it puts the planet itself on the line. Man has always struggled with the question of how to feel connected with another man as a way to stay united, given the fundamental fact that we see, hear, and touch another person but cannot actually 'experience the experience' of that person. As JK Rowling[11] pointed out, "we touch other people's lives simply by existing"—how, is the test of our character. We might also add that our existence itself is made possible by others' sacrifices. We come into the world separately and go out separately. The challenge is to 'internalize' others in ways that counteract our proclivity to scapegoating, and satiating our nihilistic and narcissistic impulses. The gap between 'we' and 'others' is now a murderous divide. For, that which we cannot 'internalize', we annihilate. But first, we must learn to 'internalize' ourselves. For that we must shift our gaze from the distant stars to our deep soul.

Contemporary evil, which is now primarily mediated by and incarnated through plutocracies, technocracies, bureaucracies, and corporations, far outweighs the classical evil perpetrated by individual humans, which captures headlines and breaking news. It has less to do with *what we do*, and more with *how we live*. And it depends on how the deed affects the environment. Nothing can be deemed moral if it has an adverse impact on the environment. Evil is so detached from the doer and so deeply impregnated in how we do anything that, as Andrew Kimbrell (*The Human Body Shop*, 1993) points out, "The very idea of our society being characterized by masses of evil people seems somewhat comical". All in all, there is a striking paucity of modern Mephistopheleses".[12] It is debatable if our serial killers and school-shooters and church and mosque-bombers and child-rapists and air-polluters qualify to be 'modern Mephistopheleses', or if they come anywhere close to John Steinbeck's character Cathy Ames, whom he describes as a woman "as close to pure evil as one is likely to get this side of hell" (*East of Eden*, 1952). But, even if it were not so, we are dangerously drifting to the place to which Satan's choice inexorably led in Milton's *Paradise Lost*: "All Good to me is lost… Evil be thou my Good". It is because evil is our good that even when we do evil we think we are being good, and, evil "has become the grey eminence infiltrating all areas of human existence".[13] Still the bottom line is that both good and evil co-exist with equal legitimacy in life and in nature. It is interesting to note that in *Paradise Lost*, Milton establishes good and evil as constantly shifting forces that both God and Satan seem to mobilize in opposition to each other.

Some scholars even say that "the conflicting discourse between the two forces redefines Heaven's God as a being capable of evil, and Hell's Satan as a creature seemingly capable of good".[14]

In turn, the moral quandary inherent in the 'twin-questions' has gained added relevance and greater rigor than ever before. Indeed, few actually agonize; many think that being good is no good for anything good; and being bad is not bad, certainly better than being dead. Perhaps more than either good or bad, or rather cutting across both, effectively we are deemed dead to all things but greed. And we now have an entirely new dimension to good and bad. Unlike in earlier times, everything man does affects the planet, sadly not for its good. Plunder and predation of the planet are the bedrock of our civilization to such an extent that many feel that nothing short of a radical roll back, if you will, can save the planet. It does not mean we have to turn our backs on industry, agriculture, and technology and go barefoot or back into the caves. It means that we need to evolve what we might call the doctrine of the 'paramountcy of the planet'—that is, what is bad for the planet nullifies whatever good there might be in anything we do. The climate crisis is a direct consequence of our twin-inabilities: not doing what we want to do (to change our predatory and profligate lifestyle), and doing what we don't want to do (polluting and poisoning the planet). These 'inabilities' affect everyone, not only the elite, the powerful, the corporates, the carbon lobby and the fossil fuel promoters. In this respect, the role of big business stands out. According to one estimate, only a hundred companies produce 71% of the world's greenhouse gas emissions. Our paralysis in the face of clear and present threats to our very existence is symptomatic of the fact that "something seismic, something utterly mysterious has happened in the human spirit and psyche at the deepest level, and equally mystifying is that we do not have the foggiest idea what it could possibly be".[15]

Not having the 'foggiest idea' and unable to find convincing answers to the twin 'questions', and perceiving a threat to its own paramountcy, the human mind has mounted a twin-strategy: self-righteousness and self-destruction. Being righteous is good, even 'godly'. Socrates, for instance, said, "Whereas, the truth is that God is never in any way unrighteous—he is perfect righteousness; and he of us who is the most righteous is most like him".[16] But being self-righteous is bad. Self-righteousness often stems from self-doubt, when we are on shaky ground.

A self-assured man is not self-righteous. As societies we are 'self-righteous because we are unwilling to accept that we really don't know much about fundamentals, have no clue or control over much that happens or prevent what should not happen. Self-righteousness gives us the cover to carry on, a bandage on an open wound. Inevitably it slips into self-destruction. The fact is that complexity underpins human nature. There is 'something' underneath our fierce survival instincts that pushes us closer and closer to the edge of extinction. Our drive to destroy is not restricted to ourselves, our lives, and our loves. It also gets externalized and forces itself upon the world. That is why we so mindlessly destroy the biosphere and exterminate other species.

The streak of self-destruction, what Freud called '*thanatos*', we have always had. Whatever is the source and the cause, the truth is that something in our consciousness seems to seek to, so to speak, dismantle us from the inside out. For all we could guess, it could be that nature might have inserted it into us as a fall-back, an ace in the hole, as it were, to curb, contain, and if need be, to put us away if we become too much of a thorn in its flesh, too intolerably hubristic. Sooner perhaps than later, nature will reclaim what once belonged to it, or it might, over time, 'scramble the coding that makes us want to destroy everything'. Self-harm and self-destruction are much broader and more insidious than being suicidal, the triggers of which are now almost the same as for any other action or reaction in everyday life; we no longer need a special circumstance or a warped mind or a wounded life. We have reached a stage when, as Camus wrote, "... in the end one needs more courage to live than to kill himself" (*A Happy Death*, 1971). We may still not be itching to commit species-scale suicide, but self-harm is now almost compulsive and contagious. And even suicide which most religions condemn as a sin—usurping God's disposition of life and death—is fast ceasing to be a loaded word or a cowardly deed. Many now posit that, in general, when people die, it is against their will, and the same is true for suicide, except that in the case of suicide the meltdown is emotional rather than biological. All through history, man's destructive capabilities were naturally contained, and even the prospect of some adverse unintended consequences was never a major deterrent, because they were never potentially apocalyptic. Human society was never under pressure to curb two of its greatest gifts, curiosity and creativity, for its survival. That safety net now stands shattered. The boundary between individual murder and the murder of humanity is getting blurred. Nuclear technologies, nanotechnologies, gene-editing, robotization, and man-machine-mergers carry grave and ghastly risks. But we must remember that all of them can do a lot of good if properly willowed and channeled; the real risk is how we use them. It is a sorry state; it is a terrible state to be in. We can't trust ourselves to do what we can and want to do. And we don't trust another human. In response, we are creating a 'super-synthetic' man, hoping to offset and overcome what we don't like about biological man. Modern science was supposed to have made God redundant, but he keeps turning up in our latest technologies. We hope that, in the words of Ian McEwan, "we might have the joyful problem of rather nicer people among us" (*Machines Like Me*, 2018). Actually, our 'marrying' the machine is only another avatar of what modern man really wants to arrange: the marriage of science and secularism. The fact is, we have for long been fascinated by machines but we have also been fearful of what they might mean. As early as in 1942, Isaac Asimov laid down his *Three Laws of Robotics*, and warned that robots must be programmed not to ever hurt humans as otherwise we would be doomed. Today, as Kevin Kelly (*Out of Control*, 1994) puts it, "The realm of the born—all that is nature—and the realm of the made—all that is humanly constructed—are becoming one. Machines are becoming biological and the biological is becoming engineered". It brings to mind what EM Forster envisioned way back in 1909, when he wrote: "Cannot you see that it is we that are dying, and down here the only thing that really lives is the Machine? We created the Machine, to do our will, but we cannot make it do our will now. It has robbed us of the sense of space and of the sense of touch, it has blurred every human relation" (*The Machine Stops*, 1909). We are the only species that goes to great lengths to create something smarter than we are, and equally is terrified of what it might do to us once it sees through what we are. Instinctively, we feel inferior, fear the worst, but still cannot hold back. It is a part of the human nature, not only to look down on those we feel are inferior, but also to dread that which we look up to, to be wary of what we worship, and yet want to be one of them like gods. That is why, merging into a machine and emerging as a god is at the apex of our agenda for the future. It should also be at the top of our worries right now.

When that merging eventually happens, we hope that, like the men of '*The Machine Stops*', we will live with 'buttons and switches everywhere' for everything we need (including a button that produces literature, and some buttons to communicate with friends). In such a dystopian world, men seldom have to move their bodies, and all unrest will be concentrated in the soul. It means that, in such a world, not only the rich, but all the rest will be infested with what Thorstein Veblen (1899) called the 'Leisure Class' parasite. Once we get infested, all of us will do what the rich do now: indulge in conspicuous waste, conspicuous consumption, and conspicuous leisure. It almost means that we want to abandon our very identity, our very humanness—which, according to Indian scriptures, a soul gains after passing through 8.4 million species (cockroaches, snakes, spiders, ants, sea creatures, etc.)—simply to be able to do nothing! It means that one of the things we prize most as humans, our ability to think of clever and original ideas and possibilities, in short, our power of imagination—which Einstein said is the 'true sign of intelligence, not knowledge'—cannot rise above becoming a 'clever' machine. And pray, what, in turn, do we hope to get in return? We hope to get everything from doing nothing: from redundancy to emancipation; from oblivion to absoluteness; from gadget to godhood.

From Pygmalion falling for his chiseled Galatea, to maverick Frankenstein marveling at his 'modern Prometheus', to the man-meets-machine fiction of Philip Dick, humans have been enthralled by the possibilities of emotional relationships with their synthesized imitations. Over centuries, automatons have evolved from simple mechanical marvels to the electronic androids of the modern age. What is new, experts say, is that it will only be a question of years before automated creatures will "feel" what we do to them, and will feel the need to reciprocate or retaliate. The upshot is that devices we once deemed cold and mechanical could soon become the objects of real companionship and outlets for human desires, including sexual. It is even being suggested that future people will be falling in love with and marrying robots, and that robots will be preferred candidates for 'arranged marriages', because they can be customized (in terms of physical and personality traits) to the liking of the parents and prospective spouses, and synthetic mates might be preferred as they could be trusted to be less jealous or more affectionate.[17] This looks like a huge stretch of credulity because in the end, a robot is still an obedient tool, not a feeling person. But the take-away point is that the velocity and virtuosity of technological change is unstoppable and unpredictable; greed and glory can seduce anyone to cross the proverbial *Lakshmana rekha*, the forbidden line. One of them could be our quest to create synthetic or new 'forms of life'—to build reproducing organisms that will do the will of man. Another is our quest for the elixir of life.

In fact, it has happened before. Of all things, gunpowder was invented accidentally in China, circa 850 CE, by an alchemist who was trying to find the elixir of life.[18] That single invention might well have paved the path for the probable catastrophe that human race is racing towards. One wonders: what possibly could be the unintended outcome of our present quest to become *Homo Immortalis Omnipotent*?

Greed and glory cause ineffable grief. Greed is wanting *more* than you need, deserve, or is good for you. Immortality is but greed. We want power for glory. But, we must realize that, as Tolkiens emphasizes in *The Lord of the Rings*, the force that distinguishes evil from good is a major corrupting influence of power. Mass killers, in the logic of their minds, want fame and glory. Today's mass culture and our own vicarious urges guarantee it. We all, in different degrees and various ways, like to 'peek' and 'sneak' and watch the flash of the blazing gun, the knife coming down, or the flesh being flayed off, and this urge to be aroused while passively participating, is almost worse than running the risk of doing the evil oneself. Wars are products of both greed and glory. Much of the disappointment and despair in human relationships stems from wanting more from each other than we want to give. If we are 'enough' for each other, as we are, then we enjoy each other, not resent each other. If 'enough is enough' then there is no need for more. It is greed that is the basis of our yearning for wealth, eternal youth, immortality; we want more than what humans are meant to have. Basically, we want to outlive our own lives. Earlier, we were satisfied with 'virtual' or 'spiritual' immortality through progeny, name, fame, and soul. Now we want 'practical' or 'sensual' immortality through our own physical body and brain. What we forget is that we are defined by our thoughts, desires, dreams, regrets, and sorrows—not by flesh or meat, or bone or blood. The big difference between scripture and science is that the former exhorts us to shed our identification with the body—which Henry Wood describes as an "animated fleshly statue, visible, sensuous and material",[19] and the Upanishads describe as 'ill-smelling and unsubstantial'—whereas science tells us that we are nothing but the body. For most of us, poor in spiritual perspective, the only practical reality is that the body—our physicality—is the only vehicle that enables our existence in the world. As Henry Wood says, man "has mistaken his own identity... believes himself material in his being..."[20] The bottom line is that we want to live on in the physical body, even if it is puffed-up and wrinkled and wretched, as a way to be deathless. Our obsession with our body, although it is now at its zenith, is long-standing. Plato believed that proportionality in the body was evidence of a divine design, similar to what could be found in the intricate and exquisite architecture in the natural world. On the other hand, the Upanishads tell us, "He who clings to the perishable body and regards it as his true Self must experience death many times". That is, even as we strive to become materially 'immortal', we are daily committing 'spiritual suicide'.

The Lure of the Forbidden and the Streak of Cruelty

Right down from Adam, we have always done what we should not have. As Mark Twain quipped, "It was not that Adam ate the apple for the apple's sake, but because it was forbidden. It would have been better for us—oh, infinitely better for us—if the *serpent* had been forbidden". To contain and channel technological change we need 'consciousness-change'. Instead of consciousness-change, what technology is trying to do is to find ways to upload consciousness into what is called the 'Cloud'.[21] That is because our consciousness is currently controlled by our mind, and as the Buddha said, "It is a man's own mind, not his enemy or foe, that lures him to evil ways". Our brains have been completely rewired for the worse due to addictive technology. As a result, the more powerful technology becomes, the more vulnerable man might be to evil. In fact, according to Andrew Kimbrell, "we are witnessing the 'technification' of evil". And if we add 'globalization' then we can understand why so many of us are unable to resist the lure of evil. Yet, there are others like Spanish sociologist Manuel Castells (*The Rise of the Network Society*, 1996) who argue the opposite, that [the information age] would dramatically increase the productivity of individuals and lead to greater leisure, allowing individuals to achieve 'greater spiritual depth and more environmental consciousness'. But such a view flies in the face of the past and present. Many in industrialized societies now have 'greater leisure', but it has not led to any greater spiritual awakening and is not helping in any way in combating the climate crisis. Although we don't notice, it is technologies like *Facebook* that are having a tremendous effect on behavior; they have, as someone said, turned us into products, into users, into their virtual employees. Our behavior is so wobbly and wacky that there are no more taboos or forbidden zones or safe havens; we can, everyone of us, might do anything anytime to anyone; when the crunch comes, we do not know whom to trust the least, spouse or stranger, relative or recluse, friend or foe, snake-oil salesman or a pseudo-spiritual guru.

Without consciousness-change, technological-change might make our streak of cruelty more socially toxic. A man like Gandhi confessed to his own cruelty, while Marquis de Sade believed that 'cruelty, very far from being a vice, is the first sentiment that nature injects in us all'. In fact, as Jonathan Glover tells us, "The festival of cruelty is in full swing" (*Humanity: A Moral History of the Twentieth Century*, 1999). And being cruel is not the exclusive trait of sadists and serial-killers or suicide-bombers. In fact, much as we want to insulate ourselves from such 'evil' people, the truth is that they are, in Philip Zimbardo's words "terribly and terrifyingly normal". David Buss strikes the same note and says, "Most killers, in a nutshell, are not crazy. They kill for specific reasons, such as lust, greed, envy, fear, revenge, status, and reputation, or to get rid of someone who they perceive is inflicting costs on them. They are like you. They are like me".[21] All of us are, in a variety of ways, sadists on the sly and metaphorical molesters in the mind, and instruments of evil. Killing is hurting fatally and it is possible to hurt as much without killing. We can, and do more than we realize, kill through spoken words. It is tantamount to involuntary manslaughter. In actual killing, there is no hurt once killed. But not in killing with words. The wound left by a word may never heal. Of all our sense organs it is our mouth that can touch other people's lives, both to hurt and to heal. As King Solomon says, "Life and death are in the hands of the tongue."[22] The Jewish Talmud says that negative speech is even worse than the sword, because it kills many people, even at a great distance. All this does not mean that we cannot do immense good or be 'effective altruists', that we are incapable of putting our lives on the line to save total strangers, even of a different faith. That is what makes being human so frustrating and challenging, exasperating and exhilarating. All of us have within us what it takes to do godly good and monstrous evil, but the trouble is we have no control over either. All of us are made of the same composite, and the same war is waging in our consciousness, and therefore any of us could be an

Eichmann[23] or a Schindler,[24] a Godse[25] or a Gandhi. Each of them in their own mind believed that what they did was not only right but also righteous.

Our mind, or our mental template, if you will, justifies or offers alibis for everything: greed or genocide, callousness to others' suffering, or unspeakable cruelty towards fellow-animals. As Dostoyevsky said, "No animal could ever be so cruel as a man, so artfully, so artistically cruel". Indeed, to adequately express what we do to and with animals, we need to invent a new vocabulary and new words. Words like cruelty, sadism, and savagery do not capture and convey what they are supposed to. The irony is that when humans act cruelly, we call them 'animals', while the truth is that only humans behave cruelly. As Thomas Edison aptly said, "Until we stop hurting all our living beings we are still savages". It is a snapshot of how amoral and callous that we, as a society, have become. And of how, what Jaron Lanier[27] called the 'culture of sadism' has become embedded in us. What we have been doing so far to other animals is now spreading to other humans. What matters to our mind is what *we* want, what *we* think is beneficial to us, and for that everything is a 'resource'; that now includes man himself, a source of supply, support, or aid. Once we develop such a mindset, it is easy for the floodgates to fly open. If man is simply another mineral resource, then like any other we can be used or discarded or dumped according to the need. And then again, if we are a resource, why do we talk of the population problem as a time-bomb? No one complains of excesses of any other resource; it is always about scarcity. Indeed, the real problem is that we have not found the way to effectively and empathetically harness human potential for common good. Basically we, unlike other species, are not positive contributors to our ecosystems. For example, ants, it is said, outnumber us and consume ten times more food than we do. And yet they are not contributing to the climate crisis because they are net contributors to their world, not rapacious extractors. It shows that with a different mindset towards the environment, we can perhaps grow to ten billion in numbers without making the planet pay for it. But for such a 'mindset' we need consciousness-change. To win the war on climate, and, for that matter, on anything else like poverty or pollution, we need to 'win' the war within.

At the root of human destructiveness is his role as a consumer. In fact, to consume is to destroy, to waste; that was why tuberculosis was once called 'consumption'. The human population is a 'problem' precisely because we are consumers; not creators, or efficient users of resources. And if a 'problem' can be resolved by 'dumping' the offending human, what can be more efficient? Instead, we must learn to view human beings as the end, and cultivate *nurturance*—emotional care and ample attention—as a skill, so that we can train ourselves to be compassionate individuals in a shared society. Compassion, it is useful to remind ourselves, is not 'condescending kindness' to a handful, but 'passionate engagement' with everything around you. To arrive at that objective, we should pursue compassion passionately, and temper our passions with compassion. One of our shortcomings relates to what psychologists call 'collapse of compassion'—people tend to feel and act less compassionately for multiple suffering victims than for a single suffering victim.[28] That is why we are quick to respond to individual suffering and injustice, and placid and passive in relation to mass suffering and injustice. We are also insensitive to intergenerational injustice like climate injustice. By our refusal to radically cut greenhouse gas emissions we are deliberately and willfully putting at risk the health and lives of our great-grandchildren. By our refusal to give up our needless comforts we are callously denying the basic needs of future generations. While we have to cultivate 'compassionate' skills, what we are perfecting are 'killing' skills. With natural death no longer acting as a creator of a level playing field—everyone in the end does not die, at least not the same way—killing has come to take its place—anyone can be killed anytime. Almost anything can be used to kill; bare hands, cars, knives, rocks, fire, pillows, ropes, and even water have all been used to snuff life out of another person. As Philip Zimbardo puts it, "Before I knew that a man could kill a man, because it happens all the time. Now I know that even the person with whom you've shared food, or whom you've slept, even he can kill you with no trouble. The closest neighbor can kill you with his teeth: that is what I have learned since the genocide, and my eyes no longer gaze the same on the face of the world".[29] We have always killed one another; we have never hesitated from taking another's life when we thought it would get us what we want. And contrary to how we view ourselves as normally moral and as a largely peace-loving species, the truth also is, as a recent study reveals, "we are the most relentless yet oblivious killers on Earth".[30] But bad as it was, killing is no longer the 'killing' of the good old bad days, when it used to be the most morally abhorrent of actions, the rarest of rare crimes, the most sinful of them all. We now kill through everything we do, the food we eat, the water we drink and the air we breathe. We kill when something we don't believe is believed by others, be it faith or ideology or even a disease like Ebola in the Congo. Governments kill, corporations kill, and all sorts of individuals kill in all sorts of ways. As for the people affected, they are reduced to numbers, distanced into numerical units, moved into a balance sheet, profit or loss calculation. The people who work in these entities do not consider themselves as doing evil; in their mind, they are just doing their job, making a living. The evil they do comes under the purview of, in the words of Philip Zimbardo, "knowing better, but willingly doing worse".[31] Our minute and specialized jobs separate and insulate us from ethical consequences of our collective work. We pretend we don't know; but it suits us not to know. As Andrew Kimbrell puts it, "Each of us is caught, therefore, in a kind of job blackmail… We sell our moral birthright in order to "pay the bills".[32] It is all the consequence of our current corrupted consciousness. Some even think that consciousness itself, rather, the evolution of consciousness, has turned human existence into a tragedy that need not have been, were it not for it. Otherwise, we would have lived like other animals, wholly, mating, eating, reproducing, and dying. That is debatable, but in any case we cannot travel back in time. At this point, nothing short of an alchemy of our consciousness can set right what is wrong with us. But we must also remember that consciousness is not our monopoly. We have a higher level of consciousness, but all sentient beings, including the vegetable and mineral kingdoms, possess consciousness. It means that everything lives and is conscious, but not all life and consciousness is similar to that of the human. As someone pithily put it, it is possible to poison a mineral and to murder it, much as you can murder a human being.

Everything is a 'part' and a 'process' these days. Nothing is whole or wholesome. What everyone does, day in and day out, is a bit, a specific part; no one is allowed or interested to know more than necessary to get his paycheck. For, 'the man who knows too much' is too much trouble. There is a growing growl that humans are 'untrustworthy and too 'temperamental'. The second lost 'capacity' is our repeated failure to see danger that is crystal clear except, or even, to the blind. Human history is replete with perils foretold and we have always 'good reasons' to disregard them. The latest and perhaps the most serious and almost insurmountable danger to mankind comes not from other species or nature, but from man himself. The problem is that human character is, as David DeSteno argues, not a black-and-white dichotomy of good and bad but a far more nuanced 'greyscale' continuum.[33] All of us at times behave in a manner that we fear we have become, as RL Stevenson's Dr Jekyll writes in a letter to his friend Mr Utterson, "a danger that I cannot name". As if that is not alarming enough, the fact is also that the causes and compulsions of all our crises are 'rooted in the ordinary, daily economic activity of our species' at this point in its history. And, that is not because, or only because, we are all 'bad' who do some terrible things now and then. One in fact wishes it were so. It is simple and surgical. Now, it is almost everything we do any time and every time to live as modern or post-modern, or some now call *auto-modern*, human beings.

Horrible as it is, actually killing in its broadest connotation is not the worst about us. When we pluck a flower, the flower bleeds, and when we uproot a vegetable, we are killing. No one doubts that trying to eradicate mosquitoes is not evil, although scientists caution us that we still don't know enough of their role in our ecosystem. But then, who cares for the ecosystem? More than killing it is cruelty that is the bigger and 'treatable' issue. Different shades of cruelty exist deep inside each of us, manifesting most often in our tendency to deliberately inflict pain, denigration, and suffering on others, although our mind usually comes up with one or the other of the three 'Es'—evasion, explanation, and excuse—to escape the guilt and consequence. It is also necessary to remember that while every act of evil is the same—murder is murder, and rape is rape, genocide is genocide, whoever the perpetrator—, every individual is unique. In fact, *why* a particular person does something is also unique, even if that reason is horrendous. Some, like Polish philosopher Karol Wojtyla, who advocated the school of thought called 'personalism', even say that *not recognizing* evil itself is evil. And, even more, not recognizing that we are the source of evil is the chief impediment to fighting evil. The Greek philosopher Sophocles said, "With so much evil stored up in that cold dark soul of yours, you breed enemies everywhere you touch." But that 'stored up' evil makes us mistake those enemies for friends, and friends for enemies. That is why some celebrity serial killers of our own twisted times invoke the Gandhian remorse as an alibi, and say it was the evil inside, or the devil within, which had made them do their terrible deeds. For example, Ted Bundy, the American mass murderer of late 1970s, is believed to have told his girlfriend, "There is something the matter with me… I just couldn't contain it. I fought it for a long, long time… it was just too strong". We have long known, more by intuition than intelligence, that inside our essential being, in some nook, corner or cranny of our soul, sinister forces lurk, waiting for an opportunity to pounce and become deeds. It is deeds that in the end matter; they shape us much as we shape them, and they affect others. A recent study suggests that "dark personality traits—Machiavellianism, egoism, narcissism, psychopathy, sadism, and spitefulness—all stem from a common 'dark core'"[34] that exists inside each of us. The study also says that while each individual dark trait manifests itself in widely different ways, they seem to have much more in common than initially meets the eye. If true, it means that we can no longer take refuge in thinking that there are evil people out there in the wicked world and the only thing to do is to flush them out and eliminate them. The fact is that we are all potentially capable, if things go awfully wrong, of behaving like that very evil 'person' we are looking for to ostracize from human society. Some killers and jilted lovers, in Nietzschean tones,[35] raised themselves above the rest of us and proclaimed that their deed is so lofty that it was 'beyond good and evil'. Some others say that this doleful world anyway is all evil, and that a particular evil action just happened to come out because of certain circumstances. Although from the mouths of murderers that could be a ploy to evade responsibility, we do know that circumstance can sanitize evil, and certain acts, while appearing heinous or abominable, might actually have been committed for the benefit of others; here, the individual is not only free from moral offense, but may even gain great merit. In short, matter does not matter; motives matter and intent is all-important.

Yet what is striking is that saints and sinners alike, heroes and villains are saying the same thing: they are impotent before a more potent inner evil force which induces them to harbor evil thoughts and to indulge in unwholesome actions. Most of us in the moral middle, too, share the same helplessness—our almost pathological inability to do good when we want to, and, even worse, the compelling inability to *refrain* from doing bad. In fact, the Upanishads say that all organs in our body are susceptible to evil except our breath. We see it all around and in every relationship; we hear the sounds of the mocking laughter of evil. Evil has become irresistible because it is seen as the short-cut to the one thing that is irresistible: making money. What we are allowed to see and hear is designed for that, bringing to mind, upside down, what George Orwell told us in his classic book, *1984*: "The Party told you to reject the evidence of your eyes and ears. It was their final, most essential command". Now we cannot even choose to 'reject' because once we see or hear we get hooked. We must avoid evil. But we do not know how and where to begin, and how to fight it. That is because what we see and experience are symptoms, not the root of the evil. It is like trying to put out the flames without putting out the fire. This tension and tussle saps our internal energy, and affects our behavior drastically and scars our psyche and personality. We all live wounded lives, troubled by our own thoughts, unable to be at peace with our own emotions, or with fellow-humans. So powerful is the devil inside that when faced with a choice or a course, so many, despite free will or in exercise of it, choose evil and so many succumb to seduction so easily. We are distraught, feel terribly guilty and blame ourselves. Part of the reason is that sometimes in despair, we look upon the evil inside as a standalone, we think there is nothing else and therefore we think there is nothing we could do. But then, we do good too. It is often said that God created man with both good and evil inclinations, the two tendencies that pull him in opposite directions, and also that it is His command that we choose good over evil. But if that were so, why is that we all feel, with little effort, the tremors of the presence of evil inside and not as much of the good? While all life is and everything we do is a binary choice—between good and evil—why is it so taxing to choose good? The truth of the matter is that human behavior is plastic, open equally to both altruism and back-stabbing. In Shakespeare's words, "The web of our life is of a mingled yarn, good and ill together" (*All Is Well That Ends Well*). Science now says[36] "nothing is either good or bad, desirable or undesirable, or anything else except that it is made so by laboratories inside us producing the emotions on which we live." The fact is that there is some evil in the best of us, and some good in the worst of us. In fact everyone, even the most creative person is a blend of seemingly incompatible qualities. That spirit is what Rumi referred to when he said, "The human being is like a jackass, with wings of angels tacked on". We are all mixtures of good and evil, light and darkness, lower than the lowly animal, and as sublime as the Supreme. There is something beautiful in the worst and hideous among us as illustrated in the story of Jesus kneeling before a stinking carcass of a dog and exclaiming "Praise be to God, what beautiful teeth this creature has". A great thinker can be a mean man and a lustful man can love dearly. No one is pure or perfect. And there is terror not only in the darkness of the unknown, but even more in the bright lights of the known.

Evil we usually associate with sadistic violence, cruelty, and viciousness. Sometimes, like in Hinduism, good and evil are equated with order and chaos, and the struggle between the two is the essence of our existence. Good and evil are extreme opposites, but they cannot do without each other. Gandhi, in his comments on the Mahabharata, said, "Human life is like a fabric woven with black and white threads—threads of good and evil"; and also that "None can be said to be evil personified". If everything is good then nothing would be good. The reality is that we all contain within ourselves the capacity for kindness, as much as for cruelty or evil. We have within us both the 'Kingdom of God' about which Christ spoke, as well as the cave of the devil. We like to embrace good and shun evil, but in the Bhagavad Gita, it is said that a *sthitaprajna* (person of steady wisdom) sees the presence of God not merely in the good and noble, but also in the wicked and ignoble. The point is that we all are capable of being self-serving and generous, callous and compassionate, cowardly and courageous, treacherous and trustworthy. Indeed, anything anyone can be, all of us are. The spiritual guru Paramahansa Yogananda called evil the 'shadow of God', and said that 'the dark shadows of evil are interspersed with the pure white beam of the virtues of God'. The idea of a 'shadow' inside each of us was famously propounded by the Swiss psychiatrist Carl Jung. According to him, it is the deeper 'dark side' of our persona that consists of the primitive, negative, socially or religiously disagreeable human emotions and impulses like sexual lust, hunger for power, selfishness, greed, malice, anger, or rage. We must also note that some emotions like anger and rage are not by themselves necessarily 'bad' or socially disruptive. If channeled in the right direction, they can do a world of good. Way back in 350 BCE, Aristotle (*Nicomachean Ethics*) wrote that "the man who is angry at the right things and with the right people, and further, as he ought, when he ought, and as long as he ought, is praised". In fact, the most pressing need of the hour is to have more good people really, really angry about inequity and injustice all around. Similarly, righteous rage can be more socially beneficial than passive acquiescence. Some, like biologist Jeremy Griffith, go to the length of saying, "What's needed on Earth is love of the dark side of ourselves" (*Freedom: The End of The Human Condition*, 2016). Our response generally is to either pretend as if such emotions and impulses do not exist or to repress them. But research and experience has shown that it only makes them stronger and erupt more intensely when they no longer can be contained. Experts suggest that by 'accepting' the reality of their reality, we can reduce the harm they can do. Then, how can you fight such an embedded evil, the sinister shadow? The answer is three-fold. One, however distasteful, we must recognize and realize that there is inside each of us, a dark patch, a part of the primordial past of our human inheritance. Second, we must strengthen the opposite goodness and Yogananda's 'pure white light' within. The way to strengthen the good within is by doing good in the world. We must always be aware of the fact that everything we do every day has a twin effect: it affects the world we live in, and acts as ammunition in the spiritual struggle between, in Steven Pinker's words, our 'better angels' and 'inner demons'. Third, although difficult to practice, we must strive to fight the evil, not the evil-doer. One of the problems why evil holds such sway over us is because we try constantly to explain it away and not fight it effectively. To fight it effectively does not mean trying to erase or expel it; it means to always retain an upper hand over the evil within. The outside world merely conforms to the moral condition of the human spirit. Evil in man is but a reflection of evil in the world, and vice versa.

Struggle for Supremacy Over Consciousness—the War Within

What we, like many generations before our own time, fail to comprehend sufficiently is that not only do we harbor both good and evil in our consciousness, but that these two, along with their allies, are constantly engaged in an epic and endless struggle for supremacy over our consciousness. What we have failed to recognize is that this 'struggle' is more than conflict or confrontation, even more than combat; it is analogous to what we characterize as 'war'. This 'failure' has been our hamartia, our tragic flaw that is responsible for so much that has gone horribly wrong in human history. We don't even know when it began—some say two million years ago, when man became a 'fully-conscious being'; some say as recent as three thousand years until the time of Homer's *Iliad*. It is one of those things 'we do not even know we didn't know'. Whenever it originated, this is an eternal internal war that goes on every minute of our lives. The two fighting forces are two sides of our own self. No impulse, even evil, in man is irreclaimable; nothing human is doomed to destruction. Man's manifest mission is to reclaim the negative dimension of his own personality. It is this 'complexity' that translates as the enigma of the 'human condition', and as the capriciousness of human behavior. No other explanation fully explains, not even, as Jeremy Griffith says, that it is a "result of us humans becoming conscious and at odds with our species' particular cooperative and loving, Edenic, moral instincts" (*Freedom Essay 3: The Explanation of the Human Condition*, 2016).

We must upfront recognize that this is not like any other war we fight in the external world, where we try to vanquish the opponent and emerge victorious; it is more like a Sisyphean internal struggle—thankless, endless, but necessary. And we must accept that our act of rolling the boulder up the hill is to make sure that neither side, not even the evil one, has to lose or get defeated. What we must focus upon is how to actively intervene and support the righteous side in this war; that is the only way to solve any problem, to better ourselves and to grow spiritually. Hiding from or avoiding struggle and conflict will only result in the triumph of evil. Merely acknowledging and 'accepting' that we all have a 'shadow' or a 'dark spot' or evil within us is not sufficient; it can even embolden and strengthen that very evil we don't want to win. We must constantly and actively ensure that it does not overwhelm the good, and the light within, in the war. But once we recognize this imperative, many things that made no sense, or made our heads hang in shame, and the very basis of our erratic behavior, will fall into place. And 'blindfolding' ourselves will no longer be the only way not to see what makes us sick in our stomach or not to go mad and slaughter each other just by seeing. But if we don't make that effort, and continue to deal with our problems as we have been doing, none of them can be resolved. And if we do, nothing else would need to be done. It is this war that the Bible alludes to, when it says, "For the sinful nature desires what is contrary to the Spirit, and the Spirit what is contrary to the sinful nature. They are in conflict with each other, so that you do not do what you want".[37] It is this war that Islam alludes to when Prophet Muhammad says the greatest *jihad* (struggle/striving) is to battle your own soul, to fight the evil within. This was the 'inner battle' that the American theologian Thomas Merton had in mind when he said that he 'felt in his bones that his own life constituted a battleground between conflicting interests, warring tendencies, mutually exclusive selves'. Actually, *we* don't battle the evil within. It is the *good within* that battles with it. For the 'we' in us includes the two sides, the good and the evil. *They* 'battle' each other, but 'we' need both for our wholeness as humans. That is what is exceptional about this war. We should ceaselessly strive to ensure dominance of the good in the war, but should never risk the defeat and destruction of the 'evil within'. We do not know the beginning, but we do know that there can be no end. It is a war in which we cannot afford either victory or defeat. For we need both adversaries, the good and the bad, intuition and intellect, head and heart, in Jeremy Griffith's explanation, "instinct and conscious intellect", for our very survival. This war goes on unnoticed because no blood or corpses come out of our body, and we think there is peace within us. This war provides a plausible platform to many things that baffle us.

Why is our behavior so erratic and at times so appalling? It offers, if not an answer at least an explanation to the laments of great men like Saint Paul and Rishi Vyasa, among others. Above all, it lets us hope for a better future, a more moral man, and a basis to overcome all the problems that torment us. And, most of all, it gives an answer to the question we all ask: What can *I* do? The response is, *win your own war within*. Anything else is, in the words of the Danish 'Tolstoy', Henrik Pontoppidan, "a lifeless thing—nothing more than a broom handle, a crutch which might help a soul to forget its lameness for a while, but could never be a life-affirming construct."[38] Many mystics have long wondered if some insidious external force is relentlessly impeding their spiritual *sadhana* or progress. Traditionally it was blamed on mysterious, malevolent beings like demons and devils. Now we know that these demons and devils are within each of us and are engaged in a fierce battle with their opposites. And, more important, yes, we can make a difference. We have long thought that we are all born with a permanent package of attributes and traits, some good and the mostly wicked, and that we have to more or less live with them, in our behavior. But, no; it doesn't have to be that way. That is only partially correct.

Recent research is telling us that we can go beyond the grip of the 'given-at-birth', and cultivate, nurture and augment our positive qualities like kindness, compassion, forgiveness, and gratitude. Cutting across all these is sharing, which we must remember, is caring. The spirit of sharing could not only make us more responsible earthlings, but also enable us to boost the kindred forces in the war within.

'Warring' is part of being human; some say it is a part of how we evolved. Indeed, man has been at war with life since its inception, and the resultant struggle is what human society reflects. Many 'wars' we have fought before, including two World Wars, and many civil, ethnic, religious, as well as wars for independence and for secession. And many we fight now, on social ills like wars on terrorism, on drugs, on poverty, on discrimination, etc., but this 'war within' is the most consequential of all. Our failure to recognize this central reality gives rise to what in French is called *plus ça change, plus c'est la même*, why things might appear to change or improve, but beneath it all they remain just as bad as before. This is the 'Mother of all Wars', the real 'war to end all wars'. This war offers the overarching theory we seek to make sense of all that happens in human life that seems so bizarre and even absurd; why we cannot do things in a way that is so self-evident. This is the war that determines how we behave and defines who we are, whether a purely material being or a spiritual being, and if it is a blend of both, which one will exercise greater influence on how we live. It is an eternal war because neither of the opposing forces can or will ever be able to, gain 'victory' or 'vanquish' the other. They are forever related in a state of perennial antithesis, each one requiring the other. The war is for control of the commanding heights of our consciousness. And whoever controls consciousness controls everything else. Everything else is secondary. Whatever happens in the outside war hinges on the ebbs and flows of this war.

It is hard to understand why we get attracted to the unfamiliar and ignore the immediate, but that has cost us a lot. Our knowledge of distant worlds—worlds outside even our galaxy—is increasing day by day, but our awareness of the world within remains abysmal. And RD Laing noted that "our time has been distinguished, more than by anything else, by the mastery, the control of the external world, and by an almost total forgetfulness of the internal world".[39] Scriptures—epistles from the gods—and the holiest of sages have tirelessly told us that everything we seek is within us; that all power is within. The Bible tells us, "A good man brings good things out of the good stored up in his heart, and an evil man brings evil things out of the evil stored up in his heart. For the mouth speaks what the heart is full of". In other words, you can discipline yourself externally, but if you have hate or lust in your heart, you are still in trouble. As Rumi said, "All inspiration you seek is already within you. Be silent and listen". Unaware of the 'world within', let alone of this perennial war within, every time a terrible thing takes place and someone does something abominable, we wonder, 'why, why?', 'who really are they?', 'how could they do such a thing?!', not realizing that perhaps those people are acting against their own will, and that their actions are a reflection of the struggle between the good and evil within their own being.

Many religions tell us that every man is born with both a good and an evil inclination, and that most men will, at some time in their lives, succumb to their evil inclination. The traditional Jewish view on this complex subject is well-defined in rabbinic literature. Man's inclinations are therefore poised between good (*Yetzer HaTov*) and evil (*Yetzer HaRa*), and he is not compelled towards either of them. He has the power of choice and is able to choose one or the other side knowingly and willingly. The *yetzer hara* is not a demonic force, but rather man's misuse of things the physical body needs to survive. In fact, a Jew's very purpose in this physical and material world is to ultimately triumph in this epic battle. Islam too echoes this line of thought. Prophet Muhammad said that 'the greatest jihad is to battle your own soul; to fight the evil within yourself'. This internal spiritual struggle, in Islam, according to many scholars, is the major struggle (*Al-jihad al-Akbar*), higher than the external 'holy war'. In other words, jihad also is what we now classify as a war within. If the major war against evil in Islam is within our soul, the Christian war is a 'war in heaven' between God and the Devil. It is also between flesh and spirit. The Bible says: "Walk by the spirit and do not gratify the desires of the flesh". Alyosha of Dostoyevsky's *Brothers Karamazov* changes the scene of action and says that 'God and the devil are fighting there and the battlefield is the heart of man', or, more to the point, the battlefield is our consciousness. Again, this is also the war between the princely cousins, the *Pandavas* and the *Kauravas*, in the Indian epic Mahabharata at Kurukshetra.

We must understand that all those who appear normal and lead seemingly sane lives are also potentially capable of committing similar deeds, for we are all made up of the same bundle of passions and react to provocations and temptations essentially the same way. And whether it is a murderer or a mahatma, it all depends on how one of our unique attributes, the capacity to judge, evaluate, or decide the right from the wrong, actually works. But, as history shows and modernity brings into sharper focus, such a capacity often can go haywire, because it is easy to find what's wrong, harder to find what's right, and often the choice is not between right and wrong, but right from right and wrong from another wrong. All of us struggle with the dilemma how to tell correctly when everything around is so topsy-turvy and chaotic. And so corrupted is our consciousness that often, through whatever process, what we are inclined to choose is the wrong one. When that 'wrong' becomes a simple mistake or a horrible massacre is hard to tell, because it all happens in the 'world within', out of sight and without our 'personal' participation. We are all equally as helpless about what is happening inside us. And 'what is happening inside' is nothing but, and nothing short of, what we call in the world outside 'war' between two sets of forces, one that comes under the rubric of good and the other evil, a war between two of our own 'selfs', better and bitter. When the forces of good were dominant in the previous ages or yugas, men were righteous. We now live in an age and at a time when the moral manifest of man is at its weakest and that translates into all the terrible things we see in the world. Men of earlier times might have been generally more virtuous and righteous than now, but evil was always waiting in the wings. That was the reason why Saint Paul exhorted us[41] to wear a 'breastplate of righteousness' in fighting evil. Evil now is not only stronger but also hydra-headed and more embedded in everyday life.

Evil is the way to grease greed and gratify consumerism, to appease hatred and abet injustice. It is not merely the absence of good or the mere shadow of light or darkness. And that was foretold in Hindu scriptures. It was written that in the present *Kali Yuga*, the penetration and infiltration of evil into the human world will be complete and unchallenged. That this would be a time when men would need a reason to be good, and none to be bad. It was written that, in this age, people will 'tend to be greedy, ill-behaved and merciless, and fight one another without good reason'.[42] The scriptures like Srimad Bhagavatam and Mahabharata even detail how individuals in various relationships behave in this age, and one must add that they are eerily accurate. The Srimad Bhagavatam says that 'wealth alone will be considered the sign of a man's good birth, proper behavior and fine qualities', and that a 'person's spiritual position will be ascertained merely according to external symbols, and on that same basis people will change from one spiritual order to the next'.[43] In fact, it is even said that since nothing is an accident, only those with *karma* appropriate to a sinful life are born in these ghastly times. These prophecies apply so aptly to current times that one is utterly at a loss. Does it mean we are doomed people fated to live in evil?

One way we obfuscate evil, and give ourselves a moral cover for our bad behavior, is by depicting evil as a monstrous act or a profound immorality, like murder or rape or genocide or mass massacre. The forensic psychiatrist Michael Welner, who studies depraved behavior, says, "Everyday evil encompasses a myriad of everyday actions... the possibilities are literally limitless". Limitless because evil is now virtually indistinguishable from our behavior. It is not merely a twisting or corruption of good. What Hannah Arendt called *banality of evil* is more true than ever before. The fact is that evil has become banal, morality is chiaroscuro. And it is not confined to the criminal realm, and it need not even be illegal. Even more to the point, the very wellspring of the legal system in a society, the State, is itself a major source of what Arendt called organized evil. And it has been for a while. Tolstoy wrote, "The truth is that the state is a conspiracy designed not only to exploit, but above all to corrupt its citizens". And so is the economic system in which we live and work and die—capitalism. Social evils like extreme poverty, extreme inequality, and exploitation are the products of capitalism, mainly though not exclusively. And technology is exacerbating ills like inequality through, for example, genomic technologies by propagating the idea that some lives or traits are not as desirable as others. The key is 'access', equal access to power, privilege, opportunity, creative expression; this is what capitalism denies and subverts. Indeed, its critics say that capitalism sacrifices humanity's well-being for private profit. Man has always been a 'working animal' and work has always been viewed as more than a means to make a living. It is what connects you to society; it is what lets you express yourself; it is what allows you to share your time and skills with others for a common purpose; it is what remains after you are, in Kurt Vonnegut Jr.'s phrase, 'stone-cold dead' (*Cat's Cradle*, 1963). But capitalism has made it a matter of life and death. In fact, in Japanese there is even a word for 'death from overwork': *karoshi*. It covers a range of ailments from heart failure to suicide, so long as the root of their cause is in working too hard. It is all about ambition, grit, and hustle. "Work, for its disciples never really stops and they don't want it to stop because it is the source of their rapture".[44] The issue goes beyond finding a *modus operandi* between work and vacation and even beyond the impact of the 'Universal Basic Income'. It relates to the issue of how to use 'time' as a resource for spiritual growth and common good. It has become an immediate imperative, what with artificial intelligence and automation threatening to throw millions out of work. Will man then become more spiritual or sensual or suicidal? How will more time spent on inane entertainment and erotic titillation affect his mind? As has been famously said, an idle mind indeed could be a devil's workshop, and could be catastrophic in societies with more guns than people. Albert Camus once quipped that 'idleness is fatal only to the mediocre' (*A Happy Death*, 1972). But then, what else are we, and even more would be, as we are feverishly working towards making the machine synonymous with excellence, and we want nothing but not doing anything in return. Indeed, so much is our ardor for the machine that it covers up mediocrity, which itself is a spinoff of our excessive reliance on the machine. The reality is that even more than what evil, both hot and cold, can do, it is, in the words of David Wong, "warm, dense fog" or the "mass of flavorless mediocrity"[45] that is a greater threat to human survival. Being the best of anything seems so pointless. Our lives and work are so intertwined that striving for excellence might even inadvertently strengthen the 'stupid boss' or the corrupt system.

To ensure that the forces of evil in the war within are subdued, we need to bring about a fundamental change in the context of human life. In this context, it is important to pay particular attention to a dimension of modern life that occupies so much of our minds, and we take great pride about: love of loyalty to one's country, patriotism. This is necessary because it contributes in no small measure to the dominance of evil in the world and that, in turn, strengthens the forces of evil in the war within. We value patriotism very highly and consider it almost a moral imperative. But many who run the State exploit that sentiment for questionable purposes; there is talk of manufacturing a patriotic cyborg superhuman, like the *Six-Million-Dollar Man* or the *Bionic Woman*. Way back in 1775, Samuel Johnson famously said, 'patriotism is the last refuge of a scoundrel'. We cannot talk for scoundrels, but even the sane and stable get their thrills in defense of their country, right or wrong. For some time now, the decline and impending demise of the nation-state has been speculated upon in the wake of globalization. Although the nation-state is not as sovereign as before, and its hold over its subjects is not as strong, it is still the most powerful political institution and the bedrock of global order and stability. It still evokes plenty of passions and abundance of emotions, and impels us to do things beyond our better judgment. It also comes in the way of cultivating a culture of planetary consciousness and an enduring sense of global citizenship. The absence of such a 'consciousness' and 'citizenship' is a major reason for our inability to solve global problems like climate change. When naturalist David Attenborough warns of climate-caused collapse of civilization, our response is not to prevent such a 'collapse' but to strive towards transforming humanity into what is called a 'space-faring civilization'.

Right now, the plutocracies that run national governments are the stubborn stumbling blocks; they believe that what is good for planetary health is downright dangerous for their political health. They get away with it because their citizens in their hearts believe that what their governments are doing is good for them even if it is poisonous to the planet! It is generally accepted, even by enlightened persons, that what a government considers to be the 'national interest' overrides every moral principle, and that governments can lie, kill or torture their own people and that is not evil, or, at the least that is a 'necessary evil'. And that if we are 'law-abiding', no evil can touch us nor can we be held morally accountable. The unvarnished historical fact is that the worst horrors and atrocities were legal and perpetrated by 'patriotic' people. And then again, the fact is that more than genocides or mass massacres, small cruelties committed by common people—who pride themselves as good and just, and benevolent—have done more than most people realize to spread and enflame evil in human society. We must also understand that we are the only species which exhibits not only malice but also *Schadenfreude*, delight at other people's misery. Researchers say that what appears to be at the core of Schadenfreude is *dehumanization*, the process of perceiving a person or social group as lacking the attributes that define what it means to be human. The daily reality these days is that most of us experience evil in social and subtle forms like intemperance, inequity, ill-treatment, ill-will, taking advantage, trampling over others feelings, exploitation, and even, in the current milieu, rabid individualism and lavish living. Interpersonal evil is still alive and kicking but it is dwarfed by institutional evil. When such unsavory traits stay dominant inside in the war within, however much we try, we do bad. We live with them;

we experience them as villains or victims—often the line gets blurred—but do not think we are evil. The way to alleviate evil is to do good proactively. The best defense against both interpersonal and institutional evil is to embed compassion into everyday living. The Dalai Lama says, "If we want to make others happy, practice compassion. If you want to be happy, practice compassion".

In Mahayana Buddhist traditions, compassion (*karuna*) is one of the primary qualities that a practitioner should cultivate. This, along with wisdom, is a necessary requirement for progressing along the *Bodhisattva* path. Compassion does not shut its doors to any one, not even to a cold-blooded killer. Indeed he needs it more because he has, in the language of the Bible, 'sprinkled blood'.[46] And we know we too need it as we too have in us what scientists call the 'dark core', which is what impels men to do evil. And no one is immune or impervious. History shows that some of our much-admired great thinkers, writers, leaders, and role models have had skeletons in their closets, that they have been callous, cunning, and cruel in their private lives. And exceptionally good men are also susceptible to very ordinary weaknesses. That does not necessarily negate their greatness or goodness; it only that they too were like any of us. It should make us more hopeful about ourselves: we too can be one of them. Despite the 'dark core', all of us are still capable of compassion, which science tells us can be sharpened like any other skill, similar to a muscle that can be strengthened with exercise, and enhanced through systematic training programs. It means that man is in no way predestined to evil, although he is constantly tempted by malevolent forces which, like a wild beast, lie in wait, ready to leap on its prey. We do not have to cringe and crawl in the face of the evil within; we can still lead a virtuous life if we muster the will and skill to do good. That will beef up the forces of good in the war within.

Even though they have not explicitly focused much on the war within, all religions and scriptures, ancient archetypes and great men, spiritual and secular, have grappled with the prickly issue of good and evil in human life. For instance, the conflict between good and evil is one of the precepts of the Zoroastrian faith, first enshrined by Zoroaster over three centuries ago. It is central to Manichaeism, an Iranian religion, which the founder called the *Religion of Light*. Manichaean theology taught a dualistic view of good and evil. A key belief in Manichaeism is that the powerful, though not omnipotent, good power (God), was opposed by the semi-eternal evil power (Satan). Humanity, the world and the soul are seen as a by-product of the battle between God's proxy, Primal Man, and Satan. The human person is seen as a battleground for these powers.[47] According to Buddhism, desire is the root of evil; and Vedanta says that ignorance of our true nature (*avidya*) is evil. Nietzsche, on the other hand, said "Not necessity, not desire, no—the love of power is the demon of men". Whatever is the source of evil in the first place, let us face it: the evil we encounter in the world is more devilish and daring. It is tinged with malice, designed not to derive maximum gain but to inflict maximum pain and misery on another person. What has happened, and is happening, is that the evil within us has gained the upper hand in the war within; it has infiltrated and corrupted our interpersonal life and is strutting triumphant in the world. We must bear in mind that life without suffering is a virtual oxymoron, and that in fact, our own body is the source of our suffering, subject as it is to decay and disease. And much of our suffering in fact emanates from our relationship with other people. What is now getting blurred is the boundary between what is called demonic or sadistic evil and everyday evil, between acts that are merely bad and those that are truly depraved. The evil we encounter today is raw, naked, unashamed, and unapologetic. That is so because it overwhelms the good inside us. And that is because the ground within is now more suitable to the seeds of evil. What evil stands for is what we want from life. That strengthens both the evil hiding in the crevices and corners of our conflicted and beleaguered soul, and in the thick and humdrum of our daily life. What is glaring is that evil-doers don't just do bad that hurt and harm others. They choose to make their actions even worse by behaving sadistically and by deliberately ignoring or intensifying the damage and suffering they cause.

It is yet another sign that forces of evil and *adharma* have gained an almost unassailable dominance in the struggle within. What many of us do not understand is that not only do both good and bad coexist in each of us, but they combine with other kindred forces to wage a war to gain the upper hand in our consciousness. And the fortunes and fluctuations in this war eventually determine our behavior, what we do and what we don't—and no amount of laws and ethical codes can make any significant difference. One pivotal factor we should never lose sight of is that we cannot be moral simply because we want to appear good. Morality *per se* cannot ward off or fight evil. And we need to widen the ambit of morality. Many evil perpetrators convince themselves that they are acting morally in doing what they are doing. We also have to rethink who qualifies to be a 'perpetrator'. Is it only the actual doer or should it include the 'mastermind'? We often ask how a mass murderer can kill innocent people and children. At least they have a twisted cause in their warped minds; what about 'official' mass murderers who authorize launching of drones to kill a 'terrorist' suspected to be hiding in the vicinity? Is the manufacture of a nuclear weapon itself or of toxic chemicals, not only their use, a sin? Or the development of technologies that we know we don't have the wisdom to put to good use? What is the best thing we can morally do, saving ourselves, or sacrificing ourselves? Is morality a matter of numbers or a question of intent? Can 'loyalty' to a family, company or country no longer be deemed to be a virtue by itself? We have to redraw the boundaries of what is right and what is wrong, and what is 'larger good' and 'lesser evil'. Should there be anymore different moral norms applicable to the rulers and the ruled, the state and the citizen? Which is a lesser evil, kleptocracy or kakistocracy? We cannot arrive at precise and 'fool-proof' answers; we have to constantly improve and improvise.

The only way to minimize errors is to cultivate the right kind of mindset. To checkmate, contain, and combat evil in the world we have to stem the tide in the war and strengthen the forces of good inside. For that, we have to aggressively enhance the good we do in our daily lives. We must remember that whatever we do all day, whatever we put into our body through any of our sense organs, serves and feeds one or the other of the 'two wolves' inside, wolves that are constantly at war with each other. Everything we ingest is 'natural' nutrition to either of them. Like everyday evil, we also have to have everyday good, a good that, in the words of the humanist William Morris, we can do with a consciousness that makes us act as if *harm to one* would mean *harm to all.* In fact, some say that it is the purpose of evil to throw things into disarray, and that it is the very reason why God created it and allows it to exist. We can do good in many ways if we recognize that in human life, luck (or whatever one chooses to call it: fate, destiny, *karma*) plays a huge role—from birth to death—, and that we should make it our manifest mission to help the unlucky, the disadvantaged, the handicapped, and to do what we could to make life less difficult for them and lighten their burden. For, as George Eliot said, "what do we live for, if not to make life less difficult to each other?"[48] And make life less difficult particularly to the less fortunate among us. No other species is as disparate and divergent as the human, and it is precisely that disparateness and divergence that offers immense opportunities to do good.

The subject of what Lars Svendsen called the 'philosophy of evil', and the fight between good and evil, has been a perennial theme in great literature like Mary Shelley's *Frankenstein* (1818), Robert Stevenson's *The Strange Case of Dr Jekyll and Mr Hyde* (1886), JRR Tolkien's *The Lord of the Rings* (1937–1955), William Golding's *Lord of the Flies* (1954), and John Steinbeck's *East of Eden* (1952). The common theme in all of these is that humanity is continuously immersed in a struggle of good versus evil. Steinbeck sums it up: "I believe that there is one story in the world, and only one... Humans are caught—in their lives, in their thoughts, in their hungers and ambitions, in their avarice and cruelty, and in their kindness and generosity too—in a net of good and evil". Steinbeck calls it, "the way in which this sense of opposed absolutes rises from deep within man, representing something profound and inevitable in human consciousness". Before Steinbeck, we have Shakespeare in whose entire oeuvre the fight between good and evil is a recurring refrain. In Hamlet, he says, "for there is nothing either good or bad, but thinking makes it so". And in Macbeth, throughout the play, Macbeth and his wife, after the murder of Duncan, are engaged in a constant combat between the good and evil within themselves. A much-acclaimed work of this genre is Joseph Conrad's classic *Heart of Darkness* (1899), which highlights the struggle that humans go through, with their own morals, and their own battles with their hidden evils. In the *Harry Potter* books, there is no magic in the world without a fight between good and evil. All things are limited to being what they are and nothing more, and the world becomes a boring and burdensome place. You have to escape to the realm of magic to make things interesting and discover the potential for human flourishing and wholeness. Not only modern literature but also scriptures underscore this issue. According to Jewish belief, the focus of the battle between good and evil is not mastery over the outside world, but over the soul of the human individual and the power it contains; a moral struggle that takes place in the heart, not in the outside world. The contestants are man's conscience against man's urges, man's spirituality against the physical life force. The Indian scripture *Katha* Upanishad says that all life is a choice between two paths—*sreyas* (goodness) and *preyas* (pleasantness)—and implores us to tread the former. The wise prefer the good to the pleasant; the foolish, driven by sensual desires, prefer the pleasant to the good. *Preyas* sizzles with sensual pleasure, while *sreyas* leads to spiritual joy. In the Bhagavad Gita, Krishna compares sense-born pleasures to 'wombs of pain and sorrow.'[49] But the reality is that all through our lives we want pleasure, which we equate with happiness, while pain we equate with misery. That is perhaps why so few are 'happy', and studies indicate the emergence of yet another inequality: *happiness inequality*. As Jeremy Bentham says,[50] pain and pleasure are 'two sovereign masters', and it is under their governance that nature has placed mankind. The two are a package, inseparable. But all life, we travail in vain to embrace pleasure and shun pain. In fact, Freud went to the extent of saying that what decides the purpose of life is simply the program of the 'pleasure principle'.[51] Some say that our difficulty to tread the path of *sreyas* instead of *preyas* is a structural shortcoming of *Homo sapiens*; that we are, as Kant said, 'made out of crooked timber'. Unable to face up to the fact, we have been living in denial and despair. That denial has become defiance in the modern era, and of late it is this defiance that is manifesting as a direct dare to the gods to stop us, if they could, from becoming one of them.

Homo sapiens to *Homo Deus*

Our longing not to be a man anymore has become a desperate cry to be a god. The crystallization of man's will to attain god-like powers is a result of his hubris that he no longer needs, in order to live wisely, what the Greek poet Aeschylus described as the 'awful grace of God'. At a time when the mantra is 'greed is good', the ultimate 'greed' cannot but be the desire to be a god. It is this genre of desire that Miguel de Unamuno implied in his book *The Tragic Sense of Life* (1912): "Every created being tends not only to preserve itself in itself, but to perpetuate itself, and, moreover, to invade all other beings, to be others without ceasing to be itself, to extend its limits to the infinite, but without breaking them". In effect, we do not want to cease 'to be human'—we don't want to be a God in the flesh like Jesus Christ or Lord Krishna—but want to extend the limits of the infinite, and become a god. Desire, as the Buddha said, is the source and cause of suffering. We already have a multitude of desires that cause so much suffering.

And we, as Adam Curtis says, "have become the slaves of our own desires".[52] God only knows if this desire is a delusion, and what it will do to us. How and why did it arise in the first place? Is it an external implant, a sinister and satanic plot, or is it part of evolutionary dynamism gone astray? 'Being like Him', as the Bible says, or, 'For is He not all but thou', as Tennyson says (*The Higher Pantheism*), or, '*Aham brahmasmi*—I am God', as the Upanishads say, has always been man's spiritual aspiration. Or, in the words of Aldous Huxley, "All is in all—that All is actually each" (*The Doors of Perception*, 1954). The theory of evolution, in saying that we all came from the same original source, rose from molecule to man, is saying the same. The fundamental difference between that 'aspiration' and what science is aspiring to do, is that the first one was a '*to be*'—a state, a condition, something which continues unchanged through time, whereas the second is '*to become*'—an event, a transformation, a metanoia, a *change* of state. 'Being like Him' is like 'being' a tiger, which is very different from *becoming* a tiger. In seeking divine status, it is really the perks that matter, not the position. What is ironic is that those very people who deny divine existence or say that He is dated, if not dead, are those who want to make man a god. Mystics, saints, rishis, and shamans throughout our troubled history have named our struggle as humans in different ways—but they all pointed to the need for us to consciously grow into our divine potential. As God within, it is, in reality He who is experiencing through them what they experience in life, both pleasure and pain, good and bad. What modern man is truly seeking is not the goodness of god, but His divine powers and perks.

God or no god, the fact is that man has always felt shackled and humiliated by his animal roots—Descartes called animals 'soulless automata'—and by his innate impermanence and imperfections. 'Being a god' is shorthand to become free from these two limitations. Some, like the great Indian yogi Sri Aurobindo, say that perfection and imperfection are the same truth seen from two sides. Some say that we are, in a sense, a species with 'perfection pending', which includes moral perfection. There could be a sinless man but not a perfect man, save perhaps a full and direct divine incarnation. Even Jesus, as perfect a man as could possibly be, before his crucifixion, said "… on the third day I shall be perfected".[53] What we want is physical permanence and bodily perfection. Many people, particularly the young, are suffering and dying under the thrall and torture of the phantasmic self they're failing to become. Our obsession with body-perfection is a travesty of the spiritual path. In fact, the *Advaita Vedanta* school of Hindu philosophy says that there is no need to try to attain anything, even perfection; each of us already *is* God. The famous Upanishadic aphorisms, *Aham brahmasmi* (I am God) and *Tat tvam asi* (You are God), are clear indications of how, at the highest level, we have viewed ourselves in our earthly existence. The Bible too has several passages that humans can become like gods. Some Christians (Latter-Day Saints) believe that our earthly experience is to progress towards perfection and ultimately realize our divine destiny. Yoga, or union or oneness with God, is in spirit the effect of attaining the loftiest layer of consciousness. Hailed as the oldest scripture, the *Rig Veda* proclaims, *Prajnanam brahma*—'consciousness *is* God'. God himself, in Hinduism, has been called *Sat-chit-ananda*, or 'existence-consciousness-bliss'. Each one of us, as souls, are individualized *Sat-chit-ananda*, according to Paramahansa Yogananda. The word *chit* is also interpreted as sentience, and *Atman* as sentient life energy.

Contrary to what Aleksandr Solzhenitsyn said, men have not forgotten God. On the other hand, in a weird way, God is all there is in the human mind. For the devout, He is the only hope, the only one that stands between them and despair and death, the only balm for their wounded hearts. For the secular and scientific, their aspiration and ambition is to erase the boundary between man and god. It is not only godly powers that we now covet; we have come to conclude that only by becoming a god can we solve all our problems. In fact, some say it is inevitable and irreversible and, even more, that it is the only way the human can reach his full potential. In short, they say divinity is our destiny, and fulfilling it is not defiance of nature but a service to its intent. But divinity is in each of us. There is nothing wrong with man wanting to actualize, or realize, God as *Sat-chit-ananda*, that is, 'truth-existence-consciousness-bliss'. What is wrong is acquiring such powers without 'becoming the being', without consciousness-change, or some kind of a rebooting, if you will. What science is tempting us with, some say, is what Satan told Adam and Eve: if they would just follow the 'promise' that Satan offered they could be 'like gods.'

To be fair, we are not that 'bad'; we don't mean to sit on his heavenly throne; 'god' is really a nickname, or code-word for want of something more accurate, for something we want to be. We don't want to be a god that appears and disappears, makes lightning or triggers typhoons, answers prayers or gives boons. We don't want to attain, much less maintain, a state of godly bliss, sanctity, and purity. For we might say, and even believe that man is a spiritual being having a human experience, but we cannot live without sin! For long we have had an idiomatic expression for those who hold our fate in their hands, gods, and that is now who we yearn to become. For instance, the ancient Hermetic discourse called *The Key* says, "We must dare to say that the human on earth is a mortal god, but that god in heaven is an immortal human". What we have set out to do is to bend fate and mend man into an immortal earthly god. Not only that, like the 'heavenly' gods, we too don't want to be accountable for our actions and misdeeds! But the 'being' we want to turn into, let us be clear, thank God, is not God; not the all-pervasive, all-knowing Supreme Being, the *Paramatman*, as He is called in Hinduism, or *Allah* in Islam or *Jehovah* in Judaism. But then, when scriptures and saints and mystics strive towards dissolving into divinity or union with God, they precisely mean that very Supreme Being. Furthermore, it is a state of consciousness when one loses all sense of the personal self, when there is no longer any *aham* or ego. It is the *aham* that leads to *ahamkara* (arrogance) and to *agraham* (anger). That is why, it has been said by yogis that 'God equals man minus ego'. Vedanta says that ego is the main culprit responsible for endless self-centered thoughts, and the root cause of pain and suffering.

Ego, or ego-consciousness, is that which drives our material life and makes us opaque to each other. It is both a necessity for survival and a barrier to *moksha*, liberation. It is the core of our identity. Spiritual *sadhana*, what Vedic rishis of India and Christian mystics and Sufi saints have strived to, is to dissolve the limiting human self into the infinite divine Self. True to our times, we have both trivialized and technicized this spiritual process. What science is planning to do is to replace the divine by blending man and machine—which some call a *satanical* machine, and some others, a *spiritual* machine—to attain the attributes of gods or angels. Essentially it means that having, as we falsely think, transcended the natural world we now aim to transcend the biological world and become a kind of transhuman-'god', somewhat similar to what Dante experienced as he entered into the sphere of the heaven, called 'transhuman-change'. Another analogy that comes to mind is Goethe's *Faust*, who feeling like a 'wretched fool' and no 'wiser than before' tried to transcend human knowledge in order to gain divine knowledge. Transhumanists expect that artificial intelligence, the advent of cyborgs, and uploading people's minds into software will converge to make the transition. Then, what do we 'become' and what will be our faith? The new 'religion' rooted in artificial intelligence is called the *Way of the Future* (WOTF), whose aim is 'the realization, acceptance, and worship of a godhead based on artificial intelligence'. And yet not cease to be man. Avaricious that we are, we don't want to give up anything we have, including all that is distasteful about us. We want to be 'smart' but still, when we choose, we stay stupid; we want to be super strong but still feel the prick. We don't mind becoming a 'silicon body', but not hold back on sex.

The model that roughly resembles what we seek is that of the Greek gods, or of the *devas* of Hinduism. What attracts us is that not only do they live forever but also suffer from some of the same flaws and desires as humans, like anger, avarice, favoritism, and jealousy, and are even able to have sex, licit and illicit. 'Gods', like us, regularly fight amongst each other and engage in petty bickering and senseless quarrels. But it is not all that novel or inventive. In fact, in our prehistoric times, the chasm between man and gods was narrow; they used to routinely talk and walk with gods. Indeed we want to do better; to acquire their traits, but with a twist. Gods are immortal; they, whether they like it or not, cannot die. We want to keep death as a choice and be able to bring the 'dead' back to life, or perhaps become the 'walking dead'. It is driven by greed, our penchant to always 'have-it-all'. We must remember that what we think we lack or view as limitations are parts of the cosmic puzzle. Different species have different lengths of life for reasons we may not know. If one species alters its life span artificially or unilaterally, then the finely tuned balance in creation and nature's design strategy that optimizes life support while minimizing the expenditure of energy, will go horribly wrong. Even imagine if dogs have the same life span as humans. Perhaps the world would be a better place but that is not possible! So is it not possible for man to literally 'become' a god or any other species. What we should aim to do is to be a 'humane-human', not transhuman. We should strive to become more whole, more holy. We must also bear in mind that every species, however minuscule or mighty, has a niche in nature. That this is particularly true in regard to biodiversity is brought home by the new finding that the world's lowly insects are hurtling down the path of extinction which, in turn, 'threatens the collapse of nature', and that to arrest it, we will need to change our ways of producing food. Furthermore, even if science has its way and *Homo sapiens* does become *Homo Deus*, it still does not mean that we will all, one fine morning, wake up as gods or that everyone born hereafter, in the lab or from the womb, will be born with the body of a god. Scientific godhood, like safaris in space, will benefit only a fraction of humanity. We are poised at a critical moment when, once again, science is unleashing its prodigious creativity without adequate engagement and careful thought. And even if we become 'gods', many may still look up to the only 'God' they are accustomed to worshipping. In the human mind, there is no contradiction between becoming a god and believing in God. As Albert Camus said, "Nothing can discourage the appetite for divinity in the heart of man". But it is also good to remember that, as Emanuel Swedenborg reminded us, "a life of kindness is the primary meaning of divine worship" (*New Jerusalem and Its Heavenly Doctrine*, 1758). In other words, we can become 'god' by being good to fellow-humans. This is what is implied in the Hindu aphorism '*Maanava seve madhava seva*', meaning service to man is service to God. It means, 'you will use your life in service; you will be in service to life'.

In the Melting Pot of Life and Death

Science is trying to hijack God, render Him redundant by taking control of the two things He had absolute hold over and we had none: birth and death. It has been, from the very beginning, that 'giving birth' is tantamount to being 'given to death'. That is what modern man is intent on changing. We might, we are told, soon be able to make life from scratch, even dispense with the male to make a baby, and eventually even bring the dead back to life, at the least, keep death at bay. We can design babies and delay, possibly even defy death. The line between life and death is getting blurred, throwing into question long-standing assumptions about what makes a sentient being alive, and we hear terms unthinkable a few years before such as being a 'little less dead'. Such a prodigious ability has led to a seminal turn of events at the deepest depths of human consciousness. As a result, the way issues and choices related to life and death are processed, assessed, analyzed, valued, and judged has radically mutated in the human mind. It has given rise to a key question: for anyone who chooses not to die, is more life necessarily better? Is existence a sufficient reason for continued existence? And what could be the reasons or causes sufficient for man wanting to continue to live infinitely? Most of all we need to bring ourselves to face the wrenching question: Has the modern human way of living itself become, on the whole, an irreversible, 'unnecessary evil' on earth? And if so, what is our duty as a self-avowed moral being? Man always wants to know what else there is on the menu. A principal reason why we want immortality is because mortality is not a choice; had it been so we might even want to choose death. In fact, that is what is happening: death, even if involuntary, is becoming an alternative to life. If man attains 'immortality', all deaths for whatever reason, will become 'premature'. All the turmoil and tragedies, slaughter and shootings, massacres and madness, callousness and cruelty we witness and that cause us so much distress and dismay, is but an outward manifestation of what someone called 'mental diarrhea'. Another, possible fallout we must take serious note of is the social impact of immortality or of an exponentially lengthened life span. Eternity is expensive, and so is dying with dignity these days.

We do not notice it, but a major stabilizing and soothing factor in human society is our belief that, sometime or the other, before us or after us, everyone in the end bites the dust—president or philosopher or plumber, powerful or powerless, rich or poor, celebrity or common folk, friend or foe, spouse or stranger. That 'reassurance' is what lets us endure and wait. That knowledge keeps a lid on resentment, indignation, anger and rage; we tell ourselves 'so what; he too will pass and meet the same fate; my misery is as impermanent as his success'. If the underclass, oppressed, and exploited, even sections of the middle class truly come to lose faith in death as the great leveler, then there is no knowing what might befall; we have never had such a situation or experience before and therefore even our imagination will fall short. Whether or not gods envy us our mortality, mortality has a huge place in maintaining order and stability in human society and in containing the darker drives inside us. We would do well to keep this in mind while plowing in tons of money into research on immortality—at the expense of other problems of greater priority, problems pertinent to what Manuel Castells called 'the fourth world', which includes sub-populations that are socially and technologically excluded from the global society. In the modern world, individual decisions on how we, particularly the wealthy, use money, do matter, because an extremely wealthy man by the very way he lives, works and plays and has fun, could impact on other lives, could help or hurt a lot of other people. We must also not forget that the actual, at least for sometime, beneficiaries of related research will again be the very plutocracy—the club of the really rich—which runs the modern state. Life used to be seen as a gift. Now it is being demanded as a right... Life is now no different from what we create on a factory assembly line. Contemporary society creates fake wants, which integrate individuals into the existing system of production and consumption via mass media, advertising, and marketing. We live in twisted times when our collective creativity focuses on creating and satiating *wants* more than fulfilling essential *needs* of human existence. Pop star Robyn's lyric "*No, you're not gonna get what you need. But baby, I have what you want*",[54] pretty well sums up what is wrong with modern culture. A stage has come now to rethink what we 'deserve to desire' and whether we are 'worthy of our wants'. A few can get whatever their worldly *wants* are—cozy comforts, slick gadgets, exotic yachts, instant entertainment, salacious titillation—but a huge chunk of humanity lives deprived of basic human *needs*—clean air, potable water, safe food, stable shelter, sanitation. What is worse is that many of us also think that our aim ought to be to empower the 'have-nots' to get the same luxuries; indeed that is what they want. We do not think their very making is immoral, that it entails the misuse of non-renewable resources which could be used to fulfill more 'basic needs'.

Our thirst for wealth is such that we don't care how we get it. We condone evil so much we don't care if we are the casualty. And yet, life has become so meaningless and frightening even for those whose 'basic needs' are more than met, that 'right to life' is now beginning to be viewed as inherent in the 'right to die', and death is being seen not as the end of life but end of pain. It is being argued that just as people have the right to live with dignity, they also have the right to die with dignity. The huge gap between 'right to die' and 'right to kill' is also narrowing, and many are beginning to see killing as a remedy, another available option. We already implicitly exercise this 'right' through abortion. Abortion takes place when parents or partners decide that bringing into life another human being does not suit their interests; instead, it creates another life-long inconvenience or problem and therefore they have the 'right to kill', or, as it were, nip it in the bud. Many now want to extend that 'right' from the womb to the world, arguing that what is moral inside cannot be moral outside. This is not a case for or against abortion; it is to highlight the fact that norms and values around issues of life and death are seismically changing. Genetic engineering, nanotechnology, robotics, computer technology and artificial intelligence might, in the not-too-distant future, enable humans to create or redesign life and produce offspring 'suitable to our taste'... Recent scientific advances from genomics to assisted reproduction have brought us to a stage when a tongue-in-cheek kind of billboard advertisement like "before you drop your beans check your genes' is not so flippant or out of context. And as a *de facto* 'god', we hope we will be unshackled from God's confining commandments and moral restraints. These are meant for those scriptural humans, not for the synthetic humans, or even to humans of the millennial milieu. Nothing happens in a cultural vacuum. And that, in turn, will generate new moral issues and dilemmas such as: How do we ensure equity in an era when intelligence can be decided by gene editing, and wealthy parents can 'customize' their offspring?

Earlier the classic moral dilemma was whether it was ethically correct to kill one to save several. Now the dilemma centers not around 'saving lives' but how many *other* lives are worth wasting to kill a wanted man. Even at the personal level, the imperative is shifting. Many feel no moral qualms to pass by a critically wounded person to be on time to keep a date, and equally in using killing to make a living or to get an exam postponed or to get something you need badly like an iPhone. What is happening at a deeper level of our consciousness is that while we still dread natural death, murder is a blockbuster source of entertainment. Our fascination stems from a desire to experience crime vicariously. What is happening at a deeper level of our consciousness is that while we still dread natural death, killing is losing its stigma and odium. If not yet stylish, it is becoming simply another lifestyle choice. The unimaginable becomes casual, the hideous becomes tedious, and the unbearable becomes ordinary. It is a seismic shift in our mindset, far reaching and utterly unnerving in its implications.

We live at a time when there is a broad consensus that, as human beings, all of us have certain basic innate and inalienable rights. One such right is the 'right to life'. As enshrined in Article 3 of the Universal Declaration of Human Rights, it means the right to life, liberty, and security of a person. There is a subtle shift to extend the reach of that right to include life without pain. Ending pain has long been the dream of man and medicine. But it is only now that it is being extended to death. For, what can be more painful than death? Assisted death is now legally permitted in some parts of the world on the premise that a humane society has an obligation to assist a human suffering from incurable and intolerable pain. Even with no particular pain whatsoever, there are some who still want to die. For them, this modern life—of coarseness, consumerism, shallowness, cynicism, loneliness, despair, decadence, meaninglessness—is the incurable disease, and death the only logical cure. Many have come to agree with Mary Shelley's words, "Let us leave 'life', that we may live" (*The Last Man*, 1826). In the face of all this pain and misery, we call ourselves lords of creation and masters of life and death. Some philosophers like Bernard Williams are arguing that endless life would have nothing in it, that it would propel the immortal forward into a future that would inevitably be beset with insufferable boredom. When asked, "What do you do from morning to night?" Emil Cioran replies "I endure myself" (*The Trouble with Being Born*, 1973). The 'disease' we have to cure is our corrupted consciousness, and the cure is cathartic cleansing. But then, what is tolerable to some is intolerable to others, and some stretch it to include the pain of living itself and suffering of any kind. One can ask: 'Pain is personal; why should I become a patient to end my pain and my life the way I wish it?' And in the minds of some who want to end their lives for whatever reason, that 'right' entitles them to choose 'assisted dying' to solitary suicide. After all, they argue, how we support the dying is central to who we are as human beings. Some 'pro-choice' people see this as a logical extension of freewill and individual autonomy over their bodies. It is a huge change from the scriptural injunction that life is God-given and you had no choice in your birth, and therefore should have no choice on how and when it has to end. It is medical technology that has empowered man to combine two of our long-standing goals—life without pain and death with dignity. And it is entirely consistent with our overall approach to life: choosing the path of the pleasant, rather than choosing the path of the good.

What we should also note at this juncture is that even as science is strenuously seeking the elixir of youth and eternal life, the rage and range of violence in contemporary human life has made man more lethal than ever before. Murder and fratricide have been around at least since Biblical times. Man has always killed another man for a range of reasons like greed, gain, jealousy, malice, and profit. But never was the trigger as trivial and casual as it is now. The revulsion and horror attached to killing is on the wane. Killing, under certain conditions, not only in war but in civil life too, is getting the legal imprimatur. A new human right is the 'right to die'. Some are even saying that if death in itself is not bad, how can killing be any different. There are many who, in the words of Thomas Ligotti, "despise the conspiracy of Lies for Life almost as much as they despise themselves for being a party to it" (*The Conspiracy Against the Human Race*, 2011), and for them death is the only refuge. Taking one's life is no laughing matter; nor does it give sleepless nights. Killing is no longer a novelty; every day, we are exposed to a media mélange of murders in graphic detail. There is virtually no one and no cause or circumstance that is impervious to murder. Anyone can now be a Cain (the first son of Adam and Eve), who disowned his responsibility, justified it with his existential pain and fear, and became a callous, corrupt, and murderous savage. But, by the same token, anyone, even if gentle, good and god-fearing, can end up as an Abel (Cain's brother), a suitable candidate for killing. Physical elimination is fast becoming the preferred mode of problem-solving, and technology is coming in handy for the deranged and distraught human mind. How any 'success', however dubious it might be, in the search for immortality would affect the murderous human mind, is hard to tell. But it only further underlines the need for a cathartic consciousness cleansing and change. Only such a change will motivate the 'immortal' man to be moral in leading his life forever.

What technology is doing to death is in line with what it does to life. Today's technology has changed us in many ways. One that is little noticed is its ability to make what is bad appear good, and turn the ugly into the beautiful. Whatever technology is doing to us and however easily we surrender to its wiles, in our hearts we still want to be moral, to do good and to avoid bad. In our personal lives, we all try to lead a moral life and make moral choices, but most fail to measure up. We adopt norms, codes and laws to keep us on the moral track as a way to maintain social order, but again they are found wanting. Even as this struggle goes on, new moral issues have cropped up. Our very existence has become a moral matter. More often than not, our actions seem to hurt and injure others even as we wish to do good. The reality is that whether we like or dislike each other, the 'us' and 'them' are still there in the human world. We all have to live with "the sin of being another being", in Simone de Beauvoir's words (*The Blood of Others*, 1945). It is because we view other beings as separate and different that we hurt each other in multiple ways. Prophet Muhammad said, "The best among you is the one who doesn't harm others with his tongue and hands". And between the two, the tongue is more cutting. The Ecclesiasticus says: "Many have fallen by the edge of the sword: but not so many as have fallen by the tongue". More fundamentally, it all comes down to our perception of ourselves in relation to fellow humans. It is our distorted perception that is the bottleneck. As William Blake says, "If the doors of perception were cleansed, everything would appear to man as it is—infinite" (*The Marriage of Heaven and Hell*, 1790). Once, when the great Hindu Advaitic sage Ramana Maharshi was asked, 'How should we treat others?'; he replied, 'There are no others'. In our highly comparative and competitive lives, the whole world is nothing but 'others': what others think of us, how to outsmart others; how to be richer than our neighbors, how to achieve relative advantage over our peers and compatriots, etc. Only highly evolved souls can blur the border between 'us' and 'others'. For the rest of us in the end, how we treat those who can do nothing to us becomes the test of our timbre, and not hurting those who cannot hurt us is the most basic of all virtues. The only permissible 'comparison' and 'competition' are with our own selves; who we are, 'compared' to who we were yesterday. Has what we have done today made the world any better than what we did yesterday? That is the only 'competition'.

It is telling but true that despite the estimated 108 billion members of our species who have ever been born and died,[55] we really do not know what both life and death are in their essence. A cynic might say that these are mutually exclusive, you are not dead when you are alive, and not alive when you are dead, so what is the big deal. The 'big deal' now is that the sense of solace is démodé. Man has never been more ill at ease being human than now; and never more hubristic about his capacity than now. He still may not know what 'life' truly is or isn't but he can 'create' life. In the world of the 21st century, the sheer weight of living has become such a crushing burden that life itself is being viewed as an irritating interlude between 'dying' and 'death'; there is no life nor are we 'living'. We have come to such a 'deathly' pass that we seem to need pessimistic philosophers like Thomas Ligotti to reassure us that 'being alive is alright'. Optimism, which

Milan Kundera (*The Joke*, 1967) called the 'opium of the people', has become oppressive. Not fully mollified, we seek reasons to live for, instead of looking for something we are willing to die for. Paradoxically, we constantly look for triggers to kill each other all the time, even killing for killing's sake, and yet we desperately desire *deathlessness*. Indeed, even the doubling or tripling of the human life span has become an intra-generational ethical issue. As someone put it, in our money-is-all-that-matters culture, the care of grandparents constitutes an 'absolute waste of the grandchildren's college money'. We live in a throwaway age, and now human life itself is seen as just another disposable good, and its termination, as a way to overcome life's problems. Now, nothing is inconceivable as a cause or trigger for killing. In a grisly way, typical to our times we are combining two words which are antithetical to each other to describe a horrific event, murder for revenge and call it 'honor killing'; a calculated murder to avenge or redeem the 'honor'—of the family, caste, ethnicity, country, religion. It is becoming more and more difficult to decide how to characterize a killing (banal or bizarre?) or how to apportion blame and empathy between the villain and the victim. How does one, for example, categorize a killing of a schoolmate to get a dreaded examination postponed? Truth is stranger than fiction, but this is exactly what happened in a high school in northern India, in late 2017. The young killer's intention was casual, but his deed was diabolic. Or, take the case of suicides by Japanese schoolchildren towards the end of summer recess, as a way to escape the ragging, bullying, and brutal school regimen. Here again, their desire to escape the pain and humiliation is understandable; but their choice of the means is a defining indictment of the world of their parents. So is murder-for-fame—committing mass murder so that 'when they spill a little blood, the whole world knows who you are'. In their own twisted minds, they are seeking, and getting, 'fame' and 'immortality' which we all seek in different ways. There will always be killings because that is a part of being human, but making a killer a celebrity is an open invitation for more mass killing.

Today, the human mind is the most murderous weapon, and the human psyche, as David Buss posits, has evolved specialized adaptations whose function is to kill. In today's dangerously deranged and destructive world, each of us is most at risk, both of being murdered and of *becoming* a murderer. One study says that "91 percent of men and 84 percent of women have had at least one vivid fantasy about killing someone".[56] Someone who we thought will die for us suddenly becomes our killer, and the deadliest incentive for cold-blooded murder is none other than the most sublime of all human emotions, love, whether it is a mother's love or a lover's love. Shocking but true, some wronged mothers are coming close to resembling *Medea* of Greek mythology—the woman who kills her own children, the 'offspring of her own womb', as a way to punish her husband Jason. In her words, she does it to 'vex his heart', for his betrayal, and says, in this play of Euripides, "Needs must they die in any case; and since they must, I will slay them—I, the mother". If murder seems advantageous, we go for it, regardless of who the person is, and what our relationship with that person is. David Buss says, "The real mystery is not why killing has been so prevalent over our evolutionary history, but why killing has not been more prevalent". That mystery is on the way to be solved. Suicides and homicides are becoming contagious pandemics.

Coming Soon—'Machines-Better-Than-Me'

Man is more murderous than ever before, but that has not halted his age-old aspiration to acquire godly powers. At the very core of our divine ambitions, indeed its very *raison d'être*, is life forever and eternal youth. Despite the billions that have died and despite the failure of all attempts to evade death, we have never reconciled ourselves to what the *Book of Common Prayer* says is our doomed lot: 'Earth to earth, ashes to ashes, dust to dust'. We want to become invincible, a kind of cyborg with a metal exoskeleton over our biological meat sack—and live forever on earth. Like much else in the realm of human aspiration and its aftermath, we could end up not as cyborgs, but as the cybernetic *Cylons* in *Battlestar Galactica*.[57] In the TV series, this android race was originally created to serve human needs (much like our machines), where the transfer of human consciousness into a Cylon's neural network leads to the evolution of sentient, self-aware beings (the Cylons), who are capable of interacting with and having intimate relationships with humans.[58] Ironically, the Cylon himself was not happy being a machine. He lamented, "I'm a machine, and I can know much more, I could experience so much more, but I'm trapped in this absurd body". Some fear that such creations might run amok, but others hope that such machines would be docile enough to tell us how to keep it under control. There is heady talk that we and our technological creations are poised to embark on what is sure to be a strange, exciting evolutionary path. According to these so-called 'prophets of pending paradise', humans will soon be able to farm the oceans, travel in starships, and reside in both lunar and Martian colonies. That is, if we get to survive emergent existential threats like climate change, our own self-destructive behavior, and if nanotech, artificial general intelligence, and robotization do not run amok. In fact, if there is any ET 'up there' observing what is going on down below on earth, the metaphor that would spring to its mind could be moths racing to a raging inferno, or Disney-style lemmings jumping off the seaside cliffs. By the year 2025, robots and machines driven by artificial intelligence are predicted to perform half of all productive functions in our workplaces, which, some fear, might trigger what is being termed a 'job' apocalypse, a social and economic tsunami resulting from automation. Several years ago, an informal group of experts at the Global Catastrophic Risk Conference (Oxford, UK) suggested that there is a 19% chance of human extinction before 2100. One wonders: why are all these dire threats coming up at this time? Is there a 'conspiracy against the human race'?[59] If there is a conspiracy; what is it about and who are the conspirators and why? We can only speculate. Like in a murder case we should ask, 'Who benefits?' Could it be the gods or nature? Gods have a reason, given our attempt to be like them and to usurp immortality. Nature too has a reason, because we are tearing ourselves away from it, and turning on it. Both have reason to believe that we are becoming reckless and too big for our boots, and that we must be put in our assigned spot in the cosmic order. And what better way could there be but to make man the enemy of man, and self-harm and self-destruction the *modus operandi* for our default mode of behavior?

We don't know which method they might choose, or maybe the actual danger might come from somewhere or something else, an unknowable unknown or something so well known that we overlook it. But the existential risks are real, and the way to avert the danger is *not* to turn tail and run away or turn the Nelson's eye. Whatever may be the nature of the existential crisis, the bitter truth is that in their day-to-day lives, many people are more worried about the problems created by the most obvious solution to the crisis than by the threat itself. The name of the game, the long and short of it is this: with the kind of mental attitude it habitually manifests, if the human species becomes immortal and interplanetary, it will then become a mortal peril to life in general in the cosmos. Unless, of course, that species can acquire a 'planetary brain', a 'global soul', or even, in the vocabulary of the war within, a cathartic 'consciousness-change'. Let alone a 'planetary brain', we don't even use our 'whole-brain'; we rely almost wholly on the left-brain repertoire. Recent neurological findings, according to David O'Leary,[60] tell us that 'without the contextual resources of the right hemisphere, the calculating, instrumental mind can nonetheless function as an irresponsible automaton'. That precisely is what we will become through our impending merger with the machine. We may berate our behavior for all and sundry of our ills, but the fatal flaw in our approach to resolve any of our daunting problems is that we really don't want to change, while believing that *everything else* must change. We don't want to change because it requires us to step out of the cocoon of our comfort zone, and that means risking our whole world turning topsy-turvy. For instance, it is hard to tell if we are 'willfully blind' or 'dangerously dumb', or if we are driven by a death-wish not to realize that the climate crisis is deadly serious and potentially putting human civilization in clear and escalating peril. Underscoring the gravity of the crisis, a new study says it could be similar to the mass extinction that happened 252 million years ago. And yet, our efforts so far, as someone said, are 'like an effort to put out a house fire with a water pistol'. We will keep on hoping, Micawber-like, for miracles or 'deified markets' or magical technologies to deliver us from disaster. We cannot be shaken out of paralyzing passivity in the face of moral precariousness by our conscience. Because, as Pope John Paul said, the fact is that conscience itself is finding it increasingly difficult to distinguish between good and evil in what concerns the basic value of human life.[61] That is because on the one hand, the boundary between good and evil is getting blurred and, on the other hand, the two are the principal foes in the war within. What we need now is to transcend both conscience and the very source of thinking. In the words of Stephen Talbott, "Man is he who knows and transforms himself—and the world—from within."[62] Many thoughtful observers say that a radical transformation and rise to a new level of consciousness is the only way to reverse the moral decline brought about by the delusionary dominance of man's materialistic mindset. Rather than treading such a measured path, modern man has chosen technology as the means—and machine as the model and ideal—to achieve this aspiration. But that is due to our ignorance, or inadequate appreciation of what we ourselves are made of, and what nature has equipped us with. We are wholly innocent that 'in our own being we are enough', and that, in order to travel on the spiritual path, we only require learning how to embrace our inner buzz and harness our inner strength.

The 'inner buzz', is "our personal idiom of experiencing our bodies, other people, the animate and inanimate world: imagination, dreams, phantasy, and beyond that to ever further reaches of experience".[63] For it is possible to be a well-fed man on the outside, but an impoverished infant on the inside. To nourish the 'infant' requires what spiritual seekers call 'inner work', diving deep into our inner self, a motley mix of our hidden feelings, memories, thoughts, beliefs, prejudices, wounds, and shadows. Without it, there can be no purging, no self-emptying, and no cleansing, healing, or true transformation. That kind of work horrifies us, and looking for easy options, our mind chooses the primrose path of merger with the machine.

Our intimacy with the machine is predicated by a huge hope—that the machine, even after being made smarter than man, will stay fair and loyal to him, as it is *his* creation, a kind of loyalty man himself seldom shows. The fact remains that man and, in Stephen Talbott's phrase, his 'mechanical offspring',[64] are bound together in an increasingly tight embrace. Yet, we have never been able to, in whatever we do as a trade-off, 'guarantee our sense of the human', to borrow the words of Teju Cole.[65] Man has always turned to technology for help when needed. The dark side of technology is also emerging into public view. A stark example is reports of recent research concerning implanted heart pacemakers. It is said that by tinkering with the software it is now possible to remotely alter the functioning of these devices using a mobile phone, possibly inducing instant death. It means that the specter of personal grudges translating into seemingly 'perfect' remote killings is no longer the stuff of fiction. Modern technology can make everything possible: make the false true and the unreal real. It at once empowers our capability and enfeebles our capacity. It enables us to cross over from the human realm, but erodes the core of being human. We turn to technology so much for our day-to-day living, to perform such ordinary tasks, that some, like Charlie Brooker,[66] fear that there will be very little room for free will—our flawed but still important decision-making capacity—that is a big part of being human. We are also at the same time trying to augment our dysfunctional capability by harnessing 'intelligence' external to us, like artificial general intelligence (AGI), virtually handing it over to the machines. In addition, our 'decision-making' ability has got greatly compromised by our exposure to media and propaganda designed solely to short-circuit our better judgment. We now have to factor in more people and considerations into our 'decision-making' than ever before, and our brains seem ill-prepared for that. Some fear that when singularity comes, AGI-powered beings might well, like in the Netflix show *Altered Carbon*, conclude that humans 'are not like us… they are a lesser form of life'. In that event, *they*, not us, will be at the helm. We must remember that, as Ian McEwan says, "if a machine seems like a human or you can't tell the difference, then you'd jolly well better start thinking about whether it has responsibilities and rights and all the rest" (*Machines Like Me*, 2019). We must also factor in another aspect. We think of artificial intelligence (AI) as external only because it is not internal. But that is not true. In practical terms, AI is another version of human intelligence, because it is created by humans and they can only create what their intelligence is capable of. Although we think AI is incorruptible, the reality is that AI systems might well result in replicating the biases ingrained in human judgements, rather than aborting them. Supposedly 'neutral' machine-made decisions often end up augmenting existing social inequalities. Like about everything else, experts disagree on the potential impact of AI. Some say it could usher in a peaceful, prosperous world, and help solve our daunting issues. Some like Stephen Hawking have said that it could eventually lead to our extinction. We now have more information, if not knowledge, and choices, than ever earlier, but our brain-damaged intelligence and skills seem hopelessly out of their depth to arrive at informed and enlightened decision-making. The bedrock of modernity is the epistemic line of thought that views the use of pure reason as the foundation of truth, and as the sole measure and means for uncovering reality. In reality though, our brain fights our attempts to be 'really rational' at every turn. It has a tendency to see what it wants to see, or listen to what it wants to hear, rather than what is really there. It hates being wrong so much, in fact, that it will adjust our memories to make us right in retrospect.[67] Not only that, our brain's ability to meet our needs, according to philosopher Bertrand Russell, could get worse. In this view, "we must expect, at any rate for the next hundred years, that each generation will be congenitally stupider that its predecessor".[68]

The essential point is not whether machines will be benevolent or turn malevolent; it is that even if they do remain 'loyal' to their creator, human malevolence could get a huge boost from 'merging' with AI-driven machines. To prevent that from happening, what we need to do is not go back to the pre-Industrial Age; we need to change the human mindset. We need not stop all research on AI; we have to 'demilitarize' it, and channel it towards the needs of the impoverished and the disempowered. Clearly we do need to do something radical and drastic. The trouble is that instead of marshaling the other sources of inherent intelligence like heart-based intuitive intelligence—which some call our spiritual wisdom and the gut instinct; or the third heart or primal wisdom—we are trying to mobilize alien intelligences. Cutting-edge research on the human heart has shown that the heart is also an independent source of intelligence, that it has its own nervous system and actually sends more information to the brain than the brain sends to the heart. Even more startling is the finding that the heart's electromagnetic field is thousands of times more powerful than that of the brain. This is, in fact, scientific validation of age-old insights. More than two millenniums ago, Aristotle believed in a 'cardiocentric' model of human anatomy, where the heart was the true center of human intelligence and not the brain. Joseph Murphy writes, "Within your subconscious depths lie infinite wisdom, infinite power, and infinite supply of all that is necessary, which is waiting for development and expression" (*The Power of Your Subconscious Mind*, 1963). Contrary to what we assume, everything we think is external, is also, in its deepest sense, internal. It is brain power that science is focusing on to achieve its ambitious agenda. One report says attempts are being made to develop technologies that bridge the gap between computers and the brains of humans and animals. Another report says a project is in the offing "to build conscious robots using insect brains". The concern and disquiet is about not just what robots might do to us, but what we might do to them, not to speak of what they might do to us because of what we already do to one another. Excessive reliance on artificial intelligence to save us or help us to evolve could be an invitation for 'double-jeopardy'—we will be relying on that which we think has been found wanting and, in addition, run the risk of, in the so-called Tech

Mogul and futurist Elon Musk's phrase, summoning the 'demon', or the dragon within. The conundrum is that the problems we want to address are brain-made, the intelligences we mobilize, internally and externally, are brain-based, and the decisions that intelligence arrives at cannot be any better. What science should be focusing on is how to activate or awaken the other two 'brains' or sources of intelligence—the heart and the gut, to bring to bear on our daily life.

The Way Forward is the Way Inward

At a practical level, we have to strive to practice empathy and compassion—the capacity to share, understand, and care about what others feel—in our everyday lives, as a part of bringing about contextual-change. The world we have built is poorly suffused with the caring and sharing instincts that allowed us to build it in the first place. It is these instincts that saved us when survival was at stake, and now, we need them once again when our very survival is under serious threat. But all is not lost; these are not frozen traits—something we are born with or not—but rather skills, as recent research reveals, that we can all augment through effort. It is also not automatic and entails making a choice to engage with others' emotions. And our choice about choosing empathy, not staying away from other's suffering, in turn, is not a 'free choice'; it depends on the state of the war within. If kindred forces call the shots, we choose 'empathy', and if not, we avoid it. Everything in life is 'contextual'. To truly understand something requires attention to its context. We must be clear about how, through our own lives, we can contribute to the change of the 'right kind'. There is no magic wand, no supreme effort, nor a single titanic thing to do or not do, to trigger empathetic contextual-change. Every day, we do multiple things and all those trillions done by billions add up as context. And it all boils down to how we view, treat, and interact with another human being, because there is always another person involved whatever and wherever we do anything, at home, on the street, at office, at play or while having fun or making money. Everything is interpersonal: the good or bad we do, the help we render and the hurt we inflict. In life, many things we do are a must and some are optional, but everything we do, it is possible to do it differently; what the French call *nostalgie de la boue*, to live a simpler, downsized, or less indulgent life. For, with everything we do we have a choice—to do it callously or kindly, maliciously or magnanimously, helpfully or humiliatingly, insensitively or compassionately. Even when hurting another person is unavoidable, it can still be done in a manner that minimizes the hurt and harm. According to the theory of karma, we have no control over what happens in our lives, but we have choices about how we react, and how we react is what creates new karma, which can be either good or bad karma. If we react with consideration, compassion and sensitivity, and try to see the situation from the other person's viewpoint, good karma will be generated, and if not, the bad. In other words, every day we make our own future. We must also remember that everything in life is a habit, and it can be cultivated and nourished and nurtured through what we do. That is why childhood and adolescence are so important, to make sharing, kindness, and compassion habits.

We ourselves have no idea how we might react to competitive situations that call for compassion. In fact, it is possible, as recent research has shown, that situational forces and group dynamics can work in concert to make decent men and women do horrible things. What you become depends on who you happen to be, and who you are intrinsically. The social setting and the 'system' can pervert anyone. But what is unclear is that while everyone is susceptible, who would be more likely to crack or snap, and why. Or, who is more likely to take advantage of the situation, or who is more likely to abuse their power. The answer lies in what goes on *within* the person in question. Our specific response to an external situation is but an indirect extension of the struggle for control of our consciousness. Not able to connect the two, we are left perplexed, befuddled, and saddened when we see how easily good people can be seduced to act immorally and rudely, which reminds us that we might not be who we think we are. We must also remember that although we view good and evil (and the Upanishadic *preyas* and *sreyas*) as two hostile forces, the fact is that both cohabit our consciousness and are constantly engaged in a power struggle, and one cannot exist without the other. It is equally important to remember that the border between the two is highly permeable, and almost anyone can be swayed to cross it when pressured by circumstantial and situational forces. A good man can do bad, and a bad man can do good.

In our troubled times, everything appears out of joint and upside down. These days, "fair is foul and foul is fair", as the witches say in *Macbeth*. All that is good or fair to others, can be evil or foul to them, and vice versa. Many people, even as they go with the flow to get along, sense in their bones that contemporary human society is descending inexorably towards catastrophic collapse, and that man himself is a ticking time-bomb. Capitalism, the dominant economic system of the day, rooted as it is in the ideology of growth for its own sake, has turned cancerous. Something must be terribly wrong with our world, when what has so far served as a metaphor for sacrifice, the selfless love of a mother, is called into question, when man is bent on making himself an appendage to his own creations, and when we seem ready to face any meltdown rather than give up the trappings of the good life—which we often confuse with having a 'good time', the *preyas* or the pursuit of the pleasant—mediated by technology. It is no longer a remote or improbable possibility. Scientists say that it is a now-or-never situation, that to contain and combat climate change we need to bring several drastic changes that include lifestyle changes like eating less meat, riding bicycles, and flying less. Barring the pro-growth fanatics, we will all applaud and agree but few, if any, will factor in climate change in their daily decision-making. That is so unpalatable that we are prepared, in desperation, to undertake highly risky experiments like geoengineering (the use of scientific methods to artificially control the environment, particularly the world's temperature) in order to deal with the problem of climate change. And it applies across-the-board to all other serious problems that require changes at the individual level. We must remember that any problem we encounter is at least partly of our own making, and the solution must also include actions of our own making. Instead of moving on in this direction, we, so to speak, pass the buck to technology and tell ourselves that it is technology that got us into this mess and therefore it is again technology that can get us out of it. The mind is the mischief-maker; it does not let us feel responsible or that we can make any difference. So it looks as though we are inexorably headed for a climate catastrophe or something similar or worse, in the lifetime of *today's* adults, not of the generations to come. But like mortality, we viscerally believe that we will escape the doomsday even if the world goes down, that fire and brimstone might fall on everyone's head but *we* will still be standing.

In fact, our addiction to convenience and comfort might well accelerate the impending apocalypse. What is worrying is that we are getting so damn good at creating addictive, attention-grabbing diversions that it will gradually become almost impossible to avoid addictions to various forms of entertainment. The key word is 'attention'. Everyone wants to hijack your 'attention'. For companies, our attention translates into their profit. Gadgets are another example. We know that excessive use is bad, particularly for children. It has come to the stage that the very people building these glowing hyper-stimulating portals have become increasingly terrified of them, and are trying to keep their own kids off them. And so could our mind-less or mind-driven (it is hard to tell) obsession with automation. For historians like Yuval Noah Harari, "The automation revolution is likely to make some areas of the world extremely rich and powerful, while completely destroying the economy of others". That would further widen the already wide chasm between the rich and the poor, the elite and the locked-out. There is a grave risk that killing could well emerge as another convenience to get out of an annoying inconvenience or to circumvent an impediment. Euthanasia—or physician-assisted death (PAD)—although still illegal in many countries, is emerging as the go-to response in an ever-increasing range of circumstances, many of which would have been considered not too long ago as not meriting the extreme step. Some zealots say that anybody who is unbearably suffering an intractable medical condition should have the option to die. No more do we believe that there are causes worth dying for but none worth killing for. We may start killing each other as indiscriminately as we now kill other species. And then, as the Greek philosopher Pythagoras said, "for as long as men massacre animals, they will kill each other". Like a wounded tiger that turns a man-eater because humans are far easier to bring down, people might find it simpler to kill one another. Killing in war, as Einstein said, is nothing short of mass murder. And there are no more taboos left—that a mother can't kill, that a child cannot kill, that love cannot kill, that a machine can't kill, *ad nauseam*... And from nature's point of view, that would be the most convenient, and the most natural. Injunctions such as *thou shalt not kill*, go against the very grain of nature. Without any killing the natural order will go haywire. And man, far from being a non-killing animal, has consistently been one of the most 'efficient'. Nonviolence, not as abstinence from violence or withholding of wickedness, but 'as a way of being present', was never integral to human life. Violence is another name for injury, and it is injury that is the essence of the human way of life. What is new in modern times, is that the likelihood of violence turning lethal is now greater than ever before, partly because the available weapons of violence have themselves become far more deadly. We can kill with bare hands but it requires more effort. Earlier, the weapons available during social upheavals were relatively rudimentary: swords, bows and arrows, and occasionally guns. And we have developed a taste for quick-fixes, much more so when we lose our temper. We have also developed a thick skin to stay alive. Every day, we are faced with a new horror or atrocity that takes its toll—spiritually, emotionally, and physically—on what it means to be human. We may mentally shrug it all off as of no direct concern to us, but deep inside, it takes its toll and strengthens the forces of evil inside, which are in a constant state of war with the forces of goodness, virtue, and righteousness. The irony and tragedy is that we are, as Dr. Zaius of the film *Planet of the Apes* (1968) says, "a war-like creature who gives battle to everything around him, even himself", while he is blissfully oblivious to the most important war within his own consciousness. And we are equally oblivious to the fact that it is the waning fortunes of good in this war that are responsible for much of the turmoil, mayhem, and misery in the world. We must always be cognizant that contradiction and collision define us both within and outside. We are always at war inside and outside. We are at once the observer and the opposing forces. How we orchestrate and oversee the war shapes what happens in life.

We are truly at a watershed in human evolution, a total rupture with all that had preceded the present. Man himself has come to be a modern-day *Bhasmasura*, the Hindu demon whose touch could reduce anything to ashes. That power was given to him as a boon by the gods. But when Bhasmasura turned around and wanted to test it on the very god, Lord Shiva, who had given him the boon, Bhasmasura was induced to put his hand on his own head, thereby burning himself to ash. Does a similar fate await us? What we are doing essentially is to dehumanize everything we touch. Many believe that things cannot continue like this forever and that the long-expected doomsday, the apocalyptic event, is now unavoidable. And that belief affects our behavior. And up front, none of us is innocent. Nothing simply is the same anymore—not human nature, not human behavior. Everything seems topsy-turvy, and all values are turning upside down. While divisiveness and acrimony pervade present human society, harmony eludes us. Man today is restless, even as he is more powerful than ever. He has always needed an anchor, a harbor, a crutch and a refuge to navigate through life. That role was for long performed by myth, magic, mythology, religion, and God. None of them are passé but they are in retreat, if not in disrepute. Our devoutness to the gods is in danger of getting dwarfed by our devotion to gadgets. And as gadgets increasingly shape everyday practicalities, there is mounting concern about the addictive nature of staring at the screen or the 'black mirror'. The concern is not only that excessive screen exposure breeds bad behavior but, even more, that it is reconfiguring children's brains and, as a result, there is growing realization that gadgets should be treated like tools, not toys. While, like with every tool, it depends on how we harness it, it is important to note that visual communication is the most magnetic and affects the brain most. The point though is that all technologies can be a boon or bane. For example, it is generally considered that video games are addictive and are bad for kids. But research suggests that empathy-training video games like *Crystals of Kaydor* can change the brain and help adolescents recognize emotions. It is never too early; studies show that including empathy into its curriculum can help even preschoolers. If we can change the mindset of the young (toddlers to youth), and make them more caring and compassionate, it can become a big part of the contextual change in the war within. So, it once again depends on us, on what goes on inside us, how we use a gadget or a game.

Technological change, powered by the fusion of traditional technology and modern science, is the most powerful force sweeping across the world. We would do well to bear in mind the cautionary words of Einstein about the dangers of technological development without spiritual progress. It is technological power that has transformed human activity on earth into both a geological superpower and an evolutionary force, whose impact on the landscape, atmosphere, oceans, and biodiversity has been devastating and rapacious. So rapacious that it is estimated that we have "managed to erase a staggering 2.5 billion years of evolutionary development by driving more than 300 mammal species into extinction". Even if (a huge 'if', by the way) "humans curbed these destructive actions within the next 50 years, it would take between five to seven million years" for mammal biodiversity to fully recover.[69] To paraphrase Thomas Ligotti, 'if everything in existence is malignantly useless, can the human be far behind?' And we are the only species about which one can say, "If this species were to vanish tomorrow, nothing in nature will miss it; nature may even celebrate".

What is obscene is that we search for life on other planets in our galaxy, and callously and casually destroy life on the only planet that sustains us. Some environmental toxicologists say that we have ushered in a chemical age that is changing the very code of life on earth through 'unnatural selection'.[70] We routinely put into our body so many toxic chemicals that it is a miracle that more of us are not sick or dead. The paradox is that, on the one hand, we want body permanence and, on the other hand, we poison our body through multiple ways. Ultimately not only what we use or ingest, but also what we make, ends up in our body, including pesticides and plastics. A recent report tells us that 'humans are now pooping microplastics'. But nothing will change; we simply eat whatever we like (in any case we really have no choice), and *hope* that it will be in someone else's poop.

Our mindset is such that we think we can do whatever we want but escape its consequences. Despite our tendency to be soft on evil, throughout our history we have long wrestled with two divergent moral variables: consequentialism and deontology. In simple terms, consequentialism holds that the ends justify the means, whereas deontology holds that what is important is the nature of actions themselves, and advocates disregarding the possible consequences of our actions when determining what is right and what is wrong, what moral rules we can break and the ones we should not. Humans have never found a way to harmonize the two opposites—even God in human form struggled. But the foundational fact is that, as William Blake says, "Without contraries is no progression. Attraction and repulsion, reason and energy, love and hate are necessary to human existence. From these contraries spring what the religious call good and evil" (*The Marriage of Heaven and Hell*, 1790). Unable to harmonize, vainly seeking to eliminate the 'evil within', and unable to contain the resultant tension, we have, in effect, become a 'suicidal' species. Our mindset about Mother Earth is both suicidal and homicidal.

What we do to the earth has a boomerang effect. The earth has become a kind of material *Kamadhenu*, the celestial cow in Hinduism that is capable of fulfilling every human wish and fancy. It was not too long ago that the earth was viewed as holy. A beautiful poem told us that "Earth's crammed with heaven, And every common bush afire with God; But only he who sees, takes off his shoes".[71] We must recreate that sense of reverence. What is baffling is that we wish for things that are palpably myopic like human replacement at the workplace, not recognizing that "without dignified, creative human occupation", people become "disconnected from life", in the words of the 19th-century British humanist William Morris.[72] We must understand that technological 'connectivity' is being achieved at the expense of human 'community'. And human community is, in its most basic sense, local community . It is knowing others and being known; it is not texting or e-mailing; it is to be able to smell each other. Someone described it as "an insurance policy against life's cruelty; a kind of immunity against the loss and disappointment and rage" that does come.[73] We have reached a stage when we should remember the age-old jest, 'beware of what you wish lest you might just get it'. Every desire of anyone is no longer 'his' alone; because the very pursuit of that wish has consequences that impacts not only 'his life', but also life in general. The character of what we wish has moved from necessity to contentment, from comfort to luxury and to superfluousness. That makes it very important to be very, very careful in what we wish for ourselves.

The way to address this issue is two-fold. First, we must change, not kill, our desire—not 'desire' as a generic force or energy, but 'desire' as a cankerworm in our life, as an impulse to acquire material objects. It was such a 'desire' that Wordsworth possibly had in mind when he wrote the sonnet, *The World Is Too Much With Us* (1807), and the line, "we have given our hearts away, a sordid boon". To get a grip on the 'sordid boon' in a consumeristic, capitalist society is not easy. We must, at this stage, flag one important point. Desire, even a material desire, is not bad; material life is not innately sinful; we don't have to renounce the world and live for the spirit and not for the flesh. We do not need austere asceticism, any more than one of, in Henry Wood's words, 'voluptuous self-indulgence'. In fact, the key to a wholesome life is balance and moderation. As Swedish philosopher Emanuel Swedenborg says, "If we would accept heaven's life, we need by all means to live in the world and to participate in its duties and affairs" (*Heaven and Hell*, 1758).

We need action on two fronts. Internally, the forces of goodness must be dominant in the war within. Externally, we need to change the direction of technological development. The right contextual change is not possible without realigning technological change. To paraphrase Gabriel Garcia (*One Hundred Years of Solitude*, 1967), we have lost direction while losing ourselves in the solitude of our fearsome power. Without contextual-change there can be no consciousness-change, and without the latter, we cannot prevail in the war within. Today's technological research and application is clearly out of sync with the ground realities, and human society itself is increasingly being described as an all-encompassing technological system.[74] We have come to see technology as the 'magic lever' by pulling which all our problems will be resolved. What we ignore is that every such 'resolution' creates new, and more intractable, problems. We need to bring under close and constant public scrutiny not only technological research and development, but also the sciences, bearing in mind that the science of today is the technology of tomorrow. For the first time in human history, collectively man has the knowhow, resources, and the tools necessary to give a life of dignity and good health to every human on earth. It is not happening, because of misdirection and misapplication, and 'insufficient funding'. On top of it, powerful corporations bend research and regulations for their benefit. We need close scrutiny and clear consensus over issues such as what we choose to research, who funds it, who undertakes it, who benefits from it, who is put at risk, and for what purposes. Organizations working to ensure that scientific research is fair and beneficial to society must be publicly funded, subject to peer review, and transparent to civil society. And society must also demand focused public investment in independent research rather than expecting that corporate funding will fill the niche without corrupting the process.

Without any such scrutiny and oversight, and starving many other worthier priorities for the masses, 'Big Science', 'Big Think', and 'Big Money' are now coming together and narrowing down the entire human organized effort around two big projects: artificial intelligence (AI) and immortality. Some, like Alex Zhavoronkov,[75] say that human immortality might be found in the hands of artificial intelligence; Some like Nick Bostrom, even predict that success in controlling AI will result in a "compassionate and jubilant use of humanity's cosmic endowment". As for cardiologist Eric Topol, AI "can make healthcare human again". It could be the very thing that could save us from death. It could be, but what is less noticed is that the two, in spirit, negate each other. On the one hand, we are aiming to merge into a machine and, on the other hand, we want to make the body last forever through technologies like cryonics. There is nothing wrong with either pursuits; the problem is our obsession with them. Such an absurdly narrow research agenda constitutes a gross mismatch and distortion of what ought to be the global priority agenda. We sometimes read of research that could make a tremendous difference, like turning carbon dioxide into fuel for everyday life, but nothing happens thereafter because they are not funded and pursued. Underfunding and inadequate attention is also adversely impacting on important issues like global poverty, glaring inequality, inequity, illiteracy, climate change, and threats to global health. None of them is entirely new. Poverty, for example, merited mention as one of the Islamic Ten Commandments. Signifying Islam's sensitivity as well as its recognition of the gravity of poverty it says, "Kill not your children for fear of poverty." That the Quran specifically identifies it as one of the Ten Commandments indicates that such an awful practice was prevalent even then. What is shocking is that despite centuries of civilization and progress, and decades of economic growth, poverty, in some form or other, afflicts one-third of mankind. What we now have is a cocktail of the ultra-rich, extreme poverty, and the rebellious resentment and anger of the non-rich. We are sitting on a powder keg, and into that we now have a new entrant, immortality.

While immortality is an age-old ambition, our fascination with AI, which some like Elon Musk say is "potentially more dangerous than nukes", is fresh and new. AI is now being seen as the magic wand to solve all of humanity's problems and achieve all our goals, like ushering a global community. Like any tool or weapon, AI can be used for good as well as for bad. But the issue is different. What does it do for us as humans? And does it hinder or help in our quest to bring to bear a new paradigm of intelligence to solve the problems created by the present paradigm? Quintessentially, it is a sort of acknowledgment and admission. It is to acknowledge that our brain is beyond our depth, that we will never know enough of how it wholly works or how to optimally put it to use. And it is to admit that despite our most determined efforts to grow, dissect, and boost brain power, we are not confident we will succeed. The fact is that AI can do a world of good provided it is carefully analyzed and applied—not indiscriminately but selectively, to *supplement*, not supplant human effort, or to lighten the effort where it is needed. We must also bear in mind that AI and computer intelligence are basically no different from the intelligence that runs our lives. It is being predicted that 'by the end of this century, the nonbiological portion of our intelligence will be trillions of trillions of times more powerful than unaided human intelligence'. We are also told that 'conscious or not, artificial systems are about to become much more interactive and personalized and, as such, will be changing our lives dramatically'.[77] But does that solve the problems we face today created by that very brain-based intelligence? On the other hand, experts warn that a future war fought by 'AI-gone-wrong' systems would be a fearful thing, bringing to mind the Biblical warning about such an eventuality, which it calls 'the Great Tribulation'. What we need is intelligence of an altogether different genre, which, with willful blindness, we fail to see is within each of us. It is none other than *heart-based* and *intuitive* intelligence. The human heart is much more than an efficient pump that sustains life.[78] Pioneering research by the *HeartMath Institute* has revealed that, contrary to what most of us have been taught in school (that the heart is constantly responding to "orders" sent by the brain in the form of neural signals), it is the *heart* that actually sends more signals to the brain than the brain sends to the heart! And that these heart signals have a significant effect on brain function—influencing emotional processing as well as higher cognitive faculties such as attention, perception, memory, and problem-solving. Our heart is also an access point to a source of wisdom and intelligence that we can call upon to live our lives with more balance, greater creativity, and enhanced intuitive capacities. We have to become, at the least, a critical mass of humans, essentially heart-empowered individuals, for a better and more compassionate world. But so smitten we are about AI, that it is being predicted, not without a tinge of elation, that in the future "the human brain will connect to online AI to become a hybrid of biological and nonbiological thinking".[79]

For generations we have prided ourselves as the species with the biggest brain, enabling it to be more intelligent than anyone else. Suddenly, man now feels inadequate in his intelligence in relation to his ambitions. And, rather than optimize what nature has gifted, such as drawing upon his heart intelligence, he has turned to artificial means. We tend to think that the machine is the opposite of man, that it brings to bear qualities we lack, and that it is immune to human vulnerabilities. There are indications that this not always true. First, the machine is nothing if not man-made. And, some studies have shown that, intentionally or not, artificial intelligence could pick up some of our worst traits like bigotry, racism, and sexism. This is important to note, since AI is emerging not as a subservient tool but as a decision-maker with equal rights. Already, robots—

and it tells a lot if we remember that the word robot comes from the Czech *robota*, which means 'forced labor'— have begun to join the boards of directors of companies. In the future, even doctors and lawyers could be robots, not only personal assistants. We are being told that soon one could buy 'sex-robots' off the shelf. Sexuality is just another commodity, a product that can be bought and sold. Concern is also being expressed on topics like 'robot morality', and about outsourcing morality to robots as easily as we have outsourced so many other forms of human labor. Some experts are talking of the *Humanoid Robotic Revolution*, and it is hard to tell if they are telling us to be excited or worried. In any case, we all know that all 'revolutions' throw up nasty surprises and unintended consequences. One outlandishly 'revolutionary' theory[80] says future humans could be 'hybrid humans'—products of a hypothetical interbreeding of aliens with humans. Such a hybrid species, it is hypothesized, could be capable of surviving future catastrophic climate conditions on earth, and could serve as problem-solvers or future leaders.

While digging his own grave on the one hand, by offering to the machine that which he denied the divine—*saranagati* or total surrender—man, on the other hand, is determined now to be immortal by becoming a god. Immortality has long been a spiritual goal of man, centered on the soul. Now, it is medical immortality and bodily survival after death that man seeks. He is not appeased by spiritual immortality. He wants to achieve it by being able to do things like freezing and repairing the brain, creating a new, artificial body, and transferring the 'new brain' into the new body. The closest parallel in nature that man takes inspiration from is the total transformation of an ugly caterpillar into a beauteous butterfly. It is based on the questionable assumption that even though it has a new body, it doesn't 'die', and yet is able retain some sort of memory of its past life. Not only do we not want to die, but we also want to carry forward the same physical frame, which means that we want to be like a winged caterpillar, not a beautiful butterfly. Without commensurate consciousness-change, we might well end up as some sort of an 'evil superman'. And why not, if MIT is able to create the AI-driven psychopath *Norman*? Like always, we go for the hybrid, a hotch-potch. There is no transformation without termination and dissolution and death. In practical terms, we want to give up nothing but get everything. Now, it is the body all the way; 'body beautiful' is a multi-billion-dollar industry. But if the body still fails, we have the brain as backup. It is expected that computer technology and artificial intelligence, biotechnology, and nanotechnology will all converge to make it possible for us to download our minds and attain virtual immortality. This is the exact opposite of what all religions have told us to *let go*, and shed the body identification and attachment. The Roman philosopher Seneca thought that death was a gift of God, and the Buddha thought that clinging to life is as dangerous as any other form of ignorance. The odds of outright immortality are beyond the bounds of possibility. As Michael Shermer pointedly says, "The whole universe runs down, so, ultimately, even if you could lengthen your lifespan indefinitely, the universe itself will eventually die in a heat death".[81] Biomedical research has helped global average life expectancy to rise by 20 years since 1960. Some say science now can give us indefinite life, but not literal immortality, not mathematical eternity. Semantics apart, practically speaking, the fact is that, even doubling or trebling, let alone thousand years of the average human life span, could have far-reaching social, moral, and intergenerational and evolutionary implications. Any extension of the life span of any particular species can disturb the equilibrium embedded in creation. And that could have cascading and calamitous consequences. And there is a growing growl that it is all for the rich at the expense of the poor and soon that growl can become a roar, and the roar into revolt, not of the voiceless poor but of the new majority in the world: the middle class. When that does occur it could dwarf all previous revolutions.

To a large extent, the fulcrum of our morality is based on finiteness. That everyone dies is the thread that keeps everything in their proper place: "Teach us to number our days, that we may gain a heart of wisdom".[82] If we truly can live forever, who cares what we do to any other? And there is no guarantee that it will abolish old age, and we may end up with no youth and extended old age, something like Gulliver's *Struldbruggs*. Faced with the ennui of eternal life, our future generations might, as in Jorge Borges' story *The Immortal*, seek an antidote that allows them to die. While most think that longevity is a blessing, not all long-lifers feel that way. One of the world's longest-living humans, at nearly 129 years, Koku Istambulova said, "Long life is not at all God's gift for me, but a punishment". Particularly if we might turn out to be a *Tithonus* (Greek mythology), who achieved immortality but not eternal youth, and who later lamented, 'Only cruel immortality Consumes: I wither slowly in thine arms', and beseeched, 'release me, and restore me to the ground' (*Tithonus*, Lord Tennyson).

It is important to remember that new technology does not merely give something new to use or play with; it changes *everything*. Einstein's warning that technology, when it surpasses human interaction, might usher in a world of idiots could not be more timely. Humankind might not end with idiocy; it could be far more fearsome. Artificial intelligence and rampant robotization would, in particular, have far-reaching consequences in the defense and military sectors. Future wars will be unrecognizable from what they are today, and technology will be the deciding factor. Moreover, war constitutes a gross distortion and misuse of scarce resources—financial, natural, and creative—that could make hundreds of millions of lives so much better, a cause worthy of moral mutiny. We need a complete overhaul in the entire process, from conception to application, including its funding and control. Context is the canvas of our way of life, of everything we do to live like a human being. That includes the web of relationships we work with, in particular nature. To sustain the cosmic balance, it is required that the benefit each individual provides must outweigh the costs they entail on the environment. By doing this, the system replenishes itself. This is true across species and ecosystems, with the exception of the human. And having made the machine more 'intelligent' than himself, man has decided to mate and merge with it, and augment and enhance the capability and strength of every faculty and organ in his body—from intelligence to genitalia. Some even hope to breed and possibly create a new species of *sapiens* on Mars!

In any case, what is clear is that man now seems determined not only to own the world, but to make absolutely sure that nothing worthwhile remains after he is gone; present-day man is doing to his progeny what Genghis Khan did to his conquered countries. Science is attempting to create a new man and a new civilization centered around the machine, and is seducing us with the promise to solve the greatest mystery of them all, the mystery of death. We have long struggled with our mortality. We have made hell on earth and want to escape to heaven without dying. The trouble is, as Milan Kundera puts it, "Man doesn't know how to be mortal. And when he dies, he doesn't even know how to be dead".[83] But such 'not-knowing' has not hindered man from seeking immortality. A famous prayer in the *Brihadaranyaka* Upanishad seeks divine guidance on three fronts: from delusion to truth; from darkness to light; and from death to immortality. Death is the creator of the world, states an Indian sacred text. But what science is seeking is very different from this type of immortality. In effect, what it is trying to do is to create and capture the power that raised Christ from the dead, and be what eluded even Gilgamesh and Methuselah—life unending. In fact, we want more; we want to make death reversible. Life forever clearly is not possible, because forever isn't several lifetimes, or a few dozen, but billions and billions of years. It means that like gods we *cannot* die even if we kill each other or if are run over by a truck. The question we have to ask is this: with man as he is, with the kind of mind-dominated consciousness he has, should he be endowed with such prodigious capability even if that capability is not immortality *per se*, but exponentially extended life span? Evil could become exponentially much stronger in the world and in our consciousness. And we would lose the war within. Human power now comes close to "power without responsibility—the prerogative of the harlot throughout the ages".[84] For the first time in history of life on earth, that is over four billion years, a single species, the human, has acquired the awesome and scary capability to fulfill his every wish and want. So much so we now face a new threat: the threat of some of our wild wishes coming true. Furthermore, it is not as though every man is equally powerful. It will further exacerbate the present inequalities, which will be concentrated in fewer and fewer hands. The plutocracy that runs the world will further dig in its heels, bolstered by the inclusion of the immortal-rich. And yet, no one is seriously talking of how to control and channel that power, and what kind of public policies and frameworks are necessary. Instead, we are making contingency plans to escape to the Moon or Mars! The current plans of Elon Musk's *SpaceX* are to send the first humans to Mars in the 2020s, and establishing a city there by 2050. More than 200,000 people applied for a privately-funded mission, estimated to cost six billion dollars, and which is to be filmed for a reality television series![85] Remember there is no return. In fact, it is not only Moon or Mars we want escape to. 'Escape' is the metaphor and mindset of modern man. How to escape from an assortment of conditions such as fear, dead-end jobs, despair, responsibility, work, restraints, frustrations, convention, commitments, etc., is what preoccupies many. To stay present to what is happening in the world is to embrace anything that promises escape. Many seek what in Greek is called *soteria* (salvation), but unable to identify from what, they focus their ire on the status quo, anything that is labeled, categorized, and institutionalized. Some feel that surrender to society is a way of escape from that very society. The point is, not only does power corrupt, but absolute power corrupts absolutely, as Lord Acton famously proclaimed. Also, a few might even have not proven equal to the power they come to possess. The person who will exercise the awesome power of being virtually free from the fear of death will essentially be a 'machine-man', driven exclusively by a brain boosted by selective manipulation and implanted or uploaded into a computer. It means man, or more aptly macho *machine-man*, will have to exercise his almost divine power with essentially the same or similar content and character of consciousness. Fact is, the human is always found wanting in handling any power. It is good to remember what Robert Ingersoll once said of Abraham Lincoln: "Nothing discloses real character like the use of power. Most people can bear adversity; but if you wish to know what a man really is, give him power". That being so, can we trust the human to be any better than what he is now? Without radical consciousness-change of the right kind, and with primordial and promethean power, this *Homo sapiens* will be a far greater menace both on earth and in the cosmos.

The potential flip side is that, like in our driven desire to solve deep mysteries we sometimes stumble upon deeper riddles, we might awaken sinister secrets, with consequences we would be unable to apprehend or anticipate. Quite apart from the risk of trespassing into the divine domain, immortality, for instance, can fan the flames of *immorality*, and make us hark back to the view held by some sophists in the fifth century, that practicing injustice was the most profitable way to live. In our times, when profit-making and pleasure-seeking are the primary impulses behind almost all human endeavor, such a view could be unstoppable. In fact, present-day man would rather seek the 'lower pleasures', mainly connected with immediate physical gratification and delight, as John Stuart Mill defined it (*Utilitarianism*, 1861), which are quite distinct from 'higher' pleasures—the cultivation and enjoyment of art, literature, poetry, and friendship. We are told that since death would not be inevitable, we would not have to worry about after-life, judgment day, and so on, and there would be no need therefore to be 'good' in the present life for a better post-death future. The Bible says that death came into the world through one man, and spread to all men through sin.[86] Science is saying there is no connection, and you can sin and do not have to die! But neither has addressed the more basic question: why is death *bad*? Is it because of what we expect happens or because it does not happen? Not only relief from the shadow of death, science is also promising that through such technological manipulations as genetic engineering, better drugs, and precise stimulation of various localities in the brain, human beings can live in a sort of paradise, in which all unsavory states of awareness would have been banished. That is the story science is telling us and selling us, as we struggle to make sense of what we really ought to do with ourselves. It raises other serious issues: is it ethical to disrupt our modern-human genetic heritage which has evolved naturally over at least the last 200,000 years?

Another sea-change concerns life as we understand it. Life was touted as priceless and the 'right to life' was deemed a fundamental human right. And that meant the opposite of death. But no longer. Across the world, especially in those parts where people have the time to worry about issues beyond the immediate, there is a simmering sense that the right to life includes the right to die, and even more, the right to *be helped to die*. Some are even arguing that everyone, including a murderer on death row, has a 'right to painless death'. The logic is that society cannot have it both ways: it cannot deny its citizens good health or a life of dignity, and also deny the right to die in dignity. Indeed, dying with dignity is being hailed by some as the biggest shift in morality in a generation. That is because dying is a part of living, and one cannot be deprived, at the time of death, of the rights and privileges one enjoyed while living. There is also a sense that society spends far too much to keep a few alive, who often are the rich, at the expense of the basic health needs of the poor. "The idea of death, the fear of it, haunts the human animal like nothing else," wrote Ernest Becker in his book *The Denial of Death*. We do still fear death but it is slowly getting compromised by the more fearsome realities of life. What we are seeing is the unheralded emergence of death as a kind of liberator. Death is asserting its independent right to be given its due on matters of life. Death has often been called the ultimate leveler. Science says that it might not soon be so. But it is a leveler in another sense. Whether one is rich or poor, well-off or on welfare, healthy or sick, it doesn't always matter; anyone can 'decide to die' and any human emotion can trigger it. Let us also note that there are a growing number of thoughtful people who think that the best service man can render to the planet—and contribute to the holy work of mending the world—is to stop any more human reproduction, and do everything we could to become extinct sooner than later. A similar view was voiced by biologist EO Wilson: "If all mankind were to disappear, the world would regenerate back to the rich state of equilibrium that existed ten thousand years ago". The meeting point is that neither is content with the present disposition—those who advocate our early voluntary extinction as a way to make moral amends, and those who, on the contrary, want to live forever. What we consider the current reality has become so morally fraudulent and egregious that, for many, the status quo is no longer acceptable or suitable. And everyone blames everyone else for their misery. As the 18th-century French philosopher and moralist Joseph de Maistre said, "It is man who is charged with the slaughter of man". Everyone fears the future, but no one is prepared to give up any of the goodies of good life to solve any existential problem, or to bequeath a healthier world to their progeny. Down the ages and through our march into modern times, we have been blessed by the noble sayings of scriptures, by the presence amongst us of great prophets, rishis, saints, and mystics. Among them were those, who "having reached the supreme God from all sides had found abiding peace, had become united with all, had entered into the life of the Universe".[87] Those wise men were generous with their instruction and advice on the path we have to follow. Even they could not arrest the moral drift of mankind.

Things have only gotten worse over time. Why have we been so impervious and hostile to what the wise have always exhorted us to do, to become better human beings? How come the precious seeds they had sown and sprinkled never sprouted inside us? They have always told us the same message: have a good heart, harm no one, help all, do to others what you would like done to you, fight injustice and evil. That is the path to both a good and virtuous life as well as a better after-life. Most prophets and sages failed in their own lifetime not because the message wasn't right, or that the messenger was flawed, but because the intended audience was not ready. They, like us, lived too much in their head and too little in their heart. The 20th-century spiritual master Ramana Maharshi said that the essence of spiritual discipline is to plunge the purified mind into the heart. The heart too must be seen and used differently. We must invest far more on exploring how to harness the effective guidance from our heart's intuitive intelligence. We have to ask of ourselves: why is the seed wrong or the soil barren? Have we, while paying lip service, chosen to ignore them, much the same way we ignore the clear signs of climate change, because it entails doing something that our mind does not want?

We are living in turbulent times when all assumptions about human life are running for cover and we don't know what to expect from each other as fellow-travelers. Most people feel besieged in their own lives, trapped in their own bodies. We have so far sought to find the causes and factors externally and intellectually, in our conduct and context of life. We need to go within—in Anne Sexton's words, "Put our ear down close to our soul and listen hard"—and ensure that what we wish to do, or avoid doing externally, is first facilitated in the deepest, fathomless recesses of our being, before anything takes shape as a thought or word or action. A thought or word or action is already an arrow unleashed. First, we must stop endlessly debating which is stronger in human nature: good or evil. We must accept that both are latent, and whether we do good or bad depends on what happens *within* at a certain time. Having said that, we must acknowledge that, in reality, we seem more and more prone to evil and sin. As someone drily noted, we don't have to teach our kids how to sin; it seems to come out naturally. But then that happens because the evil is stronger within than goodness. Thomas Moser, psychological biographer of Joseph Conrad, wrote, "In order to truly be alive one must recognize the truth, the darkness, the evil and the death within".

What we must up front understand is that nothing is cost-free—to get something, something else has to be given up. And that everything is 'double-edged', that we all lead 'double lives', and the one *inside* is where the real 'person' is. Every serious struggle, competitive action, anything we deeply desire to achieve, we call a *war*—such as, war on consumerism, war on crime, war on drugs, war on terror, war on pollution, war on black money, war on Wall Street, even War for Kindness.[88] Some even characterize the cut-throat competitive culture as a 'war of each against all others'. The truth, though, is that we think we are 'fighting' these wars, but actually, through our actions and attitudes we are fuelling them. We devour war movies and honor war heroes, who, sans the halo of war, become mass murderers. Yet, despite being suffused with war in our outer life, we know nothing of the war *within*. And we must understand that everything that happens, at least anything consequential—whether we do good or bad, how we behave and relate with the rest of the world, even how we think and feel—is but an extension, an expression of the state of the war within ourselves at a given point in time. If we accept the actuality of this war, not simply that we are capable of entertaining horrible thoughts and vile emotions, many things that seem inexplicable—why is there so much evil and suffering? why is our behavior so unpredictable?—begin to become intelligible. We must stop this futile and tiresome debate about whether we are essentially good or bad, spiritual or material, and why we behave so badly at times, and what to do to be better beings. None of these have a firm footing of their own; they change according to the vicissitudes of the internal and external wars. If the forces of good have the upper hand, we will do good, and bad otherwise. And that 'within', the inside of us, the core of our being, what Keats called 'the abyss of himself', is the spiritual space at our innermost depth. Lao Tzu famously said that a journey of a thousand miles begins with a single step. Many limitations man has overcome, but for what thwarts the journey within, he is at a loss to know how to take the first step. We are launching things into space 'like crazy' but none into the inner space. We need something like a 'spiritual SpaceX program' to explore the world within. The fact is, as Pico Iyer (*Global Soul*, 2000) reminds us, "The Inner World Is a Great, Undiscovered Terrain". With all the tremendous advances in medicine we really do not know how the various organs in our body function independently as well as in tandem with each other, how they together constitute the physical body and make the difference between life and death. We know we have a mind, but not much about what it actually is, and where it resides. We know we have a consciousness, but not much about its content or character. We know so little in the world of our inside—*adhyatmika*, in Sanskrit—because we don't think it is important to get what we want from life, and because it does not come in the way of our worldly pursuits. It does not bother us; so we don't bother about it. And then, to know what goes on within, we need a whole new wherewithal, which is spiritual, not scientific. Indeed man's chronic laggardness in making spiritual progress is because of our utter ignorance of our inside.

Even if we ritually chant the Upanishadic mantra of *shanti*, *shanti*, *shanti* (peace, peace, peace!) at every occasion and opportunity, there is no denying that we love wars. Some say that even God is "pro-war", not only us, the deeply flawed humans. Maybe that is why we have never had any extended periods of grace or peace in our history. We might quote the Jewish prophet Isaiah and repeat that 'they shall beat their swords into plowshares and their spears into pruning hooks' as an ideal and aspiration. Plowshares and pruning hooks we have always had, but not through any alchemy of swords; instead, swords have become guns, bombs, missiles and atomic weapons and autonomous weapons. It was believed that some Biblical-era wars were even declared as 'divinely-ordained'. God, in the Old Testament, for example, ordered the complete destruction of the Canaanites. About the great Kurukshetra war (in the Mahabharata), Lord Krishna declared that it was necessary, when he was admonished for not having prevented it even though it was in his power to do so. Why such a horrible bloodshed was 'necessary' he did not explain. But one thing we must understand is that we cannot apply human standards and norms to the divine. As Martin Luther King said, divine justice is 'entirely alien to ourselves'. We cannot judge that which is inherently incomprehensible, divine will. The world outside is 'incomprehensible' because the world inside is impenetrable and the factors that come into play to 'comprehend' are now far more and more complex.

Wars do bring out the worst in us, but still nothing unites a people better than a war. It raises our adrenaline, gives focus and purpose, and helps in mobilization. Experts differ whether we are the only war-waging animal on earth. Some say that ants and chimps come closest. How do we explain this self-destructive human lust for war-making? It is because war, like nothing else, offers avenues to manifest some of our deepest and darkest urges, passions and prejudices. We must understand that war is basically a form of conflict but on a wider and more violent scale. And conflict is not only natural to the human condition but is also essential to our growth. What we should seek is not to strive towards a conflict-free world which is impossible, even counterproductive, but to develop models of conflict-resolution through dialogue, and by mentally putting ourselves in the situation that someone else is in. Once we do not try to impose our will and interests on another, conflict becomes a communion. We must not also forget that all conflicts in the external world are but extensions of the basic internal conflict, the war within. If we want to resolve conflicts in our life, which are inevitable and necessary, then we must ensure that the forces of goodness and conciliation are dominant in the war. It is also useful to bear in mind the nature of this war. This 'war within' is a war without beginning or end, a civil war, an incestuous struggle for supremacy over the human consciousness. It is a war without victory or defeat. It is a weird war in which we cannot afford what we yearn for in any other war: the crushing defeat of the enemy; outright victory. It is a war in which we *do not* want to kill the enemy; for without the enemy, the other side too cannot survive.

And yet we are total strangers to this war. All living is a state of war, but the war within is the most intimate and meaningful. We believe that in life we must not stay neutral in the fight against injustice and evil, but we are mute and quiet to the fight against these very foes in our own breast. Yet, in that very breast, as William Blake tells us not to forget, "all deities reside" (*The Marriage of Heaven and Hell*, 1790). It is not that we are altogether unaware that it is in the 'cave of the heart', as the Upanishads call it, that the inner meaning of life, the meaning of all human existence, is hidden. But that very ground deep within is also the battlefield for the war within. It is a war that is often compared to the great Kurukshetra war between cousins, the 'good' *Pandavas* and the 'evil' *Kauravas*. What is special is that this war was fought with God in a human *avatar* being present to ensure the victory of the good. An intense struggle continually rages within our own soul or consciousness, but we don't know what to do, or, more importantly, we don't relate it to anything happening in our lives. We know little about this war, and we don't care to learn more, because, unlike other, external wars, this is invisible and beyond sensory experience. Even though we are blissfully unaware, we supply arms and ammunition to *both* warring sides, by everything we do every day through our sense organs. And that, although we are unaware of it, offers us a constant opportunity to change the course of the war.

Recent research tells us that even what we eat can have a bearing on the war by helping one or the other side; some foods nourish positive emotions, while some others nourish negative emotions. Indeed, the minutiae of everyday life, things like what we buy, what we wear, what we make, what we consume, could have a positive ripple effect not only on the world but also on the war within. And indeed this is the only way any change can happen. If we cut out supplies to the evil side and reinforce supplies to the virtuous front, we can ensure that the war will wage on our terms. And if this happens, it will immediately affect every war outside, and even more fundamentally, our mindset and behavior. We, or at least a critical mass of humans, could become compassionate warriors in real life, warriors who not only help everyone but refuse to hate anyone, whose sword is love and armor is cascading empathy, having the ability to put themselves in other people's hearts. But how does one attain such a lofty mindset? The Upanishads say that the way is for us to see all things in ourselves, and ourselves in all things. One wonders which is more difficult. If we can become such warriors in everyday life, we can change not only the context of life but also the character of the war within. In the end, the context of life is how we live and do our daily chores and choices. It is these myriad things, and how we perform them, that matter and make the difference between a worthy life and a wasted life.

We do not need to be *sui generis*, or do Olympian things, to change the context of life; it is enough to be humane and do the ordinary things that we do as a service to God, as the Bhagavad Gita implores us, or as a service to another fellow-humans, indeed to any other sentient being, as Bodhisattvas do. That is one way of bridging the gap between our moral values and daily actions. It is good to remember that a universal principle of the universe is that "what we focus on, multiplies". If we focus on good, then the cumulative effect can be overwhelming. One need not be a Bodhisattva to make the world a tiny bit better. And we don't have to be a Saint Paul who offered, 'For I could wish that I myself were accursed and cut off from Christ for the sake of my brothers, my kinsmen according to the flesh'.[89] It is enough to infuse every deed with what Buddhism calls 'loving kindness'. It only calls for surrendering the sense of ownership of things that we possess. Actually we don't 'possess' anything; in time, things possess us. We can only 'own' that which we can absorb, appropriate and appreciate; no more. The poet Padraig O Tuama, described as an extraordinary healer in our world of fracture, said, "Belonging creates and undoes us both". While we should shun the desire to 'own' material things, a sense of belonging is important for a fruitful life. What Hannah Arendt wrote in the 1930s (*Origins of Totalitarianism*), "The experience of not belonging to the world at all, which is among the most radical and desperate experiences of man", applies equally to the 21st century. In the middle of frenetic activity, constantly being 'busy', many are lonely, which is increasingly a trigger for suicides.

A related quandary many face is being part of what is described as the rat race: we could either get caught up in a fiercely competitive struggle for wealth, excellence, and success at the expense of moral value, or exit the race and risk social failure or broken relationships. We are smitten by 'success'; we want to be 'successful' in whatever we do, in our job, in our relationships, in making love or war, or making money. We also believe that the obstacle on the way to our success is another man. The essence of this way of thinking is that everything is justified in order to be a 'winner'—never the L-word, loser—and that means trampling over everyone else on the way. Our entire educational system and work culture are tailor-made for that purpose; indeed, they feed upon it. It is a system that trains the young to, in Einstein's words, "worship acquisitive success as a preparation for his future career". The purpose of education ought to be to know how to, as aptly put by journalist Sydney Harris, "turn mirrors into windows". In a 'mirror' we see our image and the area around, but through a window the view is limitless. Today, what goes for education even cracks the mirror and everything we see through is distorted. It even distorts our own image. Education, therefore, has to go beyond manufacturing cogs for the economic engine, beyond acquiring the skills to make money.

Although we 'work' all the time everywhere, what we call 'work' is what we do when we go, every weekday of ours, to a particular place, an office or factory, and spend the entire day exhibiting a particular skill in the company of others doing a similar thing, and for which we are paid wages or salary on a daily or weekly or monthly basis. Although it requires sharing and working together synergistically, the work culture is competitive and the driving motive is almost always profit-maximization. What we need to do is to turn competitive culture into cooperative culture, and factor in social good as a part of profit-making. Nowadays, education is designed to produce fiercely ambitious, competitive individuals who want always to succeed, regardless of the means or methods. And that inevitably colors their whole personality and social behavior and their role as family members. Soon, the whole of humanity becomes a conglomerate of cut-throat combatants, who see everyone else as someone to overcome for their own survival and success. The mantra is 'success', which is material achievement and advancement, in order to get on to the gravy train. And it doesn't matter how much suffering we cause to others and to our own selves. How can we then play a role in mitigating the stock of suffering in the world? If we are ruthless in achieving our goals, where is the room for sharing, which is one of the most important attributes that must be nurtured? The contextual-change that is necessary for consciousness-change must include measures to deal with the ravages of the rat race. We cannot seriously talk of spiritual growth if we spend all our working life, and what goes as education, immersed in a culture of ruthless one-upmanship, where one is constantly outfoxing each other. We need to learn to admit that almost every problem we face is at least partly of our own making, and that we are mad at others precisely because we see in them what we are trying not to see in ourselves. We need to find and invent avenues outside the current economic system to sharpen and strengthen man's latent better instincts and to tame, what Freud called, 'the inclination for aggression', without which, he said, man does not feel 'comfortable'. Those avenues must be such that they are attractive and emotionally, if not economically, lucrative. It must start from pre-school and continue through college, and include events like compassionate retreats and empathy workshops. One must be able to live like a normal person and make a living, and yet be a caring, considerate, and compassionate person. That must be an integral part of education. What is called for is a judicious mix of 'how to make a living' and 'how to live wholesomely'.

While the reality is that we are all sojourners on earth, each of us wants to leave footprints that don't fade with time. We always want to win, to prevail, to dominate, to control every situation and contingency. So dominant and destructive is our desire to control others that Erich Fromm has called it another form of necrophilia. Everyone except oneself, and everywhere except within. That must change. The fact is that while we have traveled very far into outer space—far into the void out there, between the planets, and beyond the solar system—and gained much knowledge of the cosmos, our knowledge of the inner space is abysmal. But what is this space, this *within* that we relentlessly refer to? The *Chandogya* Upanishad describes it as the city of *Brahman*, a secret dwelling, the lotus of the heart. It has an inner space within which is the fulfillment of our desires. The Upanishad goes on to say that whatever we know in this world, or not know, is contained in this inner space. We have focused entirely on technical tools like *Voyager 1* to wander into the far reaches of outer space, but have paid no attention to find or innovate heart-centered spiritual tools and techniques to delve into our own selves. We are expending enormous resources and human creativity to develop what astronaut Andy Thomas described as "go-nowhere, dead-end" technologies to put humans in space at the expense of basic needs, like food, water, shelter, and sanitation for a billion humans on earth. This has been our greatest failing and greatest challenge. The fact is that the methods used by mystics, masters, and rishis—like *tapas*, mind-control, intense prayer, *prapatti* or absolute and unconditional divine surrender—are not easily adaptable to our outrageous world. That must change. Plans are afoot for a round trip voyage to Mars in thirty years, but the odyssey within, we haven't even started. And that must change, too. Unless we learn to intervene and influence the internal ebbs and flows, we cannot change anything externally. All the problems, be it climate change or corrosive consumerism, the emerging pandemics of suicide and homicide, mindless militarization or moral decline will only gain speed. But if we can change the tide and ensure that the righteous forces attain and maintain the upper hand, then we can have a pandemic of peace and virtuous infection and contagion of compassion.

The philosopher Ludwig Wittgenstein once told a friend that 'all his life there had hardly been a day, in which he had not at one time or other thought of suicide as a possibility'. The Italian poet Cesare Pavese said it explicitly: "No one ever lacks a good reason for suicide". For, otherwise they wouldn't do it any way. In fact we all have 'good reasons', but for some that 'good' becomes good enough to impel them to take their own lives. Now, we don't need a reason, or every reason gets turned around to be good enough to entertain self-harm. Actually, nowadays, no emotion or thought or feeling or passion can be ruled out as a potential inducement or provocation for suicide. It has also become a soulful cry for help, an assertion of autonomy over one's own life, a way of protest or even a bargaining chip and blackmail. We also find that, in some instances, the same conditions and context that provoke a suicide in one culture, become a trigger for a homicide in another culture. In Japan, a disgraced man will do *hara-kiri*; in USA, he might more probably go on a killing spree. Little noticed and shockingly, across the world, more people die from suicide every year than from conflicts, wars, and natural disasters combined. We don't realize it, but suicides, which some call 'deaths of despair', can be contagious, like the common cold. There are troubling signs it is already happening, for instance, following a celebrity suicide. When a much-publicized suicide becomes a trigger for a 'suicide contagion', it is called the *Werther Effect*, named for Goethe's novel,

The Sorrows of Young Werther (1774). If suicide is being seen as a viable way to end suffering and sadness, homicide is being viewed as the viable way to end or avenge dishonor, harassment, humiliation, and injustice. Fundamentally, deep inside us, suicide seems to have shed its 'sin-skin', as an extreme step of the truly desperate, depressed, and mentally unstable. It is now inching to the top as the *de facto* default choice to get over any irksome situation, a route of escape from a troubled childhood or relationship or marriage, or even as a way to punish those against whom one has a grudge or grievance. And homicide is no longer the 'heinous crime' perpetrated by really bad people or psychopaths or sadists, or committed under intolerable provocation or in the heat of passion. But it is useful to remember that both the growing casualness of suicide and the seeming triviality of homicides are but symptoms of a larger malaise of the mind: *moral nihilism*. Human beings are not seen as responsible for what they do, therefore, each individual makes up the difference between good and evil. Nothing has any intrinsic value, even life, and a negation of the basic laws that society has set up—either religious or social laws—makes them meaningless or menacing. The practical way is to simply destroy everything—anyone, oneself or others, nature, planet earth, or other species. It is moral nihilism that makes us believe we can barter humanness for efficiency—maximum productivity with minimal effort and minimum time.

Efficiency, and its twin, competence, is what we seek and pursue in all walks of modern life, and this leaves no room for any weakness or stiffness. Increasing the 'efficiency of performance' is now a top scientific priority. In this mindset, a murder is merely a 'contract job', and rape another form of 'rough sex' gone a bit too far; and stealing is no different from sharing, and lying is a way to wield leverage. For someone who feels left out of school, the school itself becomes a symbol of failed society that can be 'fixed' with minimal effort. In the same way, that person's focus shifts to other symbols of society or religion—a church or mosque, a packed promenade or stadium—which could be targeted for maximum destruction. To stem this macabre trend, we must change the tides of the 'war within' through consciousness-change and contextual-change. Whatever we do, we cannot tame the tide from the outside. Something truly hideous has happened inside each of us. The point is not that technology is bad, it is the obsessive human desire to control the uncontrollable, to pursue anything that obscures the reality of man's own life. It is there, in that dark corner of the human psyche, where the monsters lurk. It is about this human tendency to take just about anything and turn it into something awful. Whether it is God's inscrutable *leela* or play, or the work of the Devil, or an 'occupational hazard', we do not know. If we fail to tame the tide, homicides will become as common as the killing of animals today. We feel no guilt or remorse in killing animals because they are not human. In the future, we humans may cannibalize each other because we are not animals. In addition to the existing killing triggers like rage, revenge, religion, greed, we will kill each other for sport and fun, as avenues of diversion and entertainment. As a society, we are constantly and endlessly 'entertained' by the preposterous, the absurd, the volatile, and the violent.

We have failed to hold a steady course and to resolve or manage the many existential problems that we confront. Humans have consistently shown that they are rather lax at any kind of risk management. We are not very good at risk/return analysis, or at narrowing down possibilities into probabilities. That is why we are always caught on the wrong foot when a crisis hits us, whether it is a natural disaster or financial crisis or climate change. It is also because experts never agree on anything and so we, rather our minds, simply pay heed to the one that suits us and ignore the rest. A clear example is climate change. Depending on who we are asking, it either doesn't exist, or is an engineering problem, or requires nothing short of global mobilization, or could be solved by simply nudging the free market into action. When it comes to risks that threaten our very existence, and we have to take measures to monitor, minimize, and control any adverse impact, our mind simply refuses to get involved. Our own behavior belies us, makes us sometimes wonder: 'Is it really *me* out there?' That is because whether it is risk management or behavior, they are the external ways, whereas the source and the cause are internal. The way to move forward is to shift the arena of action entirely from behavior and context to consciousness and its content, character, and control. It is time to pause and ponder on this word *consciousness*. Although a "word worn smooth by a million tongues",[90] it has remained the holy grail of our 'thought-tormented age', to borrow a phrase from James Joyce (*The Dead*, 1914). In one sense and at one level, consciousness is everything, a state of being, a substance, a process, a place, an epiphenomenon. It is at once individual and universal, personal and cosmic. It separates as well as unites. Consciousness is what keeps us alive; it is what makes us do what we do. Although some behaviorists have associated belief in consciousness with superstition, there is general and broad agreement that we, and perhaps all sentient beings, have consciousness. Freud said, "What is meant by consciousness we need not discuss—it is beyond all doubt". And Tolstoy once said that death is the disappearance of the object of consciousness. When we are alive, it is the force that drives us, that impels us.

Scholars have long debated about the precise relationship between brain, mind, and consciousness. Many believe that conscious awareness originates in the brain alone, more precisely in the neocortex. A growing body of evidence suggests that the heart plays a particularly significant role in this process. Many spiritualists say that in addition to the physical heart, we all have a *spiritual* heart, and it is this latent force that we need to re-awaken. They call for a heart-based consciousness, using the heart as the organ of perception. While the physical heart works to keep us alive, the spiritual heart acts as the center of control in our spiritual life. The impulse for consciousness-change must come from this center, and it will come only if the center is awakened. Recent research[91] also indicates that intelligence does not only reside in the brain, but also in the heart. And that the heart is a conscious organ, and the 'heart' of consciousness exists in the middle of the chest.[92] To achieve one of our long-standing goals to bridge spirituality and science, we need to turn to the heart, and building such a bridge must be part of consciousness-change. A critical requisite for consciousness-change is to restore the right balance between our mind and our heart. As of now, it is all about the brain, and it is through this path that science has been furthering its agenda. And that is the grievous error. With the brain as the sole navigator, anchor, guide, and beacon, we will never be able to introduce 'higher dimensions of our consciousness into our awareness', as the Chinese philosopher Lao Tzu pointedly told us. It is everyday awareness that makes us who we are, and it is at that level that true change is needed. Native wisdom and nascent research tell us that the human heart is a source and storehouse of intelligence, memory, and energy, independent of the brain. It is the pump that keeps us alive; its regression as a source of intelligence is the beginning of much of what ails us as modern humans. If, as Einstein cautioned us, the same consciousness that created a problem cannot solve it, then we need a cathartic consciousness-change and the heart must be at its center. The only revolution that can truly transform the world is that of the consciousness within. Many now believe that it is only by restoring the heart to its rightful and righteous place that we can cure our ills and evolve further. This is the true alternative to our frenzied embrace of the machine as our salvation.

But context too is critical, because whatever happens and whatever we do in everyday life in the most basic form and at the rawest level are the arms and ammunition that both sides use in this invisible and soundless war. In many ways, context is content. If we do good, the forces of good in the war will be stronger, and if we do bad, the forces of evil will gain an upper hand. Nothing we do goes in vain or without impact. Context is life, and life is not solid. It is fluid and constantly opens opportunities, new karma. In life, we pursue many things and make multiple choices during the course of everyday living, but we can't know for sure how our choices will affect the world around us. But if we look closely, almost all hinge upon and impact upon three critical 'Ms': morality, money, and mortality. Virtually every waking moment, and maybe even in our sleep, one or the other preoccupies us. Even if our actions belie, we want to be moral but on our own tricky terms; money-wise, 'having money' has become a virtue unto its own, and it has reached such a stage that is even okay to make money off actual murder. Max Weber[93] once wrote that "man is dominated by the making of money, by acquisition as the ultimate purpose of his life". Simply put, money buys whatever the owner of money wants. Money is no longer the means to the 'rational pursuit of gain'; now any 'gain' sans money is worthless. Even more, we are now told that money can get you a new body, even eternal life. And even if we still have to die, money matters even after we die. It is a measure of how much we love our children. It is by leaving lots of money that we want to ensure that they will have a 'good life' even if the world around crumbles into ruin; just as we wish to ensure that we will be able to pay their way to immortality and interplanetary existence. We will do well to bear in mind Henry Fielding's warning: *Make money your god and it will plague you like the devil.*

Today, on the moral scale, we are nosediving towards the nadir—and money (or rather, in Mark Twain's phrase, our 'rabid hunger' for money) is, in no small measure, responsible for it. Money has taken on such a mystical, *Lord-of-the-Rings*-ish quality, that the only way to escape its power is *not* to have any of it. One of the urgent tasks we have on hand is to build a consensus on what we might call a 'new morality', a new framework for ethical living. At a time when we are flooded with conflicting choices and technology is raising new moral dilemmas, we need new guidelines in making the right choices that not only safeguard the individual's interest but do not endanger humanity and the planet. Technological pursuit itself, many argue, has to be 'democratized'. The morality of the morrow must be more social and spiritual than personal and materialistic. If the present trend continues, much of mankind will remain mortal, while a small minority could afford immortality.

The way we think through and deal with the three Ms—mortality, money, and morality—has gone awfully awry and is creating tremendous negative energy in the world, resulting in untold misery. Unless we are able to bring about fundamental, drastic, and directional changes in our interface with them, we cannot bring about any meaningful change in the context of our lives. The good news is that, if we can correctly orchestrate the changes, it would lead to a world of good. Money and morality, for example, can do both good and bad to each other. Morality *minus money* can be a force for good, and so can money *plus morality*. If human life can be freed from the suffocating sway of money, man will become more moral. If its grip is loosened and if it is properly channeled, money can become a moral force, and suicides and homicides can greatly diminish. And if man becomes essentially, if not wholly, a moral being, then perhaps he will bring to bear a more measured approach to his deep driving desire for immortality. Such a moral man would desist from taking all sorts of poorly thought-over devices like merging with the machine, or turning into bionic hybrids, with 'tiny robots scurrying around his brain to help him think'. Instead, we should direct that money and mind-power to building the human and moral infrastructures. The context of human life is vastly changing, primarily due to technologies like the internet and artificial intelligence. We need a new framework for a moral life that places greater emphasis on social virtues than on personal piety, on environmental ethics than on family values. For instance, adulteration and pollution must be seen as greater threats to the social order than adultery and prostitution. For a better world or a better human, money must stop being the sole agenda. The betterment of humanity must have much to do with both morality and mortality. Death is now not so simple. Many moral issues are arising about what to do when one wishes to die or when one is no longer in a position to decide. And with enough money, we might do to death what we do to each other: *cheat*. That is, we could bounce back after a century or two from deep sleep, and possibly even play with our grandkids of our own age.

These days, everything is up for grabs, available for rent or sale. We want to take everything, give nothing. We are like a drowning man refusing to 'give' his hand but prepared to 'take' the hand of the rescuer. Nothing is off the table to get what we want, not even the womb or virginity; everything has a price and nothing has any value. We want to be upwardly mobile, not morally upright in our permanent pursuit of pleasure, power, and profit. The love of money might still be the root of evil and corrosive corruption in the world, but the real problem area is the mendacity of the human mind, not money. If money disappears, our mind will invent something else. We must also remember that money looms large everywhere because we are empty of any other moral capital—social, cultural, or spiritual. Money must be made a moral tool, and a part of doing so is to dilute the exclusive emphasis on how one makes money, and place greater emphasis on *how it is utilized*. It does not mean we are ignoring the fact that money weakens every other social bond; it only means that we cannot wish it away. When everything is conditioned by money, then the scarcity of money makes everything scarce, including the very basis of human life. Making it available to the deprived and needy becomes a high moral act, even if the means and motives are unholy and the money itself is tainted.

The big money being poured into research on immortality must be redirected to where it could improve the well-being of billions who die due to extreme poverty and human negligence. *That* is critical to winning the war within. Without contextual-change, there can be no consciousness-change, and without consciousness-change, we will continue to lose the war within. That is the only way to steer both man's mindset and earthly behavior towards righteousness and compassion for all. Both righteousness and compassion are important theological concepts in many traditions including Zoroastrianism, Hinduism, Buddhism, Judaism, Christianity, and Islam. But they must germinate and sprout within. The American psychologist and philosopher William James said over a century ago that 'the greatest revolution of our generation is the discovery that human beings, by changing the inner attitudes of their minds, can change the outer aspects of their lives'. But nothing happened since and, as a result, things are getting worse. The empirical evidence is gaining increasing clarity and credibility day by day: humanity is poised at a momentous moment, a tumultuous time, perhaps unlike any other in human history. This generation of humans faces a quandary that no one in the past has faced. Is mass suicide the 'categorical moral imperative' of this generation—an action, so as, in the words of Immanuel Kant, "not to disgrace the dignity of humanity" but to salvage whatever we still can? For we have reached a stage, in Kant's words, when life's "continued duration threatens more evil than it promises satisfaction". Let us be clear on what we have collectively done to the planet: the earth is well on course to turn into an 'orbiting cinder', and we are showing no signs of waking up from the climate coma. We have repeatedly proven that we are not hard-wired to learn while doing, and lack the courage to admit an error and to do the needful to set it right. That is why we are in this muddle, and the planet in such peril. Has our own willful exit into the sunset become the only responsible response? The choice before us is not between going down with the sinking ship or jumping off it. It is how to save the ship itself. If we want to stick around, then we have to morally mend ourselves from bottom up. Has the digital age ushered in a new context for moral living? Some say that modernity has rendered morality redundant. But the point is that even if we turn the clock back, which is impossible, evil will still be with us and morality would be in retreat. Morality, in the end, governs how we relate and treat each other, particularly the weakest and the most vulnerable. Our moral behavior is inseparable from our overall behavior. The model for such behavior has to carry the spirit of an old Irish saying about trust: "*Mo sheasamh ort lá na choise tinne*"—you are the place where I stand on the day when my feet are sore.

The man of the moment is simply inadequate and inappropriate to face the forces his own inventiveness has unbuckled. As he wades into the 21st century, man is doubly dangerous because he is at once too powerful and too enfeebled, too ambitious and too adrift, and that is a very ominous condition. To survive, the human is doing all kinds of things in the name of augmentation of his body and brain, while actually eroding his own core identity. He now looks upon himself as a sum of his parts, not holistically, and that 'I' is at the root of his lure of the machine. So besotted and in such a thrall we are with anything inorganic, mechanical or electronic, that we have adapted the adage "imitation is the best form of flattery" and decided to be one of them. Instead of symbiosis, what we are doing is to pay the ultimate tribute, offer the total surrender, which we have denied to the divine. Our imitative admiration for the machine is such that we have decided to adopt the same fragmented, piece-by-piece, limb-by-limb approach to human betterment. As a kind of throwback to what is known as de La Mettrie's doctrine,[94] man has come to believe that logically it is but right that the two—man and machine—should become one for mutual benefit. And that he thinks is man's destiny and destination, the way to New Age nirvana, to bypass 'natural selection' and become a god. Then man believes that he can shed being earth-bound and be able to live in outer space. It is outer space that modern man is now fixated upon. Going to Mars might soon be like going to the North Pole now. None of it will solve any of our problems back home and make man any less of a threat to himself and to all others around. If any, a mechanized near-immortal man would be more brazen, and the malice in his mind more metastatic. The real space sojourn is to go into 'inner space', the world within.

A man–machine merger may give us a new 'body', but what we need is a new consciousness. It is more likely that it will be the machine that will call the shots, not because it is smart but because we are stupid to try to make it smart. And it is also possible that, as Elon Musk says, if the machine "has a goal and if humanity just happens to be in the way, it might well destroy humanity as a matter of course without even thinking about it. No hard feelings". That is what humans do to other humans anyway. And then again, the man–machine merger is but the logical extension of mechanization that started with the Industrial Revolution, and, in the words of Kirkpatrick Sale[95] "the ideal of industry is to eliminate the living factor, even including the human factor". It is the culmination of what Andrew Kimbrell calls, "living fully in the technosphere". The only way to arrest this fatal attraction is to diminish the dominance of our mind in our consciousness. That change must come in the world within as a part of the broader consciousness-change. In the world outside, we have to orchestrate a contextual-change that involves, in particular, the way the three Ms—morality, money, and mortality—are currently being perceived, understood, and addressed. The three are interconnected, and have to be dealt with in tandem with each other. For example, for morality to be strong in the world, money must be weakened; and for money to be a moral tool, we need a new framework for moral life. Mortality, rather our timeless thirst for eternal life, besides running the risk of yielding unintended consequences, is emerging as a major make-or-break moral issue, a source of a new dangerous divide and potentially the last straw on the backs of the poor and powerless, the marginalized and the social left-overs.

The bottom line is that we humans, given the kind of consciousness we have, are now simply too much of a toxic baggage for nature to carry around too long. We are blissfully unaware but we are all potential 'suicide-terrorists'. Mercifully, most of us might live through and remain 'potential'; but you never know what could be the trigger or tipping point, ideology or inspiration, irresistible temptations of evil or dark impulses looking for an alibi. The point is not that we always mean bad, but we do mostly bad despite our best intentions. We can be a murderer or a martyr or a mahatma, but we have no clue which of these three will crash through our defenses. We can't get a hold on ourselves because we are wholly clueless about the fierce fight between the two polar sides of our psyche to shape and control our personality. Whatever we might call the process—mutation, metamorphosis, transformation, transcendence, transmutation—we must give way or go in, even without knowing the answer to the Vedantic question, "Who am *I*?" Because the answer to the question, self-evident as it may be, is that human intellect is not only incapable of comprehending but fully capable of subverting it. And if we keep doing what we are doing, we will keep getting what we are getting. We must now shift the gaze from "What are we?", to "What should we be?", and work out how to bring that about. It is important because who we think we ought to be affects how we behave.

The world needs a 'New Man'—a *humane* human, not a *humanoid* human, a new paradigm, persona and personality, a new mindset and a new heart-driven consciousness. It is only through that way can we bring about a blend between mind-driven rational intelligence and what in Sanskrit is called '*ritambhara prajna*', or heart-centered intuitive intelligence. Technology, versatile and invaluable as it is, cannot create such a man by blurring the boundary between man and machine. The marriage or merger might not give us a god but a demon with godly powers. We are like Oscar Wilde's fisherman who, for the love of the mermaid, shed his soul on the advice of a witch, and we could face the same tragic fate in our 'love' for the machine.[96] Our 'witch' is technology, and the one we are prepared to give up to 'marry' the machine is the very essence of being human.

The fatal attraction for the fisherman was the mermaid's ethereal beauty, and for us it is eternal life. Without consciousness-change, even radical extension of longevity can make the human the greatest menace since life began on earth. The man of the morrow has to be more a spiritual being than a material being, born within each of us, raised from the rubble of the greatest of all wars—the invisible, inhouse war in the battleground of the *Kurukshetra* of our consciousness. What we must bear in mind is that, in the end, as the Greek philosopher Plutarch said, "Whatever we achieve inwardly will change outer reality". If we can change what is happening 'inwardly' in the right direction then we can change outwardly in the right direction and bring about a better world. And as JK Rowling told Harvard grads (2008), "We do not need magic to change the world, we carry all the power we need inside ourselves already". This is the only war that makes it possible to harness such a power; everything else is a skirmish, a sideshow of the shadows. Unless we unravel the way to intervene and influence, if not control, the fortunes of this war, the world will only wind down into a more horrific place than it is now.

This book presents a mélange of ideas, options, and insights to make it possible for the good in us to prevail over the evil in this war within.

Chapter 1

Musings on Mankind

The Human Animal

The state of the world today raises deeply troubling questions about the state of man. Now, more than ever, the unrelenting refrain is 'we are the world'. For, the human is the one who is singularly responsible for everything that has gone wrong, and for every crisis the world faces. Man the Unknown, is now *Man the Terrible*, the most feared beast on Earth, feared both by man and by fellow beasts. While our ancestors have been around for much longer, about six million years, the modern human, *Homo sapiens*, only evolved about 200,000 years ago. Quite apart from prehistoric civilizations and those inferred from religious texts, human civilization, as we know it, is barely 12,000 years old, and the era of industrialization started in earnest only in the 1800s. Yet, in this blink of time, we have managed to do quite a bit! We have quadrupled our number, in a little over 100 years, to 7.3 billion—which is projected to reach 9.7 billion by the year 2050, and 11.2 billion by 2100. Although new studies reveal a continuing slowdown in the rate of population growth, due to the near-global decline in fertility rates, the matter of greater concern ought to be human behavior, not human numbers. Instead of focusing on how many we will be in the future, what we should ponder over is this: how can a being, to describe whom scriptures slip into superlatives, and science goes into raptures, how could such a being behave so badly and so irresponsibly? Although we humans are just 0.01% of life on earth, man has become the exterminator of all other life on earth, the plague of the planet. In spite of being a diminutive harbinger of death and destruction on his planet, the human animal has been the most aggressive and murderous of all. Douglas Fields (*Why We Snap*, 2016) elaborates: "Violence exists in the animal world, of course, but on a far different scale. Carnivores kill for food; we kill our family members, our children, our parents, our spouses, our brothers and sisters, our cousins and in-laws. We kill strangers. We kill people who are different from us, in appearance, beliefs, race, and social status. We kill ourselves in suicide. We kill for advantage and for revenge, we kill for entertainment: the Roman

Coliseum, drive-by shootings, bullfights, hunting and fishing, animal roadkill in an instantaneous reflex for sport. We kill friends, rivals, coworkers, and classmates. Children kill children, in school and on the playground. Grandparents, parents, fathers, mothers—all kill, and all of them are the targets of killing…" It means that human killing does not stem from our being a primate; it is endemic to our species. Not only that, we view everything in human terms, anthropomorphize animals, giving them human attributes and values.

Our attitude towards other forms of life on earth has always been at best ambivalent. With a broad brush, we can classify that attitude in five ways. One, we are directly made by the divine as an apex of creation, with the implicit mandate to deal and dispense with the other forms as we will. Two, we too are 'animals' but, at the same time, we are so uniquely endowed that we are actually a genre apart. Three, we are a 'higher-animal', and all the rest are 'lower' animals. Four, we are just like any other animal and what we think 'unique' about us is nothing but what is necessary to be a 'human animal', and every other creature has its own 'unique' attributes. Five, judging from what the human has done since his appearance on earth, we are the 'lowest' of them all. The moral and spiritual dimensions cut across all five posits. If we are already and actually 'all-divine' or made in 'His' image, we should be expected to manifest the moral qualities we commonly associate with the divine: noble, good, kind, compassionate, just, etc. If we are altogether a different 'make' of an animal, or the highest, one would also expect our behavior to be qualitatively 'superior'.

Our historical footprints indicate, at least from a moral perspective, as Mark Twain observed, that we are the *lowest* animal. Twain wrote, "… for it obliges me to renounce my allegiance to the Darwinian theory of the Ascent of Man from the Lower Animals; since it now seems plain to me that the theory ought to be vacated in favor of a new and truer one, this new and truer one to be named the *Descent* of Man from the Higher Animals". And that conclusion, he wrote, he had arrived at through a 'scientific method' and 'actual experiments' made in the London Zoological Gardens, and covered many months of painstaking and fatiguing work. He also noted that covetousness, avarice, indecency, vulgarity, and obscenity are 'invented' by the human animal.

In fact, we 'humanize' even the divine and feel disappointed when the divine does not measure up to our expectations. As biologist Jeremy Griffith puts it, "…words used to describe human behavior… demonstrate that there is a psychological dimension to our behavior; that we don't suffer from a genetic-opportunism-driven 'animal condition', we suffer from the *psychologically* troubled *human* condition". Another study shows that our violence operates far outside the bounds of any other species. A recent study elaborates that "human beings kill anything. Slaughter is a defining behavior of our species. In addition, humans do have this high propensity for proactive violence, which is basically what is responsible for war. We kill all other creatures, and we kill our own". This killing spree is gaining speed day by day. According to the World Wildlife Fund (WWF), mammal, bird, fish, and reptile populations have fallen on average by 60% since 1970. The biggest cause of wildlife loss is the annihilation of natural habitats followed by killing for food. It is not the wrath of God but the greed of man that is more fearsome. Whatever 'good' we did do was actually saving the planet from humans. According to a recent study, since the dawn of civilization, humanity has caused the loss of 83% of all wild mammals and half of plants, while livestock kept by humans abounds. And so dominant and overpowering is human presence on earth and so affected the planet's environment, geology, and climate, that the present period in human geological history is now officially called the Anthropocene era.

That honor, or dishonor, of accelerating extinction that is bestowed on us is due to what is referred to as the *Great Acceleration* of human activity, which is closely connected with the sixth major phase of extinction that we are witnessing on earth. The way we have decimated and denuded the planet is so predatory, that, in the words of astronomer Martin Rees, "the darkest prognosis for the next millennium is that bio, cyber or environmental catastrophes could foreclose humanity's immense potential, leaving a depleted biosphere" and a crippled planet. Comparison of mammal numbers of the time before humans became farmers and the Industrial Revolution began, reveal that just one-sixth of wild mammals, from mice to elephants, remain. That ruthless destructiveness equally cripples the human world. And much of all the gut-wrenching things that shock and distress us are consequences of that very streak of destructiveness of man, much of it the ruins of our path to progress, prosperity and 'good life'. It is 'destruction' that matters, no matter who or what is on the way, even our own selves. Some use 'destruction' to find themselves. In Hermann Hesse's book

(*Siddhartha*, 1951), Siddhartha, with his lofty spiritual goal in mind, says "I will no longer mutilate and destroy myself in order to find a secret behind the ruins". We do that routinely for sensual purposes. Our response, rather the lack of it, to clear and present existential threats like the climate crisis, is another form of self-harm. In fact, self-harm is the signature of our species. We seem to have almost a fatal attraction to things that harm us, even kill, especially if the substance is slow-acting and pleasure-giving. Mentally, we keep a distance and think of anything unpleasant or dangerous as 'this thing over there'. That is part of how we manage to kill ourselves without even being aware of it. The net result is that we have become a soft, suicidal and savage species; we shun pain and we seek instant gratification with little effort; we like short-cuts and quick-fixes; we want luxury and laziness at the same time; we crave for conveniences and comforts. Our growing addiction to gadgets stems from being a soft species. It is technology that has made us soft by giving us an appliance or appendage to every task, even the most routine, to help us or replace us with. There is a kind of a brewing backlash, and some parents, while they continue to be consumed by appliances of all sorts, are convinced that "the devil lives in our phones and is wreaking havoc on our children".[1] They fear that screen time is going straight to the pleasure centers of the developing brain. It remains to be seen how the Apples and Samsungs of the world will react to the trends, because, if kids actually start growing up without looking at or into screens, then these companies will go out of business. We must also be aware that if we don't use, or grossly underuse, what nature has gifted us, then sooner or later, nature will make constructional adjustments to reflect the reality. For nature abhors both vacuum and redundancy. It may even transfer our unused capacity and faculties to other species. In fact, that is implicit in natural selection. And we have in us a stubborn streak that simply turns the Nelson's eye to anything that is uncomfortable, anything that threatens our ride on the gravy train. We are now being told that we have just a 12-year window of opportunity to set right things to avoid a climate catastrophe. But how many of us are willing to loose any sleep or worry about what might happen after 12 years? We just hope that the experts are wrong or, on a rebound, make merry in the meantime. The human mind resorts to one of the three 'E's to escape from a tricky spot: evasion, explanation, and excuse. And that destructive capability is daily mounting with every technological advance. The actual 'doer' might be someone else for a certain horror, but we are all participants, perpetrators and beneficiaries. The question to ask is not 'who are they?' but 'who are *we*?'; not 'who is he?', but 'who am *I*?' This question is the mother of all questions; it is at the heart of the Advaitic Vedanta school of Hindu philosophy, and of all spiritual *sadhana* or pursuit.

We must remember that anything that we make happen in the world outside, first happens in our own mind, and in our consciousness. Man, at the morrow of the 21st century, has become so schizoid, suicidal, narcissistic and nihilistic that one wonders whether he has had evolution or atavism, ascent or descent, from our animal roots. Comparisons are surely odious, but every species has its strengths and foibles. With a mix of condescension and conceit, we tend to think that nonhuman animals are little more than clever automata with a toolkit of preprogrammed behaviors that respond to specific triggers. In fact, it is this line of thought that lets us get away with all the unspeakable and horrendous things we do to animals. The truth is that being human is to be *all-animals*; neither higher nor lower. God might have run out of ideas when it came to creating man, and He might have just jumbled up the attributes of other animals, and, feeling a little bit sorry, added a bonus—made him in His image. At different times, we can be any other animal: tiger, elephant, lamb, fox, dog, wolf, vulture, snake... We never can tell which animal or divine character we will show up as, and we seem utterly helpless about it. That is the predicament, promise and peril of 'being human'. That is perhaps why philosopher Peter Zapffe said that man is a tragic animal. For, a tiger is a tiger, or a dog is a dog, but there is no such thing as 'man is a man'. Man is exceptional not because he has any exclusive attribute, but because he has in him *all* conceivable attributes. There is one dimension of our existence that bears some attention: it is our claim that we are a 'spiritual being', implying that other animals are not. One of the things that signify our sense of insecurity, not superiority, is our almost compulsive comparison with animals—the refrain that *we* can and *they* can't; that *we* are and 'they' aren't. Firstly, to judge whether other creatures on earth are 'spiritual' or not we should have yardsticks and norms to apply, which we do not have. Everyone has their own understanding of what a spiritual life entails. Secondly, while other animals do exhibit some of our worst traits like aggression, violence and even cruelty, they do that as a part of their *swadharma*, necessary to their ordained way of life. In our case, those traits are optional, and not necessary for our swadharma or survival. And then, we alone are endowed, or blighted, with the worst of all attributes in nature: *malice* (wishing ill without any gain), and its toxic twin *schadenfreude* (deriving pleasure from others' misery). The closest in nature that resembles us in this respect, strangely, is in the plant kingdom, the *Pisonia* tree. This ruthless tree, found in the tropical waters of the Indian and Pacific oceans, produces extremely sticky seedpods that get stuck onto any bird that flies into them, either trapping it in the tree's branches or weighing the bird down so much on the ground that it is completely unable to fly. The bird usually starves to death, if it doesn't fall easy prey for crabs or other predators.

What is baffling is why this particular tree alone has this malicious streak, and what evolutionary purpose its horrible trait serves. It is all the more surprising when we bear in mind that it takes man mutations through several generations for any trait to be fully formed and become functional. In that sense, one can argue that animals minus malice are more 'spiritual' than humans. Recent research suggests that animals too can have spiritual experiences. We are all animals, birds of the same feather, but each one having a different blend of the same menu of components. But, what about divinity, which we have unilaterally appropriated to ourselves? If animals are 'better' than us in terms of how they live and die, how can *we* be divine and not them? The fact is that all sentient beings are divinely designed and it does not make any difference, if we are good or bad; in any case, no one is all good or all bad. And nothing can exist without His will, even evil. The only difference is that other animals live solely by instincts specific to their nature of life; we, on the other hand, are made of a much broader range, and live by choice. And that leads to a struggle between our own intrinsic traits, tendencies, and dispositions. The world as it is, and what each of us does in this world, are but sparks and shadows of this *struggle.*

We have expectations of a just and moral world. Man requires meaning in a meaningless world. And we don't think we are endowed enough to be what we want to be—an interplanetary immortal being. That is why we are prepared to commit mass *hara-kiri* and meld into a machine. Life is now all about 'business'. Taking a cue from that business strategy for growth, what is called 'M&A' (merger and acquisition), we want to do the same with our life. We have come to believe that by *merging* with a machine—and thus blurring the boundary between animate and inanimate matter—we can *acquire* the elixir of eternity. Every sentient being, even a worm or ant, is special and exceptional and fulfills a niche in creation. But truth be told, we are quite a heady mix. Mean, malicious, and murderous, we surely are, but also, we humans have cooperative and loving moral instincts. As Charles Darwin said, 'The moral sense perhaps affords the best and highest distinction between man and the lower animals'. But others maintain that there are no animals that are as evil as humans. It means that we have in us what it takes to be the noblest and the meanest, the most virtuous and vicious. Thus far, we really did not know when which of the two would show up in our behavior, and what we could do to contain them. Only now do we realize that the answer is *within*, that these two opposing sides, good and evil, along with their respective allies, are waging a full-blown but bloodless war, the war within. It is the flow and course of this war that manifests in our behavior as good or bad. Although the good is by no measure gone, it is evil that seems to be steadily gaining ground in the war. It is this war that Jeremy Griffith alludes to when he talks about a "battle for the management of our lives… between our already established, gene-based, naturally-selected, instinctive orientations, and our newly emerged, nerve-based, understanding-dependent, self-adjusting, fully conscious mind",[2] which, he says, began 2 million years ago when we became fully conscious.

While this fierce war wages in the human consciousness, the human condition is being transformed so fundamentally by the sweep and velocity of cutting-edge technologies that, soon, when we meet one another on the street, we will wonder if the other person is human. By the end of this century, it might well become difficult to define what *human* means, and who among us is human, and who is a hybrid, or cyborg or android or robot or a monster. The human could possibly *not* be the strongest or the smartest, and it is debatable if that is good or bad from a planetary perspective. If man's dominance on earth weakens or ends, would the world be more moral and safer if non-humans or part-humans are in control? Would nature, so mercilessly mauled by man, regain its resilience and grandeur? Some idealists might call that the ultimate altruism, while realists could condemn it as foolhardy masochism.

We really don't know, and *that* is the cause for concern. With all his endowments and accomplishments, culture and civilization, self-awareness and ability to learn, improve and improvise, why is modern man so starved of wisdom, good judgment, even enlightened self-interest? What makes us so willfully blind to the obvious, and unable to work together for meeting common challenges? The question arises: Is it all the effect of the passage of *yugas*, and the advent of the Hindu *Kali Yuga* or Dark Age, when, as foretold, righteousness is said to be in retreat and evil is both banal and bold? Indeed, paradoxes in the human context abound. We are both wild and divine, made of the clay of the earth and cosmic dust, dancing away in deep space. We are a 'self-conscious nothing' (as Julius Bahnsen said) while being a geological force to reckon with. We are all human; but few are humane. Most of us think we are virtuous; but few are bereft of vice. We are all uniquely blessed with the power to know what is important and what is immediate, what is soothing and what is healing, and yet so few of us can manifest that capability to make myriads of choices of daily life. Many of us feel we are moral and good even if, we grudgingly admit, a few times we got carried away and did things we are not proud of, but very few shrink from hurting the weak and vulnerable. We think we are peace-loving and non-violent because we have not physically assaulted anyone, though the truth is we do more hurt by our mouth than by our hand. We are endowed with the unique power of reason, *viveka* (wisdom) and *vichakshana* (discrimination), but most of us act with *aham* (ego), *ahankara* (arrogance), and *agraha* (anger). All told, the human, until he turns into something else, is quite a thing to chew over. That is why man has been called all sorts of things: the unknown; the species in denial; thinking animal, begotten by God Himself, organic machine, a work in progress, and so on. But the bottom line and the baggage we want to shed is the beast.

Empathy—Not a Human Monopoly

Our strongest claim to species-superiority is that we alone are a 'rational', moral, and compassionate species, with the unique ability to judge right and wrong. But alas, that too is now being scientifically challenged. For example, primatologist Frans de Waal has argued that "many of what philosophers call moral sentiments can be seen in other species..." Even reciprocity and willingness to follow social rules. According to him, "Dogs are a good example of a species that have and obey social rules; that's why we like them so much, even though they're large carnivores". He also says, "To endow animals with human emotions has long been a scientific taboo. But if we do not, we risk missing something fundamental, about both animals and us". Being systematically more brutal than chimps and more empathic than bonobos, we are by far the most bipolar ape. Our societies are never completely peaceful, never completely competitive, never ruled by sheer selfishness, and never perfectly moral. We are told that if a squirrel finds a baby squirrel without parents, it will immediately adopt it! In chimpanzees and other animals, we see examples of sympathy, empathy. And, cows choose other cows as best-friends and spend all their time together.

Making a huge leap forward in this direction, researchers are now reporting that some primates not only "do each other favors even if there's nothing in it for themselves", but also feel compassion for us, suffering humans. We see that trait among domesticated dogs, which we also know mourn for the loss of their loved masters long after their death; in some way maybe more than humans. The fact is, as Frans de Waal says, "no one doubts the superiority of our intellect, but we have no basic wants or needs that are not also present in our close relatives. But it does not mean that we or any other animal is a 'moral animal'; nor are we evil incarnate. The truth is that every creature on earth contains within it everything that is there in nature. Why some species and some among us are 'more or less moral, or more or less evil' is a different matter. It has much to do with the war within.

What is alarming about modern-day self-destruction is its virtuosity, range and reach, which is even beyond species-scale, as we have become the pre-eminent exterminators of all other forms of life. We are, aided by technology, not only trying to transform ourselves into an impregnable, immortal species, but we are also exterminating other species at such a dizzying pace that evolutionary natural selection is not having enough time to adapt and allow other species to survive and take their place. We are told that, despite greater public awareness "a quarter of the world's mammals, a third of its amphibians, more than a tenth of its birds, a quarter of its warm-water corals, and a quarter of its freshwater fishes are globally threatened with extinction". Only a third of wild animals now exist compared to forty years ago, and there are only 3,500 tigers still surviving in the world today!

Fact is that we have long nurtured a misplaced sense of pride that man is a one-of-a-kind marvel, that humans are unique and 'exceptional' to all other earthly creatures, that modern man is the best there is, or could be. The more we know about both man and beast, the more it is becoming clear that animals are more humane than the human, and that man is more animalistic than the animal. According to Mark Twain, who considered man as among the lowest of animals, "the passion of revenge is unknown to the higher animals".[3] Indecency, vulgarity, and obscenity are our exclusive traits. Twain also said that, of all the animals, man is the only one that is cruel. For humans, we should note, cruelty is not entirely a personality trait and a habit. In other words, even if there is another way, we choose the cruel way. It is such a 'habit' that when a word suffices, we use a cutting word. When silence is sufficient, we sneer. When we can live with condescension, we cannot resist callousness. When rebuke is relevant, we seek revenge. When envy is pardonable, we unleash malice. Even if the 'rat-race' is inevitable, we brook no 'prisoners'. To buttress his point, Twain cited two instances: one in which an English earl organized a buffalo hunting party in which they killed seventy buffaloes but ate only a part of one, and left the rest to rot; the other, in which seven calves were left in an anaconda's cage, and the 'grateful reptile' immediately ate one of them and allowed the rest to live side by side. We claim we alone have a soul. Whether or not it is true, as James Herriot puts it (*All Creatures Great and Small*), "If having a soul means being able to feel love and loyalty and gratitude, then animals are better off than a lot of humans". And quite possibly, as Henry Beston says, "In a world older and more complete than ours, they moved finished and complete, gifted with extensions of the senses we have lost or never attained, living by voices we shall never hear". The message to carry forward is simple. Whether or not other animals have a soul, or consciousness or conscience or something far more evolved, is beside the point. In fact, there is growing evidence they do. Recent research even hints that consciousness-like phenomena might exist not just among humans or even the great apes—but that insects might have them, too. Every species is one of a kind, has a special place in the cosmos. In contrast to the human animal, other animals meld effortlessly into the landscape of life on earth. Humans do have some particular abilities that others lack, stemming largely, if not entirely from our brain, the portion called the neocortex. We really do not know if that, by itself or more probably in tandem with unknown others, makes us what we are, the most complex, convoluted, cunning and confused being on the planet. We also harbor the most mixed of all bags of emotions, feelings, sentiments, and passions, and our reactions and responses are also more unpredictable. Most of them exist as pairs of opposites, like love and hate, kindness and cruelty. Since they are inherently incompatible, the consciousness itself has become a warring zone. Scientific research shows that many animals are very intelligent and have sensory and motor abilities that dwarf ours. Many animals also display wide-ranging emotions, including joy, happiness, empathy, compassion, grief, and even resentment and embarrassment. In many ways, human emotions are the gifts of our animal ancestors. As a last-ditch attempt at showing our 'superiority', it is now claimed that we alone have 'self-awareness', defined as metacognition, the awareness of one's own ability to think. Well, we really do not know. Instead of endlessly trying to discover or invent cases and reasons for our superiority over other species, the more prudent way would be to err on the right side and treat other animals as fellow-animals, and try to bring to bear on them the same qualities we expect for ourselves from our fellow-humans.

We must shed that skin of superiority not only with regard to other animals but also in relation to our own ancient predecessors. In fact, a truly 'superior' person has no need to feel superior. That apart, the plain fact is that there were similar forms of life on earth long before the advent of the *Homo sapiens*. Calling ourselves *sapiens*, the 'wise ones', is either symptomatic of, it is hard to tell, our self-righteousness, or satirical sense of humor. We are not the wise species; we are the *wild* one. While the earliest humans were not conscious of nature as something distinct from themselves, modern man has convinced himself that confronting nature is not only his 'natural' right, but also the only path to human evolutionary 'progress'. He treats nature as he treats another man over whom he has some hold, with condescension and contempt. Yet, nature, forgiving and non-discriminatory in showering its grace and generosity, has tolerated such behavior primarily because much of human activity did not, in pre-modern times, fundamentally undermine the basis of the cosmic balance. Our chosen course of confrontation with nature has brought the full tapestry of life on earth to a perilous point: just *one* species, among an estimated 8.7 million species on this one planet, is threatening to cripple nature and make the planet infertile for life itself. The startling revelation is that the food we eat, the timber we cut, and the water that man alone draws, amounts to an astounding one-third to one-half of the production of our entire ecosystem. The earth's 'biospheres' are extremely fragile, and depend on myriad interactions and interdependencies that, once broken, cannot be replaced. Human presence for long has been both transformative and terminal to nature, but it has never been as bellicose and esurient as it is today. So much so that human activity has overtaken nature as the paramount force in shaping the earth's landscapes, atmosphere, ecology, and all forms of life. The primal question that all this human rampage brings up is whether life is worth preserving at all, and whether there is no longer any choice except to extinguish human life altogether. Is that the most moral of all choices that each one of us, regardless of who or where we are, must face today?

That, in turn, brings up another thought: what about the 'mind of God'? Einstein once said that that [the mind of God] 'is all that matters; everything else is a detail'. We can only hypothesize but we do know that nature as His proxy and alter ego reflects His 'state of mind'. Whether or not there is any link between divine design and human activity, a time might well come when nature itself will have to make a choice it has never really required to make thus far: between its own integrity, and human audacity. Some still believe that a blend of détente and entente is still possible, and such a harrowing choice might not be needed yet. Even if it were so, the point of no return is clearly not too far away. This does not mean that nature is all moral and we are all amoral (if not 'evil'), or that nature is peaceable and pure, and humans are depraved and debauched. What we must never let slip from our conscious-awareness is that what sustains the order in the living, incarnate cosmos and creation is what is called *dharma* in Hinduism, our 'moral-base'. Dharma is impossible to translate; it is many-splendored and encompasses many virtues. But if one has to identify one single variable, it has to be *justice*, not mercy. If you err and commit a wrong, you must pay for it, you must be punished, no matter who or how mighty you are. That is why, in Hindu epics, all divine avatars killed the adharmic or evil people, who were not shown any mercy. In fact, that included those who were personally dharmic or virtuous, but were obligated to opt for the wicked, like Bhishma and Karna in the Mahabharata. All struggle, whether in the far corners of the world or in the deep depths of our inner being, is for the moral high ground. Any struggle implies two opposing sides: we are all made of a cocktail of dichotomies such as self/other, mine/yours, good/bad, love/hate, kindness/cruelty, indifference/compassion, worldly life/spiritual life… and trying to lead a moral life is part of the effort to extend greater support to the better half, our loving side, than to the bitter half, our hateful side, within and outside. Here, it is important to draw attention to a subtle but important point. All dichotomies (*dwandas*, as they are known in Sanskrit) are 'real' at a relative level. They are 'unreal' in absoluteness, that which the Upanishads call *purnamidam*,[4] and Buddhism calls *sunyata* or emptiness.

We need to accept and embrace ourselves in our entirety, not selectively as we do, for the simple reason that who we are is precisely what nature needed us to be, for its own completeness and fullness. None of us is an accident or an aberration. Instead of self-acceptance, so many suffer from self-loathing and that is responsible for so much of violence and unhappiness in the world. Unable to accept, we turn on others as a reflux. When this 'better-bitter-balance' is severely out-of-balance in the mass of mankind, Lord Krishna avers in the Bhagavad Gita, God will intervene to restore a reasonable dharmic 'balance'. But it still does not mean that 'evil' will be, or should be, erased from the earth. That is because there is nothing intrinsically and absolutely good or bad, positive or negative, and it is the intent and purpose that makes the difference. Even the smallest, tiniest, insignificant happenings in the world have an effect on this 'struggle', a struggle that has no end, despite periodic divine intervention.

The irony is that while man now claims to be the master over other forms of life and nature, he is too willing to surrender it all to a contraption made by his own mind. Although its import and implication is wholly hazy at this time, what is happening is this: modern man has convinced himself that to fulfill his destiny, he must be at war with nature, mate with the machine, and attain a kind of existence that will be what is being dubbed as *Life 3.0*.[5] His new creation, the machine, promises to acquire a 'mind' of its own, and mimic human brains in pace and processing capability.[6] For all we know, it might then outclass us, and possibly, even be able to have sex with an other of its kind, or with humans, like in *The Matrix*, if it so chooses, to evolve and spawn a superior species. The human of the present kind, if anyone still manages to linger and live, will then be an adjunct or acolyte of the machine. And by then, humans will be imitating machines to be more successful in life. In any event the nature of our nexus with technology in general, and with the machine in particular, will be the most fateful in human life, perhaps even more than between the divine and human. The euphoria is such that technology will, according to transhumanists and technophiles, allow *Homo sapiens* to discard the legacy of our evolutionary past, usher in the 'naturalization of heaven', eliminate aversive experience from the living world, and completely eradicate the biological substrates of suffering, and replace malaise by the biochemistry of orgasmic bliss.[7] And the divine connection could become marginal to human life. Intelligent machines would then be the new godhead, perhaps, the very avatar of Vishnu prophesied in Hindu scriptures to contain the rise of evil on earth in this *Kali Yuga* or Dark Age.[8] Whether the machine will turn out to be a 'Vishnu' or a villain, the ground reality is that the rate at which machines are evolving in capability may far exceed the rate at which society is able to deal with them. Moreover, as philosopher Herbert Marcuse noted, technology creates new, more ingenious and effective, even more pleasant forms of social oppression, making classical totalitarian control through terrorization unnecessary. It obliterates the opposition between private and public existence, and between individual and social needs. The wish to preserve life as we know it, even at the cost of dying, is quintessentially human and timeless. In an elemental sense, we are all dying all the time, but what we want to avoid is immediacy and inevitability. And dying, as Sylvia Plath said, is "an art, like everything else". We can leverage it to liberate us from the restraints of the realities of living. Mark Twain, for instance, begins his autobiography with the words, "I speak from the grave rather than with my living tongue, for a good reason: I can speak thence freely". We are encoded with the determination to remain exactly as we are, forever; and having hit a wall so far in that quest, we now feel that we have finally found not only the path but even a scientific short cut... We are so mesmerized by our cognitive creativity that we almost instinctively look for 'technical' solutions to complications created by that very technical capability, whether it is the nuclear arms race or climate change or artificial intelligence, something that Einstein foresaw and warned against.[9]

Technology is not static—it is a showpiece of human ingenuity. It can take any form we want it to. So then, why does the ever-increasing number of technological devices around us give us so little contentment and confidence?

What we need now is not so much 'technical' empowerment but moral empowerment, not technological fixation but ethical, endogenous capacity-building. In an ironic twist, those who are rooting for the machine say that it is the only way man can be more moral, that once the machine becomes self-aware and self-learning,[10] free from human programming, it might be able to more judiciously distinguish between what is 'good' and what is 'bad', and act more humanely—not humanly. With full command over what machines do, it will be free from one of our age-old helplessnesses: as a good man, why do I do bad things? The essential point to ponder over is that the value of any life lies in the kind of choices the 'being' (whether it is wholly human or hybrid or humanoid) makes with it, not only with what intention, but with what result and how that result affects others. That point now is even more critical, since science has exponentially expanded the sweep and span of human choice-making. We might soon be able to 'choose our baby the same way we pick a new outfit from a catalogue'.[11] And we can choose whether or not to continue to live, if we want to end our life, choose when to die, and choose if we want to come back, and if so when… If we can do all such magical deeds while still being human, why then do we need a machine as our mate? And what could possibly be the yield of such a union? Some say that our decision to dissolve into machine is perhaps the most enlightened and humanitarian of all decisions man has ever made, precisely because it could entail our early extinction. But, what is the expected pay-off of this mating or cross-breeding? Is it a signal that man has finally given up on himself and on God? And is the perennial aspiration of God-realization now going to be off the human agenda? Is it to save the human from implosion and extinction? Is it to give us jelly-fish-like immortality? Or is it really to unwittingly pave the way for the advent of a morally more mature form of life? What is the expected outcome here? What it translates into is that we will no longer be burdened or bothered by flesh, blood, or bones, but be just a scan of our brain on a machine, enabling it to will any form, and then live ever after. It is being predicted that before the end of this century we will be able to upload our brains to the 'cloud' or internet, essentially preserving our minds as a form of software for eternity. For long, human longing has been to rise above the animal nature; now it is to rise above human nature itself. It means we are prepared to, *de facto*, give up 'being human' to be something different—but what that should be, we don't think is important enough to know or at least be clear about. It raises a most fundamental question: what constitutes the core of being human? Is it our physical appearance and body build, our minds and our capacity to think, or is it our feelings and capacity to love or to hate, or is it something less tangible, our values and character, or is it the soul or spirit?

The brain is 'what makes *me* me'. In the words of the acclaimed neuroscientist, David Eagleman, "you are your brain". Logically, therefore, to understand human nature we only need to understand the human brain. If that be the case, why do we want to go beyond the brain for what we want to get from life? The answer again is the ease of convenience, which is what most millennials and the so-called *Generation Y* want in life. By opting to mate our 'brain-selves' with a machine, we probably hope to beget a super-intelligent and immortal generation—which can colonize another home in the cosmos, when our Earth, in about a hundred years or so, becomes unlivable. Such a storyline for so complex a phenomenon as human nature is not only simplistic but, even more, it paralyzes us from looking into the root causes. It is not just the chemistry of the brain, but that desire to cater to every craving, no matter how harmful it could be to the body, mind, society, and the planet. If there is one thing that we must do urgently, it is to move away from this storyline. When it is becoming increasingly clear that the kinds of thoughts, perceptions, misconceptions, and biases that the brain germinates, incubates, and nourishes, are not necessarily the kind that give us an accurate picture of reality, it is cockeyed to put all the eggs of humanity in the basket of the brain. And that, we must note, carries a consequence with a thick theological tone. What we have steadfastly denied to God—*prapatti* or *saranagati*, or complete surrender, as it is called in the Hindu Vaishnavite tradition—we are now prepared to offer on a platter to the machine, just when science has made us more mighty than ever before. While earlier we used to measure up a mechanism against man, now in a weird twist, we measure *ourselves* against a contraption like the computer. Some say that in about twenty years, there will be no such thing as a computer, since there will be *nothing* that is not a computer. An ironic reversal of roles, "We're *like* the thing that used to be *like* us. We imitate our old imitators, in one of the strange reversals in the long saga of human uniqueness".[12]

The Mood of the Moment

As a result, most people feel deep within, even if only fleetingly, a sense of despair, that things are not what they ought to be, that life has become both shallow and surreal, materialistic and meaningless, and that no man can be trusted in any relationship. We wonder if the 'problem' is an endemic 'design' deficiency or an exogenous 'development' default. Framed differently, are we made *that* way or have we made ourselves *this* way? Put in theological terms, is it the machinations of a 'mischievous' God or the masterwork of a malevolent mind? In more practical parlance, would man have been a 'better being' had he been left to his own 'nature', wit and whim, without the influence of any external 'knowledge', religious, metaphysical or ethical? And finally, in a strategic and spiritual sense—what should be the direction of our travail? This is a critical niche of inquiry, having a vital bearing on human behavior and destiny. Whatever resources, faculties and energy we can muster, on what should they focus upon? We know the problems; but what should we do in a way that is socially compatible and spiritually progressive? This is not a new dimension or debate in the history of human thought. For long, scriptures, sages, mystics and philosophers have grappled with it. Of late, science has joined the fray. It has acquired new or added urgency because the crisis has reached a critical point and the stakes are escalating almost daily. We know that we begin our life with a built-in 'handicap'; a design-default, one might term it. Our sense organs are designed to let us relate with the outside world; and we are told that we use but a small percentage of their potential. That has made us who we are. Aldous Huxley said that 'man is intelligence in servitude to his organs'. What is 'inside', what goes on 'down there' is the deepest mystery but it is what determines our behavior.

We must never forget that all through the trials and travails of life, our beliefs don't make us a better person; it is our behavior that is crucial. We use the words 'belief', 'disbelief', 'unbelief' and 'non-belief' to signify the state of the certitude or uncertainty of our knowledge. 'Belief' has come to be the defining divide in life and that is why we put the whole of humanity in two warring camps: believers and non-believers in God. 'Belief' is personal; behavior is social and spiritual and the link between man and God. Finally we are judged—indeed, we should judge ourselves—on how we view and treat other living beings, and how we weigh in their well-being, their rights as equal co-creations of God, entitled to the same needs and privileges that we claim for our own selves, in every choice and decision that we make. No man deserves all that he wants; and when we begin to think that we alone are entitled to something, we begin to exploit others. Entitlement can slip into 'embezzlement'.

We must bear in mind that every choice we make speaks more about ourselves than about the choice itself, and by our choice, we construct what we most fundamentally are. God is not unduly worried about how we treat Him in our mind; He will make up his mind on how we have lived, based on how we made a difference to the lives of His fellow-creations. Because, whether we like it or not we do make a difference; it is impossible not to do so; even indifference can make a difference. There is no neutrality in life. The question is, to what effect? Have we, through the myriad things we do, voluntarily or involuntarily, made the lives of others better or worse, made their burden lighter or heavier? That is the only thing that matters, here and hereafter. Although what we do matters, it is also only a visible extension of what goes on 'down there', without our knowledge or control. The body is merely a medium and the instruments are the sense-organs. Unless we can somehow get a peep beneath, get to know what happens before we speak or act, we cannot change our behavior. Many a thing we attribute to the 'inside'—brain, mind, heart, soul, spirit, conscience, consciousness, and so on. Man needs all those to work in symmetry for a harmonious life. Each has a part to play and the interplay between these gets translated into behavior. That *inside* is where thoughts originate, feelings are formed, emotions coalesce, words germinate and actions incubate.

All scriptures and wise men have emphasized the need for a clean 'inside' life, in order to live a life in harmony with the outside world. The *Maitri* Upanishad eloquently advises: "Let a man strive to purify his thoughts. What a man thinketh, that he is: this is the eternal mystery. Dwelling within himself with thoughts serene, he will obtain imperishable happiness". Gandhi echoed the same, "aim at purifying your thoughts and everything will be well".[13] The Buddha said that 'with our thoughts we make the world'. Emerson said that 'thought is the blossom; language the bud; action the fruit behind it'. Descartes famously uttered, "*Je pense, donc je suis*" (I think, therefore I exist). So, who, then, is the thinker? According to the *Kena* Upanishad, the thinker is the 'Self', described as 'bodiless within the bodies, as unchanging among changing things', the divine spark within all living beings, which is not different from the Divine, which the Upanishads call *Brahman*. The Kena Upanishad further says, "the Self is in the ear of the ear, the eye of the eye, the mind of the mind". The basic premise is that if we want a certain fruit we should sow the right seed. We cannot harbor impurity inside and expect purity to permeate outside. Hindu scriptures advocate three types of purity for a spiritual person: purity of consciousness (*chitta suddhi*); purity of nerves (*nadi suddhi*); and purity of body (*bootha suddhi*). Our 'within', the theater of our life experiences, is like a blender; what comes out depends on not only on the ingredients but also their relative weight. The brain-mind has come to occupy a huge chunk of the 'inner space' and that, in turn, has distorted human society.

Governance Deficit

Human society has never been able to arrange, organize, and manage its affairs in an orderly and harmonious manner. Whatever is 'unique' about the human, in relation to other animals, the paradox is that we alone need 'governance', and we alone are utterly ungovernable. To paraphrase Thomas Jefferson, we cannot repose "confidence in man", and we need to "bind him down from mischief in chains". But we never found a way without turning the chains into suffocating shackles. What we have ended up with is that man is more unruly than ever; man, more than ever, needs to be restrained, and all the governance experiments we have tried—from City-state to Nation-state—have fallen far short. Indeed, they have had a perverse effect. This has led to what is often referred to as 'governance-deficit', which afflicts man at once internally and externally. We are in the dark about what goes on inside, and have no control about what we do outside. Both lurch with a momentum of their own. But life hurtles on, without a pause either for the query or the answer.

The sacred word says that the solution is to explore the deepest depths of our own being, to conquer our internal enemies, to tame our dark passions, to tap into the nobler side of our consciousness. Vedanta expands it and says that to become and behave wholly human, we should know or realize, at the deepest level of our awareness, that we are wholly divine. Science has a one-word answer to all human personality problems: the 'brain'. By striving to use it better, and by dissecting and diving into its depths, science believes that the brain will empower us to fashion new technologies like nanotechnology to eventually help us become invincible, invisible, and immortal. Various technologies make us believe that we can live outside 'normative nature' and give rise to what are called 'revenge effects'. These are not merely side effects, but are consequences of technology (or of human interaction with the technology) that partially negate the advantage that the advance was supposed to bring.[14] Although in one sense all technology is enhancement of one or the other of our natural abilities, what is being attempted is qualitatively different. We are attempting to overcome our biological limitations when we try to cultivate x-ray vision, and exponentially increased the 'speed of cerebration'. This raises an ethical question: is there any point at which human 'enhancement' is just wrong? Or are these just tools like any other—and part of our inevitable future?

Helping: When Joy Comes Calling

The subtle secret, the eternal enigma of nature and life is this: we cannot control events, but we can control our *responses* to events. We cannot choose our destiny; but we can choose how we face up to it. How we react to what happens is more important than what happens. Eknath Easwaran says, "It's a perplexing paradox: so long as we try to make ourselves happy, life places obstacles in our path. But the moment we turn away from ourselves to make *others* happy, our troubles melt away. Then we don't have to go looking for joy; joy comes looking for us". We cannot do much about our own suffering, but we can do a lot to help others to absorb their suffering; when it is reciprocated, our suffering too dissolves like snow in summer sunshine. Help is service by another name. We should try to, in Swami Vivekananda's words, "look upon every man, woman, and everyone as God. You cannot help anyone, you can only serve: serve the children of the Lord, serve the Lord Himself, if you have the privilege". We can do very little to avoid getting hurt, but a lot more not to hurt others. A huge hinge of human suffering is built into the very sinew of human society; individual human beings instinctively act in self-serving ways that are not conducive to the commonweal or to his spiritual growth. That becomes easier if we remember that what 'others' want from life is the same as what we yearn for—harmony, love, meaning, peace of mind, good health. As Raoul Vaneigem (*The Revolution of Everyday Life*, 1967) puts it, the reality of our life is that "we seem to live in the State of variety, wherein we are not truly living but only in appearance: in Unity is our life: in one we are, from one divided, we are no longer... While we perambulate variety, we walk but as so many Ghosts or Shadows in it, that itself being but the Umbrage of the Unity". One of the classic dilemmas in human life arises from the situation in which multiple individuals, acting independently and rationally, will eventually deplete a shared limited resource, even when it is transparently apparent that it is not in anyone's long-term interest for this to happen. Our consciousness can only grasp what is demonstrably—and dramatically—of utility to us, and the awareness that that leads to long-term detriment eludes us.

The current crisis of climate change is an illustration. Man, in the space of a handful of millenniums, has drastically changed the composition of the atmosphere—which now contains much more carbon dioxide—and of the oceans, which are more acidic because more of that carbon dioxide is dissolving into them. And, because carbon dioxide is a greenhouse gas, we are changing the climate by melting glaciers and raising sea levels. At least 75% of the world's land surface has been modified by humans. It is human activity that is reshaping the planet's rocky material—mining and other excavation shifts four times the amount moved naturally by glaciers and rivers. As the world's population has grown from 2.3 billion in 1950 to over 7 billion today, some 3 billion hectares of the world's original forest cover—nearly half—has been lost. The world's forests, the lungs of the earth, have shrunk by some 40% since agriculture began 11,000 years ago. Three-quarters of this loss occurred in the last two centuries, as land was cleared to make way for farms and to meet human demand for wood. The World Resources Institute (WRI) reports that, of the forests that still stand, "the vast majority are no more than small or highly disturbed pieces of the fully functioning ecosystems they once were". There are now more trees on farmland than in forests, and if we were to weigh all of earth's land vertebrates, 90% of the total would be made up of humans and the animals we have domesticated. And yet much of the world is caught between climate zealots and climate skeptics. Only human 'intelligence' is capable of quibbling about what it all means. On matters not even comparable in gravity and enormity, we say 'prudence is better part of valor', or 'when in doubt, err on the safer side'. But when it comes to the very survival of the species, we opt for complacency and risk self-destruction. We assume that the earth's resilience and replenishment capacity is endless, and that it will always bear our burden and backstop human life. But we should not forget that the earth's environment has not always been so benign, and, for roughly half of the earth's history, the atmosphere lacked oxygen and was replete with noxious gases, carbon dioxide, ammonia, and methane.

Another human flaw is our chronic, if not congenital, inability to harmonize individual interest and common good, the immediate and the important, the beauty and the beast, and most of all, the mind and the heart. While Vedanta says that it is so because we fail to recognize that we are parts of the Cosmic One. Modern thinkers like ecologist Garrett Hardin (*The Tragedy of Commons*, 1968) wrote that 'ruin is the destination towards which all men rush, each pursuing his own interest, in a society that believes in the freedom of the commons'. The truth is that the myriad things that define life are such that almost none of them are possible without coming into conflict with other things equally necessary for our lives, and often for other lives. That means that at every step of our way in life we leave behind, as it were, a 'dead body' or a 'wounded soul'. Indeed no karma, or action, is possible without any kind of *papa* or sin; without causing some sort of harm to another life, perhaps even killing. That, in the holistic sense, is another dimension of interconnectivity and interdependence of all life—and death—on earth. To be alive is to live for others; the only way to get 'relief' is to make our life useful to others. In every death we also 'die' because the 'dead' were a part of the holistic 'We'. And in the 'life' of other people we also live. We are partners in the success and failure, triumph and tragedy of everyone else. We abhor death, fear death and profess *ahimsa* but it is at best an anthropocentric view; the fact is we cannot move from any place to any place, perhaps not even breathe or till without some killing. While 'killing' is deemed as the ultimate crime and a sin, the fact is that we inflict more lasting pain and suffering on others through our very way of life. One might even say we exaggerate 'killing' and underrate other forms of harm, hurt, and injury. Non-lethal physical violence can last a lifetime. Subtler forms of violence like exploitation, humiliation, abuse, neglect, indifference to injustice can cause deeper and more sustained damage and hurt. Even imposing our will on others, even if well-intended, is violence. By that test and standard, few, if any, have been non-violent. Even Gandhi, the apostle of ahimsa, was, in that sense, 'violent' as he wanted his wife and children to do what he did or follow what he said, whether or not they were convinced. 'Self-righteousness' is another implicit form; it does violence to other's views, beliefs, and sensitivities. Likewise, intolerance and inequity are alternative forms of violence.

We are also privy to different forms of 'collective violence', social, political, religious, and economic. All it means is that even with the best of intentions and due diligence and care we cannot but impair the lives of other people, not to speak of other creatures. Clearly our capacity to hurt others is immense. Scriptures are themselves replete with violence. Acts of violence are sometimes not only condoned, they are even celebrated. That is the noble premise behind a Jain ritual—*Samvastsari pratikraman* (ritual for washing away sins). Jains seek forgiveness from all the creatures whom they may have harmed knowingly or unknowingly, by uttering the phrase *Micchami dukkadam*, which translates as, "If I have caused you offence in any way, knowingly or unknowingly, in thought, word or deed, then I seek your forgiveness". Dag Hammarskjold wrote, "Forgiveness breaks the chain of causality because he who 'forgives' you—out of love—takes upon himself the consequences of what you have done. Forgiveness, therefore, always entails a sacrifice".

We must also touch upon another variable that has greatly deepened and sharpened human suffering. It springs from the age-old clash between two human impulses: cooperation and competition. In all life they coexist, and while for much of our history we were able to maintain some kind of detente, during the past few centuries our competitive drives have overwhelmed the cooperative imperative. Competition, confrontation, and conflict have come to dominate daily human life. Cooperation is necessary to achieve any objective beyond the capability of an individual, but it needs to be backstopped by harnessing the competitive energy. History has shown that a society based purely on cooperation (the Marxist model) or competition (the laissez-faire model of capitalism) is unsustainable. One might even say that we are 'naturally' more competitive than cooperative; it drives every aspect of human life. That is why we need collective restraints and that is necessary not only to contain human avarice but also to restrain human hauteur exemplified by our onslaught on nature. Our unbridled competitive impulses have also aggravated global suffering. Although we talk of competition as the essence of the 'free market', in truth there is nothing 'free' or even 'fair' about markets, or anything 'competitive' about competition. We all love oligarchy, monopolies, and domination; we brook no rival, not only in matters of market or money, but even in matters of power, love, and sex. Our instinct is to possess something or someone so completely and exclusively that they cease to exist. We want to prevail in every situation and that necessarily makes someone else suffer. In the current fierce competitive culture, there are few winners and many losers, and many, often the majority, are discarded, marginalized, impoverished and denuded of their due as human beings. That 'suffering', which affects our self-image, is more intense than 'natural' suffering. That leads to anger, envy, hatred and violence. It is not only the body that suffers; it is also the psyche. History has shown that the human mind cannot 'humanely' handle power over others. It is apt in the case of economic power, the capacity to impose one's will over others through economic means. The root of social economic power is the idea of 'private property'; the sense that one can possess, own, monopolize a piece of property, of land. Bertrand Russell wrote, "It is preoccupation with possession, more than anything else, that prevents men from living freely and nobly" (*Principles of Social Reconstruction*, 1917). And Sigmund Freud said, "By abolishing private property one takes away the human love of aggression". As someone reminded us, 'even the tiniest piece of land is four thousand miles deep, and that is quite a bit of ownership'.

Till recently, man was content with changing the inorganic environment; now he is changing and enhancing *himself*. In a sense, the trend started with the direct method: when the ape-ancestor first used a stone, he was modifying his bodily structure by the inclusion of a foreign substance. A hallmark of technology-driven culture is speed; we want to do everything, go everywhere, attain everything in the swiftest possible way, in the shortest possible time. But we also know that speed kills and shortens life. Yet, we are powerless. The Chinese philosopher Chuang Tzu wrote a long time ago that 'to a mind that is still, the whole universe surrenders'. Trotsky aptly summed up this aspect of human nature: 'As a general rule, man strives to avoid labor. Love for work is not at all an inborn characteristic: it is created by economic pressure and social education. One may even say that man is a fairly lazy animal. It is on this quality, in reality, that is founded to a considerable extent all human progress; because if man did not strive to expend his energy economically, did not seek to receive the largest possible quantity of products in return for a small quantity of energy, there would have been no technical development or social culture. It would appear, then, from this point of view that human laziness is a progressive force'. We may not know what we want to do or where we want to go; only that it must take as little effort and time as possible. Such is our obsession with speed that we might actually be accelerating the speed of our extinction, far ahead of what nature might have intended.

We might soon, if we are to believe the prophecies of some futurologists, 'sleep-walk' into a future that blurs the boundaries between living and non-living beings, and our bodies and the rest of the world. It is being said that 'our technological progress has by and large replaced evolution as the dominant, future-shaping force' and that we, humans, have 'become optimized, in the sense that we now control the future'. Some researchers peering far, far into future say that 'as genetic engineering becomes the norm, man will take control of the human form away from natural evolution and adapt biology to suit his needs'. This includes, apparently, an ever-expanding forehead to accommodate his growing brains, implanted communication devices, and eyes so large people will resemble tarsiers. Some others say the human by then might well resemble 'cyborgs (or robots) imbued with machine mind'. Many are worried if humanity can survive this century. In fact, some scientists say, "the ability to really muck about in the human genome is only decades or centuries, not millenniums, away".[15] A millennium can take its time; century is what counts. Disturbing as this is, the more practical question is what should we, as individuals whose lives have a ripple-effect, do to mend our own 'behavior', to find peace within and harmony outside? Whatever man might look like far in the future is not the matter; how he behaves is the rub. There has always been a chasm between our sacred thought and secular behavior, and between scientific solutions and ordinary lives. With the suffocating sweep of materialism on the one hand, and the growing zeal of rabid religiosity on the other, the two chasms have widened but the lines between the two have got blurred. In this logjam, through this impasse, how do we break through, get a grip on our rudderless lives, our wind-like minds and our wolfish behavior?

Packaged Pleasures

To get that 'grip' we need to get a grip on our mind. Our mind is elusive but our brain is tangible. The human brain, we must remember, evolved over almost 90% of human evolution, to adapt to the life lived by humans of that time, whom we derisively describe as 'hunter-gatherers'. In fact, the 'modern man' is no different. The men of that age hunted and gathered for survival and subsistence, for food. We do the same… the quarry being pleasure, profit, and power. Man has always craved for pleasure and shunned pain. What is new is the change in the character of modern-day pleasure. It has become what Gary Cross and Robert Procter described as a "revolution—as significant as anything that has tossed the world over the past two hundred years": packaged pleasure.[16] Modern technology has tectonically impacted upon human consumption and sensory exposure and experience. We not only ceaselessly crave for pleasurable experiences but also want them to be immediate and without any time-lag between event and experience, sensation and satiation. We want to grab and gorge on sight, 'often to the point of grotesque excess'. What is new, as Cross and Proctor point out, is that while pleasure was born in paucity and is sustained by relative scarcity, that context has fundamentally changed. The 'modern consumer culture', or 'packaged pleasure revolution', reinforced by the gale of globalization, has upset the 'ancient balance between desire and scarcity'. It has led to an unbridled onslaught on finite natural resources, which is like the 'earth eating itself to death'. Our gluttony for goods and services is also leading to a breakdown of traditional moral norms and to greater tolerance of tyranny and oppression.

We have a hunter's instinct to ruthlessly prevail, to subdue and control other people, many times sans any self-gain. The one difference is that despite being 'hunter-gatherers', those humans were more in balance than the modern ones. The parts of the brain that were responsible for 'negative' emotions were largely in a state of symmetry in relation with the parts in the brain that were the focus for 'positive' emotions. In the hunter-gatherer era, 'negative' emotions, which were centered inside and around the amygdala in the brain, were activated by perilous situations of real physical danger, such as when a tiger chased the human. The 'positives'—bonding, affection, empathy, and sharing—were also present in those times, but the 'negatives' were more needed and therefore were stronger. Today, those same neurological mechanisms are still ensconced in our brains, but our circumstances have changed unrecognizably. One of the consequences of the growing hold of the negative forces, or in the words of Adam Smith, 'unsocial passions' like greed, jealousy, malice, hatred, intolerance, lust for wealth, sex and power—the false gods—is that we have muted, in the words of Martin Luther King Jr., the 'inaudible language of the heart'. The upshot is that our stress responses are ill-adapted to the modern living context; the same reactions that a hunter-gatherer had to the threat-perception of a lurking predator are now triggered when somebody cuts in front of you on the highway, as well as in many other examples in the daily life of today's chaotic, complex society. It is these unconscious processes, what are described as 'thinking below the level of awareness', that propel us to think, speak, and act in multiple ways. What we don't know is what exactly goes on deep down there—'inside'—that makes us think in a certain way, say a particular word or behave in some way. All animals are as autonomous and interconnected as we are, although we label ourselves as the only 'social animal' and 'rational being'. One of man's great failings is that he has never found a way to realize, recognize, and organize himself as a member of an interdependent and interconnected collective community, where the well-being of other members need not be at the cost of his own. We have never been very good, Marx notwithstanding, at deep social thought—how to participate, share and optimize social 'capital'. On the other hand, despite our breathtaking contemporary connectivity—even boasting platforms like Facebook, Twitter, LinkedIn—we are assiduously eroding that very capital. Social media is powerful but double-edged. It can shatter social barriers but also strengthen sectarianism. It can foster brotherhood of kindred spirits but it also enables us to hide our true personality, cheat others and project a false image. The irony, and tragedy, is that no man who ever lived before had the means to bring about human synergy, the whole becoming more than the sum of the parts. And no one before us has wasted that opportunity more than we have.

That being said, it is easy to point the finger at technology and digital devices, but this is another ruse of our mind: to throw a red herring, a diversionary tactic. The problem is 'within', not within any appliance. What lures so many to suicide is not the smartphone; often they have one, but if they do call, they get to talk to a machine; it is because no one cares to give a shoulder to cry upon. It is because of what happens within, not because of social media, that our most charitable view of a fellow-human is as a 'necessary nuisance' or an 'opportunistic option'; more often, an irritant-fly to be eliminated. If our 'within' is cleansed, the very same devices can become bridging or bonding social capital, and we can turn that very 'problem' into a platform, a launching pad, for human brotherhood, man's eternal yearning. Our decision making, despite our much-hyped 'surgical' analytical capability, has never been our real strength. You may say that we are most afflicted with what experts call cognitive errors, which are systemic and spontaneous; the choices we make, generation after generation, are seldom innocuous, more often toxic. We can only mend the process marginally, because it is the source that is sullied. For, a certain seed can only yield a certain fruit. It is the brain that is the source and however magical, plastic, and organically adaptive it might be, it cannot, so to speak, change its spots. We know precious little about the processes at work before an animal barks or growls, grunts or attacks; but what seems to set us apart is that while other animals' insides are largely a 'collection center', for humans it is also a cauldron. 'Other animals' are largely predictable; humans singularly are not. Every mammal on this planet instinctively develops a natural equilibrium with the surrounding environment but we humans deliberately do not. That is why we are more erratic and dangerous than other animals; one never can tell how humans will, individually or collectively, react to a given temptation or common provocation. People make commitments—to a nation, faith, calling or loved ones—and endure the sacrifices those commitments demand. Often this involves fighting against natural evolutionary predispositions. One of our predispositions that is at the root of much of our misery and suffering is divisiveness, our view of everything as opposites, that the good of one is necessarily bad for the other. In short, we view life as a zero-sum journey, which we can only survive at the expense of another person. That must change if we are to stop killing each other at every opening and opportunity. But that must come from 'within'. We have for long turned to scriptures for moral guidance but, whether objectively we can agree or not, we cannot altogether ignore the fact that there is a growing sense in some 'intellectual' sections, that 'it is not possible for the religious doctrines derived from holy books to be the catalyst for moral evolvement'.[17] One might perhaps qualify it and say that this is because of the way these books are filtered by the modern mind and interpreted by the zealots of different religions. And the idea of science, or scientism, as some like to call it, the idea that any question that can be answered at all, can best be answered by science, is fast becoming another dogma. And despite its seductive claim that it can fix morality by fixing our brains, it seems more probable that by the time science is done with our body and brain, the verdict might well be: 'operation successful; patient died'.

We need to rethink, or re-feel, what 'being a person', not only being human, ought to be in today's world. And about what we tend to view as a 'problem' and as a 'solution', and the criteria and the terms of their use and application in the contemporary social and moral setting. The 'problem' is often the problem, or what we think is. If we are clear and correct about the cause of the 'problem', the solution springs forth; sometimes more than one. That is why Einstein said that 'the formulation of the problem is often more essential than its solution, which may be merely a matter of mathematical or experimental skill'. He also said that you cannot 'solve' a 'problem' with the same mindset that caused it. And, too often, the true 'problem' is 'we', not 'others'; within us, not outside us. The problem of how to deal with 'others' has long baffled moral philosophers. Should we place them on equal moral footing with ourselves? And if so, what kind of constraints must we place on ourselves in dealing with them? It is the mindset that matters most and predetermines a person's responses to and interpretations of situations. Our mindset is now the mind, and *that* is the real problem. We are using the same 'mindset', or the mind, to answer questions about itself, about the 'problem' of the mind and its place in the human consciousness. It carries huge implications; even beyond how we address global issues such as environmental crisis, climate change, good governance, or mass poverty. It defines who we are, what happens in the 'war within'. And conditions how we live, view life situations, and our attitude and aptitude, and the contours of our moral universe. Morality is now a hostage to the mind. One more thing is becoming very clear. For long, scriptures and sages have emphasized the need to control and master the mind as an essential aspect of spiritual seeking, or *sadhana*. That is still desirable but barring a handful of truly evolved souls that is beyond the reach of the rest. When a moral sense is not ingrained in a mindset, history teaches us, it is a sure sign that civilizations are ripe for decline and fall. Our attitude towards money, like sex, it too riddled with anomalies. Just as sex is a medium of both intense love and burning hatred, money is something we both love and hate almost at the same time. We talk about the corrupting influence of money, but all our life we seek that very power. We want lots and lots of money, but we don't want to be known as the 'rich'. It would take a lot of imagination to imagine what we would like to do with our life if money were to cease to be the object and the objective. If money continues to occupy the same suffocating space in human consciousness and if it is viewed in the same light as of now, it will be well nigh impossible to move towards the goal of 'humane' human transformation, or to turn the human into an essentially moral being.

Being Better Than We Were Yesterday

One of the main impediments to human 'betterment' is our practical inability to answer the question, *better than what?* or *better than who?* That kind of 'betterment' takes us into the slippery terrain of competitive comparison, which is self-defeating. Transformative technologies are expected to enable us to edit, delete, add, and replace, activate or suppress specific genes inside the human body, with which it might be possible to change the genetic basis of particular traits. Scientists are also using gene editing in human embryos. New gene-editing technologies, some scientists warn, could be turned into a biological weapon by transforming a common virus into an unstoppable drug-resistant killer. This raises once again the fundamental question: can human creativity be trusted with such awesome power? Can we just go wherever our creativity takes, where no man has gone before, not into outer space but into the more vital space of 'being human'? Techniques like brain-training, boot camp for the brain, are expected to allow us to crash through the 'cognitive glass ceiling, a number tattooed on the soul',[18] and significantly modify and enhance human 'fluid intelligence',[19] signaling a startling change from the earlier perception that they are a 'given'. But, transformative as the implications are, the more fundamental questions remain. We may become more intelligent, but does it change the way we understand, the way we ingest and digest information, the way we conduct ourselves in the interpersonal world? In short, more of the same kind or genre of 'intelligence', being bright, scholarly and intellectually agile, with high cognitive capacity, does any of that contribute, if not lead to human transformation or a nobler mindset? The fact that the 'more intelligent' persons with high IQs of 150 or more behave no better than the remainder belies the premise. Great or 'beautiful' minds are double-sided coins; their very 'extraordinariness' becomes a burden on others; their very high intelligence impacts on their integrity. Most of them have what we usually call a 'shady side', being a nasty spouse, infidelity, pettiness in private, etc. Granting that there is no perfect human and that these are generic judgments without understanding the contexts, the point is that creativity and character, intelligence and integrity are not always compatible companions. The question frequently crops up: how and what do we measure ourselves with, and what is the direction of betterment? Because if we don't know that, as Einstein said, we may be expecting a fish to climb a tree, and finding that it could not do so, conclude that it failed. Perhaps the best answer is, 'the only person we should be better than is the person we were yesterday'. And, "there is nothing noble about being superior to some other person. True nobility lies in being superior to your former self".[20] That is the only way to be better, the only way to monitor and measure our moral and spiritual progress. It is incremental and it requires constant effort for continuous improvement. And for that the qualities we associate with 'being intelligent' are not good enough; sometimes they are impediments. Many religious and spiritual leaders and saints were not, purely in terms of intelligence, different from their devout lay followers. For example, Siddhartha did not have any formal education to be transformed into a Buddha. What is becoming increasingly apparent is that for us to become better 'problem-solvers' and 'decision-makers', we need consciousness-change, and for that we need to go beyond the confines and character of what we currently consider as 'intelligence'. Even if we concede that at some point in the future we don't have to be stuck with the brain we now have, and that we could attain 'cognitive control', 'manipulate our working memory' by using 'smart pills' and 'thinking caps', and even substantially boost or build our brain power, which scientists claim might be possible biologically, in some sort of 'boot camps for our brain',[21] that is unlikely to mitigate the malaise or solve and problems we are now grappling with.

As for the 'physical body', which is what we have to cope with all our life and whose care preoccupies our mind, it is being predicted that "the future is likely to bring us astonishingly advanced, and increasingly unusual ways to enhance our bodies", giving us the capacity for 'body-modification', 'elective bionics' and 'designer babies'[22]. The vision and aim is to make the human being 'perfect' by making him impregnable, invincible, invisible at will and with x-ray vision, super-intelligent, strong like *Superman* and eventually immortal. The unstated expectation, the hidden hope, is that such a 'perfect' human, liberated from mundane worries about disease, disability, and death, will be minus malice, more moral, more responsible, and will then have a reason not to be self-destructive. The bedrock of such belief is that the brain is the sole source of 'intelligence', and what we call mind and consciousness are its other names. And by inference, 'consciousness-change' is nothing more than, and equivalent to, 'boosting-brain-power', and fixing it where necessary. This is a fatal fallacy, as other frontiers of scientific research testify—the heart has its own intelligence, memory and nervous energy, and the mind is more than the brain.

The worrisome thing is not only where such scientific effort will ultimately take shape, but also what such an effort, in and by itself, might entail and yield. And does it amount to changing the basic character of being human, equivalent to turning a cat into a dog, and if so, can we get away with it? Can humans do whatever they want to? Does it amount to changing the cosmic balance, the balance between multiple forms of life on earth, with different capabilities and vulnerabilities, each playing, even if unnoticed, a specific, irreplaceable, and positive and negative role in the grand scheme of nature? Are we crossing nature's invisible but real '*Lakshmana rekha*'?[23] Or, like in the real Ramayana, no such line is drawn or exists for our 'chosen' species? Furthermore, man has never respected any line or limits and that, in fact, is the essence of 'being human'. And then, it is often said, we should live in harmony with nature, implying that we should stay within our 'natural' limits or laws of nature. But then, all medicine, in one sense, amounts to defying the laws of nature. Such warnings have always been sounded and man still went ahead, with no ill effect, at least visible. Indeed, we are where we are because of that. And yet, in every game there are rules, and every play has a script, and every species has an assigned role in maintaining the cosmic order, disobeying which will lead to chaos. But chaos is needed for creativity. One of today's hot-button issues is: how far we can push our planet's natural systems and deplete its resources, beyond which we will incur a major blowback? Does man's tireless effort to be 'immortal' amount to one such '*rekha*' or forbidden line? By extending human longevity, are we not, in principle, crossing it? One could passionately and persuasively argue from both sides. But the essential point is this. Even assuming that scientific technology can make man a mini-Methuselah, give him angelic youth and x-ray eyes, make him 'invisible', and enhance every body-part, it cannot change the quality of his consciousness, or the way he now acts and reacts, reflects and responds, thinks and feels. And without that man will be a marauding menace. If our sensations, responses, reactions, impulses and instincts remain unchanged, then we cannot resolve any of the serious problems the world faces. Contrary to what we assume man has become, if not the 'monarch' of the earth, at least the dominant species, ushering in what has come to be called the *Anthropocene* era is but a fraction of the time we have been around, at best a few thousands out of a million. That struggle for survival and the wages of modernity have taken a huge toll on all human relationships and on human consciousness itself, and have corrupted our cognitive capacity, the very process of knowing, information-analysis, reasoning, judgment and decision-making.

For us to have the capability to move towards a cathartic change in our social behavior we must cleanse the 'entire process'. We must also at once bear in mind another crucial factor. When we talk of 'behavior' we refer to our physical activity. While ultimately everything becomes action, more often than not, it is through our words that we relate with other people. Much of the good we can do and the hurt we can inflict come from the words we use. The advice of a saying variously attributed, from the Buddha to Mary Ann Pietzker,[24] is worth bearing in mind: before we say anything we should be reasonably certain and ask ourselves, "Is it true? Is it necessary? Is it kind?". Perhaps one could reverse the order; fact is, much of what we say is 'needless', even noxious. Too often we speak when we have nothing to say; and when we do have something worth saying, words are hard to come by. As for 'truth' and 'kindness', it is also worth remembering another advice: "And never say of any one; What you'd not have said of you" and, most important, "No ill of any man to say; No, not a single word". But 'word', spoken or written, is a mighty force. In fact, Hindu scriptures say that the entire cosmos emerged from the sound '*Aum*'. Before the beginning, the *Brahman* (absolute reality) was one and non-dual. It thought, "I am only one—may I become many". This caused a vibration which eventually became sound, and this sound was *Aum* or *Om*. Creation itself was set in motion by the vibration of *Om*. The closest approach to Brahman is that first sound, *Om*. Thus, this sacred symbol has become emblematic of Brahman. The vibration produced by chanting *Om* in the physical universe corresponds to the original vibration that first arose at the time of creation. The sound of *Om* is also called *Pranava*, meaning that it sustains life and runs through *Prana* or breath. Curiously, an American neurosurgeon, who, after he 'died' and went to heaven and came back, described hearing the sound of the word *Aum* and identified God with that sound.[25]

One of the necessities of living is cleansing, a process by which we discard the filth and toxin we gather in the sheer process of living. Even in the purest of 'living' we attract and accumulate impurities through our body as well as mind. The problem has become more acute in modern times. We are constantly exposed to potentially dangerous toxins through the food we eat, the air we breathe, and the water we drink. There is almost nothing uncontaminated that we put into our bodies. Humans are the biggest producers of rubbish. Huge amounts of plastic now roam the oceans, where they threaten marine life by blocking out the sunlight that nourishes plankton and algae. It is estimated that over 100 billion gallons a year of fresh water is turned into toxic fluid that contains multiple chemicals. And the almost insane irony is that we want to live forever but still poison our bodies through everything we put into them for the sake of 'making more money'. We need to detox our body, mind, and consciousness; and, perhaps even our soul; and it has to be constant and continuous. Still, it is easier to cleanse what we put inside than control what happens inside. That is because we have no tools to go 'in'; to know what happens before we act; to know what takes place in the melting pot of our consciousness. The tools that we now have are scientific, which have made a tremendous and tectonic difference to human condition and well-being. But it has also brought us face to face with many problems the world now faces, forcing many to think that maybe we have gone too far and deep in our reliance on what is called the 'scientific method', and that we have strayed too far from the scriptural and spiritual path. There is also a gnawing unease about the nature, content and character of our very being as a living entity, that our lives are bereft of both depth and what psychologist Mihaly Csikszentmihalyi calls the 'flow'.

Superlative and seductive scientific claims are being made, and we find ourselves bewitched and bewildered. We are being told that computer software is so reorganizing the world that "with our bodies hemmed in, our minds have only the cloud—and it is the cloud that has become the destination for an extraordinary mental exodus".[26] That millions of people are finding their lovers [and mates] in the cloud, that though geographical distance separates our bodies, the distance between our minds is being measured geodesically, that is, in terms of "the number of degrees of separation between two nodes in a social network".[27] And that soon we could soon live in "cloud towns, then cloud cities, and ultimately cloud countries".[28] But then we all know that the cloud is hardly a place to build an edifice. We no longer have to be perturbed about the 'energy problem' and 'our own' sunup in the sky can bale us out… Some spiritual teachers say that this body itself is a piece of earth powered by the sun. Each one of us is a solar-powered life. In terms of the solar and lunar cycles, the human body is perfectly poised. Mystics have long believed that the sun is not a mass of exploding gas, but the gateway from the physical universe into the astral worlds from which life energy is ever pouring forth to enliven our solar system.

Another nagging problem has been the very way our brain 'thinks' that makes us bad, but we are assured that soon we will be able to 'fix' our brain and smother our meanness, that we could soon swallow a 'pill' and become compassionate, that we will finally achieve our long-sought goal of understanding human nature and even "change the way we think about each other". What are we, the non-scientist, not-so-smart people of the real world, to make of all such scientific stuff? And what are we supposed to do? If all of these do happen, substantially if not entirely, man could become, in behavior, if not in spirit, a true *satvik*,[29] a semi-saint made by science. But the real reason why we feel so reassured is not because of such a prospect—no one wants to be a 'saint', of all earthly things—but it could mean 'business as usual'; that we can merrily go on messing up the earth and environment, and feel no need to make any 'adjustments' in our parasitic lifestyle. Clearly, if there is one thing evolution and history teach us, it is that in nature and in life, short-cuts are treacherous terrains, and silver bullets and golden hammers and holy grails are ever elusive.

Scientific Insignificance and Spiritual Completeness

The dilemma is that, even if we want to move away from the 'scientific method', we see no path that is easy to tread. By making our life comfortable and pleasurable, and by minimizing our bodies and brains to have a 'good life', it has made us unfit for any alternative life. Science has also, more fundamentally, altered our perception of ourselves on the cosmic canvas. It has given us both perspective and a sense of insignificance that is further complicating our search for a choice. It is good to be cut to size, but if we are 'nothing', then what use is anything? If something is yours, whether it is body, mind, or soul, then the logical inference is that that which is '*yours*' cannot be you; and so, who are you? The truth is that, as Advaita tells us, we are 'no-thing' but 'not nothing'.[30] Zen puts it differently, 'there is no better thing than no thing', meaning that no matter how wonderful anything is, there is nothing more wonderful than no thing. Even science says that 'nothing', even empty space is nothing. In other words we are the 'nothing', or the Thing beyond all things. And that Thing is nothing but what the Upanishads, summoning the highest of human thought, describe as "the ear of the ear, the eye of the eye, and the word of words, the mind of mind, and the life of life". And as the One who sends the mind to wander afar, who first drove life to start on its journey, who impels us to utter these words, who is the spirit behind the eye and ear. The fact is that, as John Updike (1985) puts it, "Our century's revelations of unthinkable largeness and unimaginable smallness, of abysmal stretches of geological time when we were nothing, of supernumerary galaxies and indeterminate subatomic behavior, of a kind of mad mathematical violence at the heart of matter, have scorched us deeper than we know". And, "standing on our microscopic fragment of a grain of sand" (James Jeans),[31] we have stumbled into this 'terrifying universe' if not by mistake, at least by 'accident'. Jacques Monod, author of '*Chance and Necessity*' (1971), said, "the universe was not pregnant with life, nor the biosphere with man. Our number came up in the Monte Carlo game", a random happening.[32] Max Tegmark said, "Our lives are small temporally and spatially. If this 14-billion-year cosmic history were scaled to one year, then 100,000 years of human history would be 4 minutes and a 100-year life would be 0.2 seconds".[33] The philosophy of cosmicism, advocated by the scientific indifferentist, HP Lovecraft, echoes the same idea. But it is not only science that instilled the idea into our head. Eons ago, the Greek God Apollo said: "Insignificant mortals, who are as leaves are, and now flourish and grow warm with life, and feed on what the ground gives, but then again fade away and are dead".[34] Such a vision stems from what some call a "banal metaethical confusion",[35] and they persuasively argue that issues of scale have little impact on meaning, significance, and value, and if certain things possess intrinsic value, then their value is not diminished or eliminated by the largeness of anything else, even that of the cosmos. But in a different way, 'scale' does matter. One of the problems we now face is that everything is so gigantic that we lose our identity as a part of it. 'The ever-expanding scope and scale of the global economy obscures the consequences of our actions. In effect, our arms have been so lengthened that we no longer see what our hands are doing'.[36]

We may be 'insignificant' from a scientific or cosmic view point, but from a spiritual perspective, each one of us is cosmos itself; there is nothing in the cosmos that is absent inside each of us. Indeed, Vedanta proclaims *Aham brahma asmi—I am the Brahman*, the supreme Soul, the transcendental Being. Vedanta follows up with *Tat tvam asi—That thou art*, where 'that' stands for the almighty *Ishvara* or Brahman, and 'thou' stands for the *jiva*. It means that you, I, and we, they, each of us is as 'significant' as the cosmos. Even from a purely 'power perspective', mankind is far from insignificant; we now have god-like powers to create life, as well as to possibly destroy all life on earth. And we are led to hope that eternal youth—like a snake we might be able to shed our wrinkled skin and don a youthful 'second skin'[37]—and physical 'immortality' are within grasp. At the least, we hope to 'die young as late as possible'. All that still does not make a difference to our spiritual comatose existence or cosmic insignificance. The way to be fully awake and to surmount 'cosmic insignificance', and our sense of irrelevance and everyday impotence, is by imbibing the spirit of 'cosmic consciousness', which as Richard Maurice Bucke[38] put it, is "a higher form of consciousness than that possessed by the ordinary man", which is more of an intuitive knowing than a factual understanding. The Buddhist *Nirvana* is sometimes described as nothing more than being awakened to the enlightened nature of our consciousness. The Upanishads say, "those wise ones who see that the consciousness within themselves is the same consciousness within all conscious beings, attain eternal peace". It comes very close to what William James called 'mystical experience' or 'mystical consciousness'. Swami Sivananda, a 20th-century Indian spiritual guru, describes it: "This new experience bestows new enlightenment which places the experiencer on a new plane of existence.

There is an indescribable feeling of elation and indescribable joy and bliss. He experiences a sense of universality, a Consciousness of Eternal Life. It is not a mere conviction. He actually feels it. He gets the eye Celestial… The little 'I' has melted. The differentiating mind that splits up has vanished. All barriers, all sense of duality, differences, and separateness have disappeared. There is no idea of time and space. There is only eternity. The ideas of caste, creed and color have gone now".[39] Some call mystical the opposite of the 'mundane', on the analogy of paranormal and normal. Some even say that mystical or paranormal experiences are really 'normal' and 'ordinary', and that the rest of us operate at suboptimal or subnormal levels. People we variously call diviners, shamans, prophets, sages, mediums, and inspired artists are some such persons. It is also said everyone has such latent powers, but they lie dormant 'within'.

Cosmic consciousness, in one word, is perfect awareness of the oneness of life, the awareness that all living beings are parts of the cosmic body, and therefore there is no such thing as inclusion or exclusion, separation or integration. It is not an alien state; as Sivananda says, "it is an inherent, natural faculty of all men and women". But sometimes we feel like an 'alien' in a different sense. The Tibetan Lama Tarthang Tulku says (*Love of Knowledge*, 1987) that the self lives in the world like an illegal alien, always afraid that its identity will be questioned.[40] It is partly a reaction to this feeling of insecurity that makes us so possessive, predatory, and exploitative in our attitude towards the earth and our fellow-humans. In our behavior we are both 'collectors' and 'correctors': we 'collect' everything we can lay our hands on, and we 'correct' everyone else... A prerequisite to a higher state of awareness is that we must be able to rise above the limitation of everyday sensory perception. The capability is already present in us. It is inactive, or non-functioning in the majority of human beings on account of the force of *avidya* or ignorance. It is a state of consciousness that prophets, rishis, messiahs, saints and mystics have attained since time immemorial. It is that which separates the rest from such realized souls. The first step to take, on the road to cosmic consciousness, is to change our perception of our own selves, not as human beings trying to have a cosmic experience, but as cosmic beings experimenting with human existence. We not only 'exist' because we are 'conscious', but everything in the cosmos, including we humans, are expressions of cosmic consciousness. Such remembrance will also help us shed our sense of limitedness, insignificance and temporariness. However infinitesimally small or infinitely finite we might be on the cosmic scale, and however miniscule human presence might be on earth (less than 1%) in astronomical terms, "humans have become a force of nature reshaping the planet on a geological scale—but at a far-faster-than-geological speed".[41] "As species go down in our presence, we're not only altering earthly existence. We are also altering the very potential for earthly existence".[42] The paradox is that while humans might be peripheral in the natural world, human actions are not. Human beings have the capacity to influence physical reality through intentional behavior; they are 'elemental in their force'. As Mark Lynas puts it, "Our collective power already threatens or overwhelms most of the major forces of nature, from the water cycle to the circulation of major elements like nitrogen and carbon through the entire earth system. Our pollutants have subtly changed the color of the sky, while our release of half a trillion tons of carbon as the greenhouse gas CO_2 into the air is heating up the atmosphere, land, and oceans".[43] It is important to mark the last more prominently, the ocean, about which we scarcely spare a thought. Man is now turning his greedy gaze on the ocean. We are told that China is planning a massive sea-lab 10,000 feet below the surface of the sea. Perhaps of all the ravaging we are doing to nature, the one to the oceans is the most worrying, as it could lead to the breakdown of the 'mystical bond between man and ocean'. We should remember that three-fourths of the oxygen going into our lungs comes from the ocean. The acidification of our oceans—due to absorption of more than 20 million tons of carbon dioxide from human activity every day—could eventually cause the loss of biodiversity, as well as food and financial security for the entire planet.[44] One of the prime causes of the greatest extinction of our prehistory was, besides global warming, the acidification of the oceans. Is it a curious coincidence that it is happening now? The Intergovernmental Panel on Climate Change (IPCC) says that current carbon dioxide levels are highest in 400,000 years. Many seemingly innocuous things we do as a part of technology-driven modern living like emails and tweets also contribute via their high electricity consumption. A study has shown that a single email is estimated to add about four grams of carbon dioxide equivalent into the atmosphere. The bitter fruit of all this rapacity is this: whichever way we might want to look, the truth is here to behold: pristine nature—creation—has disappeared forever.

It is vitally important to dispel the delusion that man is a product of a freak accident and wholly a terrestrial creature, and of no particular consequence to the cosmos. That might be true if man is "a creature not of Earth alone, that in both a spiritual and scientific sense we should regard ourselves as simultaneously Earth citizens and 'heaven dwellers'...", and that we are "active agents of our own evolution, capable of rationally directing—or misdirecting—our human and planetary future".[45] The truth is that we are all 'historical figures' and everything we do, even the minutest, is a part of the flux of history, the stuff of the stars. That is why every choice is a cosmic choice.

Despite our delusions of grandeur and presumed preeminence, which is getting chipped away every day by new discoveries, there has always been a certain unease—'something don't feel right'[46]—about the way man makes choices that affect fellow-humans, non-humans and nature. That 'unease' has now grown into what is being described as an 'existential angst', a gnawing gut feeling that the clutch of certitudes that sustained us for so long are passé, and we wonder, 'what good would living do us?' Simone de Beauvoir aptly describes: "Men of today seem to feel more acutely than ever the paradox of their condition. They know themselves to be the supreme end to which all action should be subordinated, but the exigencies of action force them to treat one another as instruments or obstacles, as means. The more widespread their mastery of the world, the more they find themselves crushed by uncontrollable forces. Though they are masters of the atomic bomb, yet it is created only to destroy them. Each one has the incomparable taste in his mouth of his own life, and yet each feels himself more insignificant than an insect within the immense collectivity whose limits are one with the earth's. Perhaps in no other age have they manifested their grandeur more brilliantly, and in no other age has this grandeur been so horribly flouted".[47] Unable to give anything meaningful or give up anything meaningless, not knowing what the core is and what is appearance, always falling short of what they want to be, a growing number of people have begun to doubt the validity and viability of their very existence. Essentially, we 'cling' to things we should discard and 'crave' for things that give momentary elation and lasting sorrow. It is these two attributes—clinging and craving—that, according to Buddhism, are like fuel to the flames of suffering. '*Samsara*' is the process, not a place, by which clinging gives rise to suffering; if the fuel supply is cut off, the flames abate and we attain *nirvana*. In fact, it was by 'giving up' all that—which we, lesser men, would cherish: privileges of a pampered prince, comforts of heavenly palace, a devoted wife and the thrill of an infant son—that Siddhartha transformed himself into *Gautama*. Craving, we associate with material objects, but the more pervasive 'burning longing' in the modern world is for affection and love, even attention and appreciation. What most people fear most in life is rejection, a cause of a great deal of violence in the world. But our material way of life constantly replenishes the fuel of a 'comfortable life'. As a result, we find ourselves in what Viktor Frankl calls 'existential vacuum', or what philosophers and psychologists call 'existential angst', or mystics call 'abyss experience'. Whatever term we might use, it encompasses a canvas that covers emotions, feelings or thoughts that include deep disquiet, a sense of a 'sinking heart', anxiety, anguish, fear, dread, despair about not only one's own existence, but of the world at large. Are we in the death throes of a doomed species? Is this finally it, the much-anticipated or feared 'end of the world'? And, are we secretly happy that, at last, it is getting over?

Above all else, this malaise, this state of consciousness is what afflicts modern man. Almost everything else is but a symbol and a statement. It is at once a fountain and a fulcrum, cause and consequence. The irony is that what should have been an introspective inward odyssey—to know what our priorities should be in a lifetime, and how we should harness our time and space in this life—this spiritual quest is now turning out to be a life-threatening emotion and a suicidal drive. Many young people are taking their lives, desperately groping for a meaning to their existence, unable, as a Christina Aguilera lyric laments, to find a way to 'dry their tears' and become 'free to fly', or 'find a place where nothing is harder than it is'. They are coming to the conclusion that 'life meant nothing to them'. Many people, disoriented and disconnected and dysfunctional, find life, in the words of Sylvia Plath (*The Unabridged Journals of Sylvia Plath,* 200), a 'monumental, grotesque joke', and that the 'unreasoning barbaric purity' of our 'uncivilized' days were better. They are disenchanted with what they see in the mirror and disgusted with what they see around; they feel that their future is slipping out of their grasp and lose themselves, in the words of William Thomson "in an orgy of consumption, crime, and immorality".[48] They may savor the good things of life, but they do not like the way they are now accessible. What

Thomas Freidman called 'merger of globalization and information technology revolution' is also leading to what he called the 'globalization of anger'. We may add intolerance, bigotry, extremism, and racism too. Contrary to the expectation that the more people communicate and get to know each other, the more they will be accommodative of differences, what is happening is the opposite. It may well be that globalization has had a perverse effect because that is what we really are—the more differences we can discover, the easier it is to exploit. That merger, through mediums like television, Facebook, Twitter, Skype, LinkedIn, etc., has also globalized 'greed'; everyone is now exposed and naked to every enticement, to the same temptation. Everyone is exposed to what King Solomon cautioned his son against: "Greedy for gain, which taketh away the life of the owners thereof".[49] The cultural and classical moral defenses of many people are crumbling. Our dependence on gadgets and laxity in morals is aptly expressed by a Hollywood actress who said, "We live in a world where losing your phone is more dramatic than losing your virginity".[50] As one of those experiencing such angst puts it, 'Nothing provokes an emotional response anymore; fear, happiness, anxiety, are all feigned. I've truly forgotten what it feels like to love or to laugh or really to just be sincere'. That is a terrible state: forgetting how to be 'just sincere'. Sitting and staring at screens all day long is making many youngsters socially sterile face to face, inept interpersonally.

Thwarted and tormented, frustrated and frightened, they try everything from corrosive consumerism to reckless road rage, from liberated libido, to use of levitating drugs like *LSD* or *Ecstasy*, all to get some 'relief' from the draining drudgery of daily life. They want to be suffused with what they describe as 'the stream of joy', to experience the 'high'—a short-cut to a higher state of consciousness, a new and improved religious experience. And, in the words of Albert Hoffman (*LSD: My Problem Child,* 1980), to realize that 'what one commonly takes as 'the reality,' including the reality of one's own individual person, by no means signifies something fixed, but rather something that is ambiguous—that there is not only one, but that there are many realities, each comprising also a different consciousness of the ego'. That is the essence of all scriptures, and if one can really transcend to that level of consciousness, the world will be rid of all that afflicts it. Ken Kesey (*One Flew Over the Cuckoo's Nest,* 1962) elaborates: "I believe that with the advent of acid, we discovered a new way to think, and it has to do with piecing together new thoughts in your mind. Why is it that people think it is so evil? What is it about it that scares people so deeply, even the guy that invented it, what is it? Because they're afraid that there's more to reality than they have confronted. That there are doors that they're afraid to go in, and they don't want us to go in there either, because if we go in we might learn something that they don't know. And that makes us a little out of their control".[51] That might well be true; our lives are so suffocated and strictly controlled by tradition, culture and order that we shrink from anything that even appears to threaten that state. One could certainly agree that the world desperately needs go beyond 'just thinking' to a new plateau of consciousness for man to evolve and reach his full potential. The problem is that, while it might be possible to experience a momentary euphoria through experiments through synthetic drugs, it is facile to think that *that* is the route to human transformation. Instead, what seems to happen is that the *existential vacuum* implodes, the quest comes to a crash, a bud gets crushed before it can flower, fracturing its fragrance. It often leads to what French sociologist Emile Durkheim (*Le suicide*, 1897) called 'anomic suicide', a "product of moral deregulation and a lack of definition of legitimate aspirations through a restraining social ethic, which could impose meaning and order on the individual conscience".[52] Durkheim explains: "One cannot long remain so absorbed in contemplation of emptiness without being increasingly attracted to it. In vain one bestows on it the name of infinity; this does not change its nature. When one feels such pleasure in non-existence, one's inclination can be completely satisfied only by completely ceasing to exist". It makes inroads into those minds that are fragile or overly sensitive—the adolescent and the early young; and those who cannot handle either emptiness or excessive fullness. At another level of awareness, we want both 'fullness' and 'emptiness'. We have a 'secret streak', to discard, to empty ourselves, to be fully free, to feel weightless, to fly like a bird. That is why, even though there is no need to, we get naked, shed all our clothes, even ornaments, when we 'make love', give ourselves fully, to 'unite' with, to dissolve into, a beloved. If only we can show even a shade of the same 'giving' towards the rest, we can find peace within and outside. Trapped in the coils of a coarse and corrosive life they conclude that the only way out is all the way out. Durkheim elaborates: "It is too great comfort which turns a man against himself. Life is most readily renounced at the time and among the classes where it is least harsh". In the early 2000s, it was reported, for example, that suicide was the third cause of death among youth fifteen to nineteen years old, and second among college students in USA. In that country, by 2016, suicide surged to the highest levels in nearly 30 years.[53] What is alarming is not only the growing numbers but even more their all-encompassing casualness, ordinariness, and matter-of-fact-ness. The fact remains that with all the advances in psychology and ability to peep into human emotions, we still do not know what pushes one person to resort to what the papers euphemistically call 'taking the extreme step', and another person, similarly situated, to be able to cope with it. Equally alarming is that more often than not, suicides end up with homicides, often with people taking their loved ones, their own children. While explanations abound, we must once again turn our search for answers inwards, and treat this situation as yet another tell-tale sign that we are fast 'losing' the war within.

Traditional safe-havens like religion are no longer able to offer a shield against the merciless maelstrom of life. Most people might still see their roots in their religion and do what is expected of them, but that does not seem to answer the existential questions they struggle with. We are much like the pilgrim in Dante's *Inferno*, who finds himself in a dark wood, at a dead end in the midst of life, with a sense that all the ways to move forward are shut. Or like Arjuna, in the Mahabharata, who finds himself with no way out of his predicament of either killing those he venerated, or being called a 'coward' by his own divine mentor. There is a growing sense that although our brain/mind has made man the monarch of earth, it is also to blame for much, if not all that is wrong with the world. There are also serious questions about identifying the brain with the mind, and the mind with consciousness. And grave doubts if completely targeting the brain to better ourselves is a wise thing at all.

Many fear that the force within that has guided us in our march to modernity is pushing us to the brink, to the edge of the abyss, towards premature earthly passage and, in spiritual terms, to the ever-widening chasm that, in Thomas Merton's telling phrase, separates "us from ourselves".[54] And let us be very, very wary: this 'enemy' is not the enemy that Jesus exhorted us to love.[55] This 'enemy', make no mistake, is 'real' but invisible, lurks and hides deep in the depths of our consciousness, always waiting for a tempting opening to take over, make us do things we detest. Oscar Wilde quipped, "a man cannot be too careful in the choice of his enemies". Maybe, we have been—in trying to be too careful, and perhaps trying to find a 'worthy' external enemy, and not finding anyone 'suitable'—egged on by the internal enemy, and turning on each other. One explanation is the theory of *karma*; we are all 'heirs to our karma'; we *have* to do, or not do, certain things, regardless of our wish or will, because only in that way can a particular *prarabdha* karma can be acted upon. The package of prarabdha consists of very diverse components. When other people hurt you it is their karma; and how we react is our karma. To exhaust them we play multiple roles in life, as parent, spouse, son and daughter, sibling, lover, friend, foe, professional, and many other some seemingly trivial. If a certain role is not required for a particular prarabdha of a particular person, we will not play that role. For example, some remain unmarried or un-partnered; some have no siblings; some have no children; some are still born; some die in a few days; some die very young and some live long. It is because that particular prarabdha requires before it completes this life. How we perform each role and whether we give or receive happiness or unhappiness depends also on which way a particular prarabdha requires. It is said in Buddhism, "*Yadisam vapate bijam tadisam harate phalam*"—as we sow, so shall we reap. The same theme is replicated in the Bible, "Do not be deceived: God is not mocked, for whatever one sows, that will he also reap". If one suffers, then the cause lies in *him*, and it is futile blaming someone else or believe that it is the wish of an Almighty Creator God, or is due to an original sin. According to Buddhism, there are several causes for any one event or happening. Karma is a vital factor that plays an important part in the life of beings in making their life miserable or fortunate. In the *Karma Café*, it is said, there is no menu; you get served what you deserve, and until you fully partake of it you cannot leave. The other explanation is how we behave, act or react, respond to circumstances is a direct reflection of the ever-shifting and fluctuating fortunes in the 'war'. We must stop debating and wasting our energy and intelligence of every kind about 'this' or 'that'; if we are 'spirit' or 'flesh'; 'good ' or bad'; 'selfish' or 'altruistic'; and so on. We have always been, we are, and we will always be all of 'them' and more. Every one of us does some 'good' or 'bad' all the time, consciously or otherwise; we are capable of both causing and relieving pain and suffering, even saving a life or taking a life. But we still do not know when we become capable of which or what. That is because it reflects the state of the 'war', and we have no control over it. The attendant issue is, "which of the two—doing good or doing bad—is more natural, easier, more effortless, more spontaneous, and reflexive. The answer too is the war. If the 'good' opponent has a clear 'winner' in a battle, not the war, then the good we want to do occurs without much laboring; if it is the 'bad', then we do bad more banally and brazenly.

To 'survive' and to 'succeed'—these are the 'mantras' we chant and the ones we have come to accept as the only goals in life, which eclipse everything and anything else. But the Buddha offered us a model that is both ethical and practical: "To prosper in harmony, your success must not result on the failure of others. Your success must not harm others. Your success must not make others unhappy. Your path to success must be a way to nurture everybody".[56] What matters in the end is, how our 'time' on earth affects others' 'time', and that often ends as travesty or a tragedy. Joseph Addison, in his essay, '*The Vision of Mirzah*' (*The Spectator*, 1711) voices it well: "Alas, said I, man was made in vain! How is he given away to misery and mortality; tortured in life; and swallowed up in death". We might quibble about morality, but about mortality we think we are more sure-footed. We are told that we are on the verge of a scientific 'second coming', as it is being dubbed, namely 'death control'—to make death obey our dictum; to hasten or halt death, to postpone or prevent any earthly ending, to cure the 'disease' of death, not to become one not-so-fine morning as though we have never been.

Whichever way we are headed as a species, the 'troubles' are what we wrestle with every day in our mundane, meandering and muddy lives. That, according to the Bible, is what God allotted to the human lot. It says, "Mortals, born of woman, are of few days and full of trouble".[57] Perhaps to ensure that we cannot fight the 'troubles' too easily, God put the epicenter of our 'troubles' as well as the know-how to overcome them tantalizingly close, but beyond our routine reach: deep inside our own consciousness. It means that for all our 'troubles', we will have no one to blame but ourselves, nowhere need we go but inward. The fact is that before we 'behave', before we say a word or take any action, before even a thought crosses our mind, a whole lot happens somewhere within our own mortal body that determines our relationship with the rest of the world, and how we connect with fellow-humans and with other creatures. Whatever we do, whatever happens at any given point of time, depends on who or what gains an upper hand at that point. If we are doing 'good' deeds, it means that the goodness in us is prevailing at that time, and if 'bad', because the negative forces are ascendant at that time. In one sense we are much like 'programmed puppets', 'manipulated marionettes', if you will, by an internally 'external' force over which we are outwardly powerless. Perhaps puppets or marionettes are better performers because they are wholly mechanical and are free from self-consciousness. And that 'internal', 'inside', 'interior', 'within' is what we loosely call 'consciousness'. What we see and experience is the screen projected by the real action deep in the depths of our being. And, either by divine design or traits innate to the human condition, we have no insight into what we might call the 'infrastructure of our inside'. Advaita Vedanta compares it to watching a movie on a screen in which we actually see and experience buildings burn and turn to ashes, but the screen itself remains unburnt. The screen is real and the action unreal.

The Age of Loneliness

The big temptation has always been to dismiss all that is wrong with us—any behavior that troubles us too much, that makes us uncomfortable—as a random malevolence, deviant aberration, the deranged doings of a crazy nut, of a genetic freak, or as acts of momentary madness; everything except identification with our own 'untamed' selves. That has always been a grievous error, never more than now. This streak of destruction is also responsible for our assault on nature. It is important to note that human beings destroy their living environment at the same time as they destroy one another, and that healing our society goes hand in hand with healing our personal, elemental connection with the world. If our relationship with each other is rooted in what Buddhists call 'loving kindness', then our connection with nature will cease to be destructive. The defining drive in contemporary life is a cocktail of disaffection, discontent and despair, and if everyone of that ilk seeks to avenge them through destruction of those held directly or indirectly responsible, the human world will then slide into a horrific hell-zone.

While such a 'cocktail' can be a positive force for 'progress' and excellence if properly directed, the truth is that it has become another manifestation, or 'operationalization', of unbridled greed, which is now getting blurred with another 'unique' human feature: the feeling of 'entitlement'. Greed is wanting much more than you need or due, but 'entitlement' is to view what you want as what is your right. Deserving is different from entitlement, just as greed is from desire. It undermines contentment. But contentment has also a downside. It can lead to complacency and conformity, to love of the status quo, and to the 'slow but sure stamping out of individuality' (à la Dylan Thomas), to a life that is but a bargain, that is no more than, 'so much per week, so much for this, so much for that'. There are a growing number of people in the world who think they deserve whatever they want, and when they don't get it they conclude that it ought to be the fault of some other person or society. A growing number of people, covering a broad spectrum of society, not only the weak-minded or having psychological problems, are convincing themselves that that which is denied to them is their due, if not a right, be it money, love or sex, or power, and that if they cannot have it, no one else deserves to have it. It is a ploy of our mind to shift the responsibility for our failures from ourselves to another person or society. In one sense, it stems from the fear of failure, or the fear of being the loser. Like with sex, our sense of 'morality' is obsessed, and afflicted with, success and scorn at 'failure'. John F Kennedy, following the *Bay of Pigs* fiasco, rued "success has many fathers; failure is an orphan". Nothing we dread more than being dubbed as such. 'Failure', even more than the belief that we have 'failed', deals a mortal blow to our sense of self-worth, social standing, and that dread drives many towards suicide—shockingly, kids have killed themselves for not getting good grades in a school test. Such is the humdrum human mindset about 'success' and 'failure'. And both are defined and measured by immediate results and material well-being—passing an exam, getting a job, getting a promotion, a happy relationship. Most of us might not be able to put to practice Samuel Beckett's vision of 'heroic failure' as a way of life, which he expounded in his acclaimed work *Westward Ho!* (1983): "Fail again; Better again; Or better worse; Fail worse again; Still worse again! Till sick for good, Throw up for good". He himself 'failed' to hide his 'success'. No one really knows what 'success' and 'failure' in the totality of life is, but that does not deter us from venerating 'success' and vilifying 'failure'. Generally we think 'success' is to have a good career, make a lot of money, have a good marriage, or 'partners', or 'raise' a good family and so on. The absurdity and agony of human predicament is that we do not know what else to judge our life with. Our 'intelligence' is not good enough for us even to 'know' how to assess our life, in all four stages, childhood, adolescence, youth, and old age. And that failure is not an end point but an essential component of a cyclical process. So many have lived worthless lives, so many buds did not blossom, so many flowers smothered; so many have killed themselves, so many have been wrongly applauded, all because of this 'mother of all of failures'.

Education, career, home, and workplace pretty much gobble up our life, and how we do in these places has, by default, come to sum up our success or failure. If we don't do well in education—which means getting good marks in the hundreds of tests and exams we take over a period of 15 to 20 years through our childhood, adolescence and youth—then our family, friends and society will pronounce that we are, if not a failure, certainly not a success. We don't get a job, therefore we are a 'failure'. If we don't have a good career, do not get one, or don't rapidly climb up the professional ladder, or worse get laid off, we are deemed a failure. At the workplace, failure has a heavy price, can cost you the job itself. However, some researchers are arguing that venerating success and looking down on failure is shortsighted even from a business point of view. Ron Friedman's *The Best Place to Work*[58] makes the same point and suggests that companies wanting to be competitively successful and on the cutting edge of innovation need to embrace failure in their employees, and "accepting failure doesn't just make risk-taking easier, but "in a surprising number of instances, it's the only reliable path to success". Often what we call failure is part of the learning process. Thomas Edison said, "I failed my way to success". A Chinese proverb says that 'failure is the mother of success'. JK Rowling in her address to the graduating class of Harvard (2008) said, "You might never fail on the scale I did. But it is impossible to live without failing at something, unless you live so cautiously that you might as well not have lived at all—in which case, you fail by default". In fact, many great achievers—Walt Disney, Albert Einstein, Vincent Van Gogh, The Beatles, Michael Jordan, to cite but a few—failed repeatedly or were considered mediocre, before tasting success.

Success or failure also has a huge bearing on the morality of means. These two are also another *dwanda*, part of the inherent duality of life. We should not be elated by success or afraid of failure. We need take the two in their stride but should not be possessed by them. Even in our own personal lives, looking back at what we once thought was a setback would have later turned out to be a stepping stone to success, a set-up for a comeback; and what we then considered a success, we might now wish it didn't happen. Most times, it is other people's opinions that shape our own view whether we are a success or not. We should not extol success or look down upon failure. That is one of the qualities of *sthitaprajna* (steady wisdom) as detailed by Lord Krishna in the Bhagavad Gita. Most of us cannot reach those heights; but even if we cannot reach the peak, at least we can go to a higher plateau. The stranglehold of success and the burden of failure in our culture need to be loosened and lightened. That could save many innocent lives and make life way less miserable to most people. And that could be a big step towards eliminating a huge moral temptation from our lives. For too often we sell our soul for success. We might not know that but it exacts a terrible toll on our psyche. An agonizing number of people, particularly young adults, already tired to the bone with what success entails in today's ruthless world, are behaving as if they are 'constantly torn between killing themselves and killing everyone around them', and they seem to feel that these are 'the two choices; everything else is just killing time'. Such are the states of mind that breed mass murderers and lead to senseless school shoot-outs. We can't derisively dismiss them as twisted minds and crazy loonies. Too often some of them are some of our most promising; their mindset is a product of our tormented times, wages of our warped values.

The Two Journeys—Outer Space and Inner Space

Man has long had two 'dreams', both integral parts of the 'human story'. One is to go higher and higher into the far reaches of space, and the other is to go deeper and deeper inside our own selves. The outer space is the cosmos, limitless; the inner space is physically bounded but still limitless. The real 'beyond' that is most impenetrable is not outer space but the *inner* space. The *Chandogya* Upanishad eloquently explains: "As great as the infinite space beyond is the space within the lotus of the heart. Both heaven and earth are contained in that inner space, both fire and air, sun and moon, lightning and stars. Whether we know it in this world or know it not, everything is contained in that inner space. Never fear that old age will invade that city; never fear that this inner treasure of all reality will wither and decay. This knows no age when the body ages; this knows no dying when the body dies. This is the real city of *Brahman*; this is the Self, free from old age, from death and grief, hunger and thirst. In the Self all desires are fulfilled".[59,60] Advaita Vedanta says that "to keep the mind constantly turned within and to abide thus in the Self alone is *Atmavichara* (self-enquiry)".[61] The 16th-century Spanish poet and Roman Catholic mystic Saint John of the Cross described it as a journey through 'the dark night of the soul'. Marcus Aurelius described it as 'to retire into yourself'. That is a way to get a grip on our own selves, our mind, our consciousness, to awaken and bring to bear the best out of us in the service of man and God alike. This is the essence of what the Upanishads call 'Self-realization', what the Buddha implied in his vision of Nirvana, what Lao Tzu referred to when he said that 'He who knows others is wise; he who knows himself is enlightened'. It is the idea behind the Delphic axiom 'know thyself' and the ancient dictum 'man, know thyself'. Paramahansa Yogananda says that "self-realization is the knowing—in body, mind and soul—that we are one with the omnipresence of God… God's omnipresence is our omnipresence". The principal reason that none of us is content with what we have, is because we do not know who we truly are, and that is because what goes on inside us is a mystery to our own selves. We are strangers to our own selves, always surprised by our own actions, bewildered by our own behavior. We are foreigners to our own passions and the compulsions, temptations, and terrors that impel us, sometimes seduce us—to do what we do, or not do what we want to do. The world confronts two kinds of 'terror': terror for a fanatical cause; and terror of sheer 'living' with dignity. Both terrors have a single source: the *within*. Often times, we 'know' more about another person than about ourselves. In one sense, the person that stares back at you in the mirror is more of a 'stranger' than a stranger on the street. Ironically we can, if we want to, share a smile with the external stranger than the 'internal' stranger with a smirk on his face.

Human reach has extended into outer space, and peering through, say, the Hubble Space Telescope, we can see galaxies billions of light years away. And, we are told that "we can only realistically expect to send spacecraft to within the boundary of our own solar system". Going to the Moon, like climbing Mount Everest, is no longer breaking news. The destination now is Mars, the aim is to put up a permanent space colony on that planet. NASA, for example, is now mandated and tasked to 'get humans to Mars by 2033'. We have several plans to send manned missions to Mars, with a view to "eventually settling on and terraforming the planet, while utilizing its moons, Phobos and Deimos".[62] The space entrepreneur Elon Musk built the rocket company *SpaceX* from scratch, in order to take us to the Red Planet. An initiative of several distinguished scientists, including the late Stephen Hawking, aims to send a spacecraft to *Proxima Centauri b*, the planet closest to Earth outside the solar system. The motive is not only to experience the thrill of going 'where no man has gone before', but also, as Elon Musk envisions, to reduce the 'risk of human extinction' by making life multiplanetary, which he calls a 'strong humanitarian argument'... It is to jump the ship before it sinks and land on an island, so to speak. We have traveled to Pluto, and we are well on our way to the Kuiper Belt, the region of the solar system that exists beyond the eight major planets. We have even traveled into interstellar space. About our outward odyssey, with remarkable prescience, the French novelist Jules Verne had written, way back in 1865, that "in spite of the opinions of certain narrow-minded people, who would shut up the human race upon this globe, as within some magic circle which it must never outstep, we shall one day travel to the moon, the planets, and the stars, with the same facility, rapidity, and certainty as we now make the voyage from Liverpool to New York".[63] That indeed might come true and we might even, as someone predicted, be 'honey-mooning on the Moon' in our own lifetime. But that might not prevent us from burning a bride for dowry while on the Moon!

For, on the very face of it, we have made more headway on our outward journey, 'investigating the heavens', than on the 'inward' voyage, to explore the cosmos within. The Upanishads proclaim that the little space within every living creature is a replica of the cosmos and contains "The sun and the moon and the stars. Fire and lightening and winds are there, and all that now is, and all that is not". Our 'inner space' has remained more impenetrable and unfathomable; more of a black hole than those out there in outer space. But, like outer space black holes, it is the brightest spot in our inner universe. We are making more 'progress' and are able to go deeper into distant space, and know more about the stars, galaxies, and universes in the cosmos, than in our timeless thirst to travel *inside* to know what makes us who and what we are. Without 'going down', if we 'go up', as we do now, there is a huge risk; with the mindset man currently has, he is likely to behave no differently on Mars, or the Moon, or on any 'new earths' than how he behaves on this earth. The fact is we have largely exploited everything we can over here, and knowing it is going to come to an end, we are looking for another place to exploit. We will exploit other places also the same way and move on to yet another place. Unfortunately, we are looking at space exploration and human migration into space as a technical, technological or economic (how to bring down the costs) challenge. Through all his long evolution, man has been earth-bound and that is not simply a physical fact; it is also psychological and psychic. The earth is in each one of us, not simply the ground on which we stand. We are often disoriented, even if briefly, if we even relocate our place of residence. We must also bear in mind the 'mental' implications of our outreach into the womb of outer space. The human mind, prevailing for the most part in the 'war within', having, 'colonized' our consciousness, is now trying to conquer extraterrestrial space. Even more worrisome is that the 'content' of the human mind itself is under threat of radically being modified through applied neuroscience, drugs, computerized implants, brain-machine interfaces, by nano-scale devices, or other advanced technologies. There is little doubt that all these will leave an impact on human consciousness and human behavior but, unfortunately or by divine design, our 'intelligence' is not good enough to guess in which direction. Another way of putting it across is to say that that human 'power' has broken the defenses of the world beyond, but it is still knocking on the outer rampart of the inner world.

Human 'intelligence' has unraveled many 'secrets' of nature, or so it believes, but has come a cropper in regard to the 'war within'. We must remember one thing and grasp its full import. Man has become awesomely powerful and much of it is misdirected. We must remember that much of the power man has acquired is to do exactly what he wants, which often translates into what is dubbed as the 'conquest of, or over, nature'. And, as CS Lewis explains: "Each new power won by man is a power over man as well. Each advance leaves him weaker as well as stronger. In every victory, besides being the general who triumphs, he is also the prisoner who follows the triumphal car".[64] And it is inherent in human 'culture' to use every power we have, to test and use every weapon we make, even if it is self-destructive. Maybe one day, sooner than we can imagine, some nutty democrat or true dictator will 'test' our missiles on celestial objects or other planets. Control over 'outer space' without control over 'inner space' is hazardous. Although the 'Outer Space Treaty' clears forbids states from placing 'nuclear weapons or other weapons of mass destruction in orbit or on celestial bodies or station them in outer space in any other manner', clearly when a country becomes capable of doing so, it will do so. Already, there are reports that Russia is planning to build a 'nuclear space bombing machine'.[65] There is another danger. Why does man want to migrate to Mars or the Moon or whatever? Is it to escape from earth or seek new fortunes, to conquer new land, or to dig for gold? Would the lure of getting away from our seemingly doomed earth, decimated by man himself, act as a spur to further ravage our dear earth and play havoc with its ecosystem and environment? That is a real probability, given man's track record. Without getting rid of malice, if man 'colonizes' other 'earths', as some eminent scientists like the late Stephen Hawking have advocated,[66] what is being described as 'space settlement', those earths too will meet the same fate as our own. Even if we train to become the 'Mars Generation' we will, consciousness-wise, still be the same toxic humans we are on earth today. We humans have not been able to make something so simple as wishing others well an effortless habit; with what gumption do we want to spread ourselves elsewhere! Or, even call ourselves the 'most evolved' species or 'essentially spiritual' species. The same greed, possessiveness, and predatory behavior that have brought this earth to the brink will drag the 'others' too to the same fate. And if our passions remain what they are directed towards, and if we try to 'humanize' the universe, it might lead to unforeseeable and unwelcome consequences. Then there is the question: could the huge resources spent (a single space shuttle outing costs over half a billion dollars) be better utilized down here on priorities like eradicating mass poverty, cleaner environment, etc.? Whether or not *Man*, as a species, is the 'measure and mirror of all things', as we proudly proclaim, *Man*, as the individual, is certainly the 'measure' and 'mirror' of mankind. Man is his only limit and that limitation comes from within. The Sufi mystic Jalal ad-Din Rumi said, "The garden of the world has no limits, except in your mind". More appropriately, it is our 'inside', our 'within', of which the mind is but a part. Margaret Mead once said, "Never doubt that a small group of thoughtful, committed, citizens can change the world. Indeed, it is the only thing that ever has". While an individual is the basic unit, and it is not possible to affect any radical alteration on a mass scale, what is needed for a cascading and self-propelled momentum is a 'critical mass' of connected kindred spirits. For, "when an idea reaches critical mass there is no stopping the shift its presence will induce".[67] And we do not need to be heroes to align history; we only need to mend the way we 'live', 'make a living', 'deal' with other people, with other creatures and, most of all, with nature. And everyone can be an agent of change, as Mother Teresa said, by casting "a stone across the waters to create many ripples".

The Natural Need for 'Negatives'

Looking at all the horrors of the 20th century, and even more at what the ordinary, normal people—whose names, in the words of John Keats, are 'writ in water'[68]—do these days to their own selves and to fellow-humans, one wonders: How can human beings behave in ways that so thoroughly violate both reasonable and rational norms, and are obviously self-destructive? That includes not only what we are doing to each other but also to the environment, earth and nature, which can only be explained away as another form of self-destruction. But such are the laws of nature that, as GK Chesterton said, 'nothing is more effectively hidden in the farthest recesses of the oblivious than the obvious'. We blush about our own behavior, because we are blissfully oblivious and unobservant of what goes on within our own selves. Nothing seems so mysterious or a riddle or an enigma than our own behavior, both individually, collectively, and as a species. Aghast at his own behavior, man has always struggled to know why he does things he hates to do, to rid himself of his negative traits like prejudice, violence, ill will, hatred etc. The true answer is this: we are mixing up ends and means, the instrument and the direction. Nothing in life is unitary, or single-edged. Everything has a dual-purpose. In nature too, what we call 'negatives' exist, they are essential; without them creation will cease. Violence has a place, even anger, envy, rage, lust; it is the intent, person, principle, purpose, and whom it benefits that make the difference. In the wrong hands, and at the wrong time and circumstance, anything can be harmful; anything in excess, in isolation can do more bad than good, defeat the very purpose. If everyone is calm, incapable of anger, if we are all passively peaceful, mind our own business, that would give free reign to 'evil', which also is a powerful part of nature. Similar is it with another that we are advised to guard against—doubt. But often it is not doubt by itself that is a negative. We can make grievous errors if we are 'doubt-less' and too sure; Ezra Bayda tells us: "Provided we don't get lost in the negative beliefs that arise with it, it [doubt] can lead to a deepening of our quest".[69] Divine avatars never hesitated to use what we usually view as 'negatives' as means to achieve a 'positive' end. We often miss this central point. We need both 'positives' and 'negatives to survive and to help maintain equilibrium, within and outside. It is our 'behavior' that is so baffling; it is because we are not able to ensure the 'equilibrium' in the 'war within'. We have crafted a way of life, the human way, that feeds, abets and aids almost wholly our 'negatives'. There is no 'equilibrium' any more in human life. That must be restored, an exercise that some call 'spiritual struggle'.

Our 'behavior', whether 'autistic' or altruistic, benign or malign, is, in turn, nothing but a replica of the ever-fluctuating fortunes of that epic struggle. Every event in our life, every triumph and tragedy, every success and setback, the way we deal with every situation, has already happened, even if it is a few seconds sooner, before we actually 'do' or 'experience', enjoy or bemoan. All our past and present, everything that happened and is happening, every atrocity, all great human accomplishments, everything as a species we are so proud of, is but an outward projection of the state of this eternal war within, particularly of the people concerned at that particular point in time. If we can grasp this fundamental fact, nothing will surprise or shock us, and everything becomes explainable and comprehensible. The same will hold good for the future too. If we want to see that our future is better than our present, the only way is to positively affect the flow of the war.

Tikkun Olam—Healing the World

To affect the flow of the war, we have to affect the flow of our daily life. We cannot predict the future, but what history tells us is that what seems promising can become a nightmare; things can go horribly wrong and we can encounter what are called 'tail events' and 'black swans', events so out of everyday observations that we will fall short of what is required of us to meet such events. It all comes down to how human consciousness acts upon these 'possibilities' at a certain point of time and place, in the shape of certain human beings. We must also come to terms with another reality. We cannot any longer trust, or turn to, what Mark Twain called our 'sleepy conscience', what Gandhi called the 'inner voice', as our moral watchdog or as a tool to aid us in judging right and wrong. That 'sleepiness' is so deep and prolonged that it has made us virtually comatose. We need to turn our attention from *conscience* to our *consciousness*. We need such a tool to imbibe and internalize the simple message from nature: a life not useful is useless; or in Goethe's words 'an early death'. The famous motto of the Christian Methodist faith expresses this thought beautifully: "Do all the good you can, by all the means you can, in all the ways you can, in all the places you can, at all the times you can, to all the people you can, as long as ever you can". In Hebrew, the purpose of life is *Tikkun olam*, helping and 'healing of the world'. Carl Jung said that the 'sole purpose of human existence is to kindle a light in the darkness of mere being'.[70] A beautiful poem, *Another Reason to Live*, by Zen monk Seido Ray Ronci says it all: 'To hold the hand, to kiss the forehead; to wipe the face, to clean the soiled sheets of the dying'.[71] Swami Vivekananda simplified it in his usual way: 'he alone lives, who lives for others'. There is another reason why we have to make our lives 'useful to others'. Because we depend on others for our very existence, even just to be alive. Einstein expressed this thought when he said, "Many times a day, I realize how much my own outer and inner life is built upon the labors of my fellowmen, both living and dead, and how earnestly I must exert myself in order to give in return as much as I have received. My peace of mind is often troubled by the depressing sense that I have borrowed too heavily from the work of other men'.[72] Fortunately, we do not have to struggle too hard to do that. That 'being useful', that 'living for others' can take multiple forms and ways, depending on the nature of the need, not the person. The simplest way is to try one's very best, use every might, 'to see that every single act you do creates or contributes to what you care for, at least does not dilute. Whether the person is weak or strong, wretched or privileged, wicked or virtuous, does not matter. In Emerson's words, 'to leave the world a little better, and to know that one life has breathed easier because you lived here'. And we don't have to do something heroic or extraordinary. In a figurative way, we have to be 'doctors' and relieve an other person's pain and suffering; and it can be physical, mental, or even spiritual.

It is said that there's a passage in the Pali canon where the Buddha talks about himself as a doctor. He was indeed a peerless physician for the spiritually sick. Regardless of who the 'patient' is, we should simply heal and help in every way we can, and not worry about how that help is used or misused and what comes in return. That could be a good point of departure for us when we are caught up in life's balancing act. We are all bound to each other, and by helping others, we will discover an unacknowledged, undervalued part of our own selves. When we acknowledge that suffering is our common ground, it enables us to feel as though everyone we see has been our mother, father, daughter, or son or a friend or foe in one or other of millions of lives, not only in the human form. Sometimes in separate lives, some kind of a karmic role reversal takes place between husband and wife, parent and child, master and servant, even owner and pet. What in Buddhism is called the *Bodhisattva* path is dedicating one's life to the benefit of all beings, doing whatever we can to help ourselves be happy and free. According to this 'path', helping yourself, when your goal is to help others, might seem contradictory, but in fact it is the only way it can work. In the end, the notion of putting oneself last is really an inside-out form of self-cleansing. One such injunction even states, "when somebody whom I have benefited, and in whom I have great hope, gives me terrible harm, I shall regard that person as my holy guru". The person becomes a 'guru' because, by his actions, he tests our resolve and patience. The great 9th-century Buddhist Sage Shantideva taught that all the joy that exists in the world comes from wishing for the happiness of other sentient beings, not merely other human beings, and all misery from narrow egotism. He was prepared to exchange his happiness for the suffering of others, and he says, "May I become a servant for those sentient beings who need a servant". Perhaps the most impossible thing to do in human life is to be, and behave, like any *other* person, the exchange of 'self with the other', or one's life for another life. That is the ultimate separation. But, without at least bridging the gap, we cannot really fully share our life with others or look at a problem from another's perspective. Great souls, and Bodhisattvas and rishis, have struggled with this issue of how to create the space to put ourselves in someone else's skin to the best of our ability, imagining what they're going through, and how they perceive us, and identifying how we might help. A side benefit of seeing ourselves from another's perspective is that it is a great way to keep the ego in check, if not to abandon altogether. Ramana Maharshi says, "The individual being which identifies its existence with that of the life in the physical body as 'I' is called the ego… This ego, or individual being, is at the root of all that is futile and undesirable in life".[73] He also says that the common religious view of the three fundamentals as separate entities of world, soul and God lasts only so long as the ego lasts.[74] And that so long as the ego lasts, human effort is necessary, but when the ego goes, actions become effortless. One of the principal 'undesirable' manifests of the ego is to make us always look for self-gain and to desist from doing anything that could possibly be of any help to anyone.

In Einstein's words, 'only a life lived for others is a life worthwhile'. It is ancient wisdom too, as voiced by Marcus Cicero: *Non nobis solum nati sumus*— not for ourselves alone are we born. In the Mahabharata,[75] the dialogue on statecraft between Dhritarashtra and Vidura has this to say: 'One should wish for the prosperity of all, and should never set heart on inflicting misery on any group. One should pay attention to those who have fallen in distress and adversity; One should show compassion to all creatures, do what is good for all creatures rather than a select few'. Buddhism even calls for compassion to someone who tries to kill you. It says that 'when someone is trying to physically injure us, the practice is to meditate on patience for oneself and compassion for our enemy'. Martin Luther King Jr brought all this esoterism to a simple question, and said that life's most persistent and urgent question is, 'What are you doing for others?' The answer to that question, if we ponder over it for a while and be truly honest to ourselves, has to be: "what we are 'doing to others' is currently the chief source of suffering; none of us can claim that we caused no suffering to anyone". Two things are inescapable: we all 'suffer'; and we make others 'suffer'. That is Man's Fate and God's Choice. Lord Krishna calls the world of life '*Duhkhalayam asasvatam*', the place of suffering and the non-permanent. Buddhism says that all suffering is delusive like the death of your child in a dream. The great paradox, and also the great opportunity, is that it is easier to help people than not hurt them; it is easier to alleviate 'suffering' than not cause it; it is easier to be nice than not being nasty; it is even easier to save; but not nag, nibble, and negate others. In general, one might say that life is such that cultivating 'positives' is less arduous than avoiding 'negatives'.

Before we wander any further into the woods and get lost in Auden's 'lovely, dark, and deep woods', it is important to note and never forget another fact of life: that everything, all knowledge we possess and are able to have access to, indeed everything in life and life itself, is provisional, conditional and, at best, an approximation, a good guesstimate, if you will. Everything in life is impermanent, qualified, finite, but it, as Vedanta affirms, is all an 'appearance'; it seems so; not *is*. And, ironically, it is 'appearance', the way we look, the image in the mirror, that dominates modern life. It is 'appearance', not the reality, which we want to change, to 'improve', to 'augment', to 'enhance', to make whole. To cater to this 'need', to satiate this thirst, we have a surfeit of help at hand: plastic surgeons, navel and nose fixtures, fitness gurus, diet doctors, therapists, life coaches, body-shapers and fashion consultants and so on. Vedanta says that the Absolute alone is real; this world is only 'appearance', *maya* or illusion. Vedanta says the way out is to become the 'Absolute'. What modern man wants to do is to use his knowledge and intellect to not remove, but to perpetuate the 'illusion' to work on his 'appearance' and make that the 'absolute'. What he wants, in practical terms, are better jobs, a better love-life, better clothes, better cars, better relationships, better social statuses, better financial situations, etc. But at the end of the day, few are satisfied and many are bitter, angry, lonely, alienated, and disillusioned.

A World of Individuals

We must bear in mind that when we talk of the world in abstract, we are actually talking of a 'world of individuals', a conglomerate of 'units of life', each 'unique' and 'not being anything else'. It is the sum total of what the multitude of individual men and women feel, know, imagine, reason to be, and of whatever is knowable to a human now or ever. For long, philosophers and scholars have debated who is supreme: the individual, or society, the unit or the conglomerate. Some say that the liberty of the individual is the greatest thing of all, and that 'the submission of the individual to society—to the people, to humanity, to the idea—is a continuation of human sacrifice… the crucifixion of the innocent for the guilty'. Others argue that it is our inability to go beyond the bounds of what psychologists call 'individuation', described as a process by which individual beings are formed and differentiated (from other human beings). That 'individuation' is the cause, root and reason for all the travails of mankind. And, individuation is greatly influenced by 'intelligence'. We still do not know what intelligence in the operative sense means. And who is 'more' or 'less' intelligent than another person? Someone who is a genius in one field of awareness or activity might be a novice in another aspect or area. And we know all too well that a most 'intelligent' man amongst us, whose hallmark is 'reasoning' capacity, might act most 'foolishly' at times. In fact, many of the problems that mankind faces spring from the exaggerated confidence in reason. That is because we are *more* than 'intelligence' or 'intellect', and we ignore the other two dimensions: the psychic and the spiritual. The great rishi Sri Aurobindo said that a 'true transformation' of man can happen only through a triple transformation—psychic, spiritual, and *supramental*. He writes, "The forces that stand in the way of sadhana are the forces of the lower mental, vital and physical nature. Behind them are adverse powers of the mental, vital and subtle physical worlds. These can be dealt with only after the mind and heart have become one-pointed and concentrated in the single aspiration to the Divine". The aim of the sadhana is "to transform the whole nature, so that the being may live in union with the divine, and the nature becomes a field for the action of the divine Knowledge, divine Power and the divine Ananda". What is necessary for man to do is to surrender some of his individualism for the collective good. Indeed, as Tagore says, "creation has been made possible through the continual self-surrender of the unit to the universe. And the spiritual universe of Man is also ever claiming self-renunciation from the individual units".

Such are the soaring visions of realized souls—what the human form is capable of, and needs to work towards. Sri Aurobindo himself says, "He can succeed in this only if he makes it the supreme object of his life and is prepared to subordinate everything else to this one aim. Otherwise all that can be done is only to make some preparation in this life—a first contact and some preliminary spiritual change in part of the nature". Yet, at the level at which we live our lives, the connecting thread of all human thought, scriptural and scientific, sacred and secular, is veneration of life and vilification of death. Death, our 'intelligence' tells us, is dirty, dreary, dreadful, and an unnecessary—and unfair—end to being born human. And even if we have no clue what happens next, whether we go nowhere or somewhere, we believe that any sort of life with any amount of misery and depravity is better than any sort of death. We are even prepared to 'die' temporarily if we can escape death 'permanently'. That is why we abhor 'killing' of any kind or for any purpose. Without 'killing' there is no death; we are 'killed' either by bacteria, decay, and disease or by an insect, animal or an appliance, or another man. And every 'death' is at once natural and induced; 'natural' because everyone dies; induced or enforced, because no one wants to 'die', even the one who commits suicide. A suicide note often simply says 'consider my death as normal' and describes it as one's 'last wish'. Alongside the instinct for self-preservation, we also have the urge for self-destruction. Freud hypothesized that humans have a 'death drive' or 'death instinct', which he called *Thanatos*, but it appears to be accelerating. What Camus called the ultimate philosophical question, is fast becoming the ultimate 'final' solution to life's problems. It takes a trifle of an effort to 'die' than to 'live', many are coming round to feel. For a growing number of distraught and desperate people, the very thought that they can actually do something, anything—it just doesn't matter what—, that actually puts an end to an intolerable relationship, a pestering problem, a debilitating and draining condition, a crippling loss of a beloved or even of a crop, or just the fear of having to live out life in this world, is becoming a temptation too strong to resist. The searing commentary on our modern life is that suicide has become, in the minds of many, not an extreme step, but a reasoned response to the ugliness of modern life, which is defined, in the words of Aleksandr Solzhenitsyn, as "physical bloom, happiness, and leisure, the possession of material goods, money, and leisure, toward an almost unlimited freedom in the choice of pleasures". All this and the 'psychological detail' entails "the constant desire to have still more things and a still better life and the struggle to this end".

The allures of the luxuries of life, and the uncertainty of after-life, cease to be deterrents in that frame of mind. And it is seducing many young lives, not only those who are anyway at the end of life's journey. It is an issue that requires deep introspection and close attention of psychologists, religious leaders and of all thoughtful and caring persons. The basic facts of 'death' are stark and simple. The *Brihadaranyaka* Upanishad explains: "When body and mind grow weak, the Self gathers in all the powers of life and descends with them into the heart... By the light of the heart, the Self (which is hidden in the lotus of the heart) leaves the body by one of its gates; and when he leaves, *prana* follows, and with it all the vital powers of the body. He who is dying merges in consciousness, and thus consciousness accompanies him when he departs, along with the impressions of all that he has done, experienced, and known". And it offers an analogy to illustrate the process: "As a caterpillar, having come to the end of one blade of grass, draws itself together and reaches out for the next, so the Self, having come to the end of one life and dispelled all ignorance, gathers in his faculties and reaches out from the old body to a new". Simply or simplistically stated, one moment we are 'alive' and the next we are deemed 'dead'; 'life', or whatever it might be, departs, the body disintegrates and decomposes and is quickly disposed off and never again to be seen, and the rest of mankind get on with their lives till their time 'comes'. The 'dead' are 'gone' but not altogether forgotten. While some believe that the dead drift into the domain of fading photos, in some cultures and traditions, the 'dead', our ancestors, are ritually remembered through requiems; and even 'fed' every year, which it is believed is a day for the 'dead', for their sustenance wherever or whatever they might be or become. 'Death' defies logic, and there is no intelligible rhyme or reason, save, to some extent, the theory of karma, why at any given point one person is 'alive' and another is 'dead'. Maybe what we call 'death' is what we think is 'life' and vice versa. Then again, while death is 'earthly departure' in human terms, a matter of dread and regret, what about 'earth'? Is it a matter of 'relief' and 'celebration', the lessening, however infinitesimally little, of the human burden on earth? We can surmise and speculate but we cannot shy away from the fact that with all our intelligence, knowledge, scriptural wisdom, scientific insights, messages from mediums from the other side, 'we have never found either a *modus vivendi* or a *modus operandi* with mortality', a way to accept, accommodate and absorb 'death' into our earthly existence. Every 'death' of a known person intrudes into and affects our affects our lives. We visit the 'place', attend rituals, comfort the bereaved even if we really do not know what to say and say good things about the dead that you did not tell them when they were alive. The sun does rise the next morrow and we do our oblations as a part of 'being alive', and the 'dead' go wherever they go, or nowhere and henceforth they remain a part of our past.

Seminal Choice—Merger with the Machine or Evolution from Within

But the irony is that while we all blame brain-led human behavior as the source of all the problems of the world, we are also trying to solve the problem only by augmenting that very brain-power artificially. Our present mindset is that whatever we want and for whatever is wrong with us, we can get a fix through *ersatz*, artificially or synthetically. That is not confined to either organs or intelligence. It includes even overcoming our moral flaws through what is being described as 'artificial morality', a research program for the construction of moral machines. Suddenly, the name of the game in town, the flagship issue, the panacea for all our troubles is the 'machine'. Alexis Carrel suggested, "Humanity's attention must turn from the machines of the world of inanimate matter to the body and the soul of man" (*Man, The Unknown*, 1935). We are doing the opposite. The irony is that while the machine is man-made, we trust it more than ourselves. We are seeing virtues we think we ourselves lack; we think that a machine can act as a cover for our weaknesses and vulnerabilities. The guiding philosophy so far has been, in the words of Henry Ford, "for most purposes a man with a machine is better than a machine without a machine". But the question is, 'better' for what? In any event, we are about to make a quantum leap, a paradigm shift in our relationship with the machine. The accelerating advances in synthetic body parts, artificial intelligence, stem cell research, and genetic engineering, it is expected, will move us to a new era, where humans mingle with humanoids, cyborgs, and artificially intelligent robots. We not only want to make more and more sophisticated machines, appliances and gadgets to make our life 'better'; we want to go all the way like what scriptures told us to do with God—merge with it; dissolve into it. What adjustments we are forgetting is that in the man-machine symbiosis, it is man who has to make all the adjustments and compromises; the machine can't, or does not need to. It is through such a 'merger' or 'dissolution' that we want to become immortal, travel to and live in outer space, colonize the moon and Mars. Besides the machine, what we bank upon is the brain. In fact it is the blend of the two that is the magic wand to solve all our problems. The fact that we still do not have a 'fine-grained understanding of the neural structure of the brain' does not deter us from finding ways to merge our mind with the machine, which is the aim of projects like Elon Musk's *Neuralink*, the neurotechnology initiative that is reported to be developing implantable brain–computer interfaces. Instead, what we ought to be working on is how our brain and heart can better work together to broaden and better the base of our 'intelligence'.

We are now stranded in a state of 'materialistic slavery'; we have long ago almost lost what we might call the innate capability to live without some mechanical help. We rebel and fight against all kinds of slavery, personal, social, political, but we wallow in this slavery. To get freedom from this slavery too we need help, not materialistic but spiritual help. For long, having some sort of a machine allow us to do work with less muscle effort and greater speed, has been a part of human life and history, perhaps even pre-history, from the time of our human predecessor *Homo habilis,* which means 'handy man' or 'capable man'. But it has always been a supplement, complement, something that reinforces us. Now, if the present trends continue and forecasts come true, the machine might replace us; we will be reinforcing the machine, helping it to do its work better, with less 'machine' power, by offering our muscle power. There are a number of religious leaders who are greatly concerned about this trend. Pope Francis, for example, says that "work is a necessary part of the meaning of life on earth, a path to growth".[76] And we are doing it willfully, eagerly, even 'lovingly'; looking at the machine as a kind of a modern Messiah, a savior, to bale us out of our own trap, to solve every problem created primarily because of that very machine—which we now call android, cyborg, robot, biorobot, etc.—, to make us 'immortal', to take us to the next level of evolution. Cyborg might sound new and novel, but as Andy Clark points out, "human beings already are—and have been for quite sometime—cyborgs", but "not in the merely superficial sense of combining flesh and wires but in the more profound sense of being human-technology symbionts: thinking and reasoning systems whose minds and selves are spread across biological brain and non-biological circuitry".[77] And he goes on, "we cannot see ourselves aright until we see ourselves as nature's very own cyborgs: cognitive hybrids who repeatedly occupy regions of design space radically different from those of our biological forebears".[78] We are now at a crest of time facing a critical choice: to tread the path of the machine or the path of what we might call 'evolution from within'.

But what foxes us most is this: 'But WHY?' Why are we so persistent to make the machine our problem-solver, as the vehicle for achieving all that we want to achieve as human beings? We must get one thing straight: without the 'human', we are not human beings, whether it is good or bad is another matter. It is sometimes characterized as a 'great social calamity of our time'.[79] The growing role of the machine is not new. It started with the Industrial Revolution. It was well captured by Samuel Butler in his classic work *Erewhon* (1872). In that he wrote, "There is no security against the ultimate development of mechanical consciousness, in the fact of machines possessing little consciousness now. A mollusc has not much consciousness. Reflect upon the extraordinary advance which machines have made during the last few hundred years, and note how slowly the animal and vegetable kingdoms are advancing. The more highly organized machines are creatures not so much of yesterday, as of the last five minutes, so to speak, in comparison with past time". The same thing was also anticipated by Alan Turing in his 1951 paper *Intelligent Machinery: A Heretical Theory*. John von Neumann later talked about "approaching some essential singularity in the history of the race beyond which human affairs, as we know them, could not continue". Because the capabilities of artificial intelligence exceeding human intellectual capabilities and control are impossible to comprehend, the technological singularity is an occurrence beyond which events are unpredictable or even unfathomable. None of such warnings or forebodings have had any effect on the march of the machine or on the mechanization of human community.

When we think of technology we usually mean industry, or manufacture, or mechanization. But it is also equally agriculture, particularly mechanization of farming. The philosopher Martin Heidegger went to the extent of comparing the mechanization of the food industry with the "fabrication of corpses in gas chambers and extermination camps, the same as the blockade and starving of the peasantry, the same as the fabrication of the hydrogen bomb".[80] While most would agree that it was a huge stretch and a wild exaggeration, the fact should not be ignored that it was a watershed even in man's harnessing of the power of science-based technology. After the industrial revolution, technology has become the preeminent force in human life and has virtually pushed aside every other factor and force to the sidelines. Birth and death are no longer what they were a century ago. It is already possible, through a variety of prenatal tests to determine whether a child will be a boy or a girl, retarded or crippled, or the victim of some fatal genetic disorder. The question is: what does one do with that knowledge? As for death, now we do not know when we are officially 'dead', and—if science has its way—we could 'die' when we want to and come back to life in the same body at a time of our choice. Medical technology is re-sculpting the human body, and mechanization is marginalizing the role of humans in human life. One of the 'realities' that man has long been uncomfortable with has been his own body. He thinks and feels he is different, but his body is not. Ernest Becker puts it this way: "Man is a worm and food for worms. This is the paradox: he is out of nature and hopelessly in it; he is dual, up in the stars and yet housed in a heart-pumping, breath-gasping body that once belonged to a fish and still carries the gill-marks to prove it. His body is a material fleshy casing that is alien to him in many ways—the strangest and most repugnant way being that it aches and bleeds and will decay and die".[81] That is what we are trying to undo. We can now transplant almost every organ in our body. Since the first heart transplant done by Dr. Christiaan Barnard in 1967, it is now no longer so novel. Every year, it is estimated that more than 5,000 heart transplants are performed annually worldwide. Science, we are now told, might cross the final frontier—human-head transplant. In 2016, two surgeons, Dr. Xiaoping Ren and Dr. Sergio Canavero, wrote about full human head transplants being within the realm of the possible.[82] As for the goodies of 'mechanization', we are told that we can engage a *Rosie*[83] at home who can be 'primarily a personal assistant but also a photographer, security system, and household efficiency monitor'. Some reports say that it would soon be possible to have with us a 'Mother' robot that could build babies out of mechanized blocks, and then create new ones that evolve from the previous generation; robots would then be able to evolve on their own, in the same way in which animals and humans have done.[84]

It might be possible, in the not-too-distant future, to envision machines being made of bones, muscle, and skin tissue, and possessing all the capabilities of normal humans, while being man-made, with programmed brains. 'Brain', maybe, but how about, as they say, 'having a heart' and a consciousness and conscience? And let us not forget that, as John Bernal pointed out, "the human mind evolved always in the company of the human body, and of the animal body before it was human. The intricate connections of mind and body must exceed our imagination, as from our point of view we are peculiarly prevented from observing them. Altering in any perfectly sound physiological or surgical way the functionings of the body will certainly have secondary but far-reaching effects on the mind, and these secondary effects will be still unpredictable at the time when the physiological changes take place".[85] The so-called 'mind-body' problem, the 'relation between conscious experience and the physical world', has long been beyond our grasp, but some strides have been made in the past decade or so. Although it may require "revision of some deeply-held presuppositions" the obstacle to a breakthrough is, it is said, "not in our genes but in our suppositions",[86] and with that as a point of reference, some cognitive scientists and observers are hopeful of solving this riddle soon. Two other factors we must also grasp. Our 'fatal attraction' to the machine is also an adverse off-shoot of the state of the 'war within'. Two, it is not, as commonly presumed (at least not only) to relieve or replace human labor or to have workers who do not 'throw down their work and gnash their teeth', or not go on sick leave or to make our life less burdensome or boring. It goes much farther and deeper, and that is why the machine was so irresistible. Even those who are not 'replaced' are exhorted to become more machine-like, compliant, obedient, tireless, temperament-less, single-minded, or more accurately, *mind-less.* We are 'mechanizing' not only the workplace and offices, but also our homes, hotels, hospitals classrooms, communications and commerce, colleges… everywhere where human beings interact with other such beings.

Such a trend is in line with one of the fantasies that man for long has entertained—about mindless, self-propelled helpers to relieve their masters of 'toil'. It is rooted in the very core of human nature, our almost pathological drive and desire to control, no matter who or what the object is. It is to extract 'obedience' from our partner, children, fellow-humans, other species, the earth, even the skies. The human is, in his mind, a control freak. Given a chance, we obsessively try to dictate how others, particularly the vulnerable, are supposed to be, to think and to feel, and impose our views on others. We try to dictate how everything is done around others. We all, in different degrees, are 'self-obsessed' and afflicted or infected, with what psychologists call the 'narcissistic personality disorder'. The greatest temptation we cannot resist is to find fault with and 'control' every one else, except our own selves. In fact, it is our utter, pathetic inability to have any control over ourselves, over what we say or do, that makes us so aggressive in our desire to control others. The latest 'advance' in this direction is something man has long wanted: to 'control' the other animals. And scientists say that a new *brain-interface device* that helps translate brain waves into commands could let us 'control animals with our thoughts'.[87] It is the desire and ability to influence or direct people's behavior or the course of events. It is almost pathological, this temptation. Few of us are devoid of this desire. And much of the trouble in the world comes from this obsession to control: of individuals over other individuals; of groups over other groups; of races over other races; of nations over other nations. And technology is promising a 'future where everything around you can be controlled'. Needless to say, for the good of our own future, we must try to 'control' our power of control. Power and control are the two legs on which modern man walks. They are a part of everyday life, that we, in some measure or the other, exercise in every situation and setting and in every relationship. Power makes us feel superior to others, freeing us to shift our focus away from others to our own goals and desires. It can be heady, intoxicating and once tasted, or exercised over another, be it a spouse or colleague, or stranger, it can become even involuntary and addictive. Sometimes, 'being controlled' can also be compulsive, we may even derive 'pleasure', as in the Stockholm syndrome. But, properly focused, power and control can empower us to make a moral difference for the greater good.

There is no denying that technology has also given us the power to exterminate all other species on earth. We are doing this on the mistaken premise that they are of no use or consequence. As the Norwegian philosopher Arne Naess put it, "We are dependent on every, practically every kind of… every species. We don't know which species are of no consequence for us. So, the more seriously you take the non-living… the non-human beings, the better".[88] We have no control over ourselves, our desires, our passions, our prejudices, our avarice or anger but we want to control and conquer everything else. The master-slave relationship gives us another form of control. Even though formal slavery stands abolished globally, some sort of soft or subtle slavery is very much a part of human life everywhere. We just can't give it up, slavery in spirit; it is good for our oversized ego, only those who cannot do not. And man, even 'slave', is turning out to be too unreliable, too temperamental, too demanding, particularly when they close their ranks. And then, any sort of slavery raises 'prickly' issues like human rights, labor laws, unions, and minimum wages and so on. Now, with a machine no such issues arise. That is why we are trying to create a new class of 'new and improved' mechanized slaves, who are more 'efficient', and who, we assume, will be more compliant and devoted to our whims. The 'female' might even be prettier, and the 'male' more masculine than the human one, experts assure us. Slavery will stage a comeback; but no one will protest. For governments, it will give more muscle to make 'war' without human cost; for corporations it will mean more profit, more productivity, less labor trouble, and haggling with unions; for individuals, it will offer more comfort, safety, and more robust and trustworthy domestic 'help', with the likes of 'android servants'. Maybe we might then be able to clean up the environment! Our choice of the word *robot* is revealing and a give-away. The word robot comes from the Czech word *robota*, which means servitude, forced labor. We are indeed making 'progress' in that dubious direction. Thousands of patients are already reported to be using some kind of a brain implant, to treat brain-related disorders. A future robot, or cyborg, or maybe something else of the same genre, might turn the tables on us like in Karel Capek's 1920 play *R.U.R* (*Rossum's Universal Robots*).

The future that is being dangled before us is that robots might become autonomous and outnumber humans, like today's cell phones, in the next thirty years;[89] or become as common as computers even sooner. And some say that every home will own a drone by 2025.[90] As robots become more autonomous, there could be a real possibility of computer-controlled machines facing ethical decisions, like the one faced by the fictional computer character *HAL9000* in the 1968 film *2001: A Space Odyssey*. If robots are electromechanical representations of our entire selves—minds plus bodies, as some say, and if they outnumber us on earth, what could possibly be the impact on human life, or how do we define them as human? What would that do to human evolution? Could we embed ethical systems into robots, so that they mechanically make the judgments that seem right to most people. How would that affect human-to-human relationships? First, those who now hire humans would prefer robots and we cannot blame them as that is a 'logical' extension of what we prize most: rational choice. Some might even prefer a robot mate to a human partner, or a robot nanny to a babysitter. Humans could be unemployed or be reduced to helpers and semi-skilled labor. If robots are going to have the same kind of mindset that we have, then they would be no better than us; probably worse, because they will have no heart as a balance. If they are more 'intelligent' than us, and as self-destructive as we are, we can end up being *their* 'robots', or be eliminated altogether. They can become killing machines, and we would never know why, when and how they might turn killers. In 2015, a technician was killed by a robot at a Volkswagen plant in Germany. This could have been a freak accident, or a straw in the wind. But can robots be held responsible? And if they are 'intelligent', should they be treated as 'persons'?

As in Mary Shelley's *Frankenstein*, our greatest gift, creativity, in a monstrous twist, is reinforcing, in the words of Joyce Oates, "humankind's predilection for self-destruction".[91] The evidence is all around. Possibly an ultimate in this direction would be sexless reproduction; to synthetically replicate ourselves. According to a report, a Chinese company, which has the world's largest cloning factory, already has the technology needed for human replication through cloning.[92] Fundamentally, cloning is asexual—a child becomes a product of one, not two, as nature has intended, turning procreation into manufacture. Some society women feel it releases a female from what is euphemistically called 'to make out', the torture of 'someone sticking something in you… for a thing to grow in your body… which eventually tears itself out, leaving a trail of blood and destruction'.[93] We 'create' weapons, wasting precious human and scarce natural resources, being fully aware that they are too destructive to be used but which can fall into the hands of those who are too deranged or desperate not to use them. We constantly enhance the lethal power of hand guns so that one crazy man can, with every new version, slaughter, more easily and with less skill and effort, more than he could have done with the previous model of the weapon. We 'create' machines with the dedicated objective of rendering us useless. What we fail to understand is that once something gets made, it is foolish to imagine that their use is exclusively our prerogative. Machines have a 'life' and a dynamic of their own. The Creator created us; what *we* create is also *His* creation. The same thing goes for so-called inanimate objects. As Jennifer Worth puts it, "Inanimate objects have a life of their own, especially when they are the daily companions of a living soul". Our very life depends on these 'things' and therefore they deserve respect, if not reverence. That is why, in Hindu festivals, there is a ritual called the '*Ayudha puja*', where one remains respectful of all things that one commonly uses, be it a plow or a tool or a knife or a car, or a book—and in today's world, a cell phone, or a computer or a gun or drone, or a missile—depending on who we are and the work we do to make a living. We are supposed, on that day, indeed every day, bow down to that object and pay obeisance and use it respectfully.

Unless one approaches something with a certain sense of reverence, and a deep sense of involvement, it will not yield hope for an outcome. Anything that we use, we have to see it as something above ourselves, and bow down to it so that it evokes a deep sense of involvement. Once such involvement is there, we will handle it well, and will get the best out of it. But what we are unaware of is that everything in Creation, even if it is an 'inanimate thing', has a life in its own way, and is so integral and indispensable to our 'life' that it deserves respect and reverence. The two principal 'instruments', or 'implements' with which we spend all our lives, from birth to death, are our body and mind; so pervasive and fundamental they are that we have to be reverential. Being 'reverential' means both taking care and keeping some distance, or being detached. Which is what scriptures advise us to do: don't be too attached to your body and mind; they are 'your body' and 'your mind', and therefore not 'you'.

A broader question that crops up in this line of thought is this: if everything we 'create' is also God's creation, and nothing can happen in the world without His grace, does it include nuclear weapons, and weapons of mass destruction? And did God make man to be self-destructive, or did He allow the 'finest' of his creations, as the Bible says, that which is made on His image—*mago dei*—, to spend all his time on earth being self-destructive. To put it differently, how does Joyce Oates' predilection for self-destruction fit into or play out in God's Grand Scheme of creation and destruction? Just like in creation, are we also doing His work on earth in all the 'cides' we indulge in—suicide, homicide, infanticide, ecocide, fratricide, patricide, matricide, and so on? Quite logically, come to think of it: how can we—frail, flawed, slaves of our senses, venal, under the thumb of materialism and malice-filled mind—acquire the awesome capacity to accelerate human extinction and to blow up the planet if He did truly not want it? Technology, in that light, is a divine avatar, both in its ability to lift lives and to exterminate life itself. And, from this perspective, how should we view our latest 'creations', machines in general and robots in particular, that are predicted to be even more central to human life in the future, in war and peace, at home, at the workplace, in communications, transportation and in the struggle for global strategic power? Are they meant to be acts of creation or destruction? Many humanoid robots already exist like Darwin Op, Darwin-mini, NAO Evolution, Pepper, Romeo, iClub, Kuratas, etc. Some are very expensive, costing more than a million dollars, while simpler ones can be obtained for just over a thousand dollars. Robots are no longer used just in industrial environments, factories, warehouses, and laboratories. These 'intelligent' human-like machines are already becoming part of our lives, of the society we live in. The passage of time will bring lower costs and new technologies, which will narrow the intelligence gap between robots and humans and will enable their widespread purchase.[94] The question is: what is 'human-like', and what does 'more intelligent' mean? Will these creations have self-consciousness and what is their driving 'thinking force' that makes them do what they are capable of doing? And what is the glass ceiling when it comes to these robots: will man become completely redundant or be reduced to a side-kick, or will he still call the shots?

Whichever scenario might unfold, man will still matter, and the make-or-break point to bear in mind is not how versatile, 'intelligent or powerful a robot might become. The more important question is, after the tinkering and reinforcing that science promises to do with our body and brain is done with, what will be the state of 'human' consciousness of that human being? And if we 'transfer', 'upload' the brain/mind that we currently have, into that 'being', it is hard to predict whom the future has to dread more: the 'modified' man or the humanoid? Mary Shelley's Frankenstein leaps to our mind as a possible paradigm. The humanoid will be the 'monster'; and Victor Frankenstein, the 'new man'. We will be like the creator who despised his own creation and forced that form of life to behave like a monster, ending eventually in his own destruction. Like the humans of today, Victor (the creator of the monster, in the novel) in fact wanted to make one 'like himself'; certainly not the hideous creature it turned out to be. As for morality, it is arguable who was moral or who the victim was: Victor, who abandoned his own creation, or the monster who murdered many people as revenge for his creator' callousness? We are in fact a bit of both. Like Victor, we too are filled with hubris and dreams of glory, and have the power to 'play God'; and like the monster, we harbor deep longing for goodness, love and, above all, friendship, which the Buddha said is the 'whole of holy life'. The monster might have a good reason to feel like that, but, in our world too, with far less justification, everyone, even the villain, even a mass murderer, thinks he is a victim, and like Victor they too run away from any moral responsibility for what they do. We may not like to own up, but the fact remains that for every crisis the world faces, all of us or each of us, is 'responsible' for the 'disfigurement and destruction of creation'. Another character that we are increasingly coming to resemble is *Duryodhana*, in the great Indian epic Mahabharata. Duryodhana was the architect of his own destruction, as well as of his entire clan. Despite being the heir apparent of a huge kingdom, he was consumed with greed, malice, hate, and extreme ambition. Even more telling is that he openly acknowledged—which we still do not do—that he was following the path of *adharma* or evil, but was unable to restrain himself. If we can come to terms with who we are now—a hybrid or the monster, Frankenstein, and Duryodhana—and if we are still capable of some sacrifice, should we then welcome what scientists describe as the 'human-robot-symbiosis' as the road to choose at this crossroads of history?

Brain—the Beast Within

We must first grasp one central fact: whether it is a computer billions of times more powerful than unaided human intelligence, or a rogue or sentient-robot, they are all brain-bred and mind-made. But the beast within all of us is the *brain*. All of us have what is often called a 'reptile brain', that links us down the ladder to the fight–flight–freeze mechanisms inherent in all mammalian (and earlier) life. If we do not want the future to be a 'logical' extension of the present, whether and when singularity[95] happens or not, and whether or not man becomes a slave of, or merges into, a machine, for man to evolve in the right direction, human 'intelligence' must also evolve into wisdom and for that it has to be more broad-sourced. We don't have to be 'brain-dead'; for that, we would need to complement, not supplant, the brain/mind. We have to create or discover an additional source, not externally but internally. Every thought we entertain, everything we see and perceive, every word we utter and every deed we do is wholly mental. This is not a new discovery or revelation. So synonymous is mind with man and so limiting, that it has even been said by spiritual masters that 'man minus mind is God' or, positively, 'God plus mind is man'. Not only spiritualists but even some great scientists have echoed the same thought. For example, Einstein wrote that "behind anything that can be experienced there is something that our minds cannot grasp, whose beauty and sublimity reaches us only indirectly and as a feeble reflection".[96] That 'feeble reflection' must be a shining star, a beacon of bright light.

But the mind too, like everything else in life and nature, can be both 'good' and 'bad'; contingent on the 'state of mind' of the mind. The mind manifests as logic, reason, and intellect. They have played a huge role in human survival and supremacy. But they have their own character and limits. The biggest of the challenges mankind faces at this hinge of history was best summed up by Alexis Carrel (*Man, The Unknown*, 1935): 'Those who desire to rise as high as our human condition allows, must renounce intellectual pride, the omnipotence of clear thinking, belief in the absolute power of logic'. The great 8th-century Indian philosopher and theologian, Adi Sankara, assuredly one of the sharpest human intellects ever and an unsurpassed spiritual master, expressed the same skepticism when he asked, "have we not exaggerated the power and role, the clarity and reliability of reason?" He said that it is not 'cold logic' that can lead to self-realization; it is insight that we need, which is "the faculty of grasping at once the essential out of the irrelevant, the eternal out of the temporal, the whole out of the part".[97] Voltaire said, "Judge a man by his questions rather than his answers". A Chinese proverb adds: 'He who asks a question is a fool for five minutes; he who does not ask a question is a fool forever'. The poet David Whyte wrote about, "questions that can make or unmake a life... questions that have no right to go away". They won't 'go away' but cannot also be settled the way we want it. After twenty years of what he himself called 'presumptuous research', Raimon Panikkar reached his 'humble conclusion' and asked, "How can human thinking grasp the destiny of life itself, when we are not its owners?"[98] Whether our 'natural' destiny was to 'squat in caves and shiver, then die'[99] or conquer the stars and be immortal, as we dream to do, our task on earth ought to be to make the planet a safe place for future generations to live upon. And, we must acknowledge that all ultimate 'questions' have no infallible answers, and all human ability to 'know' is tightly circumscribed, for good, or godly, reasons.

We must also never allow ourselves to go soft on another central fact. While perennial questions concerning the origin of evil, what is evil, and whom we can call evil, and under what circumstances will never 'die', the reality is that in the innermost recesses of our being there are seeds of both good and evil, and that an epic struggle is constantly raging between the two for the conquest of our consciousness. And yet, one cannot exist without the other. We must bear in mind that even if it is a struggle we don't witness or feel or experience, it is real and if we want to rise to our full 'humane' potential and become a more benign being and seriously address any of the existential threats the world is facing, then we must prevail in this mortal combat—at the least manage a positive stalemate. In all of us there are two men, two personalities. One is one whom some call, a bit unfairly, the 'animal man', or more accurately 'self-centric man', slave of the senses, driven by desire and pursuit of pleasure; the other is the 'spiritual man', essentially struggling or seeking to turn his existence into a tool to be useful to others. What we call our 'behavior', which often surprises, saddens and maddens us so much—how could we, we wonder—, is but an external extension or reflection of the 'state of that struggle' between these 'two men'. Call it the karma of Kali Yuga, our current age, or whatever else, over the recent past, the personality of 'self-centric man' has become the dominant force in our consciousness. And that, we need to change, using every means at our disposal, every trick or trade, to induce and bring about an internal 'regime-change', a revolution in the psyche of every human being. But such a revolution cannot be brought about solely by any external entity alone, be it religious, political, or social. Yet context matters. To change something we must be open to change. In fact, that is a central fact we tend to ignore. Nothing in nature, nothing in life happens, or can happen, out of context, or in isolation. Everything that happens in life has to happen for something else to happen, or has happened. All morality, all virtue, all religions, all scriptures, all science, all thinking are contextual, outcomes of space and time. We venerate scriptures as sacred, and a truly religious person is expected to live by the Book. They might be the very word of God, but the medium, even if he is a prophet, is the human consciousness. Some scholars even say that different portions of the same Book have different things to say, reflecting the ethos of the time of the specific part. For example, it has been said that the peaceful Quran passages were revelations that began in Mecca, and the war-like ones were from Medina. When context changes, content changes. And if it doesn't, it becomes irrelevant and injurious. It is our constant failure to accept and adapt this truism that is responsible for so much of what went wrong in human history. We cling to ideal concepts, ideologies and beliefs that demonstrably do more harm than good. What has thwarted our aspirations to lead happy, harmonious, and fruitful lives is due to another central fact. We have been completely clueless and powerless to do anything about anything 'within' and that 'helplessness' has a huge bearing on how we lead our lives in the *karana jagat*, the causal world.

Man—Noble Savage, Civilized Brute, or Half-Savage?

If we are 'moral'—or spiritual, for that matter—then we wouldn't be so reflexively self-righteous, a trait that rationality again rationalizes. After all, the line between 'self-belief', or 'self-esteem', which we deem a virtue, and self-righteousness, which is bad, is very thin. It is rationality that draws the line. The 'moral' state of man at birth has long been a subject of scholarly and speculative debate. Some say that "men come into the world with their benevolent affections very inferior in power to their selfish ones and it is the function of morals to invert this order".[100] Others aver that we are essentially 'good' at birth and it is culture and civilization that corrupt us. Whether we are a 'civilized brute', 'noble savage' or, to borrow a phrase from the American television serial *Star Trek* (Arena) 'half-savage'—there is hope. The fact is that we have always been, are and will always be, morally mixed-up and messed up, although the make-up of the 'mix' varies from time to time and person to person, even within the same person, sometimes dramatically and drastically. Everything that is in nature—the good, bad, and ugly, noble and nasty—they are all there within each of us. They constantly collide and fight for supremacy. There is almost nothing that has always and everywhere been deemed either 'good' or 'bad'. When the necessity and context change, the focus of what is moral and what is not also changes. What might appear as immoral or cruel now, like slavery, patricide or infanticide, for example, were at another time conceived and viewed as acts of mercy and morality. Furthermore, if man had been wholly selfish or selfless, he would have been extinct a long time ago. And whether any such 'event' would have been good or bad for life in general is another question. Another point we must remember is that all morality heavily hinges on the assumption that we have a good measure of freedom of choice between good and evil. The point is that none of us is so right or righteous that we can walk through our lives sniffing and mocking at others. Our 'morality' too is double-faced. One for us and for our 'near and dear'; another for others.

Although a bit too biting, in one sense, there is still some sense in Oscar Wilde's quip that "morality is simply the attitude we adopt towards people whom we personally dislike". But even that 'double-face' is a part of evolution. Had we been entirely morally even-handed and treated everyone alike, we would again be extinct by now. That is how generations succeeded each other in an uninterrupted continuum.

What we should never lose sight of is the supreme, and subtle, secret of nature. In fact, it is no secret; it is overt, open, and apparent. It is two-fold. To harness nature we must first befriend it. Blavatsky's *The Voice of Silence* (1889), a translation of *The Book of Golden Principles* says, "Help nature and work with her, and nature will regard thee as one of her creators and make obeisance. And she will open wide before thee the portals of her secret chambers; lay before thy gaze the treasures hidden in the very depths of her pure virgin bosom". We have been exploiting nature's treasures, not by 'working with her' but by 'groping' her 'bosom'. What we see is its backlash. The 'second' is that everything in the cosmos and creation, comes as a *dwanda*, a pair of opposites, like light and darkness, positive and negative, good and evil, leaving and clinging, hardship and hope... And that, the great Sankara, the foremost exponent of the Advaita philosophy, says, is also due to the power of *maya*, the cosmic illusion, sometimes called the Indian Sphinx.[101] Everything is dual, but knowing it is not, is wisdom. The conundrum is that nothing is 'standalone', all by itself, and yet any action should be performed as if it is. In a basic sense, they are not 'opposites'; nothing in nature is opposed to another; each is different; and that 'difference' has a cosmic purpose. Each is distinct, indeed exists, only because the 'other' is out there. In fact, they create each other; like 'being' and 'non-being'. Without darkness there is no light; if there is no error there is no truth; without vice or evil there is no virtue or goodness; without a road up there can be no road down; and without death there is no life, and so on. Inside each of us and in life at large there is a dwanda. In fact, the Jewish *Kabala* describes the Infinite God as a 'unity of opposites'. Lord Krishna says in the Bhagavad Gita that He is the *dwanda-atheetha*, the One beyond any 'pair', beyond any compound. He tells Arjuna, "By the delusion of the pairs of opposites, sprung from attraction and revulsion, O Bharata, all beings walk this universe wholly deluded".[102] Becoming an 'atheetha' ought to be the goal of life. That, in effect, is a state of harmony. But then, what is the certainty that 'delusion' itself is not an appearance of illusion? The fact also is that even a 'negative', properly used, can be positive. The same snake venom kills but also saves. Context also changes the character of the same action, positive or negative, virtuous or sinful, legal or illegal. The parent of all paradoxes is that the 'parent' of all pairs, the dwanda, is the one within. The way to 'support' it is by the way we 'live', which, in turn, is greatly influenced by the balance in the internal 'dwanda'. Being different is good; being indifferent is bad. Indeed, "we are all equal in the fact that we are all different. We are all the same in the fact that we will never be the same. We are united by the reality that all colors and all cultures are distinct and individual. We are harmonious in the reality that we are all held to this earth by the same gravity".[103] People have lost interest in people; it is things that matter. We may not even notice this about ourselves, but none of us are truly interested in anyone; it is only that which we think will be pleasurable and comfortable for us to be familiar with that we care about. If we can grasp and comprehend this fundamental truth, everything falls into its proper perspective, like looking at the earth from the moon, and will give us what we need most in life—a launching pad for lift-off, an anchor to wrap ourselves around. Even our existential experience in daily life tells us that our cognitive capability is 'necessary but not necessarily sufficient' even to lead our mundane and meandering lives. We are creatures conditioned by context, molded by space and place; so is knowledge.

Has God Gotten Weary of Man?

Three of the foundational questions that have long haunted humankind are: "Who in the world am *I*?", "Why am I doing what I am doing?", and "What ought I to do to become what I ought to be?" More practically, how much of what is amiss and remiss, innately illicit, deficient, and decadent in us is our fault, and unique in particular in each of us, and what should be the source of the change from within that changes the way we relate and connect with the world? Given the inroads that the machine has made into human life and turned man into a means for its perpetuation, and given our dismal terrestrial track record, we must wonder if the 'human machine' has become so irreparable and fatally dysfunctional that we should accelerate our efforts to lighten the 'human' part and heighten the 'machine' part. Some argue that "a moral machine is better than a flawed human being".[104] Should we now actively work to install an 'autonomous' robotic-machine as our natural biological successor on earth? Are we safer with 'synthetic biology', said to be already in transition from field to reality?[105] The emerging field of synthetic biology envisions engineering the living world. Record sums are being invested in research in this direction. Although the premise is that it will deliver novel biofuels, drugs, foods, materials, bio-products like organs for transplant, chemicals, and even perfumes, clearly it will also yield unexpected other offshoots. A field of such potentially huge significance requires informed social and ethical attention.

Besides all the timeless questions of theology and philosophy, we must now add another one: has God finally given up on man, the one who, as the Bible says, was 'made in His own image'? And, has God left him naked to the malice of his own mind? We have no way to know, but what we do know is that we are getting disdainful of God. Many mock and ask "what has God done for me lately?"[106] Pope John Paul II said that "the limit imposed upon evil, of which man is both perpetrator and victim, is ultimately the Divine Mercy".[107] Is that why evil, these days, has a smirk on its face? We have performed, in Nietzsche's words, 'divine decomposition'. Whether avowedly atheistic or not, whether or not we have 'faith' and/or 'belief', we so conduct our lives as if God is either helpless to help us or to hurt us, and therefore skeptics conclude that a "God that matters, in the 21st century, is all but extinct". And an ad is out for a "God who matters and can be trusted".[108] By 'to be trusted' we mean to do our bidding, to be at our beck and call—that is what we want from God. Even if we believe in God, we have come to convince ourselves that to please the extant God we need not be good and virtuous, that by being ritualistically devout, worshipful and 'charitable' with God, we can sanitize, if not sanctify, our bad behavior, and we can wash away our evil. From the prehistoric times to the modern day in human consciousness, God, religion, and morality are, as a recent study reveals, deeply intertwined with what it means to be human, for better and for worse.[109] At the practical level, most of us no longer feel any discomfort in being 'pious' and ritualistically zealous in our theological life, while being immoral and malicious in our interpersonal universe. We are able to indulge in all this duplicity, double-talk, jugglery, and are able to get away with it, and to a large extent are able to 'have it both ways' because we are in practical terms slaves of our mind. Our mind is so cunningly nimble that it can explain away anything and turn a mass murder into a holy action. And it is not only 'fanatics', whom Vivekananda called 'the sincerest of mankind', and 'extremists' who are led to do such things; even 'responsible, 'deeply religious', god-fearing 'leaders' have justified gross evil as righteous acts, 'just wars'. Another instance is President Truman calling the atomic bombs, which he ordered to be used over Hiroshima and Nagasaki, as 'merely another powerful weapon in the arsenal of righteousness'. He did not say, as many have said, that it was a 'lesser evil' or 'necessary evil', or that he was doing his 'duty'. All his life, he never doubted why he did. The bomb was not dropped on Tokyo, where the people who were waging the war were living, and there was never a credible explanation. One view was that dropping the bomb on Tokyo would have led to 'lesser' damage, as it was already a rubble, and another very curious, if not cynical, reason was that they did not want to kill those—the war-wagers and leadership—with whom they had to negotiate surrender! Purely objectively, how can we 'rationalize' it, reconcile an individual's presumed 'goodness' with cold-blooded murder of thousands of innocent people? The mind can make us anything, and make us believe we are 'moral'.

It is our artful ambivalence about God, divine disconnectedness, and our broken relationship with nature, that has led some perceptive observers like Mark Juergensmeyer, Dinah Griego, John Soboslai to conclude what is responsible for many of our thorny problems like the current environmental crisis[110]—and most certainly for the current 'morality crisis'. Ivan Karamazov of Dostoyevsky's *Brothers Karamazov*[111, 112] says, "Without God everything is permitted now, one can do anything". Or, according to a different translation, "If God didn't exist, everything would be possible". The key word is 'if'; the premise is predicated on the non-existence of God. It does not mean that Ivan believed in that; in fact (in the book), he later confesses to Alyosha that he does believe in God. But the quote is often used to signify that sans belief in a supernatural, supreme power, we cannot anchor our moral truths or truly know right from wrong, even right from another right, and wrong from another wrong. The positive take away could be that we then know we are on our own, are socially responsible for our actions, with no alibis or evasions, nothing to explain away with. If we have full faith in God, however we visualize and wherever its, or His, locus might be, we have a solid anchor, a clear focus to 'realize' Him, to live life according to His dos and don'ts as revealed in the scriptures. Most of us are in the world in between, neither with implicit faith and belief nor with explicit denial. What we 'know' is so ludicrously little either to affirm or deny. We want the divine on our own terms in our own den; we think that God owes us much in return for our belief in Him. And we think that devoutness can be an antidote to immoral behavior and acts as a buffer to injustice and oppression. We use worship to try to placate or even bribe God into overlooking how we ill treat and exploit other people and torment and torture other species. This is not a nascent trait or tendency. One of the Hebrew prophets, Amos, for example, warned against this and posited that God's absolute sovereignty over man compelled social justice for all men, rich and poor alike.

Conclusion

Things seem so awfully out of control in the world primarily because the *human animal* is out of control. He is out of control because control over human consciousness is in the wrong hands. That is, in the hands of the mind. So long as that remains unshaken, it doesn't matter if we become 'immortal' to migrate to Moon or Mars. If any, things will get far worse. And that is why the war within is doing so badly. That is why human behavior is going from bad to bizarre. The planet itself is in peril primarily due to human activity, but man, instead of owning responsibility and redressing the situation, is making plans for lunar or Martian escape. So then, if things are like this, can it get any worse? Is the 'weary' God, to paraphrase Rick Yancey (*The 5th Wave*, 2013), divesting humankind of humanity to rid the earth of humans? Has self-immolation become the sacred and solemn duty of every caring human being, to rid the planet of what Agent Smith (*The Matrix*) calls 'the cancer of the planet', a plague? But if we don't do that and we choose to stay on the slippery course, will we become a multiplanetary species, and who could that '*we*' might well be? Will the post-modern man become the Biblical Methuselah (and live very, very long)? Or, will he become the Puranic Markandeya of Hindu scripture, and live forever? Or will he become someone like the Immortals of Jonathan Swift's *Gulliver's Travels*—people who do not die, but age and become ill, demented and hunger for death? Put differently, the darkness that is currently enveloping us the time before dawn or the time after dusk? Is it the death throes of a doomed species or, as the Bible says, 'the beginning of the pangs of birth'? Can we turn the gilded age into the dawn of a golden age? Will money further exacerbate the greed, rancor, and injustice in the world and trigger a catastrophic collapse and a social meltdown, or can we transform money into a moral tool to usher in a more just and egalitarian human society? Will morality continue to offer a cover for social ills, or would we be wise enough to consensually create a 'new framework for ethical living that is socially and spiritually topical? Will technology succeed in its goal of turning the human into a Deus or god, or will it turn us unto a hybrid of zombie and walking dead? Or will it help erase absolute poverty, mass illiteracy, and ill health from the face of the earth, and arrest and reverse existential threats like climate change? Will we continue to look for new ways to nag and nibble, torment and terrorize, divide and destroy ourselves, or realize the oneness of all sentient life, that we are all manifestations of the same Supreme cosmic consciousness, which, in the words of Richard Bucke (*Cosmic Consciousness: A Study in the Evolution of the Human Mind*, 1901) as entirely immaterial, entirely spiritual, and entirely alive? Will we continue to be the butchers of biodiversity and terminators of terrestrial life, or recognize, as William Blake said "everything that lives is holy" and that every form of life, from ant to elephant, termite to tiger has an irreplaceable niche in nature, and that their premature passing could cripple the ecosystem and life in general, and that the human, whoever technology will turn him into, is by no means immune? No one knows for sure. The answer can be anything. It depends on what happens in the womb of the world within, and how the war therein shapes up, and which side of us—divine or demonic, good or evil, wise or wild, noble or nasty—comes to control the commanding heights of our consciousness.

Chapter 2

The Two Cherokee Fighting Wolves Within—And the One We Feed

The Triad of Worlds We Live In

All of us talk routinely and reflexively of the world we live in as if it is a stand-alone, homogenous, harmonious entity. We actually *live* in three parallel, yet interdependent, worlds. And our inability to harmonize the three worlds is the source of much misery. The *first* is the world as another name for Planet Earth—seen as a pale blue dot from space—which harbors and houses over seven billion humans, and many more billions of non-humans. It is a 'dark, dreary, and dangerous' world that catches our eye and engages our attention, but we never truly believe we are a part of it, that what happens to it is of any relevance to our life. Practically speaking, we don't live in one big world. We live in a collection of small worlds. The *second* is the world of near and dear and neighbors, family, friends, and foes. This is the world that truly matters, and yet we are affected by what happens in the first world. The way we have tried to overcome this ambivalence, this 'irksome inconvenience', true to our genius, is to have it both ways: to be caring and cooperative towards a few, the ever-shrinking 'near and dear', and be competitive and callous towards the rest. Caring for the 'few', as the Dalai Lama noted, is 'emotional attachment', not 'genuine compassion'. As he puts it, "true compassion is universal in scope"—one might add, not subject to reciprocity. The Dalai Lama goes on: "The rationale for universal compassion is based on the same principle of spiritual democracy. It is the recognition of the fact that every living being has an equal right to and desire for happiness... Compassion and universal responsibility require a commitment to personal sacrifice and the neglect of egotistical desires". Jesus said, "You must be compassionate, just as your Father is compassionate". And compassion is simply 'returning a favor', a *quid pro quo*, if it is shown only to those who are 'good' to us'. True compassion comes into play when it is extended to those who do 'harm' to us. In the karmic, if not cosmic, sense, those who harm others, 'suffer' more than the others do. Human nature is such that if we do, or think we do, 'good' to other people, it is natural to expect recognition, if not gratitude, from them. And when we do not get it, as it so often happens, we feel hurt, even resentful. And that sours our own mood and mind and affects our future responses to similar situations. Expectation always leads to disappointment, and it is very hard for a person of average abilities to do anything, particularly an act of altruism, without expecting something in return, even a simple and sincere 'thank you'. Scriptures and sages tell us that we should try to transcend that spiritual 'limitation'. Prof. Iswar Chandra Vidyasagar, a philosopher, reformer, and educationist, whom the Sage Ramakrishna himself hailed as compassionate, was once informed that someone was abusing him. Prof. Vidyasagar reportedly answered, "Why so? I do not remember having done any good to him". Compassion is not only for 'others'; we need to be 'compassionate', at least 'considerate', towards our own selves. Too often people try to cope with their suffering with low self-esteem or harbor a sense of inadequacy and failure. They fall into patterns of stressful and destructive self-loathing which just multiplies into misery. Self-compassion is different from self-love, which is injurious to others; compassion, wherever it is directed, can only do 'good'. It is also different from random acts of kindness; they lull us into thinking that we are 'good', that it balances our 'bad'; which might even embolden us to be more brazen. Compassion essentially is a state of sublime consciousness, and once we cultivate it in our whole mindset, our behavior and personality changes. We do not need to become a Buddha or Christ or even a Gandhi to be compassionate. At its core must be the dictum that our lives and those of all beings are connected as in a giant web spread right across the planet and indeed beyond. If we can imbibe the sense that we are all made of the same stuff, subject to the same natural processes, all sailing in the same 'existential boat', we will naturally feel compassion towards all other life and forms of life. As the Buddha sings in the *Karaniya Metta Sutta*: "Have that mind for all the world, get rid of lies and pride, a mother's mind for her baby, her love, but now unbounded". It is relatively easy to accept this intellectually, to feel good about ourselves and stay stranded in the smug status quo. For it to have any practical effect it has to become our reflex reaction.

The *third* and the most important, is the *world within*, our inner world, invisible, impervious, and impenetrable. The first world is our only home. Although the world outside, the phenomenal world is the same geographical zone of activity, different people perceive it differently. For some, the world is wondrous and the people are good, while for others, it is, in Arthur Schopenhauer's words, 'such a miserable and melancholy world', where the people are deceitful and sinful. It is so, because the outer world is the projection of our *inner* world. But somehow, we see ourselves apart, and separate. The paradox is that everything is globalized in this world but not our mindset. We stay connected regardless of distance or culture, but lose touch with our own inner or deeper selves. Everything any of us does affects everyone else, and yet we all behave as if we are an island unto ourselves.

Deep down we just believe that the 'fate of the earth' is not our fate; and even if it is, we will *somehow* survive it, triumphant amidst the smoldering ruins and burning *ghats* of a dying earth. That is the headwater of all that is amiss with humanity today. It is this facile, if not false, faith that lets us go to sleep at night, and do all the sundry silly things the morning after and feel good. And that is why the second world is the real world we actually care about, because everyone in this world is but an extension of 'I, me and mine'. It is from this world that we derive our sense of identity, or sorrow and well-being, rather than from the first world or the third, the world within. The lives in the second world crisscross ours, give us joy or sorrow, delight or despair, make life tolerable or toxic, meaningful or malignant. It is what happens in this world that seduces us to suicide, and impels us to homicide. What is upsetting about death, in fact, is the prospect of getting separated from the second world, not the first, universal world. The 'third world' is the inner world, the most consequential and the most meaningful. It is this world that Matshona Dhliwayo calls the 'greatest temple in the universe' (*Lalibela's Wise Man*, 2014). Both the first and second worlds are but its reflections and extensions. But our inner world is invisible, and yet, as George Eliot says (*Middlemarch*), 'the true seeing is within'. The biggest change mankind has to make, is a paradigm shift in its preoccupation and focus from the external to the internal, from the without to the within, from outer space to the inner space, and, most of all, shift his focus from the wars outside to the spiritual war within. The world within is the world of our consciousness, and the 'war' that rages is for gaining control of its commanding heights.

The paradox is that there is no consensus on the definition of what constitutes this 'third world', except that it is not the much-talked-about 'Third

World', the economically underdeveloped countries of Asia, Africa, and Latin America. This is not a geographical or physical world; it is the *spiritual* world. Although we used to think that it is exclusive to the human world, many scholars and researchers are now positing that it is inherent not only in the animal kingdom, but also in the vegetable and mineral kingdoms, although human consciousness is higher than that of others. And that spiritual growth calls for attaining higher levels of consciousness. Consciousness is both universal and unique; unites and separates. Both unites and divides. All of us are fragments or sparks of the divine or cosmic consciousness. And yet, as individual forms of life, we all have our particular consciousnesses. The dissolution of the particular into the universal or cosmic consciousness is the ultimate spiritual goal. Views, however, vary on where we are consciousness-wise at this juncture in our history. Some say that although everything appears dark, grim, gloomy, and depressing, there are tell-tale signs that we are actually poised at the dawn of a global or planetary consciousness. From the other end, others argue that all the stomach-turning things happening in the world, perpetrated by us humans, indicate how depraved and debased human consciousness is. If that were so, how does one explain the good things people still do? In truth, both are true. Our individual consciousness houses all our emotions, feelings, and inclinations and dispositions and passions and, depending on their intrinsic nature, they all fall into two camps or sides or opposing sets of forces: good and bad, darkness and light, constructive and destructive, *raga* (attachment) and *dvesha* (aversion), positive and negative, righteousness and wickedness, altruism and selfishness, mind and heart. And the opposing forces battle for control of the consciousness. We do good when the forces of goodness attain an upper hand, and bad when the bad adversary dominates. The good, the bad, the ghastly that happens in the world is simply the external manifestation of this war, and it has its ebbs and flows, and fluctuations and swings. It is an intense and fierce struggle for control and conquest of this planet and the human consciousness. In spiritual terms, the fight is between our two 'selves', higher and lower. And the final goal is not to 'defeat' or 'eliminate' one or the other, the good or the evil, the raga or the dvesha, but to transcend them. That is what the Bhagavad Gita suggests—*raga dvesha viyuktaihi*, transcending the opposites—as the way to cultivate tranquility and divine grace. But in the intermediate state in which we live, the 'fight' goes on.

What is striking is that nothing grabs our adrenaline more than war; it brings out man's true nature—good and bad, noble and ignoble, heroic and horrendous. And yet, we are utterly oblivious and unaware of this deterministic of all wars within. In the words of the Christian evangelist Billy Graham, "The wars among the nations on earth are mere popgun affairs compared to the fierceness of battle in the spiritual unseen world. This invisible spiritual conflict is waged around us incessantly and unremittingly". It is our consistent and persistent failure to recognize and pay sufficient heed to this greatest of all wars, the war within, that is the root cause of all our troubles and problems, and for all the venom, virulence, and violence in the world that causes so much despair. This explains the stubborn persistence of organized violence in the human world. War-making is a major aspect of modern life, and research indicates that this has been the case for the past several millenniums. In recent decades, numerous anthropological studies have presented compelling evidence that interpersonal violence and warfare, in varying degrees, have been an integral part of humanity's history. Current studies suggest that some of the earliest humans did engage in organized violence that appears as approximations, forms of, or analogues for what we now view as warfare. Some scholars even suggest that it could have been a significant driver of human evolution.

As for the 'war within', we really don't know when it began—estimates vary from two million years to three thousand years. Many scriptures have referred to the evil within, and the paramount need to fight it, and some saints have lamented their inability to do what is right, but no one has painted it in its true colors. We have been waging all sorts of wars for several centuries, but few, if any, have realized that the most important of them all is going on right under our noses, inside the citadel of our own consciousness. We have long wondered why we behave so badly at times, but never even suspected that the cause as well as the remedy is in the sanctum of our own soul. It is a matter of everyday frustration that we are often paralyzed into passivity in showcasing qualities like what the Buddhists call 'loving kindness and compassion' in stressful situations, but it never occurred to us that it is because these very qualities are on the losing side of the war within. Human transformation has for millenniums been the aim of our spiritual *sadhana* (practice), but it always gave us the slip because we chose to ignore the fact that true transformation must rise, like the Phoenix, from the ruins of the war within. When 'breaking news' tells us of a bloody massacre somewhere in the world, we ask, like an alien up in the sky, 'what is happening to humankind?', but it never crosses our mind that it is the ascendancy of this very mind in our consciousness that is responsible. And so the capacious charade goes on: we get on with the myriad mundane things of our meandering lives, always surprised, shocked and saddened, but feel helpless even as the forces of anarchy and evil gain strength, fed by our own actions. The answer to the question why we do nothing individually, even as a blind man can see that the climate crisis is real and potentially capable of making the planet uninhabitable, is that without consciousness-change, climate change, like the ill-fated *Titanic*, is headed towards its own iceberg—our willful blindness.

All too often, we feel overwhelmed and besieged by what life entails, and we get stricken with a sinking feeling, like a raft let loose in a stormy sea. It is because our gaze, attention, and energy are wrongly directed. We gaze at the stars instead of 'seeing within'; we voyage to outer space, instead of 'going within'; we marshal all our forces to wage all kinds of wars, driven mainly by ego, avarice, and malice, instead of directing out attention to the 'mother of all wars', the *War Within*. And this war, unlike other wars, has two frontlines: consciousness inside and context outside. We really do not know when this war began. Some say it was there all along, and that it gained speed and shape only with modern man. Others say it began when human evolution evolved to the present self-aware level—what Julian Jaynes calls the 'breakdown of bicameralism'—about three thousand years ago. But the fact is, whether it was a war or not, a struggle or fight between two sets of intrinsically inimical forces, good and evil, light and darkness has been a constant through the ages. To 'win' this war—which is to facilitate the ascendancy of the forces under the rubric of good over those of evil—we need to induce and orchestrate a radical modification of the character and content of our consciousness in the contemporary 'human way of life'.

Forward—Outward or Inward?

Framed differently, the question is: is the way forward *outward* or *inward* ? Do we turn our gaze and energy to engage with the universe within, or do we exploit and enjoy the world without? Almost instinctively, we view them as separate, even alternatives or opposites. The idea that everything in nature comes in pairs of 'opposites' permeates Greek philosophy too. The most prominent is the 'Table of Opposites' of Pythagoras, which, among other items, includes good and evil, and light and darkness. Such examples are 'day and night' in Heraclitus' philosophic theory, 'justice and injustice' in Anaximander's, and 'love and strife' in Empedocles' philosophy. The paradox is that both 'opposites' are two primal cosmic energies, two poles which are opposite but, at the same time, complementary to each other and which are both manifestations of the one and only reality. How to harmonize the two without destroying either is the challenge we face, which is at the heart of the war within. We tend to think that science deals with the world 'outside', and spirituality with the realm 'within'. We assume that the within is a given, but unknowable unknown, about which we can do little. But the outside, we feel, is within reach, which we can mold and manipulate to our advantage at will, to make human presence on earth eternal and unchallenged. The fact is that they—the worlds within and without—are holistically connected, even functionally interdependent; neither can exist without the other. And the 'world within' is a veritable gold mine of all that we seek and long for. In the Indian epic Mahabharata, queen Gandhari, who willingly marries the blind king Dhritarashtra, chooses to blindfold her own eyes for the rest of her life, to show her oneness with her husband. Henceforth, she does not see the world without, but she receives the "choice blessings of the world within" and acquires great spiritual powers, strong enough to throw a curse on Lord Krishna himself. The macrocosm is within the microcosm, as much as the microcosm is within the macrocosm. That is the central message from the Upanishads. Swami Vivekananda explained, "The microcosm and the macrocosm are built on the same plan. Just as the individual soul is encased in the living body, so is the universal Soul in the Living *Prakriti* [nature]—the objective universe". The inward–outward dichotomy is also used to define the man–God interrelationship. Meister Eckhart wrote, "The more God is in all things, the more He is outside them; the more He is within, the more without". Everything that comes out is but an extension, reflection, and projection of what is already inside. And the 'already inside' is itself an outcome of an internal struggle. We may think that only wars of the world are real, but spiritual warfare too is very real. Warfare happens every day, all the time inside us. Whether we believe it or not, all of us are in a state of war. Eknath Easwaran says, "Spiritual life too is a battle. Mystics call it the war within; the clash between what is spiritual in us and what is selfish, between the forces of goodness and the powers of destruction that clash incessantly in the human heart". He also says that the subject of the great epic Bhagavad Gita is "the war within, the struggle for self-mastery that every human being must wage if he or she is to emerge from life victorious".

The arena, the theater of operations, where we can find any leads to solve our problems can only be within the microcosm—the individual man. WB Yeats wrote in his poem *Cuchulain's Fight with the Sea*, "I only ask what way my journey lies". Jalal ad-Din Rumi said, "Everything in the universe is within you. Ask all from yourself". But the outward-to-inward journey is more complex; it requires more effort. For, how we live in the world outside influences what goes on inside. The inward journey has been characterized as the longest journey, the path to God, the internal pilgrimage, etc. The 'inward' is the world beyond perception, the world of intuition, emotion, and feeling, the world of seekers and noble souls. The destination is the *nihitam guhayam,* the One hidden in the 'cave of the heart', the *Atman*, the Self. And the obstacles are the senses and 'mind-body-identification'. In the Bhagavad Gita, Lord Krishna draws the analogy of a tortoise to convey the message. He says, "When, again, as a tortoise draws in on all sides its limbs, he withdraws his senses from the objects of sense, then is his understanding well poised".[1] Just as our brain and body are connected, so are our inside and outside. We are fairly clear that what appears as the outside is the phenomenal world in which we exist, work, play, live, and die. The conundrum is that while we must undertake a journey inwards, we do not know the way; we only know the way outward, but it leads nowhere. We must transcend our robot-like existence that devours all our energy and attention, even imagination, mostly just to stay alive, to fulfill our obligations, to earn a living, to raise a family, to have fun. In the end, we feel only inadequate, going from crisis to crisis, while time ticks away to an end that ends it all. Most thoughtful people concur that what mankind needs is a cathartic cleansing of consciousness. With our consciousness composed of different stages or levels, some say we are now at the stage that manifests as the 'me-first', materialistic, and aggressive behavior; but there are signs that we are on the threshold of a leap up the ladder to a consciousness driven by 'trans-rational intuition'. Scientists tell us that man is certainly at the same time the most aggressive and altruistic animal. In other words, different individuals, or the same individual at different times, can respond differently to different situations, and temptations and provocations. It is said that "evolution didn't just shape us to be violent, or peaceful, it shaped us to respond flexibly, adaptively, to different circumstances, and to risk violence when it made adaptive sense to do so. We need to understand what those circumstances are if we want to change things".[2] If we want to tame human aggression we have to create appropriate circumstances. Many might argue that the circumstances we are shaping will make us more aggressive; others opine that once the consciousness threshold is crossed, man could become a more introspective, tolerant, socially sensitive, and environmentally harmonious person. When that threshold is reached, consciousness does not dissolve; it is the *limits* that dissolve. The final stage, reached by prophets like Jesus, Muhammad, the Buddha and Mahavira, by mystics like St. Teresa and St. John of the Cross, by masters like Ramakrishna Paramahansa, and by teachers like Sankara and Swami Vivekananda, is when we are able to erase the boundary between the creator and creation, between one living being and another living being, and reach a level at which humanity itself becomes one tribe, living in harmony on sacred Earth. We might indeed all have clairvoyant consciousness, dormant but extant, with which the living can talk to the dead. While we can speculate about the evolution of aggression of the human, the two critical factors that everything hinges on are consciousness and circumstance.

Our chief living limitation is our instinctive interpretation of our own selves as limited and lone beings. It is our inability to comprehend the import of the Upanishadic mahavakya, '*Tat tvam asi*', (Thou art that), and come to terms with what Martin Buber[3] called the '*Ich und Du*' (I and Thou) relationship. We think, feel, and behave as autonomous individuals; all pleasure and pain, happiness and misery is experienced by our 'standalone' selves. However, most religions tell us this is the greatest misconception. The truth is that everything is united, everything is connected, nothing is separate, and the substratum, the ground underneath is all divine. What we have to overcome is not a malfunctioning brain or a wayward mind or even a corrupted consciousness; it is to move into a different realm of reality. The realm we are comfortable with is the one that is physical, observable, measurable, and repeatable; in short, borne of the scientific method. We have ignored the spiritual realm. We possess all the pieces of the jigsaw puzzle but it is so huge that we never see it as whole.[4] And we wonder why. Could it be because of the brain that nature has given us? The brain—the 'three pounds of strange computational material found within our skulls'—is master of the body. For happiness and harmony it should work in tandem with the body, but for over a million years of our evolutionary struggle for survival, the left-brain, which is the seat of what we call reason and logic, became the dominant part, and the right-brain, the source of emotion, intuition, love, and empathy, became a passive passenger. We are now poised at a momentous crossroads. The kind of intelligence we will nurture towards what direction and purpose will shape human destiny. Intelligence is the one thing that separates man and other species, and man from man, and contributes to making us how successful we are.

The aim of artificial intelligence (AI) research is to develop thinking machines that outdo and overtake all human cognitive capabilities; leaving mankind, in the words of Donald Michie, Britain's leading AI researcher, "living in the interstices of uncomprehended, incredibly intelligent electronic organisms, like fleas on the backs of dogs".[5] The irony is that we are increasingly more comfortable in the company of thinking machines than of thinking men. There is growing concern that technologies like the internet are not only intrusive, but might be making information so easy to obtain that it is atrophying our very ability to think.[6] In effect, it means that 'we have two people living inside our heads, the person you call 'you' and a total stranger who lives in the other half of the brain'.[7] Another view is that it is not that we have two brains but actually two minds, 'one of which has far greater powers than the other'.[8] A certain sort of 'ancestral harmony' existed in human evolution between the 'two minds' that allowed smooth flow of communication between them, and enabled man to lead reasonably well-ordered and symmetric lives. Problems started when this flow was interrupted, or became one-way, from the objective to the subjective. Einstein said, "The intuitive mind is a sacred gift and the rational mind is a faithful servant. We have created a society that honors the servant and has forgotten the gift". A radically different viewpoint is that it is not a matter of two minds, but a matter of head versus heart. We have two autonomous but inter-reinforcing sources of energy, memory, and intelligence, centered around the mind and heart; and that until recently it was the heart that was the dominant partner, and man was a happy and harmonious being. For reasons not quite clear, the mind acquired ascendency, the heart went into eclipse and all our troubles started. Such a view is no longer confined to scriptural thought; it is now emerging as a scientific possibility. Julian Jaynes called the 'dual-centered' human consciousness a 'bicameral mind'. We all know that we have something that we have come to call 'consciousness', but we do not know what it really is and how it operationally relates with the brain, mind, and heart. Yet another hypothesis is that we all have a 'Laurel and Hardy type of consciousness', two different selves that constantly spar with each other. In addition, we also have, according to this view, a third person inside, a robot, who or which performs all repetitive tasks of life.[9] Some argue that we all have hidden, dormant, occult powers. These are more pronounced in some people, and were possessed by our ancestors but have been lost as they were no longer needed. While we live in the visible physical world, there is another invisible, 'normal, original, eternal, spirit' world.[10] Our ancestors were in constant contact with the 'spirit world', and literally conversed with the gods. The complete severance of this communication is responsible for our diminished human lives. Rudolf Steiner even says that if we do not get closer to the world of spirits, "something completely different from what ought to happen will happen to the earth".

As if we are not sufficiently befuddled we are also told that that what appears remote and marginal is "often what the soul inwardly needs".[11] But then, some researchers tell us, about 'the power of thinking without thinking',[12] that more often than not, right decisions are taken not after deliberative thought, but by instinct and blind feeling. Chesterton wrote that you can only know truth with logic if you have already found it *without* it. Whether we rely on intelligence or intuition, the question that arises is that if life's road, in the harrowed phrase of Emily Bronte, 'winds uphill all the way', a Sisyphean struggle, then why not quickly slide down and end it all? To whom should we turn for help—the 'you', the 'stranger', the 'robot', the 'hibernating heart', the 'hidden self'?—and for what purpose, and how? Does the solution to all our problems, personal and civilizational, lie in harnessing our hidden powers, described as 'a sign of our evolutionary potential'?[13] And if so, how? How do we untie the knots that hold us back? If we want to turn our lives around and become modern-day 'mini-mystics' or 'miniature-mahatmas', or simply men without malice, what is the road map?

Consciousness-change and Contextual-change

The real suffering, and its only solution, is embedded 'within' each of us. And, *each of us* requires *each one of us*. The deepest secret of sentient life, particularly human, is very simple. We can achieve everything, fulfill every desire, and dream, not directly but through a detour; not explicitly but implicitly, through the medium of another person. Anything done solely for self-gain is pyrrhic; anything we do for another's well-being is a win-win; you benefit more than the beneficiary. Only by sharing can we become whole; and make life less difficult to someone else, anyone from spouse to stranger. All our life, we search for a meaningful life when the 'elephant' is next to us. We seek the divine everywhere when our true 'identity' is the divine within, the immortal aspect of our mortal existence, the *Atman* as the Upanishads call it. It is something that we cannot 'see'. There is a growing realization in the world today, especially in the New Age movement, that the only way to avert a cataclysmic catastrophe is a gradual shift in global consciousness, that without such a paradigm shift nothing else will work, nothing else will save us… Before we even ponder over such weighty issues, it is important to offer some cautionary caveats. Like in all issues relative to the future of *Homo sapiens*, it is possible, even highly probable, that all our best answers are tantamount to tilting at windmills; for the truth is beyond our mind-mediated capacity of perception. The capacity we need is to be able to 'see things, ourselves, other people… differently', *à la* Beau Lotto.[14] But this much is still true: whatever might possibly happen in the future is contingent and congruent upon the direction of the transformation not of the world around, but of our *inner* life—a process that spiritualists call 'consecration'. And just as in worldly life we don't win or lose, but live, so it is with our life within. We cannot 'survive' either victory or defeat, triumph or capitulation. What we should aim at is a constructive stalemate, a favorable deadlock. All creativity is transformation. In fact, without transformation there is no life. The key question is transformation from what to what, and how. While we are witness to and passive participants of external transformation, we are wholly clueless and utterly unaware of what goes on inside us, and that results in a disconnect between the two: external transformation and internal transformation. As a direct consequence, many of us try to deal with this 'disconnect' by resorting to all kinds of distractions and amusement. American writer Scott Fitzgerald portrayed the 1920s as a decade that began with 'the general decision to be amused'. This applies even more sharply to the 21st century. What is important to note is that these distractions and delusions do not end at amusing or entertaining us; they act as nutrients to our internal destructive passions, and feed the 'wrong' army in the war within.

One of our biggest obstacles to bringing about a holistic approach to address the challenges of our time is that, although we talk of 'one humanity' and 'one world', we all exist in our own personalized worlds, which are specific and special to each individual, a fraction of humanity. As the Mexican saying goes, *cada cabeza es un mundo* ('every head is a different world'). In fact, it is the head that gives form and shape to everyone's world. And that is the chief problem man faces. We mistake it for an answer, whereas it is really a question. It is the main handicap and hindrance to better the human condition, and stands between morality and man. Perhaps the greatest 'delusionary illusion' is to think and act as if there is an unbridgeable chasm between our life's inside and outside. The fact is, for something to happen outside in the external world, that activity has to be caused by something inside in our internal world, and vice versa.

The war within is also the answer to the question why, despite being essentially a 'spiritual being', man has become an economic animal. If we can change the direction of our desires, it will change the direction of human effort and creative power. We will then be able to radically alter not only the context of our life, but even the content of our consciousness. However, the 'consciousness-content' cannot be changed unless the 'context-content' is changed. And then again, what does God, up from the sky or deep inside each of us, think of all this? While it is sheer stupidity or utter naivety to rule out any possibility, a note of caution will be in order. Logically then, we should all somehow cling to life, hang on for a quarter century, by which time, it is expected that people will start lives that could last a thousand years or more. The down-to-earth reality, however, is far more modest and matter of fact: so far, whatever science has done in this field is to prevent premature deaths and thus increase the average life span; it has not really extended our actual life span, which is generally believed to be 120 years, even by a single year.[15] The irony that eludes our acumen is that on the one hand, man, unable to come to terms with the demands of modern life, is struggling to find reasons *not* to die, and, on the other hand, science is dangling the carrot of immortality before us. Perhaps the greatest indictment of contemporary life is that so many are finding it easier to end life than to continue living. If ever the era of immortality does descend, we might well see a reversal of roles; just as we now long for immortality, men then might yearn for mortality.

What we are outside impacts on what happens inside, and what goes on within our consciousness makes us who we are. Most of us live outside and strive to achieve some goal, some ideal, through our external effort. But the truth is that there is nothing 'out there' unless it already is 'in here', within the confines of our consciousness. We may not know exactly what consciousness is and its link with the brain and mind, but we do know that it is, in large measure, the difference between being alive and being dead; and that it is what both unifies and differentiates us as living beings. If we want compassion to be our compass in navigating through life, we need a compassion-dominated consciousness, and for that we need to nurture a compassionate context of life. What we need right now is a new compass to set our direction and steer us through the stormy seas of our own consciousness. And, it is important to note that it carries some basic evolutionary implications. Natural selection has been a governing principle in creation for over four billion years. As Elizabeth Kolbert points out in her book, *The Sixth Extinction: An Unnatural History* (2014), whether we intend to do it or not, we are deciding which evolutionary pathways will be shut off forever, and which can be left open to flourish. We are moving towards what is being described as 'evolution by intelligent direction'.[16] We are also being told to brace ourselves for the seismic possibility that the human, or whatever remains of him, is about to transcend Darwin, and that evolution will be, in the future, mediated by man, not natural selection, which has held sway for over three billion years. What does it all amount to? And what does that mean for the much-talked-about *New Man of the New Millennium*? If the species has been static on the evolutionary scale, since the monkey became a man, and if an equally seismic man-mediated change that rivals such an event is coming soon, how should we react and, more importantly, try to influence such a change? If we are approaching a tipping point in which all things that were hitherto impossible suddenly become commonplace, and if everything we wish we could actually make it happen, then are we yet again eating another forbidden fruit? And does this prove or disprove the all-knowing, all-powerful Almighty? Whichever answer appeals to whoever, the stark fact of the matter is that mankind is tottering on a balancing beam, and there is a more than a fair chance that it is about to get thrown off the beam. And man is not even sure what is down below. The scary thing is that while the outside world is brimming with hair-raising events, profound mutations are happening *inside* our consciousness, even as we go about living, working, mating, multiplying, murdering, and, most of all, making money. And that entails much more than going to work everyday and getting a periodic paycheck to buy groceries and gadgets; it has an enormous ecological cost. Even spiritually we are all at sea, as uncertainty meets us at every step. Is mortality the sinful fruit of our Biblical fallen nature? Or is it a golden gift of life, the envy of the angels, or an epiphany liberating us from life's *fait accompli*? All this rumination within trickles down to three matter-of-fact matters: world-weary as we might well be, how do we live so that life is worth its whole? And, on the individual level, as long as *I* am alive, how should *I* relate with other sentient beings who are anyhow as alive as I am, both in its limited and larger sense? And then, what is this *I am* that is so intrusive and insolent, at once threatened and vulnerable? So, who is that 'I' (or 'me' or 'mine') that we so pathetically and pathologically cling to as sentient beings? According to the Vedanta school of Indian philosophy, all troubles start the moment we utter the '*I*'; everything else is an illusion.

To this ageless list of questions we need to add one more, probably the most momentous, the most fateful of them all: can such issues be considered academic or superfluous now because we might not after all be around for too long? We seem to be, in our preternatural hubris and inebriated haughtiness, crossing two dangerous thresholds—the Darwinian and the Divine. The first, by trespassing into the forbidden zone between animate and inanimate beings and trying to turn machines into 'conscious beings', or living things. The second, by seeking 'death-less' life and mimicking, or mocking, God. Once man himself was described as the 'ultimate machine', a 'complex machine created through nature by God'. The tragedy is that, instead of optimizing and fine-tuning, harmonizing fully what this natural 'machine' is endowed with and is capable of, we are diverting our entire energy and creative power to making *external* machines to get what we want from life. We must understand that every form of life is a blend of attributes, and trying to enhance any particular 'ability' might be counterproductive, and could upset the balance in nature. That applies even to the length of life span. It is said that we are on the verge of uncoupling intelligence from consciousness, and machines might come to know us better than we know ourselves.[17] Whether that 'knowing better' is good for us or not is a wholly different issue. Now, man wants to create 'conscious machines'—possibly moral machines[18]—outside the realm and reach of nature, and turn himself into a 'god' by linking up with it. A huge chunk of man's ageless effort has been to go beyond being human, or to be more than human. That 'more than' has now crystallized into becoming a 'god'.

If there is one common thread between all religions and most cultures, it is the sanctity of human life. It is based on the premise that 'life' is priceless and the human is special, closest to the divine. Scriptural injunctions like the Jewish Talmud say, for example, that since all mankind is descended from a single person, taking a life is like destroying an entire world, while saving a life is like saving an entire world. But these have largely ceased to be serious restraints to taking a life... While we are, on the one hand, trying to achieve breakthroughs in living without ageing, and living as long as we wish to, without regard to cost and consequence, we seem, on the other hand, to have lost our nerve and self-confidence. Such is the depth of our self-belief that we have, for all practical purposes, given up on ourselves and our own internal power, and cast our lot with external powers, be it artificial intelligence or thinking computers or robots or androids or cyborgs, to help us out. And it is not science-fiction—about 4000 Swedes are already "cyborgs", part human and part machine. Implanted in their hands is a tiny identity chip, which they can use instead of ID cards or credit cards. We have cognitively concluded that without hooking up with an external contrivance we will not be able to achieve anything. The surprising thing is that every time we have to believe something, say God, we want proof, but when it come to technologies like artificial intelligence, we trust them even if we don't understand how they actually work. And although we associate proof with rationality, not everything can be proven true or false. In Kurt Godel's words, "You'll never be able to prove every true result... you'll never be able to prove every result that is true in your system". The 'fact' is that facts on their own don't tell you much; in fact, they can lead you astray. It is only when coupled with what you desire and with whatever gives you pleasure or pain, that they can guide your behavior. That is why it is so important to desire the right desire, and want the righteous want. In real life, the dividing lines between proof, fact, opinion, and truth overlap and crisscross. It is important not to underestimate the power of hatred, like love, in the world and within all of us. It gives, albeit depraved, a sense of purpose larger than life, of working for the greater good. Purpose is highly personal and subjective, and yet it always develops in a social milieu and a consciousness-context. To have a right purpose requires a right mindset and that requires the right balance and mix in our consciousness. It means that what we need now is not a cognitive but a 'consciousness revolution', powered by both cognition and intuition, mind and heart in the *right* combination. While the two have to work in harmony, not in hostility, we must make sure the command and controls are with the heart. A sprinkling of brilliant minds can vest us with promethean powers, but a few beautiful hearts are not enough to ensure that we are worthy of having them. The new word to put us in our proper place is that humans are organic algorithms.

Literally everything around us today runs on *algorithms.* They power the internet, make all online searching possible, they direct our email, work silently behind the scenes when we use our GPS systems, etc. Smartphone apps, social media, software… none of these things would function without algorithms. Altruism itself is based on algorithmic calculation of cost and expected payoffs, which are vital for self survival. The humble algorithm is now being anointed as the New Almighty of the techno-religion, omnipotent, omniscient, and invisible but all-pervasive. As Yuval Harari puts it, "More than a century after Nietzsche pronounced Him dead, God seems to be making a comeback. But this is probably a mirage. Despite all the talk of Islamic fundamentalism and Christian revival, God is dead—it just takes a while to get rid of the body".[19]

The Power of the Heart

The power to effect a consciousness revolution must rise from *within.* And that 'power' is none other than our own heart. We learn early in life that it is good to have a kind and caring heart—and it feels good, too. The intuitive intelligence of the heart could tilt the scales in the war within. The spiritual story of the 21st century will be, at a deeper level, the drawing and redrawing of the battle lines of the head and heart, between what you know and what you feel in the war within, of how *Homo sapiens* is trying to broker a kind of détente between the two, to ensure the survival of both but in a different blend. We live in a world where the logic of the head is at odds with the emotion of the heart. For a wholesome and harmonious life, we need to listen to both the heart and head, but too often, the voice of the head almost silences that of the heart. We are now pretty much focused on our head, or brain, which James Watson[20] called the 'grandest biological frontier, the most complex thing we have yet discovered in our universe'. While pretty much ignoring, and taking for granted, the even grander frontier—our heart. The relatively new concept of 'coherence' is emerging, pioneered by institutions like the HeartMath Institute;[21] it is a highly efficient state in which all of the body's systems, in particular the heart and mind, work in sync, ensuring that the whole of us is more than the sum of our parts. To be fully human, we must ensure the development of the heart and the head. It is in this spirit and with this objective that initiatives like 'activating the global heart' are being taken to bring about a shift in the content of global consciousness, a work in progress. In his work *The Celestine Prophecy*, James Redfield, for example, wrote that 'over the past half century, a new consciousness has come to the human world'.

We need to blend both our strengths and weaknesses in the right proportion to have the right consciousness. The renowned 20th-century Indian philosopher Jiddu Krishnamurti said that "intelligence comes into being when the mind, heart, and body are really in harmony".[22] He also underlined the utter inadequacy of thought and thinking. He believed that it was thought that gave us religion, and it is thinking that separates us as individuals from one another. But to overcome the impediment of their 'insufficiency', we don't have to abdicate thinking and eliminate the mind. What we need is a new balance and baseline in our consciousness between the two primary sources of intelligence and energy—the mind and the heart. We must also bear in mind that everything in the cosmos, from trees to humans, is energetically connected. But like in every situation and between any two things, there cannot be perfect equality; one or the other has to be a dominant partner even if it constantly changes. And it applies to the head and heart, too. We have to make a kind of choice no man has ever been called upon or required to make: which of the two must be at the commanding heights of our consciousness—the head or the heart? Science is working in both directions, although the bulk of the effort is brain-centered. And that has to change; science must have a greater heart-centric focus. Only then can we achieve what we glibly call a paradigm shift, and move towards what some mystics call transcendental consciousness, or cosmic consciousness, which induces awe, supreme joy and the highest, unalloyed felicity, free from pain, sorrow, and fear. It is, in its effect, a divine consciousness, a state of sublime spirituality attained by prophets, ancient rishis and great saints and sages. The Upanishads proclaim it as all-embracing, one that keeps the stars, the sun the moon… all in their place in a state of close communion. Most of us cannot attain that state, but we can certainly move towards it in different degrees. That is the kind of consciousness-change that mankind should strive towards. Only that will enable and empower us to see ourselves differently about our place on the planet, and only then can we alter the causal course of human creativity. If we do that, and if we do let the heart control the mind, then 'we are off to the next galaxy, both inward and outward'[23], and will almost permanently prevail in the perennial war within. Man by himself is incomplete for that task. In Hindu scriptures like the Vishnu Purana, it is said that the final or tenth avatar of Lord Vishnu, called the *Kalki* avatar, will not only restore dharma to its rightful place on earth but also awaken the minds of those who live at that time. Our age is that time and it could mean that the advent of the next divine manifest on earth could well entail and result in a profound consciousness-change. That is because, unlike in earlier divine avatars, evil on earth is not personified in some of us. As Nwaocha Ogechukwu says, "No one can deny that each one of us has an aspect of the devil within us" (*The Secret Behind the Cross and Crucifix*, 2009). But for God to restore dharma on earth, He cannot simply slay modern-day rakshasas (demons), which most of us are in different degrees. He has to help us win the war within, and that will lead to a consciousness-change. And that is the only way to what the ancient Chinese philosopher Lao Tzu called, "the introduction of higher dimensions of consciousness into our awareness", which theosophist Annie Besant compared to the snake shedding its skin and the butterfly emerging from its chrysalis.

As a species we are at a critical crossroads and have to make a decisive directional choice between two divergent paths. The *Katha* Upanishad speaks of the two-fold path available to mankind: the *Pravritti marga* (path of material and bodily pleasures), and the *Nivritti marga* (path of goodness and righteousness). We can frame it differently for the 21st century: today's *pravritti* is augmentation of cognitive intelligence through artificial intelligence (AI). And, *nivritti* is exploring and energizing the awesome but dormant power of the heart's intuitive intelligence. AI is now clearly at the cutting edge of our creativity (and big business, too), whereas we know very little about the heart as a source of intelligence and energy independent of, or in tandem with, the brain. Heart intelligence is 'the flow of intuitive awareness and inner guidance we experience when the mind and emotions are brought into coherent alignment with the heart'.[24] The inner dynamic working of the deep consciousness is altogether different from the dynamics of the rational mind, which we are familiar with. We have been conditioned to perform all our cognitive, analytical, and synthesizing activities of knowledge at the rational level. This conditioning is so deep that we have forgotten the faculty of intuition that we possess inside our heart intelligence. That is why our choices and decisions are so skewed. Recent cutting-edge research suggests that the "heart also is an access point to a source of wisdom and intelligence that we can call upon to live our lives with more balance, greater creativity and enhanced intuitive capacities."[25] Both the brain and that thumping organ in our body are powerful tools that not only sustain life, but help us experience the world in a profound way at a deeper level. A proper alignment of the heart and mind can help us make better decisions and live more balanced and peaceful lives. And that calls for a fundamental change in the content and balance of our consciousness. Consciousness is the master key, and every crisis the world faces—political, economic, climatic, social—is but a reflection of a 'crisis of consciousness'. It is, in Jiddu Krishnamurti's words, "a crisis that cannot anymore accept the old norms, the old patterns, the ancient traditions. And considering what the world is now with all their ill will and destructive brutality, aggression, and so on, man is still as he was: brutal, violent, aggressive, acquisitive, competitive, and he has built a society along these lines".[26] When Pope Francis said that the "ecological crisis is also a summons to profound interior conversion",[27] he meant consciousness-change, a fundamental shift in the command and content of our consciousness. Climate change is more than ecological crisis; it a mirror to what is wrong with the human way of life.

Nothing deters us from dreaming to be the masters of the universe, of birth and death, of brain and body, and willing to be, as Thoreau once said, 'the tools of our tools'. Some may not flinch from death, but they still want to make our lives free from fear, worry, pain, and anxiety. The fundamental question this generation of humans must ask itself is, what must we desire or hope to have? For hope is no longer so harmless, and desire can be decisively destructive. Earlier, in the main, our dreams and desires, hopes and aspirations and ambitions were largely individual-centric and local, and our failures and setbacks were individualistic and isolated and the fall out was also limited and contained. To meet, to really connect, and to encounter another as deeply as possible—this has been an abiding and enduring human aspiration. Now we can have the unlimited ability to technologically communicate, combine, connect, and cooperate on a species-scale. But that immense 'ability' to better the human condition largely remains untapped. But it is not merely technical or technological; it is spiritual too. In Karen Armstrong's words, "We urgently need to examine received ideas and assumptions, look beneath the sound-bites of the news to the complex realities that are tearing our world apart, realizing, at a profound level, that we share the planet not with inferiors but equals".[28] What we ought to strive towards is consciousness-to-consciousness, and heart-to-heart communion, not mind-to-mind communication and microchip-implants.

To arrest the drift and drag, and to change the course of our civilization, we need another internal revolution: a consciousness-revolution, an inner alchemy that allows us to go beyond the boundary of thinking itself and restores or reawakens the role of heart intelligence. The very evolution that led to this impasse has to be re-directed within. We have to contain the predominance of our mind in molding the way we live and that requires drastically diminishing the mind's internal monopoly. For that, we need an internal counterweight, which can only be the heart in its role as a major source of energy, memory, and intelligence. The real reason why we have failed to make any breakthrough in the face of problems that threaten our very future—like climate change, terrorism, moral paralysis, runaway mechanization, materialism, and militarism—is our abysmal inability to take cognizance of the fact that there is a whole universe within, and that what happens there has a decisive bearing on what happens in the world in which we are born into, live and die. Spiritual literature is replete with words like 'inner world', 'inner self', 'power within', 'inner seeking', 'inner awakening', 'inner journey', and so on. We have been repeatedly told that we can find everything we search for if we can reach inward into our heart: truth, strength, love, hope, happiness. And inward is not a direction or depth but a dimension. As Rainer Rilke said, 'the only journey is the one within'. For Rumi, we enter 'a mine of rubies and bathe in the splendor of our own light'. All such are noble thoughts and wise advice, but the reality is that we are stranded at the gates of our own skin.

We are living at a time when events around us are occurring at such a dizzying pace in many parallel and diverse directions, that our cognitive capacities are unable to put them all together, to clear the detail from the design, the structure from the substance, and read the portends and grasp their true significance. Our evolution has not equipped our brains to handle such a blinding blitz from so many quarters simultaneously. We no longer know if the ground beneath us is solid earth or swirling sand, and the more we know, the more we come to know how little we know. Our very sense of reality, even the feeling that we ourselves are authentic and 'living' is in question in our own mind. Is reality itself real or relative? Are the feelings, thoughts, emotions, perceptions, and situations that make up our ordinary human experience obstacles or opportunities, or alarm bells to our growth as essentially spiritual beings? According to the Upanishads, 'The wise man should hold his body steady, with the three upper parts—chest, neck and head—erect, turn his sense, with the help of the mind, towards the heart by means of the raft of the *Brahman* to cross the fearful torrents of the world'.[29] In short, if man wants to change his behavior for the better or to make spiritual progress or move towards a higher level of consciousness, the way of the heart is the only way.

The Evil Within

While we externalize the clash between good and evil, it actually is an incestuous affair. As Carl Jung puts it, "Nothing is so apt to challenge our self-awareness and alertness as being at war with oneself."[30] Even if we do win all external wars, it will be a vacuous victory; it would be, as the Bible says, tantamount to losing the soul.[31] Among our contemporary great thinkers who have pondered long and hard over this war, the one that springs instantly to mind is Aleksandr Solzhenitsyn. In his monumental 1973 work, *The Gulag Archipelago*, he brings out its immediate context and its intricate complexity, and writes, "If only it were all so simple! If only there were evil people somewhere insidiously committing evil deeds, and it were necessary only to separate them from the rest of us and destroy them!". And he goes on, "In my most evil moments, I was convinced that I was doing good; and I was well supplied with systematic arguments. And it was only when I lay there on the rotting prison straw that I sensed within myself the first stirrings of good. Gradually it was disclosed to me that the line separating good and evil passes not through states, nor between classes, nor between political parties either—but right through every human heart, and through all human hearts. This line shifts. Inside us, it oscillates with the years. And even within hearts overwhelmed by evil, one small bridgehead of good is retained; and even in the best of all hearts, there remains… an un-uprooted small corner of evil. Since then I have come to understand the truth of all the religions of the world. They struggle with the *evil inside a human being* (inside every human being). It is impossible to expel evil from the world in its entirety but it is possible to constrict it within each person".[32]

These are very weighty and wise words. We can 'constrict' the evil within each of us only if we can positively influence the war within. However, we have almost convinced ourselves that if we do not want to end up on the scrapheap of scapegoats, or be labelled as a loser, we must at the very least acquiesce to evil. Once we allow ourselves to wallow in that line of thought, the temptation becomes too much to resist to cover up for all our misdeeds; 'necessary' becomes 'necessity'. Such a necessity is the necessary evil that even if we behave badly towards other people, we still think we are 'good' people. Our moral nonchalance and ethical apathy to what happens around us—which is unfair, unjust, exploitative—and our inability to instinctively or impulsively respond to other's suffering, has become so ingrained in daily life that it has taken a tragic toll on human personality. Thomas Hobbes tellingly wrote that 'all in their natural condition are possessed of the will to injure others, to tyrannize over other men; each has thus to fear the other'. And by ignoring the within, we are injuring ourselves, putting our well-being, even health, at risk. It is now even being said that 'cancer is thus a breakdown from within'.[33] It means that not only evil, but illness too is within. A Rwandan proverb reminds us, 'You can out-distance that which is running after you, but not what is running inside you'. The world outside is the periphery, but the epicenter is within. We can control the periphery if we control the center. What we do on the outside influences what happens inside, but it is the center that prevails. We talk of good people and bad people, and that if we can get rid of the baddies, the problem would get resolved and the world will become a place of peace and harmony. One actually wishes there are identifiable bad people; it would then be easy to exterminate them like what we did with smallpox and polio. Alas, that is not only too simplistic but also false. We know that all of us are both good and bad at different times, or to different people at the same time. And we do not always feel bad about being bad to a person who is not considered bad. Our idea of someone being good or bad hinges purely on how that person behaves towards us, not on what others think. The burden of our suffering often is to 'suffer' others. If everything about morality is so sliding, slippery and subjective, or as-you-like-it, how then can we know how we're doing, and if we cannot, how can we become better? Contrary to what Spinoza tells us that 'to act in conformity with virtue is to act according to the guidance of reason…' it is a good which is common to all men, and can be equally possessed by all in so far as they are of the same nature. And contrary to what TS Eliot said, "So far as we are human, what we do must be either evil or good; so far as we do evil or good, we are human; and it is better, in a paradoxical way, to do evil than to do nothing: at least, we exist",[34] we do both 'good' and 'evil', and evil today is so stomach-turning that 'doing something' to combat is better than 'doing nothing'. The accent here is on 'doing', not 'being'. It simply means that every time we do anything, we must try to do the 'good' thing that is good for our soul and does no harm to anyone else. But to do that does not depend on 'us', the breathing, walking person who stares back at us with a smirk in the mirror; it depends on the 'war within', inside our own deepest depths. The truth of the matter is that inside each of us "Dragons are there, and there are also lions; there are poisonous beasts and all the treasures of evil. But there too is God, the angels, the life and the kingdom, the light and the apostles, the heavenly cities and the treasuries of grace—all things are there".[35]

We must bear in mind that this is not something metaphorical or symbolic or figurative that we can ignore or condescendingly nod our head and do nothing about. Starkly put, everything we do in our life, agreeable and disagreeable, good, bad, ugly, has an effect on the War Within. In the language of worldly war, they are the 'supplies' and logistical support that gives the wherewithal to both sides to wage the war. This War is as literal, real, actual and authentic as any other on the ground; if any, it is even more tangible, as it underpins every other war. It is not a 'star war', or 'war of the worlds', or some remote 'tribal war' about which we can, in the comfort of distance, read in the papers or see on a screen, be entertained or get our adrenalin worked up, and feel smug that we are not on the frontline or have to bear the collateral consequences like in the external wars. Everything about this war is about us; the place, the fighting, the forces, the fallout, they are all 'us'. This 'war' rages inside each of us with every breath we take, all the time, without a lull or break, relentless, remorseless, with no shut-down at sundown. And more ominously, every shift in the course, and the flow and every turn of the tide impacts on us in every thought, word or act that we entertain or engage in. Every 'happening' or activity in what we tend to call 'our everyday life' affects the war. It determines 'who we are' and what and how we do, and what we create and for what purpose. We tend to think that what we think is 'life' is different from our 'everyday life'. We want our life to be 'beautiful', but lead everyday lives in ugliness, pettiness, and perfidy. We view everyday life as some kind of a prison and yet we crave for eternal life of the same genre. Our 'within' is both a 'black hole' and a 'war zone'. The 'black hole' inside each of us, the blacker and darker, is more impenetrable and more difficult to get in than any in the cosmos. The perplexing part is that, unlike in any other war, we have to take sides in this war; help one side any way we could, but we cannot let the other side get annihilated. God can sit on the sidelines with a smug; that is why he is He and we are not. Nothing happens to Him, everything happens to us. All our problems arise because, for a long time, the 'other side'—the evil within—has gained dominance. There are clear tell-tale signs. Some of these are the steady surge in senseless suicides, cutting across all ages, particularly children, the casualness of homicides, mass murders, and suicide-bombings. Every religion has projected its own vision of God and we have had so many religious wars—some people even blame organized religion for most of history's killings, and Christianity alone is blamed for the deaths of some 17 million people[36]—but what is needed now is a change in our perception of and posture towards God. Scriptures and sages have told us to treat God as our savior, refuge and shelter, and to surrender to Him wholly—called *prapatti* or *saranagati* in the Vaishnava tradition of Hinduism—and absolutely, but now we want Him to submit to our 'strength' and we ask 'clever' questions such as 'what has God done lately for me?'. This line of thought is closer to what the great anarchist Mikhail Bakunin said—"If God really existed, it would be necessary to abolish Him"—than to Voltaire's aphorism, 'If God did not exist, it would be necessary to invent Him'. We turn to god-men and gadgets to help us out, not to God. With them we have more patience, and even faith, than God. All this is due to the fact that, wittingly or unwittingly, both by what we do and, perhaps even more, don't do, we are doing the opposite of what we want to do—lending support to the endogenous forces of immorality, wickedness, and evil. What we should constantly strive to do is to support the nobler part of us so as to empower it to have an upper hand over our nastier side. Henry Miller wrote, "every day we slaughter our finest impulses". We 'slaughter' by constantly singing the '*sutra* of success', which usually translates into academic excellence, professional progress and making a lot of money. 'Success' is also associated with 'control' and 'power', and we act on the premise that 'every increase of power means an increase of progress'. Sometimes our success might be similar to what Mary Shelley wrote about Victor Frankenstein's 'success' in creating a monster: "Success would terrify the artist; he would rush away from his odious handywork, horror-stricken. He would hope that, left to itself, the slight spark of life which he had communicated would fade; that this thing, which had received such imperfect animation, would subside into dead matter".[37] But like Frankenstein, we too cannot escape from the 'success of success'. We can 'succeed and fail' and 'fail and succeed', and we can never really know, if in either case we are failing or succeeding. That is because both are relative and contextual. Our obsession with 'success' is so overpowering that when 'failure'—the antithesis of what success stands for—stares us in the face, be it a term test in school, or in keeping a job or in love, and the whole world crumbles, life itself becomes both worthless and wearisome and the 'sutra' turns out to be one for self-destruction. The 'success sutra' is exacting a terrible price from society. The lead character in Greg Egan's story *The*

Infinite Assassin (*Axiomatic*, 1991) proudly defines himself as "'I' am those who survive and succeed. The rest are someone else". That 'rest', that 'someone else' is, above all, the stranger within, the alien inside. But 'success' is a measure as decided by others, which we ourselves deploy when dealing with others' success. We must also bear in mind another little-noticed factor. It is about what we take for granted almost routinely: 'everyday' existence; what it could do to us; its grind and drudgery, what it entails, how much of our psychic and physical energy it extracts. In modern society, an individual cannot see himself, as Albert Camus wrote, beyond the routine and the ritual. All life is nothing but so many 'everydays'; every new sun a new beginning. Everyday has a name, a particular day of the week, and a number on the calendar; the day and date is the setting for every triumph, the mundane and the magical. Nature gives so many chances to relive our lives; it makes every morning a new birth, to start all over again, and to die when we sleep. And no matter what we do, or don't, the War goes on.

The 'war within' is not only a war for the control of our consciousness; it is also *within* the consciousness. In fact, they are the two aspects of the same war. The fight is really between 'mind-controlled consciousness' and 'heart-incubated consciousness'. This 'war' is crucial for mind-control, and crucial for the cathartic cleansing of our inner cosmos. And for better behavior and for a world in harmony with itself. Unlike external wars, the aim cannot be to ensure 'permanent' victory or total defeat of either of the two 'blood-brothers'. The human genus cannot afford the luxury of total and comprehensive victory of either of the two. Were that to happen, sooner or later, the human will be extinct. Not only do we need love, compassion, generosity, altruism but also things like anger, aggression, avarice, at the proper time and place. If they are not necessary they wouldn't be there in the first place. Duality is not necessarily hostility. We have the tendency to view and label things either 'good' or 'bad', and wish to get rid of the 'bad'. They are as much a part of us as our 'better' ones. They are essential for the existence of the other. Without chaos there can be no order; without darkness we cannot experience light. In fact, even the so-called 'negatives' if rightly redirected, can do us a world of good. If we are all and only 'good' inside then too there will be trouble. What's good may not always be good, and what's bad may not always be bad in the world outside. On that most can assent. Some say that 'being kind and caring is a good thing—as long as the person you are kind and caring towards deserves your kindness'. Being forgiving may produce contentment—except when the forgiven has no plans to make amends. Even that may sound sensible. But in the crucible of give-and-take living, we find it very difficult to forget our hurts and forgive our tormentors. But as Jack Kornfield puts it, not-forgiving is tantamount to 'giving up all hope of a better past'. In that sense, forgiveness is really not about someone's hurtful behavior; it is about our own relationship with our past. All this sophistry misses a central moral point. Why do some people go out of the way to help someone whom they hardly know, and why do many others pretend not to see or turn a Nelson's eye?

The tragedy of our life is that it might well be possible to live a life without consciously helping anyone, but it is not possible to live without hurting, intentionally or unintentionally, anyone anytime. All of us, sometime, hurt someone or the other, almost routinely and almost every day. We need to forgive and be forgiven. A withering glance, a wounding word, even killing one's own self can hurt another human being. It can happen anywhere, at home or at work. Anyone who has suffered a grievous injury knows that when our inner world is disrupted, it is difficult to concentrate on anything other than the person who caused it. Forgiveness is easy because it is unilateral, an act of compassion towards the person who, not you, has to pay the price. The 'good' we feel about ourselves, many psychological studies have shown, is tremendous. But in practice, we find it very hard to 'forget' or to 'forgive'. And that includes forgiving ourselves, sometimes harder than forgiving someone else. Instead of forgiving, we play the blame-game. In fact it is easier to 'forgive' than to 'forget'; for forgiveness comes from the heart and forgetting from the mind. Indeed, the heart is the fountain not only of forgiveness but also of love, kindness, and most of all of mercy. If we can manifest these qualities in our life we will also be strengthening the 'virtuous' forces in the 'war within'. If, for example, as Pope Francis implored, mercy—which he described as the ultimate and supreme act by which God comes to meet us—becomes 'the basis of all our efforts'[38], then the very 'context' of our daily life will become compassionate. The opposite of compassion, we must remember, is not cruelty; it is complacency, which is what afflicts the most 'good'. Sometimes we face questions such as these: Can we be compassionate without taking sides in a dispute? In other words, can we be compassionate for both sides? And does that amount to encouraging evil? A thorny issue that all of us, even God, face, is how to balance mercy and justice, and which assumes paramountcy, in the infinite possible variations of human life. Mercy too at a point becomes unjust. Jesus, when asked how often one should forgive, said, up to 'seventy times seven'.[39] Lord Krishna, in the Mahabharata, promised that he will forgive Sisupala ninety-nine times and slays him the hundredth time. Simply put, what we do and what happens has a huge bearing on what happens after death. This message comes out strongly in what has been called the *Myth of Er* in the last chapter of Plato's *Republic*. Socrates says that not only do justice and justness and injustice and unjustness, good and bad, play a huge role after death, but also implies that Er was chosen to be the messenger to humanity about what he has seen take place between death and new birth. In the words of Socrates, "For each in turn of the unjust things they had done and for each in turn of the people they had wronged, they paid the penalty ten times over, once in every century of their journey… But if they had done good deeds and had become just and pious, they were rewarded according to the same scale".[40]

We can also see the 'war within' in the form of a clash between 'mercy' and 'justice', or 'intuition' and 'intellect'. Einstein once said, "The intuitive mind is a sacred gift and the rational mind is a faithful servant. We have created a society that honors the servant and has forgotten the gift". That again is a fallout of the internal war. What we need is a harmony and 'positive' balance in the consciousness. If we can shift the center of gravity of our consciousness away from intellect to intuition, our vibration begins to change; we begin to feel greater levels of peace and well-being in our life. If we can induce such a 'shift', as it were, we will begin to realize that we are a powerful spirit, experiencing 'being human' for a period of time, and not a human being striving for a spiritual experience. The stakes are simple but stark: whether the human continues to be the most malicious creature that ever walked on earth until he implodes or immolates and cripples earth itself, or if he will mend course through a 'conscious' consciousness-change and becomes a benign being, a soothing, 'spiritual' presence on earth. Many great thinkers have long recognized that imperative and some have predicted an impending leap in human consciousness. In 1974, the American professor of psychology Dr. Clare W Graves wrote an article for *The Futurist* magazine, titled *Human Nature Prepares for a Momentous Leap*, which he described as "The most difficult, but at the same time the most exciting transition the human race has faced to date. It is not merely a transition to a new level of existence but the start of a new 'movement' in the symphony of human history".[41] Some predict what Terence McKenna called *The Archaic Revival*, of the emergence of a 'Global Tribe'. Everything else other than 'consciousness-change', the shape and form it will take, are but mere details. But then, as is said, often the devil is in the detail. Those 'details' are our daily deeds, what Coleridge describes as the "petty things of daily life".[42] As for 'God', man's mind has effectively rendered him an 'opportunistic option'; no longer even a 'necessary nuisance'. We have turned the aura of 'divine sanction' to whip up our darker urges and come to believe that if we are 'pious' we do not need to be pure at heart, if we are devout we do not have to be decent, and if we try to get closer to God we can be callous to human suffering. Nobody wants to 'suffer'; everyone shuns it except those who see it as a way to constantly seek God. In the Mahabharata, the mother of the virtuous Pandavas, *Kunti*, prays to Lord Krishna to bless her with perpetual sorrow, as she realizes that if sorrow deserted her, she would cease to seek Him. It brings to mind what Keats said about sorrow: "But cheerly, cheerly, She loves me dearly; She is so constant to me, and so kind: I would deceive her, And so leave her, But ah! she is so constant and so kind… But now of all the world I love thee best" (*Ode to Sorrow in Endymion*, 1818).

Once we recognize and accept and come to terms with this bedrock reality of this 'war within', and its implications and impact on our life, all contradictions, confusion, and conundrums will dry up. Our task will then become very simple and straightforward: to do all we can and could to help the kinder, gentler, better-half be the dominant partner. The ebbs and flows of the war are so continuous and shifting that we become unsure of everything because our fortunes and misfortunes reflect the state of the war at that time. That keeps us always in an ambiguous state, always on the edge, and prevents us from 'making up our mind' and to act upon what we even know to be the right thing. To illustrate, even assuming that 'being moral' is good for our own well-being, we are plagued with nagging questions. Is it universal and timeless or is it subject to time and space? And if it is both or neither, how does one distinguish the timeless from the time-bound, and the perennial from the particular? Does a 'higher' moral end justify 'lesser' immorality, or in *dharmic* terms, should we sacrifice the 'lesser' dharma that is enjoined upon fewer people at the altar of the 'greater' dharma that contributes to the cause of the 'greater' good? This is the question that emerges out of the Indian epic Mahabharata. So much scholasticism has accumulated on this subject that there is a whole winnow of metaphysical knowledge, generally called moral philosophy or ethics, that deals with questions such as the right and wrong of what we do and how we ought to live our lives. And it is so closely interwoven with religion that morality without religion is deemed not only dangerous but also blasphemous. The entrenched belief is either God crafted the moral sense during creation or inspired religion to show us the path to morality. There are others who argue that there is nothing divine about morality, that habit is purely a human expediency and an atheist can be equally, if not more, moral than a theist.

One cannot deny that religion has helped man to become a better person, but we must not also ignore that the corruption that has engulfed religion has also sapped the moral sensitivity of man, and a great deal of evil springs from the realm of religion. And it springs not only from religious zealots, or as we call 'fundamentalists', but, even more, from all of us. The real problem is not any religion *per se* but its selective attribution and misinterpretation, looking for isolated passages to do what we want to do and turning it into the Only Truth. More fundamentally, religion, like any knowledge, is corrupted because it is filtered through our consciousness, which is dominated by the human mind, and the attributes of the mind—malice, self-righteousness, intolerance—get attached to religious practice. No moral self-righteousness and intolerance is as lethal as the religious type because it is clad in the authenticity of God. Of all the human attributes, perhaps the only one which is not double-faced, which scorches what it touches is, malice. If malice is our defining signature and if we are the most endowed of all forms of life on earth, then what human or creative purpose does it serve? Einstein once said that 'the Lord God is subtle, but He is not malicious'. But how does one explain our inherent divinity with our unique attribute of malice?

A major watershed development over the past century is that human power, which for long has maintained some sort of balance between its constructive and destructive dimensions, is now out of sync. One of our greatest failings as a species is our inability to live in a state of cooperative cohabitation with other members of our own kindred kind. We find it so hard to work with others, labor and live together as a cohesive species, something that other not-so-intelligent species seem to do almost instinctively. Even worse, we alone are capable of willing each other harm, even without any expectation of self-benefit. Although biologically we all belong to the same species, in practical terms our main qualification is that we still interbreed, out of which come out future humans. We must learn that sometimes compassion takes the form of stepping aside, letting go of our need to be right, and just being happy for someone. Now we can ill afford ill will. The Buddhist *Medha Sutra* meditation says, "Let none by anger or hatred wish harm to another". Now, not 'wishing harm to others' in itself, is no longer lofty as it is, a moral precept; it has become an existential 'essential'. The choice between 'harm' and 'help' in our social life is no longer a 'personal' or 'private' matter, to be judged elsewhere or hereafter. Edgar Cayce alluded to the rewards of hereafter when he said, "You'll not be in heaven if you're not leaning on the arm of someone you have helped". That may well be so; indeed it must be so. Modern life, with all its downsides and drawbacks, coarseness and insensitivity, carries a huge hope. It has changed the motive and dynamic for helping each other into an imperative; it is no longer an option. Every one of us is now indispensable for all of us to be what or who we want to be. In one sense, each one of us is the proverbial 'hundredth monkey' to all of us, potentially a critical member whose behavior could help us reach the tipping point. Technology has so intertwined our lives that our actions affect others and others' actions affect ours. Technology accelerates everything, and has, according to some psychologists, a 'profound effect on the way we experience time'. Technologies like communication technologies shrink time and distance and inform us instantly about any happening anywhere and empower connectivity for any cause, noble or noxious. The speed of intercontinental travel—soon, we are being promised, we can go around the globe in sixty minutes—is also turning infectious diseases into pandemics, and also creating a level playing field of potential victims. Pathogens with the means to travel respect neither class nor position, neither race nor religion, neither the rich nor the poor. When it comes to susceptibility to new organisms and biological weapons, in a hyper-connected world, we are all equal prey. In fact, technology is slowly but surely replacing human interactions and has come to mean so much that "we actually expect more from technology and less from each other"[43]—probably even from God! Since we think that technology will 'fix' every problem, our behavior is also becoming more reckless, profligate, and predatory. Even what we used to do earlier like conservation we are not doing now. Technology is also relentlessly replacing human labor, which happens when, in the words of John Keynes, "unemployment due to our discovery of means of economizing the use of labor [outruns] the pace at which we can find new uses for labor". It has profound consequences, far beyond the ambit of economics; it goes to the very root of 'being human'. Although we have reduced work as wage-earning, it is a tonic to both body and brain. Mass scale and prolonged human idling can become another existential threat. An idle mind, it has been said, is a devil's workshop, and if a man's hands become idle what would the world be like? The ever-accelerating technological change, in particular digital technology and automation, threaten to idle millions, even billions, depriving not only the means to make money but also depriving identity and dignity of life, potentially triggering a kind of catastrophic social conflagration. We no longer can be sure who is a neighbor and who is a stranger, who is a native and who is a refugee. It essentially undermines our humanness—what makes us who we are as 'persons'—and of being the human species—who we are collectively. It is distrust that drives automation. And automation, as has been said, breeds automation. Fundamentally, our love of the machine comes down to one thing: we don't like others who we have to live with or work with to be who we are, and exhibit the same qualities we have—be he or she a spouse or servant, colleague or a concubine, worker or a whore. What is being called 'digital damage' is affecting nearly every kind of human relationship, and the 'digital divide' is wider than the economic divide, cutting across every society. Too much digital participation, it is feared, is corroding human empathy. For, as Baroness Susan Greenfield, author of the book *Mind Change*, says, "If we don't speak to each other, it is harder to establish empathy". Empathy, the ability to comprehend and share the feelings of others, is central to moral life. Everyone needs it, rich or poor, powerful and powerless, villain and victim, and if we let that go then any hope for human betterment would become a mirage. For empathy is more basic than sympathy or compassion.

The Three 'M's and the War Within

While consciousness-change entails altering the current content and character of our consciousness so that the very dynamics that drive our thinking, feeling, and experiencing change, contextual-change encompasses change in the way we create our living context. In that context, at this tumultuous time, the three most important constituent parts are the triad of the three 'M's—morality, money, and mortality. Unless we are able to totally and comprehensively rethink, reconfigure and renew our conception and understanding of what they ought to mean in modern life, we will continue to lose the war within. On all three fronts, we need to go back to the drawing board, so to speak, to break out of the box and turn the three obsessions into openings and opportunities to tilt the scales in the war within. These are so intricately embedded in human consciousness that there is nothing we can do without the underpinning of one or two or all the three. Of the three, it is the magnetic might of money that is now at the frontline of both human transformation and planetary destruction. And the time has come to comprehensively rethink its role in human destiny. Invented as a means of exchange, money has no intrinsic value, but allows us to ascribe relative values to all things. Money is more portable, more durable, more easily exchanged and hence more sought after than other goods. It is almost a cliché to say that time is money, but time is also life, and we ought to demur at putting a price on our own lives. Money's very pervasiveness and transformative power also makes it a translucent instrument, a spiritual tool. Money, righteously earned and shared, can make the world so much better. There is no doubt that 'money makes the world go around'. The deterministic role of money was long foreseen in scriptures. In detailing the traits of the age of Kali Yuga, it was written several millenniums ago that 'In the Kali Yuga, people will seek only money. Only the richest will have the power. People without money will be their slaves'. And even more tellingly, 'The leaders of the state will no longer protect the people, but plunder the citizenry through excessive taxation'. There is hardly a moment in our life when money ceases to be a factor in earning, saving, spending and even more in thinking. We will have to rack our brains to think of anything bereft of a money angle. And there is hardly a crime without a money-motive, and money is a big factor in many suicides, even homicides, that occur these days. It is man-made but it has become the most 'finite' of all finite resources and everyone is short of it, individuals, business, countries and the material world.

Money is hydra-headed, each head sensitive to the purpose and circumstance. It is salary when an employer compensates you for your work, wages for your sweat; dowry if a father pays it to get his daughter married; bribe if it is illegally paid to do a favor; dividend if a company pays it to a shareholder; interest if a bank pays for keeping your money; donation if it is given to charity; ransom if given to kidnappers; alimony if it figures in a divorce, and so on. In multiple ways we discriminate race, caste, color, religion, ethnicity, but they all vanish if one has 'enough' money. It gives respectability to everything we seek, and every position and power—political, social, economic—comes within reach. Making money do what we want, and not doing what it tries to make us do is morality. In reality, man is now marginalizing morality and trying to overcome mortality. When one does not have 'money', the only other alternative, as some are discovering, is to go back to the body; use it to trade for money to live, and to 'make a living'. Mortality has been called the ultimate leveler in human life; that all men are finally 'reconciled' in death. That whatever we achieve or fail to achieve, rich or poor, powerful or powerless, acclaimed or anonymous, everyone will end up the same way, become a cold corpse, which the living hasten to destroy lest it linger and not let us live. Money is now threatening to undermine that central tenet. If you are really rich you can afford to extend your life span far more than that of others, if not to become immortal. Money can *make* man do anything, even murder one's own 'near and dear', a spouse, one's own child, a friend. And money by itself can *do* almost anything, can empower a life of dignity, erase social deprivation, even save a life; or make us greedy and gluttonous, erode sensitivity and compassion. Money and murder are increasingly getting interconnected, and no 'relationship' is immune, intimate or professional. Spouses have killed each other, children their parents, friends their friends, business associates their colleagues, and so on, when greed turns deadly. What are called 'dowry deaths' and 'contract killing' are murders for money. The insatiability of money is such that no one feels he has 'enough' to satisfy his desires, dreams, and delights. The 'limit' that worries our mind is not things like 'limits to growth'. Everyone feels 'limited' by money, individuals, the ultra-rich to the dirt-poor, corporations, even nation-states. It is at the heart of every crisis we face, environmental, economic, and moral. It is to have 'more' money that we put poison into the air we breathe, into the water we drink, and into the food we eat, and at the same time to become immortal. Fritjof Capra makes a telling point when he says, "We accept ever-increasing rates of cancer rather than investigate how the chemical industry poisons our food to increase its profits".[44] And yet, it is but a tool, an instrument, a means, and a medium, although of late we have made it the end in itself.

Money occupies our mind but it doesn't have a mind, at least not yet. As of now, the master is the mind, what Swami Vivekananda described as a demon-possessed, scorpion-bitten, drunken monkey. Buddhism uses the psychological metaphor of 'monkey-mind'. Adi Sankaracharya, in his famous poem *Bhajagovindam*, called it *mudhamati*, the 'foolish mind'. It is such a 'monkey' that controls our consciousness, and is at the helm of our life. If our mindset, or as some like to say, 'mindsight', remains frozen about the 'three Ms', and if consciousness remains static, then both 'changes'—consciousness or contextual—will remain static. Because, if we do not learn to deal with them differently, one might say 'spiritually', then it makes no difference what else we can do. We must also at once note another dimension. It is that the very place and position of man in the cosmos has fundamentally changed. The human is no longer merely another biological being. He is now an 'ecological serial killer',[45] 'the deadliest force in the annals of biology',[46] a geological force. And humans are "running geologic history backward, and at high speed".[47] In biologist Edward Wilson's words, man is a "geophysical force, swiftly changing the atmosphere and climate as well as the composition of the world's fauna and flora". That is happening alongside another important 'happening'. That very force that made man 'such a force' has also biologically enfeebled him, as compared with his ancestors,[48] and the trend appears to be accelerating. For instance, we are told, today's 'children are growing weaker as computers replace outdoor activity'.[49] Not only our bodies but our brains too will become weaker with computers and other gadgets doing much of what we used to do before, and they will leave us even stupider.[50] The irony is that we are trying to become more efficient 'decision-makers' and aiming to go 'beyond the brain' and, at the same time, the 'brain' has come to the conclusion that being 'beyond' in situ is too much of a bother and, in line with man's lure of short cuts, it is easier to go external.

And that also fulfills another craving of the human—the urge to mate or merge with, or dissolve into something or someone like the divine or the beloved. Now, we say the divine and the beloved are too troublesome, too opinionated, can be too demanding, and in any case, life is short and we have no time to waste on such loony pursuits. As a rebound and as an extension of our materialistic mindset, that 'urge' is manifesting as the machine. For, unlike the 'beloved', we can embrace it without being rebuffed, and unlike the 'divine', we can insult it without inviting its wrath. The ultimate spiritual aim and end of all life, even creation, is unity, merger, and dissolution, to lose one's distinctive identity. It manifests in many ways both spiritually and sensually. Prophets and wise men aim at 'dissolution' to serve humankind. Some call transcendence spiritual dissolution. The 5th-century Chinese philosopher Lieh-Tzu said that division and differentiation are the processes by which things are created. Since things are emerging and dissolving all the time, you cannot specify the point when this division will stop. Indeed death is dissolution; we dissolve, or merge into the elements. One such 'sublime' experience while we are alive is what we call 'being in love'—we say things like 'I am you, we are the same one'; 'I am thee also now. You are me now'. We just want to dissolve, merge or vanish into the one we are in love with. Man's ultimate goal is the same: to dissolve into the divine. Indeed that is the purpose of human birth, which, therefore, makes it very important not to waste it, or 'leave it empty-handed'. Modern man, exasperated with his fellow-humans and disenchanted with the divine, has 'fallen' in love with his own child: the machine, much like Pygmalion, the Greek mythological figure. That process is called whole brain emulation (WBE) or mind-uploading—simulating a human brain in a computer with enough detail that the 'simulation' becomes, for all practical purposes, a perfect copy and experiences consciousness. Pope Francis described this as turning human beings into 'ghosts trapped inside machines'. The apprehension that people might actually fall in love with their smart pet appliances like 'responsive robots', with whom or with which they spend far greater amounts of time each day than with humans, is now being taken seriously by psychologists and social scientists. Incredible as it may seem, according to one study, men cannot stay away from their smartphones for more than 21 seconds, while that time-lag is 57 seconds for women. John Lennon once said, "If everyone demanded peace instead of television sets, then there *will* be peace". Now, we should substitute 'smartphone' for a TV set. And we tend to think that peace is for politicians to worry about, not us. But the truth is that what we 'demand' depends on what happens in the world within.

We need to ponder over where human creativity (technological in particular) is headed. We have become so addicted to technological 'appliances' that life is unthinkable without them. In fact, the aim is to 'exploit human vulnerabilities to engineer compulsion', to create an 'app that both triggers a need and provides a momentary solution to it', to 'cement into habit as users turn to your product when experiencing certain internal triggers'.[51] The underlying idea and strategy is that 'reducing the thinking required to take the next action increases the likelihood of the desired behavior occurring unconsciously'. Clearly, machines can never substitute a human partner for the deepest form of biological love. But given man's present muddled mindset and disillusionment with what biological mating and marriage entail—temper tantrums, kids, divorce, alimony, violence—he might well find that 'romancing with the machine' might be the closest he can get to, to cater to his need for bonding, intimacy, and companionship. So far, man had no choice, but among the many choices that technology offers, is this one too, which is to end human monopoly over 'benign love'.

Technology is also messing up all the three 'M's and pushing humanity headlong into murky, unchartered waters. Death is thus far the final finality, and must be dealt with first among the three. It is also at the frontline of the scientific agenda. It is to confront and defy nature and negate the three things that nature has ordained for all animate life on earth: decay, disease, and death. That we cannot escape it is exemplified by the lives of prophets. A particularly good one is the life of the Buddha. On his way to becoming the Buddha, he conquered the mighty *Mara*, which actually means killer, liberating himself from the frailties and forces within him that rendered him mortal, and yet he too suffered the pangs of old age, and finally died from disease. Even Lord Krishna, revered as the complete personification of godhead, died stricken by the arrow of a hunter due to mistaken identity or, as some say, to pay for an adharmic act in his previous incarnation as Rama... Science is, in effect, saying that what avatars and prophets and sages could not surmount, *science* can. Not only that, we can have it both ways: we can be both 'be dead' and 'be alive', and even if a loved one is clinically 'dead' we can 'virtually' keep that person alive in a machine and be able to interact with him or her, whenever we want! It is also claimed that "the avatars would be created using a process called 'photogrammetry' which can accurately reconstruct a virtual 3D shape of a human being from existing photographs and video. Computer voice synthesis will take into account local and regional accents to deliver a more accurate representation of what they sounded like. The digital lifeform would also be linked up to social networks and large databases so they would be kept 'up to date' with their relative's activities and could communicate with them about their day".[52] All this is still 'science-fiction', but by now we should be wary of such stuff; they can surprise and show up. But all this once again raises the question: What constitutes a 'person' and which of that is to be 'uploaded'? Are we a clump of molecules moving and interacting in a way to create what we call '*Homo sapiens*', 'brain', 'personality', 'you', or is there an unknown X-factor? What about consciousness? Will that be 'transference' or 'transformation'?

The Cherokee's Two Wolves

But no new moral reconstitution will even remotely become probable unless we go 'within' and shift the fluctuating fortunes of the 'war within', the greatest, the longest and the most fateful of all wars. The idea that even as we fight external wars we ourselves are a war zone, that two sides of our own psyche fight for supremacy, has long been a part of ancient wisdom and indigenous folklore. Notable among these is a Cherokee story, in which a grandfather tells his grandson that inside each of us, a constant battle goes on between two wolves. He says that one 'wolf' is Evil: it is anger, jealousy, greed, malice, resentment, inferiority, lies, and ego. The other 'wolf' is Good: it is joy, peace, love, hope, humanity, kindness, empathy, and truth. Hearing this, the boy ponders for a while and asks which wolf will eventually win. The grandpa replies, 'The one you feed'. In another version, the grandpa says, "If you feed them right both will win", because a starving wolf will become more dangerous, but 'make sure the 'good wolf' is fed more'. This is how the battle unfolds in our 'within'. We feed the 'wolves' inside us by the way we live, the way we relate with other living beings, and that in turn, depends on who calls the shots inside us. We must realize that every day we make choices, important choices that are liable to be overlooked as being trivial—and these choices define us; they constitute the 'feed' to the wolves. They are a statement of who we choose to be in this life and what impact we will have on the world around us. Philosophers like Marcus Cicero put it differently: "the enemy is within the gates; it is with our own luxury, our own folly, our own criminality that we have to contend". We are left bewildered by our own behavior. We could discuss and debate on moral principles and ethical objectivity and on how to anchor our conduct, and if that should be the greatest good of the greatest numbers or by the application of a universal 'litmus test', or by balancing conflicting moral obligations and duties. That is futile as we have known all along because the methods and means we mobilize for the task are themselves inadequate, even improper. That is why most of our choices and decisions are flawed. For, the real 'choices' and 'decisions' would already have been made in the cosmos 'within' before we get down to it. It is like trying to put a Band-Aid on an internal bleed, or closing the stable door after the horses have bolted. If we are to find a way forward and make man a better being and even to make earth a less endangered planet, we must shift our gaze within and recognize that the most seminal of all struggles is in our own self. The nearest yet farthest space is inner space; the most impenetrable barrier is the periphery of our very body. The tragedy is that we all have the answers to all our questions within ourselves; it is just that we haven't learnt how to get in touch yet. It is like starving with the food we need in a locked room next door, and the key lost in the ruins nearby. We have to find the lost key or break through the wall. For that we must 'go within'. A Buddhist saying goes, 'Look within, thou art the Buddha'. Marcus Aurelius said, "Look within. Within is the fountain of the good, and it will ever bubble up, if thou wilt ever dig". To dig within or, in Yeats' poetic phrase, 'entering into the abyss of himself', or in the words of Tennyson, 'temple-cave of thine own self', is a recurrent refrain, and a central message in all religions. Jalal ad-Din Rumi described it as the 'long journey into yourself'; and for the poet-philosopher Iqbal, it was to 'pass from matter to spirit'. Carl Jung said, "Your vision becomes clear when you look inside your heart. Who looks outside, dreams. Who looks inside, awakens". Many simply call it 'spiritual journey', the journey which, as human beings, we are expected to go on, a journey not to go somewhere but, in Aldous Huxley's words, "in the dissipation of one's own ignorance concerning one's self and life", which is "the finding of God as a coming to one's self". It is only through such a journey that we can achieve the greatest of all conquests, the conquest of the self, and the highest of all freedoms, the freedom of one who has overcome himself. It is only through such a venture that it will become possible to, as ancient wisdom exhorts us, 'rouse thyself by thyself'. It is only by undertaking, at least consciously choosing to 'go within' that we can discover the kind of alchemy we need most of all, the ability to cleanse our consciousness.

Some evolved souls experience 'divinity' by cultivating what has been called a 'two-fold existence'. Swami Mukteswar, the guru of Paramahansa Yogananda, explains that "saints who realize their divinity even while in the flesh know a similar two-fold existence. Conscientiously engaging in earthly work, they yet remain immersed in an inward beatitude". He described the interior of our being as an 'Eden within'. It is also the darkest and brightest of places; dark as it harbors of our negative impulses, and bright as it not only offers a home to our positive feelings and emotions but also to the Almighty. According to the Upanishads, transcending the bounds of knowledge into the realm of realization is the spiritual journey man is born to embark upon. 'Bounds of knowledge', in effect, means overcoming or overpowering the hold of the brain/mind over our consciousness. This is the trick or prank that nature has played on us. On the one hand, it has given us the marvel of a brain, which has enabled and empowered us to outflank, outsmart, and prevail over physically much stronger species. On the other hand, it has ensured that our overwhelming dependence on this very 'marvel' keeps us confined to those very 'bounds of knowledge' that we should cross to fully realize human potential. And, as William James noted, we live 'half-awake' and 'habitually fail to use powers of various sort'.

Mind Over Mind

The key is to go 'beyond' our five senses, which, as the scriptures never tire of telling us, hold us captive. They say that unless we can subdue, if not master, our senses, we cannot make any significant spiritual advance. Some commentators say that the secret of the Bhagavad Gita was that Lord Krishna was exhorting Arjuna to pick up his *gandiva*, his mighty bow, not so much to fight the Kauravas arrayed on the battlefield of Kurukshetra, but actually to fight with his five 'enemies' inside. But these five are themselves not free; they are captives of the mind. The mind is a major constituent of our consciousness. The other major constituent is heart intelligence. Neuroscientists have recently discovered that there are over 40,000 nerve cells (neurons) in the heart alone, indicating that the heart has its own independent nervous system—sometimes called 'the brain in the heart'. In addition, the heart has an electromagnetic energy field that is far greater than that of the brain, and this field can be measured up to 10 feet beyond the physical body. This provides support for the spiritual teachings that tell us that humans have energy fields that constantly intermingle with each other, enabling healing (or negative) thoughts to be extended and exchanged. The heart is increasingly being seen not only as the organ that keeps us alive but also as the one whose intelligence is independent of the brain, and the one that keeps us on the moral path. It is, in fact, the imbalance between the brain and heart that has warped human personality. The war within is also then a fight between the heart and brain for control of consciousness. One of the most important challenges both spiritualism and science are concerned with is how to enhance the role of heart intelligence and diminish that of the brain/mind. At the same time research is also underway to boost brain power and to acquire 'mind control' (called *sama* in Sanskrit). While the scriptures have talked of 'mind-control' as a spiritual tool to control one's own behavior, science is now trying to break into other people's minds, to manipulate their thought processes and induce them to do what others want them to do.

Man has long sought the power of mind over matter. Mark Twain quipped, "Age is an issue of mind over matter. If you don't mind, it doesn't matter". Now, man is seeking the power of the mind over mind. It is an awesome power. Politicians, corporations, industrialists, even terrorists want it to achieve their ends. Politicians want it to govern without dissent, to get elected and re-elected. Corporations and managers want to improve worker productivity and to earn more profits. Terrorists want to penetrate the minds of their recruits to turn them into 'killer robots'. However, we must realize that if mind-power gets more potent, then the 'negatives' will receive more nourishment and become stronger. But let us not overly get carried away with this dichotomy about the 'goodness' of good and the 'badness' of evil. The 'negatives' are as essential as the 'positives'. Indeed we would have been extinct long ago in their total absence. A lot of people think like Mr. Spock (the half-human, half-Vulcan character of the television serial *Star Trek*), that some people become exceptional leaders because it is their negative side which makes them strong, that their evil side, if you will, properly controlled and disciplined, is vital to their strength. While clearly it is our mind-power that drives our lives, we are also told that humans have, or have had, finer faculties. These are variously called intuition, the sixth sense, paranormal powers, occult energy, psychic abilities, anomalous experiences, and so on. Some theosophists say that such powers, latent but now dormant, are not supernatural or abnormal but natural; and the layer at which we are functioning instead is subnormal and unnatural. We are below par, below our potential.

They predict that such game-changing capabilities will one day be used as a natural means of cognition and navigation, and once that happens, it will be a giant step towards human spiritual transformation. But that depends on the state of our consciousness. It is also generally believed that the locus of these intuitive powers is the human heart, which is a tremendous source of intelligence, energy, and memory independent of the brain. What happened, however, in these modern times is that as the brain grew bigger and tightened its hold on man, the heart went into enforced eclipse and became simply a pump that we only want to keep ticking without ever stopping. That, in turn, has disturbed the inner equilibrium and strengthened the negative forces in the internal war, which has corrupted, if not conquered our consciousness. In his book *Shambhala: The Sacred Path of the Warrior*, Chogyam Trungpa Rinpoche says, 'It is not *what* you fight against that matters as much as knowing what is worth fighting for. Wake up and dream'.

The Quicksand 'Within' the War Within

The war within, unlike other wars that end at a certain time with a victor and a vanquished, is a continuous continuum, and will never come to a definitive closure. It is a war with millions of mini-wars, or little battles that are fought every day, every hour or every minute, in which there is a transient winner. Such is the level of our ignorance that what we are surmising about the war within is actually internalizing what is happening in the world outside. That is the basis for the premise that it is an epic struggle between good and evil. We may not know much but we do know enough to know that what goes on deep down inside, shapes what we are, and how we behave, and it has a vital bearing on what goes on in the world beyond our bodies. It is this war that decides if we will rise up to our noblest potential or go down to the lowest, meanest depths. What we call our 'behavior' is purely a reflection, indeed a mirror image, of the seesaw battles with fluctuating fortunes. How we behave, how we act and react are all mini manifestations of the state of the war at that point and time. We do not see the battles or the rubble; we don't feel it or experience it; we hear no rumblings of guns blazing, or the shouts of the winner or the screams of the loser. Life goes on with innumerable chores and choices, delights and disappointments, triumphs and tragedies and all the while we think these are all our doings—of our free will, or of Fate or God. Yet, they do play a part, pull a string or two in the '*karmic kathputli*' (the karmic puppets), but they do that in the internal theater. All that we witness in the world—all the terrible horrors, insanity, cruelty, terrorism—are but a display of the state of the war within and the perpetrators. And all the wars, conflicts, wickedness and viciousness in the world are but sparks and skirmishes in comparison with this insidious internal incinerator. Being at war has been the state of the world. According to one estimate, during the last 3,000 years, the world has been at peace for only 240 years; that is less than 10% of the time. This is but an enlarged reflection and extension of the internal war. We must understand that there is no question of winning this internal war. We need the negative as much as the positive to continue to exist within us to survive in the world outside. The ideal state of this war is a state of stalemate, with the virtuous forces having an edge in most of the daily battles within the war. If we somehow manage to ensure that the good that is in us prevails in these mini-wars, then all the intractable problems we are grappling with will become manageable.

The universe within, we variously call mind, consciousness, sub-consciousness, soul inside, and so on. The locus and focus of our effort has to be in that bounded but limitless space. That 'space' is also sometimes compared to dry quicksand; every step we take to get out gets us deeper down. As Jess Scott says, "It was alarming, how humans could spend entire lifetimes engaged in all kinds of activities, without getting any closer to knowing who they really were, inside" (*The Other Side of Life*). Without such cathartic cleansing and churning and looking within, we cannot morph the fundamentals of what it entails to be human on earth. We cannot go forward on any of the problems and issues, or mend our behavior unless we recognize that the greatest and most tenacious of all wars is taking place right within each of us, and we are barely even conscious of it. Even 'external' wars and 'natural disasters' are brought about by the inner vibratory balance of good and evil being disturbed by an ascendancy of harmful vibrations and resultant human actions. If we can rectify and restore the 'inner equilibrium' in each of us, or at least in the 'critical mass' of mankind, then such outbreaks will be far fewer. But we need minimal but sufficient numbers to succeed, to change the direction of human endeavor. Swami Vivekananda said, "A few heart-whole, sincere, and energetic men and women can do more in a year than a mob in a century". How many are those 'few', and what the threshold is, crossing which unleashes an unstoppable momentum, we do not know, and perhaps will never know. That 'threshold' can be any of us, and so we must believe and behave. There is also an important change in the dynamics which we must take note of. Human evolution has entered a new phase, a new direction: the blurring of the boundary between individual and community. Henceforth, things can get done, problems get resolved only through men living in tandem for the common good. Even the next 'avatar', the cosmic savior, might be a conglomerate, not an individual entity. The Buddhist monk and author Thich Nhat Hanh in fact foresees that: "it is possible that the next Buddha will not take the form of an individual. The next Buddha may take the form of a community—a community practicing understanding and loving kindness, a community practicing mindful living. This may be the most important thing we can do for the survival of the earth". An individual is necessary but not sufficient for human transformation.

The most 'negative' of all—the main malaise of man—is malice, which is the most destructive of all emotions, distinct from envy and jealousy, and perhaps the only truly 'unique' thing about this animal. There is nothing 'self', or even 'selfish' about malice; it is all about 'others'; wishing them ill without any self-gain; capable of feeling unhappy about others' happiness; of rejoicing in another's misfortune. In that sense, unless we can get rid of the malice in our mind, we are not even equal to other animals emotionally. Recent neurological research has revealed that in many individuals, the amygdala and its associated systems in the brain, which are responsible for the 'negative' emotions, are becoming prominently enlarged, at the expense of other areas such as the hypothalamus, which is responsible for people's sense of well-being and happiness. We have always had within both the 'negative' as well as the 'positive' emotions like love, kindness, tenderness, compassion, sharing, solidarity, and connection to others. But they were for long in large measure evenly matched, in a state of balance. It is the breaking of the balance, starting a few millenniums ago, that marked the beginning of corruption of the human condition, alienation from nature and solidification of the sense of separateness. The tragedy is that although, as neuroscience tells us, our brain's very design makes it sociable, inexorably drawn into an intimate brain-to-brain linkup whenever we engage with another person, our competitive culture has come to identify our very identity with separateness. In a practical sense, we have different bodies; therefore we are 'separate'. There is inevitably some 'distance' between any of us, but that gives an opportunity to share the space in between. But it has become a crippling disability that deters complementing each other. We exist, work, and live always with other people, but we have not found a way to build bridges between being 'near each other' and being 'together'.

The madness and mayhem on this planet is largely due to our inability to achieve a balance within, and with, ourselves. For a more harmonious and happier human being, the restoration of this 'balance' is an imperative. For better human behavior, we have to ensure that the 'positive' emotions prevail in the process of decision-making. The only way for that is to alter the course of this eternal internal war. Outwardly, the 'war within' manifests as a moral injury or trauma, which is the clutch of the throat, twitch in the stomach, which we feel whenever we violate what each of us considers right or wrong. But we quickly put it away, lest it become too bothersome. That, in turn, translates into the plethora of ills that we experience in everyday life: indifference, intolerance, injustice, callousness, cruelty. All or some of them have existed in human society from time immemorial, but never before have all found a safe haven at the same time in our 'within', nor has their virulence been so scorching. The war is fought not only between two forces; its influence and impact are also two-fold. The war, and the myriad battles within, affects, even determines the content of our consciousness as well as our earthly conduct. And, on the side, we can influence the course of the war through our will and behavior.

Another contributing and complicating factor is that the very 'intelligence' that propels our personality itself is not of the right kind. The paradox is that it was the evolution of 'intelligence' that marked the arrival, and eventual ascent of man. Other non-human animals too had brains, some even bigger (dinosaurs, for example). It is the relative proportions of brain and body that matters. It was the 'neocortex', the so-called 'gray matter', which enabled the human to perform complex functions, sensory perception, logical and deductive reasoning, and conscious thought. While that kind of 'intelligence' empowered man to survive, prevail and ultimately acquire the power to lord over all other forms of life on earth, once that stage was reached, it became not entirely appropriate for his further growth and stability of the human world. One of our paradoxical perplexities lies in that part of our consciousness which gives rise to what is often called 'collective intelligence', the 'combined intelligence' we bring to bear as members of a group, or community. Although we are not fully aware of it, the fact is that we are the sum total of our previous past and of the people we interface and interact with in the world, our family, peers, or co-workers, even the man on the street. And what we learn, all comes through the doors that other people open for us. It is also being said that a sense of shared identity—that thinking as *we*, rather than as *I*—is good for our mind and body. Life-expectancy is reported to have declined in modern societies in which people live isolated lives. On the other hand, the reality also is that although we are often described as 'social animals' we lag far behind other social organisms like ants and termites in the way we organize and live communally. In our case, unlike ants, for example, the whole, or the cumulative energy and intelligence, has often been less than the sum of the parts. Not only have we fallen short in converting individual energy into social synergy; we expend a good chunk of our energy to undermine others. That is the primary reason why we have never found a perfect formula, or model for a 'just' society. We are 'social animals', but we also fail most as constituent parts of society, of a collective whole. And that is why every 'constitution', which often ironically starts with soaring but shallow words, 'We, the people', have all been found wanting. From the 'city-state' to 'nation-state', from kingdoms to empires, from oligarchies to ochlocracies, theocracies to dictatorships, to democracies, they have all failed. That is because there is no way to predict, preempt human wantonness and wickedness, no way to curb individual avarice and evil while giving autonomous 'social space' to every individual. Man cannot be trusted with any 'authority' or power over other people. The conundrum is that the human being is too complex a form of life to be contained, but contained he must be, for the good of others. That 'complexity' also stems from the fact that we have no clue or control over what happens inside each of us. While the arena for action, change and control is inside, we focus on our external behavior. Although scientists and theologians might argue why there is something rather than nothing and what is it that proves or disproves, nothing for sure comes from naught and the fluctuating fortunes of the 'war within' determine how we act and react, how we treat each other. And if we, as individuals, have no hold on our own behavior, how then can we be 'governed' externally, which essentially calls for sharing and complementing and willingly subjecting ourselves to external controls for the larger good. In the words of Swami Vivekananda, "external nature is only internal nature writ large". If we do not have internal coherence and internal peace, we cannot have peace and order in the world. The Buddha said, "Peace comes from within. Do not seek it without". The men that 'govern' as well those being 'governed' are human, subject to the same foibles and limitations. For, as James Madison once noted, "If men were angels, no government would be necessary. If angels were to govern men, neither external nor internal controls on government would be necessary". While external governance depends on internal governance, internal 'good' governance hinges on the course of the 'war within'.

Some of us can be 'super men', or even achieve 'supra-mental intelligence'; but we can never become a super-organism (broadly described as a collection of agents which can act in concert to produce phenomena governed by the collective, phenomena being any activity that 'the hive wants', such as ants collecting food or bees choosing a new nest site). We are essentially unable to 'get it all together', what we have within each of us as a species; or, 'get along with each other' synergistically. Adding to our woes, we make use of, in the words of William James, "only a small part of our mental and physical resources"—one might add of our spiritual potential. Nor have we achieved 'intelligent' internal coherence. Our 'intelligence' is fractured inside and fratricidal outside.

Human 'intelligence', or intellect' as some like to call it, is multidimensional and includes not only the cognitive power, but also emotional intelligence, intuitive intelligence, and spiritual intelligence. We are way off the mark even with regard to the source of our innate and operative 'intelligences'. It is, contrary to the popular view, not all centered in the brain; the heart has its own independent but interdependent intelligence; the gut has its intelligence; perhaps even the cells in our body. All 'intelligences' are designed to work synergistically for a human life of harmony. Somewhere, sometime, things went horribly skewed, the mix got messed up. And the power of 'rational thinking', or of the 'left-brain mode' of thinking, identified with critical thinking, logical reasoning and objectivity, has come to dominate, or even monopolize, our conscious lives, at the cost of other innate but dormant or underutilized capabilities like emotional thought, intuitive insightfulness, and spiritual awareness. Consequently, man has become a dysfunctional and destructive being. Unless we can rejig the 'mix' and configure a new blend of our 'intelligence, we will, as Eckhart Tolle says, "always end up re-creating the same world, the same evils, the same dysfunction".

But then the essential point is that we cannot behave like ants or bees because we are human animals, not eusocial mammals, not even chimps. Just as we cannot be a tiger or a leopard, so we cannot be an ant or a bee or a butterfly or a bird. We can certainly learn from the way they submerge or sacrifice their 'individuality', and become, to borrow a phrase from René Girard, *interdividuals*, for the good of the colony or hive, but we cannot do what a caterpillar can: become a butterfly. That which is in the lowest, more accurately different, state of existence, like the mineral, has no right to grumble, saying, "O God, why have You not given me the vegetable persona?" In the same way, the plant has no right to complain that it has been deprived of the attributes of the animal world. And an animal cannot complain of the want of the human qualities. Every form of life or existence is unique in itself, and has an irreplaceable place in the theater of creation. In the Bible, it is said, "But who are you, a human being, to talk back to God?" Shall what is formed say to the one who formed it, "Why did you make me like this?" Does not the potter have the right to make out of the same lump of clay some pottery for special purposes and some for common use? What we should focus upon is how to optimize, harmonize what we have, and who we are as human animals, to the last detail to achieve the goals and guideposts we set ourselves to achieve. We cannot 'evolve' into something like a 'cell in a giant social body', from an individual into a colony, with a perfect 'division of labor'. We cannot, either as individuals or as a species, be any other, but we must be true to ourselves and be the best we can as we are. But what is truly, unchangeably, exclusively human 'capability'? It is difficult to codify as it is, on the one hand, timeless and, on the other hand, changes from time to time. And then we have different 'capabilities': physical, mental, spiritual and so on. And it varies from person to person. Given all these difficulties, as a species we must learn to emulate the behavior of 'colony organisms', and drastically reduce conflict, enhance cooperation, develop and nurture a 'hive mind' or collective consciousness', a shared identity. Not knowing how to handle conflict has been the source of strife and sorrow. Conflict is everywhere in nature. Conflict is both internal and external. There is conflict in our consciousness, which is the war within. In fact, it is this internal conflict in Arjuna's consciousness that has given us the great Bhagavad Gita. Externally, diversity means difference, and difference leads to disagreement, and disagreement into argument, and argument into acrimony, and acrimony into anger, and anger into, as the Bhagavad Gita says, to loss of control over the senses and to ruination. It is self-righteousness, the *I-know-it-all* and *I-am-right* feeling, that is the cause of conflict. And that does not let us see the other or alternative point of view. That does not let us concede or compromise or yield. Conflict becomes bitterness, violence, hatred, and war. Conflict is now embedded in our mindset, now the prism through which we view everything. Our consciousness itself is in a state of conflict and that is why we have the war within.

Technology and the 'War Within'

Whether technology *per se* is ethically inert or morally malevolent, its power and potential has other implicit consequences that we barely take note of. The anti-technology mass murderer Theodore Kaczynski (also known as the 'Unabomber') explained in his manifesto: "Due to improved techniques the elite will have greater control over the masses; and because human work will no longer be necessary, the masses will be superfluous, a useless burden on the system. If the elite are ruthless they may simply decide to exterminate the mass of humanity. If they are humane, they may use propaganda or other psychological or biological techniques to reduce the birth rate until the mass of humanity becomes extinct, leaving the world to the elite". That scenario is certainly a possibility; so are potential risks in technological advances and frontier technologies like genetic re-engineering, nuclear power, and so on. But there are dangers in the current 'low' technologies also, indeed even in 'primitive' technologies. How we use any technology, or any technique or tool, depends on who the user is and how it is harnessed. To be fair, there are a number of thoughtful and spiritual persons who think that modern science-based technology could do wonders to mankind and that the much-dreaded 'marriage' of man and machine might be for the mutual good. The Dalai Lama recently quipped, probably in a lighter vein, that he would not rule out the possibility of one day reincarnating as a computer! He says that man is also a 'machine with a consciousness'. Now, if a man-made machine, with man's help, acquires something akin to what we describe as 'consciousness'—ability to feel emotions, for example—then will it transform into a 'living entity' like any of us? The question is not if technology, like everything in the universe is God's creation, and therefore spiritual. And not also, as the Dalai Lama says, that man too is a 'conscious' machine. Both assumptions and inferences might be true or false; it does not matter much. The essential question is: what kind of 'consciousness' might it have and how does it get it? If it is from man (probably) and if its 'consciousness' is anything like what man has now (most likely), then we are doubly-doomed. What kind of 'machines' we might make and how we put them to use all depends on the state of human consciousness, particularly of those who are on the frontline of scientific research and spiritual search. We know that technology has not only been the defining force behind the 'military-industrial complex', but it has also unrecognizably altered the character of war and made the enemy-land (there is no such thing as warzone anymore) into a theater of massacre, an open-ended graveyard, a smoldering giant burning *ghat*. Even 'spirituality' can be a negative force, if it is practiced by the wrong people.

Everything we do, even how we harness human creativity, depends on the state of the 'war within'. A huge chunk of that creativity is not in the arts or letters, literature or painting, but in technology. The debate whether technology is double-edged or not, boon or bane, will never be settled. What is increasingly becoming apparent is that human consciousness, at the level at which it is operating, seems more hospitable to its negative power because consciousness itself is corrupted. As a result, technology is being put to use for elitist and divisive and destructive purposes. It is widening the chasm between plutocracy and the people, the elite and the masses to such an extent that some say that a no-holds-barred global class struggle is inevitable, spearheaded this time not by the working class but by the middle class. We are living at a time when serious people are seriously saying that "there is not a single aspect that doesn't have the potential to be totally transformed by these technologies of the future". The decisive impact that technology will make on our future hinges on this epic struggle inside. Our tireless and ceaseless endeavor should be to reinforce and strengthen the 'positive' forces like love, caring, compassion, sharing, humility, gratefulness, tolerance, and temperance that are caught in an epic struggle in our consciousness. Some say that the real combatants are gods. They say, "There are gods at war within each of us. They battle for the throne of our hearts, and much is at stake". This is why idolatry is the most discussed problem in the entire Bible. Behind every such struggle that you and I have is a false god that is winning the war in our lives. Don't give in to the myth that gods are only statues that people of other cultures or people of long ago worshipped. Pleasure, romance, sex, money, and power are just a few of the gods that vie for our allegiance in today's society. Loss of self-control, both as individuals and as a species, has always been man's biggest problem, but never more needed or absent than now. It is at the root of all problems, from casual sex to catastrophic climate change, gluttony to the greenhouse effect, broken homes to social breakdown. No one seems to be in control over their lives, emotions, feelings, desires, dreams, and drives. The less control we have within, the more we need it outside. And that lack of inner control is at the core of concern about our behavior. But there are some who worry what might happen if we are able to gain control over ourselves, that is, if we are able to intervene, meddle, and manipulate what goes on inside our consciousness. If we are free to make ourselves however we wish to be, if we are able to modify our motivations, what would we do? If we have the power, on whose side in the 'war within' would we tilt towards? Would we become more 'humanely' human or more 'inhumanly' human, more compassionate or more callous?

The bottom line is that our 'behavior'—which in practical terms means the kind of things we do to stay alive, to share the living space on earth with fellow-beings; to make a living, to amuse and entertain ourselves, to compete and to progress—defies our claim to be a rational race, or as the species with a *carte blanche* direct from God to rule over all life on earth. The irony, and tragedy, is that no other species and no other man of any other time, with all the dazzling add-ons at his elbow, is more 'busy' than man of this day and age. Yet his life, after it is done with 'being busy', is more barren and bereft of 'meaning' than of any one before. Man has long wrestled with the question: Life being 'given'—a blend of 'divine beauty', brutality, and barbarism—what then should I do with myself? Carl Jung, in his autobiography *Memories, Dreams, Reflections*, agonized over this question. He wrote, "I know only that I was born and exist, and it seems to me that I have been carried along. I exist on the foundation of something I do not know. In spite of all uncertainties, I feel a solidity underlying all existence and a continuity in my mode of being". He quotes Lao Tzu, "All are clear, I alone am clouded", and interprets it as Lao Tzu being a man with superior "insight who has seen and experienced worth and worthlessness, and who at the end of his life desires to return into his own being, into the eternal unknowable meaning". He ends with a hope: "Life is—or has—meaning and meaninglessness. I cherish the anxious hope that meaning will preponderate and win the battle". The battle, or the 'war', is in his own being, his 'within'. If Jung, with his great insight into the human psyche, was left with nothing more than 'anxious hope', what hope do we have?

Many, particularly the very young, often referred to as Gen-Y, are experiencing the pangs of the terrifying gravity of inner emptiness, the 'unbearable lightness' of heavy hopelessness, the dreary drudgery of 'making a living'. And many feel, looking at the coarseness of contemporary society, a numbing sense of moral despair at the enticing trappings of our soul-less civilization. We are more on the move than moving towards where it matters. We produce to discard, and what we consume does no good to anyone. We 'take' and 'take', and 'take' everything that appeals to our senses, give no thought to how what we 'take' comes from, from where, and what it entails. If it is in the 'market', and if we have 'money', nothing else matters. How many fellow-humans are exploited, how much child-laborers are involved, how many trees are cut, and how many animals are tortured and slaughtered to get the things we 'take' from the market place or the shelf of the store, we give no thought to. Our clothes, fine or cheap, are our second skin and reflect our personal sense of style, taste, personality, culture, and even beliefs and values. But do we know, or care to know, how and where they are made? It is a huge industry, and the world clothing and textile industry (clothing, textiles, footwear, and luxury goods) generates several trillions of dollars annually, backstopped by sweatshop labor of women and children in poor countries or totalitarian states, who work long hours in toxic environments at abysmally low wages. Fast fashion is the second biggest polluter in the world, second only to oil. We don't see them and we don't know them and we don't care. We feel good wearing 'sweat-and-blood'-soaked fancy clothes, and we have enough money to get them, and that is all that matters. The moral alibi is, that which is not within the immediacy of our knowing we cannot be held accountable for. Everything is a matter of 'marketing' on the mass media. Everything that happens, and even every image of horror, has to compete not only with other 'horrors' but also with images of consumer goods, toothpaste, cameras, luxury houses, etc. Because our attention span is limited, and sometimes seconds on the fleeting screen can cost millions, the 'image' must grab our eye and mind instantly or else the money goes bad and all in vain. Repetitive exposure to such viewing has a numbing effect, and we need—and the sponsors and the marketing-gurus, who 'specialize in the production and specialization of such an image' know that—each next time more gripping and more 'horrific' horrors. And watching them is when we relax, enjoy and be entertained! Distance mass production and mass marketing gives us the cover not to think of the process of production—where, how and by whom it is made—and of the attendant moral and ecological costs, and then we think that what stands between the image and an item is only money (if we have it we can get it) and the moral aspect gets marginalized.

Court of Conscience

It is again the mind that chooses how to put technology to use. The same robot that can be used in warfare can also enable a paralyzed man to lead a life of dignity. Since many remote areas of the globe lack all-weather access, scientists have invented transportation systems that use electric autonomous flying machines to deliver medicine, food, goods and supplies wherever they are needed. The message down the ages and across the oceans is always the same: everything in nature and everything man can make could be used constructively for the common good or destructively for collective doom. It is the make-up and mix, character and content of human 'intelligence' that is the arbiter. The problem is not either with scripture or science, culture or civilization. It is the nature of the beast, intelligence. And one of the drawbacks in our left-brain intelligence has been its inability to break the barriers between different religions, philosophy and science and to inject what Abraham Maslow called 'being values', or meta-values, into other attributes like 'logic', 'devoutness', 'sincerity', 'passion' and 'fervor'. That is how the religious personality can live in comfort with cruelty and callousness towards other people, and an 'honorable' and 'upright' scientist can, in 'good conscience' make weapons that kill thousands of people whose names and identities he will never even know. And the rest of us can lead normal lives with multiple personalities, which allows us to use a mask to cover our inconvenient faces! We are living in unsettling times and our mind-driven consciousness has annihilated, or abolished, what we used to call our 'conscience'. No one considers he is accountable, in Gandhi's phrase, to the highest court of conscience. We feel no moral ' pricks', hear no 'voices', no tugs of our gut; and it is not because it is all 'quiet on the inner front', but because all our seeking, all of our journey, our hunger for adventure is outwards and upwards. After all, we only want a good life, good sleep, good carrier, good recreation and eternal life even if we are already dead within.

And we have failed to notice that what we are searching for in the universe is right within the 'inner universe': within our own selves. Ancient traditions and many religions have long told us that our heart and our gut are independent, though interconnected, sources of intuitive intelligence, which many animals too have, but have become comatose for hundreds, if not thousands, of years. Scientists say that there are more neurons in our gut than anywhere else except within the brain, signifying that it is more than a place of ingestion, digestion, and excretion. The gut, along with the heart is called the 'intuitive brain'; these two organs are separate but are holistically connected with the 'brain' in our head. If we can somehow awaken and activate them—the heart and the gut—they can, along with the brain, bring about the right blend in our 'intelligence'. We have chosen to set aside the 'help' available within and we have lost the 'dart of longing love'. What our creativity is laboring upon is to harness the machine to overcome the inadequacies of our brain-incubated 'intelligence'. The rationale that is often offered is that the human brain is increasingly unable to cope with the complexity and contradictions, range and scope of factors that need to be harmonized for sound decision-making in the contemporary context, and, as a result, we have little choice but to rely on computers to supplement or even supplant human intelligence. And that computer systems that have access to, and are able to store, analyze and process, mountains of data almost instantly and objectively, can be better at decision-making than humans with their foibles, prejudices and with their tendency to look at every issue through the prism of personal benefit. The fact, they say, is that most people are severely limited in terms of the amount of information they could process at any particular moment in time, and are unable to carry out the mental operations necessary to make calibrated decisions. While that is a reasonable inference, the question is: are computer-aided or computer-made decisions truly objective non-human decisions? Some experts say 'not necessarily'; they say that it is wrong to think that computers are neutral and that algorithms reflect the biases of their creators, which means they too are subject to the same limitations of human decision-making capabilities. This means that whether it is scientific activity or political problem-solving or computer-aided calibration, the orchestrator is the brain, and the intended purpose of insulating or marginalizing our choices and decisions from the weaknesses and vagaries of our brain/mind will not be achieved. That again means that if we want to improve human problem-solving capabilities we have to induce and orchestrate a paradigm shift in the very infrastructure of our intelligence that drives our lives. And such a shift has to happen 'within' generations.

In embarking on this adventure, we must also realize that what we call 'intelligence' is not the monopoly of man. Every creature from ant to ape, from a plant to a dolphin has its own insignia of intelligence, 'unique' to that form of life, created in its own world, called *Umwelt*. There are as many 'umwelts' out there as there are organisms, perhaps even many more, although they all share the same environment. We 'think' that we are the most 'intelligent', an assumption increasingly in question. It is now reported that crows, ravens, and rooks possess higher intelligence. We do not know about other creatures but man has multiple 'intelligences'. We wrongly identify 'being gifted' with having a high intelligence quotient (IQ). So prized is the IQ that even one-year-olds are being subjected to tests to determine their score, so as to enhance it as a way to stay or succeed in the endless, self-defeating, or pointless pursuit. We want our kids to be smart, in fact smarter than others, as we believe that that will empower them to prevail in our highly competitive world. The key factor in life, we have come to believe, is to be 'smarter' than others. And we credit our very survival as a species to that single attribute. For many millenniums, we humans have considered ourselves superior, primarily due to our large brains and our ability to reason, that we humans are exceptional by virtue, that we are the 'smartest in the animal kingdom'. It has been believed that human superiority is the decisive definition of man's place in nature and that it is ingrained in the genetic code of all of us. Even Aristotle, whom *Encyclopedia Britannica* called 'the first genuine scientist in history', echoed this view and wrote that nature had made animals for mankind, 'both for his service and his food', and 'there is no such thing as virtue in the case of a god, any more than there is vice or virtue in the case of a beast: divine goodness is something more exalted than virtue, and bestial badness is different in kind from vice'. Spanish philosopher Ortega Gasset reassures us that 'the greatest and most moral homage we can pay to certain animals on certain occasions is to kill them'. If 'killing' is a way to pay 'homage'—it may well be so, from nature's point of view—then why not humans? And that, incidentally, is what we are doing!

There are different voices too about human 'uniqueness'. Some say that we might not be as smart as we think, and that animals can have cognitive faculties that are superior to those of human beings, and that "the fact that they may not understand us, while we do not understand them, does not mean our 'intelligences' are at different levels; they are just of different kinds".[53] If further substantiated—and even if not generically more 'intelligent', if it can be established that our animal-cousins can do some tasks more 'efficiently' than human animals—this could be one of the most sobering of 'spiritual' revelations. Even more far-reaching and profound, it indicates the desired direction of evolution of human thought. It is to focus our attention on ways to bridge the abyss between human and non-human animals, to learn to treat them as full-fledged forms of life, like our own kin and kindred, not inferior beings deprived of all feelings, emotions, pain, empathy, and camaraderie that we are capable of. That is another path to realize and 'know' God, the common Father and creator.

Whether or not we are the most 'intelligent' and smartest of all animals, cognitively or functionally, is not really germane to the instant point. It is that our current brand of 'intelligence', which is left-brain incubated, is a big part of the problem, and not the solution. At its most basic level, it has not enabled us to cooperate and complement each other, at least to simply 'get along' with each other. What we need to do, and what we should do to our kids, is not to deepen our extant 'intelligence', but to broaden it to include others like emotional, interpersonal, social, and spiritual intelligences. The fact is that which particular 'intelligence' dominates at any point determines what kind of 'world' we create, live in, experience, even imagine. Change of 'intelligence' changes everything. In our case, it is the intelligence of the brain/mind that dominates us and the 'world' of our experience, marginalizing others like emotional and spiritual intelligences. But it was not always so and it need not be forever. So if we want to change the world for the better we have to change the brand of our 'intelligence' that drives our lives. It is not a matter of becoming 'more intelligent'; it is about being 'differently' intelligent. And that source of 'differently' must be *in situ*, germinated within our own selves, not exogenously or artificially, but outside the ambit of what we call the 'mind'. The measure of how intelligent we are—our intelligence quotient—is what essentially differentiates man from man, the upshot of whatever we do as 'conscious beings'. While a high IQ has obvious advantages in the human world, the idea that higher IQ is better, and that a certain level of IQ is required to achieve certain goals in life, has been proven wrong again and again. Ironically, a very low IQ, too, can be a life-saving alibi; it can literally save one from the gallows. Whether it is high or low, intelligence has come to mean the difference between success and failure, recognition and ridicule, genius and garden-type. Most of all, 'intelligence' is prized for its problem-identification-solving capacity. The basic assumption is that our intelligence enables us to assemble and analyze all relevant facts, to take into consideration all the pertinent factors, and allows us to frame and make right choices for the right course of action. At this pivotal point in human history, which itself is a chronicle of human bungling and faux pas, and attempts made to cover them up, where many are aghast at what man has wrought on earth and where he is headed, it is this dimension that calls for careful study and reflection. First we must recognize that the scope for our 'choice-making' is very narrow. On the really important issues we have no choice. We have no choice over our earthly arrival: to whom we are born to or the place and time of our birth. We have no choice over the birth of our progeny. We have no choice over the time and place, even the way, of our earthly departure: death. And yet all our life we try to ward it off; and sometimes to embrace. If death is predetermined, then is our drive towards physical immortality tantamount to divine defiance, a dare to nature?

Even within this meager 'menu' the actual 'choices' we make are highly circumscribed and conditioned; they appear as 'choices', but we are, in reality, the executors, the instruments. 'Choices' make us more than we make them, and over time, we *become* what the real 'choice-makers' want us to be. Jean-Paul Sartre simply said, "We are our choices". We make a 'choice' among the choices offered to us, and they themselves are loaded. What is not on the table doesn't really exist and the 'table' itself is so crowded with such pseudo 'choices' that the difference between them is actually, 'Twixt Tweedle-dum and Tweedle-dee'. Still, every choice has a ripple effect, both on our character and, something we scarcely are conscious of, on society.

The most worrisome aspect is that we have turned out to be, with all these caveats, poor 'choice-makers' and 'problem-solvers'. In fact, we tend to identify intelligence with 'problem-solving' capabilities and that the better we are at problem-solving the more intelligent we are. 'Problem-solvers' are usually highly regarded and rewarded. Yet the fact is that all through our history, problem-solving has been our weakest spot: skewed-prioritization, flawed decision-making, faulty harmonizing of competing demands. It is this that has led to all the problems we have faced, all the wars that we have waged, all the misery we have endured as a species. If we want more harmonious humankind and a more stable world, the 'problem' about problem-solving has to be addressed. The real problem is that often we cannot even agree on what the 'problem' is; let alone how to 'resolve' it. Basically the 'problem' is that our brain, more precisely the left-brain, consists of many specialized units designed by the process of evolution by natural selection for fragmented tasks. While these modules occasionally work together cooperatively and seamlessly, they don't always, resulting in impossibly conflicting beliefs, vacillations between patience and impulsiveness, transgressions of our self-supposed moral imperatives, and pompous views of ourselves. We have always been reasonably good at narrow advocacy and compartmental conception, and weak on holistic 'thinking', integration, and harmonization. In modern times it has gotten worse, because today's problems are more complex and convoluted, and require precisely those very skills we lack, or we do not possess in sufficient measure. To the point that we are unable to agree on what needs to be done to address any of our issues, what Shakespeare called 'sea of troubles'—political, social, economic, technological, environmental, psychological, and cultural. For example, what we see around us is chaos, creeping shadows, darkness, and horrors, but what we cannot make sense of is what the mute message is. We are lost in the darkness, but whether it is the darkness before dawn or the darkness at the midnight of the new moon, whether or not the 'darkness' is of the 'maternal womb of a new consciousness', or of the chilling confines of a cold coffin, we can only surmise.

That mankind is on the threshold of an epic transition, we all concur. The trouble is that we are confused if what we see and experience in the world presages the dawn of a Utopia or the dim darkness of a Dystopia. Views vary if, as many fear, we are experiencing the death-throes of impending self-extinction or the faint birth-pangs of a new 'Axial Age' of 'spiritual unfoldment', which could lead to a profound consciousness-change or when 'singularity' comes calling. Human brains are chipped, or linked to computers, and a kind of 'man-machine' merger is occurring. These three different scenarios appear, all are plausible, but there is no way to tell which one will be the 'winner'. Here again, it depends on who, or which attributes, prevail in the 'war within'. During the long length of human pre-history, our brain and our emotions were by and large, in tune, in a state of subtle balance. That 'balance' was between what we call 'positive' or 'negative'. Our negative emotions such as anger, fear, anxiety, hate, and aggression were used for survival and hunting, and for the defense of the group or community against predators and rivals. They were entrenched and embedded within long after their need was not so strong, and have become more powerful through the inputs received from the outside world. The positive emotions such as love, kindness, compassion, and solidarity to others were brought to bear as a means to synergy in the community. And they have become weaker as they were starved of the nutrients from the external world. The principal reason for much of the aggression, wretchedness, wickedness, and hatred, which seem to be on the rise every day, is the growing ascendancy of the 'negative' forces in the ' war within'.

A Stinging Word and a Withering Glance

The core issue though is this: is human aggression and violence, in its destructive and demeaning sense, genetically hard-wired, or is human violence the somber 'software' of our struggle for survival in the 'living world' and the worldly wages of our culture, civilization and modernity? Opinions vary, and we will probably have no up or down answer. What we must recognize is that mankind will never be free from all violence, and the fight to overcome violence is part of the war within. Just as peace is not merely an absence of war, non-violence is not simply refraining from violent acts. We instinctively associate violence with physical actions, but in truth, non-physical violence, hurting without hitting, is far more pervasive. The medium need not be the hand; it can be our mouth, even eyes. A slap on the face may be less hurting than a stinging word. A looks-can-kill glance can send shivers down the spine more than a whiplash. Taking advantage of the other's vulnerability is violence. Gandhi said 'poverty is the worst form of violence'. It can be an abuse, psychological, emotional or verbal, or a deliberate snub, a scalding scolding. *Gaslighting*—mental abuse in which false information is presented with the intent of making a victim doubt his or her own memory, perception and sanity, is violence. In fact, "people ganging up on someone by spreading rumors, humiliation, and verbal abuse are just as bad as thugs who physically beat someone to cause injury or death… People are comfortable using non-physical violence because their actions cannot be measured like physical injuries".[54] The same action or speech or gesture can be 'violent' or even 'affectionate'; it depends on the intention and attitude. A curt and dismissive word can hurt, but simply listening with empathy can heal. There is a vast difference, for example, between mercy killing and murder, between contract killing and the executioner's execution, between consensual sex and commercial sex, even between seduction and rape. Even in the same relationship, the same act can be violent or loving. Some even say that "Violence itself is not physical, though the delivery system very well may be. Violence is energy—invasive, penetrating, abrupt, creepy, and unrelenting. It is the filth you cannot wash off with a shower".[55] Even 'passive resistance' and every form of 'protest' is a form of violence, in the sense it tries to force people to do something that otherwise they will not. But violence is sometimes needed for the voice of moderation to be heard. According to Hannah Arendt, "Violence… is a much more effective weapon of reformers than of revolutionists".[56] The argument against violence is that, although justified and even necessary under certain conditions, it is often counterproductive, that it leads to more violence, and that, in Arendt's words, the 'means overwhelm the end'. Non-violence can be cowardly in certain situations and 'being truthful' can do more harm than good at times. If we are 'kind' to a psychopathic killer and do not tell the truth we might be responsible for the murders of more people.

Every religion has recognized and warned us of this 'war within'. Zoroastrianism calls it a war between the god of light and god of darkness, and it advocates the simple formula of 'good thoughts, good words and good deeds'. Its founder Zoroaster was, in the words of Tagore, the "first man who gave a definitely moral character and direction to religion and at the same time preached the doctrine of monotheism which offered an eternal foundation of reality to goodness as an ideal of perfection".[57] And he 'showed the path of freedom to man, the freedom of moral choice'. Christianity describes the 'war' as a fight between God and Satan. However one might view it or call it, deep inside all of us there is struggle, tension, fight or war, which determines how we act or react, how we behave. There is in everyone a Dr. Jekyll and a Mr. Hyde; and perhaps many 'Jekylls' and 'Hydes', particular to every situation and relationship. The 'universe' is within and the forces are internal but the stakes are universal. It is not confined to the well-being and liberation of each of us; it directly and decisively affects the whole of humanity and the fate of the earth. The fact of the matter is that if we cannot control what happens inside we cannot control what happens outside. A 'suicide' is also an outcome of a 'war within'. When some people say that something 'broke inside', what they mean is that they lost the battle, and that, in turn, led to 'ending it all'. The irony is that while we have no qualms about species self-destruction, we have always been ambiguous about individual self-destruction. Our stance has wildly wavered between 'noble', 'heroic' and 'honorable', to 'mortal sin', 'heinous crime' or 'cowardly', between an 'act of genius' to a ' form of insanity'. On the species-scale not many agonize, because the individual mind cares as much or as little about the human as any other. The 'war is within', so are the barriers. Rumi wrote, "Your task is not to seek for love, but merely to seek and find all the barriers within yourself that you have built against it". The chief barrier is our own mind. Joseph Campbell said, "The ultimate dragon is within you".

All 'wars', between individuals or tribes or nations, are 'within' our own selves, and we have to win that 'war' for the future evolution of mankind. The Preamble to the Constitution of UNESCO declares that "since wars begin in the minds of men, it is in the minds of men that the defenses of peace must be constructed". Those 'defenses' have to be erected within. War, it has even been said, is a "biological necessity of the first importance... not only a biological law but a moral obligation... an indispensable factor in civilization".[58] Similarly, "War is not a pathology that with proper hygiene and treatment can be wholly prevented. War is a natural condition of the State, which was organized in order to be an effective instrument of violence on behalf of society. Wars are like deaths, which, while they can be postponed, will come when they will come and cannot be finally avoided".[59] At the outset of the First World War, Thomas Mann wrote, "Is not peace an element of civil corruption and war purification, a liberation, an enormous hope?"

All 'wars' of all sorts, in the ultimate reckoning, are about 'control'. It is our irresistible urge for control that consumes our lives and causes so much misery and mayhem in the world. Control gives the feeling of power, satiates the desire to prevail, it allows us to humiliate and to feel superior. We want to control through knowledge, through privilege and position. In every relationship, there is an element of control. Through control, we exploit each other and it is innate to every dimension of the human way of life. The fact of the matter is that we virtually cannot live without exploiting someone or the other sometime or the other; at least we should not heap humiliation—the feeling of being put down, made to feel less than one feels oneself to be—not rob them of the dignity, not to invade and violate their personal space. Deep inside our psyche, almost everyone harbors 'humiliation'. Wayne Koestenbaum (*Humiliation*, 2011) says, "I have lived with humiliation all my life, as I think all human beings do". WH

Auden wrote in his work *In Solitude for Company*, "Almost all of our relationships begin and most of them continue as forms of mutual exploitation, a mental or physical barter, to be terminated when one or both parties run out of goods". What Donald Klein calls *The Humiliation Dynamic* is, in his words, "a pervasive and all too often destructive influence in the behavior of individuals, groups, organizations, and nations… from an early age, inescapable". As Klein puts it, it is not only the 'experience' of humiliation but also the 'fear of humiliation' that dominates human lives. It is implicit in every relationship of mutual dependency. The fact is that there are many things we do in life which serve no purpose or self-interest except to humiliate others and get some 'kick' out of it. Essentially it is a show of power, of sadism. It can be belittling and berating and browbeating of the defenseless. It can be as simple or 'innocuous' as raising one's voice, finding fault, admonishing, giving a dirty look, a withering glance; anything that hurts or injures another person's self-respect and sensitivity is humiliation. And much of it comes from the near and dear; more from the 'near' than the 'dear'. Prolonged proximity removes the veneer we hide behind and oftentimes brings out the worst in us. We become naked not only in the bathroom or bedroom, but also in the immediacy of intimacy and that can rob one of respect. Power corrupts more when the other person seems powerless. Imposing our will on anyone, even if for 'their own good' can trigger a feeling of humiliation. Gandhi said, "It has always been a mystery to me how men can feel themselves honored by the humiliation of their fellow beings". But there is a catch here. Sometimes we may be thinking we are honoring someone by our actions while in fact we are humiliating that person. Gandhi himself is a paradox. He imposed his will on others including his wife, and in one instance, coerced her to clean toilets. He might have been nobly motivated, but was he right to make someone do what they did not want to do? Perhaps there is no perfect answer. We do impose our will on someone or the other, sometime or the other, knowingly or unknowingly, for good or bad reasons. If no one tries to 'control' anyone else, does not impose their will on others, there will be no conflicts, no exploitation, no violence, and no wars. But that is as much an ideal as a violence-free world. But the difference is that while violence is inherent in nature, *à la* the big fish eats the small fish, 'control' seems to be endemic to the human species. Perhaps with few exceptions, other animals kill their prey primarily for food, not to seek to control or humiliate or hurt for their own sake. But 'exploitation', like violence, need not be only physical or materialistic. It can be—indeed it is more—psychological, mental, emotional.

Sexuality, Gender-neutrality, and the War Within

At a fundamental level we are caught between twin 'realities'; our identification with our physical self, and our urge to 'connect' with other humans. What we call family, friendship, relationships, and society are means to couple the two. Our sexuality is another instinctive drive towards the same end. Few areas of human life appear as confusing, contradictory, and convoluted than sexuality. It is at once the greatest mystery and the most magical. It is a 'mystery', as we really cannot figure out what God primarily intended it to be, to amuse us or to do His work of creation. It is 'magical' as we cannot decode how such a 'messy' act can yield such ecstasy. It is all around but no one has 'enough'. It is supposed to 'free', needs no capital or investment, but it exacts a heavy price in every way, and kind, we get it, on the marital bed or in the marketplace, straight or surreptitious. Whether sex is like any other drive, desire or attraction, and if not, how it differs, has long been discussed and debated both scripturally and scientifically. For example, in Jewish law, sex is not considered shameful, sinful or obscene. Sex is not thought of as a necessary evil for the sole purpose of procreation. Although sexual desire comes from the *yetzer hara* (the evil impulse), it is no more evil than hunger or thirst, which also come from the yetzer hara. In Hinduism too, sex is not a taboo but sacred. Not only do many Hindu temples explicitly depict sex—and the celebrated *Kama Sutra* is still on the frontline of erotic books—but even the Upanishads have explicitly referred to it as an act of worship. The Brihadaranyaka Upanishad, for instance, refers to a woman's lap as the 'sacrificial altar'. More mundanely, or as a matter of fact, sex is sometimes compared to other desires, attractions and basic needs. Marquis de Sade, from whose name the words sadism and sadist are derived, wrote that 'sex is as important as eating or drinking and we ought to allow the one appetite to be satisfied with as little restraint or false modesty as the other'. But there are obvious differences. We do not die if we are deprived of sex for a prolonged period; but, on the other hand, the sensation of orgasm is a 'little death', which the French call *la petite mort*.

Whether it is pristine or profane, passion or instinct or impulse, drive or urge, it is most creative (creates another human being) and destructive (sexual jealousy is highly destructive), and acts as a kind of temptation that few can resist. Even saints and religious men have been seduced by women. Many powerful people and celebrities have confessed, or were later exposed. Some highly creative people are known to be heavily sexual, raising the question if there is any connection. Beside its outward attributes, sexuality is the closest we can get to erase separateness. It is an unquenchable longing, to unite 'flesh and spirit', to join another human being so intimately and intrusively that at least momentarily the two become one, and, in so doing, become an instrument of nature and to give life to another being. Charles Eisenstein says, "when we humans engage in sexual intercourse, we recover, for a few moments, a state of being that was once the baseline of existence in a time of greater union and less separation". Incidentally, we are now being told that it was not love that led to sex, and that our sexuality has, literally, if you will, fishy origins, that as far back as 385 million years ago, armored fish called placoderms, discovered, or stumbled upon intercourse.[60] Whoever might have started it first, after all these millions of years and billions of copulations and procreations, we still have not figured out if sex is sacred or simply a skill, whether it is doing god's work of creation or merely another bodily function. Sexual behavior is seamless, a driven desire to 'unbound' oneself, to liberate oneself from the confines of one body and one life. The great paradox of life is that we can go to the moon, cross the stars but we cannot cross the barrier and boundary of our own body, but much of 'being moral', being caring and compassionate requires precisely that: to go beyond and beneath our body. And that is what 'being in love' means and empowers—to put another human above us, to subordinate our pleasure and happiness to someone else's. Eisenstein says, "When we 'make love' we let down our boundaries on many levels. The euphemism is appropriate, love being nothing other than a release of the boundaries that separate us from another being".[61]

It is the 'sensual' version of spiritual longing, for wholeness without conscious awareness, a sharing of sexual energies to achieve 'oneness', and to ensure the continuum of creation. What sexually we do instinctively and passionately, we require supreme effort to replicate it in a social, non-sexual setting. When it comes to sex we are less fastidious of these divisions, barriers, boundaries, and borders. All walls that create so much tension, intolerance, violence and hatred do not matter, or become porous, when it comes to sex. Those whom we consider 'inferior', in terms of race, religion or faith, or ethnicity, or social status, whose men we are prepared to slaughter, are welcome where sex, the most intimate physical contact, is concerned. In war, men are killed, and women are raped, and only then killed or held captive. Masters have gone to bed with their slaves, including the great Thomas Jefferson. No one is an untouchable. Even someone who is considered an 'untouchable', a *Sudra* in Hinduism, is not untouchable where sex is involved. In that sense it is a leveler, a unifier. Those with whom we might not even be willing to share a meal, we do not mind uniting with in bed. We don't mind deriving 'pleasure' from those we hate. And the 'sex-goddess' Marilyn Monroe simplified it "Sex is a part of nature. I go along with nature".

What then really did God/Nature intend? Did it create two sexes primarily for sex? Could it not have found a more elegant way to tempt man to multiply himself than virtually creating two 'sub-species', who had to spend much of their lives trying to figure out how to deal, mate, and outflank each other? Why is it so difficult to complement each other instead of copying? Is there any hidden agenda? Is sex only heterosexual, as same-sex sex cannot make babies? Is sex all physical, sensual, and orgasmic? Is it nature's insurance to ensure the uninterrupted cycle of creation? What is 'natural', or 'unnatural' sex? Maybe nature wanted to have some fun at our expense, creating us individually with a hidden hunger for unity, and then watching us struggle to satisfy our hunger, in the process making an ass of ourselves. And to ensure that we never get 'enough' of it, or get tired of it, it has invested it with intoxicating recreational pleasure. And having done that, it felt 'safe' enough to link it with procreation, as the Bible puts it, as the way 'to multiply' mankind. Or, is there a more subtle, more profound purpose beyond our depth in the cosmic scheme of creation? All these questions are now assuming moral, political, nationalistic, and demographic overtones. Sex between members of the same gender, long considered as illegal, illicit, and immoral, are now accepted in many societies through the legalization of marriage within the same sex, male or female. The question if it is meant primarily for reproduction or recreation has become a hot button issue in many advanced countries. On a global scale, it is generally believed that the current human population of nearly 8 billion is excessive, and that to satisfy our appetite for natural resources at the current levels we might well need another earth. But the very countries that advocate 'population planning', a euphemism to pervert, or drastically reduce, future growth, and to reduce the overall numbers, are aggressively urging their own people to increase their birth rates.

This issue, along with the climate crisis, dramatically illustrates the dichotomy between national and global perspectives, that what might be good for the world might not be good for a country, and when there is a clash the national need prevails. And it underscores the ills of 'nationalism' and the imperative of a strong and effective global institution whose decisions are mandatory. Many 'developed' countries are worried not only about declining birth rates but also about changes in the 'sexual-profile' of their people. While on the one hand, modern society is sex-suffused, many are starved of sex, which some say is more than food-starvation. Some talk of 'an epidemic of sexless marriages'. One report goes on to say, "In the midst of a sex-saturated culture, overflowing with dramatic images of the female anatomy, a new phenomenon has developed: men losing interest in sex"[62] Many young people are eschewing not only marriage but sex altogether. One study found, "Japan is in danger of heading for extinction after researchers found that more and more of the country's young people are shunning the idea of marriage and having children. One in four unmarried men and women in their 30s say they have never had sex, and the majority of young women prefer the single life".[63] In 2007, Russia declared 12th September as the *National Day of Conception*, hoping that a day off to do a 'patriotic duty' will reverse the trend. Scandinavian countries, long known as some of the most liberal, tolerant, and progressive societies, and as responsible members of the global community, have left one's sexual preferences and purposes to individual inclination, based on the idea that a sexually 'satisfied' population is a hipper and more productive society, and, in so doing, implicitly underplayed sex as a means of procreation. But things have changed. Alarmed that the birth rate is below 2.1 children per female, the number required to replace the current population—the Danish birth rate is 1.7—many are openly egging couples to have more sex, and offering financial and other incentives for more babies. From a global perspective, and a more egalitarian alternative—and a more cost-effective way—would have been to welcome and encourage more migration and immigration from 'poorer' countries. That they did not choose this way is a reminder that the ideal of common humanity and global citizenship are as far away from realization as ever before, despite globalization and communication technologies. Technology has also revolutionized human attitude to sex. One can have secret trysts with strangers through the web, or buy sex toys in the anonymity of online shopping. Condoms, contraceptives, and pills… we now can have sex freed from both fear and responsibility. Recreation has won over procreation. Wherever there is a new technology, the sex industry is quick to adopt it. It does seem that modern man is content with the ecstatic pleasure that sex provides, which has so far stood the test of time; here too gadgets, toys, dolls, and tools have made inroads and threaten over time, like robots in the workplace, to replace the human in the bedroom, and to indulge our kinks. It is said that 'the previously taboo, everything from hook ups to queer sex and kink, have become more accessible'. A time may come when people find it less of a hassle and less taxing and more effortless to 'buy' a 'mate' of latex than go through the grind to get a human partner. It is being predicted that future sex is going to feature lots of sex with robots, and that 'it is going to be perfectly normal that people will be friends with robots, and that people will have sex with robots'. And no one will need to actually physically touch each other ever again. Technology could eventually eliminate the need to be in the same room with your sexual partner ever again. No ones knows whether all this innovation in the bedroom will make us sexually enlightened or lead to a dystopian future where humans give up on biological sex. Some experts have commented: "If a robot can give you more pleasure than a human, maybe the human should be trying harder". Try harder—to do what, to be who? The defining question of the next 10 years, we are told, is likely to be whether technology is used more to maintain intimacy with partners over great distances and enhance relationships, or create insular worlds where we can please ourselves—and to dispense with human intimacy for sexual satisfaction.

In one sense, our 'obsession' with copulating is perhaps symbolic of our desire to undo our accidental or intentional or enforced separation from each other in being born alone. In truth, we began as One, became multiple and in the end go back to the One. The first 'life' burst out in the tiniest little cell. The single cell organisms started combining and working together to form multicellular organisms, not through aggregation or aggression but through a magical complex of interrelationships maintaining a perfect cooperative co-ordination of disparate functions. The enduring tension between separateness and singularity, unity and multiplicity is perhaps symbolic of this 'original' separation and the yearning to become 'one' once again. The physical 'separateness' between man and man cannot be eliminated; two 'bodies' cannot fuse into one; what truly separates one from another is mental and psychological, which manifests as selfishness, self-centeredness and self-righteousness, slander and malice. In short, on pursuing the spiritual goal of 'oneness' of all forms of life with the awareness that we are all waves of the same ocean, the sparks of the same flame, we must realize that a giant step towards that 'goal' would be to eliminate, at least greatly diminish, the 'psychological space' between one man and another. For that, we should devise mechanisms to deepen and strengthen our emotions like consideration, compassion, kindness, and altruism so that physically we might remain different and distinct but functionally and emotionally we banish the various forms of divisiveness in the human world.

Our present times are considered, particularly in Western countries, sexually most liberated and promiscuous and permissive, and teenagers feel that sex is not only normal, but expected in any relationship, almost immediately. It is said that today's young people are the first generation 'raised' on pornography—there are an estimated 4.2 million porn sites in the world and the number is ever increasing—and many teens are less inhibited than they were 20 years ago. Sex has become pervasive and embedded in every walk of human life, be it social, political, for entertainment or marketing or media. And yet, one survey says that only 44% are 'sexually satisfied'. Sex is increasingly interwoven with violence and crime; it seems to draw out our darker side. We read news reports of children as young as two or five being 'raped' and murdered. Many working women, including in the armed forces, are complaining of sexual harassment by superiors and colleagues. Human sexuality increasingly appears out of control, and more and more people seem unable to resist their darkest desires. Although all statistics are questionable, many share the view that sexual violence is on the rise and that it is taking different forms including ethnic rapes and religious rapes. Another emerging trend is blurring the boundary between the sexes, leading to what is called 'asexuality' or 'neutralization of mankind'. There are few truly masculine men and feminine females. Men are showing feminine qualities and women male traits, thus acting against nature, which intended that the sexes, by being constituted wholly different in body, brain and bent, do not normally come into rivalry and antagonism in the fulfillment of their respective life-roles. We are, in effect, trying to refute a fundamental basis of creation: everything exists as a 'pair of opposites', the most fundamental of which is male and female. It is on 'duality in unity' that the cosmic order operates. It is hard to imagine what would be the evolutionary consequences of this phenomenon of gender-neutrality?

Sex, and its attendant rituals, have always been a very important part of all ancient cultures, and some customs are bizarre, but the most noteworthy feature is that it is the female who is given more options and choices. Whether or not what we generally consider as sexual 'fidelity', or 'exclusivity' are hard-wired or not is arguable. Some researchers, based on surveys and on anthropological records, as well as their study of the behavior of our closest primate cousins, chimpanzees and bonobos, make the case that humans actually evolved to be promiscuous. They attribute our modern sexual malaise to the mismatch between our Paleolithic libidos and the monogamous straitjacket into which we have forced ourselves. Technologies of all kinds like the internet have been central to the ways in which sex is understood and experienced in contemporary societies. And we can now connect with one another with unprecedented ease. Prowlers can see more potential mates in an hour on *Tinder* than any of our ancestors encountered in their lifetimes. Although one feels greatly distressed at such terrible happenings in today's world, it is no comfort to be told that much of this was foretold in ancient Hindu texts like the Ramayana, Mahabharata, Srimad Bhagavatam, Linga Purana, etc. These were written in the context of descriptions about moral decay in the current 'age' of *Kali Yuga*, described as an extended period of increasing sin. Some of the following predictions seem to fit into the contemporary scene with uncanny accuracy.

> The desire for sex in this age of Kali Yuga will be one of the most captivating of all preoccupations of the human race. It will distract most of society from the real spiritual purpose of life. People will want to satisfy themselves in this way and then use up so much energy, physical and otherwise, to meet their sensual desires. It will sap them of their time in life when they could be using this existence in much more important ways. Even pre-teenage girls will get pregnant. The primary cause will be the social acceptance of sexual intercourse as being the central

requirement of life. Men will have lustful thoughts, and so will women. Lust will be viewed as being socially acceptable. Prostitution or frivolous sexual activity will take away one's sense of bodily and mental cleanliness. It will increase addiction to trivial bodily pleasures, which will accelerate degradation and disease in society. For quick profits, debauched men and even women will capture and force many young girls, and boys as well, into a life of prostitution, which will often leave them hurt, wounded, diseased or ruined for life. Such exploitative culprits, who engage in human trafficking and force others into such an existence of engaging in the sex trade, will multiply like a virus in this age. And like any virus, if they are not destroyed completely, they will only reappear later in a different place. Womanliness and manliness will be judged according to one's sexual expertise. Marriage will cease to exist as a holy union. Men and women will simply live together on the basis of bodily attraction and verbal agreements, and only for sexual pleasure. Women will wander from one man to another. Young women will freely abandon their virginity. Some men will violate the wives of others and some, in the indiscriminate rage of lust, will go (wherever she may be) with any woman.

We can engage every single word in the above expose to describe the prevailing scenario and situation in the world today. It makes us wonder how anyone can so vividly sketch what is going to happen several thousands of years in the future. So, what does this, and other dire forebodings, mean? Having been born in these times, are we simply fated to be immoral and evil, that we are being driven by forces of implacable fate in everything we do? Does it, therefore, absolve us of feelings of shame and guilt? The question that needs to be thought through is this: how will our libidinous behavior impact human future and evolution? Will carefree copulation become the 'chosen' instrument of ultimate self-destruction? Will humans ever be liberated from the basic biological needs, especially sex, that drive our evolutionary past, and how will it affect human behavior? Will human sexuality, unbridled and on the rampage, further corrupt, enfeeble and defile human passion and personality and accelerate decay and destruction? Or will we find a way to direct that awesome energy towards human redemption and renewal? And, as many now are saying 'humans are still evolving today', how will the current dedication of so much of our mental and psychic time and energy for sex influence that evolution and our desire to be better than we were yesterday? For, our desires and passions know no reason nor respect any bounds or boundaries. For long, they were driven by the struggle to survive. Now that it is not so compelling, how will they reflect and react? How will the imminent 'sexual revolution' play out? Will mechanization of sex relieve us of the tension of human sexual pursuit, and release psychic and spiritual space? Or, will it, coupled with intra-gender sex, make us more mad in our mindset as it is not the kind of human sexuality that nature has intended, and further strengthen our destructive impulses?

The bottom line is that our sexual behavior is but a part of our overall behavior, and our 'behavior', as we have been stressing, is but a reflection and extension of the state of the 'war within'. Sex being a primal passion is more susceptible to its influence and impact than other aspects of human life. Every human attribute and emotion gets magnified manifold in the company of sex. Pleasure, pain, passion, jealousy, revenge, they all are more intense than in any other state of awareness. They can make man a maniac and, if properly propelled, a mahatma. The fact is that we are all sexual beings; it is through that very route that we are all born, but we are more than that. The path of sexual transformation is not about rapidly indulging in sex, denying sex, running away from sex, or even overcoming the desire for sex. From ancient times, many have envisioned transforming sexual energy into a spiritual tool, more than as a means of recreation or procreation. Besides Tantric and Taoist sexual energy practices, there are several other references to the secret powers within sex. The Jewish Kabbalah for instance, refers to sexual desire as the deepest spiritual expression, and in yoga, our sacred sexual energy lies dormant until awakened through what is called the *Kundalini* way. Psychologist Carl Jung wrote about the notion of sexual alchemy (similar to Freud's sexual sublimination). All of this implies that, with the right will, we can transform the raw passion from our libidos into sublime creativity. But, sadly, all that is happening in matters of sex offers, more than any other, evidence that the fortunes of that which is good, noble and righteous in us, is waning and getting weaker, and the evil in us has gained advantage and ascendancy. It is but natural that it affects the most basic of all urges that has always been a dominant force in human affairs, even in prehistoric times. If we want to gain some control over our sexuality, without which we can have no control over the direction of human development, the only way, and a powerful way, is to reverse the fortunes of the war by strengthening the forces of good. It is a critical key to 'winning' the war.

Our Two 'Hearts' and the War Within

The question about morality of war has long been discussed. Morality is a crucial dimension of human life. We have long agonized over what we ought to do, should do, must not do, or may do, to make our life fulfilling and at the same time, make sure that it does not jeopardize others' lives. Is 'morality' man-made, a social convenience and necessity, or is it a divine injunction? If so, where is it codified and what is its irreducible essence? What is moral behavior and when is it morally right to do wrong things? Is a religious person inherently 'moral'? Should any 'war', which necessarily is violent and involves mass killing and maiming, be deemed moral, immoral, amoral, or evil? It has been said that 'morality has no place in the assessment of war'; or perhaps, more factually, we can say: morality, by definition and design, has no place in war. And hence the question of 'assessment' does not arise. In fact, one might say that man invented 'war' precisely to abandon 'morality' of every kind; to give license to evil of every imagination. But almost all religions that do not condemn war *per se*, sanction war, if not glorify it, in certain circumstances. There is also an implied sense that wars, which essentially entail the sudden death of large numbers of human beings, are necessary as a way, or the only way, to maintain the life-balance on earth. It is a part of the package of 'being human', nature's ruse to counter the human survival capacity. Basically 'war' is really a composite of two of our worst traits: avarice and aggression in an organized and virulent form. Some have argued that human beings, especially men, are inherently violent and, while this violence is repressed in normal society, it needs the occasional outlet provided by war. When we are not actually at 'war', our inherent urges like avarice, aggression, and violence get exposed in other non-war-like ways, no less lethal and more embedded in our daily life. Many have suggested that war-making is fundamentally cultural, imbibed by nurture rather than nature. Still, we cannot say it is another animal instinct; like that of a tiger, who needs to kill to live. It means that it is not germane to being human but is now as much 'human' as anything else. What is intrinsic is the 'war within'. The 19th-century Tibetan Lama Jamgon Kongtrul characterized the 'war' thus: "From the outside, we appear to be genuine *dharma* practitioners; on the inside, our minds have not blended with the dharma. We conceal our afflictions (called *klesas* in Sanskrit) inside like a poisonous snake. Yet when difficult situations arise, the hidden faults of a poor practitioner come to light". In fact, the 'war without' has become such a huge part of human history because the wrong side is winning the war within.

What incubates inside is 'perception' and what happens outside is 'behavior'; both of which influence each other reciprocally and simultaneously. What we perceive is what we become. The ancient rishi *Ashtavakra* says, "The reason why we grow old, age and die is we see other people grow old, ageing, and dying. And what we see we become". Our predicament is that we do not know exactly what goes on inside us, but we do know that some kind of turmoil is constantly at work. We seem pulled by different forces, even from 'outside' we can sense it and feel it; as if someone other than 'we' are calling the shots. We do not know exactly how but we do know that our brain, body, and behavior are connected and even our heart. We use almost involuntary expressions like 'I just feel that way'; I am in two minds; I have the gut feeling; I hear voices within or an inner voice; and I cannot prove it but I believe it, etc.—all symbolic of the 'war within'. When Hermann Hesse said he listens to 'the teachings my blood whispers to me' he was referring to a voice from within. When we say 'I doubt it', it could well be someone suggesting what we call a 'second opinion'. When we say 'I am not so sure', it could be a word of caution offered by a more sober internal impulse. The trouble is that the inner voice talks to us in a soft whisper, and we cannot hear it in the downpour of the din of modern life. That is why many mystics and saints stay silent, to be able to listen to what the Bible calls the "still, small voice within". Our external 'wars' are bloody events interspersed with periods of 'peace', or *absence* of a war. The 'war within' is a continuum, without any interregnum or interruption, sometimes intense and fierce, and sometimes subdued and subtle, but always involuntary and effortless. If we do not know who is fighting whom and what the rules of 'warfare' are, how can we take sides or try to influence the outcome? But, maybe, it is extreme naiveté to think of the inner struggle as a 'fight' or 'war', in the sense in which these words occur in the external world. Both imply that one side must vanquish or destroy or decimate the other side, or the opponent, and that we would be 'better off' if we manage to eliminate the 'bad' side. This is a unique kind of 'war' that should not conclude with a total victory or defeat of either of the two; that would be a greater catastrophe than the war itself. 'Both sides', the 'good' and the 'bad' have legitimate roles to play as they are the two sides of the dwanda, and it would be a catastrophe if one side manages to totally wipe out the other. Indeed, one might even say that one can drive creative power from the tension of the opposites, from the dialectics of dwanda. What has gone awry and what needs to be promoted is 'cooperative co-existence' and 'inner harmony'. This brings up the timeless question: why do humans fight when they can share and live in a spirit of synergy? Is it biological or evolutionary? We fight because we don't like sharing, whether it is food or shelter, fame or fortune, success or glory. It is this inability to partake that is at the root of all friction, conflict, and war in the world. We want to possess, own everything. Our mind likes exclusivity, not inclusiveness.

Nature is providing us within our own selves what we 'rationally' seek in daily life: choices, and alternatives before we 'make up our minds'. The only difference is that what we decide outside is a 'conscious' act, and what happens within is opaque and impervious to our will and wish. We do not know whether it is also 'conscious' but at a different level or depth of consciousness or the 'unconscious', which also is in fact another dimension of consciousness. Whichever is the way, we have to reckon with two realities: we have almost no say in what transpires in the womb of our being, in the vortex of our vitals; and whatever happens there manifests in the way we perceive, relate and connect with everything external to our own selves. The key therefore is to get some hold on the war within for a better world. That is why the Buddha said, "It is better to conquer yourself than to win a thousand battles. Then the victory is yours. It cannot be taken from you, not by angels or by demons, heaven or hell".

Kurukshetra—Arjuna's War Within

An analogy often invoked to mirror the war within is the great *Kurukshetra* war in the Indian epic Mahabharata. This war, which lasted 18 days, took place at a place in North India called *Kurukshetra*. What is unique about this war was that it happened in the direct presence of the Divine, Lord Krishna, the only perfect incarnation of Lord Vishnu. It resulted in all that horrific bloodshed, killing of a brother by a brother, of a student by a teacher, of a grandson by a grandfather, not to speak of tens of thousands of others. It was a war that not even Lord Krishna could prevent, although it is open to question whether really He could not or did not want to prevent. In the very end, Krishna asks Arjuna, "O Dhanajaya! Conqueror of wealth, have you heard it with an attentive mind? Have your ignorance and illusions been dispelled?" Of course, Arjuna said 'yes'. It is important to recognize that what dispelled Arjuna's moral qualms about fighting was not the answers and arguments of Krishna, but the absolute and unconditional surrender of his ego at the Lord's feet. It is also important to digest the truth that Krishna's real target audience was not just Arjuna, but all humanity for all times. The goal of the Bhagavad Gita was not only to induce Arjuna to 'win' his war within, but also to help us 'win' our own inner spiritual wars.

The Kurukshetra war offered an opportunity to Lord Krishna to propound the great Bhagavad Gita, which has served as a beacon and a balm for tens of millions of people, some of whom, paradoxically, were pacifists like Tolstoy and Thoreau and Emerson. Thoreau called it the 'First of Books'. Gandhi said, "I have received more nourishment from the Gita than my body has from my mother's milk". Tens of thousands, including the '*Narayana sena*' (Krishna's own army), were killed, through means fair and foul. Here is an important moral issue worth noting. Krishna gave His own army to the evil Duryodhana, when the latter, along with Arjuna, came to seek Krishna's help. The intriguing question is, why didn't Krishna refuse to provide any assistance, and say that He would only help the righteous side? The answers to such questions are that there are no absolutes, even when it comes to good or evil, and one must choose sometimes among conflicting compulsions. The right course for one person might not be right one for another person in the same circumstance. And it is possible that for the same question there could be more than one right answer, which is what quantum physics now tells us. Each one must decide for oneself. That is why, it is so important to have the right consciousness, and that is why, consciousness-change is so important for correct decision-making. The moral message is that whether we do good or bad, it is the motive and purpose that matters, and has to be done regardless of whatever consequences, good or bad, that might follow. To a limited extent, it does mean that the question of end versus means has to be resolved contextually, governed by the overarching principle that the larger good should prevail over the lesser need. That was why the grandsire and 'godly' Bhishma, who was duty-bound, fought for the evil side and justified his own 'unfair' defeat as his penance, and as necessary for the safety of Hastinapura, his motherland. It was Bhishma, not only Krishna, who could have prevented the war had he forsaken his vow of obeying whoever sat on the throne of Hastinapura. Bhishma held his personal honor higher than what was best for society. That was why, despite being a great man and despite having the gift of choosing his own death, he had to experience such a painful death, lying on a bed of arrows for 58 days, with the arrows protruding from his own body. Bhishma's moral quandary holds lessons for us. It means in our own daily life, where we all play limited roles, as employees or workers, in large organizations, we are still morally responsible for the final outcome, based among others on our own contribution and work. It means who you work for is as important, if not more, as what you actually do. In other words, even if you have no control over what you do, whatever you do in your own narrow niche carries moral accountability.

It was said that where there is dharma there is Krishna, and where Krishna is there is victory. The Kurukshetra, both in mythology and in the popular mind, symbolizes the victory of dharma or righteousness and justice over adharma, evil and injustice. The first verse of the Gita refers to the Kurukshetra as the *dharma-kshetra*, or 'the field of dharma'. One wonders how a place of war, bloodshed, and massacre can be called a holy place. The implication is that nothing is either good or evil *per se*, nothing is sacred or sinful on its own. Everything is relative, contextual; even mass killing. It is the intent and the purpose that determine what it is. But then, who determines? In the minds of both opponents waging the war, it was 'justified' and 'necessary'; or else there would have been no war. And it does mean that at times the ends do justify the means. And Kurukshetra was not just the location of the brutal carnage. It is also the birthplace of the Bhagavad Gita, about which the great Adi Sankara said, "From a clear knowledge of the Bhagavad Gita, all the goals of human existence become fulfilled". Albert Einstein said, "I have made the Bhagavad Gita the main source of my inspiration and guide for the purpose of scientific investigations and formation of my theories". In turn, it was expounded by Lord Krishna to help the prince Arjuna to 'win' his own 'war within'—between the forces of doubt, despair, demoralization, apathy, and moral ambivalence, and the forces of resoluteness, decisiveness, ethical duty, and moral clarity—so that he could wage and win the war between dharma and adharma, between good and evil, in the external world.

Gandhi called the Gita an "Allegory in which the battlefield is the soul, and Arjuna, man's higher impulses struggling against evil". Swami Vivekananda further remarked, "This Kurukshetra war is only an allegory. When we sum up its esoteric significance, it means the war which is constantly going on within man between the tendencies of good and evil". We must remember that all the characters are flawed one way or the other, and the war is not for the triumph of flawless good over absolute evil, but of the lesser evil over the greater evil. And as Carl Jung noted, "in the last resort there is no good that cannot produce evil, and no evil that cannot produce good". Inside each one of us there is a Kurukshetra; and all the characters in that epic are also within each of us: a *Dhritarashtra* (willfully blinded by *moha*, undue attachment), a *Duryodhana* (knowing what is right, but unable to resist the wrong due to jealousy), a *Sakuni* (scheming and trying to settle scores), a *Karna* (noble at heart, but ruined by misplaced loyalty), an *Arjuna* (righteous but wavering), a *Dharmaraja* (noble but vulnerable), a *Kunti* (virtuous but fearful of society), a *Draupadi* (who was born through fire, whose humiliations act as a trigger for the battle of Kurukshetra). And perhaps a mini-Krishna, too. No character is flawless, just as no human can be. Which particular character, or a mix of characteristics, manifests at what time is hard to tell. At the end of the Kurukshetra, what remained were the decimated Kauravas, a despondent Dharmaraja, the bereaved Pandavas, a 'cursed' Krishna, and a river of blood. And Krishna justified all that, and even the use of unfair means, for the triumph of dharma. It is sometimes said that great wars take place to reduce what is called '*bhoobharam*', the burden of Mother Earth. If that be the case, and if a horrendous war like the Kurukshetra was required then, in the *Dwapara Yuga*, what might be needed now, in this *Kali Yuga*, the most immoral of all yugas, with most of over 7.7 billion humans choosing the path of *preyas* (pleasure) over the path of *sreyas* (goodness)?

The archetypal meaning is that within each of us a battle rages between selfish impulses that ignore the claims of justice and justness, and a realization that ultimately we are all connected in a unity that embraces all humanity and the whole world. Arjuna is our conscious mind, which must make the choice of how we will live. The wicked cousins are our impulses to self-centeredness, lust for wealth and avarice, and anger and hatred. Krishna is the divine essence within us, our higher Self, which is always available to rein in the horses of our feelings and thoughts, and to guide us in the battle of life, if we will only surrender and seek that help. It tells us that we each have within ourselves the answers to all our questions and confusions. We only have to call upon that inner power to discover who we are, what we can trust, and how we should act. Sri Aurobindo compared Arjuna to a 'struggling human soul'. The Kurukshetra must be viewed as a gripping and gory battle between dharma and adharma, good and righteousness and evil. Just as the Pandavas and Kauravas were first cousins, so are our inherent 'tendencies'. Like the Kurukshetra, our 'war within' too is a fratricidal war, both are endogenous and both are legitimate. In the spiritual sense, as Swami Nikhilananda says, "Arjuna represents the individual soul, and Sri Krishna the Supreme Soul dwelling in every heart. Arjuna's chariot is the body. The blind king Dhritarashtra is the mind under the spell of ignorance, and his hundred sons are man's numerous evil tendencies. The battle, a perennial one, is between the power of good and the power of evil. The warrior who listens to the advice of the Lord speaking from within will triumph in this battle and attain the Highest Good". At the end of the battle, the 'evil' Kauravas were defeated and destroyed and the 'virtuous' Pandavas, led by Yudhishthira ascended the throne of the Hastinapura kingdom. In that battle, the real 'hero' or the '*Sutradhari*' is Lord Krishna, who, without himself bearing arms guides the Pandavas to victory through a variety of ruses. How do we apply that principle to our time and age? We face two moral imperatives. On the one hand we do see raw and ravenous evil even in our daily lives; on the other hand, our moral choice-making has become extremely complex with competing priorities and claims: family, professional, social, national, economic, ecological, religious, and so on. The human mind has never been good at harmonizing conflicting obligations; it is now all at sea. The more perilous development is that we are unable even to separate 'evil' from 'good'. Thomas Merton says, "The greatest temptations are not those that solicit our consent to obvious sin, but those that offer us great evils masking as the greatest goods".[64] And the 'self-righteousness' of individuals, races, religions, and nations is a primary source of a lot of evil. Our 'righteousness' about self-righteousness is awesome, blinds us to others' righteousness, and breeds conceit and callousness and robs us of a robust sense of guilt. We must also not forget that 'it is the evil that lies in ourselves that is ever least tolerant of the evil that lies in others'. The inference we should draw from our history is that much of evil has been committed not by those people who wallow in evil, but by those convinced of their own righteousness and equally of the evil of their victims.

We experience this phenomenon in our own lives. That is how we are able to carry on with our lives while hurting, humiliating, and trampling over other people. If we are convinced of the righteousness of our own unrighteous actions, then we feel no guilt; indeed we think we are the 'victims' and the 'victims' are our oppressors. The other aspect, often underemphasized, is what is called 'institutional evil', committed by 'conscientious' individuals as a part of or on behalf of, institutions in legitimate discharge of their duties. A recent post explains: "The institutions seem to be set up to put pressure on underpaid district managers, to make cheating easy, and to make it easy for the corporations to turn a blind eye to what's going on. The culpability of the whole is greater than the sum of the culpabilities of the parts".[65] A huge slice of contemporary evil is in this category, and the institution that ranks first is the State itself. The workplace, more than the home, is the locus of evil, and the institutional evil, more than the explicit individual evil, is the instrument. Although everyone condemns 'evil' most also agree that an evil-free world is impossible. After his 'experience with God', Dr. Eben Alexander writes, "Evil was present in all the other universes as well, but only in the tiniest trace amounts because without it free will was impossible, and without free will there could be no growth—no forward movement, no chance for us to become what God longed for us to be. Horrible and all-powerful as evil sometimes seemed to be in a world like ours, in the larger picture love was overwhelmingly dominant, and it would ultimately be triumphant".[66]

We cannot get rid of 'evil'. We must live with it in some form or the other; everyone is capable of some sort of evil sometime or the other. So few seem capable of declining an 'invitation of evil'. Evil is not alien to any of us; the war within is the war between good and evil. All this is a truism but what does it mean in our daily life? We cannot willingly become an instrument of evil; we must fight tooth and nail both within and without, not because God wills it but because 'being bad' doesn't let us feel 'good' about ourselves. As a balance or a counter we must nurture and cultivate 'love' which man is capable of 'naturally'. Love is so enchanting that "for the sake of love heaven longs to become earth and gods to become man".[67] Rudolf Steiner says that "spiritual beings must love; but only human beings can choose to". Viktor Frankl (*Man's Search For Meaning*) wrote, "Love is the only way to grasp another human being in the innermost core of his personality. No one can become fully aware of the very essence of another human being unless he loves him". Erich Fromm (*The Art of Living*, 1956) says, "Love is not a sentiment which can be easily indulged in by anyone, regardless of the level of maturity reached by him". It is an 'art' that has to be learnt the same way any other art has to be. Whether love is an art or science, an emotion or energy, the fact is applied in daily life extremely narrowly or divisively. Love is giving, not taking; it is inclusive, not exclusive, and not reciprocal. Much of 'love' has come to represent what it is not supposed to be. We love someone but loathe someone else that person loves; we love our religion but decry another religion; we love our country but at best we are indifferent to any other country. We 'love' humanity but very few people we actually are able to love. That is why there is so much insensitivity, intolerance and hatred in the world. And that is why evil is both banal and brazen in our world.

Brazen, stark, direct, revolting evil most of us can and must avoid; but we must strive ceaselessly to refrain from banal evil. And to be on guard against what Hannah Arendt wrote about the 'interdependence of thoughtlessness and evil'. But human life, perhaps all life, is such that it is impossible to 'live' without hurting anyone anytime, consciously or unconsciously. What one could do is to minimize and mitigate it and 'make it up' by helping anyone that needs and wants help. And it is useful to bear in mind what Dante said, "He who sees a need and waits to be asked for help is as unkind as if he had refused it". Even if we cannot always be able live up to that soaring standard that ought to be the direction of everyday effort. Martin Luther King Jr. said, "Life's most persistent and urgent question is, 'What are you doing for others?'" He also said the moral question is not, 'If I stop to help this man, what will happen to me?', but, 'If I do *not* stop to help this man, what will happen to *him*?' The practical question is: under what circumstances are we, individually and as a generation, morally justified in violating norms and ethics, and for what kind of higher causes or ends, in today's context? Who is to make the call? But when once we accept, one moral transgression justifies and permits another, even if 'minor' immorality, then we lose all control over our behavior, which is what the 'war within' is all about. The key is constant, willful, relentless effort. Martin Luther King said, "In the final analysis, God does not judge us by the separate incidents or separate mistakes that we make, but by the total bent of our lives. In the final analysis, God knows that his children are weak and they are frail. In the final analysis, what God requires is that your heart is right. Salvation is not reaching the destination of absolute morality. But it is being in the process and on the right road".[68] What are important are right intention and right effort, which also happen to be two of the eight elements of the Buddhist Eight-fold path. Hinduism calls them '*chitta suddhi*' and '*abhyasa*'.

There are three important differences between the battle at Kurukshetra and our own 'war within'. One, while the war of the Mahabharata was an eighteen-day bloody battle, the war we wage is a continuum, without a break; in fact a chain of billions of battles. Two, as there is no final end, so is there no final victor or vanquished. It is a see-saw battle, with fluctuating fortunes, and with different 'victors' even every day and in every situation. Three, there is no Krishna, to guide and help the 'Pandavas' of our consciousness. And just as without Krishna the Pandavas would have been defeated, so is it now. There is another 'troubling' outcome of the Kurukshetra that we should not ignore, but out of which it is difficult to draw any clear message. In one sense, there was no 'victor'; no one was 'happy'. King Yudhishthira went into deep depression after realizing the carnage the war caused, including the killing of his own elder brother Karna (he did not know then). And the real finale of the war was not the coronation of Yudhishthira but the destruction of the entire clan of Lord Krishna himself by their own hand, caused by a curse of the queen Gandhari, the mother of the 'evil' Duryodhana and his ninety-nine brothers. So, if the war was nothing but wholesale killing, not only of the evil forces but also of the dharmic or virtuous, then what does it mean and what lessons should we learn from it? At one point, Krishna justifies the massacre as necessary to lighten the burden on *Bhoomata*, that is, Mother Earth. So, was it evil people who constituted the 'burden'? And if so, why was it that the righteous too had to be sacrificed? And if it was simply a question of reduction of human 'numbers', which was minuscule at that time as compared to present times, should we 'welcome' another war or a nuclear Armageddon? Some scholars even say that the world's macabre fascination with nuclear war is just the latest repeat in a series of blunders that human technology seems obsessed with repeating, and many of today's deserts were the pre-historic battlefields of 'nuclear' wars. Perhaps, dreaded weapons such as the *Brahmastra* were actually nuclear warheads, at least what we very recently termed weapons of mass destruction. Without such weapons, it would be highly unlikely that in eighteen days, millions could be killed with swords and primitive arrows.

Whether or not any of this is true, the point to ponder over is this: if the Almighty—about whom the Quran says, "To Him belongs what is in the heavens and what is in the earth. He is the Lofty, the Mighty"—was at that time 'directly' and 'physically' present and still a wholesale slaughter was unavoidable to restore the moral balance on earth, what about now, with over seven billion humans hell bent on destroying nature and directly endangering earth, the very Bhoomata to save which Krishna said the great massacre was needed? The Mahabharata war, it was said, was caused by Duryodhana's greed, jealousy and hatred of the Pandavas. Those three attributes, plus malice, are now running amok on earth and have seeped into the deepest crevices of human consciousness, and have fundamentally altered the human psyche itself. And this time around, Mother Earth herself is in the direct line of fire. The fact is that none can tell if we are all, each of us in our daily lives and in the minutest choices we make every day, simply playing our deemed parts towards a pre-ordained end, as everyone in the Mahabharata did. Could it be that, like then, so now, there are no 'villains' (or everyone is) and no 'heroes' (or perhaps everyone is)? If everyone is playing a pre-ordained part, whether that 'part' was a 'reward' or 'penalty' for what we did before or what Fate ordained for us as a part of a Cosmic Play, what can we do now, except to play that part as well as we are supposed to and derive as much 'pleasure' as we are allowed to have? It means that we should do everything 'professionally' and not take anything 'personal' too personally.

Empathy vs Reason

One can sketch many utopias and dystopias about the future of humankind, but two things are increasingly becoming clearer everyday. One, we must get some kind of grip on technology and on its seemingly unstoppable momentum and direction. But that need not be, even should not be, what Bill Joy described as 'technological relinquishment', that is to abandon all technological research, to save us from otherwise certain early extinction. Two, it is now becoming increasingly clear that the human organism, as it has evolved, is simply not suited or equipped to make the kind of adjustments and sacrifices necessary to solve any of the 'existential risks' humanity faces, like climate change and potential pandemics of suicide and homicide. There is also an enhanced awareness that sensory capacities alone cannot impel us towards empathetic engagement with others. Adam Smith articulated that view and wrote, "Though our brother is upon the rack, as long as we ourselves are at ease, our senses will never inform us of what he suffers. They never did and never can carry us beyond our own persons, and it is by the imagination only that we form any conception of what are his sensations. His agonies, when they are thus brought home to ourselves, when we have this adopted and made them our own, begin at last to affect us, and we then tremble and shudder at the thought of what he feels".[69] It means that our mode of perception, our sensory experiences, our impulses and reflexes, which condition our way of life, do not by their own momentum lead or let us become empathetic beings. We do not know whether or not there is another world, called *Noumenon*, a realm beyond our sensory capacities. It exists, so it certainly seems, as Kant opined, 'completely unknowable to humans'. As a result, some have suggested that the only way humanity can overcome the present potentially cataclysmic crises is for man to re-engineer himself—'to fiddle with physiology and tinker with the inner mechanisms, mechanics of life at its most biologic level'—into a 'new man' who will be not a 'bionic man' but a 'better being', more empathetic and less environmentally demanding. In other words, to 'fiddle' and 'tinker' with what nature intended; which is what medicine is all about. We do not let the disabled and the sick die 'naturally' without any external interference so that nature eventually produces more suitable and better specimens down the line. The effort so far has been to make man stronger, smarter, angelic, and empower and enable him to live eternally or make every man a potential modern-day equivalent of Bhishma of the Mahabharata, who was given the boon to determine when he should die. The problem is that that will not equip us any better than the 'existential threats' we face. If any, they will probably turn them from potential to probable. If our purpose is to so re-make man so that he is 'most probably' more capable of becoming a 'problem-solver' then 'problem-aggravator', then we need to alter the direction of our dreams. Such a 'man' will have to have a body smaller in size with a built-in aversion to meat eating, and automatically and effortlessly capable of living with fewer resources, capable of withstanding hardships like heat and cold without air-conditioning and heating... Some suggest what is called 'pharmacological enhancement of empathy and altruism', as a way to overcome that which retards positive personal change, which will empower us to conquer 'weakness of will', about which Arjuna and St. Paul complained, and enhance our empathetic and compassionate capabilities through drugs. It is even being proposed that if humans could be 'fitted' with cat-like eyes, we would not need so much lighting in the night, and we could greatly reduce global energy usage![70] The basic premise is that the only way to make our behavior socially, environmentally and generationally sensitive is to radically mutate our body and brain. Some scientists say, drawing on the analogy of computer hardware and software, that 'it is possible to reverse-engineer the biological software and then modify it however we like. This means we can re-engineer the human body to behave however we want (or at least, to do anything that is physically possible)'. But the essential question is: does it amount to consciousness-change, which is what is required?

We are really in a fix. We know that if we are really and wholly left to our own wits and 'wisdom', most of us cannot change in the direction we want to change. Our minds are too feeble, too conditioned and corrupted for us mobilize the 'iron will' we need. We need to cleanse our consciousness of a multitude of toxins but we do not know how, and even if we do what they entail is simply beyond the capabilities and resilience of our body and brain. No longer can the proverbial prick of conscience save us from moral temptations. We have long been told that goodness and good feelings, empathy and benevolence never go in vain, and those who show them benefit as much, if not more, as the recipients. While that has been traditional wisdom, exemplified by the statement 'evil is empathy erosion', researchers now offer as usual a mixed picture, confusing our already confused minds. As a case in point, empathy fits very well. Even if we do not lead a life of empathy, we do instinctively believe that what the world badly needs is more 'empathy'.

We have recently had a flurry of books making the same point, two among them being, *The Empathic Civilization* (2010), by Jeremy Rifkin, and *Humanity on a Tightrope* (2012) by Paul Ehrlich and Robert Ornstein. They make the powerful argument that empathy has been the main driver of human progress and that we need more of it if our species is to survive. Ehrlich and Ornstein want us "to emotionally join a global family". Rifkin calls for us to make the leap to "global empathic consciousness". But some who spend a lot of time and thought on the subject say that empathy can do a lot of good, but also lot of bad too, and that it is ill-suited to confront today's problems like genocides and global warming, and that "empathy will have to yield to reason if humanity is to have a future".[71] Psychologist Paul Bloom complains that empathy is "parochial, narrow-minded, and innumerate". But it is 'reason', not empathy—the brain, not the heart—that made human decision-making so flawed and human society so fragmented. The implication in the 'case against empathy' is that empathy is good but empathy can induce, or seduce, us to make moral judgments or support social policies that might be harmful. The anti-empathy logic posits that empathy is such a powerful and potent moral emotion that, instead of being an uplifting force it can be a destabilizer, and that it can draw away our attention from more important issues to less important, narrower cases of specific individuals or groups. The premise is that empathy cannot cover the whole of humanity, and the problems we face are worldwide and therefore empathy is not the appropriate tool. Put differently, our 'empathy' to a few, usually the 'near and dear' can be potentially deleterious to the rest. Our very reaction to death differs from the near and dear to the rest of mankind. Their death shakes us and we are not consoled by the reality that it is the common lot of humanity. Tennyson wrote, "That loss is common would not make; My own less bitter, rather more". The divide between the two—the ones we care for and those we don't give a damn about—is morally the most corrosive of all. All our life is consumed by immediacy and intimacy. We cannot ensure equal treatment of all and it is natural to be partial towards those who are a 'family' or a friend. But it need not lead to callous indifference and to behavior that is toxic to the rest of humanity. The fatal flaw of this thesis is that empathy is treated as a finite resource, and that an empathetic individual is not socially relevant or can be an input into collective effort to solve common problems. On the contrary, such a person can be a more powerful agent to create and coalesce a kind of consciousness and mindset, which is indispensable for any species-wide transformation. 'Empathy' is not like fossil fuel; it is like sunshine. The epicenter may be local but its reach can be global. And contrary to the postulate that empathy and morality are not connected and that the less empathetic are not necessarily morally apathetic, the two are mutually reinforcing. If we can enhance and deepen 'empathy' we can make ourselves better beings, more sensitive, more responsible and responsive, and that certainly will be helpful in solving global problems. 'Empathy' might not be the 'open sesame' or the magic bullet, but to say that with more 'reason' we can change our lifestyles, be energy efficient, turn away from the use of fossil fuels and become 'global citizens' does not stand to any test of 'reason-based' reasonable assumption. The mother of reason is our brain/mind, and at least for the past three thousand plus years we have been virtual slaves of our minds. That which dominates us cannot but be responsible for what and where we are as human beings; it is our exclusive reliance on logical reasoning, capacity that caused the problems. 'Empathy' comes from the heart and it is to the heart we now have to turn, for our very survival.

Of Head and Heart

The real problem that has thwarted all attempts towards finding a *modus operandi* for human transformation is that the human is neither inherently 'moral' nor 'rational'. Had it been otherwise, the world would have been a different place. Rationality in broad terms is to hold ourselves answerable to the relentless rigor of logic and evidence, even when it is uncomfortable to do so. When we are rational, we try to avoid our natural biases and preferences, like paying heed only to evidence that supports our preferred options or selfish interests. We have long claimed uniqueness on both fronts. Morality is about the character of our actions and how they affect other people. Being moral is to shift the focus of concern from the self to another, not to do to others what you wouldn't want done to you. And to always factor in the larger cause and common good. Neither being rational or irrational is a sufficient test of human character. Our boast has long been that 'other creatures may have wings or claws or sharper eyes, but none… have this unique power of reason, not even a weak or low variety of it. We alone have science, morality, and philosophy, and through them wisdom, for we alone are rational'.[72] But science itself also says that "There are inherent limits to logic that can't be resolved, and they bedevil our minds too".[73] And we associate 'reason' with 'reasonableness'. But as Bernard Shaw rued, "The reasonable man adapts himself to the world. The unreasonable man adapts the world to himself. All progress depends upon the unreasonable man. All my life I have refused to be reasonable". Adapting the world to yourself 'swimming upstream' can be stimulating and challenging, but then has very little to do with being unrighteous.

While this has been the general refrain, there have always been doubters and dissenters even among philosophers and men with high reasoning capabilities. David Hume, for one, held that 'reason is wholly inert, and cannot by itself alone move us to action, as it would have to do if it were to be truly practical'. Bertrand Russell minced no words and stated, "Man is a rational animal. So at least we have been told. Throughout a long life I have searched diligently for evidence in favor of this statement. So far, I have not had the good fortune to come across it".[74] Hume also wrote, 'Reason is, and ought only to be the slave of the passions'—we might add senses. If that were so, how can that be 'rational'? It means that practical reason alone cannot give rise to moral motivation; that we don't and cannot always act reasonably or logically. Emotions can get the better of us and override logic. The fact also is that our senses do not alert us automatically about what is good for us or evil, what furthers our life or endangers it, what goals we should pursue and what means will achieve them, on what values our life becomes better, what course of action it requires. This means we do not have *in situ* capacities to be either purely rational or wholly moral. Most of the time we fall, so to speak, between the two stools, unwilling to choose, and often ending up with the worst of both. Deep within we are not sure what really and actually we are, living lives 'rationally', by the exercise of our logical and reasoning faculties, which means purely brain-driven or morally, which means where necessary to deny one's own interests and to struggle, to live a life of service, sharing, and usefulness to someone or the other most of the time. But such a life of *seva* or service must be faithful to the principles of justness and fairness. Stealing, for example, is also a kind of 'sharing' but it is not considered moral. But we have someone like Saint Thomas Aquinas telling us that "It is not theft, properly speaking, to take secretly and use another's property in a case of extreme need: because that which he takes for the support of his life becomes his own property by reason of that need". That sounds 'moral' but the devil, as they say, is in the detail. Considering that almost everyone has some 'extreme need' sometime or the other, how and who should determine? Even if we bring the 'extreme' down to the 'basic' like food, shelter and clean water what kind of food or roof over the head is an entitlement, the absence of which becomes an 'extreme need'? But the spirit of Aquinas' statement is sound; which is that while a society is governed normally by settled norms it is morally permissible to violate them at times of dire need and in extreme circumstances.

Much as we might squirm and wiggle, even a cursory glance at the human cannot but fail to tell us that we are both selfish and self-destructive, if we are not otherwise restrained and influenced. Even we do not know, as 'intelligent' individuals, how we will react if tempted or provoked beyond an invisible threshold. If we are 'rational', we would not have, for example, the climate crisis, nor would we have, just to make some more money, polluted and poisoned the air we breathe, the water we drink and the food we eat. If we are 'naturally' moral we would not have had sadists and mass murderers like Elizabeth Bathory (the inspiration for Dracula), Talat Pasha (architect of the Armenian massacre), Attila the Hun, Genghis Khan, Caligula, Ivan the Terrible, Adolf Hitler, Joseph Stalin, Mao Zedong, Pol Pot, and so on. They were human; had the same body and brain and heart, crafted from the same timbre, made of the same flesh, blood and bone; capable of similar emotions and feelings. It is because evil is banal. And there are no moral conundrums or revulsions, and what concerns us is legal correctness, not moral character. It is because human nature is 'ordinarily' obnoxious and inordinately irrational, that human behavior is so unpredictable and so revolting and man so ungovernable. Philosopher Immanuel Kant argued that it might well be possible to govern a society of devils if they were rational and clear about their long-term self-interest. The point is that we are not 'devils' (at least not all the time) nor are we 'angels'; nor dogs or dolphins; elephants or eagles. It takes us away from the right path to human fulfillment for us to try to describe, depict and define him by any single attribute or predisposition. That is why the human is so fascinating and frustrating, and even frightening. We are all a bit and blend of everything—divine, diabolic, rational, whimsical, intuitive, intelligent, noble, moral, immoral, evil. Everything that is in the cosmos we have within each of us. In the words of Rudolf Steiner, "For what lies inside the human being is the whole spiritual cosmos in condensed form. In our inner organism we have an image of the entire cosmos".

How, when, and what comes out and becomes behavior even the gods can't tell. It hinges heavily on the state of the war within. What we, humans, try to do is to bring rationality and morality closer, try to be 'rationally moral' and 'morally rational' in making decisions and choices. In fact, there are some who posit that we all have reason to be moral if, and only if, we live in a society whose moral order is in fairly satisfactory shape, because being in it offers a good chance as every member can have of leading a life that comes as close as possible to a good life according to their (internally flawless) conception of it. One way of facilitating this is to bring about a kind of entente between our two independent but interconnected 'intelligences': of the head and of the heart. We must bear in mind that in the war within these two are in opposing camps but we need them both. Our rationality comes from the head and morality from the heart. It is wise to keep in mind what Nietzsche said, "One ought to hold on to one's heart; for if one lets it go, one soon loses control of the head too". We take the 'heart' for granted; we worry about our head, the brain. All that we want is that the heart should keep ticking. We want to be 'brainy', which means to be more 'intelligent'. We don't say more 'hearty'. Our brain is amazing; so is the heart. Our 'heady-intelligence' is so intelligent that it is not good enough to even let us know where we are headed as a species: early extinction or spreading itself out into the solar system. But it is good enough to constantly invent new ways to divide and decimate each other, and make man a 'wolf to his fellow man'. The tragedy is that man is nothing but mind, and mind is the principal problem. Instead of addressing this problem we struggle with the problems created by the mind. And the way to address is to dilute, if not erase, its grip and hold on the human consciousness. That 'way', that source is also within each of us, a part of what constitutes the human package, in our heart. Contrary to what we usually assume, the human heart is not only an awesomely powerful pump but also a tremendous source of energy and intelligence. Every day you are alive, your heart creates enough energy to power a truck for 20 miles of driving. Your heart pumps blood to almost all of your cells, quite a feat considering there are about 75 trillion of them. During a normal life span, the heart will pump about

1.5 million barrels of blood, enough to fill about 200 train tank cars. The first heart, a tiny group of cells, begins to beat as early as when a pregnancy is in its fourth week. Humans form an emotional brain long before a rational one, and a beating heart before either. Heart intelligence is really the source of emotional intelligence. The heart has its own independent complex nervous system known as the 'brain in the heart'. Its 'intelligence' is independent of, but constantly in communication with, the brain, and the source of much that is good about us. Heart intelligence is the flow of awareness, understanding and intuition we experience when the mind and emotions are brought into coherent alignment with the heart. Antoine de Sainte-Exupéry said, "It is only with the heart that one can see rightly; what is essential is invisible to the eye". It validates the idea that people can be smart in a way that doesn't have anything to do with IQ scores.

What we should worry about is not only how to avoid a 'heart attack', but equally how to make our hearts rule our lives, or at least have a greater say in what goes on inside us. For, as Blaise Pascal said, "the heart has its reasons which reason knows not". And as an extension it implies that if we can learn to listen to those 'reasons', or rumblings, we can become less confrontational and more caring in making choices in our lives. However new research is indicating that intelligence and intuition are heightened when we learn to listen more deeply to our own heart. It's through learning how to decipher messages we receive from our heart that we gain the keen perception needed to effectively manage our emotions in the midst of life's challenges. The more we learn to listen to and follow our heart intelligence, the more educated, balanced and coherent our emotions become. Without the guiding influence of the heart, we easily fall prey to reactive emotions such as insecurity, anger, fear, and blame as well as other energy-draining reactions and behaviors. Such 'wisdom' can be now validated or legitimized by emerging science, but mystics have always known that true intelligence is a blending of head and heart, of thought and feeling. Our heart needs the help of our head to generate and act on more skillful emotions. Our head needs our heart to remind us that what's really important in life is putting an end to suffering. 'Intelligence' has to be holistic and the next phase of human evolution must include this dimension. Then alone can we live as 'we are one another' and be able not to 'stop at our skin'.

Restoring the Heart to Its Rightful Place

Looking at all the unsettling and unsavory things happening in the world, a growing number of people have come to believe that, as Steve Grand[75] puts it, "there is a strong possibility that we've got everything horribly wrong". They are beginning to see more clearly than before when the 'wrong' began. It began with the virtual monopoly of intellect in orchestrating our lives and the sidelining of our intuitive heart intelligence, or as some call it, 'heart's consciousness'. The heart is now emerging as a key to a better human future. The beginning is to shed the sense that the heart is simply a superb hydraulic pump that pushes blood through the arteries, capillaries, and veins to deliver oxygen and nutrient-rich blood, and evacuate waste products to and from the tissues of the body. Recent research indicates that it is not merely a pump and that our heart is 'more intelligent than the brain'. It means that those feelings we have are 'intelligent' feelings and that strengthens the fact of all of us having inherent psychic abilities and intuition. If we could shed our brain-fixation and tap more of our 'heart intelligence' we might make more headway. Contrary to what we now assume, the 'organ of intellect' was not always known to be the brain. In fact, for long, there were two competing views regarding where the intellect is in the body: the brain or the heart. Even Aristotle argued for a cardiocentric (heart-centered) model, that the heart is in fact the primary organ of intelligence. In this, he differed from his teacher Plato, who subscribed to the encephalocentric (brain-centered) model, and posited that the "eyes, ears, tongue, hands, and feet act in accordance with the discernment of the brain". It is the heart, not the brain, which is the major energetic organ of organization and integration of the human body, and the physical and spiritual energy link up in the inner heart.[76] Our heart, in fact, has its own nervous system where the neurons are connected differently and more elaborately than elsewhere in the body, and while they are capable of detecting circulating chemicals sent from the brain and other organs, they operate independently in their own right. Having its own mini-brain is the reason why heart transplants work, given the fact that severed nerve connections do not reconnect in a different body. Furthermore, this elaborate nervous center in the heart has more functions than simply regulating the electrical activities of the heart to keep it pumping. It is interesting to note that while the heart can be influenced by messages sent from the brain, it doesn't necessarily obey them all the time. Furthermore, the heart's mini-brain can send its own signals to the brain and exercise its influence on it. Charlie Chaplin, who wrote a beautiful poem on turning seventy[77] which, *inter alia*, said "When I started loving myself I recognized, that my thinking can make me miserable and sick. When I requested for my heart forces, my mind got an important partner. Today, I call this connection heart wisdom". And lest we forget, "connections are made with the heart, not the tongue"—nor with the mind.

"Perhaps the heart path represents a different way of interacting with the world than our current brain-dominated approach, a path many of us might want to explore and one that is based on sensing the energy that resonates within everyone, than always trying to master and control things, people and the cosmos".[78] We have to review our ideas of intention, intelligence and intuition. The French philosopher Henri Bergson, for example, posited that intuition is deeper than intellect, and said that the next human quality to develop is intuition. The theosophist Annie Besant brought in the spiritual dimension and said that intellect has to be "subordinated to the higher spiritual quality, which realizes the unity in diversity and therefore comes to realize the divine Self in man. That is the next step forward, looking at consciousness". [79] And that way we could accelerate both 'consciousness-change' and 'contextual change'. Sri Aurobindo declared that for "man to come face to face with the realization of all that has remained his dream and his aspiration through the ages, [he must] emerge into a higher stage of consciousness". Such a higher stage of consciousness has to be in a state of better balance between mind and heart, between brain-based intelligence and heart-intelligence.

"Cardio-energy not only maintains the very interactive cellular structures of the body, but interacts with other hearts and energy systems as well, creating an ever-increasing unity of ever more complex systems of energies which are constantly in communication and interaction with each other. Therefore, it is the individual heart which receives from outside itself, sources of information its related mind organ cannot access on its own, and in turn, transmits information to other hearts multiplied exponentially by the countless sources of cardio-L energy which contribute to its own 'wisdom'. In so doing, the individual heart becomes a microcosm of the larger macrocosm of cardio-energy of which it is a part, and to which it contributes, thus, in a most significant manner, participating in the creation of its own reality. This notion of the 'wisdom of the heart', not only in the sense of what the heart knows and intuits, but also from where and to where its wisdom travels, and with what effect, is a central theme in Kabbala and Hasidism".[80]

It is also suggested that "it would be a serious mistake to view congestive heart failure and its treatment merely from the materialist perspective of physical organ dysfunction. Rather, such ailments of the heart must also be understood within the context of the heart's very own L energy and therefore, and most importantly, from the perspective of the heart's own energetic and spiritual effects upon itself". Some like Rabbi Nachman "speak not only of the role of the heart in terms of one's own health, but also that, the good thoughts in the heart are the good inclination, through which good deeds and attributes are revealed. This is a formation for good. Thus, when a person thinks good thoughts, he purifies the Space of Creation".[81]

If we can manage to harmonize the three independent but interconnected intelligences that we have—mental (IQ or left brain), emotional (EQ, or, right brain), and heart (HQ)—then, only then, can we change what and how we think and feel. Without such change, our behavior will not change and we will not win the war within. Only by that harmonization can we truly improve the quality of decision-making. Only then can we "foster a new level of understanding of the phenomena of life in the biological sciences, and enable physicians to rediscover the human being which, all too often, many feel they have lost".[82]

Conclusion

The question why humans kill one another so needlessly has tormented the minds of philosophers, sociologists, and psychologists. Why is peaceful, amicable, and constructive conflict resolution so difficult in daily life? Why has diversity, instead of enriching, become so divisive and destructive? Will we be ever able to make sense of human behavior and truly understand the human condition? Are we innately violent, as Thomas Hobbes hypothesized in the 1650s, or is our bearing and mien influenced more by nature, as Jean-Jacques Rousseau theorized a century later? Can we ever become truly moral beings?

While we will never have clear answers because there are no clear answers, one thing is clear. As Carl Jung said, "wholeness for humans depends on their ability to own their own shadow". The 'shadow' we have to own is 'the black box inside of humans they can't go near'. The box contains all that we don't want to own, even admit: violence, cruelty, sadism, hate, bigotry, etc. That many saints and mahatmas have confessed to these failings should only enhance, not diminish their saintliness. We have long lived with the agony of the good vs evil affliction and how to resolve it. The great philosopher Nikolai Berdyaev wrote, "There is a deadly pain in the very distinction of good and evil, of the valuable and the worthless. We cannot rest in the thought that that distinction is ultimate... we cannot bear to be faced forever with the distinction between good and evil" (*The Destiny of Man*, 1931). What we have not sufficiently recognized is that our behavior, whether we do good or evil depends on what happens 'within' our consciousness, which in turn is in a state of war between these very forces: good and evil. Although recent studies do suggest that there are "good grounds for believing that we are intrinsically more violent than the average mammal", we should not forget that we are also, on the other extreme, equally capable of supreme sacrifice and highest altruism. Fact is that if there is evil within, there is goodness too. Along with 'selfish' genes we are also hard-wired for empathy and compassion. That is why we are also the most complex form of life on earth. Our range of emotions are far wider and most exist as pairs of opposites, love and hate, cruelty and compassion, indifference and empathy, malice and altruism, etc. Our consciousness is also more evolved and that makes it more of a player in our lives than of other species. The result is that co-existence of 'pairs of opposites' in our consciousness turns into conflict, and conflict into a confrontation, and confrontation into a no-holds-barred war between two sets of forces, dharma (righteousness) and adharma (wickedness). And this *War* is all that matters, all there is to do. To 'win' the war, rather, more to the point, help the forces of good to prevail in this war, we have to do good in our daily life, helping and not hurting, and by ensuring that whatever gets into our body through our senses is wholesome for the forces of righteousness. In other words, the war within can be 'won' by leading a virtuous or dharmic life. But the conundrum is that to lead such a life we have to 'win' the war within. It is a two-way process and we have to work on both fronts at the same time. Internally we must learn how to enhance the role of the heart intelligence and externally by performing our actions and activities in the spirit of what the Bhagavad Gita calls *nishkama karma*, to do one's actions without expectation of any reward. Expectation not only causes disappointment, but also colors and corrupts the action and the result. Freed from self-interest, our actions automatically become righteous. In turn, they become suitable to serve as 'feed' for the forces of goodness. In short, the doctrine of nishkama karma not only sanitizes our external life but also helps us to 'win' the war within.

To sum up, to 'win' this war, we need to adopt the following nine-point agenda: (1) recognize, at the level of our collective awareness, that there is a whole world within; (2) recognize that the most consequential and the most important of all wars is taking place in that world; (3) recognize that all our current problems and hopes and dreams for our future hinge on how the war wages and its ebbs and flows; (4) recognize that although invisible and inaccessible we must find a way to intervene in this war and help the 'good wolf'; (5) recognize that the only tangible way to do so is by changing our mindset and our behavior; (6) recognize that for that we need the twin changes: consciousness-change and contextual-change; (7) recognize that our comatose heart-intelligence has to be awakened in our consciousness as part of such a change; (8) recognize that to bring about the required change in our context of life, we have to follow the spirit of the doctrine of nishkama karma in our daily life; (9) recognize that given the way and extent the triad of the 'three Ms'—morality, money and mortality—shadows and dominates our lives, our particular attention has to be bestowed on these subjects.

Chapter 3

Money—*Maya*, *Mara*, and *Moksha*—All-in-One

Money, *Homo economicus*, and *Homo consumens*

Money's precise moment of birth might be diffused and difficult to pinpoint, but its might is unmistakable. For, might itself is a problem in the human mind, not a perk, but it is many times multiplied by money. It is at once a master key and a magic wand, the ultimate illusion (*maya*), the ultimate temptation (*mara*) and the ultimate liberator (*moksha*). Money is at the center of the mindset that asks, 'if everything has a price, does nothing have a value?' The hold of money over our mind is formidable; nothing else comes even close. Other than malice, it is money that separates us from other animals. Mind with money is a man-eater; and without it is a toothless tiger. Recent research has shown that thinking about money undermines our sense of social connectedness. Obscene opulence adds social isolation to what is described as the psychological solipsism of power. Whether or not money can buy everything, the fact is, as Emerson said, it costs too much. Money sugarcoats everything, including murder; in fact, it has become a major incentive for killing. Money rides roughshod over sex, qualms, restraints, or relationships. Some experts are beginning to see a link between inequality and rates of homicide, and find that inequality predicts homicide rates "better than any other variable"[1] and the *perception* that it can, makes money matter the most. Money too is at the heart of the crisis of morality. There is a general belief that all money tends to corrupt, and that absolute money corrupts absolutely. And that it has destroyed all vestige of civic virtue. And there is much truth in that. While money inherently is value-neutral, it is also true that it takes lot of effort to be moral in handling money at all levels and stages. It is very difficult not to be unfair, unjust and not deny someone else's due, if not legally, ethically. And that has become far more extensive and invasive in modern times. The point of departure is this: the world has transited from a *modus vivendi* where most of humanity had no need of money at all, to a *modus operandi* in which much of mankind struggles to survive on extremely small amounts of money. This 'transition' has profoundly altered the role and place of money in human life.

The moral perils of being rich were made clear in many scriptures. The Book of James warns the rich: "The wages you failed to pay the workers who mowed your fields are crying out against you. The cries of the harvesters have reached the ears of the Lord Almighty. You have lived on earth in luxury and self-indulgence. Money is now the median and measure of success, fame, and fortune. Whether or not money can buy happiness—a subject on which many have said much—it certainly has much to do with our acute anxiety, high levels of stress and the rat-race, a metaphor for our modern life of Sisyphean struggle without satisfaction, sometimes described as the 'dog-eats-dog' culture.[2] And money is the fulcrum of the 'market economy', which philosopher Michael Sandal says has turned into 'market society'. The dynamics of this 'society 'are seriously distorted, resulting in intolerable injustice. As a recent Oxfam report shows, in several countries, wage inequality has increased and the share of labor compensation in GDP has declined because profits have increased more rapidly than wages. While the income share of the top 1% has grown substantially, many others have not shared in the goodies of economic growth. And much of decision-making, personal to businesses and national—is now economic and the result is money crowds out motility in our everyday life. The use of money as the primary, often the only, measure of success puts enormous pressure on even those who are not directly involved to toe the party line, to echo the chorus.

Money is the one thing having which nothing else is needed and not having which everything else is valueless and vain. There is almost nothing man does these days without the shadow of money looming over. Its hold on man now is vice-like and vicious. For reasons still unclear, money seems to draw out of us some of our worst traits like greed, envy, jealousy, and malice. Some say money corrupts; others, that it is *man* who corrupts money. Some argue that money is only "a tool of exchange, which can't exist unless there are goods produced and men able to produce them, and therefore it is neither virtue nor evil". Some say that it is the instrument of the strong to exploit the weak; others say that it offers a chance to become strong by virtue of intellectual exercise and effort. Some say it exacerbates inequality and unfairness; others, that it gives inherent value and worth. Essentially, it is money that separates the so-called 'one-percent'—the ultra-rich—and the rest. It is money that could keep you healthier and live longer, even become immortal. Money is power in its barest sense. The British historian and essayist Thomas Carlyle 'described its power in the following words: "Whoso has sixpence is sovereign (to the length of sixpence) over all men; commands cooks to feed him, philosophers to teach him, kings to mount guard over him,—to the length of sixpence".[3] But what is indisputable is that money's essential character has changed from exchange to enrichment, from a means to obtain the basic needs of life, to itself becoming an end. And, perhaps above all, it has turned man essentially into a consumer, which has bred a culture of instant gratification and one-upmanship. There is lot of money to be made on 'body-upgradation', the latest fashion-statement. We are being sold on the need to upgrade all parts of ourselves, all at once, including parts that we did not previously know needed upgrading. According to one estimate, the so-called self-improvement industry rakes in ten billion dollars a year. Money is the most pressing moral issue now. If we can handle money well, and do not allow it to mess with our mind, much of the rancor, friction, and violence in the world will become manageable. Everyone thinks that to make or earn money to feed a family, for example, nothing is bad or immoral, even cold-blooded murder. For instance, according to police in New Delhi, India, anybody can be a contract killer, including a mother of seven, a science graduate, and a property dealer. How desperate they are and for how little they are willing to do such a terrible deed is indicated by the fact that the money in question, for the 'killing contract' was a mere Rs.49,000 (less than $1,000). For some others, hired-killing is a moral short cut to get rich, a snapshot of collapsing social norms and value of life. In other words, both the need and lure of money can trigger a mercenary and murderous response in us; if we can get it right with money, everything else will fall into place. With the rise of *Homo economicus* as the primary human persona, the emblem and analogue of human values, everything else, even health, has taken a back seat. Recently, the Director General of the World Health Organization warned the world that putting economic interests over public health is leading the world towards three gradual health disasters: climate change, the failure of more and more antibiotic drugs, and the increase in so-called lifestyle diseases caused by poor diet and exercise. And with the advent of industrial production as the primary way to multiply money, the utility of every man, woman, and child to society, became how much he or she spent as a consumer, what economists call 'potential purchasing power'. Economics, materialism, and money have become synonymous. We value our material life more than our moral life. As a result, today's politics, which is a means to acquire power, is dominated by economics. In 'democratic societies', the political power obtained through periodic elections is often financed by rich donors who want their pound of say in what the elected do later. Even the so-called charitable organizations, in some affluent societies, are supported by what is called "dark money"—unlimited donations obtained by nonprofit organizations and spent on influencing elections, without disclosing the identity of the donors.

And much of the way we entertain and amuse ourselves, and almost all of sport, is about big, if not dark money. From *Homo economicus*, we have turned into what Erich Fromm called *Homo consumens*—a total consumer in a paradise conceived as an infinite warehouse, "where everyone can buy something new every day, buy everything he wants and even a little more than the one next door to him but transfigures us into an empty cipher—anxious, passive, profoundly discontented and bored".[4] That gnawing feeling of deep 'discontent' is spreading to all human inventions and institutions that have been painstakingly built up and which hold humanity together—family, community, marriage, markets, traditions, state, religion, etc., foundationally altering our social and moral life. Whether it is *Homo economicus* or *Homo consumens*, the bedrock of the identity is money. What we give value to is how much money we earn regardless of how much we are left with to do things that give us comfort, convenience and control over other people. As the Chinese statesman Deng Xiaoping famously said "It doesn't matter if a cat is black or white, so long as it catches mice". We don't care who the ruler is, what system of governance it is, or what 'ism' it follows. All that we want is to have plenty of money in our bulging pockets to get all the material goodies we see on the screen and on the shopping malls. It increasingly appears that ethical behavior and efficient markets are rarely compatible, a point implicit in what Adam Smith said in *The Wealth of Nations* (1776): "It is not from the benevolence of the butcher, the brewer, or the baker that we expect our dinner, but from their regard to their own interest". With all the euphoria surrounding 'free markets', which really is an oxymoron, there is a growing sense as articulated by thinkers like Harvard's Michael Sandel that markets alone cannot define a just society, that there are moral limits to markets. The fact is that markets "do not just produce what we really want, they also produce what we want according to our monkey-on-the-shoulder tastes".[5] Well, we know what a monkey does whether it is on the back or the shoulder, or in the mind!

The difference lies in a mix of 'more' and 'less'. In earlier days people led simpler lives, with limited wants and with more of a moral mindset. That made people generally 'more' hesitant to appease the monkey' in, or on, them. And then their reach was limited to the local store and they were 'less' subject to temptations like seductive ads on TV. And those who had 'more' money did not feel the need to buy 'more' things. Earlier, wealth was finite, primarily spread and exchanged, and having it in excess was considered sinful. Generosity and charity were associated with wealth earned through righteous means and through *swadharma*, doing one's own dharma. People were generally open about their wealth and worth but they did not flaunt it. Now people are more open about their sex lives than about their wealth. The hypnotic effect of money and wealth was foretold in the scriptures in the context of describing the effects of the *Kali Yuga*, the most immoral of all ages. They describe the effect and attraction of money in these terms: "Men will devote themselves to earning money; the richest will hold power. Wealth alone will be considered the sign of a man's good birth, proper behavior and fine qualities. Property alone will confer rank; wealth will be the only source of devotion.

The fundamental transformation came when the mind married money, as it were; when money was turned into a major fault line in human life—the divisive line between the 'haves' and 'have-nots'. It came into being, as Aristotle noted, when the various necessities of human life could not be easily carried about and people agreed to employ in their dealings something that was intrinsically useful and easily applicable to the activities of life, like iron or silver. The value of the metal was first measured by weight and later, to avoid the trouble of weighing and to make its value obvious at sight, kings and governments devised coin money. It has come a long way since. Its primary purpose of exchange was sidelined and money became a symbol of social status and a major means for separation, discrimination, and exploitation. But unlike in a barter economy where savings and investment were very difficult, modern money—paper currency and the bank note—opened the doors to economic growth. By itself, paper money has no value; it rests on trust and it offers fluidity, flexibility and, for the creative mind, opportunities for speculation, savings and investment. Of all the things in the world, it became the most sought after possession: to obtain, protect and keep money, people go to extraordinary lengths. They plan and scheme and use every subterfuge; they steal and kill for it; they expend more time, energy, and effort for its sake than for any other purpose. Much of a person's life consists of no more than earning, saving, and spending money; and the remainder of his life is spent caring, tending, and preserving the possessions purchased. No sacrifice, no relationship or human bond is spared when it comes to making money. Alan Greenspan, a former chairman of the American Federal Reserve Board quotes a friend as saying 'I understand the history of money. When I get some, it is soon history'. With it, man is a monarch; without it, subhuman. With money in abundance, man can overcome 'natural' or inherited limitations; but without it, one can scarcely obtain what is needed to be wholly human. Ironically, man cannot do with or without money. Just as man has evolved, so has the character and color of money. Moderation and the middle path have given way to gluttony and greed. There are those who have come to believe that striving for inner balance and tranquility will erode their competitive ability, who see a dichotomy between being wise and worldly-wise.

Epiphany of Modern Man—Money

Somerset Maugham famously said, "Money is like a sixth sense without which you cannot make a complete use of the other five". Voltaire put it differently when he said that when it is a question of money, everybody is of the same religion. Thomas Jefferson said that money, not morality is the principle of commercial nations.

Cicero said that endless money forms the sinews of war. Indeed violence, warfare and wealth are intimately connected. Men are violent for money and money makes violence possible. Money is both the tool and purpose of violence. Money is a principal factor in most of suicides and homicides, not only among the poor and poorer regions of the world but also in affluent societies, Glyn Davies in his *A History of Money from Ancient Times to the Present Day* writes that 'ever since the invention of coins, monetary and military history have been interconnected to a degree that is both depressing and surprising.' He even paraphrases Clausewitz's famous dictum and refers to war as the continuation of monetary policy by other means, quoting 18th-century William Davenant: "Nowadays that prince who can best find money to pay his army is surest of success". Davies concludes that the military ratchet was the most important single influence in raising prices and reducing the value of money in the past 1,000 years, and for most of that time, debasement was the most common, but not the only way, of strengthening the 'sinews of war'. Whether it is making love or war, some mavericks say that "we are evolving unto a society with much in common with that of insects: ants, termites, hornets, etc. Something analogous to social behavior makes us swarm in towns and cities like ants in their dark colonies". The instinct that compels us to behave like that, the theory continues, is money, which is "to us what genes are to ants", and which "will govern human evolution in the future more than DNA". Selfish economics rather than selfish genes govern human evolution; in the richer nations, "we are no longer evolving according to the principles of natural selection", and "we have swapped our life-giving queen for cash", and the root of all evil. The human race has greedily sold its soul to the Devil. There is little doubt that money, much like technology, has had a transformational effect on the human condition. By empowering man to acquire convenience, comfort and gadgets for every need, money, together with technology, has made man a 'soft species' and eroded considerably the strength and resilience of the human organism. And technology is also raising money-made moral issues. For example, who should a driverless car choose to kill in order to save its passengers: a money-less man in rags or an executive in a business suit? How should we program for such an eventuality?

The very fact that our desires often transgress the bounds of biology or balance of life on earth, and that our social life goes beyond the demands of sheer survival, requires a medium to harmonize and optimize the diverse capacities of human society and makes synergy socially possible. That was the origin of what we call 'money', initially designed as a medium of exchange of products, services, and talents, facilitating human interfacing, an input into the making of an orderly, if not an egalitarian, society. The transformation of money from what it was intended into what it has become—our all-consuming passion—is perhaps the single most destabilizing development in human history; it has created not only a 'new class', but even a new breed of men. Money is more than the coin, paper or plastic to acquire goods and services. Money is linked to complex emotions, feelings and behaviors. It has a huge influence on what we call 'quality of life' and on the pursuit of the three Cs and Ps that consume much of human life—comfort, convenience, and control; pleasure, profit, and power.

Mind and Money

The mind invented money but, in turn, is enslaved by its own invention. The mind views and relates to the entire world of life through the prism, and prison, of money. Money is broadly defined as 'any marketable good or token trusted by a society to be used as a store of value, a medium of exchange, and a unit of account'. In *A History of Money*, Davies defines it as anything that is widely used for making payments and accounting for debts and credits. Money has been called many things by many wise and 'otherwise' men: like muck, not good unless spread (Francis Bacon); like manure, which spreads around does a lot of good, but piled up in one place, stinks like hell (Clint Murchison Jr); the most important thing in life (Bernard Shaw); equally important to those who have it and who don't (Galbraith); one of the great inventions of mankind (Alan Greenspan); and a myriad more. Since prehistoric times all sorts of things have been used as money and Davies lists some of these: amber, beads, cowries, drums, eggs, feathers, gongs, hoes, ivory, jade, kettles, leather, mats, nails, oxen, pigs, quartz, rice, salt, thimbles, umiacs, vodka, wampums, yarns, and zappozats (decorated axes). Davies says that money did not have a single origin but developed independently in many different parts of the world.

Today, scholars say that money's origin had little to do with trading, as popularly believed, but arose in a social setting, possibly as a method of punishment. Barter was probably the earliest form of human exchange when humans were essentially hunter-gatherers, fishermen, and farmers. Stone Age man, according to anthropological evidence, used precious metals as money. Silver was first used as coins in Lydia (Iron-Age kingdom) or Turkey in 3 BCE. In Babylonia, a form of rudimentary banking was prevalent. In 118 BCE, banknotes in the form of leather money appeared in China and in 800 CE, printed paper currency also appeared. According to Marco Polo, the Mongols adopted the bank note as 'legal tender', i.e., it was a capital offense to refuse them as payment. Only in the 17th century, did coinage become standardized and certified. Paper money, first in fiduciary form (which promises to pay specified amounts in gold and silver), and later in its own right (where the paper did not promise payment in some other form), became the mainstay of money in the late 18th and early 19th century. An obsession is essentially a consuming desire, a compulsive craving; so compulsive that it becomes the center of one's existence to the utter exclusion of all the rest; it transports the obsessed to a different state of consciousness and to a different moral mindset. While it could hamper and hinder regular life, through our obsessions, we are often seeking redemption or relaxation. As the Buddha said, if desire itself is the supreme disease, then obsession can eat our very vitals and its cessation is itself *nirvana*, 'the stopping of becoming'. Some scholars interpret nirvana as "letting go of clinging, hatred, and ignorance, and the full acceptance of imperfection, impermanence, and interconnectedness". Some scholars say that Buddhism tells us what nirvana delivers us from—suffering, *dukha*—but not what it delivers us into. A Buddhist master and scholar, Nagarjuna, even says that a desire for nirvana, as enlightenment, is itself an obstacle to nirvana. He also makes a distinction between 'longing', which he says we could have, and 'desire', which he asks us to eschew. Longing, it is said, is about 'here and now'; and desire is a future state, what Jiddu Krishnamurti called 'future psychological time'.[6] In that state of obsessive desire we are no longer balanced; we do not calculate profit or loss; we just do it because that is the only thing that matters. Without the obsessed object or person, the whole world seems empty; and with it, we do not need the world. Although most often viewed negatively, 'burning obsession' is the driving force behind much of human creativity. In some, obsession can turn into depression; but that very obsession-driven depression can trigger great creativity.

The description of love in the Bible is the opposite of 'obsessive love'. It says that "Love never gives up. Love cares for others more than for self. Love doesn't want what it doesn't have. Love doesn't strut, doesn't have a swelled head, doesn't force itself on others, it isn't always "me first," doesn't fly off the handle, doesn't keep score of the sins of others, doesn't revel when others grovel..."[7] Sometimes we hate someone we wish to love but cannot love; sometimes we do not even know what the driving force behind our obsessions is. It is possible that there is no single source or trigger but we cannot insulate such people from the world around them, a world that sustains their life. The world now worships 'success' and scoffs at 'failure'; in fact, as David Brooks says, we fear 'failure' more than we desire 'success'. Our deepest desire, the desire to love and be loved, is not immune to the crippling 'fear of failure'. Our reason-centric, "post-modern" culture puts emphasis on the hedonistic pursuit of happiness, freedom, individuality, and self-centeredness. It seeks contentment through achievement, enlightenment through escapism. In this 'culture', 'failure' in love becomes the ultimate admission of incompetence, an unbearable humiliation, a negation of one's right to be 'happy'; an intolerable insult to one's self-image. Unable to accept the humiliation or digest the insult, the affected individual turns his revengeful ire onto the subject or object of his 'obsession', and the world at large is held responsible.

While we might still primarily associate 'obsessive revenge' with 'failed love', being 'obsessed' is almost universal. We are all obsessed at some point by someone or something—a person, pet, movie star, a guru, a place, love, sex, guns, sport, a TV show, a gadget... Some obsessions are hidden, we are afraid to even admit them to ourselves; some, we never tire of dreaming of, whose very existence makes life worth living, and any burden worth bearing. Obsession can take different forms with different results to the obsessed and the affected. An 'obsession' with God has a different effect than one with a gadget, for example. Positively, 'obsession' can make us focus more, or give us dogged determination. Negatively, it could blur our moral vision and lead to great destruction. It has been said that "passion is a positive obsession; obsession is a negative passion". While there are myriad personal 'obsessions' that consume much of our life, as a species too our evolution has been defined by the pursuit of many collective obsessions. Some of these, in no particular order, are God, sex, body, wealth, death, convenience, comfort, control, fame, food, clothes, shopping. And we are obsessed with not only what we have—and do not have—but, even more, with what others have and should not have. Among these, the three that are likely to align the course of human destiny and the evolution of human consciousness are the 'three Ms'—morality, money and mortality.

The Three 'M's

On all three fronts, we are in the throes of cathartic convulsion. We associate human 'goodness' with 'morality', but on one thing most agree—the 'difficulty of being good'. Whether or not man is a 'moral animal', most agree that we are in a state of moral free fall. Not a day passes without our hearing or reading news that rudely reinforces this inference. Horrible things are happening so routinely and repetitively in every part of the world, it makes us wonder whether man has gone mad or evil has finally triumphed on earth and taken over man, the supposed regent and agent of God. Now, no one can think and say even to himself "Evil can't touch me; I am good and cannot be seduced or tempted or provoked to do such things". We cannot, on the one hand, talk of unity and oneness of all, and then wash our hands off others, who are just like any of us. We must bear their cross too. As for the second M, we all know, and have been repeatedly warned about, the corrupting influence of money on the human mind, yet are unable to escape its clutches due to its pervasive and penetrating place in human society. Tragically, it seems that money has got into the very make-up of man at the most elemental level. How often have we seen a child clutching money and calling it *his* 'pocket money' or simply '*my* money'! An illustration of this point comes from a letter written by a child to God which reads: "Dear God, If you give me [a genie lamp like] Aladdin's, I will give you anything except my money or my chess set.—Raphael".[8] If a child, still enchantingly innocent, does not want to exchange 'his' money even to God, that speaks greatly about both man and money. It tells us that money is now not merely currency or a medium of exchange; it is now part of our DNA; and integrally defines us. Angelic eternal youth and immortality have long been the elusive human universal aspiration. But in recent times, science has brought them into the realm of possibility with consequences too unpredictable for human imagination. The question is, can humans attain eternal youth and not destroy the planet? And, "can we avoid the scale of human population growth that would turn us into a seething viral infection on Earth's skin that completely destroys it? Or, more likely, us?"[9] If we do achieve outright physical immortality, then "earth will decide she's had enough of us, and shrug us off—like the pesky little germs that we are".[10]

Not everything 'alive' in nature is mortal, although the few life forms like bacteria that did not and still do not reproduce sexually can be considered immortal, barring accidental death. So, we do have a 'precedent'. If 'primitive' bacteria can, why not we, the most 'intelligent' and innovative life on earth? In our tumultuous times, it is becoming increasingly difficult for laymen to decide how they should react to research on issues like human immortality. Money has much to do with it. Firstly, money is flowing into attendant research at the expense of far more important and urgent provision of basic needs for billions of people. Second, the fruits of that research will not be equally accessible. It is being openly said that by the year 2050, man can become technologically immortal but only the rich will be able to afford it. In other words, it will be money which will be the deciding factor on who has to die and who doesn't have to, money being the deciding dice. That, in turn, could create one more source of tension, friction, and divide, and it could easily reach the boiling point. Already many are saying that the next apocalypse might be economic, not nuclear; that the current grotesque global inequality—just eight men own the same wealth as the poorest half of the world—is unsustainable and morally abhorrent. So offensive to any semblance of justness, which is central to morality, that not overturning it is tantamount to inciting evil? But secretly we all want to be, and hope we will be, sooner than later, one of the one-percent and so we watch and wait for our day. This along with the large privatizations has fueled the rise of wealth inequality among individuals. By any reckoning, we are living in the times of the ultra-rich, a second 'gilded age' in which a shimmering surface masks crony capitalism, serious social problems, and crass corruption. While there can be no perfect equality in any human institution or relationship in any walk of life, the present situation in which a CEO earns more than 1000 times his employee clearly violates every canon of fairness and fair play. But then, whose morality is it anyway, of the master or slave, of the rich or poor The CEO thinks it is moral because he has earned it by leading the company, and he has not cheated anyone. The worker thinks it is obscene because the value of his work for the company is much more than the glaring gap indicates. But perceptions are important and there is growing groundswell that that we are at a flash point and, that sooner than latter the non-rich will revolt and when that happens it could dwarf all earlier revolutions in its intensity and destruction. Clearly the world needs a new economy, radically different economy, which some call 'human economy, designed for the 99%', but how to bring it into being without violence and bloodshed is the moot point. The answer again is the same. We cannot transplant it externally. The transformation must happen within. Which means winning the war within.

Another imponderable is the growing seamlessness between man and machine and the gnawing sense that the world, perhaps even we, are better off with machines running the world. If, for example, man and machine become intelligently indistinguishable, which means that the human population gets doubled or trebled in terms of brain power and behavior, what kind of world will this result in? It is being predicted that by the year 2029 machines will pass the Turing test, that is, they will be indistinguishable from human intelligence.[11] Does that constitute human progress or machines-coming-of-age? Does that pave the way to the next step of human evolution or are we creating perhaps another kind of life built on the ruins of human life? Since it affects us and our children's lives, shouldn't we have some say in such matters? The project *2045 Initiative*, funded by Russian billionaire Dmitry Itskov, aims to create technologies enabling the transfer of [an] individual's personality to a more advanced nonbiological carrier, and extending life, including to the point of immortality. It envisages the mass production of lifelike, low-cost avatars that can be uploaded with the contents of the human brain, complete with the particulars of consciousness and personality. Itskov's goal is to make "a digital copy of your mind in a nonbiological carrier; a version of a fully sentient person that could live for hundreds or thousands of years".[12] Not a virtual but an actual 'human' immortality. Avatars, we are reassured, can have sex as an artificial body can be designed to receive sensations. Not only that, the project also aims to "actually save lives" and "to help the disabled, to cure diseases, to create technology that will allow us in the future to answer some existential questions". Such as, what is the brain? what is life? what is consciousness? and, finally, what is the universe?

Money—*Maya*, *Mara*, and *Moksha*

The issue is not whether or not some sort of money is necessary for human life. It is both necessary and noxious; it depends on how we earn it, how much we retain of it, and how we disperse and dispose of it. Indeed the discovery or invention of money has been described as arguably one of the greatest, on par with fire and the wheel. All religions recognize the need for it, but they also warn us to be wary of excessive attachment to it. On the one hand, they treat it as a blessing, a blessing that God wants to bestow upon us in plentitude. On the other hand, they describe it as an obstacle to faith, and a mortal menace. At the same time, scriptures also talk of 'spiritualized wealth', and of money as a 'divine tool'. The key is to ensure that it flows in the right direction—without stagnating, or being used for obscene ostentation—and that it is put to use as an instrument to lift the lives of the impoverished millions dying for want of dignity.

Money that is made at the expense of others gets tainted, because it is energetically used in an egocentric, selfish way. No money is too small to make some life-saving difference to someone or the other. One of the *purusharthas* (human aspirations) in Hindu philosophy is *artha*, or material wealth. *Artha* means that which is an asset or that which is meaningful. Most important, it must be acquired or possessed in a dharmic way, which also means not hurting or harming others and not unjustly depriving others of what is their dharmic due. The question is what the quest for money makes of us, and what it makes us do. In its material sense, it provides the wherewithal to enable people, families, institutions societies, and nations to have the basic material needs of life. Yet, money and wealth can also offer humanity more than existential value. Rightly conceived and understood, it can improve the human condition and even bring joy, beauty, and leisure to life. Lack of money can impoverish life, enfeeble the body, denude dignity, and make human life a living hell. On the other hand, if wealth becomes an unprincipled obsession placed above our duties to God and society, it becomes perverted and devoid of its power for the good. Money in some form or the other has always been a legitimately important and moral factor in human life. The Quran says "How excellent wealth is! Through it I protect my honor and get closer to my Lord". The Bible does not call money the root of evil; it is the love of it or obsession with it that leads to evil. What is new is the preeminence of that very 'love' of, or obsession with money in human life, and its emergence as almost the sole means to achieve all human aims, aspirations, expectations—prosperity, well-being, security, control, comfort, power, fame, to be good, even to acquire a good after-life. We can no longer ignore money in any serious reflection of anything human—politics or philosophy, economics or ecology, science or spiritualism, morality or evil, mortality or immortality. The villain is not money, it is the mind. Technology, as a medium of the mind, has accentuated the evil that the love of money can do. Only the rich can afford life-extension technologies, at least in the short term. From pocket money to pensions, making a living to standard of living, savoring good life to the joys of philanthropy, obscene opulence to abysmal poverty, conspicuous consumption to pragmatism, it is all about money.

Money creates problems when we do not have it, and yet, even more problems when we *do* have it. Money has become a major test of human character. How we 'manage' when we do not have it, and how we 'behave' when we have it, speaks a lot about our moral mettle. Money makes us both master and slave. Our power over money is real only inasmuch as we are able to understand its power over us. For centuries, if not millenniums, man has sought to digest the essence of money. Philosophers and economists, statesmen, writers, even poets, have written about money. It has been acclaimed and cursed; dreamed of and disparaged. Money is capable of creating and destroying, of uniting and dismembering. Like God, if we have money in our corner nothing and no one else is needed; for we can 'get' everything else with it. It can be exhilarating, intoxicating, magical, and mesmerizing. It can make people both partners and parasites and can impact the fate of individuals and whole nations. Here comes the unfortunate bit: what was meant as a medium of exchange has turned man himself into a medium—to make money. Those who possess money are in fact possessed by it, overcome by the passion to multiply it by any means and at any cost. And this change, unless corrected, could destroy human society. The crisis in the global financial system is but a symptom. The time has come to face up to the fact that any agenda for human transformation must include how to change the way money is perceived, generated, and utilized. A great virtue of money as a commodity is that it simplifies and facilitates one of the greatest requisites of spiritual life: sharing and giving. If money is properly shared and spread, there would, for example, be no extreme poverty in the world. When it comes to rousing our conscience, statistics have lost their sting and pinch. Yet they provide useful insights. The World Bank says that at least 80% of humanity lives on less than $10 a day. According to UNICEF, about 22,000 children die each day due to poverty. And they die quietly in some of the poorest villages on earth, far removed from the scrutiny and the conscience of the world. Being meek and weak in life makes these dying multitudes even more invisible in death. And, according to Oxfam, the surge of $762 billion in the wealth of the world's 2,043 billionaires, in the year 2017, was enough money to end 'global extreme poverty seven times over'.[13] Another shocking statistic is that only 5% of all new income from global growth trickles down to the poorest 60%. Grim and bad as it might seem, it also offers a ray of hope. Never before did so many people need so little to lead healthier lives, and never before could so few people do so much for so many. Money's very concentration makes it easier to diffuse it in the right direction, with the maximum effect. What is needed is consciousness-change in these billionaires.

Try as we might, it is hard to understand money's grip and gravity; how it came to be the building block of human happiness, the fulcrum around which human life revolves. We can understand the lure of sex, or of power, or pursuit of pleasure, or fear of death; all of which are somehow related to biology and human nature. How could money grow to be such a sinister shadow under which we spend all our brief time on earth and waste all our energy? It looks as if money is the ultimate temptation to drag us down to our doom, to bring to the surface our darkest instincts. Money plays the role of both *Maya*, the Vedantic illusion—the euphoric feeling that with money we need nothing else; and the Buddhist *Mara*—as it tempts us to follow the unrighteous path to acquire, amass, and enjoy wealth. The truly intriguing, even exciting, thing is that in this very area of darkness, it can be a source of liberating light. The much-derided material wealth can also be a means for *Moksha*, not in the sense of breaking an individual's cycle of birth and rebirth or death to death, but in helping each other to break out of their cycle of misery and dehumanization. It is so essential, its absence can cripple life to such a degree, that providing the means to acquire it to the truly needy can become transformative and benefit the 'giver' more than the 'taker'. Although baneful in its effect on the mind, it can also be a conduit for compassion. 'Blessed are those who have money; for they have the power to make the everyday lives of so many so much better'. John D Rockefeller, one of the richest and most philanthropic men of modern times, expressed it aptly: "God gave me my money… I believe the power to make money is a gift from God, to be developed and used to the best of our ability for the good of mankind. Having been endowed with the gift I possess, I believe it is my duty to make money and still more money and to use the money I make for the good of my fellow man according to the dictates of my conscience". This Rockefeller quote was described as a kind of partnership between God and

Mammon. Mammon lords over the accumulating department, and God over the giving and spending department. It also means that different rules govern the two departments. Rockefeller himself was described as 'money mad, money mad, sane in every other respect but money mad'.[14] He didn't pay much heed to means and morals while becoming very, very rich but channeled a good bit of it for charity. How do we rate him as a 'moral man'? Was the world better off or worse off with Rockefeller as he was, lock, stock, and barrel? The fundamental fact does not change: wealth righteously earned and shared generously can help lift many lives; wealth, ill-gotten and unshared, is corrosive. Although we tend to conflate the two, wealth is not another name for money. Wealth is fundamental and is the stuff we need to live: food, clothes, houses, gadgets, travel, land, and so on.

One can have wealth without having money. Wealth is as old as human history. Far older, in fact; even ants have wealth. Money in its current dominating form is but a comparatively recent invention. Leave alone money, making wealth is not the only way to get rich. In fact, for a huge chunk of human history it was not even the most common way. Until a few centuries ago, the main sources of wealth were mines, slaves and serfs, land, and cattle, and the means to acquire them were by inheritance, marriage, conquest, or confiscation. Money gives the false feel of easy access to pleasure, power, and pelf. It makes us feel 'powerful' and paves the path to possessing 'power'.

The Many Faces of Money

The baneful influence of money on humanity was foretold in Hindu scriptures like the Mahabharata, Srimad Bhagavatam, and Ramayana. In Srimad Bhagavatam, for example, Sage Suka says, "In the Kali Yuga, wealth alone will be the criterion of pedigree, morality and merit". In the Mahabharata, Sage Markandeya tells King Yudhishthira "… and wedded to avarice and wrath and ignorance and lust, men will entertain animosities towards one another, desiring to take one another's lives". While all that might have been true when money was not so central to human life, it is no longer fully correct in today's society in which money is irreplaceable and indispensable for orderly life. Indeed what was once said about the mind can now be said about money. The mind, it was said, is the cause of bondage but can also be the source of liberation. Money dominates human life so much that, while the love of it can be the source of evil, its extreme absence can cripple life and deny dignity, an essential attribute of the human condition. DH Lawrence wrote "money poisons you when you've got it and starves you when you haven't".[15] Bob Dylan crooned "while money doesn't talk, it swears".[16] But its hypnotic spell also contains a silver lining. It has, on the one hand, deepened the ill effects of 'love of money'; no relationship, no moral scruple, no sensitivity, is immune to its lure; no crime or sin is unthinkable. In contemporary society, we have bestowed almost godly powers upon money, and whilst money's necessity makes it irreplaceable and universal, it is its deification that makes it a 'religion'. However in religious terms, 'money' and 'wealth' *per se* are not always deemed bad or evil. In Hinduism, the consort of Lord Vishnu is Lakshmi, the goddess of wealth and money.[17] The important point is that money and wealth are viewed in a broader context than in pure monetary terms. They are 'sacred' too and even God Vishnu needed wealth to get himself a wife on earth and had to borrow it from Kubera, the God of wealth.

Apart from its magnetic lure, and because it is deemed so vital for human life, money also attracts many superstitions. There are superstitions surrounding every aspect of money, from getting it to saving it. Some rose from plain old-fashioned common sense while others were rituals based on natural phenomena that were seen to be omens, auspicious and ominous. There are even conflicting superstitions, depending on the culture. In Argentina, finding money in the street is considered extremely lucky. As long as you never spend it, it will bring you more money. But in Trinidad and Tobago, finding money in the street could bring evil spirits into your home. In some countries like Greece, it is believed that money attracts money and so it is bad luck to completely empty one's pocket or wallet. The ancient Greeks threw coins into their wells to keep them from going dry. In Japan, snakes are viewed as symbols of prosperity and therefore purses made with white snakeskin are popular. The ancient art of *Feng Shui* advocates several practices to make money. In England, putting money in new clothes is supposed to bring good luck. According to Mexican tradition, making a cross on the floor after picking up 'found money' will bring even more money. In some countries even bubbles in a cup of coffee or tea are associated with money; elsewhere, if a bee lands on your hand it indicates wealth is on its way to you or if you write with green ink, profits will flow from your hand.

The impact of money goes beyond what we can do with it, what it can buy or procure; it defines life itself, feeds our ego, vanity and viciousness. Money breaks all moral barriers. We might serenade *à la* The Beatles that 'money can't buy me love', but the fact is it is so vital for life, it could even prompt some to take lives in its name. There is almost no crime without a money trail; all crime is, in the end, crime for gain—personal, national, or international. There is growing recognition that controlling money flow is the key to controlling crime. On the other hand, it also became an easily available instrument to better people's lives. The good thing about money is that we do not need a lot of money to do good; even small amounts, properly channeled, can make a significant difference. The same amount can have a varied impact on different people; for some marginal, and for some others life-saving. Properly channeled, money can be a powerful 'compassionate' conduit to alleviate pain, suffering, and misery in the world. It can be a boon and a bane, a blessing or a curse, contingent on how we come to possess it and spread it. One could even go the extent of saying that a person's moral stature is more enhanced if he makes every effort to earn lots of money righteously than if he chooses to eschew any contact with money, even if it were possible. But it is moot if the choice is between earning money unrighteously and using it righteously, or not making any effort to earn any money and not spending any money to help others.

We may fitfully fantasize about transforming human society into a *Shambala* or *Shangri-La*, an *El Dorado* or Utopia, but the crucial challenge before man is to move from the mind-dominated mindset of 'money-mindedness' towards a more just social order and 'spiritual alchemy', which, in the words of Karen-Claire Voss, is "a form of illumination, a means of transmutation, a method for experiencing levels of reality that are not ordinarily accessible, since they exist beyond the level of everyday reality". It is to fundamentally alter the coordinates that drive human consciousness. What becomes unmistakably clear, as we struggle with the pressures, pitfalls, and pulls of modern life, is that the Rubicon that man has to cross is reason itself, what TE Lawrence called 'thought-riddled nature' (*Seven Pillars of Wisdom*). The Sufi saint Jalal ad-Din Rumi said that "it is reason that has destroyed the reputation of the intellect". It is with a blend of inductive reasoning (from the specific to the general) and deductive reasoning (from the general to the specific) that we think through, to deliberate, to deduct, to distinguish the real from the unreal, good from evil, to judge and evaluate the ethical. But the conundrum is that 'reason' is not good enough to *reason* about reason. It does not allow us to be 'reasonable'; it tries to exclude every other source of 'thought'; it makes us feel so smug and sanctimonious, so human-centric. For every moral trespass or callous act, it gives us a 'because' and prevents us from learning from our own life. But at some level of conscious reflection we all, even if grudgingly or fleetingly, admit that there are 'limits to reason' and that we need, in the words of the Polish philosopher Leszek Kolakowski[18] a 'deeper level of engagement with reality' to live life well and truly. But we do not know what these limits are in actuality and since no other tool is on hand we stay faithful to reason and live a life defined—and diminished—by it.

Reason has not even let us be clear-eyed and candid about where man is currently positioned in his own evolution or as a being in the cosmos. Those that are expected to exert the highest human intellect—the pundits, the experts, the specialists—cannot agree among themselves about what is in store for the human race. A case in point concerns the earth's atmosphere. Generally it is believed one of the impending threats to human life on earth is 'global warming', that the planet is dangerously getting hotter and hotter primarily due to human activity. But there are other scholars who contest that the real danger is 'global cooling', not global warming. For example, according to the geoscientist Shigenori Maruyama, we are at the terminal point of the warm interglacial period, and the next glacial age may start at any time, probably by the year 2025.[19] With all our expertise, insights and tools, if we cannot arrive at a consensus on such a life-threatening issue, how can we take any corrective actions, which will need to be tailored to the threat perception? Another example is the strategy for poverty reduction. Some say that the way out is through sustained economic growth; others that it is through dedicated direct targeted programs. Ironically, or tragically, both sides on every contentious issue cite the same 'facts' yet come to completely different conclusions! If the experts and specialists who have the necessary tools and skills cannot come to a consensus, what are we—the novices—supposed to do to take care of our common future?

We live in an age of specialization, super-specialization, and miniaturization. We need specialized knowledge, but specialization should not lead to generalization. We cannot view a human being only in terms of biology or geology or psychology. Man is too complex a being to be explained away in any particular way. While there are many variations, broadly speaking, we are presented with two diametrically contrasting scenarios. One view is that there are those who see in the world, in the words of Viktor Frankl, 'nothing-but-ness'[20] (as distinct from nihilistic 'nothingness'), who find nothing right in the modern world, and believe that our civilization will soon implode; that "humans in our present form will cease to exist, replaced by other species quite unlike our present selves. A beautiful doom, but doom for us nonetheless".[21] Others take a diametrically different view, insisting that ours is a better time than any other, that we are on the launch pad of a planetary civilization, what Joseph Campbell calls 'planetary mythology', an interplanetary habitation that will make man not only immortal but also a true master of the universe. Then we have the theory that whatever is happening is natural and pre-ordained and in that sense we cannot help our behavior, selfish and destructive as it might be. While we play our doomed parts, they tell us, stop 'beating your breast, and instead go with the flow and try to extract as much juice and joy as you can squeeze while you can. But what they forget is that it has also been said that precisely because things are so 'bad' it is also possible to make a big difference through very little effort. Because the world around is so dark, even a tiny candle lit or any small good deed can light up a larger domain and touch more lives than ever before. As Helena Blavatsky, cofounder of the Theosophical Society and author of the classic *The Secret Doctrine* puts it, "Thus, by bearing all the manifold troubles of this [Dark] Age and steadily triumphing, the object of [man's] efforts will be more quickly realized, for, while the obstacles seem great, the powers to be invoked can be reached more quickly". It is also said that the elusive goal of God-realization, is easiest and fastest in this age by simply chanting the divine-name, *nama sankirtana*, as it is called in Sanskrit. It means that the very sweep of immorality in present times can be turned into an opportunity to achieve what man has long sought. It was said that the great Radha–Krishna devotee Chaitanya Mahaprabhu often recited this verse from the Bhagavad Gita:[22] "… one who always keeps Your holy name on his tongue becomes greater than an initiated *brahmana*. Although he may be born in a family of dog-eaters and may therefore, by material calculation, be the lowest among men, he is still glorious. This is the wonderful effect of chanting the holy name of the Lord. It is therefore concluded that one who chants the holy name of the Lord should be understood to have performed all kinds of austerities and great sacrifices mentioned in the Vedas. He has already taken his bath in all the holy places of pilgrimage, he has studied all the Vedas, and he is actually an Aryan" (one who does not boast, but is an actual devotee of God or one who is advanced in spiritual knowledge). Righteous human conduct can be more productive than at any time in recent human history. Science can also be a catalyst to dispel darkness. It has already rid man of much age-old suffering associated with debility and disease.

Money—from *Summum malum* to *Summum bonum*

We all know that money is not only the most valued thing in the world, but human life itself would not be possible without money. On the other hand, although as the Greek philosopher Protagoras said—'Man is the measure of all things: of the things that are, that they are, of the things that are not, that they are not'—money certainly is the measure of everything human, and its 'non-existence' makes human life functionally meaningless. It, above everything else, is responsible for the moral meltdown of man. We also know that for the sake of 'more' money there is nothing man will not do, no barriers he will not cross, no relationship beyond sundering, no crime too heinous. But money, in essence, is only a medium and a tool. It will, like a carriage, take us wherever we want to go, but it will not replace man as the driver. It will give us the wherewithal to satisfy our desires, but it will not *create* our desires. Money gives material shape to the principle that men who wish to deal with one another, must deal by trade and give value for value. When we accept money as a return for our effort, we do so only on the assumption that we will be able to exchange it for the product of the effort of others.

Money cannot purchase happiness nor can the lack of it lead to unhappiness. It is also a question of degree. Daniel Goleman says, "The rich may experience more pleasure than the poor but also require more pleasure to be equally satisfied".[23] It is the mind that makes the difference. As Ayn Rand puts it in *Atlas Shrugged* (1957), "Money will always remain an effect and refuse to replace you as the cause. Money is the product of virtue, but it will not give you virtue and it will not redeem your vices". And, "Money is so noble a medium that it does not compete with guns and it does not make terms with brutality". She goes on, "So long as men live together on earth and need means to deal with one another—their only substitute, if they abandon money, is the muzzle of a gun". It is the mind, not money, that calls the shots. It is the way the mind manipulates money that is responsible for the ills ascribed to money, such as the skewed distribution of wealth. For example, it has been reported that 'the bottom half of the world's population owns the same as the richest 85 people in the world'.[24] The real problem is that money becomes baneful if it flows in the wrong direction, from workers to nonworkers, from the poor to the rich, from the creative to the noncreative. The reality is that the creators are often impoverished and much of the money is held by the work of others, not their own. Money itself would be good if it were our servant, not the master as it is for most of us. Money itself would be a great social stabilizer if it represented goods, labors, and creativity, but it does not.

But strange as it may seem, in this immoral age, money can be made sacred too. It could become a potent moral tool and spiritual bridge. Contrary to popular belief, money *per se* is not innately evil or dirty. It is the mind that matters. Money can be anything: power, freedom, temptation, provocation, the root of all evil, the sum of all blessings. If we use it for the right purpose, it is moral. We must separate earning from spending; just because the money we possess is lawfully earned does not mean we can spend it as we wish for our wants. We must view money too, like morality and mortality, indeed like everything else in the contemporary social context, which includes the stark reality of abysmal poverty and awful living conditions of over a billion people. And money alone, in whoever's hands it might be in, and however little or large, can alleviate, if not erase poverty. And making money should not be seen simply as a zero-sum game. We must revive the spirit of philanthropists like Andrew Carnegie, who maintained that 'no man can become rich without himself enriching others'. In this regard, the rich and poor are alike. The rich can do more but, no one is too poor to help someone poorer or in greater need. Joseph Murphy says, "I like money, I love it, I use it wisely, constructively, and judiciously. Money is constantly circulating in life. I release it with joy, and it returns to me multiplied in a wonderful way". For the *rich* to do more, we need to loosen the grip of what is called 'lifestyle money', money we dispense with to conform and maintain our comparative style of living, and the attitudes, activities and habits that come with it. Indeed much, if not most, of our money goes in that direction, consumed by what is expected of us by the industry and advertisers. The need to live up to our lifestyle leaves very little. For money to serve the social good, we must free ourselves from the assumptions and expectations of a 'good life. But then, some tricky issues crop up. For example, is it okay to rob a bank and distribute the money to the poor? Is corruption justified if we give the money to charity? What takes precedence, righteous earning or righteous sharing? Do ends justify the means insofar as money is concerned? Buddhism lays stress on what it calls 'Right Livelihood', which implies that we cannot work for or participate in socially harmful activities. In any case, its very pervasive indispensability—no one can live without any money—offers an opening. If morally earned and properly channeled, it can make a life-or-death difference; it can lift the poor from the margins of deprivation and destitution to a life of decency and dignity. Through money, at this time in history, one could do more good to more people than through most other means. In other words we now have a window of an opportunity to transform money from *summum malum* (the greatest evil) to *summum bonum* (the greatest good). If we can succeed in this effort, the world will be transformed from what Thomas Hobbes called "*bellum omnium contra omnes,* the state of 'war against all', of 'every man against every man', which is the condition of current society, into a happier and harmonious place.

The source and the use of money demands the highest judgmental skills. It has come to be unjust and exploitative because of the way we 'make it' and mobilize it and marshal it. In the process, our negative passions come into play, like greed, avarice, and malice. These have dominated our mind-driven consciousness and, unless we change the composite of our consciousness, money cannot become a force for good. The result is a human society aptly described by Ayn Rand: "When you see that trading is done, not by consent, but by compulsion—when you see that in order to produce, you need to obtain permission from men who produce nothing—when you see that money is flowing to those who deal, not in goods, but in favors—when you see that men get richer by graft and by pull than by work, and your laws don't protect you against them, but protect them against you—when you see corruption being rewarded and honesty becoming a self-sacrifice—you may know that your society is doomed".[25] But if we can somehow bring to bear on our personality our 'positive' passions like compassion, sharing, sensitivity and justness, then money too can become a creative power. We must also bear a central fact. It is that throughout our lives we do myriad things as members of society, and, despite our best efforts, we can never be sure that what we receive is proportionate to our effort and inputs, that our share is just and that we are not living on someone else's labor, and that our rewards are not ill-gotten. Many theories have been put forth by social scientists on how to ensure fairness in distributing gains from social cooperation but none of them have proved beyond leaks and misapplication. The simplest way is to constantly and consciously make every effort in every context and situation to give more than what we get, to always be on the lookout for even the most trivial opportunities to help and heal and not let go any such openings, regardless of who the recipient, or the occasion, might be. And the simple fact is that there is no other way; nothing else works to give us a sense worthiness and fulfillment—and to solve every problem the world faces—than giving, caring, empathy, compassion, going beyond ourselves and our family, crossing out of our comfort zone to serve others. Let God, not you, be the judge whether they deserve or not. Thank God that He has given you the mind and means to give. That is His gift. The good thing about giving is that you do not need to have anything; you have yourself and that is more 'givable' than anything else. To love you need to give, but to give, you do not need even love. We simply need to have a heart.

The Great Moral Issue of Our Age—Money Management

The medium of money and the act of 'making profit' sanitize any ill effects of what goes on in an office or shop floor or boardroom. If we want to raise the bar of morality in human society we must not exclude any place from moral responsibility. Adding insult to injury, so to speak, the fact also is that most people do not like, let alone enjoy, what they do to make money. In other words, they get no joy in this world and are accountable in the afterworld. We must also address what has come to be known as the 'doctrine of lesser evil', that sometimes we have to deliberately choose an alternative that violates our own moral sensitivity and do things against the grain, as the only other choice would be to condone or allow something more horrible to happen. For example, suppose the state has in its custody a suspect who has information about a horrific act, and does not reveal it despite cajoling and persuasion. Would the state be morally justified in torturing him? While it is true that often choices are between different grays, not between white and black or good and evil, we must not forget that the 'lesser evil' is also evil and that we are morally culpable. It also underscores the truism that there are no absolutes in nature, not even in morality. Each case has to be judged on its own merit. We must constantly reconcile contradictions between concrete contemporary conditions and absolute, non-historical, universal values. That can only be done by an 'active subjective judgment'; by means of a 'monologue in our mind' and a 'conversation in our consciousness'. All morality comes down to that. That is why the key to everything is consciousness.

We want to live our lives without inconvenience, without discomfort and without any pain, and we want good health and a good life. And, we have come to believe that to have these, we need *plenty* of money. And for that no price is too high, no sacrifice too sacred and no sacrilege too profane. Andrew Carnegie, the American philanthropist and once dubbed one of the richest men in history, said that the proper management of wealth was a great moral issue of our age, that nothing debases more than the worship of money and that "a man who dies rich dies disgraced". For many—too many people—money is a measure of their identity and self-worth; it makes them feel powerful, on top of the world, and conversely, its absence or limitation makes them feel impoverished, if not existentially impotent. Nothing else matters more; nothing else gives us more thrill and satisfaction, when one has it, and nothing causes more despair, when one does not have it. Nothing else is ever enough, and nothing else casts a more somber shadow over human life. Money can buy or get anything, so we say, but there are exceptions too. Mata Hari, the famous female spy and seductress during the First World War said that she would prefer to be the mistress of a poor officer than of a rich banker! Was she then less money-minded and more moral?! After all, she was just doing a job, a refrain that is a constant in modern life. All our life is consumed by whatever it takes to get a job, to keep a job, not to lose a job, to change a job. And we cover many moral omissions and transgressions by saying 'I am just doing my job'. The principal reason to do a job is to make money. A job lets us make money, which, in turn, lets us make a living, often at the expense of making a life. We work, we study, and we live with money 'as the object'. Philosopher Alan Watts used to ask his students, "What would you like to do if money were no object", and "How would you really enjoy spending your life". The answers were to be poet, writer, painter, and so on. The tragedy is that most people spend their life engaged in a professional activity that is *not* their passion. And there is nothing more limiting and mentally more destructive than doing things one does not like. But the greater question is that if money is no longer an object, would we really spend the day in the sun with a pen or a brush or a shovel? More likely, we would be sitting in front of a screen! Even if we do not have to 'make' or earn money, money must still be spent, whatever we come to have in any way. How we use, spend, share or spread money still remains as a moral matter. What we need to do is to change the mindset.

A big chunk of contemporary human effort is to do what the ancient Indian sage Yagnavalkya (in the *Brihadaranyaka* Upanishad) told his wife Maitreyi cannot be done: to buy immortality with money. Scott Fitzgerald famously said,—'Let me tell you about the very rich. They are different from you and me…' They are different not only because they have more money, which enables them to live differently and live in 'refinement, utmost refinement, total refinement' as Siddhartha Gautama described his life before his awakening, they even think differently of death! They are different from the rest but they are also different from each other in the way they see, gain, and use their wealth. Although money has a corrosive effect on human consciousness, money can also make a difference between a life of dignity and a life of indignity and degradation. Being very poor can rob a person of what it takes to be human. And the very rich can lift the very poor from that subhuman state. Not doing so can be as sinful as slow murder. That is why all religions extol charity. Charity is not meant only for the rich; it is sharing, and sharing can be done by everyone, even the poor because there is always someone else richer and poorer than us. No one can become rich only through solitary effort or that they are the most deserving of them all. For the very process entails unequal and disproportionate effort. In that sense it is a reasonable assumption to go by that no one is 'rich' because he has righteously earned it and charity is not giving but giving back; it is paying back in money what we borrowed in kind, as sweat and skill, time and energy of other people.

There have always been economic gaps, and some have had more money than others, and men have always desired to live in the lap of luxury. Today, the gap between the rich and the poor is becoming wider and sharper than perhaps ever before, which could become a major source of social tension. Human experience over millenniums has shown that human ingenuity is far better at creating wealth than sharing and distributing it. In 2011, *The Economist* magazine, usually an ardent advocate of economic growth as the panacea for the ills of humankind, identified this issue as a primary trigger for global instability. In its special report, it noted that there are more high-net-worth-individuals and millionaires than Australians in the world. About 1,000 billionaires happen to control one third of global assets; the richest 1% of adults control 43% of the world's assets; the wealthiest 10% have 83%, and the bottom 50% have only 2%. Those at the bottom, particularly those at the 'bottom of the bottom', the absolute poor, the marginalized, the downtrodden, the oppressed, are those who lead lives that deny them the full biological human potential, and yet it is they who allow the rest to lead 'human' lives. The leisure class and the mainstream mass and the middle class, depend on the marginalized, for the goods and services that backstop their luxury, leisure, entertainment, even to live in their opulent homes. The growing gap between the leisure class and the working class has widened social divisions. It has given rise to those, particularly in the rural areas, who are called left-wing-extremists, who argue that those at the top are rank exploiters and cruel predators and that only through violence would it be possible to endow, enable and empower those at the bottom and restore a better economic balance in human society. Their aim is to overthrow the tyranny of plutocracy and install the reign of the proletariat. Because of the widening gap, on the one hand, and because the poor are now able to actually see through the mass media how the rich lead their lives at their expense, their creed is increasingly finding favor with the rest of the 'bottom' in many countries. If money continues to play the same deterministic role in human affairs, and the new class of the nouveau riche, which includes national and transnational corporations, continues to control the levers of economic and political power, there can be little doubt the economic divide of the world could become a source of catastrophic conflict in this century.

There is another downside to this division. With sheer bodily survival and subsistence consuming so much labor, effort, and time, the human has long dreamed of leisure as the route to *nirvana*, allowing him to do more worthwhile things that are good for his soul. We commonly identify affluence with luxury,

luxury with leisure, leisure with entertainment, and entertainment as a way to eclipse our misery. These days, nothing holds our attention except what comes to us as entertainment. Entertainment is today's enlightenment. It gobbles up almost all the time left after making a living, all the time released by traveling faster, and working with, even being replaced by, a machine. For entertainment stimulates; and without stimulation, our mind wanders away, looking for something more juicy. We watch the news only if it is entertaining and graphic. A celebrity or high-class murder is the perfect fix—in one go we have glamour, sex, violence, and mystery. Earlier, people used to dread natural disasters as their lives and homes would be in danger. Now, secure in the thought that we are insulated and insured, the excitement begins the moment we hear of any impending storm or cyclone; we are even inwardly disappointed if it passes by without event. The real tragedy of human life is that we are at sea both in the state of work and at leisure; in earning a livelihood and in enjoying leisure. The Mahabharata reminds us that *kala* (time) cooks all beings. As life ebbs and every passing moment brings us closer to death, the cosmic question crops up: after biology is done with, what should a living being do with every waking minute of earthly life? Since nothing is purposeless, what did nature intend when it created the human form of life? The affluent have luxury but little leisure, and no time other than to make more money and to keep it safe, not even the time to enjoy the luxury, let alone provide food for the soul. They are not worried about their own growth; they want their money to grow. While money appreciates, morality depreciates. Topmost on the menu of what parents want to leave behind to their kids is money in its various avatars. What we now have is a desire for the lap of luxury. The kind of things that some want—and have—are outlandish and obscene, not only when compared to the poor and deprived, but also in terms of what it means to the earth. Morality apart, that kind of human life, albeit limited to a tiny minority of men, carries not only serious economic implications but also potentially perilous ecological, environmental, and civilizational consequences. In one sense, the milieu of their lives is not human anymore. The rest are 'doubly-disadvantaged'—they do not get to share the spoils, yet they pay the price. This leads to bitterness, hatred, and violence. The irony, and tragedy, is that in our craving for the luxuries of life we are compromising and corrupting the necessities of life. What the poet Edward Young said of kingdoms applies equally to civilizations, and perhaps to species—

on the soft bed of luxury most kingdoms have expired. That very perceptive philosopher Thoreau also puts it well: "Most of the luxuries and many so-called comforts of life are not only *not* indispensable, but are positive hindrances to the elevation of mankind".

We can erode but not erase economic inequity, let alone inequality. We cannot bridge the so-called development divide or eliminate the exhibition of obscene opulence if we treat the issue only in economic or political terms. Even conceding that perfect economic equality is impossible and that that inequality is a part of diversity, the fact in its extreme forms has a pernicious effect on societies, "eroding trust, increasing anxiety and illness, ... encouraging excessive consumption".[26] And, that "for each of eleven different health and social problems: physical health, mental health, drug abuse, education, imprisonment, obesity, social mobility, trust and community life, violence, teenage pregnancies, and child well-being, outcomes are significantly worse in more unequal rich countries".[27] Inequality is bad both for the very rich and the poor, and for the in-betweens. It is bad for the rich as it robs them of their capacity for empathy. It is bad for the poor because their minimum material needs overwhelm everything else, distorting their priorities and diminishing their human potential. But the more important point is that, even if we want to, we do not have the means, or the methods, by which we can justly apportion the fruits of any common labor in any collective work. Let alone put to practice the Marxist maxim 'from each according to his ability, to each according to his need'. It is also because the nature and quality of labor of different constituent persons is so different that it is not possible to objectively weigh their contributions; and if we cannot do that how can we determine their 'fair bite' of the collective pie? But still no one can say that a CEO getting 110 times more than an employee, at a time when money is what matters most, is nothing but socially incendiary and morally repugnant.

Even if one practices the adage 'frugality is morality', the essential point is that what we do with money—quantum being immaterial, and the poor not excluded—and how we earn it and live with its tantalizing presence or paralyzing absence, is the true test of morality. Money has also a critical bearing on man's two other, in the words of Prof. Darshan Singh Maini, "cruel despoilers of life's bounties and largesse":[28] sex and power. And sex has a strange power over us. It is a great leveler like death, and breaks through all barriers of gender, age, relationship, blood ties, position, and privilege. No one is an untouchable when it comes to sex. A master would not even touch a slave or share a meal with her, but is eager to engage her in the most intimate exchange and seduction. A billionaire would not care to glance at a destitute, but if she is deemed 'desirable', he would pay anything to buy her body. Where is the hypocrisy? Is this nature's way to ensure that sex never gets outdated or outclassed by any other power or temptation, including money? We have come to believe that with enough money we can control everyone, buy anything and anyone, barter everything—from virginity to maternity; from societal adulation to angelic immortality. In a sense, wanting to be good and not wanting to be dead are natural desires; it is money that makes man a monkey, makes him do things he would not otherwise be tempted or possibly persuaded to do. And money accentuates the veneer of vanity that clouds our vision. Although money has come to play a deterministic—maybe even terminal—role in human affairs, its power of seduction has long been recognized. The *Panchatantra,* the ancient Indian text long considered a *nitishastra* or text book of wise conduct and good behavior, says, "money causes pain in getting; in the keeping, stress and fretting; pain in loss, pain in spending; damn the trouble never ending... money can only get what money can buy—not happiness, not sleep; wisdom, etc."[29] It also says that "No treasure equals charity; content is perfect wealth; no gem compares with character; no wish fulfilled, with health".[30] The Bible says that, 'The love of money is the root of all evil.' Christ elaborated, "It is easier for a camel to pass through a needle than for a rich man to pass through the gates of heaven";[31] and "If you want to be perfect, go and sell all your possessions and give the money to the poor". And again, "No one can serve two masters, for either he will hate the one and love the other; or else he will be devoted to one and despise the other. You cannot serve both God and Mammon".[32] It is not that all rich are evil; it is that money must be righteously earned and it is that those with a lot of money are more likely to expend much of their energies towards protecting their riches and their expansion.

Like much else that scriptures, prophets and sages have enjoined upon us, these too have fallen on deaf ears. Instead of giving away, we want to grab, and our appetite for acquisition is insatiable. We want to be perfect while still being greedy and part with nothing for the marginalized. With matters of money, earning, storing, saving, and spending have become the primary, if not sole, preoccupations for the best of men. Morality, we believe, exacts too heavy and high a price; it becomes a burdensome bore, an obstacle to sipping the sweetness of life, a needless needle in an already complicated life. Yet, despite their different trajectories and governing dynamics, man has been able to maintain, until the advent of modernity, some kind or semblance of balance between the triad of his three deepest desires—to be moral, to make money, and to ease into immortality. Each was able to hold its own and assert its own legitimacy, without inordinately or improperly encroaching on the other's psychic space. Man's desire to be moral did not stifle his desire to be materially well-off; his desire for material well-being, in a large measure, was morally moderate; and his desire to be death-less was not overly influenced by his moral or monetary standing. It is this balance or symmetry that is now seriously disturbed and distorted. For men of this century, *moksha* or liberation comes down to one thing: to be free from the hypnotic hold of money and thus be able to share it. Put differently, without freedom from money, or rather from the things that money lets us afford, no other freedom is of much use on the spiritual path. Indeed it is becoming clearer every passing day that the economic, environmental, and social problems of the world are, at their very core, moral issues that need to be addressed at the micro level; not only at the individual level, but even at the microcosmic level of the mundane chores of daily life. At the root of morality is money. In one sense, we have made morality mortal, and mortality amoral, and money the metaphor for man. The minimal goal, the bench mark, so to speak, has to be that we must be able to lead full and productive lives, work for a living, raise a family and savor the goodness of life without worshipping wealth, exploiting each other, trying to cheat death, exterminating other forms of life and ravaging nature. And in so doing, we must let the *Buddha* inside the womb of each of us to come to life.

Money, it has also been said, has "the power to blind us even to our better selves".[33] Marx, in his *Economic and Philosophical Manuscripts* (1844), gives the dialectical and existential perspective. Among other things, he writes that 'by possessing the *property* of buying everything, by possessing the property of appropriating all objects, *money* is thus the *object* of eminent possession. The universality of *its property* is the omnipotence of its being. It is therefore regarded as omnipotent... Money is the procurer between man's need and the object, between his life and his means of life. But *that which* mediates my life for me, also *mediates* the existence of other people for me. For me it is the *other* person'. He calls money the '*distorting* power both against the individual and against the bonds of society, etc., which claim to be *entities* in themselves. It transforms fidelity into infidelity, love into hate, hate into love, virtue into vice, vice into virtue, servant into master, master into servant, idiocy into intelligence, and intelligence into idiocy'. And again 'that which is for me the medium of money—that for which I can pay (i.e., which money can buy)—that am *I myself*, the possessor of money. The extent of the power of money is the extent of my power. Money's properties are my—the possessor's—properties and essential powers. Thus what I *am* and *am capable of* is by no means determined by my individuality. And further 'money is the supreme good; therefore its possessor is good. Money, besides, saves me the trouble of being dishonest: I am therefore presumed honest…'. Marx, citing Shakespeare, calls money the 'visible divinity', that it has the ability to transform all human and natural properties into their contraries; and that it is 'the common whore, the common procurer of people and nations'. He then asks, "If money is the bond binding me to *human* life, binding society to me, connecting me with nature and man, is not money the bond of all bonds? Although Marx writes intensely about money, albeit tinged with an implicit warning, perhaps the most euphoric description of money comes from the pen of Ayn Rand, who writes, in her magnum opus *Atlas Shrugged*, that money is 'the barometer of a society's virtue', 'the creation of the best power within you and your passkey to trade your effort for the effort of the best among men'. Ayn Rand says that 'money rests on the axiom that every man is the owner of the mind and his effort', that 'when you accept money as payment for your effort, you do so only on the condition that you will exchange it for the product of the effort of others… your wallet is your statement of hope that somewhere in the world around you, there are men who will not default on that moral principle, which is the root of money'. Further, according to her, 'Money demands of the recognition that men must work for their own benefit, not for their own injury, for their gain, not their loss—the recognition that they are not the beasts of burden, born to carry the weight of your misery—that you must offer them values, not wounds—that the common bond among men is not the exchange of suffering, but the exchange of goods. Money demands that you sell not your weakness for men's stupidity, but your talent for their reason…'. Rand says that 'money is the product of virtue, but it will not give you virtue and it will not redeem your vices'. She adds "but money demands of you the highest virtues, if you wish to make it or keep it" and proclaims that the proudest distinction of Americans is the coining of the phrase 'to make money', which she says 'holds the essence of human morality'. Rand is breathtaking and makes one breathless too. If all that she says is true, man, at least an American, must have become an angel by now, and the Western world, at least America, a land fit for gods. That it hasn't happened nor is it likely to should give us some food for thought.

That kind of 'thought' is articulated by those scholars and spiritualists who have chronicled, what they call, the perils of money. The reality is that, as the writer Louisa May Alcott put it, "money is the root of all evil, and yet it is such a useful root that we cannot get on without it any more than we can without potatoes". John Stuart Mill once said that money is a machinery for doing quickly and commodiously, what would be done, though less quickly and commodiously, without it. Metals have been used as money throughout history. They became useful when the various necessities of life could not be effectively carried out, and, as a result, societies agreed to deploy in their dealings with each other something that is innately useful and easily applicable. The value of the metal was in the beginning measured by weight, but, over time, rulers or sovereigns put stamps upon it to avoid the headache of weighing it, and to make the value recognizable on sight. While money always played an important role in human civilization—metallic money was in use over 2,000 years before the birth of Christ—its power increased enormously with the advent of paper money in the late 18th century and since then man has not been the same. It fuelled the contemporary culture of consumption and a mindset of materialism. The arrival of electronic money and what is called e-commerce in the late 20th century unhinged money from the constraints of space and time. Money has transformed human personality more than any other single factor. It became the sole criterion for judging a person's worth and success in life. The pervasive influence—mostly negative—of money and materialism on human psychology is well documented in a recent book called *The High Price of Materialism* by Tim Kasser.[34] Kasser offers a scientific explanation of how materialistic values affect 'our everyday happiness' but also makes the point that the effect is not only on the psychological well-being of man but also on his physical health.

Money, Body, and Brain

In today's world, the underscoring belief is that nothing and no one is without a price tag, in cash or kind; nothing we can summon is beyond barter for pleasure and progress. The driving force is money. A growing number are turning to their bodies to earn extra money, or to make both ends meet, not as a last resort but as an easy option. Today's utilitarian man argues: why must we exclude, as a resource, the body that is the only thing we unquestionably own, and over which no one else can lay a claim? If one can 'morally' and legally sell or mortgage our brains to make a living, which is what much of what we call 'work' or doing a 'job' is, why can't we sell or put to use our own body and its parts to make a living? In the age of 'marketing' for money, specific parts are marketed for cash. For instance, in Japan, one advertising agency paid young women for *thigh-vertising*—wearing a temporary product tattoo on the bare skin between the hem of a short-skirt and the top of a knee-sock. Then, an enterprising young man in America launched *Lease Your Body*, to entice good-looking people to 'lease' space on their bodies to advertise and market commercial products. Of course, there are innumerable other ways in which one could market his or her body for a living—selling one's hair, sperm or eggs, breast milk, bone marrow and blood, renting a womb, modeling naked, etc. We generally consider that some of these practices, particularly prostitution, to 'make a living' as signs of moral degeneration, but we are soft and silent when it comes to selling one's skills and souls, talent and ingenuity for the sake of promoting armaments, alcohol, cigarettes, and drugs. It means that the body is sacred and the brain is secular. In fact, we can do more harm by lending or leasing our brain for the wrong purposes than the body. Body vending primarily affects the individual whereas brain misuse impacts on society itself. It is very difficult to inject morality into this matrix. One could forcefully argue that there is nothing wrong, that the individuals are only making use of whatever nature has endowed them with. They are harming or hurting no one. If anyone 'suffers' it is only they, and society cannot have double standards between brain and body. The critical ingredients in whatever work we do are intent, sincerity, honesty, diligence and being useful and helpful, not harmful.

After all, it is with the body that athletes and sportsmen earn money and glory by being 'auctioned' to represent or play for the highest bidder in games such as cricket. Then again, if selling sex is the culprit, what about marrying for money? Many sell their body, and arguably their soul and autonomy, in an institution like marriage. It is also said that 'prostitution' is not simply selling sex; it includes any action that compromises one's beliefs and values to obtain another thing, whether money, security, or even a promotion. The other view can be that all religions prohibit the use of sex for a living. This view holds that the sex organ is not like any other organ, that sexual intimacy is of a different genre than any other human interfacing, that commercial sex is often exploitative and that, as it is associated with procreation, it is sacred. For long, experts have debated why the human race is so aggressive, bloodthirsty and kill-happy. Is the 'villain' the gene, our hormones, or the environment? Why do we destroy that which gives us shelter and which keeps us alive, the earth? Why do we starve ourselves and build weapons that kill us all many times over? Are we diabolic, or demented or deranged? Contrary to what one might infer from today's horrific cruelty, massacres, and mayhem, the idea that humans are peaceable by nature and corrupted by modern institution, has always found a voice in authors and intellectuals. Take, for a small example, José Ortega Gasset ('War is not an instinct but an invention'), Stephen Jay Gould ('*Homo sapiens* is not an evil or destructive species'), and Ashley Montagu ('Biological studies lend support to the ethic of universal brotherhood'). There are some scientists who say that, in the ultimate test of altruism, "we are better at putting ourselves in other's shoes than we used to be" and that we are actually more evil in the cause of antiquated morality (e.g., religious morality) than from "amoral predation and conquest".[35]

The principal reason why we cannot agree if we are 'morally' better or worse-off is that we cannot agree on what human well-being is or ought to be, and if there is anything we can all embrace as an all-weather 'moral truth'. And it all depends on what we bring under the rubric of 'violence'. Although there is a decline in the number of armed conflicts and resultant casualties in this century, it should not lead us to obscure the bigger picture. We must remember that 'violence' is a multi-headed monster and manifests in multiple ways. The time has come to broaden its ambit beyond the 'intentional use of physical force or power, threatened or actual'; it must extend to mental, psychological, social, and moral dimensions. We might not go as far as the Jain scripture that says that "all sins like falsehood, theft, attachment and immorality are forms of violence which destroy the purity of the soul". But we must include several other forms of violence besides the physical, and also acts of omission, indifference, intolerance, and injustice. For example, violence by the word is far more insidious and degrading of dignity than violence by hand. Hurting, humiliating and wounding other's sensibilities and sensitivities, taking undue advantage of others' vulnerabilities and helplessness, deliberately slighting, a cutting word and obscene opulence in the midst of acute poverty are also forms of violence, more lasting than physical harm. From this perspective the world today is more violent than ever before. Indeed modern life is unlivable without some sort of 'violence'. Thomas Merton wrote half a century ago that the "rush and pressure of modern life are a form, perhaps the most common form, of its innate violence". That innate violence, in the past five decades, has turned into 'infectious' violence. Today, to be violent is the use of any kind of force intended to control or exert power over another person to make him act in a manner contrary to his volition, and to hurt, intimidate, inhibit or dominate another person. It may take various forms: an action, spoken words, written words, humiliation, etc. The modern world is also seething with 'collective' forms of violence like genocide, ethnic cleansing and race riots. We have crafted a society that values, even worships, both work and entertainment, and people use technology to switch off one form of 'being busy' and switch on the other. This is a form of violence. It causes violence first of all to the human persona and psyche, because we cannot either know or become our true selves if we don't have periodic periods of reflection free from distraction. Second, 'being busy' in both work and entertainment serves primarily material purposes at the cost of moral and spiritual underpinnings. Our obsession with corrosive consumerism is a form of violence; so is our relentless onslaught on the earth's ecosystem. But we do not think, even the best among us, that we are violent; it is insidious. We are all 'violent' in one form or the other but perhaps the most violent of all is the very instrument—the State—which is meant to offer security and safety to those who are victims of the more powerful and exploitative among us. A monopoly over the legal use of violence is deemed a *sine qua non* of the modern State. Violence and state power are inextricably intertwined, with the state operating simultaneously as a limiting and restraining force and as a perpetrator of systemic use of violence and force. To put it differently, a state inflicts violence against another state and other organized groups (warfare), it can direct violence against its citizens (State violence) as a way to exercise control and political power, or it can wield its monopoly of the legitimate use of force to constrain or contain the use of violence within society in the name and guise of maintaining public order.

Whether or not we are 'natural-born-noble savages', as Rousseau described, we cannot ignore the unmistakable truth that the factors that inseminate and impregnate violence—avarice, anger, animosity, self-righteousness, possessiveness, intolerance—are 'natural' to our psyche. We must first acknowledge this insight. PD Ouspensky once wrote that "so long as a man is not horrified at himself he knows nothing about himself". It may be that in today's world, a popular form of entertainment is no longer, like in 16th-century France, cat-burning, in which cats were hoisted in a sling and slowly lowered into a fire, while people watched and cheered; but we still use dogs for target practice. Slavery as a labor-saving device might be illegal but we still have bonded labor. Most people see not much difference between entertainment and enlightenment, sensory satisfaction and salvation. Rape is still a lascivious part of the spoils of war; but it also is more intrusive and pervasive, touching almost every human relationship—we now have things like date-rape; marital-rape; child-rape; revenge-rape, gang-rape and incest-rape. And unlike in the past when the casualties of war were confined largely to the battlefield, what we see now, euphemistically called collateral damage, is the murder of civilians far away from the actual arena of fighting, accounting for more killings and mutilations than that of the actual combatants. Killing has always been integral to the human psyche. It has always been viewed as the ultimate punishment, deterrent, or manner of settling scores. Since Cain went nuts and killed Abel, there have always been those humans who, for one reason or another, forcibly and violently ended others' lives. The Roman Emperor Tiberius enjoyed throwing victims off a cliff on the Mediterranean island of Capri. Gilles de Rais, a French knight and ally of Joan of Arc during the Middle Ages, went crazy and ended up murdering hundreds of children. Just a few decades later Vlad the Impaler, the inspiration for Dracula, was killing people in Transylvania in numberless horrifying ways. History is replete with mass murderers from Genghis Khan to Mao Zedong to Pol Pot. And every war is mass murder. In every society, there are individuals who feel an urge inside them to kill not only those they have a grudge against, but total strangers. What does it all mean? What has happened is that there has been a seismic shift in the psychology of killing in the mind of man. Virtually our entire civilization is built on killing and death—for fun, for pleasure, or profit, and even (supposedly), "for God!" It is no longer the ultimate deterrent or act of cruelty, or punishment. More and more people are associating killing, the self or others, as an easy way to accomplish their life goals, to eliminate what they fear, or as a facile 'problem solver'. And technology makes it easier; 'distant killing' allows you to stay in comfort somewhere and take lives far away. Are such people less or more guilty than one who fears for his life, real or illusory, and kills a neighbor? We should also refocus our priorities of culpability and criminality and bring to the forefront what are called social or 'white collar' crimes. Our love affair with the miracle of the marketplace, and the resultant gross economic injustice, is 'killing by emaciation' and deprives and devastates more people than killing the old-fashioned way. Companies that advertise products known to be slow killers are silent killers. There are those who adulterate food, air, and even medicines for profit and *de facto* kill, cripple or endanger the health of more people than mass murderers, but such people are often envied for their riches and lifestyles. It may be time to revisit and rethink 'direct' killing.

It is noteworthy that, in Hindu mythology, God and his avatars never hesitated to kill the 'evil' person, not only as a punishment for his evil deeds but also on the premise that his continued 'existence' was not in the interest of the world. One could even argue that if death is no 'big deal' as the scriptures tell us—it is but another rite of passage of life—then why should killing, which is another form of dying, be held so heinous? Even now, many societies allow euthanasia, which is killing with consent. Today, killing is taking more mundane but macabre forms, not very different from lying, cheating, and robbing. The everyday happenings we read in our newspapers are hard to square up with the premise that human violence is on the wane. It is of little comfort that the occurrence of such horrible things was foretold in this age, the Kali Yuga, in the epic Mahabharata: "In the dark age (of Kali), morality mixed with three parts of sin liveth by the side of men". We have now rampage murders or spree killings: a lone man, normal and nondescript, for no apparent reason, suddenly starts killing total strangers or his own family members. Such killings have always been a part of our horrific history, cutting across continents, race, religion, ethnicity, and economic and social status. While that is true, it would be a grievous folly not to recognize their contemporary civilizational implications. For the new breed of mass murderers, killing is just another way to assert their self-identity, to vent their rage or grievance or redress an injury, perceived or real. In 1999, two high school teenagers went on a killing spree at their school in Colorado, USA. One of them, Eric Harris, apparently wrote in his notebook, "Humans are as dispensable as fungus in a petri dish… I have a goal to destroy as much as possible… I want to burn the world… no one should survive". It is easy to dismiss such people as psychopaths, psychotics or sociopaths or simply as sadistic human freaks. But they too are children of our time and temper, germinated and incubated in the same melting pot of human culture.

The 'Good' That Money Can Do

In essence, and in its effect, money is power, the most powerful and potentially polluting of all. If the power of money cannot be wished away, what do we do? Should we use all our energy, attention and activism to curb and contain its role and influence, or can we turn it around and use it as an instrument for doing good, to help others in dire need, to use it as a social leveler ? Whether we like it or not, we have to acknowledge money's magnetic hold on the human mind and yet strive to see how to salvage some time and synergy for our spiritual growth. We do not have to choose whether it is the 'root of evil' or 'necessary evil', divine gift or devil's ploy—it may be all or none. We don't have to agree with the assertion that "until and unless you discover that money is the root of all good, you will ask for your own destruction. When money ceases to be the tool by which men deal with one another, then men become the tools of men".[36] One of the more important questions is: in a world controlled by money, how can we make or earn it *dharmically*, and spend and spread it bearing in mind that much of what we come to have is more than our moral right? To make money moral, it must flow in the right direction; it must be shared and spread. Is the Robin Hood way, the moral way? That is, the redistribution of wealth, what most governments are supposed to do under the cover of legality.

Money is now the measure, motive, metaphor, and means of everything we do, desire and dream of in life. It is also a measure of self-worth and self-respect. As an *ABBA* lyric intones, 'Money, money, money; always sunny in a rich man's world'.[37] In the poor man's world, its lack is marked by the three deadly 'D's: desperation, deprivation, and death. In fact, there is no such thing as 'rich man' or 'poor man'; every one is both richer and poorer than someone else. But that doesn't change the fact that our fascination with wealth knows no bounds, with some even being addicted to wealth. Some have confessed that earning bulging bonuses running into millions of dollars causes something similar to an alcohol or drug addiction, prompting rage and an uncontrollable desire for more, risking to destroy themselves and their companies rather than be satisfied with the millions or billions they already have. Money does indeed make the world go round but most of us want the best of both; we don't want to be rich and be the subject of envy, derision and disdain but, as Pablo Picasso quipped, we want to 'live as a poor man with lots of money'. Although it is impossible to define the rich, and although we want to have what the rich have, we don't want to be 'different from you and me', which is how Scott Fitzgerald famously described the very rich.[38] As for living like the very poor, we would rather die. We would rather be a Gabriel Garçia Marquez, who said, "No, not rich. I am a poor man with money, which is not the same thing". What he implies is that he wants to have his cake and eat it too; exercise power without responsibility. Money has many functions, purposes and attractions. But it is most irresistible as power, in its essence and in its effect.

Money and the mind are made for each other; together they are playing havoc on human life. Money and commerce have become the analogies through which all our human experiences are mediated. In a 2010 survey in the USA, some 77% of the youngest people polled said they are more concerned about outliving their money in retirement than about death itself.[39] The make-or-break importance we attach to money was foreseen. In the Hindu scripture Srimad Bhagavatam, it is written that 'a person will be judged unholy if he does not have money, and hypocrisy will be accepted as virtue'. Whether or not it is the love, or lack, of money that is at the root of evil, the reality is that we don't own money anymore; *money* owns us. Money is the bedrock of materialism; the backbone of capitalism; indeed, the essential to any economic 'ism'. It is the measure of meaningfulness, of well-being, of good feeling; of health and happiness; but not necessarily of goodness or of a virtuous life. Socrates said, "I tell you that virtue is not given by money, but that from virtue comes money and every other good of man, public as well as private". Money has, left to its own genius, had a baneful influence on morality. Possessing, earning, amassing, even spending it, is so overpowering that anything that comes in its way is brushed aside. A study revealed that "as a person's levels of wealth increase, their feelings of compassion and empathy go down, and their feelings of entitlement, of deservingness, and their ideology of self-interest increases…", and that wealthier individuals are more likely to moralize greed and self-interest as favorable, less likely to be pro-social, and more likely to cheat and break laws if it behooves them".[40] The findings of the study also revealed that 'People who make less are more generous… on the larger scale'; 'rich people are more likely to ignore pedestrians'; and 'poverty impedes cognitive function'.[41] Another study indicates that 'more money makes people act less human or, at least less humane'.[42] As one writer put it, 'Money can weaken even the firmest ethical backbone. Money sows the seeds of mistrust. It ends friendships. Experiments have found that it encourages us to lie and cheat'.[43] 'The simple idea of money changes the way we think—weakening every other social bond'.[44] As Marx remarked, "money, then, appears as the enemy of man and social bonds that pretend to self-subsistence".

Everything in this life is a mixed bag; so is money. Its total identification with modern life, its all-embracing scope, and the depth of its penetration has made the power of money transformational. While its immense potential to make man do horrible things has long been known, what is emerging is its transformational potential to do good. Given how irreplaceable it has become, money can make, if righteously earned and judiciously channeled, a decisive difference between life and death, between destitution and dignity. It could be a fairly accurate moral barometer of, in Ayn Rand's words, 'society's virtue'. This is not a novel idea. A distinction on how money was earned and the purposes for which it was utilized was a part of ancient Greek thought. Aristotle, for example, distinguished between the making of money to satisfy real needs (which he considered to be a virtuous activity) and the accumulation of money for its own sake (which he considered to be a deleterious activity). If the essence of man is morality, the purpose of mortality is to give meaning to life and increasingly, for good or bad, that 'meaning' of meaning is coming close to how we share each others' life, materially and spiritually. But the more basic question remains.

Should we at all allow the make-or-break role money is playing in human life? We can now 'buy' everything, including insurance for immortality, which, we are told, is cheaper than normal insurance ($78 per month for a 'cryonics term life insurance').[45] We can obtain the rewards of morality by being altruistic and donating money to noble causes. Perhaps even a passage to heaven. If money is spent in a socially beneficial manner, can that be a substitute to care and compassion, to what we consider as 'good behavior' and give us what in Hinduism is called *punya*, the rewards of virtuous actions? On the other hand, if money is used for wrong purposes or not properly shared, does it result in *paapa*, the fruits of evil deeds? But is that right? Ideally no one should be enabled to have more than what one needs, or left in a position to decide how to discretionally dispose of the 'surplus', even if it is done philanthropically. But is that possible? If society removes the allure of excess money, as wages, income, or as inheritance and takes over the responsibility of providing a person's living needs, will anyone work at all to their potential? One reason communism never had a chance as an egalitarian experiment was this insuperable impediment. Inevitably, we are left with the only imperfect alternative: to focus not in the direction of crushing or curbing the earning capacity of individuals, but in the direction of equitable distribution and social stimulants for sharing, altruism, and philanthropy.

We have to bring into our economic thinking the moral dimension. To be moral, money must move from the affluent to the middle class, from the middle class to the lower class. One way could be to inject what was once known as *georgism* (also known as geoism and geonomics) which is an 'economic philosophy holding that the economic value derived from natural resources and natural opportunities should belong equally to all residents of a community, but that people own the value they create'.[46] That philosophy attracted great thinkers like John Locke, Spinoza and Tolstoy. It relies 'on principles of land rights and public finance which attempt to integrate economic efficiency with social justice'.[47] It is based on the premise that many of the problems that beset society, such as poverty, inequality, and economic booms and busts, could be attributed to the private ownership of the necessary resource, land. It is in this light that in *Progress and Poverty*[48] Henry George argued "We must make land common property" and he drew a distinction between common and collective property. Such ideas are worth a serious look at a time when there is heightened alarm about economic inequality, so starkly brought to light by the Oxfam report mentioned earlier: the "world's richest 1 percent control half of global wealth". Those eight men now own the same amount of wealth as the 3.6 billion people who make up the poorest half of humanity. Such revelations might have sparked a revolt, if not revolution, in our better, more moral times, but now we are too numbed even to react.

And yet, we should not lose sight of our dream. The fulcrum of our existence and life must be what Abu Ibn Tufayl's solitary character Hayy ibn Yaqzan challenged himself to do: 'never allow himself to see any plant or animal hurt, sick, encumbered, or in need without helping it if he could'.[49] That is a distant dream, but dream we must. Kant's formula to 'treat every [person] as a spiritual means to thine own spiritual end and conversely' could also be a useful point of reference. Our idea of morality must not be contained by personal virtue; it should include what is known as the 'product's level of virtue'.[50] Much of our moral sense revolves around attributes such as loyalty, fidelity, honesty, and truthfulness. They are important but often verge on exclusivity. They become monopolistic; if you love someone you can't love anyone else. If you are loyal to your country you are expected to hate another country. On the one hand, we say that separateness has to be erased, that all of us are interlinked, that sharing is important, and yet we want to possess, to monopolize everything and everyone. And when we talk of society, it must include those who produce and market goods and services and the vast apparatus of the State and Government. What we face is not moral decline in the classical sense but a foundational crisis of morality.

Killing Kids for Money

Spurred by his insatiable desire for money, man conceals within himself a sinister 'mass murderer', who does not directly kill with a knife or a bullet, but who is capable of far greater damage to the human spirit and vitality. Such is this murderer who deliberately, methodically, and single-mindedly pollutes, poisons, and adulterates the food we eat, the water we drink, and the air we breathe; not to make a living, but to make *more money*, to earn more profit. The reference, obviously, is to the ever-increasing use of chemical agents in the foodstuffs we consume. Fruits like mangoes are ripened with ammonia; vegetables are treated with carcinogenic pesticides; chicken and cattle are injected with overdoses of antibiotics; fish is preserved with formaldehyde (the chemical used to embalm corpses); spices are mixed with dung, sand, and saw dust... From fruits to vegetables, from milk to sodas, from clarified butter to edible oils, from wheat flour to pulses, from spices to sweets, even the medicines we take, chances are that we are consuming products that are injurious to our health, in effect, slow poison. Food that is supposed to give us nourishment has now become the source of our enfeeblement and endangerment; so is the air we breathe and water we drink. In some countries, what passes for milk, which school books describe as complete food, contains high levels of urea, detergents, and cheap edible oil. For the record, let it be said that no other species deliberately feeds its offspring food that it knows is putrid. Only human beings would not hesitate to do anything for profit, for money. The poison we put into everything we ingest is also consumed by our children and grandchildren, which means that, for money, we don't mind maiming or murdering the ones we profess to love the most, and for whom we will sacrifice anything, and for whose sake we earn that very money.

Whose job is it to see such things don't happen? The 'rulers', of course. But power is what motivates them to do *nothing* about it. The general public are helpless as they have no alternatives to eating and drinking whatever is made available in the marketplace. They are too much in love with the good life; and while on other issues of far less import they organize, agitate, and manage to change the perpetrating system, in this case they are apathetic, refusing to believe and to decisively and collectively act. And while they are prepared to pay exorbitant prices for luxuries and fine goods, in the case of food and water they want affordable prices, forcing the producer to choose adulteration over authenticity, poison over purity. So, everyone has a stake in this: the producers profit and consumers enjoy lower prices. Everyone makes a 'ritual' protest but is not prepared to fight or make any sacrifice; we are all both villains and victims. It is like death: everyone thinks that they are somehow untouched and only others will get affected. Yet another example of willful blindness of the consequences; and blind faith in their personal invulnerability. These synthetic chemicals contribute to subtle and gradual dysfunction in the human body. They not only cause slow and more painful death to far more people than rampage killers, they also jeopardize their vitality because an enfeebled generation cannot but beget more enfeebled, and endanger the next generation. Adulteration, like adultery, is time-tested, is a very old practice for profit. But it used to be relatively innocuous, like mixing water with milk, adding lower grade oil with more expensive oil, and so on. Today, however, harmful chemicals are mixed with foodstuffs as a way to spend less and to earn more. Then, it was cheating; now, it is mass murder or 'generational genocide'. Synthetic chemicals, or what Randall Fitzgerald (*The Hundred-Year Lie*)[51] calls 'chemical synergies', that is, the combinations of these chemicals stored in our bodies, are major sources of mass murder or mutilation. Modern man lives and dies in a cocoon of chemicals; almost everywhere he lives and everything he inhales and intakes is laced with such synergies, which are now embedded into the mainstream of the food chain and are integral to and inseparable from leading what we have come to call 'civilized life'.

While chemicals are inherent in nature and are indispensable to life (water is a chemical, and so is oxygen), synthetic chemicals have different effects and are potentially toxic and carcinogenic. Prolonged and sustained exposure and ingestion of toxic chemicals can not only affect our health and potentially 'disrupt healthy neurological development in unintended ways'[52] but through chemical inheritance could be injurious to the health of humans yet to be born. Just as the exposure three generations before reprograms the brain so it responds in a different way to a life challenge, as suggested by recent research at the University of Texas at Austin, so too would be our addictive appetite for the toxic chemical soup. And environmental contamination might well leave a 'chemical signature' on our genes and influence the DNA and genetic make up of our descendants three generations later. Another study shows that "the old ideas that genes are 'set in stone' or that they alone determine development have been disproven".[53] The same study also pointed out that the epigenetic changes that occur in the fetus during pregnancy could be passed on to later generations, affecting the health and welfare of children, grandchildren, and their descendants. We are also told that "evidence is emerging that the environment triggers and even alters DNA to serve purposes that transcend the individual".[54] It means that what we eat, drink, or breathe or the chemicals that get absorbed through our skin can impact the brain and binaural development of our great, great-grandchildren. While swearing by science, why do we ignore such scientific evidence and dire warnings about the toxic threat that exists within and around us; continuing with our obsession with chemicals, not only making ourselves vulnerable to diseases like cancer and mental illness but also putting on the block the lives and sanity of generations to come? There seems to be an acknowledgment that without chemicals our entire way of life will collapse, and since we cannot even contemplate that, we will accept and accommodate, and pay any price, much of which will be charged to the account of unborn humans. We might have the right to choose cancer over chemicals, but do we have the moral right to condemn future generations? To condemn them to being a 'mutant species'?

Our unrelenting onslaught on nature in the name of growth, progress, and development is not only an ecological issue but also a moral matter. We treat nature, more specifically Mother Earth, as at once a doorman, to be at our beck and call, and as a dustbin, to dispose of the waste of our civilization. Whether man is a noble savage—intrinsically peaceful but corrupted by culture—or a controlled brute, whether he is a being made in the direct image of God or a microcosm of the cosmos, the fact is that man is no longer what nature made him to be or intended him to be. What the recklessness of human behavior underscores is that the composite of the human prototype, as it matured or mutated over time, is such that no man can be trusted enough to be left to the mercy of his own mind or to the dialectic of his volitional choice-making. Cooperation is not the natural mode of man's mind. Not even competition. Indeed, the mantra of man is 'control'. Much of our life, it is this power we pursue. The power of power is irresistible, even for the gods. The lure of arrogance is intoxicating. We all exercise some power over something or someone all the time. Power is a fact of life but how it impacts on our behavior is not beyond our power. Lord Acton famously said "Power tends to corrupt; absolute power corrupts absolutely. Great men are almost always bad men". They are more likely to become bad because the blend of absolute power and a brilliant mind is a heady mix. Even the most ordinary of men tend to use power to dominate and impose their will over others, especially those who lack power themselves. We want to control everything and everybody, no matter if it is another individual or a nation or nature. Predispositions, preferences, predilections—it is these that make up much of our behavior and therefore cannot be given a free reign. Nor can any man be a real man or rise up to his potential if he is hemmed in, hovered over, controlled and conditioned externally. The quest for balance, for harmony, to tame the savageness of man and to make life on human earth softer and gentler, has been elusively timeless. In the age of unbridled *greedism*, intemperate individualism, and galloping globalization, that futile quest has turned into a ticking time bomb that threatens to undo whatever man has achieved thus far. We have not been able to discover or design the tools that help us to determine what we *should* do—or even should *want*—in a manner that is morally compatible, a behavior that contributes to the common good without compromising individual integrity and dignity. We have not found a way to express our free will (which many say is an illusion in itself) without affecting the freedom of others. Indeed, to be alive in any form of life, not only human, is to affect another life in some way or the other just doing what it takes to keep the body breathing. Only the dead are harmless to anyone. But is death itself a cause for mourning, or celebration, or both? Is every parting a little death, and death a longer parting? Even scriptures are ambivalent on this matter. The ambivalence comes from ignorance about the true nature of either birth or death. Essentially, our reaction to birth or death is personal; how it affects our life, the loss, or gain that might ensue; it has little to do with what is good for the dead or the living. Prophet Muhammad said that no one must wish for death for any worldly affliction but if one must wish for it they must pray, "O, Lord; keep me alive so long as life may be good for me; and cause me to die when it is better for me so to do".

The mind created money to manipulate, if not to enslave, man. To ensure that man will never become a true moral creature. The original functions of money were both revolutionary in character and evolutionary in its utility. Revolutionary, as man discovered that, through money, his excess energy of one day can be used for another day or can be preserved over a length of time. It became an evolutionary instrument in bringing men to act together and create a social collective of economic energy. Money is a symbol of human energy. It organizes that energy and its movement across the society in time and space. It is created by the individual's trust in the other individual and in the collective. But the mind has the power to make money 'good' if used for a good purpose, and 'bad' if used wrongly. The fact is that our obsession with money has loosened the strings that connect one human being to another. It incubates and induces an intoxicating sense of independence, an arrogant euphoria of autonomy and makes us believe that if we have it in amplitude we become 'complete' and life will be under control. From the earliest times, money in some form or another has been central to organized living. Over millenniums, money has reflected the changes in habitat of human society; but it also helped bring about these changes. Increasingly, money shapes the foreign and economic policies of all governments. There is little that man is not willing to compromise with—from virginity to marital fidelity, friendship to patriotism, personal honor to professional probity—for money. The dilemma is that with money we are subverted, and without it the world will descend into chaotic disorder. The fact is that in spite of its antiquity and ubiquity, its rightful place and proper management has eluded the ingenuity of the human mind. It has become synonymous with pleasure, pride, and power. Throughout history, the people who have had most power have almost always been rich. It has developed into a principal means of human-to-human interfacing, the glue that holds human society together. The economist Alfred Marshall maintained that the history of money is synonymous with the history of civilization. The smooth functioning of the money economy enables society to raise its standard of living by increasing production and equitable distribution through the medium of exchange. Money is central to the processes of production, consumption, distribution, and purchasing power. It makes people believe that they are free as long as they have the supposed freedom to consume and the money to pay for it. It is through money that we satiate our greed, avarice, and ambition. Will Rogers sums it up well: Too many people spend money they haven't earned, to buy things they don't want, to impress people they don't like.

The extent to which money has come to dominate human life is such that the way we think and relate with money is now a tool and touchstone to find out who we really are at our core. What we do with money, and how we live with money's pervasive presence, tells a lot about our values and essence. Money is all there is—medium and measure; means and end; symbol and substance of life. We love it (when we have it) and we hate it (when we don't). Somerset Maugham quipped that money is like a sixth sense and you cannot make use of the other five without it. Money is often perceived as a lifeless object separated from people, in reality it is man-made, imbued with the collective spirit of the living and the dead. It is also an 'instrument of collective memory'. Money has its own character, in the sense of having particular attributes, especially moral and ethical, which differentiate a person, a group or a thing from another. Over time, and more sharply in modern times, it has radically changed the personality of man; but in so doing it changed its own character. In the humdrum of everyday life we often find ourselves asking the question: how can we juxtapose money and morality in the same sentence and not come face to face with an ethical contradiction? As Osho put it, 'either you will be consumed by your desires or you have to consume your desires'. While it is true that a wholly contented man is a dead man, and that it is discontent that fuels creativity, it is also true that it is avarice that turns man into a menace. Socrates said that one who is not content with what he has is not likely to be content with what he would like to have.

There have always been broad twin obsessions about money. Those who are enslaved by it, and compulsively want to acquire and accumulate more and more. Others who are equally enslaved in their ascetic abhorrence of money. In both cases money is not a service to acquire the means for a material life; the individual comes to be at the service of money. Preoccupation with money becomes an end in itself rather than the means of achieving other goals in life. The entire complex of money today is biased against ethical values because it was developed to serve the interests of people who wanted greater power and wealth for themselves. But, as many sages have told us, power that does no good to others is pointless, and wealth unused might as well not exist. Money can both virtually and actually buy, if not bring, happiness and long life; perhaps an insurance for immortality. The Boswell quote of Samuel Johnson captures the spirit: all other things being equal, he who is rich in a civilized society must be happier than he who is poor. Jesus condemned money-changers and St. Augustine taught that money must be controlled by what is right and wrong. Dante in his classic poem *The Inferno* describes money-lenders wailing in the lowest forms of hell. Islam forbids lending money with interest. But for the deprived, the want of money turns the earth into hell. Without money we cannot have purchasing power and without it we cannot have what we need, the goods and services, to be alive. That is why Bernard Shaw said "the lack of money is the root of all evil". It is not so much the lack of money which is the problem; the problem is that without money we are denied things and services that are essential to, so to speak, keeping the wolf at bay. Both love and lack of money are detrimental to the human spirit, and money, if properly channeled, can also be an input to make human society more egalitarian and give a hand to those who are denied dignity and the basic needs of humanity. Culturally, money has always been viewed negatively as a corrupting influence; it still is, and indeed more than ever before. But its very indispensability and overwhelming presence also offers a unique opportunity to transform it into a potentially positive agent of change. It can not only make man resort to unspeakable evil; it also offers more openings to man to become a Good Samaritan, to make a difference to more lives than ever before. No free man can afford the luxury of the Spartan disdain of money. Money is too pervasive, too irreplaceable, and too intrusive in our lives to be scoffed at; we must turn it around and make it a positive tool to materially alter the lives of marginalized people.

Money, Poverty, and Morality

While pundits can debate what 'poverty' is—and below what income levels one could be called 'poor'—what we should focus on is helping anyone or all those who are in economic need of help. Obsession with money might be evil, warping the human personality more than anything else in life. But human life is virtually impossible without it, and its paucity can cripple life more than anything else. With money we can feed the hungry, provide medicines for the sick, and shelter for the homeless. This reality opens a door to do good through the evil of money. Money is now what the Upanishads said about the mind; it is the source of our bondage but it also, if properly channeled, could be the route to our redemption. By giving money to those who need it, we can make a greater difference to their lives than by giving anything else. The question that arises is this: Is it morally okay to play Robin Hood, to rob the rich and give to the poor? Does it make a moral difference how we earn the money if we spread it properly in society? The Mahabharata gives an answer. Vidura, the erudite and wise minister, tells his king: "O King Dhritarashtra, one should never think of earning material wealth through wrong means like falsehood, bribery, corruption or stealing, not to speak of practicing such evils. Wrongly earned money pollutes its possessor to such an extent that all the activities done with such sinful wealth result in harmful troubles. Even praiseworthy acts like charity and worship, and sacrifices done with such sinful income, produce undesirable results. No amount of purification can set right the defects of ill-begotten wealth". The Bible[55] says, "Ill-gotten gains do not profit/But righteousness delivers from death; He who profits illicitly troubles his own house/But he who sows righteousness gets a true reward; Bread obtained by falsehood is sweet to a man/But afterward his mouth will be filled with gravel; The getting of treasures by a lying tongue is a fleeting vapor, the pursuit of death". But if we are confronted with a choice between ill-gotten wealth well spent, and well-earned wealth ill spent, how should we choose? Does the critical importance of money in today's world sanitize how it is earned if that money saves or gives dignity to other lives? In any event, how money is allocated and utilized in the future, both individually and collectively, will become a major moral matter. And the glaring fact is that our priorities are pretty distorted. We are spending trillions of dollars on big-ticket items like immortality, artificial intelligence and the Internet Of Things (IOT), and too little on global health and sanitation. The other question is: what is ill-gotten wealth? Does it concern only how we make money, or does it include how we inherit it or how the one who gives us money for services rendered earns it? Is an employee morally responsible for how his employer generates the money he gets? In other words, are the means marginal in matters of money as long as the end is worthy and socially relevant? Does tainted money become holy if offered to the divine or for charity, and absolve them of the sin of acquiring illicit money, or at least lessen the severity of sin? One can also argue that the larger good—helping the needy who otherwise might be impoverished and incapacitated for want of purchasing power—justifies or overshadows the lesser evil, money made unethically, which could also tantamount to depriving others of what they might have ethically earned.

A person who suffers from poverty might have been less sad, angry or revengeful if poverty did not exist amidst plenty. The fact that poverty co-exists with affluence has made its victims not only sad but also angry with the wider sociopolitical power structure that determines the kind of life they lead. At the same time, of all typologies of suffering, it is economic suffering that is also the easiest to mitigate or eliminate. The existence of extreme poverty and luxurious living and income disparities is not only unjust but also immoral. It is 'economic justice' that stands at the frontline of social justice. Elizabeth Ann Seton simplified it: 'Live simply that others might simply live'.[56] 'Simply' means a life of simplicity, frugality, and moderation, with a mindset that it enables others, less fortunate, to live likewise. As the writer Stuart Wilde said, 'Poverty is restriction and as such, it is the greatest injustice you can perpetrate upon yourself.' Economics absorbs such a huge slice of our life that one must come to believe (to paraphrase Martin Luther King Jr.) that economic injustice anywhere is a threat to human dignity anywhere. Our instinctive tendency is to have little to do with things that disturb us, banish them from our lives, homes, and even thoughts. Poverty is also a problem of money: it is caused by lack of and maldistribution of money; and it can be ameliorated by both a 'bottom-up' and 'trickle-down' approach, by the empowerment of the poor and by public policies that transfer money from the top to the bottom. The rich view the presence of the poor as a law-and-order problem, a potential peril to their well-earned affluence and market-value of their homes. The 'not-rich' and 'not-poor' are united in the view that cohabitation with the poor means a problem of sanitation, public health, and 'bad company'. John Stuart Mill wrote way back in the 18th century that a distinctive mark of the 'modern age' is the determination to put far away from our sight anything ugly, disturbing, and disagreeable we find. That is one way not to feel threatened, or not to feel any sense of shame or guilt; out of sight is out of mind; out of mind is to be rid of culpability. The god-fearing, pious people would rather leave the poor to God; who are *we*, they say, to intervene where *He* does not? Global poverty is also a critical factor in good governance. Confucius said "In a country well governed, poverty is something to be ashamed of. In a country badly governed, wealth is something to be ashamed of". When both abject poverty and obscene opulence coexist and we go about our lives unruffled and unfazed, as we all do, it is a clear indication that something is awfully 'out of joint' in our consciousness.

We must bear in mind that the moral claims of the poor rest not only on community membership, but on membership of the commonwealth of the human species. We must bring back their presence into the social and spiritual mainstream. We need daily reminders that such people exist, that they suffer while we prosper, so that it might stoke the embers of a dying conscience. Being the weaker and more vulnerable, their right to live, their right for public space, and their right to be protected from poverty and low purchasing power are paramount. It is economic 'sharing' that ought to be at the vanguard of alleviating suffering in the world. We have long debated the question of responsibility: are the poor responsible for their condition, karmic or contemporary, or are *we*, the rest, responsible for creating or condoning the conditions that created poverty? What should the poor do, and what should *we* do? Such is the dominance of money in human affairs and such is the depth of desperation and loss of dignity. Economic marginalization can adversely affect the human psyche and erode self-worth. The issue of alleviation of economic suffering must be at the top of the global political and economic agenda, and of all human spiritual quest. While the rich and super rich have to bear the lion's share, almost everyone (excepting the very poor), can offer a helping hand through direct help or through support to organizations and schemes designed to help them to climb out of the poverty-trap. In today's globalized world, almost anyone can help anyone, anywhere in the world. While all this might appear like modernist humanitarianism, in fact most religious traditions such as Judaism, Islam, Hinduism, Buddhism, and Confucianism exhort the same. Whether it is a question of 'economic justice' or 'social equity' or spiritual salvation, it all comes down to one issue: the indivisibility of all life. Gandhi said that 'the whole gamut of man's activities… constitutes an indivisible whole. You cannot divide life, social, economic, political and purely religious, into watertight compartments'. For Gandhi, the poor were *daridra-narayana* (*daridra* means poor, and *Narayana*, God). Vivekananda said, "So long as the millions live in hunger and ignorance, I hold every person a traitor who, having been educated at their expense, pays not the least heed to them". Our current approach to poverty alleviation, as William Easterly writes, is 'based on a technocratic illusion: the belief that poverty is a purely technical problem amenable to such technical solutions as fertilizers, antibiotics, or nutritional supplements'.[57] To make any headway we must view the problem of inequity and injustice as a virulent virus in human society.

Materialism, Market, and Morality

While we could afford the leisurely luxury of debate, discourse, and dissent on these matters in earlier less turbulent times, with no necessity for immediate action, what we now face is an altogether new context that calls for a different approach and urgent action. As Steiner said, "Materialism has cast man into such depths that a mighty concentration of forces is necessary to raise him again. He is subject to illnesses of the nervous system which are veritable epidemics of the life of the soul".[58] Materialism—the premise that what matters is matter only and what we perceive through the senses is the only reality—has undermined morality and made us virtual captives of comfort, convenience, and consumerism. We just want these three 'Cs' at any cost, by hook or crook, and we are ready to beg, borrow, or steal, or even kill. What has so far been an endemic economic deficiency, an obsessive irritant, a character flaw, a psychological outlet, has now become a major theological concern and a planetary threat with cosmic consequences. And it has become central to what has come to be called 'the modern way of life'. As Paul Crutzen[59] puts it, humankind, or rather human presence on earth, is now playing a central role in biology and ecology. Whatever we wish to call our planet earth (Bill McKibben prefers to call it *Eaarth*, signifying that our 'old' earth is virtually dead), the damage we are doing to the planet is not merely an environmental or economic issue; it is at its heart a *moral* issue. We cannot be moral if we ravage and vandalize our own mother. Nor if we mindlessly burn the building that we are inhabiting as tenants. As if this is not bad enough, man is now venturing where no man has dared before: encroaching on the preserve of gods and creating 'man-made' life. Creating artificial life might now be a major goal of scientific creativity, but man has for long been living an artificial life, eons away from what nature intended. So artificial and adulterated is the modern human being that one might even say the 'old' human is dead and we are almost a new species, far more malevolent than our 'predecessor'. So polluted and chemicalized are we, some experts tell us, that there is a real possibility that man-eaters might not find our toxin-sated bodies palatable anymore!

The earliest form of money that we are exposed to is *pocket* money. Parents intend their children to learn the basics of money management, but this soon becomes a slippery slope and a sense of entitlement gets embedded in their psyche. Educational experts say that there has probably been no aspect of family life that has been the cause of greater strain and stress than the problem of the child and his money. The last thing a dying man is supposed to do is distribute the wealth of a lifetime to his progeny by a will, so that, hopefully, they won't kill each other fighting over it! Some even put away money for their funeral, lest their kids short-change them and deny them their due. Life between birth and death is spent under the shadow of money. Money has become the measure of man. Philosophers like Seneca might have held that a great fortune is a great slavery; but most men today would prefer that kind of slavery. Benjamin Franklin might have said 'man does not possess wealth, wealth possesses him', but most prefer being so possessed. Schopenhauer said, "Money is human happiness *in abstracto*; consequently he who is no longer capable of happiness *in concreto* sets his whole heart on money".[60] Money and 'more' are synonymous. From a beggar to a billionaire, the endless desire is to have more of money. Thomas Jefferson said, "Money, not morality is the principle of commercial nations". Jean-Jacques Rousseau described wealthy men even more harshly: "The rich are like ravening wolves, who, having once tasted human flesh, henceforth desire and devour only men".

Scriptures generally view money like flesh, as an impediment to spiritual progress, and all saints have shown not only detachment but also disdain towards money. The Hindu concept of *artha* or wealth emphasizes that money must be earned, stored, and spent dharmically, i.e., through righteous means. Money may be neutral in its nature but it is either good or bad in relation to how it is generated, garnered, and expended. In that sense, money is energy; money is power; and money is a form of life-energy (*prana*) contained in paper, coins, silver, or traditionally and most importantly, in gold. The underlying philosophy is that bad money can never do good deeds; nor can good money used wrongly reap right results. Good money is righteous money, derived from a righteous source, earned by helping, not hurting, people; by serving, not cheating, people; by making people happy, not adding to their misery. Bad money does bad things; it is money earned through the making or selling of harmful things like alcohol, arms, cigarettes, and drugs, taking bribes, and taking more than one's legitimate share. The 2,000-year-old spiritual classic *Thirukkural*, written in Tamil by the South Indian saint Thiruvalluvar, distills the basic tenets of dharmic money: "The worst poverty of worthy men is more worthwhile than the wildest wealth amassed in wicked ways. What is gained by tears will go by tears. Though it begins with loss, in the end goodness gives many good things. Protecting the country by wrongly garnered wealth is like preserving water in an unbaked pot of clay.

Riches acquired by mindful means, in a manner that harms no one, will bring both piety and pleasure. Wealth acquired without compassion and love is to be eschewed, not embraced. Finding delight in defrauding others yields the fruit of undying suffering when those delights ripen.[61] Even after two millenniums, human ingenuity cannot do any better than this to codify a more moral way of handling money.

Another equally ethical and morally progressive view of money is advocated in Islam. Its perspective on banking and lending best symbolizes this view. As one article put it, "for millions of Muslims, banks are institutions to be avoided. Islam is a religion that keeps believers from the teller's window. Their Islamic beliefs prevent them from dealings that involve usury or interest (*riba*)". The Quran explicitly prohibits interest or *riba* on money lent. The Islamic view of money is based on interesting principles: any predetermined payment over and above the actual amount of principal is prohibited; contrary to modern banking, the lender, the provider of capital, and the user of capital, the borrower, must equally share in the profits or losses arising out of the enterprise, what we call shareholders or stakeholders; uncertainty, risk, and speculation (*gharar*) is also prohibited; and, perhaps the most important, capital or investments should only support practices or products that are not forbidden or discouraged by Islam.[62] In the *Katha* Upanishad, when the young Nachiketa persists in knowing what happens after death, a reluctant *Yama*, the Lord of Death, tries all ways to dissuade the boy. Yama tries to 'bribe' him by offering unlimited wealth (rather than reveal the secret of death)—'large estates, gold in abundance, horses, elephants, etc.' When Nachiketa doesn't fall for the bait and persists, Yama is finally pleased and tells him the secret that even the gods do not know. Among the attributes of a moral conduct enjoined in the Quran is the teaching that one should not squander wealth in wantonness. Whether it is the Katha Upanishad, the Thirukkural or the Quran, the message is therefore the same. Money should be earned and used only in permissible ways; money is not an end but a moral means for moral ends, meant for communal good. In the Bible, it is said that 'the love of money is the root of evil'; wisely channeled, it can root out, at least out flank, evil'. Man cannot worship God and Mammon at the same time. Brian Hathaway, in his article *Money and the Kingdom of God* says, "If the overarching theme of Christ's message was the Kingdom of God, then the single most talked about topic within that theme is our use of money and possessions. Any attempt to live within the principles of God's Kingdom will bring us face to face with this topic and will shine a spotlight on our attitudes towards money and possessions".[63]

It is a truism to say that it is the bond of money that connects man to man in the contemporary world; the difference between one country and society to another is only a matter of degree. Scott Fitzgerald, author of *The Great Gatsby*, said the rich are different from other people. But they are different only because they are rich. If we become rich too, we would be no different by way of what we do. When the inherent avarice of our mind and the magnetism of money come together, it changes the state of our consciousness. An incisive and stimulating snapshot of this phenomenon is drawn in the book *Money and Class in America* by Lewis H Lapham, the editor of *Harper's Magazine* and a thoughtful commentator. Although it is an exposé of the American love affair with money, and some statements appear rather apocalyptic, it reflects broadly money's sway over man's mind today: "The avarice of the rich testifies not to the fulfillment of their appetite but to the failure of their imagination… In an increasingly somnambulist state of mind, they discover themselves herded into a gilded cage from which they find it increasingly hard to escape. It isn't money itself that causes trouble; but the use of money as votive offering and pagan ointment. Imagining that they can be transformed into gods, they find themselves changed into dwarfs".[64] The gilded allusion is from Edith Wharton who describes the asylum of wealth as a gilded cage, "sumptuous in its décor but stupefying in its vacuity".[65] According to Lapham, "In a rich man's culture, the wisdom of the rich consists of what the rich wish to hear and think about themselves. The protocols of wealth govern the distribution of society's awards and punishments. People seeking redress for their grievances or compensation for their sorrow have no choice but to translate their grief into a specific sum of money, people come to be valued for the money they command, not for their deeds or character… people who define their lives as functions of their wealth display their affection, or rather the lack of it, by withholding both the substance and the symbolism of money". Lapham traces the effect of money on the arts and humanities that shape man's sensitivity. He says, "A good author is a rich author and a rich author is a good author…. The romance of the artist as an impoverished seer no longer commands belief… The phrase 'poor artist' stands revealed as a contradiction in terms… The definition of money as the sublime good… results in the depreciation of all values that do not pay. What is moral is what returns a profit satisfies the judgment of the bottom line. Freedom comes to be defined in practice…as the freedom to exploit. This commercial reading of the text of human natures gives rise to a system that puts a premium on crime, encourages the placid acquiescence in the dishonest thought or deal, sustains the routine hypocrisy of politics and politicians as inviolate the economic savagery otherwise known as the free market or freedom under capitalism". Many thoughtful commentators now are suggesting that one possible cause for the new-found love of what is dismissed as superstition and 'unscientific', religion, is a rejection of the modern capitalism-centric society.

While struggling to create a new framework for a moral life, we cannot ignore the buzzwords we hear everywhere these days: 'mantra of free market'; 'magic of the market place'; 'markets know best'; 'what cannot survive in a market need not survive', and so on. We cannot also ignore the fact that an exploited workman cannot be judged and valued according to the criterion of his exploiter and the oppressor. Some even say that the truth is that, as there exist two classes in society, so there exist two moralities. According to the social critic Max Nordau, 'the natural or zoological morality affirms that rest is the supreme merit and does not define labor as pleasant and glorious except that it is indispensable to material existence'. But this morality is of no use for exploiters, whose interests mandate that the masses toil more than what is necessary, and produce more than what they need. That surplus product is precisely what the exploiters want to appropriate. It is the latter type that has come to be the mainstream morality, which extols toil and castigates leisure and idleness as the source of social ills. Whether one agrees with all such statements, this issue needs renewed attention in the context of evolving a new paradigm of a moral society. The muted message from the mainstream is that, along the refrain of the boast that economics is 'value free', morality has to be marginalized for markets to set right all that is wrong in this world, and to create a level playing field. It is also argued that free markets are necessary for getting the most from resources, to maximize production and profits, which leads to growth which, in turn, lifts the poor from poverty. The fallacy, as Pope Francis noted, is that this model does not factor in 'the cost of future resources', or 'the health of the environment', and 'businesses profit by calculating and paying only a fraction of the costs involved'.[66] By expressing such views, the Pope is emerging as the global conscience-keeper and a moral anchor and a messiah of the meek. But it is not only people like the Pope who are arguing on these lines. It is to be noted that "even those who accept the superiority of markets at generating material comforts commonly see that superiority as so morally tainted that they are sympathetic to political action to restrict normal market practices at the cost of considerable market efficiency".[67] Mikko Arevuo says "It has become increasingly difficult to make a case for the morality of markets even though free market capitalism has been unequalled in reducing poverty and discrimination, and in creating opportunities for social and economic advancement".[68] Some say even Marx recognized the good that capitalism has done to humanity, as he wrote in the *Communist Manifesto* (1848). It is hard to imagine these words came from Marx, the father of Communism: "The bourgeoisie, during its rule of scarce one hundred years, has created more massive and more colossal productive forces than have all preceding generations together. Subjection of nature's forces to man, machinery... what earlier century had even a presentiment that such productive forces slumbered in the lap of social labor?"[69]

But Marx also said, "The need of a constantly expanding market for its products chases the bourgeoisie over the entire surface of the globe. It must nestle everywhere, settle everywhere, establish connexions everywhere".[70] Essentially, the problem is that 'free market' is not the same as 'fair market', and market-mechanisms, as pointed out by Arthur Okun (*Equality and Efficiency: the Big Tradeoff*, 1975), offer no guarantees that they serve larger public interest like fair distribution of wealth and income. He wrote that "given the chance, [the market] would sweep away all other values, and establish a vending-machine society". In actuality, there are no fully free markets anywhere, without any restraints or regulations, which often serve the interests of the ruling classes, a commanding component of which are big businesses and giant corporations. The powerful use the 'market' to gain monopoly. Markets have no self-correcting safeguards and therefore cannot be left to their own dynamics. And the greatest, and perhaps the most perilous proof of this in modern times is climate change. Some like William Nordhaus[71] say that our inability to effectively tackle climate change is due to the problem of pricing, that is, of low or zero pricing of carbon dioxide emissions. That might indeed be a contributory cause in economic terms but the real issue is far deeper. Markets, totally unregulated and fully free of the underlying principles, might be safe for angels, or even for some animals. But not for humans, as long as they are controlled by their mind. Market and mind are made for each other but not for morality. At best, the human being is a blend of good and bad and, given total freedom, there is no assurance that he will not be 'bad' to make more profit in lesser time and with lesser effort. In the human mind, the immediate prevails over the important: tomorrow more than the day after, money over morality. That is the only explanation why we are so self-destructive and why so many of us still do nothing about any of our existential threats. While the efficacy of free markets as instruments of economic equity and social justice is a larger matter, what is important to note is that the tendency to view the market as the mantra to solve all our problems (like climate change) is unwise and could worsen the situation. And that, in fact, the way they function—whatever be the concept and intent—markets are likely to strengthen our 'Jungian shadow', the meaner and darker side of our personality, which, in turn, reinforces the forces of evil in the 'war within'.

Morality and Money

It is important to make everyone feel that there is more than money that can act as incentive to human betterment. Right now, what is moral in business is what returns a profit. Under the rules of a society that cannot distinguish between profit and profiteering, between money defined as necessity and money defined as luxury, murder is occasionally obligatory and always permissible.[72] By and large, the rich have the temperament of lizards, and their indifference to other people's joy or sorrow has always been evident. Among all the emotions, the rich have the least talent for love. It is possible to love, say, one's dog, but a human being presents a more difficult problem.[73] Assigned at an early age to the care of servants, surrounded through most of their lives by enemies who they mistake for friends, the children of the rich tend to become orphans.[74] The man besotted by a faith in money believes that if it can buy everything worth having—that if it can prolong life, win elections, relieve suffering, make hydrogen bombs, declare war, hire assassins, and so on—then surely it can grant him the patents of respect and triumph over so small a trifle as death. Despite the miracles of modern science 'we feel the glory of revelation only when presented with the embodiment of unutterable wealth'. Lapham compares American society to others and says, "The restlessness of American experience lends to money a greater power than it enjoys in less mobile societies. Not that money doesn't occupy a high place in England, India, or the Soviet Union, but in those less liquid climates, it doesn't work quite so many wonders and transformations".[75] Objects (or individuals) retain their value only insofar as they represent money. Lapham almost demonizes the rich: "The substitution of money for all other value becomes so complete as to change them, if not into gold, at least into stone. To describe the rich as people is to make a mistake with the language. Rich nouns or pronouns perhaps, not people. The rich tend to identify themselves with a sum of money and by so doing they relinquish most of their claims to their own community.[76] He goes on to say that "the obsession with money dulls the capacity for feeling and thought I think can be accepted as an axiom requiring no further argument".[77] Much of the critique of Lapham and his ilk centers around the culture and context of the lives of the rich. If that is all that there is to it, we can groan and bemoan and say a few sorry words and get on with our not-so-rich, 'thank-god-for-that' lives. But we have no such camouflage. Money casts its shadow over a much wider humanity than the rich, practically the entirety of humankind. For the poor, almost one of three, money is the essential means to feed, clothe, and shelter the body or dependent bodies, and to lead a life of dignity. It is the effect of money on the huge and growing middle class that is of mounting concern. It is due to the corrosive influence of money, that the middle class, which traditionally in all societies had been a moral bastion, is now, with its large numbers, in the vanguard of the moral decline of modern societies. Money and consumerism have a noxious nexus.

Money feeds, Lapham asserts, the appetite for consumerism; and consumerism in turn increases the thirst and need for money. Together they erode the moral insides of man. The need for a certain sum of money for a certain standard of living becomes overpowering enough to overcome the moral means of making 'both ends meet'. The lure of obscene opulence becomes irresistible to all but the morally most stubborn. For some people, having and spending money becomes an emotional and psychological irreplaceable; any diminution or deprivation can unhinge them emotionally. The character of money also changes according to those who possess it—inherited or acquired, easy or earned. Inherited wealth with few exceptions is more morally debilitating. Usually, not having undergone the travails of making money, the inheritors tend to spend it in ways that are personally and socially destructive. It induces a mindset of license, laxity, and lasciviousness. The caution and circumspection associated with old-fashioned frugality and need-based living becomes a casualty. An illustrative, possibly apocryphal story is told in America about John D Rockefeller, the founder of the Rockefeller business empire, and his son. Whenever the father came to New York he used to stay in a rather spartan hotel. When the son came, he used to stay across the street but in a far more luxurious and expensive hotel. The father was asked about this telling difference. He supposedly replied, 'Because I stay in a place like this, he could stay in a place like that'.

The effect of money on the mind also depends at what stage in life one gets to be rich. In the normal course, it is around middle age that one's income reaches the peak in line with professional progression. That is also the time when the senses are somewhat subdued, man is more reflective, and riches are less likely to lead astray. That is the time when man acquires a certain perspective on money and morals. If, on the other hand, large sums of money suddenly come in hand, either through inheritance or even accomplishment, early in youth, the effect on the mind could be very different—often deleterious to sensitivity and sense of proportion. More often than not, riches and youth form a potent brew. Unlike earlier times, today it is the youth that come to have sudden fortune and affluence. If not the consequence of a death in the family, the windfall could arrive through stunning success in fields like business, sports, and entertainment. This brings fame too. A young mind has many admirable qualities: freshness, idealism, vigor, drive, and determination; but to wisely handle wealth, sudden success, and fame, different qualities are needed. The gap between success and failure is nowhere larger than in areas in which human excellence is the basic raw material. If one fails, one is instantly discarded, called a loser, and ridiculed. If one succeeds at a relatively young age, one could even become a billionaire. We associate success with happiness and failure with misery. But as Viktor Frankl points out there could be 'despair despite success' and 'fulfilment despite failure'.[78]

In America, when the mantra was 'greed is good' in the 1980s, there were three 'Michaels' who epitomized quick and stunning success and fabulous riches—Michael Jackson, the pop star; Michael Jordan, the basketball wizard; and Michael Milken, the Wall Street insider trader who later went to prison. They had three things in common: youth, genius, and luck. Of the three, only Michael Jordan remained a role model largely unaffected by the adulation and awesome affluence. Making good in the entertainment business always meant big money. A close second is sports. Given the pressures and frustrations of modern life, many people turn to a favorite sport for emotional escape and to transport them to another world where someone else is under pressure. Seeing movies one gets proxy pleasure; watching sport one achieves vicarious excellence. The problem is not only the accrual of easy money but also the mixing of our ideas of a celebrity and a role model, 'goodness of life' and the 'good life'. Those who attain intellectual or ethical excellence by the lives they lead, their creativity and legacy, serving as a candle in the dark, are hardly noticed, much less rewarded. They ought to be the real role models for the young and restless, and society should do everything possible to facilitate that process. Artists, writers, and musicians languish in obscure poverty, while a sportsperson barely out of his or her twenties is extolled and idolized by society and showered with gifts and goodies. It is not so much the lionizing of sportspersons that is the problem. The message that comes out is that social recognition can be obtained only through such sports. Even more, many of these sports icons, because of the wealth they control, lead lifestyles that are far from worthy of emulation and adoption. But in the public mind, their lifestyles and their achievements are indistinguishable. The result is while their fans rarely achieve their idol's professional success, they copy their lifestyles. In its raw essence, our adulation of movie stars and sportsmen is our fixation with money.

A major manifestation of money is property, which feeds our instinct for accumulation. Other species, particularly predatory animals, may have a sense of territory, but man alone has a sense of property. Mankind, by virtue of its brute power over other brutes, has come to *own* Planet Earth, which is now divided between nations and individuals. Traditional people and tribal societies could not understand how land, which belonged to God, or to Mother Nature, could be sold. Maybe it was because they believed that land belonged to nobody that the Native Americans 'sold' large tracts of land like Manhattan for a pittance. Since in any case it was not yours, whatever you got was a bounty! The irony is man is acutely aware and insecure about his property. Our sense of property is so strong that the only ideology that even theoretically advocated abolition of 'property'—communism—withered away. It is now a respectable and much-coveted engine of economic progress, and a barometer of social success. Property is progress. But it has made man more discontented and society more fractious. Property rivals passion as the prime cause of crime. For the sake of property, some risk their own health and lives. A few years ago, the northern Indian state of Haryana witnessed a spate of craniotomies that were eventually linked to local property disputes. In a bizarre trend that was reported as 'skull'duggery, people willingly bribed doctors and the police to have serious injuries inflicted on their own skulls and immediately arrange surgical fixes in secrecy. The injuries were to serve to frame their opponents in property disputes and have them imprisoned for their 'crimes' for long periods (life-threatening injuries are non-bailable offences in India), so that the disputed lands could be encroached upon![79] Many great men have spoken about property, in particular, private property. Marx said: "The theory of Communism may be summed up in one sentence: abolish all private property". But this is against the grain of human nature and that could be the reason why 'communism', clearly one of the most idealistic and influential ideologies of all time, never had a chance. It did not fail; it just was never put into practice. Perhaps it is possible in the animal world, where no one owns any property, but certainly not in human society. Wherever society took the shape and form of human governance, it turned into state monopoly, yet another form of ownership, another tool of exploitation that led to the emergence of what Milovan Djilas called a 'new class', another ruling elite.

Precisely because man is mortal and could be dead the next minute, property becomes, next to progeny, the means to permanence. Property gives him a feeling, even if fleeting, of security in this life, and it gives him a piece of immortality. But the downside of security is daunting. As the British political theorist Harold Laski said, "Those who have security often luxuriate in a life devoid of meaning; and those who are poor can sometimes know the rarest things that life can offer… Those who have security may, in fact, live a life as solid and as pointless as the ugly mahogany with which they are surrounded. But at least their existence is freed from the specter of fear (of poverty)".[80] To live a life of dignity, society gives one no choice except to acquire property, moveable or immovable. And, like in most other things in life, man loses the balance and property becomes the end and the means, the purpose and the process. Soon, instead of him owning property, property begins to own him. Private property is the heart of capitalism. Some even say we live in an 'Age of Intellectual Property'. The American Constitution guarantees, along with the right of liberty, the right of property which, some say "has contributed more to the growth of civilization than any other institution established by the human race".[81] Others like Russell say, "It is the preoccupation with possession, more than anything else, that prevents men from living freely and nobly". Freud said that by abolishing private property, one takes away the human love of aggression. And Plato wrote in his *Republic* that no one should possess any private property, if it can possibly be avoided; secondly, no one should have a dwelling or storehouse into which all have not the right to enter. But Aristotle, his disciple, said that it is not the possessions but the desires of mankind that require to be equalized. Aristotle was right that property is only a means to fulfill desire, but possession of property also whets and whips desire. Property may be inanimate but not neutral. Plato did not condemn property, only private property. He underestimated human ingenuity. Public property, if anything were to be really called that, does not fare much better with the public mind; the arbiters of that kind of property are 'public people with private minds'. Their public position offers easier access and a short cut to possession of unearned property. It seems to be that in the proximity of property, morality runs away from the mind. The Bible says that it is harder for men who trust riches 'to enter the Kingdom of God'; and Oscar Wilde said that in the interest of the rich we must get rid of property. To both the rich would say 'Thanks, but we would rather keep our riches and take our chances'.

One of the minor mysteries of human life is that we all know we are transitory in this world, but we still want to 'own', to 'possess' everything we come into contact with—whether it is a spouse or child or an employee, a piece of earth, or a house, even God. In fact, as Erich Fromm[82] pointed out, modern man gives more importance to 'having' than 'being'. So many battles and wars are fought over ownership of land. Rousseau wrote that "the first man who, having enclosed a piece of ground, bethought himself of saying *This is mine*, and found people simple enough to believe him, was the real founder of civil society. From how many crimes, wars and murders, from how many horrors and misfortunes might not any one have saved mankind, by pulling up the stakes, or filling up the ditch, and crying to his fellows, 'Beware of listening to this impostor; you are undone if you once forget that the fruits of the earth belong to us all, and the earth itself to nobody'".[83] But Rousseau goes on to add, "But there is great probability that things had then already come to such a pitch, that they could no longer continue as they were; for the idea of property depends on many prior ideas, which could only be acquired successively, and cannot have been formed all at once in the human mind". Kingdoms, empires, and nation states, the rich and the poor, are all defined, and constrained, by ownership. It is through this kind of ownership that most people make much money because, as they say, land appreciates, which means if you hoard it, its value only increases over time. The urge to own is insatiable and insidious. John Steinbeck says "If a man owns a little property, that property is him, it's part of him, and it's like him.... The property is the man, stronger than he is. And he is small, not big. Only his possessions are big—and he's the servant of his property".[84] We own, and ceaselessly want to own, everything: land, house, goods, gadgets, and people. Actually, you can only buy and sell the rights to use; you can't actually own. But the idea of servitude, fidelity, loyalty, love, and even employment comes from ownership. People owe you their time, skills, attention, and exclusivity. When these are shared with someone else we say we were 'betrayed'. And that leads to possessiveness, jealousy and, as in love, to bloody revenge. The words 'my' and 'mine' imply we own something. All our life is spent 'owning' and 'being owned'. In reality, we don't 'own' anything that we cannot part with; that thing owns 'us'. And in truth, we don't even 'own' ourselves; we owe so much to so many people that very little is left to ourselves. But perhaps in death alone we finally own something, some property—at least in the traditions in which the dead are buried—a tiny piece of barren earth, which is all ours, whose price ironically appreciates over time, but is of no use to us, the dead.

And the question of property is inseparable from money; they are interchangeable. Without money there can be no property, and without property money is useless. Money lets us own and possess property and property multiplies money. Money lets us own not only physical property like land, buildings, and goods but even people. French anarchist philosopher Pierre-Joseph Proudhon described property as theft, because no one can own anything without depriving something, even a person, from someone who needs it more. Our passion for property, for ownership, and for possession, which are linked, has now taken a new dimension with our craze for the machine. It is the new status symbol—what machine we own, whether or not we need it or even know how to harness it. We are zealous, if not jealous, about our gadgets, appliances and mechanical add-ons. We are almost, if not actually, 'in love' with them and in love everything is fair or foul. And, as in love, it is fair not only to keep what we have, but to get what another has, if we take a fancy for it.

Money, Good Life, and Goodness of Life

No act happens in its own exalted solitude; more than one person is invariably involved or affected in everything that occurs and the fallout, too, is a blend of the good and the bad. The problem comes when we want, in every situation, the good for ourselves, and the bad for others. Although we do not still know what kind of a life is a 'well-lived' life, and what is a 'wasted' life, the mantra in modern society is 'good life' and 'growth', with idioms like 'standard of life' and 'quality time' thrown in between. And money is central to them all. The fact is, as Anthon St. Maarten put it, modern society has generally 'lost the plot'. The place where we 'lost it' is not in the marketplace of materialism, as many commonly believe; it is within the confines of our own consciousness, when it came under the undue influence of our own mind. While we will perhaps never get any conclusive answers to all that we ask or seek to know, the time has come to do some soul-searching on questions such as what is the true value and purpose of money? what is affordability? how do we judge the moral worth of our work?—and, what is a life 'well spent' or a life that is 'wasted'?

To be 'alive' is distinct from 'goodness of life', which again is different from 'good life'. This differentiation is what distinguishes the human from other animals. To be alive on earth, one needs very few things from nature, and in that condition, entails more giving than taking. Except man, other creatures instinctively lead that kind of life. That is how nature maintains its own overall equilibrium, and stays 'alive'. Why nature or God gave a 'different' treatment to man and endowed him with the faculty of willful choice we do not know. Has it overestimated or underestimated man? How does it intend to make amends to its 'mistake'? One theory is that in the 'original' man, all his endowments, faculties, powers, and abilities were working in harmony with each other and his 'way of life' was not very different from the rest. Somewhere, that 'harmony' was sundered and then man wanted more than 'to be alive', and 'money' came in handy. We came to believe that 'what we cannot be, our money can get for us'. And that 'money' can offset whatever nature has denied us. It has come to mean more than what it can actually do, its value more than its worth. John Stuart Mill wrote, "Its worth is solely that of the things which it will buy… Yet the love of money is not only one of the strongest moving forces of human life, but money is, in many cases, desired in and for itself".[85] Psychologically speaking, it has been described as "our projection onto coins, bills, bank accounts, and other financial instruments of our beliefs, hopes, and fears about how those things will affect who we are, what will happen to us and how we will be treated by others or by ourselves…".[86] Put differently, "because money is the solution to poverty, it can make us believe that we are impoverished only by lack of money. So money becomes a kind of greedy symbol for anything and everything we might want".[87] Pope Francis, in one of his addresses, noted that many of the problems the world is facing are rooted "in our relationship with money, and our acceptance of its power over us and our society… The worship of the golden calf of old has found a new and heartless image in the cult of money and the dictatorship of an economy which is faceless and lacking any truly humane goal".[88] Human cognitive and creative capacities then crafted a 'civilized life', which also meant 'living well' with material conveniences and comforts. With technology making inroads into our daily life 'consumerism' came into being. The cocktail of 'culture', 'civilization', and 'consumerism' is what we call 'good life'. In the process, man changed from a 'net-taker' to a polluter and predator, and increasingly, from a consumer to "consumer goods which can be used and thrown away".[89] To get the inputs needed to make earth fit for 'civilized human life'—or 'good life'—man has turned his greedy gaze and the tool of technology on earth and nature, even if it meant wrecking the very ecosystem, biodiversity, and environment that sustains life on earth.

The concept of what is 'good life' has changed over time. Initially it was the same or close to what we now call 'goodness of life'. It was in this line of thought that Socrates said, "not life, but good life, is to be chiefly valued". The problem is that our 'values' are our valuables. Confucius said, "Consideration for others is the basic of a good life, a good society". Instead of consideration, we have callousness. Down the line in our own time when Bertrand Russell wrote that a "good life is one inspired by love and guided by knowledge". Love, today, is bereft of two of its essential attribute, selflessness and sacrifice. And the knowledge we pursue is for power and privilege and to be successful. But for most humans, 'good life' has come to mean lots of leisure, luxury and lust, what Thomas Merton calls devoting ourselves to the 'cult of pleasure'.[90] It is not pleasure *per se* that is pernicious. The question is, *whose* pleasure? If it is directed at others it can cleanse our soul. Gandhi said, "To give pleasure to a single heart by a single deed is better than thousand heads bowing in prayer". Giving pleasure gives us pleasure but too often, as, Aldous Huxley said,[91] it is a way to exercise our power and to feel good about it. The four words 'money cannot buy happiness' is a cliché and conventional wisdom but, true to our times, even that is under attack. Richer people in any country are happier than the poorer people. Clearly, happiness levels are in positive correlation with the amount of wealth a person accumulates, and, contrary to popular belief, happiness does not level off when the assets reach a certain threshold. We equate 'happiness' with 'quality of life'. What remains hazy is the true nature of happiness and how one can measure. One can also say that 'smarter spending' can give us happiness.[92] Whatever 'smarter' is intended to be in this context, it is true that if altruistically used or spent, money does give happiness. If we can make others happy, the happiness we can and will obtain is immeasurable. One does not have to be a billionaire or Bill Gates; even the poorest can spend or share their money and give happiness to someone else.

Happy or otherwise, everyone, rich or poor, wants to make more money, save more money and also *spend* more money, the interplay of which economists call growth, and the inability to juggle with it is what makes us miserable. The bottom line is that after millenniums of his love affair with money, man is now even more confused if it is inherently 'mean' or simply 'means', good or bad, hurdle or help, in his timeless struggle to make himself a better, more responsible and responsive being. Can we say, as Laurence Olivier said towards the end of his life, "nothing is beneath me if it pays well", or should we be more concerned about 'how' than about 'how much'? Do we continue to debate Protagoras' famous statement 'man is the measure of all things' (*Anthropos metron panton*, in Greek), or should we conclude that man is simply one, albeit more cunning and predatory, of many mammals on earth? For long, wise men have wondered what the true test of manhood is, what constitutes a heroic life, what is worth dying for, and what we can give up 'just to live'.

The New Gilded Age and the Emergence of the 'One-Percent'

In the days of yore, most gloomy forecasts for man's future came from religious texts, soothsayers, crystal gazers, and occultists. Modern man came to dismiss such end-of-the-world scenarios as mere mumbo jumbo. However, if science had for a long time predicted and promised 'happy days ahead'—that the human would live as long as he wished, and would be equal to a virtual 'god'—it, too, is now finding itself nodding its head in consonance with the Doomsday Brigade. Some scientists warn that modern civilization is heading for collapse within a matter of decades due to growing economic instability and the pressure exerted on the planet by industries' unsustainable appetite for resources. People of the world are waking up to the rude realization that a select few extremely wealthy fellow-humans are enslaving the rest of us and even endangering the planet. Economic inequality is increasingly seen as a red flag, symbolized by the global gross distortion of capital, wealth, and income, and the rise of a new plutocracy dominated by the super-rich, or the 'One-Percent', which some are calling the dawn, not of the Golden Age, but of the 'New Gilded Age'. So glaring is the disparity that, for instance, in USA, the top 1% own 40% of the financial assets, and the top 10% own upwards of 85%. Moreover, while extreme inequality is fuelling climate change, the richest 1% of the world's population produces 175 times as much carbon dioxide per person as the bottom 10%, and the richest 10% produce fully half of all carbon emissions.[93] Money matters in everything, even in disproportionately being exposed to climate change and air pollution. The 'materialist menace' might be a modern phenomenon but matter, as separate from spirit, has always been a part of the human condition. So has been the spiritual aspiration to be relieved from the coils of matter. It is that one-percent that controls power and public policy making. That is the reason why governments are unresponsive to the plight of the poor, and contribute to culpable failure of the state and its laws which are tilted to favor the interests of the influential in society and are detrimental to the basic needs of the minorities and the marginalized, the homeless and the landless. The plutocracy that rules the world is not only leading to the accelerated extinction of other species, which, if unchecked, will make human life unsustainable on earth, but also to the casting away of vast sections of society to the vultures and wolves of penury, destitution, and deprivation.

Much of what we seek in life, much of what human life has long been associated with, is coded in one word: progress. Henry George wrote in his classic *Progress and Poverty*, "Many of the characteristics, actions, and emotions of man are exhibited by the lower animals. But man, no matter how low on the scale of humanity, has never yet been found destitute of one thing of which no animal shows the slightest trace, a clearly recognizable but almost undefinable something, which gives him the power of improvement—which makes him the progressive animal".[94] But what denotes progress? In common usage, it signifies the movement forward, an improvement, or advancement towards a goal. What is the goal that humans should seek to reach? It is the improvement and advancement towards material well-being that is commonly construed as progress. Such identification has long been in the works but it took a decisive turn with the Industrial Revolution where we paid, and continue to pay, an apocalyptic price. Instead of trying to achieve 'moral' movement, we got ensnared in an insatiable, maybe insane, drive towards satiation of both inane and wanton wants. How to reverse the course and change the coordinates and compass is the central challenge. If we can meet this challenge, other challenges like climate change, social disintegration, and social and moral entropy will, at the least, lose their bite. We have to learn to radically refocus, redirect, realign our intellectual, psychic, scientific, technological, even spiritual resources to face up to the realities of the emergent world. And if we can do that no problem is insurmountable. We don't have to go back to the Stone Age or become neo-Luddites. But we must give up this craze for speed, smart phones, cyborgs, and endless automation, which exact a huge environmental cost. The more we rely on appliances the less capable we will become to act without them. And automation, it has been said, breeds automation, and human beings become optional, or unnecessary, to get human work done. How can the most 'intelligent' creature on earth be so stupid as to choose self-destruction through self-replacement? The answer comes from writer Sue Halpern: "the priorities are clear: money first, people second".[95] Put differently, we are prepared to downsize, de-skill, and de-dignify ourselves to empower companies and make businesses more profitable and the rich richer. But can we blame it all on money? What about our much-touted free will and freedom to make choices? Frankly, and really, we don't know.

One thing we need to get straight. We tend to think that the pervasive predatory role of money is a part of the modern malaise. The truth is that money or wealth was always integral to human existence, a kind of thorn in the flesh, an evil, but necessary nonetheless, like evil itself. The message from the scriptures is mixed. One the one hand, we came to terms with the reality that, as a social animal, we have to live with it. On the other hand, we also recognized its addictive, divisive, and corrupting character. The Gospel[96] says that Jesus cautioned his disciples about the seductive power of money and said, "It is easier for a camel to go through the eye of a needle, than for a rich man to enter the kingdom of God". And an ancient Hindu text, the classic *Arthashastra* by Kautilya (who is also known as Chanakya) states, '*Dhanam moolam idham jagat*'—the world revolves around wealth. This aphorism is much quoted and also equally misunderstood and misapplied to justify reverence for money. It actually conveys the contrary caution, that one should live for better ideals than for basal desires and worldly pleasures. But it is also important to learn that ancient wisdom and traditions also recognized the reality of money in human life, provided it is pursued righteously. Times and things have dramatically changed since the time of Kautilya, who is believed to have lived in the 3rd century BCE. But money remains supreme and unrestrained, if any, stronger and more intrusive and invasive. It has given birth to an assortment of 'isms' like materialism, consumerism, capitalism, communism, etc. And it has driven technology in the wrong direction, towards the mass production of goods, gadgets, and gizmos for the well-to-do and the tech-savvy bourgeoisie.

One of the greatest challenges we now face is to induce and orchestrate a sea change in our relationship with money. In fact, if we could develop the mindset and means to ensure that it is spread equitably and justly across competing needs and priorities in the human population, it will have a tremendous boost to a fairer and far less fractious world. On the one hand, it will lift over a billion people out of acute poverty, and on the other hand, it will make it possible to do research and development on technologies that are currently still-born for want of funding, and which are critical to solve any nagging and pestering social problems like climate change, mass illiteracy and ill health. We must move from grudging acceptance to recognition without reservations that it can do a world of good to the world. One of the hotly debated issues now is about a 'world without money', and how, and if, such a development will be a bane or a blessing. The hope is that such a world would be fairer, kinder, and gentler. There will be no rich or poor, and no money-power. It is hard to tell how such a utopian world might actualize. While other mechanisms like UBI (universal basic income) are worth intellectual pursuit, the more practical pursuit is to try to turn money around from the Biblical root of evil to a 21st-century catalyst of social justice. We must believe that money and *moksha*, like science and spirituality, are not antagonistic but capable of coexisting. In other words, make as money as one can, but ensure that it is spread and shared as broadly and deeply as possible. And make sure it reaches those corners where it can flower the potential of the downtrodden and the dirt poor. Financial technologies can help bridge the gap between social mission and profit motive. Public policies and social norms must support activities that induce money to flow where it is needed the most, and turn society itself into what we may call a 'sharing society'. Money need not always be morally corrosive or socially disruptive; it can be morally uplifting and socially equalizing, if channeled properly. There are other motivators besides money, but money by its weight as a critical need in today's world can be a powerful inspiration. We need a new genre of social entrepreneurship that is capable of merging 'public purpose and private profit'. Along with the other two 'M's—morality and mortality—, it is another, perhaps the most important, dimension of contextual-change. What is now perceived as an impediment has to be turned into an instrument for social empowerment. For the real obstacle to common good and human enhancement—which science is focusing all its energies upon through the medium of the machine—is not money, but our own unchecked mind. Money is neutral; not the mind, which is both monkeyish and malicious. Money can do both good and bad, but as long as the mind dominates our consciousness, money is likely to do more harm than good. Which means that without consciousness-change, we cannot expect much good to come out of money. In short, we must fundamentally change the place money occupies in our conscious mind as a giver of good things of life to a catalyst of an orderly and just human society. We need a critical mass for such a change, and that must come from the millennials who are tech-savvy, but morally adrift, wandering around, trying to find some meaning for why they are alive and what they should choose to do with their time. If that happens, the world will be a far better place, less fractious and more peaceful, less miserable and happier. And that will certainly make every human relationship and institution more stable and synergistic. More than anything else, it will greatly aid the forces of good and virtue in the 'war within'.

Chapter 4

Towards a New Vocabulary of Morality

Malice and Morality

One of man's enduring aspirations is to become an authentically moral being. And the single most important obstacle has been the malice entrenched in our mind. Living in a brutal world like ours, one of the very few things that gives us some satisfaction and a hint of hope about our future is that, although we arose from brutes, we are better—better because we can judge right and wrong, and therefore we are, or can be, more responsible and responsive in our earthly conduct. It is another matter that none of such assumptions are any longer accurate. We live in a morally ambiguous and ambivalent world, in which everyone wants to be moral, and most think they are, and yet morally macabre things continue to be done and no one feels responsible or remorseful. But to begin with, in such a compromised and corrupting world, what should one do to remain rooted to our moral moorings? How this has come about is a subject of scholarly discourse, whether it is hard-wired by nature or acquired through evolution. Some say that morality is simply an instinct just like sexual desire. Theologists like William Craig posit that, "If God does not exist, objective moral values and duties do not exist". Philosopher Patricia Churchland argues in her book *Braintrust* that it is a 'false dilemma' to claim that 'either God secures the moral law or morality is an illusion', because 'morality is grounded in our biology'. And atheists like Sam Harris attack both moral absolutism—that some things are absolutely right or wrong no matter the circumstances—and moral relativism—that moral or ethical statements, which vary from person to person, are all equally valid and no one's opinion of 'right and wrong' is really better than any other—, arguing that moral values are in reality moral facts, and as facts they can be scientifically understood by studying brain and behavior. All this inevitably raises the matter of the 'problem of evil'. In fact, it is a double problem of evil. Some ask: what is the essential nature of this evil and wounded world, and is there any way out of this woe and misery? From the other side, some ask: why should this essentially good world harbor any evil, and how can we live with it wholeheartedly? Is evil a perennial characteristic of finite existence, or are we responsible for the experience of evil? We must remember that, much as we might wish, we cannot get rid of evil. For, as Socrates said, "Evils, Theodorus, can never pass away; for there must always remain something which is antagonistic to good. Having no place among the gods in heaven, of necessity they hover around the mortal nature, and this earthly sphere". Science, which so far left such matters to religion and philosophy, is now trying to step in and make a difference. Recent research by neurologists like Michael Stone (*The Anatomy of Evil*, 2009) indicates that violent criminals have amygdalae (the region of the brain believed to play a key role in the emotions) that are smaller or that don't function properly. Views of people like Sam Harris and such findings are in sync with the current scientific chorus: everything, good, evil, empathy, compassion, aggression, love, addiction, even mind and consciousness, is simply a matter of our brain. If it is malstructured or malfunctioning, or the internal balance is disturbed, things go haywire and we misbehave. Other experts argue that our brain is a big part of us but *we* are bigger than that. Indeed, our over-reliance on the brain, to the exclusion of everything else, in particular the heart, is what is inducing us to take the wrong route. If we want to strengthen and sharpen the kinder and gentler side of our personality, and make morality our default mode of choice-making, for example, we need to more than tamper with parts of our brain.

Whether man was born crooked or as a 'blank slate', or as a Noble Savage, or became a civilized brute, the fact is that man has always struggled to give birth to his 'Baby-Buddha' within. The 'birth' is a struggle because the wicked in us does not let it go. And we need morality precisely because we are not (wholly) moral. That for man to be wicked is easy and to be moral is difficult was recognized by all religions. That was why they all tried to pin us down to moral codes of conduct such as the Biblical Ten Commandments, the Seven Laws of Noah, and the Quranic Ten Instructions. By following and practicing these precepts and prohibitions, the expectation was that man would tread the moral path. While the very rationale of religious life was the assumption that it would keep man morally circumscribed, what has happened is that religious zealotry itself down the ages became a source of unspeakable evil and triggered the barbaric Crusades of the Middle Ages. And that continued through the ages, with some ups and some downs. Religion is closely associated with God, and God, through His every revelation, clearly instructed or implored man to lead a moral life and laid down the path to take. How then could religion itself rouse such intense emotions and feelings of intolerance, hatred, sadism, and blood thirstiness in the minds of millions of otherwise 'good' and 'god-fearing' people? Is there anything in the genre of religious knowledge that is tailor-made to arouse the worst in the human mind, subverting the good in us? Or has the evil inside us become so strong and virulent that it is looking for opportunities to express itself, and religious trigger is just one of them? And does the current state of religious bloodletting reflect the waning fortunes of the good against the evil in the war within?

Although externally it has not always been so, in the war within, morality, however weak, has always been a force for the good. Experts differ on the origins of morality. But it does appear that, very early after his advent on earth, man realized that simply to stay away from the throat of another animal he needed the help of others around him. While it still did not mean they did not cut each others' throats, it did sow the seeds of morality. It is morality, not the bigness of the brain, that empowered man to outwit other much stronger and ferocious animals. Contrary to what is generally assumed, what allowed us to escape extinction was not the survival of the fittest, but as Darwin himself posited in his book *The Descent of Man*, it was the survival of the kindest. Darwin also wrote that natural selection favored the evolution of compassion, a statement of great contemporary significance. Morality evolved initially as a means to cooperate for the common good, and as a biological device to place the 'us' before the 'me' in small groups. We now need that too, not to survive, but to turn our individual energies into collective synergy. The moral axiom 'act so as to elicit the best in others and thereby in thyself" could serve as a point of departure. If we can do that, there are no limits to what we can accomplish. They say we are angels who have only one wing, but we can still fly by embracing each other. The choice is ours. It does not mean that we were not mean, malicious or murderous then; far from it. But it does mean that the moral sense in us became more manifest in response to the realization that it was the only way to prevail in those cut-throat conditions. Sadly, in today's cut-throat context of life, we have done a reversal: we have adopted embraced the maxim of the 'survival of the smartest' in place of 'survival of the kindest'. And, instead of natural selection it is now 'unnatural selection'; fittest is smartest. And there is a growing concern that morality is in free fall, illustrated, for example, by the perception that Mammon matters more than morals. Some say that what we are facing is nothing less than a moral meltdown. Some are asking the agonizing question: have we come to such a perilous pass where morality has lost its raison d'être, lost the power, in and of itself, to motivate us towards good behavior? And, are morality and modernity an 'odd couple' or inherently hostile forces? Is there any scope and space for a futurist in a terrified, compromised, morally wounded world? What is the right moral option for a human being when he concludes that the world and the planet are safer without human presence? Does the present paradigm of modern life constitute the choice of what the Katha Upanishad called the primrose path of *preyas* (the pleasant), at the expense of *sreyas* (the good)? The path of preyas implies that any action that is pleasurable is good, to live his or her life in search of the next pleasurable thing, with no regard for attaining any higher purpose for his or her life. But then, the question arises: is it impossible to be good while leading a good life, a life of affluence, luxury, leisure? Some are posing 'the mother of all moral questions': do we, as a species that has done what it has for so long, have a moral right and legitimacy to inhabit this planet? What is the right moral thing for a human being to do in a world that seems to sink deeper and deeper into moral quagmire? We need a morality that is suitable to the future challenges and a force that deepens our interrelatedness and interdependence. While these issues do matter and need to be pondered over, we must not think that we are left only with a Hobson's choice between morality and modernity. Fact is both are indispensable and irreversible. We cannot reverse the tide of history and roll back modernity or allow morality to be the fall guy or a pushover. Actually, one could say that modernity already is passé and that we are living a in a postmodern world. Clearly, morality too needs to be revisited and re-conceptualized to serve as a force for unity and sanity in a world which can only be characterized as a 'man-eats-man world'. If properly handled and guided, modernity, the fulcrum of which is technology, could be a huge help to strengthen the forces of morality within and without. But technology itself, or the *technosphere* as some describe it, now constitutes the widest crucible for morality and throws up new ethical challenges. Some thoughtful observers like Andrew Kimbrell "see a dramatic dichotomy between evil as it occurred in the social era of human history and evil as incarnated in the current technological sphere... the technosphere has created a technological, institutional plane on which 'the system' [not the individual] effectuates evil in circumstances where individuals and their emotions, ethics, or morals play no significant role".[1] It has nurtured a milieu in which, as Scott Peck (*The Road Less Travelled*, 1978) puts it across, modern evil is that which "one percent of the people cause, but in which 100 percent of us ordinary sinners participate through our everyday sins". He says that evil straddles the line between a personality disorder and spiritual disorder, and an evil person knows that they are doing evil, while a sociopath does not, even though their actions may be very similar. New dilemmas confront us. For example, who should we program an autonomous car to save: a pedestrian crossing the road, or the passenger in the car? And does it matter who the pedestrians are? Every technological advance invariably raises deep and wrenching moral issues, and it is not possible to have universal moral values because they are culture-sensitive. The more technology becomes autonomous, the greater is the need to design them properly. This coincidentally was underlined by the world's first robot citizen *Sophia*. We must find a way to embed ethics into technology. And when robots increasingly replace humans, questions such as 'robot rights' will arise. As robots develop more advanced artificial intelligence, empowering them to think and act like humans, new moral issue will arise. But for this, we do not have the consciousness necessary to direct technology for the long-term and inter-generational justice and greater good. Similarly, morality can significantly offset many of the negative aspects of modernity. On the other hand, if misdirected, modernity could be a huge hindrance to making human life more moral. And morality, in its form and structure, is not sufficiently suitable to make the human world a humane world. What could make the difference is the war within.

The moral context today is vastly different from the times it helped small groups and tribes to cooperate for survival. Our brain cannot extend that necessity to the current global scale. The moral choices and dilemmas we have to make and face are vastly different. *WE* must bridge the gap between moral and social. What Nikolai Berdyaev said about spirituality equally applies to morality. He said, "The question of bread for myself is a material question, but the question of bread for my neighbor is a spiritual question". We have to bring together the social and the spiritual. That is the way to contain the contagion of materialism. Concern is mounting that our materialistic mindset is not only leading to a destructive lifestyle but also creating mental problems. Recent studies link materialism to a variety of mental health issues, including anxiety and depression, with side-effects such as selfish attitudes and behaviors, putting kids particularly at risk. We now have to deal with and interact with nonhuman personas like robots, artificial intelligence (AI) systems, and cyborgs, and we have to make moral choices in relation to them. We not only need a new understanding of morality, we now need the tools to design and program it in a manner suitable to the digital age. The digital revolution has shrunk the world into an electronic village while, at the same time, widening the distance and distrust between man and man. It has also made raising kids 'with a conscience' more complex and difficult. But the ushering of a new morality must start with us. We cannot expect teenagers to lead lives of empathy if we ourselves do not lead such lives. We must first embody and exhibit the qualities we want the soon-to-be adults to show. Be the good we want our kids to be. Show the sharing we want them to imbibe. Early moral development is crucial for a moral society.

For, in the digital age, man is, at the same time, a solitary being and a social being. What technology has done is to make man both isolated and intertwined. It is even being boasted that technology will allow us to 'ditch speech and communicate using nothing but our thoughts' by 2050. As an isolated individual, living with minimal human touch, man's actions are more prone to be more self-centered and anti-social. But the reach of the impact of his decisions, distractions, and actions can be far reaching. We make myriad, mostly minute, choices in everyday life and they have moral ramifications. The context raises new ramifications but our consciousness has remained the same. The moral context cannot be separated from our overall living context, just as our moral behavior cannot be understood without juxtaposing it with our generic behavior and conduct. And like everything else, how we behave, morally or wickedly, is also an extension of what happens inside us, in the war within. Indeed the two principal opponents in the war are morality and immorality, *dharma* and *adharma*. If morality and dharma are dominant, then we behave morally with love, kindness, and compassion. If they are on the wane, then our behavior will be tainted with avarice, aggression, hatred, and intolerance. If we want to avoid a moral meltdown we need to make morality more compatible to the contemporary context.

Enlarging the Circle of Compassion

Our incapacity to factor in 'compassion' into our daily life is a major contributory cause of our enfeeblement and the coarsening of contemporary human society. The two things we need to nurture and manifest in life are passion and compassion. We need to be passionate with compassion, and compassionate with our passions. 'Compassion' in fact symbolizes the highest virtue. Through the sharing of suffering, we can help each other to become better beings. In the Bhagavad Gita, it is said that 'When [a man] sees all beings as equals in suffering or in joy because they are like himself, that man has grown perfect in yoga'. The principle of compassion lies at the heart of all religious, and ethical and spiritual traditions, calling us to always treat all others as we wish to be treated ourselves, to strive ceaselessly to lighten the lives of others, to refrain from inflicting any sort of pain on all creatures. And yet even those who are reputed to be 'good' and 'decent' and even 'generous' among us have always found it difficult to make compassion a passion, that which gives us irresistible pleasure. It has always been a struggle and now more so than ever. As Jack Finley, the science fiction writer reminds us: "This is a time when it becomes harder and harder to continue telling yourself that we are still good people. We hate each other. And we're used to it". That 'hate' shows up in multiple ways, irritation, intolerance, anger, aggression, suicide, murder. Not being able to 'hate' anyone anytime is a quality human beings have yet to imbibe. It is said that, when asked for a summary of the Jewish religion in the most concise terms, the 1st-century Jewish leader Rabbi Hillel stated, "That which is hateful to you, do not do to your fellow. That is the whole Torah. The rest is the explanation; go and learn". The *Ishavasya* Upanishad says, "He who sees the entire world of animate and inanimate objects in himself, and also sees himself in all animate and inanimate objects, because of this does not hate anyone".

That is a lofty ideal, but even without reaching such heights we can find no utility for hate. Hate is so wasteful, so utterly useless, that it is hard even to rationalize it. Martin Luther King Jr. said, "I have decided to stick with love; hate is too great a burden to bear". But that is a 'burden' in different degrees, shapes, and avatars that we all carry. But personal, religious, ethnic, and racial 'hatred' is in the very air we breathe in and out today. 'Hate' has become so acceptable in our language that we use this word without always intending it to be that. Even in ordinary conversation, we involuntarily say, 'I hate this' or 'I hate him'; even if it is really not in the sense of hatred, which is the intense desire to destroy another person, even if not necessary, it is malice in action. Even love, if unreciprocated or obstructed, can turn into murderous hatred. The way to counter it is to cultivate compassion, learn it like any other skill. Engaging with another individual without expecting anything frees one from the confines of 'separateness' and of one's ego. It is not only a spiritual *sadhana* but also a social imperative at this juncture in our troubled world. Einstein said, "Our task must be to free ourselves by widening our arc of compassion to embrace all living creatures and the whole of nature and its beauty". 'Compassion' is more than helping out people in distress or disability; more than generosity or mercy. As Mackie Ruka of New Zealand's Waitaha Maori tribe says, compassion is an act of power, of *transformative* power. It is our inability to harness that power that impoverishes us mentally and spiritually. We seem more capable of passion than compassion, zealotry more than moderation. We need both passion and compassion, but we should try to be passionately compassionate, and compassionately passionate. When we are passionate or obsessed about something, like being in love, we become single-minded and driven, and everything else becomes secondary or non-existent. All related actions become involuntary and automatic. We must bring that 'state of mind' to compassion.

For the theologian Matthew Fox, 'compassion, in its broadest sweep', is more than moral commandment, it is 'but a flow and overflow of the fullest human and divine energies'. It has been described as the 'keen awareness of the interdependence of all things (Thomas Merton); as 'the ultimate and most meaningful embodiment of emotional maturity'. It is through compassion that a person achieves the 'peak experiences' and deepest reach in his search for self-fulfillment. Eckhart Tolle says, "Compassion is the awareness of a deep bond between yourself and all other creatures". All religions extol compassion as the highest value and virtue, both as a way to alleviate suffering and as a tool of salvation, *nirvana,* or *moksha*. It is called daya in Hinduism, and *karuna* in Buddhism, although both terms are interchangeable. Compassion has been called the transcendental and experiential heart of the Buddha's teachings. It is one of the four tenets of Buddhist doctrine of *Brahmavihara*: loving-kindness; compassion; empathetic joy; and equanimity. Compassion for all life, human and animal, is the very soul of Jainism. In fact, so identified is Buddhism with compassion, that the Buddha himself came to be known as the 'Compassionate One'. In Christianity too, compassion is given great importance. Jesus tells his listeners in the Sermon on the Mount, "Blessed are the merciful, for they shall obtain mercy". In the Parable of the Good Samaritan, he holds up to his followers the ideal of compassionate conduct. True Christian compassion, say the Gospels, should extend to all, even to the extent of loving one's enemies. As far as Islam is concerned, each of the 114 chapters of the Quran, with one exception, begins with the verse, "In the name of God, the Compassionate, the Merciful". The Arabic word for compassion is *rahmah*. A good Muslim has to commence each day, each prayer and each significant action by reciting *Bismillah ir-Rahman ir-Rahim*—invoking "God the Merciful and the Compassionate". In practical terms, compassion is two-pronged behavioral manifestation, one affirmative, the other avoidance: to help everyone who asks for or needs help; and not to hurt anyone by word or deed, if not in thought. That is the distilled wisdom, the backbone of all religions. Sin, it has been said, is hurting others unnecessarily; every other 'sin' is invented nonsense. The Dalai Lama said, "Our primary purpose in life is to help others. And if you can't help them, at least do not hurt them". It does not make a difference if one is a theist or atheist. If we 'believe' in God, we are doing His work, as his proxy. And if we do not, if there is no God to help or protect the suffering, then there is all the more reason for another man to step up and help a fellow-man. Plato said, "Be kind, for everyone you meet is fighting a harder battle". We think that our 'battle' is the hardest because we cannot feel, or experience, the nature or the ferocity of the battles of others. We 'hurt' others and are wary of helping because of the 'mine-thine' mental divide, but which, Einstein told us, is 'an optical delusion of man's consciousness'. We forget that, as Herman Melville wrote, "our actions run as causes, and they come back to us as effects". It is not that most of us are incapable of being viscerally or compulsively 'compassionate'; we are compassionate selectively and inconsistently. Many sensitive souls have long doubted whether true compassion exists at all in the human essence—or whether it is inherently rooted in self-interest. Our terrible, bloodstained, savage history gives no comfort. Indeed, the merciless message of human history is that, although man is capable of great good, he can be more easily seduced by unspeakable evil. Carl Jung wrote, "When [our shadow] appears… it is quite within the bounds of possibility for a man to recognize the relative evil of his nature, but it is a rare and shattering experience for him to gaze into the face of absolute evil".

We are all a blend of good and evil, malevolence and magnanimity, virtue and vice, and a host of other pairs of opposites. It is pointless to endlessly debate which is 'natural' and embedded, and which is not. If they are not natural or innate they wouldn't be there in the first place. We are home to the noblest and vilest, sacred, and sordid, of emotions, feelings, and thoughts. Which of these, or a combination of which, comes out and affects behavior depends on the course of the war within. Compassion is not empathy or altruism, though the concepts are related. While empathy relates more generically to our ability to take the perspective of and feel the emotions of another human person, compassion is when those feelings and thoughts extend to a desire to help. Altruism, in turn, is the kind, benevolent behavior often prompted by feelings of compassion, though one can feel compassion without acting on it, and altruism is not always motivated by compassion. Although we tend to think that compassion or empathy or altruism are about 'giving' and being 'selfless' that is not always true. We gain far more than we give, both physically and spiritually. As the Dalai Lama puts it, 'the first beneficiary of compassion is always oneself'. He goes on, "If you want others to be happy, practice compassion. If you want to be happy, practice compassion". But we cannot be compassionate outside if there is no 'contentment' inside. If we are discontented within, then we will try to find 'contentment' outside, which means fulfilling desires. The focus will then be on that effort, not on helping or being compassionate towards others. In the modern world, most persons are trapped in a state disquietedness, disaffection, alienation, and existential angst, and that is the reason why they find it so herculean to be compassionate in their behavior. It is because they are discontented with so many unfulfilled desires that they are so avaricious in their behavior; they want to find 'contentment within' by filling it up with material things. It is like trying to put out a fire by pouring fuel into it. In compassion, one wholly gives, and is thankful for being given the opportunity to give.

Compassion is not only good for one's soul, but also one's body. Recent studies of compassion reject the inevitability of self-interest. These studies support a view of the emotions as rational, functional, and adaptive. Compassion and benevolence and altruism, which are the hallmarks of all religions, this research suggests, are an evolved part of human nature, bedded in our brain and biology, and ready to be cultivated for the greater good. The study suggests that "the brain, then, seems wired up to respond to others' suffering—indeed, it makes us feel good when we can alleviate that suffering".[2] New research has shown that "when we feel compassion, our heart rate slows down, we secrete the 'bonding hormone' oxytocin, and regions of the brain linked to empathy, caregiving, and feelings of pleasure light up, which often results in our wanting to approach and care for other people". They also indicate there is a biological basis for compassion, and there are physical benefits to practicing compassion—people who practice it produce 100% more DHEA, which is a hormone that counteracts the ageing process, and 23% less cortisol—the 'stress hormone'. They are in accordance with the view held by Charles Darwin that 'compassion and benevolence are an evolved part of human nature, an intrinsic part of our brain in particular, and biological system on the whole'. Studies indicate that "compassion is not simply a fickle or irrational emotion but rather an innate human response embedded into the folds of our brains". This "suggests that being compassionate causes a chemical reaction in the body that motivates us to be even more compassionate". Another research tells us that "Our findings support the possibility that compassion and altruism can be viewed as trainable skills rather than stable traits". Specifically, they report that taking a course in compassion leads to increased engagement of certain neural systems, which prompts higher levels of altruistic behavior… Brain scans revealed "a pattern of neural changes" in those who had received compassion training, including "neural systems implicated in understanding the suffering of other people, executive and emotional control, and reward processing".

'Cast Out the Beam Out of Thine Own Eye'

Under what circumstances and conditions should an individual be refrained from what he chooses to do? Philosophers have long debated and differed on this question. Some have argued that it should only be when his intended action is a potential threat to others. By extension, it means that an individual is the best judge of what is 'good' for him and that no one else can be a surrogate. Others have expanded to include the individual's own well-being, positing that, in point of fact, most people do not act, even if they do know, in their own interests, and tend to emphasize the short term over the long term, a premise that is the basis of much of social legislation. The question is: while legality can, to an extent, serve both purposes, prevent harm to others, and protect an individual from himself, what about such 'behavior' of the species? Human behavior is now a grave and growing peril to the lives and interests of other species, in addition to its own. Albert Schweitzer paraphrased it aptly: "Man has the lost the capacity to foresee and to forestall. He will end up destroying the earth". Man is exhibiting three lethal tendencies: self-absorption, self-righteousness, and self-destruction. All three are interconnected and interdependent. We are so self-absorbed that every event in the world and in others' lives is judged by its effect on us. We are single-minded to a fault in finding faults in others. Perhaps next only to temptation, the most 'tempting' thing which few can let pass, even if a half-chance comes along, is not to find fault with others. That is a sign of both insecurity and hubris, born out of a desire to control. After a while that becomes involuntary, another habit that looks for openings and opportunities. The truth is, as Rumi reminds us, "Many of the faults you see in others, dear reader, are your own nature reflected in them". Jesus exhorts us, "Thou hypocrite, first cast out the beam out of thine own eye; and then shalt thou see clearly to cast out the mote out of thy brother's eye".[3] Besides self-righteousness, we are single-minded to a fault about self-destruction; we leave nothing to chance in our drive to do things injurious to our well-being. We are, deliberately, and for something as ephemeral as profit, polluting the air we breathe, the food we eat, the rivers, the oceans, and filling the air with enough toxic fallout to put poison into our own children's bones. The eighteen-fold increase in the global economic output has not only deepened the divide between the elite and the masses, but also created the present environmental crisis, potentially cheating our children of their future. We are not even sparing the mighty oceans. It is said that our oceans are 30% more acidic than they were a bare thirty years ago. Scientists tell us that 'just the acidification of the oceans, by itself, is enough to wipe out life on this planet'. And that the acidification of the ocean today is proceeding on a greater and faster basis than anything that geologists can find in fossil records for the past 65 million years. Another existential risk, experts tell us, is the "release into the atmosphere of methane. Its effect on global warming is 23 times more powerful than that of carbon dioxide, over the course of a century, and even worse in the short term of about 10 years. The National Science Foundation (USA) has recently warned that "Release of even a fraction of the methane stored in the [Arctic] shelf could trigger abrupt climate warming".[4] As if we haven't had enough of dire warnings, we are told that, of all things, jellyfish are 'taking over the oceans' which could accelerate climate change.[5]

None of such stuff scares us; it causes not a ripple in our smug consciousness, and nothing nudges us from our frenetic pursuit of the 'good things of life'. All those warnings, however prescient or forbidding, might well be addressed to another species on another planet. It is doubtful if the authors of such reports themselves make any changes in their daily life. Clearly no other species is so hell-bent and clear-headed in this 'death-wish'. Over a million people every year take their own lives for reasons that are almost funny if only not so deadly; many, many more make the attempt. The World Health Organization (WHO) says that over the past 45 years, suicide rates have increased by 60% worldwide. Suicide is now one of the three leading causes of death among males between the ages 14 to 45. Children as young as six have reportedly killed themselves. What we are not sure is if this streak is constitutional or civilizational, a desperate cry for concern and affection, or some kind of nature's revenge for our rapacious and predatory conduct. What can trigger murder or suicide, sadism or savagery, remains a mystery. While the majority relate to personal problems, frustrations, and provocations, some arise as reaction to all that is wrong and wretched in the world. They reflect what Antigone tells the King of Thebes, Creone: "And if I have to die before my time, well, I count that a gain. When someone has to live the way I do, surrounded by so many evil things, how can she fail to find a benefit in death?"[6] Every 'suicider', potential or actual, might not look for a benefit in death; but they see no point in prolonging life the way it came to be. Theories abound, but the truth is that we just do not know why we go on 'living' or when we think 'enough is enough'. But all this death-wish, suicidal, and murderous tendencies do not dull our unquenchable hunger for immortality, for a life not limited by the body. Man is not content to live within his 'natural' limitations, but at the same time, he is systematically atrophying what nature has endowed him with. And the 'mystery' of what transpires within our own bodies as we go about living, or rather, dying, is deepening, even as our lives are turning more and more shallow. We do not know the 'why' of many things and sometimes we ask 'why' when it ought to be 'why not'. Questioning reality as it appears to be is a human trait. The German mystic Angelus Silesius wrote, "The rose doth have no why; It blossoms without reason; Forgetful of itself, oblivious to our vision".[7] It might be 'oblivious of our vision', but we do know that at some deep depth under the largest organ of our physical body, our skin, there is some sort of melting pot that houses and harbors a host of things like thoughts, feelings, emotions, instincts, and impulses, but we do not know how they interface and interact and become understanding, comprehension, imagination, prejudice, analytical capacity, choice-selection, decision-making, etc. All those disparate but intertwined things collide, coalesce, and bubble up and gush out as 'behavior'. We talk of behavior as if it is some kind of a mystery wrapped in a riddle, something for psychologists to break their heads about. There is no unified theory of human behavior but, in practical terms, it is the way, or ways, we connect with and conduct ourselves relative to other people, to other creatures, to Mother Earth, to Nature, and to practically everything in the universe, seen and unseen. Our behavior is embodied in the myriad things we do in the normal course of every day, at home, at work, on the street, and as a partner in multiple relationships. The *Maitri* Upanishad puts the subject in context: "As one acts and conducts himself, so does he become. The doer of good becomes good. The doer of evil becomes evil. One becomes virtuous by virtuous action, bad by bad action". Perhaps we will never know for sure why man does evil, which is different from not doing the right thing, but we can say that it is not at least always. As Plato's hypothesis implied, "Evil man is evil only through error, and if one free him from error, one will necessarily make him good". It depends on what is meant by 'evil' and by 'error'. Slitting someone's throat for not parting with a penny or raping a three-year-old child and strangling the child thereafter cannot be called an act of 'error'. But no man is all 'evil' or all 'good'.

What is important in life is *what* is 'right' and what is 'wrong'; not *who* is right and who is wrong. And if we want to better our behavior, we need to put in place two things—sincere *abhyasa* (ceaseless effort) and *chitta suddhi* (purity of consciousness)—to ensure that in every circumstance, we 'give' more and 'take' less. For, every event is an amoral equation, every individual is at best an amoral 'time bomb'; and every action is a pebble thrown into the cosmic ocean. And everyone deserves, indeed is entitled, to be treated well, including you by your own self. However much we might try, there is absolutely nothing we do, or can do, that does not involve or affect, directly or indirectly, another living being. We are all fellow-travelers and the safety and salvation of each of us hinges on the attitude and actions of others. That being the case, all that we need to do, or try to do to the best of our ability, is to ensure that our inevitable impact on others' lives is helpful, at least not hurtful. And if we cannot but hurt someone, we should 'make up for it' by immediately thereafter helping another person. We are instinctively not much attuned to the happenings within, or to how our mind or consciousness works, or to whatever that lurks within us—out of sight, but all in the mind, one might say. We are only concerned about what we do outside, individually or as a group. But we *know* that the two—inside and outside, within and without—are connected, in a sense, mutually dependent and inseparable. While such a view until recently was the stuff of metaphysics and mysticism, emerging areas of science are coming round to this line of thought. As the physicist Jason Dispenza puts it, "We have been conditioned to believe that the external world is more real than the internal world. This new model of science says just the opposite. It says that what is happening within us will create what's happening outside of us". The external also influences the internal. Some scientists say that the neurobiological processes in our brain control our behavior and some others say that it is 'microbes residing symbiotically inside our bodies'.

It is as difficult to find a man without vice as it is to find one without any virtue. What induces us to choose virtue or vice, good or evil is the state of the 'war within' at the time of the choice. If we want to be virtuous and moral in our behavior, we must ensure that the 'good guy' inside dominates in the war. If we were not to default to a selfish stand, as John Rawls[8] argued, we normally would, and change (the 'biasing of genetic kin' in the current evolutionary language), then we need to tilt the scales within. If we were to operationalize Rawls' 'difference principle'—that social goods (money, jobs, property) must be equally spread unless unequal or differential distribution benefits the most marginalized groups—we have to alter the dynamics of the internal power sharing. Personal and social transformation go hand in hand. Internal change is not all internal. What we do, how we live, even whatever we pass through the five 'gates' of our body has a bearing on the internal change. We cannot truthfully and truly better our behavior unless a similar betterment occurs within. The way to get through is to adopt the advice of the ancient Chinese philosopher Lao Tzu: "The journey of a thousand miles begins with one step". That one step is really a twin: intimately inward; outwardly incremental. In both directions, we need to take several small steps, so small and so silent that we hardly notice, to shift our gaze from what we could, to what we can, from what we should not do, to what we ought to do. At the very outset, we need to will ourselves to be our own objective 'observer', or 'witness', consciously review what we do every day, the most routine and seemingly most mundane things, and see how we can marginally 'better' them, with a wee bit more sensitivity, consideration, and empathy. The synergistic effect will translate and acquire critical mass, and that, in turn, might seep through our skin, so to speak, and, over time, change the nature of the 'change' within. The more we change within righteously, the more we will change in what we do, the faster will be the pace of the internal change.

Despite all that we have accomplished to make morality our default mode, were are nowhere near what 'we could become'. There is no point looking for scapegoats or sacrificial lambs like religion, culture, civilization, technology, modernity, and so on. They all have had their part, but they are symptomatic and symbolic of a deeper source. It is not, as we tend to say, 'all *in* the mind'. It is *the mind*, plain and simple, lock, stock, and barrel. The wrong step we have taken is that we have put the wrong 'person' at the helm of our lives—our brain- and mind-driven 'intelligence'. What Einstein called "our limited mind", which has caused, in his words, a "weakness of our intellectual understanding of nature and of our own being". We have done this both willfully and by default. Willful because we are always fully in the flow of the 'nature of the beast', of what our mind is and is not. Default because there is no one else, so to speak, 'on the bench', no substitute or alternative. Our cognitive skills and abilities that are embedded in every human thought, word and action, and in mechanisms of how we learn, remember, problem-solve, however much we fine-tune and boost them, are, in the words of Henri Bergson, "created (as they are) by life, in definite circumstances, to act on definite things…"; they are incapable of "presenting the true nature of life, the full meaning of the evolutionary movement".[9] Some say that the laws of physics may well prevent the human brain from evolving into an ever more powerful thinking machine.[10] But optimists say that we might be able to, over time, find ways to target-train our mental muscles and specific parts of our brain the way we do now our biceps, to dramatically enhance our cognitive capacities and also acquire the capability to turn other people into 'extensions of our brains'.[11] Present-day gurus are of the opinion that 'There is no discernible difference between human mental functioning and its simulation by a suitably programmed computer. Computers, in principle, can think'.[12] We already have in some cities what is being called a gym for the brain,[13] a fitness center for brain-exercise. It is said that "The very act of interacting with others or working with smart devices will help us continue to develop our brains, and as our brains develop, we will in turn be able to use increasingly sophisticated devices and rely on people in more complex and powerful ways".[14] But, more fundamentally, what is 'thinking' and what is 'thought'? We identify both with the brain/mind, which is true. We also associate it with 'computation', calculations per second, and the number of potential computational pathways; and that is how we 'think' about a computer 'thinking'. A machine might do what a 'thinking' human might do in certain respects, but what about 'consciousness'?

'Being moral' should not be at the expense of being social or fighting injustice. The ability to judge right from wrong is of no use if we don't carry it forward. Although we tend to think that there can be no dissenter of something as 'good' as morality, there have always been voices who viewed 'morality' as an instrument to legitimize oppression, which is also the Marxist view. Trotsky, for example, wrote, "Morality, more than any other form of ideology has a class character. The ruling class forces its ends upon society and habituates it to considering all those means which contradicts its ends as immoral". He wrote, "The capitalist class could not have endured for even a week through force alone. It needs the cement of morality". But what Trotsky and his likes considered as 'morality' might not be very different from what 'morality' ought to be. Morality, in its true meaning, must be an abiding concern for the well-being of the world beyond our own, for sharing one's good fortune and others' handicaps and suffering, for showing empathy for the weak and compassion for the marginalized, which is the essence of 'from everyone according to their capacity and to everyone according to their need'. Morality and Marxism are certainly not synonymous, but it is possible to draw from both while looking into the future. The good news is that scientists say that they have found a 'biological footprint for compassion'—which is at the very core of morality. The *vagus* nerve in our body, in their opinion, 'appears to be intimately tied to experiencing compassion towards other people's suffering,' and it 'affects whether or not we can handle the feelings provoked by another person's suffering—and whether or not we will feel concerned and motivated to help'. And to put it in perspective, we are also told that empathy and sympathy are not a human moral monopoly, and that even mice are empathic beings that feel the pain and suffering of other mice, and that whales have emotions and do express gratitude. And 'gratitude' is important to humans too, to lead a moral life. Every day, even every minute we have a cause to be grateful to someone or the other, and not acknowledging and acting upon it negates the essence of morality. As Maya Angelou puts it, "Let gratitude be the pillow upon which you kneel". The meaning and message is that "compassionate relationships with animals are integral to a more compassionate world". And we should fundamentally recognize that "animals have active minds and deep feelings" and that "we must 'mind' them as their caretakers in a human-dominated world, where their interests are continually trumped in deference to ours".

The Doctrine of *Dharma*

The concept of *dharma* is the bedrock of Hinduism, its most important doctrine. There is no corresponding word in any other language. Hinduism itself was originally referred to as the *Sanatana dharma*, or 'ancient righteous way of life'. If diligently followed, dharma is said to give man both worldly happiness and *moksha* (liberation) from the eternal cycle of birth and rebirth. But how is dharma defined, and where is it codified? And what is *adharma* (that which is not in accord with dharma)? There is no clear and concise translation of the word 'dharma', although it is generally interpreted to encompass attributes like morality, ethical conduct, righteous behavior, justness and justice, discernment, etc. Dharma is also closely identified with two other words, *niti* and *niyama*, broadly translated as ethics and morals. The Indian epic Mahabharata discusses dharma at length. One verse says, "It is most difficult to define Dharma. Dharma has been explained to be that which helps the upliftment of living beings. Therefore, that which ensures the welfare of living beings is surely Dharma. The learned rishis have declared that which sustains is Dharma". Lord Krishna famously proclaimed, in the Bhagavad Gita, that 'when dharma on earth is terminally threatened, He will incarnate as an avatar to restore dharma to its rightful place'.[15] He even justified the slaying of righteous persons like the great Bhishma, when they chose to side with adharma or unrighteousness. This principle carries profound consequences, and it means that for the greater right it is okay to adopt morally questionable means.

The broad scope of dharma is mainly threefold. Firstly, it is designed to ensure the order and regularity of the world. It is sometimes described as "that which contains or upholds the cosmos". Secondly, it ensures peace and happiness by guiding people in the right direction. Thirdly, it provides necessary guidance to people so that they can overcome their impurities and deficiencies and work for their liberation. It is said that to really grasp the essence, meaning and governing principles of dharma, we have to refer to fourteen sacred texts collectively referred to as the *Dharma pramana*, or the true knowledge of dharma. These texts are: (1) the four Vedas (Rig, Yajur, Sama, Atharva); (2) the six Vedangas or auxiliaries of the Vedas (*siksha*, pronounciation; *vyaakarna*, grammar; *chandas*, meter; *nirukta*, etymology; *jyotisha*, astronomy); and (3) the four *Mimamsas*, interpretations of Vedic texts (*nyaaya*, logic; *purana*, mythology; and *dharma shastras*, codes of conduct). *Itihasas* or epics such as the *Ramayana* and *Mahabharata* (which is referred to as the *panchama veda*, the fifth Veda) are meant to make understanding and harmonizing of the four *purusharthas*—dharma, artha, kama, and moksha—easier to the lay person with limited intuitive capacities. They offer a more practical way to adapt dharma to everyday life by carefully studying and grasping the conduct of the epics' two central characters, *Rama* and *Krishna*. Here again, we are told that we should do what Rama did, and follow what Krishna said. That is perhaps because Rama was a *purushothama*, 'the greatest or most perfect of men'; whereas Krishna was a *poorna or sampoorna avatara*, the 'fullest or complete manifestation of God'. God is governed by different dynamics and can do things that no man can, however perfect he may be; but a perfect man can be emulated. Krishna's words must be listened to because He is supreme and is the perfect teacher; we must behave as Rama did because his actions were human and are within human reach.

Both epics are replete with dharmic dilemmas, and also raise for the human intellect some troubling questions. For example, Rama was a divine incarnation, but he was a man and he 'died' like a god—he just walked into the river Sarayu and ascended to divinity. Krishna was God himself on earth but he died like an ordinary man. Krishna's way of dying was variously explained or explained away, but the fact remains. In the Mahabharata, it is said that where there is dharma, there is Krishna, and where there is Krishna, there will be victory. Krishna was on the side of the Pandavas not because he was fond of them or related to them, but because dharma was on their side. Such instances are worth examining more closely. Duryodhana, the eldest of the Kauravas, was considered as *adharmic* or evil, because he was envious of the Pandavas and denied their claim to the Hastinapura throne. He also tried to physically eliminate them. Duryodhana's argument was that he was the eldest son of King Dhritarashtra, and therefore, by tradition, he was entitled to succeed him. The counter argument was that Yudhishthira was elder to him and—had his father Pandu, the younger brother of Dhritarashtra and the 'original' king not abdicated the throne in favor of his elder brother—he, Yudhishthira, would have been the successor, and Duryodhana would have had no claim. To that, Duryodhana argued that his father was elder to Pandu and should have become king in the first place. Duryodhana argued that in any case Dhritarashtra, his father, was the king and therefore his claim to the throne was stronger than that of Yudhishthira.

It is clearly a very complicated matter and not a clear choice between dharma and adharma. So, why did Krishna side with the Pandavas and ensure their victory even at the cost of a terrible war and, even more, why did he not hesitate to transgress the *Yuddha dharma* (the dharma of war) in the killing of Bhishma, Drona, Karna, and Duryodhana? Krishna justified that anyone aiding adharma or evil is himself adharmic and evil, and killing that person becomes an act of dharma. It means that the ends justify the means. Perhaps the answers to these *dharma sankats* (conundrums of dharma) are beyond the grasp of human intellect. And the dharma that accompanies us beyond our death need not be some superhuman sacrifice but a conglomerate of the minutiae of myriad chores and choices of daily life. We do not have to be heroes or do extraordinary deeds to seek either wholeness or moksha (liberation from sorrows) or nirvana (end of suffering), or whatever one likes to describe that state.

What comes to mind is the famous Hindu dictum *Dharmo rakshati rakshitaha* ('If you protect dharma, dharma will in turn protect you'). While the idea that 'if we lead a life guided by principles of dharma then we are insured of its protection' is logical and clearly intelligible, what is intriguing is the latter concept that implies that dharma also needs our protection, and even further, if we do not protect dharma, we cannot expect protection from dharma. How can we protect the very thing we are seeking protection from? It is a very subtle and important point. It is the recognition that while dharma holds the cosmic balance and order, there are also antithetical forces and 'negative energy' in nature. After all, everything in nature is *dwanda* or a pair of opposites; nothing exists by itself, not even dharma. One way to protect dharma is by protecting dharmic or righteous people. We cannot ignore the horrific reality of evil in human history. Evil is as much within us as without, and it manifests as the *arishadvarga*, the 'six passions'—*kama* (lust), *krodha* (anger), *lobha* (greed), *moha* (delusion), *mada* (arrogance) and *matsarya* (malice). So long as we are captive to them there will be adharma in the world—evil, lawlessness, immorality, chaos, disorder, falsehood, violence, etc. Even in the best of times, the best of men were amenable to evil. The great rishi Vyasa, towards the very end of the Mahabharata, laments: *"When people can satisfy all their desires like wealth, prosperity, etc., by treading the path of righteousness, why do they choose adharma?"* That Vyasa (who not only wrote the epic but was also an important participant in that story) should ask such a question, after the triumph of dharma over adharma at the battle of Kurukshetra, is a telling commentary on human nature. The other question that then crops up is: 'When God solemnly promises that when evil reaches a level that threatens the cosmic balance, He will Himself appear on earth to destroy evil and restore righteousness to its due place, why should *we* do anything to protect dharma?' If God should do everything, then why do we exist? Let us not forget: Krishna, believed to be the complete manifestation or incarnation of God that ever existed on earth, could not—or chose not to—prevent the great massacre of war. Likewise, we have no answers to questions like why God allowed the extermination of millions of Jews by Hitler, or for that matter, many other blood-curdling atrocities or even more pertinently individual evil actions. The fact of the matter is that we have to lead our mundane lives without knowing the 'mind of God'. Modern life is so multilayered and multicentered, and we do so many things just to be alive, relevant, and competitive in the world, that it is almost impossible to know what one's own individual dharma is. Not knowing what our primary passion and cosmic calling in life should be, is like being just adrift like a reed in a stormy sea or a leaf in a gusty gale. Another complicating factor is that there is more to becoming a righteous being than doing righteous deeds. Not acting when action is not required, not wounding with a cutting word, not humiliating and hurting others, not taking advantage of another person's vulnerabilities, are also essential elements of a righteous person. Almost everything we do either hurts or helps another person; the trick is to turn our hurt as a way to heal others. It has to become a 'way of life'; how we originate and incubate thoughts, how we use the power of speech, and how we perform the tiniest of actions, and how all of them affect the cosmic order.

In the divine calculus, where does the world stand or rank today on the dharma-scale? How far are conditions ripe for divine descent? How much time do we have, and who will invite divine wrath and who will be worthy of His protection? Who are the 'righteous' in today's world and who are the 'wicked'? Is a religious person a righteous person, and is 'religious' rage a 'just cause'? Does divine thought neutralize bad behavior? Can prayer protect the oppressor and the exploiter? Can one be both 'rich' and 'moral'? Given that there was never a time, and there never will be a time, when the earth is completely free from adharma or unrighteousness, what is the tipping point that could trigger divine intervention? Is every criminal 'wicked'? Does having no criminal record entitle us to be called righteous? Could one be moral and a criminal at the same time? We must remember that a 'righteous' person could be different from one who does the 'right' thing, not only because the same person could do both 'right' and 'wrong' at different times, but also because our 'right' or 'wrong' is largely a matter of legality or social legitimacy. Is a law-abiding citizen a virtuous being who deserves divine rescue while a petty thief is fit to be a divine quarry? Will God protect or punish a religious zealot who kills and/or sacrifices himself to avenge dishonor to his God? Mind you, those who get killed by God are said to be the blessed ones—they are liberated, not necessarily the only ones saved! The shortest way to get to heaven, in one sense, is to get killed in *yuddha* or war—*veeragati*, as they say. Heaven must be, if that is applicable across-the-board and down the ages, a pretty crowded place with all those dead in modern wars. Or is that honor reserved only for those killed in a 'just war', *dharma-yuddha*, and if so, who determines that? What about a soldier who simply obeys orders and kills or gets killed? We must also reexamine the oft-repeated statement that wars kill 'innocent' people. People can be ignorant but no one can be innocent in the karmic sense. And, in the end, every death is a kind of 'killing', even a suicide. The cause or trigger can be bacteria or a bomb, the arena, either one's own bed or the street, hospital, or home.

Our goals in life cannot be divorced from the slew of obligations, responsibilities, and duties we have towards others, but at the same time, these cannot be allowed to become obstacles to realizing fulfillment. The 'duties' in life, direct or implicit, that we need to fulfill has long been a subject of thoughtful introspection as well as scriptural scrutiny. According to the Vedic scriptures, an individual is born with three kinds of debts—*Deva-runa* (debt to God); *Rishi-runa* (debt to the sages, saints); and *Pitru-runa* (debt to one's parents, ancestors)—debts that must be repaid during his or her span of life. These debts are like mortgages on one's life, but not liabilities, as they constitute an attempt by the scriptures to create an awareness of one's duties and responsibilities. Special importance is given to one's debt to *Bhoomi Devi*, Mother Earth. On waking up in the morning, every Hindu is supposed to seek forgiveness through the prayer, *Samudra Vasane Devi; Parvata Sthana Mandite; Vishnu Pathni Namasthubhyam; Pada Sparsam Kshamasva Mae* ("Salutations to the divine consort of Lord Vishnu; who is clothed by the oceans; and is adorned prettily by the mountains; forgive me Mother for setting foot upon you"). The Hindu 'doctrine of duty as debt' is a very important dimension of human morality. What is significant is that it stretches the ambit of our duties and obligations beyond the immediacy or intimacy of terrestrial interpersonal relationships, and includes our duty to the dead who gave us life. Death does not terminate our duty or debt. During the *Bhadrapada* month of the traditional Hindu calendar, a specific period called *pitru-paksha* is set aside for ancestor-worship and veneration of the dead.

During this fortnight, people donate food to the hungry in the hope that their ancestors will also be thus fed. The idea that a life on earth has an obligation not only to our fellow-humans but also to those who lived before us is a major contribution to moral philosophy and ethics. The premise is that repaying the debt to ancestors is as important as repaying the debt to God, nature, sages, and society.

Moral Progress and Animal Rights

We must also factor in Gandhian morality, and particularly Gandhi's famous dictum: 'When we are in doubt about a course of action, try to imagine the face and life of the most miserable person we have seen, and then decide what course or choice could make that person's life a little less miserable'. The other useful guide could be the observation often attributed to Gandhi, 'The greatness of a nation and its moral progress can be judged by the way its animals are treated'. Views differ on this score, too. Most, judging by what we see and read and experience, would probably argue that we are 'regressing', and science, in the name of 'animal testing',[16] has made it worse. It is now a part of perfecting 'militarism', and the modern state's endless quest to improve the efficiency of destructive weapons. So much so that, "Killing and maiming is not enough, great importance is attached to the scientific nature of the weapon's effect. Whether it is by burning, poisoning, suffocation, infection or attacking the nervous system, each method is meticulously 'refined' on sentient, unconsenting lab animals."[17] The justification for such 'testing' has long been that animals and humans share similar biological processes; that the data obtained from animal models can be extrapolated and applied to human conditions; that every major medical advance has been based on animal testing; and therefore that whatever immorality that might entail is unavoidable and well worth it. The additional justification offered is that animals too have benefitted from research through laboratory animals. That very rationale is now being questioned, and researchers are of the opinion that it can even be *dangerous* to apply animal-derived data to humans.[18] Still, animal research has not slowed down; in fact, in countries like UK, research activity has gone up.[19] In USA, the use of animals in experiments at leading federally-funded labs has increased nearly 73% in the past 15 years.[20]

Ultimately, it is a matter of money. The fact is that there is far too much money involved for it to be given up. The question is not if such testing is inescapable or not for human healing. The real question is, does an animal qualify to be deemed a 'person'? On what grounds can we morally differentiate between the life, safety, and well-being of humans and nonhumans? If 'intelligence' is the criterion, would we substitute a mentally retarded man, or a baby, in the place of another animal with the same IQ? If it is the faculty of experiencing pain, there is not much difference between humans and some animals. The basic point is that we have always assumed—and even most major religions have concurred—that humans are the acme of creation, that they are inherently a superior form of life, and that they have a God-given right to use the earth and every creature on it for their own pleasure and progress. All of us in our personal lives practice this principle. On what other rationale do we keep pets, or ride on the backs of animals like an elephant and horse? The best among us, save perhaps some rishis, are incapable of 'non-discrimination' between human animals and other animals. Whether or not 'other animals' agree or not we have no way of knowing; but they are powerless.

While morality in its broadest meaning is universal, in its specifics it is relative to each society, to each epoch, and is, above all, relative to the interests of the different social classes. No idea or ideology is immune to time, nor can it exist outside of the social context from which it has emerged. But it cannot become an escape from one's moral, even social, obligations and turn relativism into a masquerade for the moral malevolence of modern man. The practical reality is that since right and wrong are relegated to matters of opinion at worst, or are purely subjective at best, any talk of morality becomes just that—talk. Some principles are universal and will be timeless, like respect for the integrity and dignity of another person, and consideration and compassion for all and under every circumstance, though in their application one should be sensitive to context, culture, and class in its broadest meaning. Some ask the question: does that 'all' include even the evil, the wicked, and the villain? If we want to 'comfort the afflicted', must we 'afflict the comfortable'? If we want to help the poor, must we hate the rich? What about justice, and, perhaps even more, *justness*, the combination of which is called *dharma* in Hinduism and *dhamma* in Buddhism? These are taxing questions that have troubled great men, avatars, saints, and rishis, and there are no cut-and-dried, across-the-board answers. Ultimately, each situation has to be handled situationally but based on principles. But generally we should strive to be kind, caring, and empathetic to everyone unless that causes harm to another more deserving being. The larger common good prevails over narrower needs. One can also argue that the virtuous do not need our compassion; it is only for the wicked that it makes the greatest difference. We should also remember that all of us do good and bad deeds and no one is 'all-good' or 'all-bad', and that everyone is subject to karmic influence. Who are we to 'throw the first stone'? Sorrows and wounds are healed only when we touch them with compassion. If we 'pick' and 'choose' then it becomes selective and selfish. Classical or 'old-fashioned' morality—honesty, integrity, prudence, frugality, fidelity, generosity—is still necessary, but not sufficient on the morrow of a new millennium. We need to inject what is called 'civic virtue', that it is the cultivation of habits of personal living that are important for the social order and success of the community. That should also be reflected in what and whom we reward and punish in society. It revolves around 'thou shalt' and 'thou shalt not'. Our sense of 'common sense' about morality must move from *thou* to *them*, from *don't* to *do*. Character should not mean, as it is often said, only what we do when no one is watching, or when no one is there to impress. What we do in public is equally, perhaps even more important. Personal ethics are not irrelevant but they fall short of social good. Being a 'faithful' spouse and a doting dad are good for a good home, but by themselves are not sufficient to function as a responsible citizen, much less as a planetary being. Many ruthless dictators were loving fathers, and quite a few serial killers were good family men. To be fair to 'monsters' and mass murderers, all of us, in different degrees, exhibit the same trait: good in one relationship and bad in another; even as a good spouse and bad parent, a good sibling and bad friend. And it can change from time to time in the same relationship also. Proximity and intimacy can change the personality. Partly because our goodness or badness depends also on the goodness and badness of another person. And then, there are no across-the-board criteria to differentiate good from bad. In addition, the concept of family as a source of morality is on the wane—modern man channels much of his time, energy, and attention away from home. That is why a major ethical imperative of the 21st century is to shift the moral essence towards what is called civic virtue, that is, contribution of citizens to the common welfare of their community even at the cost of their individual interests. Restrictions, regulations, and fear cannot be dispensed with, but we must move beyond and cultivate compassion not merely because it is good for others, but also for the sake of our own tormented soul. It is not sufficient to be a good neighbor; one should become a genuine global citizen, and be 'globally responsible'. It is not good enough to be 'good'; we must be good for something beyond ourselves. It is good to try to be an 'agent of change', but it is better to be an agent of healing. Our moral concern must include what we do for a living, how we spend and spread, what we earn and acquire, how we entertain ourselves, how we travel, even what we buy. These are, in effect and in their effect, moral statements.

We assume that choices and decisions are made by the individual. What happens if we do not? The American psychologist William James said, "When you have to make a choice and don't make it, that is in itself a choice". In making a 'choice' or making a 'non-choice', who is the real 'maker'? Whether we make it or not make it, what about the consequences? Sometimes by making a wrong choice we might be aiding a wrong end; equally sometimes, by not making a 'non-choice' we may be denying aid for the 'right' purpose. Philanthropy is noble, but if it is not given to the 'right' cause, and is instead given to the socially 'wrong' one, it does more harm than not giving at all. A case in point is the use of fossil fuels, a major contributory factor in global warming. Many humanitarian foundations give generously to uplifting purposes, but also have huge investments in fossil fuel industries such as coal and oil companies, indirectly negating what they do otherwise. But in all probability in their decision-making, in either case, they don't factor in the other dimension. That is true for most of us. That is the nature of the human brain; it is a good lawyer but a poor judge; good at advocacy and not good at harmonizing.

Morality and Duty

Man is arguably the most complex creature on earth, and that in turn leads to, and manifests as multiple identities and multiple personalities. We are so conditioned by multiple relationships.[21] Identity is 'the meaning through which we define ourselves, and others define us, as particular kinds of people'. In substantial measure our 'sense of who we are' is conferred on us by others in the way they treat us and by their expectations and, in turn, theirs by us. Our 'identities' are diffused and diversified and, actually, we play multiple roles in a single play, not sequentially or separately but at the same time in the same scene. William Shakespeare wrote, "All the world's a stage, And all the men and women merely players; They have their exits and their entrances; And one man in his time plays many parts".[22] Shakespeare was referring to the multiple roles that we play as we age, what he called the 'seven ages'. In fact, we do more than that. Even in a single age, we play different roles in different relationships. These identities, personalities, and relationships frame our life and embrace our life as an individual, as a spouse or a parent or a child, as a member of a community or society, as a part of making a living, as a citizen of a state, and as a global citizen and a constituent unit of the *Homo sapiens* species.

These days, everything is 'work'; just being alive is so much work, often doing things you don't like. As the novelist Philip Roth said, "The road to hell is paved with works-in-progress". Almost everything we do is in pursuance of related duties, obligations, and responsibilities. Sometimes they complement each other, but more often they collide and clash, and that is when we fumble and falter. The human mind is singularly single-minded and narrow-minded. As Lovecraft put it, "The most merciful thing in the world, I think, is the inability of the human mind to correlate all its contents".[23] It is 'merciful' because that way its maliciousness can be more contained. It is good at advocacy and aggressive articulation but not reconciliation, renunciation, and harmonization. And we do not have universally or socially acceptable norms, models, modalities, and mechanisms. But choices have to be made, and we make not necessarily the right or most deserving choices, but the most expeditious, most pressing, and the softest ones. In the process, we not only morally err but also miss the big picture, and as Joel Primack said, "without a big picture we are very small people". Multiple roles compete for our attention, with time spent on one role often coming at the expense of time spent on another—sometimes creating a win-loss situation for the various roles. Additionally, recent research indicates that role-conflict and attendant spillovers can lead to stress, exhaustion, burn-out, and lower life satisfaction, not only for those of us experiencing the conflict, but also for others in our lives as well. In short, our exhaustion and conflict can spill over to others. We admire actors who play double or multiple roles in movies but all of us play more demanding roles, even if not consciously. The quality of our 'acting' is not so much how we play any particular role, but in so doing how we do not compromise what is needed in playing other roles. If we are 'perfect' in one particular 'identity', and neglect other identities and responsibilities, then overall we fare poorly. If and when we are finally judged, if we proclaim proudly 'I was a perfect parent', or a family man, the Cosmic Judge might counter and ask: "That was only a bit part; what about your social persona? And were you fully human and humane in the totality of human interconnectivity?"

We need to also bring a moral dimension to another of our most pressing identities, as a worker, an employee, a professional, as a means to 'make money', or 'make a living'. The absence of this dimension lies at the source of much evil today. Most of us are privy to and participants in its furtherance, and we are all aware of this in different degrees. And we feel no pangs because of that magic word that sweeps away all sin: duty. Much of what we do in public these days is 'doing duty'. That is what we do all our life, doing our duty in multiple identities and capacities. More narrowly, it is what we do to make a living, to earn money. It devours much of the most active, productive part of our life, in our youth and adulthood, till we die, or till we 'retire'. Doing duty might have become a dubious, if not dirty, word now, the way we use it as an immoral cover, but the idea is not novel or new. Even mass murderers like Adolf Eichmann and extreme religious fanatics claim the same cover. It is linked to the concept of karma yoga, as well as to the doctrine of nishkama karma—doing one's duty or any work without attachment to the result; in its broadest sense, 'duty that is due to humanity, to our fellow men, and especially to all those who are disadvantaged and more helpless than we are ourselves'.

Duty is at the core of theosophy. One of the attributes we value most in contemporary life is professionalism, which can be broadly defined as performing whatever work we do with dedication, honesty, and diligence. And we cannot apply 'moral *exceptionalism*' to the workplace, on the plea that being professional requires doing any job regardless of how anyone else is affected. This is one of the most acute moral issues of our day: How to meld morality into what we do for a living? To what extent does our public persona and professional duty give a cover for moral transgressions? And that has a huge bearing not only on our private life but also on the war within. Work, doing one's duty, and professional life now consume and absorb so much of our living space, time, and energy, and impact on the lives of so many others that we cannot adopt different norms and standards of morality, for example, one for home and another for workplace. Most people separate their work from their personal life and follow their professional code of conduct. To what extent it is driven wholly by professional considerations and to how much of it is giving vent to their hidden inclinations is hard to tell. What is more important in today's world is what we may call public evil, or paid evil, that is, evil that comes from the 'workplace', be it a government office or a business or an organization or industry. This evil is far greater than purely personal evil, the evil we do off-duty. And moral offences that impact on the health and well-being of the community must attract more severe penalty than those that cause suffering to a few. For example, adulteration of food or drugs that harm the multitude must be dealt with greater severity than adultery. Moral offences like lying, cheating, and greed become far more injurious when perpetrated on the social scale. Cheating while building a bridge, for example, put in danger the lives of thousands. We may even have to concede that morality is not confined to choice-making, but permeates our whole way of life from social life to sports, from education to entertainment, from how or where to channel technology, and how and where we spend money. Should one have babies and if so how many, raises moral issues. And can we apply different standards to different places based on richness and poverty? Abortion is a moral issue. Some issues span geography and gender, and some, generations. If certain parts of the world like sub-Saharan Africa cannot sustain high fertility, why not encourage emigration to other parts which need more children? Some are even suggesting that some forms of sport, like American football (not only playing but even watching), and some kind of entertainment, like violent video games, should be branded unethical. The scope of morality must include actions necessary for saving the planet from our own toxic hands, that is, environment-friendly actions. The time has come for a 'new narrative' on climate change, which impels us to view anything done to protect the environment and roll back climate change as moral and sacred, and anything that has the opposite effect as immoral and shameful. Conservation should be treated as consecration. There is growing realization that we have to change our perspective on the climate crisis from an economic or ecological matter to a moral issue. That is why it being called 'climate justice', and justice is a big chunk of morality. Climate justice is a vision to dissolve and alleviate the unequal burdens created by climate change on the poor and vulnerable. Philosophers like Mary Robinson characterize the climate change as a human rights issue and environmental justice. Water has to be given the holy tag, bearing in mind the prediction that future wars will be *water wars*. The distinction between social and spiritual needs has to be blurred.

Beyond a point, we cannot separate our personal and interpersonal lives and values, and the 'bad' things we do seep within and contaminate our consciousness, and offer ammunition to the evil forces in the internal war. In venturing into this minefield we face several moral anomalies and paradoxes. There is widespread worry about corruption and moral laxity in public life. Everyone bemoans the fall in public probity and ethical standards, but in so doing, we exclude ourselves. Freud said that '... at bottom no one believes in his own death'. In other words, "in the unconscious, every one of us is convinced of his own immortality".[24] Science is now trying to turn that 'conviction' into a reality. One expert, Dr. Ian Pearson, claims the really rich people born after 1970 should be able to live forever. This, along with the other major preoccupation of science, perfecting Artificial General Intelligence (AGI), together might destabilize human society like nothing else before, by making us unnecessary in our own world and by atrophying our own senses. The certainty of death, not only our own but even more of others, has been a moderating and unifying factor. That everybody—our rivals, competitors, enemies, adversaries—finally dies is what keeps a lid on our grudges, grievances, injustices, oppression going out of hand. And if it turns out that the rich will have access to immortality and not the rest, it will be adding insult to injury, a red rag to the already enraged bull. Once that lid is removed and we think that our tormentor might not die but we will die, human behavior, already bizarre and brutal, will more vicious and violent than we can even imagine. And if we cannot kill or kill ourselves, then what would we do to settle scores? We can be tortured but not to death. Clearly, if robots take over, we will be condemned to eternal slavery. Would an 'immortal' man survive a nuclear war or would he have to live 'eternally' exposed to radiation with a mangled body? What would be the impact on human institutions like marriage?

Clearly, even if eternal life is impossible, even exponentially extended life spans of 300 years or more will present serious existential risks that our mindset has not evolved yet to handle.

We live in a world in which there is a great deal of nebulousness and uncertainty about basic norms and values, and, as a result, many decisions that confront public officials these days are much more morally and ethically complex. Even the best of us find ourselves ill-equipped to handle and resolve moral dilemmas in everyday life. Everything is condoned, and the premise is that morality is entirely selective, subjective, and situational. We hear a great deal about acts of nepotism, favoritism, venality, fraud, bribery, and downright theft from the public purse. Alongside this there is a general concern about maladministration, incompetence, and inefficiency in the public sector. Although the public sector gets much attention, we also know that the private sector or the corporate world is no less vulnerable and venal. It is hardly private; it is funded essentially by public money. Something seems to be going terribly wrong wherever power (economic or political) is held and wielded. Issues of conflict of interest are brushed aside and the course chosen is what is most lucrative to the key players. The basic question boils down to this: is it possible in today's world for someone to perform one's work-related duties without violating universal moral principles and still make 'moral money' and attain and retain professional excellence? The broad principles are four. One, our work should not result in harming other people. Two, those who work in the 'public space' should treat other people as ends in themselves, never as means to their own ends. Three, the implementation of the utilitarian principle: our work should be an input into achieving the greatest good for the greatest number. Four, we should act only in ways that respect the human dignity of everyone we work with or for, and the dignity of other stakeholders. While most people might agree in general about these principles, the more difficult part is what these require us to do or refrain from doing. That in turn shifts the emphasis from 'what *I ought to do*' to 'what kind of a person *I should be*'. The answer is subsumed in one word, moral integrity, which can be codified as being true to one's own self and to do any job, at any time, anywhere and everywhere, to the very best of one's ability without fear or favor, without any expectation of self-gain, and with the sole aim of contributing to a larger cause.

Yet so much of what we do we call *work*, or duty, social duty, religious duty, etc., and they embrace so many often conflicting moral nuances and ethical dimensions. Which should take precedence when, is hard to generalize. One question that crops up is, whether 'doing one's duty', or *karthavya*, is tantamount to doing what is called *swadharma*, in Gandhi's words, "one's natural duty, dictated by one's natural state of being, one's true self and one's station in life". It is difficult to draw a line between what we are professionally obligated to do, and what we should morally resist doing. How should we decide? The attendant question is: are we exempt from the restraint of morality if we do something that is immoral or unethical, something that is harmful to other people, as long as it is done as a part of our 'duty' at work, under the 'orders' of a superior? Does the moral character of an action differ if it is performed under one's free will or if it is done in an obligatory manner? If a soldier, for example, can kill as part of his professional duty (an act that is deemed neither a crime nor a sin), and for which he 'goes straight to heaven', then why should far lesser transgressions like lying, cheating, polluting at the workplace make us morally culpable? After all, one could argue that such 'immoral' actions are performed without personal gain and for 'common' or corporate good. If, for example, actions arising from duty, as philosophers like Kant have argued, have moral worth, how can doing wrong things or 'just doing one's job' be reprehensible? Work is the main source of 'making money', which is now the primary occupation and preoccupation of most people. Almost everything is 'work', and everyone is a 'worker' of some kind or the other these days—home-worker, domestic worker, office worker, factory worker, blue-collar worker, white-collar worker… We are always 'doing something'. But that 'something' often comes at a high cost, and has become a health issue in recent times. What is called 'stress' has become a modern 'disease' and our body's inability to handle it has become a major cause of heart attack. But what is startling is that this too was foreseen and written about in ancient texts. Hindu scriptures, for instance, mention that "men will find their jobs stressful and will go to retreats to escape their work". So, even our holiday retreats and time-shares were anticipated.

But there is no 'escape' from work. Living itself is work. Every living creature and being is working all the time. And so does God. In the Bhagavad Gita, Lord Krishna says that even *He* works although He doesn't need to, and there is nothing in all the worlds that is not His. TS Eliot wrote that the lot of man is ceaseless labor, or ceaseless idleness. In today's world, it is *making money* that is ceaseless. We work for money; money does not work for us. The workplace is no longer merely a place where one works for a few hours a day, to make money, to earn a livelihood. It is the epicenter of one's life, where the one with a job spends most of his waking time trying to market his merit and personality, where he meets most humans, forms lasting friendships, but also comes of age and comes face to face with some of the worst human traits like ill will, envy, deceit, aggression. A place where one makes more moral compromises than anywhere else without any unease or embarrassment. We are told, and tend to believe, that work-culture and work-ethics are a genre apart, governed by different principles and standards. Not only workers but most who work at workplaces have become, as Marx said, mere cogs in a machine operating blindly according to its own moral dictates. A person who is completely honest about everything may not be viewed as an effective worker or a good team player. For the sake of the company or employer, a worker is often obliged to sacrifice much of what he values as an individual, such as integrity, truthfulness, and non-cheating. The implicit hypothesis is that since we are paid for our time and effort, failing to do whatever we are asked to do—with all our mind and might, regardless of its implications and impact—will tantamount to professional and moral turpitude, which is not too different from the 'philosophy of the prostitute'. The so-called white-collar workers exchange their brains for money, while blue-collar workers primarily offer their brawn and body. In most jobs, there is a measure of coercion and exploitation, in the sense, as Marx noted, of the value added by our work and what we are paid. And that is the philosophy of profit, whose governing principle is calculating and paying only a fraction of the real costs involved. Immanuel Kant condemned prostitution and wrote that "human beings are, therefore, not entitled to offer themselves, for profit, as things for the use of others in the satisfaction of their sexual propensities". If we substitute the word 'sexual propensities' by 'profit-making', the rest of the sentence applies to most modern workplaces. If 'prostitution' means engaging in sexual activity primarily to make money or against one's will, don't most of us do the same at the workplace? We all use our body, our hands, our feet, our eyes, ears, our mouth and brain to do any job, any work at the workplace, which often we do not like or which otherwise we would not do. But that is not considered as immoral, let alone illegal.

The president of a country would be just doing his 'job', his 'constitutional duty', in authorizing the massacre of thousands of civilians half way across the globe, if that is inevitable to get a hiding 'terrorist'. An assassin does his 'job'; he has no ill will for the murdered. A suicide bomber also does the same. The one who pollutes the atmosphere and the one who adulterates our food are no different; that, in their minds, is their assigned task. If we are what we eat, as the cliché goes, it is even truer now to say that we are what and for whom we work for. The advice Confucius offered was simple: "choose a job you love, and you will never have to work a day in your life". The tragedy of modern life is that so few get to *choose*, or to do what they love, or even like; even worse, they would rather do what someone else is doing. In effect, doing what we love is 'play', and wanting to do what someone else does, or treating the job purely as a means to making a living is 'work', if not slavery. Arnold Toynbee made it more practical and said that the 'supreme accomplishment is to blur the line between work and play'. The fact is that nowhere else are we more comparative and competitive, and see another human as an obstacle on the path to our prosperity. And that acts as a canker within, causes high anxiety, stress, low self-worth, deep disquiet, and hypertension. And it sullies both the world within and the world outside the workplace. Goethe wrote, "The human race is a monotonous affair. Most people spend the greatest part of their time working in order to live, and what little freedom remains so fills them with fear that they seek out any and every means to be rid of it".[25] All such musings change when we bring to bear a different vantage point. In the karmic sense, life itself is 'doing a job'. We are all playing a part, a role, or multiple parts or roles, as a spouse, a child, a worker, a citizen, and so on. We must have been every other person in every relationship we are in, in this life. How we perform depends on the particular part of our *prarabdha karma* (the collection of past karma that influence one's life in the present incarnation). That might require us to be sometimes, or in relation to someone else, pleasant or unpleasant, helpful or hateful. No relationship, intimate or casual, is an accident and every relationship is karmic. That is why sometimes, even without our meaning to, the worst in us comes out, not necessarily because we are bad or the other party is bad, but only because that 'being bad' is necessary for both to pay for their prarabdha karma. The bulk of our prarabdha, which is a blend of both good and bad, is exhausted in our present life through the web of relationships that connect and bind us to each other, and the bulk of that is through intimate relationships, spousal and parental partnerships. And the precise format and nature of a particular relationship change, sometimes reverse, from life to life. And it is through the medium of relationship that we get an opportunity either to do immense good to others and to relieve their pain and suffering, or to cause intense misery and unhappiness. And in everyone relationship, there is a give and take, which itself is a part of the prarabdha, and whoever gives more and takes less earns good karmic points. It is also useful to remember that the effect of giving is not necessarily dependent on the size or the value of the gift. The same gift 'from different people giving' signifies and symbolizes differently. A beggar offering his only begging bowl to serve as a lamp has more value than a golden bowl from a wealthy man.

How we do the job of living inclusive of its multiple 'mini-jobs' is a part of the wider continuum. In today's world, where everything is a 'job', it somehow seems to absolve us of the moral consequences of what we do 'professionally'. If you are a worker in a factory that makes drones, and one of your drones is used to kill children at school, you do not feel responsible; well, you say, "I have nothing to do with it", and if you are the one who actually pressed the button you will say, "I did not intend to kill the children, I wanted to get the 'bad' fellow". If you are a worker in a factory that makes chemicals that are used to adulterate food that maims and stunts the lives of a multitude, you are guiltless. If we work for a Wall Street firm that heavily invests in a company that uses child labor or animal testing, we feel no moral qualms. Given that so much of our life is spent in making money, and at the workplace, how our brain and body are put to use, to what purpose and with what consequences for society, must become a major factor in the moral balance sheet of our lives. The moral masquerade we deploy in order to do immoral, even horrible things, is 'simply following orders'. Although 'following orders' and 'obedience and disobedience' are associated with the 'working world', they are part of life. Indeed all our troubles began, according to the Bible, with our 'not following orders' and disobeying divine orders (not to eat the fruit of the Tree of Knowledge in the Garden of Eden), and led to our expulsion from heaven and to our conversion from immortal to the mortal. What science is now trying to do is to undo the expulsion, and unmake, as it were, the Bible. In the modern world, obeying is also a part of working in order to live. The human mind is comfortable with either giving orders or obeying orders. Once it realizes that it is in no position to issue orders, it quickly surrenders and tries to get maximum mileage from the situation: a pay-rise, a promotion, or a heightened sense of security. In life, many things make us sick in the stomach just because we are commanded by a superior, a boss; his job is to give such orders, and he, in turn, might have been ordered to do so. And our moral defense is 'just doing my job', or 'my job requires that, and not doing that might cost me that very job'. What is happening in contemporary human society is that millions of ordinary people, in 'just doing their job', are becoming partners in terrible destructive processes, even when they are fully aware of what their work leads to. It would be perfectly natural to find a pacifist engaged in a job that involves making weapons of mass destruction. In obeying orders, when it becomes clear that such obedience can lead to disastrous consequences hidden from public knowledge, one faces a dilemma: to continue to do one's part, or refuse and face punishment. Most people choose to simply go along and not risk uprooting their whole life. *Doing a job* and *following orders* are moral evasions that allow us to appear moral and yet evade the cost of being moral. They let us do many a wrong without feeling any prick, to 'make a living' sans any guilt for any wrongdoing. Together, they have turned us all into dogs of war, mercenaries or soldiers for hire, while giving us a moral mask. Such moral evasions account for the biggest chunk of evil that takes place in the world. They insure us against any guilt or remorse and they let us get on with our immoral lives with impunity. Most of all, we do not feel, even the best of us, any responsibility for the consequences. But in truth, such explanations, or excuses are not entirely untrue. What we call the 'system' is so gigantic and is so driven by a dynamic and momentum of its own, that everyone, even the ones perched on top of the pyramid, are unable to direct all that happens under its aegis.

Satya*, *Himsa*, and *Ahimsa

The time has also come for us to take a deep breath and do some soul searching about our oft-repeated abhorrence for violence and the love of truth. The questions that have long troubled both sacred and secular thought are: When are we permitted to take a life? When are we in the right even if we tell a lie? What is truth? And then, is there any connection between morality and violence? Let us address the last question first. Generally we think that the two are antithetical and a moral man is a peaceful man. We think violent people are immoral, evil, sadistic, and lack empathy. This is not always true. People who commit violent acts such as mass murders are 'moral' in their mind; they think that it is morality that compels them to do the dastardly deed. Indeed, according to some researchers like Tage Rai, "The purpose of violence is to sustain a moral order".[26] Of course, that 'order' is one that is particular to the person, the violation of which the perpetrator wants to set right. It means that it all boils down to a personal narrative about how a person views himself or herself in relation to the world, how, in their mind, the world should be, and what their role is in making it happen. Put differently, morality, contrary to what we assume, is not a hedge or hindrance to immorality or evil. Under the cover of morality, one could commit a mass murder and feel no shame or remorse even when one is poised on the gallows... To prevent mass murders and other extreme violence, we have to revamp the architecture of our moral infrastructure like education, upbringing, work ethics, and understanding of success. It means "doing everything we possibly can to break down the current obsession with the individual ego 'self' and its petty stories and needs and create a more global perspective".[27] All scriptures universally exclaim and extol truth. The Rig Veda says, "Truth is one; the wise call it by different names". All religions believe that truth alone triumphs; not falsehood. As the Buddha said, "Three things cannot be long hidden: the sun, the moon, and the truth". But a host of questions crop up. What is truth? At what level or depth must we bring it to bear, and should we include thoughts and emotions? Is it absolute or relative? Is it 'a transcendent fundamental or spiritual reality'? If we do not lie or cheat and if we are faithful to a fact as perceived by our senses, are we living in 'truth'? One Indian scripture puts in perspective: 'Where speaking a lie protects people's lives, untruth is truth, and even a truth can be a falsehood'. We are similarly faced with questions about *himsa* (violence) and *ahimsa* (non-violence). When are both untruth and violence morally justified? Who are the 'people' whose lives are to be protected even at the cost of untruth and violence? One way to outwit all such quibbles is to take the Wilde-line, 'the truth is rarely pure and never simple' (*The Importance of Being Ernest*), and drown ourselves in a world of 'shaded truths' and 'true-lies', and tell ourselves that, as Byron quipped, truth is stranger than fiction!

It is physical valor that we have always prized most. The spectacle of one man overpowering and killing another person in combat excites us. That is because deep inside, that is what we want to be. It manifests in multiple, more subtle killings: to win every argument, to prevail in every situation, to dominate and control others, etc. Most of our heroes are 'war heroes', those who have killed total strangers because it is their dharma or duty, Even the most pious and kind of such men never feel guilt for having done so, even when the cause they would have fought for was unjust or downright evil. If a soldier refuses to fight, he would be called a traitor, and if he turns his back, a coward. Our attraction to violence goes beyond not being a coward; it goes beyond the need to fight injustice and oppression. It is because without violence human earthly existence is about as possible as deathless existence. But the important point is that we are morally wrong not in being violent, but in being violent *for the wrong causes*; even more in not being violent for the *right* reasons. Violence for fighting injustice of any kind, economic, social, religious, is moral; and being passive and peaceful is immoral. All killing is not always bad. Without any killing, even of the 'innocent', life is impossible. We think that killing other animals, insects, and other creepy creatures is okay because they might make our life difficult, even if they are 'innocent'. Only human killing, we smugly think, is bad, unless sanctioned by the State and sanctified by war. What we don't realize is that every species has a niche in nature and its abrupt extinction could affect all life. Even the lowly insects, according to biologist EO Wilson, are "the heart of life on earth".

Another, even more magical word that we use, most often as a snapshot of high virtue and desirable goal of life, is 'truth'. Being truthful is deemed to be a critical part of morality. Our yearning for truth rages "over the troubled soul of mankind, not refreshing and invigorating, but scorching, consuming, absorbing the last vestiges of strength still left to the afflicted one in this gloominess of the present time".[28] The practical problem is two-fold. We cannot codify 'truth', and we cannot say that 'not telling a lie' is always 'being truthful'. Nor can we say that 'telling the truth', that is, simply saying what we know, is not at times the highest evil. We must also understand that truth too is limited by what our sense organs can perceive and comprehend, and we all know too well how finite, fallible, and fallacious they are. But 'truth' has a hold on us. As a Chinese proverb goes, 'life is a search for the truth; but there is no truth'. Gandhi said, "Morality is the basis of things and truth is the substance of all morality". A popular saying in India is that if a man speaks truth uninterruptedly for twelve years, whatever he speaks thereafter becomes the truth. Mark Twain said, "If you tell the truth you do not have to remember anything". The relationship between truth, morality, and modernity is important in a world in which lying, chatting, deviousness, and deceit are almost deemed essential to survive, if not to be successful in life. George Orwell wrote, "In a time of universal deceit, telling the truth is a revolutionary act". It is so ingrained in our consciousness that even when we do not have to lie and it offers no advantage, we lie almost reflexively. The problem also is that we have some idea of 'deceit', but we have very little about 'truth'. While scriptures extoll truth, they also tell us not to make a fetish of truth in its narrow or literal sense—sometimes truth can be deadly and destructive. We have never been able to tread the middle ground where lying becomes moral and truth immoral; nor are we able to harmonize 'not lying' and 'not always speaking truth'. Most religions are 'conditionally critical' of lying. While one cannot precisely define lying, one could say that a lie is an untruth, a deviation from what is known to be real or factual; a false statement deliberately offered as being true, misrepresenting a situation or giving a totally wrong impression about something. But religions do give us some honorable exits from telling what, in jurisprudence, is called *'truth, the whole truth, and nothing but the truth'*. In Judaism, to save a life, one may lie and violate almost all of the commandments of the Torah. Judaism allows us to lie to avoid hurting the feelings or upsetting another person or causing a breach in a relationship. Many great men did not flinch when falsifying or telling a white lie or downright untruth when that was necessary to save lives or to achieve nobler goals.

All lies are not the same. The 'truth' of lying is this: always telling what one sees, hears, knows, and thinks is the truth, that everything and everyone else is untruthful, can be both dangerous and destructive. We must understand that what our senses and faculties perceive is limited and severely circumscribed. In the package that nature has empowered us with, we have peerless ability to inquire and to ask, but not always to find the right answer. That is reserved for the gods. Since our ego cannot accept that limitation, we lie compulsively. Perhaps there never has lived a man who has never lied, or not misrepresented the truth, regardless of whether it was unintentional, or told so that someone else's feelings would not be hurt. According to Virginia Woolf, the pursuit of truth without consideration for other's feelings is an 'outrage of human decency'. The greater outrage is that for the modern man, lying has become pathological, and integral to social interfacing; a psychological need to cope with the drudgery and dangers of contemporary life. The mantra is, if you do not lie, you are dead. We shade the truth in these instances either to gain a financial advantage, or just to keep out of trouble. In other words, we want to save our money, or avoid punishment, and so we alter the truth. Saint Augustine wrote two books about lying, *On Lying* (*De Mendacio*) and *Against Lying* (*Contra Mendacio*), and divided lies into eight categories, listed in the order of diminishing severity: lies in religious teaching; lies that harm others and help no one; lies that harm others and help someone; lies told for the pleasure of lying; lies told to 'please others in smooth discourse'; lies that harm no one and that save someone's life; lies that harm no one and that save someone's 'purity'; lies that harm no one and that help someone.[29] Clearly, the second category is the most malicious and malevolent. It is pure negative energy and harmful to the universe. But perhaps even more destructive, and not listed by St. Augustine, is lying to one's own self. It is this lying that allows us to live in 'peace with ourselves'; to get through the grind of life without committing suicide, or becoming a nervous wreck. A prerequisite for spiritual growth is to be true to one's own self, which involves both accepting what we care about, as well as growing over what we are. Then again, all lying is not always immoral or all truth moral. The intent is very important. A false assertion without the will to deceive might not be immoral, and a purely factual statement that causes harm might not be moral.

'Moral Crisis' to 'Morality in Crisis'

Instead of introspecting on those lines and exploring ways of retooling our mindset, and cleansing our consciousness, we ask questions that can be answered both in the affirmative and negative, to embrace questions such as: Is the present plight of man an offshoot of the inner divinity in eclipse or the death throes of a dying species? Is man 'born to be good' or a hard-wired Good Samaritan, or, in the words of Paul Rusesabagina, the Rwandan humanitarian hero, "a shark, just sleeping, lying on the bottom of a sea, which can emerge any time and break a lot of boats"?[30] Moral philosophers and perceptive people have long ruminated on issues such as the evolution of human morality, origins of virtue, and the link between sexuality, morality, and mortality. Scholars and social scientists have long debated who the authentic human is—egocentric or altruistic, acquisitive or generous, parasitic or philanthropic—and, of late, the scope has been broadened to include such questions as whether the present behavioral crisis in modern society could be described as a 'chosen blindness' or 'moral escapism'. We have long wondered about the origins and biology of morality and about the raison-d'être of mortality, just as much as we have wondered about who we really are on the canvas of the cosmos, and about the roles of genes and culture in shaping human personality. And most of us agree with what Einstein said: "The most important human endeavor is the striving for morality in our actions. Our inner balance and even our very existence depend on it. Only morality in our actions can give beauty and dignity to life".[31] Although we reflexively assume that 'good' is good, and 'bad' is bad, there have always been introspective individuals, not all 'bad', who pondered about why being good is 'good'. Sarada Devi, the spiritual consort of Sage Ramakrishna asked that if grief itself is a 'gift of God', then why can't we be bad and give that 'gift' to others? At a more fundamental level, the question is: Which is more 'moral' in terms of nature and natural selection? If we want to be moral and magnanimous, should we go beyond nature, as Thomas Huxley, for example, argued, or should we navigate a return to nature and try to emulate the ants, bees, and wasps? And what, in effect, constitutes a 'moral life'? Who does it benefit? How do we judge if an action is moral or not? Is goodness the same as morality and if so, good for what and whom? These are timeless questions and many moral philosophers have extensively written about it. Generally, in lay language, we use the word 'good' as the opposite of 'bad', and 'moral' as the opposite of evil—and the test is our behavior. In actuality, we view all life as either being or doing 'good' or 'bad'. Although, in the very nature of human life, nothing is good in and by itself, and almost everything we do is a blend of both. Moreover, when we say something is 'good', it actually translates as good 'for ourselves'. The primary, if not exclusive, focus has to be on personal piety, probity, integrity and on virtues like truthfulness, self-restraint, simplicity, loyalty, faithfulness, honesty, helpfulness, and adherence to codes of conduct and religious commandments.

Despite ups and downs from time to time, they have stood the test of time as measures of moral life. We must also bear in mind that our sense of morality, like human evolution itself, developed in a very local, confined 'world', and the intended beneficiary was the individual and that very limited world. But the world today is global and this 'contextual-change' has dealt a mortal blow to morality. We need to bring forward the central question: Being moral is to do what, and how does it help or hinder the common good? Now, it is hard to find something to do that has no global impact. When the moral context changes, the morality content too must change, in order to be relevant. We need to find new ways to judge what is moral and what is not, in the changed dynamics. That ought to thrust the whole of morality into the melting pot, and draw from it a fresh framework for an ethical living. We don't need to discard the extant guidelines; we need to shift the focus and priorities to serve the emerging need. What is good between two individuals or in the privacy of personal relationships, does not always contribute to the good of society. In fact, a major moral issue now is how not to let our personal obligations towards our loved ones, and towards our professional call of duty, dilute or distract us from leading a moral life. This issue has now become more critical given the widening gap between what is required to lead a good life, to be a good family member and have a good career, and what is required to resolve serious social and global problems. We cannot treat everyone in our life alike and perfect impartiality is not humanly possible. At the same time, we have to exercise self-restraint to ensure that we are not overly influenced by such 'natural' feelings and avoid to the maximum extent hurting other people. The thrust must be to support and serve social needs, so that an individual life becomes an input to address social problems, instead of being inimical. For long, what has been called *utilitarianism*—to choose a course of action that results in the greatest utility to the greatest number of people—has been viewed as a good moral yardstick. That has to be radically revisited since most people would like to lead a life of comfort, and what that entails has turned out to be hazardous to global health. Actually, while many of us think and often pride ourselves as leading passively moral lives, the fact is that the world is full of largely avoidable or significantly reducible suffering caused by our behavior, and the perilous state of the environment caused by the kind of lives we lead.

The ascendancy of what is often described as scientific rationality of a perception that the environment is but a pool of inexhaustible natural resources, and our wholesale identification of good life with goodness of life, and of progress with material progress, has altered both the context and contours of morality. Indeed, our reckless onslaught on natural resources has become so predatory and plunderous that we cannot any longer keep it within the margins of a moral life. In future, being moral must include the three 'R's in the use of resources: restraint, reuse, recycle. Restraint includes self-restraint. The ethic of self-restraint must be chanted and imbibed in every classroom and home and workplace. That will go a long way in dissolving every crisis the world currently faces, including the climate crisis. And without it nothing else will suffice. Technology can help, but it cannot be a substitute or surrogate. What are needed are directional changes in its use. What are called *toilet-to-tap* technologies have to be developed that could turn waste into water. We must also buy or purchase what we truly need, not because we have the money to buy the latest model we see in a commercial or in our neighbor's home. We must cultivate the culture of 'use it up; wear it out; make do without'. More than ever before, we must practice the adage 'frugality is morality', and morality is moderation and conservation. We must remember that, as the catch phrase goes, "There is no Plan(et) B; and global warming is not cool". Most of all, we must remember that what we are doing to the environment is what we are doing to ourselves, even more to our kids and grand-kids. And what good is leaving them money, property, and estate if they are going to inherit a death-enhancing environment? Money is now at the heart of modernity. It has become so piercing and subversive, and occupies so much of our thought and time that its shadow shades much of morality. We must somehow find a way to rescue morality from money, and the way to do it is not to undermine it but try to transform it into a benign instrument.

Another lodestar can be what philosopher Schopenhauer suggested, that only actions that stem from compassion have moral worth. An important point of reference is to judge what people do, not what they are, because everyone is a 'moral mix'. And no one can be pronounced wholly 'moral' or entirely 'evil'. Everyone can be, and is, both compassionate and callous, kind and cruel, considerate or condescending, petty and generous. In the cauldron of everyday life, every mundane choice is a moral choice, and every moral issue is at its heart a *money* issue. Every living minute brings death closer, but the length of life and nature and the time of the tryst with death are particular to every individual. Whether it is nature of our time or yuga or the flowering of our own nature, we have turned everything upside down including our morality and mortality; they no longer play the roles that they are supposed to do—to temper and lighten our darker dimension and to facilitate the perennial flow of life on earth. We want to be ethical in our behavior but we suspect each other's bonafides; we seem hopelessly helpless against the lure of evil; we want to live in amity but murder is very much in our mind. And money has much to do with this turning away from nature. And money makes a big difference to dying; how we die, what precedes death and what follows death. If we have enough money, we are told, we can turn death into prolonged sleep and wake up when we want to, perhaps we can make more money and then live 'happily' forever. The goal of modern man, on the morrow of the millennium, is, in short, to double or treble his present life span, to experience the languorous delights of seamless youth, flawless skin and perfect limbs; little labor and lot of leisure; instant lust and unrestricted personal liberty—all regardless of the morality of means. The chosen way is to be a part of what JK Galbraith called *affluent society*, and Thorstein Veblen called the *Leisure Class*, the bedrock of which is the abundance of money. And that is the rub of the matter, the virus of the malaise of modern man. The effect of that havoc is not confined any longer to the human society; it is planetary, even interplanetary. The human 'way of living life' is depleting natural resources at such a pace that, it is estimated, if an average citizen of the world were to live like an average resident of USA, then we would require, according to the World Wildlife Fund's *Living Planet* report (2010), a 'bio-capacity equivalent to 4.5 Earths'. It all raises the fundamental question: Have we drifted away from what we ought to have been or are we simply being true to our own immoral selves, needlessly or masochistically suffering with self-inflicted guilt, shame and remorse for what we are?

That might be the most important contemporary issue—how to make compassion or, in the words of AC Grayling (*What is Good*, 2003), the 'culture of moral concern' our primary companion, and goodness our natural, normal, ordinary and habitual response to the circumstances and compulsions, temptations and travails of human life. The new moral desideratum or principle should be 'the elevation of the particular human being other than me as the ultimate goal of action'. Even granting that we live, in Tzvetan Todorov's words in an 'Imperfect Garden', we must apply a new moral yardstick—the greatest advantage not to the greatest numbers but to the least advantaged—and factor it into our daily life. We should transform what is now occasional, exceptional, and extraordinary into normal and ordinary outpouring. 'Moral concern' must be embedded into the fabric of human needs values and ethics. And if there is one lesson from our history of horror—and the lives of millions of generations and tens of billions of humans that preceded us—it is that for man to come any closer to be a genuinely caring and compassionate being, the classical 'prick of conscience' cannot be either the anchor or the navigator; we must incubate and induce a new blend in our consciousness. But first we must move away from our comfort zone of complacency and self-righteous smugness. It is being stuck in that 'zone' that drags us down, makes us reluctant to give up the 'familiar', clinging to safety and 'surface-living'. It is that 'reluctance' that is thwarting all efforts to combat climate challenges like change.

We cannot insult, ill-treat and humiliate another person and think we are moral because we have not done anything to overtly harm them. We cannot harbor malice within and be moral in our behavior. We cannot be moral, mean, good, and greedy at the same time. Nor can we be rude and righteous at the same time; nor be pious and petty… And we cannot be deemed 'moral' unless we are 'just' and cannot separate the rudiments of a 'moral life' from our relationship with the divine, especially of others' faiths. And we cannot any more consider ourselves 'good' unless our thoughts and emotions are devoid of guile, bile, and spite, and individual actions are driven by integrity and goodwill. We have been wrestling with these issues for ages and the time has come to raise a more fundamental question, to borrow the title of an article by Colin McGinn: *Is Just Thinking Enough*?[32] Although the context of McGinn's question was different, we can use the question to explore a much broader domain. 'Just' can mean either 'only', or it could be 'fair', 'right' and 'moral'. And can we be just and compassionate at the same time in the same situation? Some thinkers argue that if only we can get our thinking right and if we can boost more of our brain power, we can solve all our problems, and the world would be a wondrous place; and then hope that science could show the way. While this is the mainstream modern view, others, even some scientists, demur and posit that thinking or rather the source of our thinking, the structure of our thought, an activity of brain/mind, is the central problem, and that unless we can find a way to remove the monopoly of our mind on human intentionality and our moral sense, we cannot exorcize the malaise and maladies that afflict mankind. It is a critical issue not only for us, the current inhabitants of the earth, but also for the future generations. For we are told that the human species, contrary to what we were led to believe, is still evolving biologically, which means that the construct and content of the future man can be influenced by the 'culture of our conduct' and the 'environment of our behavior'. This means that the milieu and minutiae of our mundane lives, how we relate with and treat other people and other creatures and how we use and misuse nature—the crux of morality—can become inherited attributes of future humans and shape the genetic mix and make-up of the human organism and complete—or at least take forward—the unfinished evolutionary process. The time has come to broaden our 'narrow and individualistic conception of sin', and the idea that 'harming God's creation is tantamount to sin'. The environment is at the heart of God's creation, and any action or non-action that leads to its contamination becomes a 'modern-day sin'. In his encyclical *Laudato Si'*, Pope Francis, quoting the spiritual father of the Eastern Orthodox Christians, Saint Bartholomew, said that the destruction, exploitation of the earth by humans has risen to the level of sin, and that we humans need to, as the Pope paraphrases, "replace consumption with sacrifice, greed with generosity, wastefulness with a spirit of sharing".

A growing number of thoughtful people are recognizing that what we call environmental, economic or financial crisis is really a values crisis, a moral crisis. But we must take it beyond the point of a crisis to opportunity. It is not a question of ethics or personal morality. We need a new frame of reference, a new point of reference and a point of departure, a new reason to be 'moral'. What is important at this juncture is to recognize what 'being moral' has come to represent, is out of sync with what is necessary for social transformation, and to mend the human mold. And, to paraphrase Martin Luther King Jr., for the human moral arc to bend towards justice, we have to go down to the roots of what a 'moral life' ought to signify. When we say someone is 'moral' or mean—and when we use terms like good and evil, right and wrong—we emphasize qualities such honesty, integrity, thrift, rectitude. It is anchored on the premise that each person has an intrinsic and singular worth, that he is an agent of his dedicated destiny, and that it is for *him* to choose between right and wrong and to suffer the consequences of his actions. But 'right' and 'wrong' are not static; they are filtered through the human mind. Their understanding is different in the mind of a psychopath and in the mind of a priest. And sometimes we do 'wrong' with the intent to do 'good'. Moral philosophy has long wrestled with the questions: Does the end justify the means, or can the right path take you to a wrong destination, the right end? Are consequences the ultimate basis of judging what is right and what is wrong? There are no 'right' or 'wrong' answers to these questions because there is no single 'right' or 'wrong' answer. In the end, the 'end' has to be what is beneficial, not baneful, to society and to sentient life. Scriptures send us mixed messages. Each time we have to struggle to make the correct calling. Ultimately, like everything else, it depends on the state of consciousness, more particularly if it is mind-driven or not.

What we call humanity or society is a composite of such 'person-centered' people. For society to be 'moral', its individuals—if not everyone, at least the 'critical mass' of them—must be moral. And yet, the context of human life, the very society of which the individual is a constituent, has so changed that a 'person-centered' code is perhaps necessary but certainly not sufficient. 'Being moral' is really to 'behave better'. But to 'behave better' and to contribute to a 'better, more moral, society' man has to broaden the contours of morality. It is not a question of replacing one code for another but to shift priorities, with the accent on behavior that more explicitly serves the common good and social stability, and which does not endanger the common home and its life-supporting environment. Another problem is now on the front burner: Is it at all possible, or necessary, to have any such thing as a 'moral code', however flexible? There are those who argue that there is no value, or norm or an ethic that is universal, absolute and eternal in nature and life. On the other hand, there are those who call it a side door to naked evil. Pope Benedict XVI described it as a "dictatorship of relativism which does not recognize anything as an absolute and which only leaves the 'I' and its whims as the ultimate measure". In addition we have a tendency to view every issue as 'either-or', 'up-or-down', 'for-or-against'. Which means in moral terms we are either good or bad, virtuous or vicious. The truth is that in nature everything is an amalgam, a blend, a package. Therefore we can be, at different times, or under different circumstances, a monster or a mahatma, saint or sinner, murderer or savior. We remain the same 'person' but behave like different persons. If we can ingest that thought deep inside, our moral perspective will change. We will refrain in pronouncing any one as good or bad, and be more charitable and circumspect and compassionate even when combating whom we consider them as more or less evil. Abraham Lincoln, who fought a savage civil war to preserve an entire nation and to abolish slavery, said that "they (the slave owners) are just what we would be in their situation". The fact of the matter is no one can be sure how we would act if we find ourselves in someone else's shoes, in the same environment and at exactly the same moment when he or she does something we find horrific. The paradox is that any of us might do what anyone else does, good and bad, in the words of the Thirukkural, "delusion's dual deeds".

Moral Gangrene and Unbridled Evil

We feel, at least we ought to feel, choked with the waste of 'moral effluvia', the spin-off of 'moral gangrene'. The horrific things that we see almost every day jolt even our slumbering sensibility, and we wonder if modern-day evil is no longer hiding behind the description of 'not being good', that of being the 'other side of the same coin'. We wonder if it has audaciously acquired a life, legitimacy, and lethality of its own, and is now unstoppable and all-conquering. Afflicted with a 'plague', we look for a panacea and a pill. With a pandemic in the air, we want to survive with a closed nose or a mask. With a tornado howling outside each one of us, we think that our thatched roof will stay intact. But our crafty mind, afraid that we will blame it for all our malevolence and misery, throws up a seductive crumb: Have we all got it all horribly wrong? Are we missing the wood for the trees? And contrary to all that depressing detail the media highlights, are we, as some 'optimists' argue, actually better placed than ever to act for the benefit of humanity as a whole? Do we believe that violence is on the wane, and a subtle spiritual renaissance is on the rise? We must also note that at the core of what has come to be called the New Age Movement, which seeks to harmonize science and spirituality, and mind, body and spirit, there is also a visceral, sometimes violent, reaction to the suffocating sweep of what we deem as 'good life'. But, more fundamentally, it encompasses another deeper tenet, namely the thought that this life, this world, is not the entirety of existence, but merely one step in an infinite voyage; that our personal consciousness is but a fragmentary projection of a much greater wholeness. That the 'divinity' is 'within', intrinsic and all-pervasive. And that all forms of life, including animals and plants, have their own intrinsic value. That bait is what draws so many of the young and the restless, and 'today's dead-end kids' to obscure metaphysical bookstores, to cults and gurus, swamis, lamas of all hues, spiritual workshops and seminars and meditation and mystical retreats. To go out of the way, to think out-of-the-box, has always been the way out in all turbulent times and in times of great change. That is at once a potential promise and a seductive peril, an opening and an obstruction. It could be a promise if we introduce greater clarity and make it more in tune with the tasks and challenges the world faces which require changes in our individual lifestyles. It could then be 'transformational' in its depth and scope and melt away the malice and meanness, hatred and hubris that blight human life. On the other hand, it could be a peril if it is turned into a cover for pleasure pursuits by charlatans and charismatic self-seekers. Most of us are poised on what is called the 'hedonic treadmill' and have to keep walking, and making more money. So overpowering is money that we cannot seriously contemplate any contemporary issue without reference to it. And if we do, it will fail because it is inextricably interwoven.

One can with equal passion posit both ways, as our very understanding of 'being better-off' and what 'violence' itself is, is blurred. For every moral misconduct or ethical impropriety our mind offers an excuse or an explanation and that enables us to lead 'normal' lives. All this agonizing thought, in Thoreau's phrase 'quiet desperation', has given birth to a new branch of science called the 'science of morality'. Joseph Daleiden, Sam Harris, and Patricia Churchland, among others, have argued that society should now consider normative ethics as an important domain of science, and that it might be possible, using disciplines like neuropsychology and metaphysical naturalism, to outline a generic basis for moral life, or, to paraphrase JK Galbraith, to "search for a superior moral justification for selfishness". But there are some who say that, contrary to popular perception, for a moral life, it is not only a matter of following moral principles and codes and applying them to daily life. It is, or ought to be, a process of determining what kind of humans we should be individually and collectively. Einstein, who described himself as an agnostic said that without 'ethical culture', there is no salvation for humanity. The practical question is that while making choices and decisions in life how do we differentiate the moral from the immoral, good from bad, right from wrong. Even from a purely selfish point of view, the problem often is that, as Rousseau said, "Our will is always for our own good but we do not always see what the good is". The new factor is not only 'what good' but 'whose good'. Most agree that a moral or virtuous life too is a means. It is about the end that views widely vary, from honor (Homer), to justness (Plato), to happiness (Aristotle). Religions generally say that being moral or good is good for you to go to heaven, and it will be handy on the Judgment Day. While by and large it was possible to describe and discuss, analyze and find remedies and solutions to 'moral' problems in earlier times, it does not seem possible now. The present 'crisis' constitutes a different class, not different degree. In the contemporary context we do not know what is moral and what we need to do to be moral, and also if certain actions are under any conditions should be deemed wrong, or if they *become* wrong because of their consequences. We are increasingly unsure if an individual is entitled to his 'moral space' which is sacrosanct and immune to others' invasion and how to balance it with an increasingly elastic common good. But the essential question is: How best could we contribute to it? The answer is stunningly simple: whatever you are good in, do it for the common good. The problem also is most of us really do not know what our 'signature' strengths are; we are more aware of our failings and foibles. That requires a conscious and sustained work; it can emerge as an epiphany, a sudden revelation or incrementally, but we will know. Then the task is to channel and harness them to service something that is higher and larger than your desires. We need to energize our energies, and also the 'moral context' of human effort has radically changed. Every effort, however tiny and small, goes not in vain. *The Book of Golden Precepts* says, "Learn that no efforts, not the smallest—whether in the right or wrong direction—can vanish from the world of causes. Even wasted smoke remains not traceless".

The dilemma of human life is how one can be moral when all of us are potentially equally capable of doing both good and evil. And we have no way of foretelling what each of us might actually do under a similar temptation. Compounding the dilemma is another reality: we are all made of the same mud and mix but no one can ever be anyone else. As Zen master Kodo Sawaki said, "You can't even trade a single fart with the next guy". We might sometimes succeed in putting ourselves in someone's shoes but not *become* someone else. That 'jeopardy' becomes even more complex by juxtaposing another variable: in the words of Shannon Alder, "No two persons can learn something and experience it in the same way". As a result, we can never, ever, be certain how any of us will respond to any particular situation. Most of us are 'bad' because we have convinced ourselves that that is the only way we can survive. Another emerging factor is that the fountainheads of immorality and evil have shifted from primarily private behavior to public performance, to governance, and practiced by those who are supposedly there to save us. The greatest evil is not now done in those sordid "dens of crime" that Dickens loved to depict. The locus is not even concentration camps and labor camps. There it was visible. Instead of Auschwitz we have Abu Ghraib. Instead of the Gulags, where people were worked to death, we have professionals; in the words of CS Lewis, "quiet men with white collars and cut fingernails and smooth-shaven cheeks who do not need to raise their voices".[33] Those who don't flinch in dispensing death as a part of their duty, and are conceived, ordered and managed in clean, carpeted, warmed, and well-lighted offices.These are not only, in Lewis' phrase "nasty business concerns" but, even more, in elegant White Houses, Downing Streets, Elysée Palaces, Kremlins, Zhongnanhais,[34] offices of secret services and nondescript offices of apparatchiks and bureaucrats. The State is now the chief source of evil, as much as those it vows to eliminate. It oppresses as much as it claims to protect, uses violence, fearless as it is lawful, brazen because there is no earthly higher power. Historically, in the interests of the common good, most people, including great philosophers like Plato, have exempted the State from the rigor of personal morality, and gave it, for example, the 'license to lie'. But it has now gone far and the common good is no longer the primary motive, which is now the interest of the ruling class, the politico-bureaucratic-business nexus. The Hobbesian premise that the State is necessarily evil to protect self-motivated individuals from other self-motivated individuals assumes that the rulers of the State have no vested interest other than ensuring fair play, and to protect the weak and vulnerable. That is no longer a valid presumption. There are some like David Graeber who even say that the State is a demonic force thwarting human freedom. Clearly it is a dangerous hyperbole since it ignores many positives that stem from the State. Without anything approximating a State what we call 'society' will implode in time.

The closest parallel to a state of society without a State is what has come to be known as the 'Paris Commune', which offered to the masses—who were increasingly disgusted with the soulless capitalist mechanization and utilitarian State socialism, and were looking for a 'humane alternative'—a beacon of hope of participatory self-governance. But how it degenerated and disintegrated provides a clue to what happens to human society sans any structure or enforcing power. It illustrates what the dialectic between the 'desirable' and 'desired' ought to be and is. We must not ignore that violent social conflict is as innate and spontaneous for humans as social cooperation and accommodation. Furthermore, those who are capable of handling State power wisely do not come to power even in democracies, let alone dictatorships. Instead, those who come to power soon develop a lust for the perks of power and they shed all principles to hold on to power; power ceases to be a means and becomes the end. No system of governance, since at least the Greek city-states, has been able to insure against this eventuality.

Whichever way it might be, the prudent course is to recognize that evil remains a concrete, clear and transparent 'moral problem', an ordinary aspect of contemporary human life. As Lars Svendsen[35] puts it, "Evil should never be justified, should never be explained away... it should be fought". We must not also ignore that the "forbidden truth and unspeakable taboo", as Joyce Oates reminds us, is "that evil is not always repellent but frequently attractive; that it has the power to make of us not simply victims, as nature and accident do, but active accomplices".[36] No one is wholly immune to the allurements of evil; nor has anyone exclusive rights over virtue. Evil is not, as some say, a parasite on the good, implying that it has no independent existence; rather, it exists because the good tolerates it, it is now a primary passion. Whether the human beast can best be left alone to his instincts and impulses, dreams and desires to lead a worthy life of utility, to his own self and to his fellow-humans, or if the focus should move to the 'circumstance' of his daily life to influence his choices and actions, is moot. But that circumstance, good or bad, in itself and in its yield, is not entirely a happenstance; it happens for a reason, to fulfill our own soul-driven desire. This question is a signature snapshot of the fallacy of dichotomous thinking in terms of binary opposition, such as either-or, black or white, good or bad, or all or nothing, which is how the human mind perceives the phenomenal world. Of all the messages that spring from Creation, the governing axiom is the 'principle of polarity' or of 'pairs of opposites'. It is called the dialectical doctrine of dwanda in Hindu philosophy, and in modern usage it is often phrased as the principle of polarity, aptly described in *The Kybalion: Hermetic Philosophy*:[37] "Everything is Dual; everything has poles; everything has its pair of opposites; like and unlike are the same; opposites are identical in nature, but different in degree; extremes meet; all truths are but half-truths; all paradoxes may be reconciled". At one level of perception, the difference between things that appear to be diametrically opposed to each other, like 'in' and 'out', 'within' and 'without', heat and cold and light and darkness, is merely a matter of degree. Opposites are the extremes of the same thing—love or hate, good or bad, moral or evil… and they can easily exchange places. And our looking at everything as either of the two is itself a chief source of human misery. As Lao Tzu, the founder of Taoism, explained, "When people see some things as beautiful, other things become ugly; when people see some things as good, other things become bad. Being and non-being create each other; difficult and easy support each other; long and short define each other; high and low depend on each other; before and after follow each other". In short, the wise man sees unity in duality. Tzu sums it up and says, "What is a good man but a bad man's teacher? What is a bad man but a good man's job? If you don't understand this, you will get lost, however intelligent you are. It is the great secret". The Bhagavad Gita says that a highly evolved man, who is called a *sthitaprajna*, transcends the three *gunas* of *sattva*, *rajas*, and *tamas*, makes no distinction between the opposites, and is "*balanced* in pleasure and pain, self-reliant, to whom a lump of earth, a rock and gold are alike; the same to loved and unloved, firm, the same in censure and in praise, the same in honor and ignominy, the same to friend and foe, abandoning all undertakings—he is said to have crossed over the qualities".[38] Jalal ad-Din Rumi compared 'being human' to a 'guest house', and exhorted a person to be open to whatever life brings us, internally or externally: "Welcome and entertain them all… even if they are a crowd of sorrows who violently sweep your house; [For] He may be clearing you out for some new delight; The dark thought, the shame, the malice, meet them at the door laughing, [because] Each has been sent as a guide from beyond".[39] Every experience, everyone we meet, whether or not they give us joy or sorrow, are meant to bring in something else or someone else into our life, and since we cannot foresee the future we can only welcome the present, however painful it might be.

Evil is not only globalized but it is also ghastly. It is globalized because its tentacles cut across all borders and have global reach. It is ghastly as we no longer have any moral safe havens. What were so far considered as safe even from evil, are now in its clasp. We read about mothers killing their own children, a father molesting his own daughter, a son killing his father for his job or for property, a *pujari* (temple priest) swindling temple treasure, a *swami* (holy man) sexually exploiting his disciples, and children slaughtered in their classrooms for the heck of it, people being blown up while in deep prayer in their places of worship, to avenge the affront to 'a' God and so on. Nothing is too intimate, sacred or loathsome for evil. Every human, even divine relationship is now susceptible to its insidious influence. That is the awesome moral challenge mankind faces; to get a new understanding of the dynamics and dialectics of evil, bearing in mind that the very institution that is supposed to insure security and justice, the State, is now a source of evil, and that the very branch of knowledge that is supposed to help us stay on the moral path (religion) now incubates evil. Unless we comprehend how it works we cannot contain or confront it. We cannot talk about the evil that the State is, in abstract terms, as if it is some distant third party. For, the fact is, as Karl Jaspers reminds us, "Everybody is responsible for the way he is governed". The State justifies every evil as a 'hard choice', unpleasant but unavoidable. Even the death of as many as 500,000 Iraqi children due to economic sanctions, designed to dent the will of a 'dictator', to make it so difficult for unarmed citizens to revolt, and do what the mighty 'sole superpower' could not do: overthrow the 'dictator'. There are no moral qualms, no regret or remorse; the bottom line is that everything is justified to avoid bringing the 'body bags' back home. Almost every State indulges, in varying depths of devilry and deviousness, in similar acts either at home to suppress dissent or to insure 'internal security', or externally over weaker adversaries.

Citizens, otherwise honorable, decent, god-fearing people, acquiesce, so long as it does not disturb their lives and of their near and dear.

Our moral quandary at this juncture is four-fold. First, while trying to be a 'moral man', being fuzzy about what 'moral' means, human creativity has, as Reinhold Niebuhr argues (*Moral Man and Immoral Society*, 1932) crafted an 'immoral society'. In our 'collective life', we seem singularly incapable of adhering to the very principles and norms that we value, though not adhere to, in our personal lives. Second, we have not been able to design the moral tools to apply in the 'immoral society'. Three, sans such tools or a moral compass, much of our life is spent in trying to find what is right and moral, and what is not, in a given situation. Finally, the most unnerving and daunting is that even after knowing what is the right thing to do in practical terms, we are often driven and drawn towards the opposite. The fact of the matter is that evil as moral infringement or injustice is embedded in human culture, and horrible things happen that bring into question our only claim to be the highest, if not the noblest, form of life on earth. We can hedge, we can quibble, we can say, 'it is too sweeping, too generic and general' but we cannot set aside the history of human horror. That everybody is not evil or that there are good people and that the human race has also produced prophets, saints, and sages should not lead us to shift our gaze from the malaise of man. It is like saying all snakes are not poisonous; we do not cuddle-up to them. The fact of the matter is why certain people actually become evil, while in others the evil lies dormant. No stereotype applies to every crime and no sin is beyond the pale of possibility to anyone. Man has wrestled with evil in the best of times, when being dharmic or righteous did not require an epic struggle. What is appalling is that we are indifferent to and intolerant of everything in the human world except evil. Depravity of some kind man has always lived with; now, it manifests also as deprivation. Such is the devastation wrought by extreme poverty and so different are the lives of the poor, compared with those of the rest, that all those that facilitate those conditions have to be treated as abettors of evil. Economic and ecological evil must take precedence over personal evil. The age-old anchor of morality, family, has crumbled under the onslaught of 'globalized evil'. We must come to terms with the new face of evil that stares at us in the mirror and we experience in the world. Unable to comprehend or to come to terms with human callousness and cruelty, desperately and determinedly running away from the historicity of human behavior, we drift into denial and shroud our sensibility, even rationality. We wonder what turns a man into a monster, and why, in some people, something terribly goes awry and impels them to do things that wreck other lives. Not a day passes without a horrific incident happening somewhere in the world, wrought by human hand, and we wonder about the lowest depth and depravity that a human is capable of. And we wonder about the meaning and mind of God that lets such things happen whichever way one characterizes the moral core of man. The somber reality is that the way human life has come to be organized after over a million years of evolution, millenniums of culture and centuries of civilization, it is almost impossible not to do things we do not 'want to do', unless those are the very things we ought not to do. It is a shattering thought, a blinding reality: what we desperately want to do, our deepest longing is simply to be able to do the good things we want to do, and not do the evil things we do not want to do. That what should be so 'simple' is so difficult is the moral story of mankind.

Morality and Modernity

Modernity, to which we sometimes ascribe many an unwelcome thing in our lives, is not the incubator of the internal war. The war is timeless, ageless, constant, and eternal. What distinguishes our 'times' from prehistoric times, is that while in those ages or *yugas* there was always a kind of stalemate or impasse, with no clear victor or vanquished, and with fluctuating and transitory fortunes between the opposing forces, it now appears that the tide is turning in favor of the forces of darkness and decadence. They are prevailing and winning most of the myriad mini-wars or battles that take place every time we choose to do something, or make decisions on any kind of mundane or momentous matters. It is, in effect, an invasion from within, and its every wish is our command. That could be the principal cause and source of much of the unease, disquiet, anger, anxiety restiveness, rebelliousness, and self-destructive impulses that so many of us sense. And that could be behind the gnawing 'gut-feeling' that the world is, in Gandhi's words, poised on the 'threshold of a twilight',[40] that our lives are adrift like a reed in an ocean, that we are inexorably moving towards the edge of the abyss. Despite our 'feel-good' culture and material affluence, we do feel that a malaise afflicts mankind but we are clueless what it could be. We know we are lost in the dark woods but uncertain how deep; we realize we are adrift but we are foxed to where we should head; we agree that the present time is a huge historical hinge, but sense that history is slipping out of our hands. We yearn to find ourselves at a place like Shangri-La or a time like the Golden Age, but what we do is to make a hell of our home. Most of all, deep down, we also realize that to arrest the drift and decline and decay, all of us and each one of us, must rise above ourselves from the "individualistic concerns to the broader concerns of humanity",[41] whose actions and habits could tilt the scales decisively. What we need above all is a clear appreciation of the behavioral drivers that paralyze humanity from changing its course from one headed towards a potential collapse of human industrial civilization, to one moving towards sustainable human behavior. A long time ago, the Buddha phrased the issue very well: "What is the appropriate behavior for a man or a woman in the midst of this world, where each person is clinging to his piece of debris? What's the proper salutation between people as they pass each other in this flood?" In short, how should one deal with and how much room must one give to another person on this crowded place called Earth while 'living' one's own 'life'? The real problem is that the way we 'understand' most often when we face moral choices, is wrong. We worry and fight for 'rights'—all the way from human rights to conjugal rights—not how to do the 'right' thing. That good people do 'wrong' things does not make the wrong any less wrong. We cannot any longer fall back on our conscience—called the vice-regent of God—to bail us out. As we live on in this society, actively taking on its spirit, our conscience gets more and more persuaded to 'go along to get along', to be 'realistic'. In fact, our inability to 'get along', not to 'suffer each other', to accept, not tolerate, each other, to complement, not nibble, each other is the primary cause of suffering. Another cause is our inability to view society as a moral community, not a social conglomerate.

The growing power of the State, of globalization, of ruthless randomness of terrorism, and of mass media adds a new dimension to morality. Anybody can be a victim; anybody can be deprived of dignity; anyone can become a refugee; anybody can be uprooted from their local milieu and support of traditional groups, family, friends, and neighbors. We are living in times when sometimes only 'distant strangers' in cyberspace, watching flickering lights and fleeting images on a tiny screen, could become our saviors. Our neighbors might become 'strangers' or enemies, impelled by caste, class, or religious zealotry, and strangers far away, whom we never even come to see or speak, can come to our aid on humanitarian grounds. It is through the arousal of global conscience, what Michael Ignatieff called "ethic of universal moral obligation among strangers" that, at times of need and peril we could get help. Traditionally, morality has been personal and local, bounded within the family, tribe, community, religion, and nation. The idea of needing or helping strangers, showing compassion and seeking support, half-way across the globe, because we are all in the same leaking boat, to face the dangers of the day is new but its time has come.

Moral Ambivalence and Serial Fidelity

The crux of the human dilemma is three-fold: man can conceive of a kind of moral perfection that he cannot attain; he is unable to live with his bodily impermanence. That is perhaps why one Buddhist *sutra* says, "the best of all meditations is the meditation on impermanence". And, despite all the insights he can summon, man is incapable of erasing the sense of separateness that divides one living being from another. Perfection is only in the province of providence. Transience is the law of nature, and no one is immune to its sway, not even the human. Our modern culture encourages us to look upon another man not merely as a separate being, but as a competitor to be confronted, to be cut to size, to be nibbled into nothing. Man wants to have it both ways; he wants to live and die at his will, and he wants to wield the power of extinction and de-extinction at his whim. Even as we ruthlessly exterminate other species—current extinction rates are 1,000 times higher than during pre-human times—science is trying to bring back to life long-extinct animals like the mammoth. And, on top of it, we claim that 'with de-extinction, we have the means to repair some of the damage we have done. The bottom line is: to have it all. No giving up of any 'good things'; to grab what we want and when—to be rich and charitable, powerful and benevolent, competitive and caring. We have, as it were, the world at our feet, and yet we expect much more than what the world can offer and feel deceived and disappointed. TS Eliot captured the dreary mood: "Birth, copulation and death; that's all the facts when you come to brass tacks". Behind such a gloomy view of human life lies the dysfunctional disconnect, or myopic mismatch, between knowledge and knowing, knowing and doing, precept and practice. Man is simply unable to behave the way he wants to behave, *just* to do the 'right thing' regularly and reflexively. It is important to underscore one dimension at this moment. However much we are prone to temptation, most of us are capable of *doing* the 'right things' in life. But it is not what we do once in a while that matters in 'being moral'; it is what we do consistently and routinely that matters. Similarly no one is insulated, or immune, from 'doing bad'. Everything in life is relative, selective, and subject to who the 'doer' is and when, where, and how any act is performed. That includes 'morality'. The rules and restraints applicable at one place are redundant elsewhere. For example, the rules on the road do not apply to the home; even at home, a bedroom is different from the drawing room. What is a man who, once he dons a uniform, becomes 'morally' different from the same person sans the same dress? A soldier is 'morally' justified—it is in fact what he is hired to do—to murder in a war situation. He is even hailed as a hero, but is court-martialed for the same act in a street brawl 'for conduct unbecoming of a soldier'. We look and yearn for uniformity and simplicity and end up with specificity and complexity. Just as you cannot bathe in the same river twice, we cannot experience the same experience twice, although nothing is original in life.

Whether or not moral 'tendencies' are integral to human nature, and whether or not morality has a neurobiological basis, an adaptation that our brains have evolved in order to cement social ties, we do harbor 'vicious and cannibalistic' tendencies, "dark things that swim deep in the waters of the unconscious".[42] We are an ambivalent species, blessed as well as doomed, capable of self-sacrifice and of sacrificing others for self-gain. And whether or not our ancestors became 'moral' by choice, as biologists like Thomas Huxley posited, and whether or not it is a slim veneer camouflaging our otherwise selfish and evil nature, the fact is that there is within each of us a streak of morality, however thin or strong it may be. Recent research[43] supports this inference. It suggests that dark personality traits—Machiavellianism, egoism, narcissism, psychopathy, sadism, and spitefulness—all stem from a common, 'dark core'. In other words, if you exhibit any of these tendencies, you're also likely to have one or more of the others. It also indicates that "While each individual dark trait manifests itself in widely different ways, they seem to have much more in common than initially meets the eye".[44] In practice, this means that an individual who exhibits a particular malevolent behavior will have a higher likelihood in engaging in other malevolent activities. This dark core or 'D-factor' is the evil within about which scriptures and mystics have spoken. We now have some scientific backing. It is this 'factor' that is fighting the forces of good in the internal war, for control of our consciousness.

Despite our tendency to echo what Oscar Wilde once quipped, "the only thing I cannot resist is temptation", we do feel bad when we do bad things. It is said that humans "have the ability to understand the evolutionary basis of human emotions: betrayal, compassion, empathy, envy, fear, greed, honesty, jealousy, loyalty, lust, revenge, and trust. But we still lack the ability to control them. Unfortunately, rather than use our intelligence to become god-like stewards of this planet, humans have instead chosen to rape and destroy the only Earth we have".[45] But nothing *ipso facto* is 'moral' or even 'legal'; everything we deem as a 'crime' or 'sin', including killing, lying, is permissible under certain legitimate and cultural contexts. For example, killing is permissible if done by the State in self-defense. Sexual 'morality' is vertical, not only horizontal. We are allowed to have sexual intimacy with any number; the only limitation is one at a time, one by one and according to the law of the land. In today's euphemism, we can have such 'serial sex' as dating, which is defined as the "human mating process whereby two people meet socially for companionship, beyond the level of friendship, or with the aim of each assessing the other's suitability as a partner in an intimate relationship or marriage".[46] We can date, online or offline, any number but sequentially. They do not have to be 'in love'. This is very different from the practice, in some tribal societies, in which girls are encouraged to sleep with many men before selecting one to marry. After marriage, one can divorce and marry many times. Polyandry and polygamy are perfectly moral in some societies and cultures. One is considered 'moral', upright and honorable if one 'dates' or marries several partners, and immoral and promiscuous if he or she has simultaneous sexual contacts, or 'cheats' while being married. But the same 'sequentiality' is frowned upon if money is used as a direct trade-off on the grounds that it violates human dignity and "proffers a monetary substitute for mutual desire". Others argue that while force and coercion are bad, there is nothing inherently immoral if the subject consciously and voluntarily chooses to be helped momentarily, since without money one cannot live, and further very few, if any, things are truly voluntary and without some consideration, in cash or kind. The point is that sexual activity *per se* is neither sacred nor sordid, neither moral nor immoral; like much else about morality, this too is time-sensitive, contextual and cultural.

Context changes the character and its perception. The wrong place and wrong time can ruin. A 'soldier' is honored if he kills on the battlefield, but could get killed if he kills on the street or at home. Sex in marriage is sacred, but a sin if indulged outside of it. In the name of the State and God, man does many horrible things that he would not otherwise do, and yet does not feel bad. The rulers are allowed to use force, even unjustly but not a private citizen, even justly. A hangman who is slated to execute a certain person is held guilty if he does the same act elsewhere at a different time. Dying while fighting in a battle can book a berth to heaven, but if a man dies elsewhere he can well go to hell. There is nothing that we cannot do that is absolutely, uniformly, universally prohibited as human beings, either by the scriptures or by society. Everything is 'possible' in life. Short perhaps of turning into a mermaid or an angel with wings or a *Ravana* with ten heads and twenty arms, we can be 'good' or 'bad'; be a Good Samaritan or a cold-blooded killer. We can turn earth into an El Dorado or living hell. What we must strive to do ceaselessly is to turn the 'possibility' of 'being good' into a 'probability', if not certainty in an everyday circumstance. That is to say, to make caring and compassion, not carelessness and callousness, our normal reactions. What stands in the way is our self-righteousness that does not let us accept, even in the light and clarity of hindsight, that we were wrong, that we were instrumental in causing hurt and pain to someone else. That robs us of remorse, and prevents us from trying to repair the damage done to another person and from trying our very best not to repeat it. In the words of George Orwell, "We are all capable of believing things which we know to be untrue, and then, when we are finally proved wrong, impudently twisting the facts so as to show that we were right". The problem is that *right* or *wrong* are so subjective, specific to a person, position and situation. For example while killing is bad, only soldiers or policemen are authorized to kill if the context requires, and even they cannot kill 'off-duty'. While stealing is bad, the State can. While sexual promiscuity is bad, and different cultures have different norms. Even about what we eat there are varying 'moral' prohibitions in religions. While for long a family was the microcosm of the society and there was hardly any clash between the good of the family and that of mankind, human life has now become so complex and multifaceted that no single institution is any more representative of the overall good. And to be 'good at' is not necessarily *being good.* Indeed most of us are 'good at' something or the other, but few are really good in the true moral sense. The desires, dreams, and priorities, even the passions, emotions, and thoughts of a 'garden-type' human being are increasingly not in congruence with that of the human cause, much less of the cosmic cause of continuance of life on earth. To be truly 'moral', it is not sufficient to be scripturally or socially restrained from doing some 'bad' things like stealing, murder, and adultery. A murderer does not always have to have hands dripping with blood. Stinginess, swindling, killing by neglect and adulteration of food and pollution of the environment do more havoc to social tranquility and human health.

To transform into a positive force in human affairs, morality has to mature from its almost exclusive focus on individual 'code of conduct' to imbibing in our mindset what Immanuel Kant called the 'Formula of Humanity', namely that we should treat what he called the *humanity in human beings*—which is distinct from human beings *per se*—whether in ourselves or in others, not only as a means but always as an end in itself. On the contrary, what we now have in the human world are human beings without *humanity*, viewing another person only as subjective means to our end and not as the objective end in their own right. Everyone should be treated as a conscious being with real feelings, needs, and interests; not as 'human instruments'. That means showing that rare thing in life, respect to the dignity and integrity of other people—indeed to all other cohabitants of earth; above all to nature. Respect rules out deception, duplicity, coercion, force, and violence in human relations. Emerson said we are as respectable as we respect others. While we talk a lot about the lack of love what is more destructive is the respect-deficit in our lives. No one respects anyone or anything. In fact we love—even like—more people than we respect. Respect is harder to earn than anything else; and that is the most glaring deficiency in the world. Lack of respect is the direct road to intolerance, injustice, and evil.

Every Minute a Moral Minute

While rationality can be rationally observed, if not explained, morality is more muted, nuanced and nebulous, ambiguous, and ambivalent. The fact is that no one wants to be, or thinks or believes he is, evil. All of us want to be 'moral', 'good', and 'decent', even if there happens to be malice in our minds, or blood on our hands. That mindset blocks any moral betterment. The misconception that also hinders our moral progress is that we think that morality means abandoning all the 'good things' of life, and to do some extraordinary things that take away the fun out of life. In its true spirit, moral means doing what we supposed to do, swadharma as Hindu scriptures call it, to the very best of our ability, and in a manner that causes least inconvenience or hurt or pain to anyone else. It is embedded in everything we do all the time. In that sense every minute is a moral minute. Every choice is a moral choice. Some, like CS Lewis (*Abolition of Man*), say that morality is our very reason for being, and if man ceases to be a 'moral agent' he will cease to be man. Others affirm that morality and being human are incompatible, and that without a backup of rewards and regulations, incentives and injunctions, man is more likely to choose the immoral or evil path. This debate is another example of the 'either-or' mindset, and the truth is, as we noted before, man is neither 'moral' nor 'evil' and how it translates into action depends on many things. As Lewis puts it, "In a sort of ghastly simplicity we remove the organ and demand the function. We make men without chests and expect of them virtue and enterprise. We laugh at honor and are shocked to find traitors in our midst. We castrate and bid the geldings be fruitful".[47] While morality in the sense of what is right or wrong is immune to time and space and is very close to natural laws, there is no 'across-the-board' or universal or rule-of-the-thumb code of moral behavior. It was perhaps best expressed by Freud when he said that men are more moral than they think, and more immoral than they can imagine. More 'morality' applies to our personal and private behavior, and we are more 'immoral' in our economic, professional, and social, behavior than we even are aware of, or care to admit. We are 'more moral', in our relationships with 'in-group', than 'out-group'. The gap between the two 'mores' is ever widening. The fact is that most of us feel like a 'fish caught on a hook', and the hook holding us is our deep spiritual longing. We spend most of the time struggling, not wanting to be reeled in, not wanting to let go of all the things that we are desperately holding. While we often know that spiritual training will take us in the right direction, we say to ourselves, "But I need to do this", or "I must have that".[48] By the time we do 'what we need to' and have had 'what we must have' we are so exhausted, sidetracked, and adrift that we lose that 'longing'. In effect, it means that the direction of our moral life ought to be to promote the good and eliminate the bad within ourselves. For, as the Sikh guru and spiritual master Guru Gobind Singh says, "The greatest comforts and lasting peace are obtained when one eradicates selfishness from within". If we can cleanse the 'within', the world itself will be at peace. It is because we are at war within that we have so little peace in the world. Instead, everything about us is 'external'. Our perception, our vision, our dreams, and ambitions are external. Our 'successes' and our disappointments and defeats are external. Our wars are external. Even God is external. Our primary preoccupation, the focus of our endeavor should be a paradigm shift from the external to the internal if we truly want a world of peace, harmony and happiness. And our essential sadhana or practice ought to be to 'internalize' God as the 'core and goal' of our life's journey. That could help rid religion of its divisiveness and zealotry and be a titanic step to transcend from what Swami Vivekananda called[49] this "miserable little prison-individuality" to "infinite universal individuality".

What then, in sum, is the state of mind of modern man? The human being has become, as Edward Wilson tells us, a 'biologically homicidal species'. Man has always been, perhaps alone amidst all forms of life, as Niels Bohr said, both a "spectator and actor in the great drama of existence". The human is now assuming the character of a choreographer and nothing he does now misses affecting others on earth. So pregnant is human behavior, which includes his personal, social, ecological and spiritual dimensions, that the smallest of human actions can now trigger enormous environmental impact. Our behavior is beyond our depth, and is driven by forces we can barely even visualize. But, thankfully, this is not so with our ability to envision the direction of our effort. And it has endangered the habitability of life on earth. Our powers are far more than we realize or even imagine; much of them are 'hidden'. And what our ancestors once had, we have either lost, or they lie in a deep state of somnambulism since we no longer need them to lead contemporary lives. The level of consciousness at which we operate is at the most superficial, the outermost or the bottom-most layer or level. That is the task and challenge: to at once deepen and elevate our consciousness. The way to deepen and elevate our consciousness is to connect our 'outward' and 'inward' worlds; we need to go deeper within and awaken or reawaken the dormant—some might call 'occult'—faculties. *À la* TS Eliot, 'We are the hollow men; we are the stuffed men'; we are the plastic people of the universe. We need to balance two things: reach the highest heights of human experience and, in the words of Edmund Burke, "turn the soul inward on itself".[50] But we need also a 'base camp' to climb the mountain, and a 'point of departure', which has to be, in the words of Whitall Perry (*A Treasury of Traditional Wisdom*, 1971), to pull ourselves "out of the dusk and dust and debris of our tottering civilization—and learn to manifest that which the Bible calls the *Abomination of Desolation*—faith, truth, and righteousness".[51]

Kith and Kin—And the Rest

The boundaries of our moral universe, whose canvas hitherto covered only the local community, are now blurred; and they encompass, or at least have the potential to encompass humanity as a whole. Our moral sense has long struggled with the question of how to relate to strangers and what justifiable differentiation there could be, if any, between family, friends, and strangers, or casual acquaintances. It is not humanly possible to relate with everyone equally, and different relationships require different moral attributes. It is the evolutionary baggage we carry, which is our natural tendency to favor our near and dear and, conversely, to view others in other tribes with suspicion, xenophobia, and hostility. Can we shed this 'baggage' and learn to treat everyone alike? If not, how much leeway or leverage or 'favoritism' are the kith and kin entitled by virtue of their relationship? The ancient Chinese philosopher Mo Tzu taught that the needs of 'distant strangers' should rank as high as those of family and clan. But the other side of the coin is that sometimes it is easier to show civility to a stranger than to a spouse, for the simple reason that a stranger comes into our life once in a while, while the spouse is a constant, and familiarity does lead to condescension, if not contempt. Prolonged intimacy can be corrosive whereas distance lets us hide our combative nature.

The institution of 'family', is not exclusive to humans, and probably is pre-human, but it is more firmly entrenched in human culture than in other species. For much of human history, family life has defined who we are as human beings. In families, we have nurtured the young and tended the old; we have passed down the religious and cultural traditions of our ancestors; we have celebrated life's joys and faced life's sorrows; and we have given structure and meaning to human sexuality, to the relations between men and women, and to the intergenerational ties between parents and children. The family has also been, and still remains, a critical economic institution—the first and primary place where the rising generation acquires the habits and skills to earn a living, and the first and primary safety net for loved ones in need.[52] It is revered and even sanctified in scriptures. For example, the ancient Tamil text Thirukkural says, "There is no greater dignity than that of the man who declares, 'I will never cease in laboring to advance my family'".[53] The foremost duty of the householder is to duly serve these five: ancestors, God, guests, kindred, and himself. As the cliché goes, one can choose one's friends, but the family is a given. That is used as a license and a *carte blanche* to cut moral corners and ethical short-cuts. Since everyone has a family, it snowballs into a moral snowstorm in human society. While on the one hand we do things for our 'family', we won't even think of doing for others. At the same time, we cherish what we call 'family values', which are "traditional or cultural values (that is, values passed on from generation to generation within families) that pertain to the family's structure, function, roles, beliefs, attitudes, and ideals".[54]

One of the things we bemoan is the 'loss' or erosion of these values. Family, in human culture has become critical due to a range of factors such as the long gestation period, the need to nurture and protect the human infant over an extended time, the religious and social arrangement of marriage, and so on. What has happened over evolution is that 'family', as a basic unit of human society, has both weakened and become an impediment to human solidarity. It has become a huge moral divide. It violates the principle that 'all humans have an equal basic moral status'. For family's sake we do a lot of things that we don't otherwise do; we feel justified in crossing many moral boundaries. We feel no guilt or embarrassment in so doing. We derive great pleasure—and greater pain—from family, particularly what we call the 'immediate family', spouse and progeny. In karmic terms, a family is a confluence of karmas and much, even more than half, of our intense karma is expended through this interaction alone. Some karmas require an adversarial relationship and that is why we see so much turbulence in some families. That is why we see marriages breaking up, children harboring animosity towards their own parents, even killing them. But in general, the institution does raise serious social and moral questions. It leads to unfairness, injustice, nepotism, discrimination, and disproportionate distribution of our energy, attention, earnings, and wealth. It clashes with one central moral imperative: to make ourselves useful to humanity as a whole, or as widely as possible. Implicitly we condone, if not justify, applying different moral standards to family as we explicitly do for the state. As someone said, to do things you hate is the measure and meaning of family. Family, particularly what has been called the 'extended family', has long been viewed as a stabilizing factor, the bedrock of human society. It is family that makes humans less selfish and more sharing, that puts others, even if they are own blood and bone, ahead of us in making choices, and serve as a model for an ideal human society. What we now face is a paradox. On the one hand, 'family values' have declined and the family is arguably in a septic state of crisis. On the other hand, family, especially filial, partiality and breeding dynasties have assumed epidemic proportions, cutting across politics to academia to businesses to entertainment. Families will always prefer their own, and parents will always do whatever is in their power to secure a future for their children. None of this is inherently wrong; indeed, these are the same impulses that have perpetuated the human race. What has changed is that this has become a source of injustice, depriving many others their due from society. But fundamentally, it is unrealistic to think that the institution of 'family' will remain intact and unchanged when everything in society is in a state of turmoil and turbulence. We want to preserve 'family values' while pursuing different 'values' in society that are in direct conflict. Our craze for money, success at any cost, has taken a toll. A family wants more money; therefore both parents, or partners, work with little time to 'raise a family'; even kids are encouraged to earn money, not because the family needs it, but as a part of 'upbringing'. Essentially we have sacrificed 'family life' for a 'good life'. It is primarily the overpowering role of money in human life that has eroded the family as a moral nucleus of human society. We organize our society in the service of wealth and we still expect our young adults to be 'less-money-minded', less 'cut-throat' and more sharing.

In that 'web', or vortex, of relationships of what we call 'family' is an important element, perhaps the most tangible and important. It is supposed to bring out the best in us—love, caring, sharing, sacrifice, putting someone ahead of us in making choices and so on. But it also brings the worst too. The family is always identified with nepotism, discrimination in favor of relatives, or kith and kin. But it also is now the most single source of violence and wickedness in society, ranging from slaps, slighting, humiliation, jealousy, beatings, rapes, torture, and murders. In fact, among the causes for homicide the most casual and trivial are those that occur in the family, like simple scolding, scuffle over sharing TV access, sibling rivalry, spousal quarrels and so on. A parental scolding for low grades in school, or for a skimpy dress, used to evoke a sulk earlier; now, it could lead to suicide. A father taking to task a wayward son could be an invitation for a cold-blooded murder. Ill treatment, exploitation, tyranny and torture can be domestic too. In addition to outright violence, what is far more pervasive is indirect, subtler, vocal 'violence and mental torture'—constant nagging and nibbling, bullying, constant 'put-downing' and fault-finding, deliberate humiliation and so on. These take a heavier toll on self-respect and cohabitation. Repeated exposure to such actions can be mind-numbing, and lead to loss of dignity and self-worth. Unlike similar acts at work or on the street, there is no room or way to seek redress or relief. That makes their perpetrator more 'fearless' and emboldened. The 'victim' can be a spouse or a sibling or a servant; can be a child or teenager, or an adult or aged. The point is that in a confined and controlled setting like the home, even small acts both of kindness and cruelty acquire added intensity and effect. Few of us are truly not guilty of any kind of 'mental' violence or cruelty or torture in our life. Intimacy, it would seem, is no recipe for goodness. On the contrary, there is strong evidence that prolonged proximity, seeing each other without the cover of civility, sharing limited space becomes necessary, and the tendency to take each other for granted, to 'own' each other, and the feeling that we can get away with our bad behavior, might evoke some of our dark passions that are at war within. In modern families, the bond that held together old-fashioned extended families is now missing: respect for age and elders; common pooling of incomes and expenditure, helping each other in times of crisis and so forth. The children are left adrift. Theories and views have always varied on the natural state of the minds of children and adolescents: if they are moral or amoral; selfish like the rest, or a blank slate; hard-wired with 'moral grammar', or susceptible to allurement. Some put the child on a moral pedestal, and say he or she, until adolescence is instinctively empathetic, feels and responds to any pain, not only to his own, while others say a child is simply an-adult-yet-to-be. Some say our so-called 'upbringing' is really 'down-bringing', and that the best thing we can do, if we really care for our kids, is not to impose our imprint on them but help them to help themselves. Our practical experience does not lend itself to any generic judgments about how to raise a 'moral child'. In earlier times, parents and relatives were moral teachers; they used to tell moral stories, recite scriptural passages and epics and showed by their example how to judge right from wrong, and the worth and value of hard work, frugality, and integrity. It is no longer the case. Most parents are too busy with their own lives, work, parties, and pastimes. Children spend more waking time away from home and are more heavily influenced by their peers and friends. The syllabus, subjects and studies have little relevance or utility for moral grounding, character building and conflict resolution. The school teacher, an institution in earlier times, often a role model and counsellor no longer plays that part. He or she is often a subject of ridicule and derision. We dream of universal brotherhood but actually fratricide is one of the top homicides in the world. We cannot fall back upon the 'family' as a model for morality, nor should we project the 'nuclear family' on a global scale.

One of the words that often crops up in any serious discourse on aspects of modern life is 'crisis'. We talk of financial crisis, economic crisis, environmental crisis, climate crisis, political crisis, governance crisis, and so on. Every crisis is a moral crisis and every issue a moral issue, even death. We read about moral reasoning, moral judgment, and moral matrices. Morality, we are told, both binds and blinds: it binds us into groups, and blinds us to opposing groups and views. In today's world, morality is so adrift at sea that rarely does anyone admit even to one's own self that he is not moral, and if one does so, he intuitively lays the blame at someone else's door. If one is truly cornered, the escape route is to say that the other moral alternative is even worse. We have sought to replace our moral sense with moral reasoning. As Jonathan Haidt says, "We are just not very good at thinking open-mindedly about moral issues, so rationalist models end up being poor descriptions of actual moral psychology". In fact, what we face is not a moral crisis but a *morality in crisis*. Morality is in crisis because the very subject of morality, the human persona, has radically altered. Haidt says that today man is 90% chimp and 10% bee; the chimp representing selfishness, and the bee, sociability. We don't know what the blend was before, but today's mix is toxic. What is required at this point in human history is nothing short of a new conception and understanding of morality.

Morality is also in crisis because it has, on the one hand, become so fuzzy that we no longer can tell who is moral and who is not; and, on the other hand, almost everyone is compelled to be a participant, directly or indirectly, in immoral actions that hurt, humiliate, and harm other people. And technology has completely changed the moral context, making some obsolete, and raising new issues. Today, our temptations and provocations are different; how to handle them must also be different. We have to ask ourselves: if most of us are decent, caring and God-fearing, then from where is evil finding its sustenance and becoming stronger every day? If most of us are moral, even in the broadest sense, how come there is so much indifference, insensitivity, intolerance, indignity, bigotry, and pettiness in our world? Where is the 'good' going, leaving the world a planet where day after day horror after horror takes place? Our 'conceptual myopia' and moral ambiguity is a contributory cause. We posit that morality is time and space specific, that it has varied, and continues to vary, from culture to culture, and what is sinful in one context, is permissible in another. Hindu scriptures have long predicted the steep fall in moral conduct of man in the Kali Yuga. If it were so, how can there be a moral crisis in human conduct? In short, is marginalized morality, or being essentially evil, the natural condition of the contemporary human?

The real problem we face is that we are unable even to know how to distinguish moral crisis from moral failure, moral masquerade, moral activism, and moral cowardice. Most of us fall into the category of cowards according to Confucius, for often we know what is right but do not adhere to it. Much of our morality is simply legal. If we get the law on our side, whether by conforming to it or by bending it, we feel we are invincible and we do not fear evil-doing. A Chinese proverb says, 'Laws control the lesser man; right conduct controls the greater one'. We are also unsure what our rights and obligations as law-abiding-citizens are, as distinct from moral rights and duties. We have to bear in mind that while nature is, in and by itself, morally neutral, we must not see human morals as artificial, but as a legitimate part of the natural landscape. And given the fact that existence is nothing but a continuum of choices and chores, from the minute to the momentous, the question is: how do we inject the moral norm into normal life? If we cannot factor in morality or moral judgment into daily activity, our behavior will not change in the desired direction, and if that were to come to pass then both humankind and planet earth will remain gravely endangered. A good starting point, as a frame of reference, could be a Thoreau quote: "Do not be too moral. You may cheat yourself out of much life so. Aim above morality. Be not simply good, be good for something". That something can be many things; the connecting thread has to be to go beyond our own immediacy and importance. To rise 'above morality' is to rise above ourselves; to simply exchange places in every human situation; to put the common good ahead of personal pleasure.

No one can doubt the need to restore integrity in public life. But, like in the doctrine of dharma, conflicts and collisions crop up in the dust and din of competitive life. For example, how do we reconcile personal probity and professional integrity? And if one must choose between them, which one comes first? We must also address another critical issue, which concerns situations such as conformity, obedience to 'superior orders' and 'simply doing what we are paid to do'. So much wrong-doing, exploitation, suffering and evil is occurring in today's world that it requires special attention. It is not a new issue. Historians have long pondered over it, particularly when horrific events like the Holocaust, genocides, and ethnic mass murders take place. How could a small group of people exercise the psychological and ideological power over otherwise ordinary people to allow killing, torture, etc.? Such questions are also part of the larger issue of 'why do we behave badly'? What do we get out of it? But 'doing bad' for personal reasons, due to reasons like greed, passion, profit or vengeance is different from committing unimaginable atrocities like organized massacres, exterminations, revenge rapes, religious barbarity, and ethnic conflicts. Do men do such things because deep within they want to, or are they helpless, faced with an unacceptable alternative? Is it really necessary, or is it our appetite for more than 'our pound of flesh'? Is it just conventional obedience or is it our deep and dark longing for guts, gore and blood? Or, is it our inability to "make an omelet without wading thigh deep in the blood of chickens and wearing their entrails as a necklace".[55] We must also consider the issue of indirect or implicit moral culpability for the actions of other workers or employees in an organization, and of the acts of the institution itself. For instance, if you are an accountant in an arms factory, or in a company that makes pollutants and poisons which are then added to the food we eat or consume, can we be considered culpable, even if only marginally and peripherally? Diffusion and division of labor does not dilute, not to say negate, our share in guilt for what the collective entity does. One could also posit that we have to bear our share of the moral consequences since whatever is the nature of our work, it constitutes an input into the overall work of the company or entity. On the other hand, it can also be argued that one's actions are in no way connected to the harmful things the company makes and therefore one is freed from all consequences.

Our moral predicament, draining as it is, offers also an opening. However much we want to insulate ourselves, we are bombarded every day with moral issues. And we feel woefully inadequate to face them and do the right thing, which is what we want both instinctively and intellectually to do. Too often, before we have the time to think, time marches on and the decision gets made, but we have to live with the consequences. And too often we realize *ex post facto* that the decision or choice made should have been different in the light of the consequence. Many times, we are not even aware of all the factors that should have been weighed. Even when rational and carefully calibrated decisions are taken, they leave out important moral and ethical dimensions. We keep repeating, time and time again, the same action, as we do not know how to integrate a moral and ethical perspective into the decision-making process. The need of the hour at this stage in human evolution is what we might call 'moral decision-making', which comprises choices and decisions made on moral values, not necessarily, or only, on legality. The essayist Nassim Nicholas Taleb says, "My biggest problem with modernity may lie in the growing separation of the ethical and the legal". Our behavioral focus has shifted from the 'moral' to the 'legal', for the simple reason that crossing the legal line could be costly, whereas taking liberties with morality could allow us to 'let our hair down' without fear.

We have long been baffled by how exactly we reason through moral problems and how we judge others on the morality of their actions. Some seem to find it easier to resolve problems morally while others find it excruciating. What is even more intriguing is that the same person acts differently to similar temptations and provocations. Science is trying to solve the puzzle by studying the 'network of brain regions involved in mediating moral judgment'. The real answer is that it is a reflection of the ever-shifting state of the eternal 'war within'. Paradoxically, we can 'decide' morally by behaving morally. That is the way to intervene and influence the ebb and flow of that war.

One of the most often cited words in modern human discourse is 'law': law of the land, law-abiding, rule of law, fear of law, and so on. If we are on the right side of the law, we feel safe. It is the lock-up room and the prison cell we do not want to be in. If we were asked to choose between the pleasures of heaven and not going to an earthly jail, most would prefer the latter. The truth is that if we are content with legality, we are more likely to end on the side of modern-day evil, which is not technically illegal. Indeed, we must be prepared to be more moral than lawful. Every decision is situational and based on available and known facts, and every one of them involves and entails moral implications. Moral decision-making stretches, or modifies where necessary, the facts to include the potential and probable, but avoidable, harm or injury to someone else, or to the environment or nature, and to future generations. In making such decisions, we are often forced to choose between two values, such as choosing between telling the truth or saving a life; between the best interests of a family or of a community; and the interests of humanity and of the world as a whole. One has to harmonize context and content, keeping in mind the larger or common good. We might also have to choose between, or balance, our different duties, rights and responsibilities in different relationships and situations, like parents, family, friends, citizens, workplace, professional, religious, and so on. But however daunting this task might appear, at this time in human history, it is too critical to be sidestepped. For, as Dante Alighieri wrote in his *Divine Comedy* (1555), "the darkest places in hell are reserved for those who maintain their neutrality in times of moral crisis". Whether morality is innate or imposed, it (or the absence of it) has a huge bearing on human social behavior. Even if it is not part of human nature, it could be a part of *evolved* human nature. Further, complicating the issue, we also know that evil could emanate as much from intended good as from unintended evil, often inescapable despite the best of intentions. The question then arises: Must we be reconciled to, and surrender to the 'inevitability of evil'? Are we, the good men of the world, to reconcile ourselves to, to borrow a phrase from Albert Camus, 'mild, benevolent diabolism'?[56] Or can we truly become a moral, spiritual species, outgrow our animal roots, turn our passions into compassion, overcome divisive hate, learn to build bridges between man and man, and in so doing erase the chasm between man and God? The answer is simple: whoever we might be, even if what we see outside is but a reflection of what is inside us, we must fight evil, whatever its source or nature, with all our might. But we hardly make any effort—evading, explaining away, or excusing every evil. Even worse, so numb is our sensitivity that what most of us are worried about when joining forces with 'morality' or evil', is not whether it is right or wrong, but what our chances are of getting caught.

We need, if we are to proceed forward, some kind of benchmark and a point of both reference and departure. And we have to frame it in the broadest and farthest cosmic and evolutionary contexts. We must balance two imperatives: evolutionary theory is a theory of nature, not a moral prescription. But equally, no moral sense or moral theory can successfully ignore evolution's insights. One of the best summations comes from the pen of Thomas Huxley. He wrote: "The practice of that which is ethically best—what we call goodness or virtue—involves a course of conduct which, in all respects, is opposed to that which leads to success in the cosmic struggle for existence. In place of ruthless self-assertion, it demands self-restraint; in place of thrusting aside, or treading down, all competitors, it requires that the individual shall not merely respect, but shall help his fellows; its influence is directed, not so much to the survival of the fittest, as to the fitting of as many as possible to survive. It repudiates the gladiatorial theory of existence. It demands that each man who enters into the enjoyment of the advantages of a polity shall be mindful of his debt to those who have laboriously constructed it; and shall take heed that no act of his weakens the fabric in which he has been permitted to live. Laws and moral precepts are directed to the end of curbing the cosmic process and reminding the individual of his duty to the community, to the protection and influence of which he owes, if not existence itself, at least the life of something better than a brutal savage".[57]

The two practical principles ought to be: to avoid, if not minimize, any kind of harm to any sentient being; and strive to do the 'greatest good to the greatest number'. For moral decision-making, what we need is the trigger of moral motivation. And for that, what we require to do is to engage not only our logical/reasoning and deductive cognitive capacities of our brain, but also the intuitive, emotional, and latent spiritual capacities that spring from the energy and intelligence of our heart. We have to nurture consciously and continually within each of us a moral mindset, a mindset or a consciousness that is not hostage to the mind and which instinctively includes moral input into the process of decision-making. And we need to do it not only alone, but also collectively. Stray individuals or isolated groups, well-intentioned though they might be, are necessary but not sufficient. Most of us are moral sometime or the other, and some more often than others. Where we err is the lack of consistency. We need a critical mass for cultural change, which spreads not in a linear fashion but in a viral way. We need an elusive and indeterminate assemblage of men and women above an unknown threshold that, once crossed, generates self-propelling momentum and positively infects minds like a pandemic. We must also face up to a fundamental fallacy. Like much else that is human, here too we apply double, or even multiple standards. Most of us, as Bertrand Russell noted, have two kinds of morality: one we preach but seldom practice; the other we practice but do not (dare) preach. We even accept, if not acquiesce to, the massacres of civilians as *jus bellum justum* (the just war doctrine). Although we might think that it is governments that fight wars, we, as primary stakeholders and shareholders, are morally responsible. Although one might concede that some wars are ethically inevitable, the moral point also addresses when such wars should be brought to a close—what is called *jus post bellum* (justice after the war). Most politicians and decision-makers know more about when to start a war than how to wage it (*jus in bello*), than how and when to end it. As a result, they sow the seeds of more wars, as in the case of the First and Second World Wars. The circumstances that led to the latter are commonly attributed, among other things, to the harsh terms of the Treaty of Versailles of 1919, which brought an end to the First World War. And citizens, as 'owners' of governments, have a moral obligation to insure and ensure such fairness and humanness in a war.

We need a basket of rewards and penalties, incentives and disincentives to ensure that our individual actions contribute to the common good. Self-sanction is thus an implicit input for the common good. The specifics of shackles must also change in tune with changing times. At this juncture, we are by and large clinging to a moral code that no longer serves the purpose—which is to tame the 'natural' nature of man and make his participation in human society constructive, not destructive. Our understanding, even our cognizance of what is acceptable and unacceptable, what is appropriate and inappropriate, what is decent and deviant, what is good and what is bad, must mutate. It is because, with all our vulnerabilities and venality, most people want to play by the rules, as far as possible, and feel that they are decent people, and that their behavior is not immoral. And if our comprehension of morality remains static then our behavior will remain rooted in the current zone of comfort. If we do not believe that our way of life is socially injurious and morally offensive, then the best of us will stay the course, and avoid a course of behavioral mending and bending. We must bear in mind that in deciding what is moral, the simplest and safest choice is the 'larger good'. In the Mahabharata, the distinguished Vidura sums it up: "To save a family, abandon a man; to save the village, abandon a family; to save the country, abandon a village; to save the soul, abandon the earth".

On a parallel track, we have to design and nurture a new base and basis, a new fulcrum and foundation, a new paradigm and pattern, new rules and benchmarks of social adulation and opprobrium, recognition and rewards, adulation and ostracism, heroism and depravity. It must offer enough elbow room for individual initiative and self-interest, but must be subordinate to social interest, order, and justice. While we must strive towards a new moral platform, implicitly, unknowingly and even unconsciously, we are already adopting a different moral (or immoral!) code in our behavior that condones things like lying, cheating, cursing, profanity in public, gossiping, groping, malicious conduct, causing intentional in jury to others, and so on. But we still do not look at ourselves as 'bad' people. We are privy to and practice much of what we condemn by telling ourselves that these are 'social' evils, which have nothing to do with us. We lament the fall in values and standards, but adopt the same brand in our behavior; we can do that because our mind protests: 'What can I do; it is systemic!' We remain trapped in our mind and in our behavior. We must become better before we can behave better, and we cannot become better unless we behave better. The silver lining is that there is also a worldwide yearning — cutting across continents, political or ideological leaning, and social and cultural identities—for a new, less materialistic, more moral mode of life that revolves around compassion.

Monetary Affordability and Moral Accountability

Another emerging money–versus–morality factor with far-reaching implications is our ability to afford things which we could not afford before. Technological advances have drastically curtailed the costs of manufacture and we now need less money to acquire things we dreamt about before. The downside of these advances is the boost to consumer culture and to an economic system that relies on and encourages selfishness and runaway consumption; which has also meant a mad rush on earth's finite resources, particularly fossil fuels. With less money being needed, more people are travelling more often across the globe—we are even told that many of us might be able to buy a round trip ticket to the moon in twenty odd years! And, more people are buying more needless things more often. We are no longer satisfied with local produce or food; we want to taste the cuisine of distant lands. Goods and services produced in one part of the world are increasingly available in all parts of the world. We are no longer content to read or hear about them; we want to experience them ourselves. Some even argue that the accumulation of capital is the accumulation of environmental degradation. The root of the problem lies in our mode of production. Capitalism is an economic system that is impelled to pursue never-ending growth, which requires the use of ever-greater quantities of resources. It is not simply, as we might assume, a question of our having enough money, legally or illegally, earned or inherited in any economic activity. It has ecological, environmental, and intergenerational implications on a cosmic scale. Although we cannot altogether desist from acquiring or travelling, it is important, however, to bear in mind that it might well have an effect on the depletion of nonrenewable resources—such as oil, iron ore, bauxite, zinc, and the rare earths (used in many electronic gadgets, including smart phones as well as smart bombs). It is not merely a matter between 'me' and 'my' money—the third party is the world at large and its future sustainability. In fact, whether there can be any such thing as 'mine' is itself questionable. The fact is that not only does money *not* grow on trees but also, there is no correlation between division of labor and distribution of dividends. There is always someone else, more than one in most cases, involved in any activity through which we earn money, and what we think of as 'my money' comes out of common labor. How can we ever be sure that that money is not actually stolen from the rightful share of another person? For example, every luxury purchase is tantamount to taking food away from the mouths of thousands. For every year, it is estimated, 10 million people die due to hunger-related causes, and every few seconds a child dies due to starvation. Both from the environmental perspective and moral point of view, all expenditure, save what is necessary for meeting basic needs, is 'theft'. Careful examination on such lines should be an input into every decision-making process.

The seductive shadow of money also falls on spirituality. Generally money is viewed as unspiritual, tainting, and dirty. Jesus said "For what shall it profit a man, if he shall gain the whole world, and lose his own soul?" We have seen how corrupting money has been in the world of fake gurus and pseudo-*sadhus*, but even with serious spiritual seekers. Money is still a means for survival, but it somehow is more corrosive and muddying in the earthly spiritual world. It starts slowly but soon it backstops and overshadows everything they do. The need for money increases even as these 'spiritual godmen' get more and more money from more and more 'moneyed' men of marginal integrity, and money-flow and money management become their main preoccupation, sidelining their spiritual quest and teaching. At the same time, the scope for more money in the hands of truly spiritual masters is enormous. Although spiritualism is not immune to the corrupting influence of money, there is one redeeming feature. Many of the rich and ultra-rich, who are normally tight-fisted and are far from philanthropic (barring some honorable exceptions), are generous when it comes to donations to public places of worship, and religious, spiritual, and humanitarian causes. Whatever might be the motives, money, even if ill-gotten, then gets sanitized and sanctified and flows in the right direction. It serves one of the most important imperatives in public policy today: to shift money being spent for ostentatious living, to satiate consumerist appetite and military purposes, towards helping the needy, disadvantaged, marginalized, and for spiritual growth, which then becomes better behavior. The human predisposition is never to be satisfied with satiation. As the Buddha once said, even if it rained gold coins we wouldn't have enough to satisfy people's desire for sensual pleasures. Still, we should be wary of excessive backlash. Undue fear of today's pseudo-spirituality—about which Hindu scriptures warned of in the context of moral decline in our current Kali Yuga—could also turn out to be throwing the baby out with the bath water. We cannot turn away from the spiritual path but we must bear in mind that the path is to find the way within. According to the Dalai Lama, "Spirituality is food for the mind, and different religions are very necessary for different mental dispositions". Spiritual advancement is not necessarily an unworldly, esoteric objective. It could, by making us more balanced, also empower us to use that which distinguishes modern civilization from its predecessors—technological, or 'mechanical power'—even more efficiently and in the right direction. The essence of spirituality is simplicity, service, and living in harmony. It is closer to the psychic than the purely physical. It is to 'have' without owning or possessing, 'doing' without expectation, 'leading' without seeking to control. It must serve social priorities and alter our condescending, if not contemptuous, attitude towards nature.

We must bridge the gap between a responsible and responsive social life and a spiritual life. If one's way of living is socially irrelevant or injurious, then that person cannot qualify as a truly spiritual person, however deeply religious or 'good' he might be. That is what the scriptures themselves proclaim. It is said that 'they serve God well who serve His creatures'. Mother Teresa, in our own time, had put this to practice. One of the oft-quoted Indian aphorisms is *Manava seve madhava seva*—service to man is service to God. Gandhi wrote, "I am endeavoring to see God through service of humanity; for I know that God is neither in heaven, nor down below, but in everyone". All these are noble thoughts, but we all know that most people find it much easier to serve God than man. We find it less wrenching to give to a place of God than to a school, or a hospital, or orphanage, or an old-age home. It does not matter that the very man we don't 'trust' stands between divine 'donation' and its earthly use. That is partly because deep inside we do not trust our fellow humans. If we are not 'giving' to God, our mind suddenly throws up questions: is it a genuine cause? How can I be sure that my money will be well spent, for the dedicated purpose?

Money can be very spiritual in its essence—everything is. It is up to each of us to cleanse our intentions and motivations surrounding money. We may profit financially if our intention is to add to the prosperity of the world. In this way, making a profit can actually be beautiful and moving—we can touch and heal others, and in turn we can equally be reciprocated. When we have more money, we may be able to do more to increase the global sharing of prosperity—not just for ourselves and our immediate families, but for everyone in our town, our city, our country, our continent, and perhaps even the entire world. We could build hospitals and schools, provide medicines to the poor, fund important research, or simply be able to give more products and services away for free to those who have less money than us. The possibilities are limitless.

The spirituality the world needs calls us to connect, to commit, to live life fully, to charm and make sacred every activity, in the understanding that there is nothing that can exist away from the governing principle of the 'Great Ground'. The spiritual in our life is not only defined by the kind of action we take but by the mindset with which we do it. It is about living each moment completely, mentally, emotionally, and physically, giving of ourselves and turning our attention and innate power to each action, giving this quality even to the most routine and minutest things. Everyone and everything is connected, and springs from and finally merges into the 'Great Ground', variously described as the Divine, Nature, Universe or Cosmos. The direction and goal of human effort have been derailed by the paralyzing asymmetry and the deep divide between our material mastery and spiritual malnourishment, and what we might call inclusive ambivalence about the sacred and the secular. We have among us many who believe in what is called superstition and the supernatural, but who also call themselves modern and scientific; and there are scientists who believe in things they cannot prove. As Martin Luther King Jr. said, we must realize that "enlarged material powers spell enlarged peril if there is not proportionate growth of the soul".[58] And that sacredness does not lie in any out-of-the-world or religious experience but in the chasteness and purity in everything we do in this very world. Any act can be either sacred or secular, or profane, depending on what it is meant for. As King said, "When the 'without' of man's nature subjugates the 'within', dark storm clouds begin to form in the world". We have to work from both directions, without and within. Although both the worlds, the one within and the one outside, are intertwined, the headwaters clearly are within. As the Arbinger Institute's book *The Anatomy of Peace* puts it, "So if we are going to find lasting solutions to difficult conflicts or external wars we find ourselves in, we first need to find our way out of the internal wars that are poisoning our thoughts, feelings, and attitudes toward others. If we can't put an end to the violence within us, there is no hope for putting an end to the violence without".[59] Man's longing for peace (*shanti* in Sanskrit) is timeless and it will remain so. The fact is we will never have a state of permanent peace outside unless there is peace within. For, "ultimately, we have just one moral duty: to reclaim large areas of peace in ourselves, more and more peace, and to reflect it towards others. And the more peace there is in us, the more peace there will be in our troubled world".[60] To have more peace in us we need to find ways to go within and help contain and combat the evil that lies there.

As the book *The Anatomy of Peace* says, "Seeing an equal person as an inferior object is an act of violence". We have to rein in the demands of the material world; we have to awaken our spiritual side. With relentless bombardment from so many different distracting sources, we have become dysfunctional. Our ability to focus is severely impaired and our 'attitudinal skills are fundamentally under siege'. We are, despite our delusions of glory and grandeur, 'brainy weaklings', or in Colin Wilson's words, 'thinking pigmies'. Isaac Newton rued that we are like children amusing themselves playing with pebbles on the beach while the great ocean of truth lies all undiscovered before us. And that is so because it is supposed to be so. Whether we are a 'fallen god' or 'god in the becoming' in the words of theosophist and founder of anthroposophy (the wisdom of human beings), Rudolf Steiner, we have no way of knowing. Truth be told, with all the weight and might of scriptural thought, the uncommon ability to distance ourselves from our selves and to objectively look back at what man has wrought on earth since his debut days of descent from an earlier creature some three million years ago, the human is a disillusioned animal. He is not sure if he is intrinsically a 'civilized brute' or, as Prof. Higgins sums up, "we're all savages, more or less". Man is perplexed about his own behavior. But that 'disillusionment' is itself a delusion: the delusion about our 'natural' nature and unvarnished identity. Billions and billions of words exist, some very profound, and others banal, about who we are at our core, about our divine essence and original sin, about the wages of evolution and costs of culture. But none of them stick or satisfy even our severely stymied powers of perception and reflection. We don't know but want to know; that is because 'knowing' is not always the way. As Taoism puts it, 'you can't know it, but you can be it'. Not only that, but the instrument with which we want to know is itself skewed. That instrument is the brain/mind, which is inducing and enticing us to do things that channel our vital energy in the wrong direction. None other than the Buddha, who delved deeper into the causes of human misery than anyone else, said, "All wrongdoing arises because of the mind. If mind is transformed, can wrongdoing remain?"

Schadenfreude, the Modern Pandemic

Whichever way we might act or react contextually, man is essentially a pleasure-seeking animal; we instinctively yearn for pleasure and avoid pain. That does not stop us from mixing the two; deriving pleasure from pain, and pain from pleasure, and getting addicted to both, or to a blend of the two. Masochism (pain from pleasure) and melancholy (pleasure from being sad) are connected. It also often happens that in life, one man's pleasure causes another man's pain. From the ancient Greeks, through 17th- and 18th-century British philosophers, to 20th-century psychologists, this hedonistic or pleasure principle has come to dominate efforts of scholars to understand people's motivation. Epicurean philosophy sprang from the attainment of pleasure, which was described as 'the beginning and the end of blessed life'. It is the basic motivational assumption of theories across all areas of psychology. While it is commonplace and conventional wisdom to say that we turn towards pleasure and turn away from pain, in actuality, human motivational behavior is more complex. Although we tend to view them as opposites, they are the two sides of the same coin. One can easily switch from one state to another. Alfred Hitchcock, the master of suspense, said, "Give them pleasure—the same pleasure they have when they wake up from a nightmare... Always make the audience suffer as much as possible". Scientists say that actually parts of the neural pathways for the two perceptions overlap. We are among the very few in nature who deliberately derive pleasure from others' pain. For us, it is not enough to succeed—others must fail. It is this twisted trait, our greatest moral failing, which has come to play a stellar role in contemporary life. From the Roman gladiatorial blood-and-gore combats to public hangings that people travelled from far to participate in, to our latest terrorist beheadings of hostages and the popularity of gruesome YouTube™ videos, we all show a voyeuristic streak of getting a kick out of others' torment. It is not only interesting but also titillating. This was what Edmund Burke possibly had in mind when he wrote, "There is no spectacle we so eagerly pursue as that of some uncommon and grievous calamity; so that whether the misfortune is before our eyes, or whether they are turned back to it in history, it always touches with delight".[61] Burke held that the pleasure we derive from others' suffering—our 'aesthetic pleasure in the terrifying'—was a 'brute and perverse fact of human nature'. The only thing we can question is the association with the brute: we are brutal, not brute-like, in our behavior.

Studies have shown that the feeling of joy at seeing someone else fail or suffer is so commonplace that we would be inclined to believe it is a basic biological response in humans. It was always a part of human propensity. The *Book of Proverbs* has this caution: "Rejoice not when thine enemy falleth, and let not thine heart be glad when he stumbleth. Lest the Lord see it, and it displease him, and he turn away his wrath from him". The modern malaise is *Schadenfreude*, a German word that literally means 'harm-joy', or pleasure derived from the misfortunes of others. The philosopher Arthur Schopenhauer remarked, "... it is *Schadenfreude*, a mischievous delight in the misfortunes of others, which remains the worst trait in human nature. It is a feeling which is closely akin to cruelty, and differs from it, to say the truth, only as theory from practice".[62] To feel envy is human, but to enjoy other people's misfortune is diabolical. While humankind and human culture have long harbored sadists of all sorts, their numbers have greatly multiplied in modern times, and they have become more sophisticated. We encounter sadism in movies, entertainment, even sports. Our fascination with crime and horror stems from this. Glory and gory are mixed up. In modern sports, in even the so-called 'gentleman's game' of cricket, people have been seriously injured while playing. Yet, the rules of the game have remained unchanged. In 2014, an Australian cricketer died after being hit on the neck by a bouncer. There was much shock, tears, and touching ceremonies but the lethal delivery of the ball stayed and the game goes on. Experts argued that without such a risk the game would lose its sheen. Put differently, people won't turn up at the stadium, or turn on the TV, and the sponsors and cricket boards will lose money. No matter it might happen again and more people might die. The blame is put on the players: if they did have protective gear, then their reflexes have slowed down! The audience, the spectators who fill the stadiums, and those sitting before the TV, that is 'we, the people', don't want changes. They, and we, like it, even if 'occasionally' someone else gets killed—that is part of the game, like a soldier going to battle. And if the rules are changed, it would mean terrible losses and we will be deprived of the visual and visceral thrill and thrall of anticipating someone getting hurt or slain right before our eyes. The 'extremeness' of American football (*National Football League*, NFL) is well known. A report said that "nearly every current NFL player can expect to suffer from chronic traumatic encephalopathy, a degenerative disease that leads to memory loss, impaired judgment, depression, and dementia".[63] Turning to the media gives us a thrill and takes our mind off the tedium and irritation of daily life. The games are not safer but we still want to voyeuristically partake in the violence on the screen, perhaps partly to avoid facing up to the far greater mayhem churning all around us. In fact, in a strange way, we are more compassionate on the screen in front than in the real world before us. Many of us often walk or drive past horrors and tragedies without even a second glance, while we are moved to tears watching similar events on TV or in the theater. The screen makes the experience 'hyper-real'. Whatever we experience while watching, it does not end when we turn it off. All those thoughts and feelings seep into our consciousness and adversely affect the course of the 'war within'.

The main message of all this is two-fold: one, increasingly, the main source of the appeal of competitive sport and the mainstay of entertainment is a shade of *Schadenfreude*; two, the participation, visually or vicariously, in acts of cruelty has become pleasurable, even necessary for man to face the drudgery and decadence, the ennui and emptiness of daily life. For, as author JK Rowling said, 'to hurt is as human as to breathe'.[64] That is perhaps why all of us should fervently put our hope in Tolstoy's words—"Here I am alive, and it's not my fault, so I have to try and get by as best I can without hurting anybody until death takes over" (*War and Peace*). A central feature of the pleasure-in-others'-misfortune notion is the belief that the other person *deserves* his or her misfortune. What is truly unsettling is that we cannot dismiss this phenomenon as an aberration, or dub people who entertain such thoughts as deviants or mentally twisted people. They are among us; they *too* are us. According to psychological scientist Erin Buckels, "Some find it hard to reconcile sadism with the concept of 'normal' psychological functioning, but our findings show that sadistic tendencies among otherwise well-adjusted people must be acknowledged. These people aren't necessarily serial killers or sexual deviants but they gain some emotional benefit in causing or simply observing others' suffering".[65] Most of us watch movies with a lot of violence, killing, cruelty, and blood-letting. And when we read reports of some favorite celebrity getting into trouble our instinct is mostly wicked titillation, rarely empathy. Does it mean that deep within we are all infected by the malaise of *Schadenfreude?* One of the most basic conflicts in the human psyche is the friction between selfish impulses and self-control. When we see something good happening to someone else, many of us would stop and mutter to ourselves: *Why not me?!*

If God Does Not Exist...

In popular perception, God, morality, and religion are virtually inseparable and indistinguishable. The fact though is that they are not identical, but intertwined and interdependent. It is possible to believe in God without being religious, and to be independently moral without any kind of allegiance. There is no one 'God', although most agree on His attributes; and when it comes to worship, every religion depicts a different picture. There is no general definition of religion, or of what true religion is, and of what false religion is; nor is there any agreement relating to valid religious values. Nor even about what we mean by the truth of religion. Yet, what we conjure as 'religion' plays a huge part in human life. The same thing goes for morality, too; we cannot agree what it means; nor on any criteria to judge moral behavior. Even if we do not know most often what is right and what is wrong, we still want to be, or known to be wanting to be, moral, good, upright, and so on. Without getting bogged down with questions such as when, how and why religion gained its foothold in human consciousness, we can safely say that it has been a part of human history. The same thing can be said with equal force about morality. We cannot pin a date of its entry or what need it was intended to fill. More important is the question how the three—God, morality, and religion—have affected each other. Some say that a principal purpose of religion is to enable man to lead a moral life. And that man stumbled upon morality as a way to survival as a tribe or community. If religion is understood to mean, in Alfred North Whitehead's words, "a system of general truths which have the effect of transforming character when they are sincerely held and vividly apprehended",[66] then one must conclude that it has not yielded the desired result; man remains untransformed, or one might say 'mis-transformed'.

Some say that religion is both necessary and sufficient to lay a moral foundation for an ethical life; some say that it necessary but not sufficient; others, that it has no need or place as a moral base. Some might be tempted even to argue that religion, or the way that it is put into practice, makes people dogmatic, intolerant, and that it actually subverts morality. Some scientists suggest that 'religious experiences shrink part of the brain' and some other studies show that 'having a strong religious belief acts as a buffer against anxiety', and that it has a calming, egalitarian effect. The fact is that the way such views are expressed bristle with value judgments, and it depends on what we consider as religious mindset, as distinct from any religion, and what we qualify as moral behavior. The essential question is what we might call religious outlook: Can we say that, 'if one is disposed to be good, religion helps'? And, on the other hand, 'If one is already drawn towards bad, would religion actually make that person more of a menace'? The way it is churning in our mind and the extent to which it is sundering the social fabric in the world, this is a vital issue to ponder over in the context of the war within. Which side is religion on? How are the religious people in the world influencing the endogenous war? Whom are they aiding and abetting? Are they, through their beliefs and behavior, pouring fuel onto the fire, or are they moderating and alleviating human passions like anger, avarice, and aggression that are so much in the play in today's world? Do religious traits and practices like prayer, pilgrimages, worship and other rituals soften our ugly side, or do they make us feel intoxicated, condescending, special, superior, and safe, that our relationship with other people actually gets worse? While it is unfair and sweeping to say that religion makes people bad, or that it strengthens the evil inside us, what we cannot ignore is that, in the words of Blaise Pascal, "Men never do evil so completely and cheerfully as when they do it from religious conviction".

Of all 'savageries', it is the religious kind that is hardest to understand. We cannot also ignore that religion has immense potential to make us confuse self-serving with 'serving God', confuse prayer with piety, self-righteousness with self-esteem.

An element of the paradox is our relationship with God in human life. Throughout the ages, many of the world's greatest thinkers have wrestled with the concept and question of God. While the vast majority of people in the world proudly proclaim themselves as men of faith and as believers, and undertake many activities in that capacity, a growing number, at the same time, seem prepared to incur divine wrath and after-life punishment in the pursuit of materialistic possessions and the good things of life. And they are many who are devout and immersed in many religious rituals with sincerity, and who hurt and humiliate fellow-humans, selectively or routinely, and see no conflict between the two. Many people identify morality with theistic belief but not with benign behavior towards other people, particularly those who cannot retaliate. The Nobelist Steven Weinberg said, "With or without [religion], you would have good people doing good things and evil people doing evil things. But for good people to do evil things, that takes religion". Some suggest that "It's not so much that religion makes people do evil, it's that it provides a convenient excuse for nearly anything, and that lowers the bar for committing bad behavior we might otherwise avoid. So while religion isn't required for people to be jerks, it may perpetuate jerky behavior and make it more widespread".[67] We also seek and find explanations and excuses for our own prejudices and polluted minds in what religious texts say, or are interpreted as. Today's terrorists, not only the religious types, too, echo the same line. The point is, right or wrong, if we believe we are fighting for God, or that God is on our side, or that we have earned God's support, then any of us can become a savage or a saint, a maniac or a mahatma. God plays multiple, sometimes contradictory roles in today's human society: He offers both hope and escape. We pronounce Him as both eternal and dated, as both timeless and the one whose time has passed. Many have so much faith in His justness and justice that they put up with rank injustice, which also allows the greedy and guilty to go scot-free. He is within us all and witnesses the battle between good and evil but He does not take sides and thus allows us to be evil. What on earth can we do with Him?! Voltaire famously said, after seeing the havoc the French Revolution had wrought on France, "If God did not exist, He would have to be invented". Can we say that now? For one, God very much 'exists', there is no need for invention. If a time comes when man really and finally gives up on God, tens of millions will be dead or killed almost overnight.

It is unlikely that any new revelations or insights could be raised any more now. We will never have conclusive and universally accepted answers to questions such as whether God created man or not. Or, if He exists or not. Or, why He 'allows' evil in the world. The more pertinent point is that the 'idea' of God can play a transformational role in human life. Whitehead said that 'the purpose of God is the attainment of value in the temporal world'. The question of value is at the heart of morality. Whatever has been the impact and influence of religion on the human mind and human history, the fact is that many religions do have value frameworks regarding personal behavior in the form of *shastras* (laws), commandments and codes of conduct, meant to guide adherents in determining between right and wrong. These include the Triple Gems of Jainism, Judaism's Halacha, Islam's Sharia, Catholicism's Canon Law, Buddhism's Eight-fold Path, and Zoroastrianism's 'good thoughts, good words, and good deeds' concept, among others. These frameworks are outlined and interpreted by various sources such as holy books, oral and written traditions, and religious leaders. These have remained mainly in the domain or religious and spiritual spheres, but they have faced serious obstacles when trying to enter the 'temporal world'. A principal reason is that it is through the medium of the mind that we have sought to relate to them. Another cause is that we have distanced and differentiated God from man and come to believe that so long as we are nice to God it doesn't matter if we are nasty in our behavior.

We cannot long wander around any serious metaphysical speculation or even materialistic mindset without encountering the age-old questions: Must morality be grounded in God? And can there be 'religion' without God? Has science made religion obsolete? Some say that goodness is good enough, a life well-lived is a good life, and that God is at best an add-on that makes it easier to be virtuous. Some, like Einstein, say that they believe in God not as a person but as an 'illimitable superior spirit'. Dostoyevsky's Ivan Karamazov says, "If God does not exist, then everything is permissible". The implied statement is that 'God must exist, because morality is a must'. Some also draw a distinction between 'is permissible' and 'ought to be permissible'. Nietzsche took a different stance, and by pronouncing the death of God he implicitly said morality too need not exist. What all moral philosophers and humanists have grappled with is where and how to draw a line in our conscious behavior in the absence of universal and unchanging moral values. We must also keep in mind that the ultimate purpose of 'new morality' is that in any attempt to create a fabric of human destiny we cannot escape, however elusive and effervescent it might be, the moral dimension. Nor can we take off the table what Armand Nicholi called 'the question of God', independent and irrespective of religion. The point is we will never be short of people who can passionately and persuasively argue in favor of or otherwise about the existence, nature, purpose, and power of the divine. Even if one sees God, another can dismiss it as a visual hallucination. In very simple but profound, even poignant, terms, the sense of God for the vast majority of mankind is nothing else than another name and form of hope, as much a part of their lives as any other living person; and this is so despite all the hardships, misery, inequity, and injustice they might experience in their lives. If God is dead, they too are dead. And it is so too, regardless of who we are individually, sinner or saint, villain or victim, oppressor or oppressed, rich or poor. And their faith in the relevance of God is larger and higher than their allegiance to any religion. They are not interested in issues such as religious atheism or theistic irreligion. Or, in issues like whether God is a person or a force, entity or energy, or about the attributes of God and how to reconcile the relevance of the divine with the reality of the wretchedness of the world. God is beyond religion; in one sense, He is infinite, impersonal, abstract; in another, He is particular and very personal; even if He will not talk, He listens, as opposed to humans. We cannot see Him but He can—and does—see us. Those who know nothing of the substance of any religion or even of their own religion, those who know nothing of any scripture or sacred text, still bow before God, sometimes seek nothing, oftentimes the smallest thing. The important thing is that they feel God's 'presence', and feel equipped to face the world, solaced, comforted, renewed, ready to endure suffering. God may have sworn to protect the righteous but the unrighteous too can seek God's grace or mercy or help. Hindu scriptures are full of stories where the demons pray to God and obtain boons which, so to say, boomerang on Him!

One of the striking paradoxes of contemporary life is the coexistence of a world soaked in materialism, selfishness, avarice, and bigotry, and the growing popularity of places of worship. We can look at it, or rationalize it, in various ways. One, that a sinner needs and turns to God more than a saint. Two, for God, everyone is the same. Three, there is no good man or bad man; only good deed and bad deed. Fourth, we are all playing different roles in the cosmic drama. Lastly, this is all the mischief of *maya*; it is all appearance, our mistaking the unreal for the real. And so on, so forth. Whichever is the truth, the fact is that those who defy the dictum of God—who are corrupt and unethical, and who commit every conceivable crime or sin—do not find any qualms or contradictions in seeking God's help while violating His word. The weak and the meek, the wretched and the ostracized, the downtrodden and the deprived, they are the ones who have reason to cavil, but they don't. Although being the ones most victimized, they don't ask questions like 'How can we reconcile the apparent ascendancy of evil with the existence, omnipotence or justness of God?' It is not that they have no expectations, frustrations or unfulfilled desires, but none of that shakes their divine disposition. They may not see or speak to God; they might not be able to recite a single verse from any scripture, but He is simply integral to their lives. They forgive Him even if their prayers are not answered in the way they wish. In one sense, God is more a part of the lives of those who negate or mock Him than of those who believe in Him. For, one needs more knowledge to disbelieve than to believe. Belief is a matter of the heart; disbelief is a matter of the mind. In either case, the divine has always been inseparable from human consciousness. As biologist Edward Wilson says (*Consilience*, 1998), "The human mind evolved to believe in the gods. It did not evolve to believe in biology. Acceptance of the supernatural conveyed a great advantage throughout prehistory when the brain was evolving". What Wilson calls 'mind' could also be described in broader terms as 'consciousness'. It is another matter that that very 'consciousness' now calls God dated, defunct, even inefficient, and wants to take His place. And since he does not know exactly how God looks like, man does the next best—make himself into a form of life variously described as supernatural being, supramental being, superman, transhuman, overman, etc. Some say that man is an unfinished product, a transitional being, deliberately left that way by God as a kind of challenge to human ingenuity and sagacity.

Underlying all conceptions of the divine is the tendency to look at everything with man as the epicenter and the center of creation, which leads us to look at God also in human terms, to imagine Him in a human form. For example, in Hinduism, God's earliest avatars are other creatures like the fish (*Matsya*), the tortoise (*Kurma*), the boar (*Varaha*), and half-man-half-animal (*Narasimha*). God could have chosen, omnipotent as He is, to do what He had to do but instead opted to take the form of non-humans to tell us that all creatures are equal to Him and that He has no particular preferential form. This can also be viewed as symbolic of the path of evolution which envisions that animal life first appeared in the ocean, then turned amphibious at some point in time, and from these developed terrestrial life of lesser orders, to more advanced forms of carnivores, to less advanced humanoid forms, and finally to man today. But in general, the message from both scriptural and scientific thought is that man is the God's finest—and highest—creation, and, at the same time, as Thomas Aquinas famously described, God is man's 'beatitude', his highest blessing, and aspiration. They also say, in varying degrees of emphasis and equivocation, that the final aim—indeed the manifest destiny of human life—is to unite with god, not in flesh and blood, but in spirit or as a soul, which we also say is exclusive to the human. No other form of life, however virtuous and noble, can at death dissolve into divinity. From that perspective, god is the logical 'satisfaction of human desire'. We are not striving for the imperative of consciousness-change; we are aiming at erasing bodily imperfection and impermanence, which science in essence equates with 'being god'. In short, while admonishing God as a 'failed god', we are turning ourselves into 'fake gods'. The fact is that our quest for bodily invincibility and existential eternity is directly against the laws of nature and is bound to deeply destabilize the direction of human evolution.

Whatever are the underlying factors, everyone, even the worst of offenders, bemoans the decline of moral values of modern society, that the world is in a bad shape, that man has become more self-centric than ever, that evil is both banal and brazen, that money rules the roost, and so on. The primary reason why everyone, both the virtuous and the wicked, can, as objectively as they could, say such things and still lead guiltless immoral or amoral lives is because we all have different perceptions of what morality is, or could be, in the modern world. We lead such conditioned lives—conditioned by society, by law, by culture, by time, by religion—that the question comes up: How much moral space does an individual really have in organizing and conducting his or her life and in dealing with other people? Whatever we are witness to in the world—the lawlessness, crime, callousness, cruelty, depravity—, is that all because of or despite the conditioning? Are we like the animal in the zoo, more violent in confinement than in the wilderness? Put differently, are we less human because of what culture, State, and scriptures induce or enforce us to do? Are we, in Rousseau's celebrated phrase, a 'noble savage' or a 'civilized brute', which means in either case we are not our true selves? But then, one could also argue that being different from the original is not necessarily unwelcome; the question is, what has that difference made us out to be? If we, for example, had remained hunter-gatherers or agriculturists, would we—and the world—have been better off? That again raises the question: what is 'better-off'? Few will demur that the physical quality of human life, in terms of what we need to do to stay alive and to ward off disease and debility and hard labor, has incomparably improved.

The debate is about morality, the implicit assumption being that modern materialistic human society is more violent and evil than that of any of our predecessors. Some disagree with this presumption and say that even prehistoric humans were not exactly peaceable creatures and clobbered each other. On the contrary, according to people like Steven Pinker, ours is the most progressive and peaceful of times. But the irony is that they also say that we face more existential threats than ever before. How a society at peace can face threats to its own survival is strange. As they say, facts are stranger than fiction. In any case, the fact is that morality *per se* is not static, and is sensitive to the passage of time. And the fact also is that the sheer act or art of living entails doing things so radically different from our ancestors that moral values and norms must also stay in step for an orderly society. But at the same time, we cannot get away from the reality that we are human, and we must consider what that means in terms of morality. Although we too are animals, higher and haughty, clearly all through evolution the character of human society has been fundamentally different from that of other creatures. For example, however much we might admire and be inspired, we cannot function like an anthill or a beehive, simply because we are not ants or bees. Since we claim that we are the highest form of life on earth, our conduct should also be commensurate. There is also a general sense that the traditional values and criteria we have long used to divide 'good' and 'bad' behavior need a complete overhaul. The classical contours that defined good and bad are more blurred than ever before. One of the major reasons is that almost everything we do, wrongly do, or even do not do, can have a global, even generational, impact. The old saying concerning ecological connectivity, that the flap of a wing of a butterfly in the Amazon could trigger a tidal wave in the Andamans, offers a snapshot even to human life. Nothing is personal, private, isolated or insulated anymore; we no longer have the comfort of autonomy or anonymity. It is the realization that the human way of life, emanating primarily from the construct of the human form of life, is, in the very scheme of nature, 'naturally' and fundamentally different from that of other animals. While that has been the underlying intent, the specifics have varied from culture to culture, community to community, country to country, religion to religion, and from time to time. What is crime in one corner is not necessarily a crime everywhere, and what is sin is not always a sin—it can even becomes sacred in the eye of another. Blood sports were not only legal but major forms of entertainment in ancient Rome. Killing for pleasure has always been a favorite pastime in human culture. Many societies have also legalized extreme forms of public torture and execution, as was the case in Europe before the 18th century. History records many cultures that condoned painful forms of body modification.

Nexus with Nature

A major dimension of our awakened sense of morality relates to our nexus with nature. Nature itself is essentially amoral. Much of our misery and many of our problems largely stem from our alienation and estrangement from nature. The words we hear often are that we have 'mastered' or 'conquered nature'. Man will be less than man if he succumbs to nature; but if he tramples upon it he risks inviting its mighty fury. We have come to identify our sense of pride and progress, supremacy and superiority on earth as being synonymous with defiance, even degradation, of nature. In the words of the anthropologist Loren Eiseley, "It is with the coming of man that a vast hole seems to open in nature, a vast black whirlpool spinning faster and faster, consuming flesh, stones, soil, minerals, sucking down the lightning, wrenching power from the atom, until the ancient sounds of nature are drowned in the cacophony of something which is no longer nature, something instead which is loose and knocking at the world's heart, something demonic and no longer planned—escaped, it may be—spewed out of nature, contending in a final giant's game against its master".[68] The governing principle of Mother Nature is interconnectivity, interdependence, harmony, and coexistence of all kinds of life on earth, and sharing of its space, predator and prey alike… what biologists call *biodiversity*. While plurality and diversity is the hallmark of nature, our signature is to undermine and erode this very biodiversity. To some extent, a measure of exploitation of nature and its bounty is unavoidable for even the primitive way of human life. More than what man actually does, it is the *way* of his doing that is the problem. Ancient societies and native communities also harnessed nature and its biodiversity to eke out a livelihood. But, even while killing their prey, they were respectful. Instead of showing sensitivity, the 'civilized' man is condescending, if not contemptuous. Instead of reverence, he is arrogant. And unless we set this right, nothing else will yield the desired result.

Humans arose from nature, and lived in the natural environments to which evolution had adapted them. But, as human community and culture developed into the complex, intensely technological milieu of the modern day, humans have become increasingly separated from nature in their daily lives. Whatever might be our civilizational accomplishments, we must acknowledge that, after the nearly-two-million-year march since the advent of our species on earth, we are no longer the 'living being' intended by nature, or would have been in the natural course of evolution. We are on a collision course with nature. Even if that itself is the intent of nature or God, the fact remains that human life has so fundamentally altered over time that it has disturbed the balance of nature and its capability to adjust to such disturbances. 'Environmental crisis' is not only cataclysmic climate change, rising sea levels, pollution, resource depletion, unseasonal weather, and growing vulnerability to droughts, forest fires, flash floods, *et al.* At its core, the crisis revolves around our conception of nature 'as a service economy, dedicated to providing tolerable weather, edible food, drinking water, and breathable air to humans'. And one might add, 'to make available inexhaustible resources of minerals and metals, and to ungrudgingly accept and absorb all that humans choose to discard or excrete'. Even if one does not believe, as the Gaia hypothesis argues, that the earth is a single 'living' organism, we know that without the earth we cannot stand on our two feet. And just as we want to take care of the building we live in, similarly, the earth too needs to be taken care of.

Scientists have been talking about 'self-aware artificial intelligence (AI)', telling us that robots and humans could fuse, that we could, somewhere in the not-too-distant future, 'download' our consciousness into a machine and be independent of our body, and that the future doesn't need us, the man of the moment. But the point is, what kind of robot or AI will merge into what kind of human? We can now obtain a gifted 'artificially-intelligent' personal assistant that mimics natural human conversation, and autonomously makes restaurant bookings—*Duplex,* an extension of *Google Assistant*™. Or take the case of Massachusetts Institute of Technology's 'psychopath AI creation', *Norman,* which 'sees' blood and gore in abstract images. What happens if AI 'Norman' merges into a real-life Norman? While all this tinkering is going on, information technologies are radically altering the dynamics of human discourse, the way humans have traditionally stored, organized, synthesized, and transmitted information, which influences the choices we make on every issue, from the sacred to the sordid. These technologies have also impacted the moral values involved in issues like privacy, trust, fidelity. Environmental degradation is intimately germane to the pandemic of consumerism, which, in turn, is symbolic of moral barbarism, materialism, and hedonistic superficiality. It is not only *how* we use technology that has moral implications; the very design capabilities of information technologies influence the lives of their users, and the moral mindset of the designers of these technologies can shape the course society takes. Several scholars are talking about 'machine ethics', and 'moral machines', and the 'human use of human beings'. Maybe the world will witness moral machines and immoral men! That is because it is easier to design and manipulate a machine than to influence human consciousness. In David Hume's 'is–ought' analogy, man might represent the 'is' and machine the 'ought'—or, perhaps, ought *not.* In any case, neither man nor machine would, by impacting on each other, be the same. Life has become so heavy and man so 'soft' that we entertain anything only if it 'entertains', which means titillation, satiation of some dark desire; even news about horrific events has to be gory and gripping to hear or read about 'seriously'.

All this, in concert, leads to a state of moral malaise. The environmental crisis, the political and economic exploitation, the erosion of social sensitivity, are but manifestations of the malaise. These challenges are herculean, and solutions to them will require deep moral reflection and a whole-hearted commitment to social justice. Whether or not the machine will become more intelligent than man, whether or not man and machine will fuse into each other, whether or not robots will relieve us from much of the drudgery of daily labor and free us to pursue higher goals, there can be little doubt that human 'capabilities', human predispositions, and what they will be instinctively inclined to do, will dramatically change, giving rise to a new human context of life. We need new bearings, new compasses, new benchmarks, and new criteria to judge 'good' and 'bad', a fresh foundation for ethical conduct, a base to judge ourselves.

The individual is the very foundation, and no structure can be sound if the terra firma begins to sink. Also, human beings have never before been as isolated and intertwined at the same time. There is virtually nothing anyone does that does not affect other people, locally or globally. While the way we lead our 'personal' public lives enables us not only to earn a living, it can impact upon the safety and quality of life of more people than ever before. The distinction between public and private life is not unique to modern societies, but the emergence of new communication media in recent times has altered the very genre of the public and the private, and of the relations between them. In one sense, it is a throwback to pre-industrial times, when the locus of human life was in villages, where everyone knew the morals of everyone else. The world, in the wake of the digital revolution, has become a virtual world, and is often described as a *global village*,[69] although the inhabitants do not behave as old-fashioned villagers. Interdependence is virtual; individuality is actual. This has huge moral implications. We now have the means to turn sharing into synergy, but we expend all our energy in trying to prevail, control, and be successful. Many people prefer to call themselves 'spiritual', not necessarily 'moral'; because 'spirituality' is more fuzzy than 'morality'. A lot of people, particularly the young, do not know what they want from life, but they do know that 'this isn't it'. There are so many overlapping and contrary strands in contemporary life, and any process of fashioning a new framework for morality has to be multidisciplinary, multifaceted, and multipronged. While, traditionally, issues of morality have been dealt with by religious leaders, theologians, spiritual masters, and moral philosophers, the latest advent is science, which is treating this subject as a 'property of the mind'. According to the neuroscientist Sam Harris (*The Moral Landscape,* 2010), "the scientific study of morality is the lever that, if pulled hard enough, will completely dislodge religion from the firmament of our concerns. The world religions will land somewhere near astrology, witchcraft, and Greek mythology on the scrapheap. In their place we will have a thoroughgoing understanding of human flourishing, which will include even the most rarified and traditionally 'spiritual' states of human consciousness".[70] Such a view is symptomatic of the problem with science; everything in life and the cosmos is subsumed and consumed by the brain/mind. If the matter of our moral sense is the matter of our gray matter, then we come back to where the 'problem' begins. It is our *mind* that is the mischief-maker, the source of our most vicious streak, and of what is wrong with us as we are. What we need to do is not try to put our brain in a coma, or our mind in deep sleep, but to lessen our exclusive dependence on them as sole sources of cognition, perception, intelligence, memory, and energy. Instead, we must find ways to awaken our dormant intelligence of the heart, which we are told, science is increasingly coming to realize is independent of the brain/mind. It is wrong, and even suicidal, to think, as is being argued by some neuroscientists, that simply by manipulating our brain, and activating specific parts of it, we can, as it were, one fine morning, wake up as moral beings; that we can, by that process, become compassionate and kind, and rid ourselves of all that mankind has wrought on earth; that we, finally, can usher in the Golden Age of perfect peace and harmony.

Morality and Mundane Manners

We must also give thought to the issue of habits—good or bad—and morality. The human is essentially a creature of habit, the routine and the ritual. If we have 'good' habits, are we necessarily moral, and if they are 'bad', are we necessarily immoral? By good or bad, we usually refer to things associated with personal behavior. Most of us are a bundle of good and bad habits. We must first note that habits are very important in life and at some level, they can be cultivated or acquired by practice. Some people are, as the lyric goes, 'sweet on the inside',[71] and sour outside; some are impeccable outside and malicious inside. What habit does is to reduce, even eliminate conscious effort; it almost becomes independent of our volition. We are essentially creatures of habit. In fact, the simplest way to be good is to make what it takes to be good a habit, if not an addiction. The import and impact of bad habits is more nuanced. A bad habit might often be bad for the person concerned, but not always so for others; it might even make a person a better social being. If someone smokes, gambles, or drinks too much, or is promiscuous, we say he has bad habits, and if someone is sexually faithful, habit-wise teetotaler, truthful, pious, etc., we tend to applaud him. But experience tells us it is not as simple as that, perhaps not even totally true. A drunkard can be, and often is, a good man, not mean-minded, a gentle and giving soul. A pious person can be perfidious in his dealings with others. It does not necessarily mean that those who are sober, straight, and simple are evil. Perhaps there is some sort of connection: maybe the same bunch of genes, or the same slice of brain, that predispose some towards habits might also make them more likely to be good, decent, and generous. What it implies is that morality has to be considered not in the context of *who* the person is, but in relation to the act and its impact on society. And personal habits are marginal, though not irrelevant, in judging the ethics of anyone's actions. Our moral behavior must be viewed through the prism of social behavior. Scientist Rupert Sheldrake says, "Habits are subject to natural selection; and the more often they are repeated, the more probable they become, other things being equal. Animals inherit the successful habits of their species as instincts. We inherit bodily, emotional, mental, and cultural habits, including the habits of our languages.[72]

The bottom line is behavior; what matters is how we conduct ourselves in the give-and-take of everyday existence. As the Buddha told us, "However many holy words you read, however many you speak, what good will they do you if you do not act on upon them?" We must also bear in mind some fundamental facts. No one really knows why humans do what they do. What we do know is that nothing comes from nothing, nothing is as it seems, nothing goes in vain, and nobody is a stranger. Without and within are reflections and extensions of each other. Paramahansa Yogananda says, "Only those who partake of the harmony within their souls know the harmony that runs through nature. Whosoever lacks this inner harmony feels also a lack of it in the world. The mind in chaos finds chaos all around. How can one know what peace is like if he has never tasted it? But he who has inner peace can abide in this state even in the midst of outer discord".[73] But the moot point is that we do not have to fight a 'war' for it. Author Deepak Chopra says, "The secret of inner harmony is that it already exists. You don't have to work for it". We just have to uncover it, remove the façades and obstacles. What we perceive as behavior often relates to our conduct towards our fellow men. In fact, it is much more; it includes how we treat other creatures and also earth. The ancient Jain scripture *Acharanga Sutra* says, "… A wise man should not act sinfully towards earth, nor cause others to act so, nor allow others to act so. He who knows these causes of sin relating to earth, is called a reward-knowing sage". One of the great tragedies of the human condition is that our much-valued intelligence has not been able to grasp the fact that just as we do not burn the house we live in, so is the case with Planet Earth. Simply calling it 'Mother', or 'sacred', does not make any difference. If we cannot grasp this self-evident fact, we do not deserve to boast that we are the highest intelligence in existence. Whether or not we are bad, we certainly *seem* mad.

Most of us are not bad but we do behave badly, and we do not know why. This is the crux of the human condition. The problem is that we want to *behave* better without *becoming* better. Einstein wisely noted, "I must be willing to give up what I am in order to become what I will be". We always want to get, not give up. A creepy crawling caterpillar cannot become a winged, beauteous butterfly if it wants to retain its multiple legs and just wants to add wings to its body. The searing sense of not being what we want to be, is not something that harasses and haunts the lesser man alone. Many great men and saints have rued the reality that their flesh refuses to follow the requirements of a moral life, and what they despised they obeyed, and what they yearned to do they were paralyzed from doing. Our dilemma is two-fold. The first is our inability to do what we want to do. The second is our inability to refrain from doing what we detest doing. Saint Paul wrote, in a letter to the Romans, "I do not do the good I want, but the evil I do not want is what I do". He also lamented, "Wretched man that I am! Who will set me free from the body of this death… So then, with the mind I myself serve the law of God, but with the flesh the law of sin".[74] Whether behaving badly is tantamount to sinful behavior or not, the fact is that all religions exhort men to strive to be good and moral in their earthly conduct. Many religions emphasize this aspect. Jainism, for example, includes right conduct (*samyak charitra*) as one of the three parts to salvation, called *Ratnatraya*.[75] It is noteworthy that three of the elements in the Buddha's Noble Eight-fold Path, *Atthangiko maggo*, are right speech, right action, and right effort. And conduct is not the same as obedience or conformity. Mark Twain said that laws control the lesser man; conduct controls the greater one. For right conduct, we need right thinking, and for right thinking we need the right kind of blend in our consciousness.

Kierkegaard wrote that 'a human being is a synthesis of the infinite and the finite, of the temporal and the eternal, of freedom and necessity, in short, a synthesis'.[76] That synthesis, or the melting point, if you will, manifests as behavior, which is only the external expression of an inner content. Goethe wrote that 'behavior is the mirror in which everyone shows their image'; and, one might also add, our inner space. But not everything that occurs inside manages to come out; in a war, only the victorious emerge; the casualties do not count. At the human level, the fight is about our psyche and our behavior. The Buddha said, "It is better to conquer yourself than to win a thousand battles. Then the victory is yours. It cannot be taken from you, not by angels or by demons, heaven or hell". Science can tell us with reasonable certitude what our gross body consists of, about our internal and external organs, our body parts and what roles each of them perform separately and in tandem to keep us alive. But what happens inside is not merely an automatic functioning of these organs and parts; it is also how all these diffused units manage 'functional unity' that, besides keeping us alive, also influence and impact on how we view and act and react in the world at large, which is what we do every moment till death releases us from that chore. We do not know how we choose or decide the way we do, and life is nothing but myriad, motley choices, mostly minute but life-changing. We do not know how information is assembled and processed and transformed into decision. The question that has been asked for thousands of years is: Why is our behavior so often at variance with what we would like to do? This was the question Arjuna asked Lord Krishna on the Kurukshetra battlefield in the Mahabharata.[77] This was the question Saint Paul agonizingly asked.[78] We know that our 'behavior', even our personality, is an amalgam of apparently unrelated but actually intertwined factors, but we do not know how they coalesce and cohere, collide, mix and churn within our bodies.

Then, why are we so miserable, unhappy, discontented, and destructive in our deportment? Why is 'separateness' so stubborn? Why is it so herculean to put another person ahead in our choice-making? Why is it so Sisyphean to try to live inside someone else's skin? At a more conceptual and cognitive level, our problem with compassion is like the 'difficulty of being good'. We know that 'being good' is good for us, but we often find many good reasons not to do good. In fact, it is easier to do good, which most of us do, sometime or the other, than 'being good', which is not 'doing bad', which really is more difficult. It is instructive to remember what Jesus, surely as good a man as is possibly possible, said, "Why do you call me good? No one is good except God alone"[79] If Jesus himself did not (out of modesty or candor) or could not claim to be a good person, who are we even to debate the issue? Most of us think we are good because we 'do good things', but the real test is to desist by word or deed not doing any bad, not causing hurt or harm to any sentient being. Similarly our experience shows that compassionate actions make us feel good about ourselves, but we still find that callousness and indifference are more reflexive. Whether it is willful blindness or sheer selfishness, we have become indifferent to the distress of others, and to the woes of other species. We can pass by a critically wounded man with scarcely a sigh and still find good reasons for having done so, like telling ourselves 'it is not my job, or 'someone else will take care', and so on. Our stomach rarely churns when we hear and read news about the rape of, say, a little child, or when we read about a mother murdering her own kids to get back at her spouse, or about the sadistic crimes of serial killers and mass murderers. We tell ourselves, 'we are not them', and the truth that those persons are also human beings matters not. We feel safe in our home and under our skin. Ideas and idioms like solidarity, brotherhood, and 'one in all and all in one' are good sound-bytes but mean nothing. And we feel no sense of guilt at all about the atrocities committed by our own governments in the guise of 'national interest'. We feel no awakenings of remorse or pangs of virtuous shame, and can rationally explain away why we do nothing in the face of economic inequity or social exploitation. Our mind provides us with evasions, explanations and excuses for our *un-compassionate* behavior. And rather than view ourselves as insensitive, much less callous, we hold the 'system' responsible. When it comes to sharing the spoils, we ask *'Why not me?'*, and when it comes to fighting the same system, we ask *'Why me?'*

To be compassionate is to reach a deeper level of consciousness. For that, we need a two-pronged approach. We need to shift the center of gravity internally from the mind to the heart. Externally, we need a compassionate environment. But that environment itself is of our own making, the projection of what goes on inside, the 'war within', over which we have no control. It means that we must somehow get a hold on that war if we are to be considerate or compassionate or even responsible in our behavior. What we *do* every time is itself the result of the war, the outcome of a constant *Kurukshetra*, if you will. If we want to do right and be a good person, we must somehow go deep under own skin and ensure that the things we value—morality, consideration, compassion, kindness, sharing, and so on—come to prevail over forces we *do not* like, such as envy, jealousy, indifference, intolerance, injustice, etc. Even if there is a biological base, not just a moral motive, for compassion, it is not sufficient to make us moral in our day-to-day living. But we also know from our own experiences that constant exposure to compassionate environments softens our rough edges and enables us to be more sensitive to suffering. It also means that with some rebooting and reengineering, and with some internal cleansing, by tapping some of our dormant energies and by creating a congenial external environment, we can make compassion our 'natural' and 'normal' response. And we do have inside us what it takes to convert the 'feeling' into active action. The desired change cannot be left to our sense of 'good sense' or spontaneity, or sense of fair play or justness, or to the proverbial pangs of conscience. That is the menu or mix that now prevails, and the present mindset is its child. We cannot also brush it aside and say 'it is a state of mind'. It is much more than that; it is a matter of the level and content of consciousness. And that can be inculcated and imbibed incrementally, almost on a daily basis, event by event, so that, after a while, it becomes a reflexive 'habit', even an effortless addiction. For, as Aristotle said, 'we are what we repeatedly do'. That is the only way we can become a truly moral or an essentially spiritual being. But the troubling question we must first address is this: 'If all religions advocate and extol compassion, if we have all that it takes for us to be compassionate and if 'being' compassionate does not really require any extraordinary effort, then why is the human world so soaked with so much divisiveness, desperation, depravity, enmity, and hostility?'

Active acceptance of one's own self—and of others as they are and as elements of the Cosmic Whole—is the prerequisite for personal growth, which is not the same as physical growth (which is self-driven). As the prostitute Sofya tells the murderer Raskolnikov in Dostoyevsky's *Crime and Punishment,* "Accept and achieve atonement through it—that is what you should do". That kind of acceptance is not very different from *prapatti* in Hinduism, the unconditional and absolute surrender to the divine will. If we bear in mind that everyone is both a villain and a victim, or put positively, that no one is all evil or all virtue, or in Vedantic terms, that all of us are a part of the same cosmic consciousness, it becomes easy to be compassionate, even towards those who harm us. In the karmic context, those who inflict hurt on us are helping us and harming themselves; we are spending some of our 'bad karma' and they are acquiring it. And they being bad to us is a part of our prarabdha as much as theirs. Whichever way one looks at it, the bottom line is that it is almost impossible to lead a minimal human life without hurting, which means also *being* hurt. Since we cannot help but hurt, what we can do is to do the opposite—heal. And we can do that in multiple ways: just being there, offering a kind word, giving a supportive hand or shoulder, simply listening, sharing one's space, time, labor, wealth, etc. We can heal a wound with the warm touch of a tender hand and a gentle hug. Sometimes, just being with someone is enough, without even a touch or a word; to help the person get the feeling that he or she is not left alone in this wicked world. One can hurt or heal even through thought. Even a sincere and strong desire can help or heal. Just as self-destructive behavior can cause harm to those that love and care for us, equally we can help and heal others by helping and healing ourselves.

The Five-Point Formula for Decision-Making

Every crisis the world faces—ecological, economic, ethical, moral, and spiritual—is a result of the poor decision-making capacities of our human 'brain-based intelligence'. We are just unable to get it right, get a grip on what causes them, and what is required of us to resolve them. These are also an extension of the internal crisis, inner struggle for supremacy—the war within—in our consciousness. While we are busy toning our 'disaster-management' skills to face up to 'natural disasters', which are increasingly 'man-made' than 'natural', the turmoil in our 'inner world' gets no attention, or even recognition. Firestorms, tornadoes, typhoons, volcanic eruptions, and earthquakes are taking place within our consciousness, more turbulent and tempestuous than the ones we experience in our outer world. The Indian mystic Osho said that to find harmony and happiness in life one must shift the gaze from the 'objective' to the 'subjective', and try to 'look deep into our inner world, the world that is absolutely private to us'. Just as our physical acts affect the outer world, similarly the play of forces that control our consciousness directly affects the inner world. Our 'world within' and our world outside are intertwined and they mutually reinforce and reflect each other.

The outer world is a mirror of our inner world. Trouble is that we have been trying to focus all our attention and ingenuity on the extrinsic world without paying any heed to the endogenous world. At the basic level it is a question of how we look upon ourselves in relation to nature. We abuse and ravage, plunder and pillage the external world because we think it is 'separate' from us and that what happens in the world has nothing to do with us. There are unmistakable hints and portents that we are very near to what Nietzsche called "the hour of the greatest contempt",[80] an hour at which one asks: 'What good is my happiness?' and 'What good is any *good?'* and 'Why is bad *bad,* when it makes me feel so good, and when few, if any in all of humanity, seem worthy of respect, let alone reverence?' 'Happiness', or 'human flourishing', what the Greeks called *Eudaimonia,* is the magical word. That is what everyone, all the time, seeks, strives for, pursues and prays for but never seems to have it, or enough of it for satisfaction. It is because we want to monopolize it and identify it with satiating our desires and dreams. Once someone said to the Buddha, "I want happiness", and the Buddha replied: "First remove 'I', that is Ego; then remove 'want', that is Desire; what you are left with is 'Happiness'. Buddhism says that anytime we identify with a sense of 'I'—as in: "I feel something"; "I have lost something"; "I am lost"; "I have done it"—we are identifying with the wrong person. We are identifying with the ego, with our pain body, not with our pure nature. The famous Buddhist saying, *Sabbe dhamma nalam abhinivesaya* (nothing whatsoever should be clung to as 'I' or 'mine') is considered as a summation of all teachings of the *Tathagata* (the word that Gautama Buddha uses when referring to himself in the Pali Canon). The Buddha says that if you have heard this phrase, then you would have heard everything there is to hear. In 'moral decision-making', that is a very handy point of reference. In practical life, we cannot confine happiness to a few crisp words but we can experience it, even if ephemerally. Whatever it is and however much it varies and is elusive, the bottom line is this: true happiness is never either or; it doesn't diminish if we spread it. Even our daily experiences tell us that the 'happiness' we can get by making another person happy is immeasurable. And it lies not only in 'doing good', but also in realizing that there is nothing we gain by 'being bad', even to those who are, or at least we think are, bad to us. Returning 'good' for 'bad' is smart one-upmanship, the recipe to dissolve 'bad karma'. The attitude of others towards us often causes unhappiness, but seldom do we realize that it could be a reflection of and reaction to our own attitude. If you deny others their happiness, you are wasting your own power of happiness. Sadly, most of us have become incapable of respecting those who can be of no possible service to us, or to treating with consideration those who can do nothing for us, or are so positioned that they cannot return our rudeness. We tend to look down on people who we think are intellectually 'inferior', socially 'low-standing' or economically disadvantaged. 'Looking-down' is, at a deep level, another attribute of the mind; the mind instinctively looks up at someone it thinks is stronger, and looks down on those it considers so weak that it can exercise control over them. What we should always remember is the sage advice, "Never look down on anyone unless you are helping them up". Ours is a time when a growing number are coming to feel a deep disgust with our 'wretched contentment', or *à la* Nietzsche, with our life of complacent comfort and languid ease amidst numbing poverty and pervasive filth. And the 'filth' is both within and without, in the content of our consciousness and in our living context.

We can improve the quality of human 'decision-making' through a five-point formula:

(1) In considering what its consequences might entail, go beyond our family and friends, kith and kin, and bear in mind the dictum of Peter Singer that "Any preference for [one's] own interests must be justified in terms of the broader impartial principle". While what is called kin might have developed as a part of survival strategy, we should not let our love for family do injustice to others. Our task

must be, as Albert Einstein said, to free ourselves from this prison [of being separate from the rest] by widening our circles of compassion to embrace all living creatures and the whole of nature in its beauty. This is in line with ancient wisdom. The Maha Upanishad, while describing the *lakshana* or characteristics of a great man, says that the "discrimination 'this one is a relative, this other one is a stranger' is for the mean-minded. For those who are known as magnanimous, the entire world constitutes but a family". Baha'u'llah, founder of the Baha'i Faith, wrote in his *Tablet of Maqsud* (1882 CE) that "the Earth is but one country, and mankind its citizens".

(2) A very good practical test is Gandhi's advice about imagining in your mind's eye the most miserable person you saw in your life, and then choosing a course of action for yourself that would make his life a little less miserable. In other words, it is not only the larger good but the good of the underdog that must be furthered.

(3) It has been said that the human brain is incapable of factoring a timeframe beyond at most fifty years. That might be a handicap now, but it was a huge advantage, indeed a survival need, in the words of sociobiologist Edward Wilson, "during all but the last few millennia of the two million years of the existence of the genus *Homo*". And, "so today the human mind works comfortably backward and forward for only a few years, spanning a period not exceeding one or two generations". At a time when we face grave threats to our very existence, and the problems are global in nature, which can only be resolved with a long-term perspective, this 'handicap' could be a crippling flaw. That is at the root of, for instance, the crisis of climate change. That being the case, the way to go beyond is perhaps to imagine your great-grandchildren and factor in how this decision, or choice, might impact on the quality of their life: if they will have cleaner air, water, and food to live on, and what kind of earth they will inhabit, and what you can do about it.

(4) Inject the moral dimension. Will our decision-making cause pain and suffering to any living creature? And which choice of ours will alleviate or reduce the global stock of suffering? When spending

money, imagine which other use it can be put to that would be socially more appropriate. In today's world, the way in which a man spends money is often one of the surest tests of character. It is good to constantly remind ourselves that each one of us is a trustee—not an 'owner' of anything, not even of the money we 'earn'—of the 'trust' that is entrusted to us by society and nature. We are entitled to our fair share of the earth's bounty, but since we can never know what that fair share is, it is safe to go on the premise that we are using more. Our 'moral' share from what we possess and enjoy in whatever form—wealth, property, even leisure—is always different from our 'monetary' entitlement. It means that we must make every effort to share and spread as widely as possible, whatever and however much or little of it we might have. One does not have to be rich to do so; even small amounts can make a big impact on someone else who is in greater need. It is not at all a pious pipe-dream; nor does it necessarily entail any sacrifice. A Harvard Business School study found that spending money on others actually makes us happier than spending it on ourselves. The findings showed that those who reported spending more on others (what the study called 'prosocial' spending) reported a greater level of happiness, while how much they spent on themselves had no impact on happiness. Another study also revealed that "people who spent the money on themselves that day weren't happier that evening… but people who spent it on others were. The amount of money, $5 or $20, didn't matter at all. It was only how people spent it that made them happier". These only reinforce what we all in our own mundane and meandering lives experience: helping others by giving money, or by any other means, makes us feel a bit good about ourselves. In other words, we can enjoy and give at the same time. But when making choices, we sideline this factor; we assume that 'giving' is giving away and diminishes what we have. We have to find a way to factor this awareness into our myriad decisions of everyday life.

(5) Last, we must try to complement our brain-incubated intellect with heart-centered 'moral intuitions', which enable us to 'determine most

of our everyday decisions about how to act'. Most of our behavior as good or bad people takes place routinely, without reflection; it is only the occasional moral dilemma or very novel circumstance that requires us to stop and reflect. If we can bring to bear in mind the five factors and weigh everything we do, buy, sell, acquire or dispose of, there is a good chance that we can not only enhance our decision-making capabilities but also enable us to be what man always wanted to be: a moral being. It is not that we are incapable of 'being moral'. We are. We do good when the going is good; but to be a 'moral being', 'being moral' has to be natural, normal, effortless and consistent, though not continuous. Let us be clear what that effort is tantamount to. It is to go beyond biology, against the grain of the ruthless process of natural selection that brought us to where we are. And for that we have to do something that we have never been able to do before: find a way to take sides and tilt the scales in the relentless 'war within' between our better passions and nobler instincts and our darker and meaner ones. We cannot any longer afford to sit on the sidelines, stay neutral or be an observer or a witness to that which defines and frames who we are and how we take decisions in our daily life.

The Age of the Anthropocene?

While scripture and science differed on almost everything under the sun, they were on the same page about one important subject, at least until the other day. It is that, according to Hinduism, out of millions of forms of life on earth, the human is the chosen, the exceptional, the special and the superior. But science, in the past couple of decades, has been methodically chipping away at this assumption. It turns out that for almost everything we have or are capable of, there exists another animal that is even better endowed. It does not mean we are not unique; but then every species is unique too. We do have two exceptional attributes, one negative and one positive: malice and morality. On malice, we truly are *superior* and *sovereign*. Defined loosely as the will to wish of another without any self-gain, we alone harbor that emotion in abundance in our mind. Malice, for the record, is not the profound absence of empathy or conscience; it is more toxic because an ill-wisher actively works to cause distress or despair just for that sake, as he knows all along there is nothing in it that could be of any use to him. It is the evil in the 'evil within'. It is not simply a matter of malfunctioning synapses and neurons in some people's minds. It is mainstream, not the monopoly of monsters or of crooked minds. In fact, mind and malice are cut out for each other. Together they form a formidable foe. C Joybell C (*The Sun is Showing,* 1864) says that a mind full of malice and hate is able to actually attack another's body and mind and thus prevent good from taking place (or at least delaying and disrupting the good). Why man alone is endowed with this toxic trait when not even a tiger has it, is something to ponder over. Is it, too, one of those noxious needs of survival which linger long after the need is not there? If so, how is the intent to do harm to another person, knowing in advance it would do no good to you, help 'survive'? On the other hand, experts say that morality itself arose in response to the need to get others' help to survive. Whichever way, the very fact that man alone is capable of harboring malice has persuaded some like Mark Twain (1896) to say that we are the 'lowest', not the highest animal. Philosopher Arthur Schopenhauer puts it across when he says that 'men are the devils of the earth, and the animals, the tormented souls'.

The more pertinent point is, can a being with natural inclination towards malice even stake a claim to be a moral being? We must understand that it is morality that governs how we are together and rests on how we conceptualize right living. At first sight, malice and morality negate each other. A more measured relook reminds us of one basic bedrock of nature: the doctrine of dwanda, or dualism, that everything in creation is a part of a pair of opposites. Malice and morality are another pair. They do co-exist, albeit in a state of constant combat. Still, we can take some heart from recent research by organizations like *The Greater God Science Centre,* who have uncovered evidence that humans are biologically wired for moral attributes like compassion and generosity, and that they are good for our health and well-being, not simply social virtues and spiritual tools. But, be it as it might, what we do to animals itself calls into question our moral credentials. It is the extreme expression of our selfishness, arrogance, cruelty, and sadism. The other question is, in the narrative of creation, is it exclusive to us? There is mounting evidence that it is not. Some other animals do have the essentials of what we consider is morality, like empathy, selflessness, and sacrifice. Dale Peterson, in his recent book (*The Moral Lives of Animals,* 2011) argues that ultimately, human morality is like animal morality, an organ residing in the limbic system of the brain. He identifies the profound connections—the moral continuum—that link humans to many other species, and shows how much animal behavior follows the principles embodied in humanity's ancient moral codes. All said and done, in the words of Robert Wright (*The Moral Animal,* 1994), "Human beings are a species splendid in their array of moral equipment, tragic in their propensity to misuse it, and pathetic in their constitutional ignorance of the misuse". In other words, even if we assume we do have some social moral capability, we are prone to misdirect that power and, what is worse, we cannot make amends because we are incapable of being aware of it. We must understand that both the 'propensity' and the 'constitutional ignorance' stem from our consciousness, and unless we engineer a consciousness-change we cannot overcome them. And then again, right and wrong are not static issues; they are always in flux.

In a society such as ours with a bewildering array of priorities—economic, environmental, social, political—making the right moral choices has proven to be beyond our cognitive capacity, particularly because we do not have any solitary litmus test. And we cannot have any such 'test' because it is often not a choice between right and wrong but between right and right, or rather balancing two or more 'rights', to choose the greater good or lesser evil. What matters most morally are the consequences. How and whom do they affect? Perhaps the best one can come up with is the utilitarian dictum 'the greatest good of the greatest number'. That brings up the question: What is 'good', let alone 'greater good'? How about the evils of majoritarianism? Perhaps we can modify it as consequences that allow us to create all the happiness we can create and remove all the suffering we can remove. And that is not a favor to another. For, in the uplifting words of philosopher Jeremy Bentham, "... for every grain of enjoyment you sow in the bosom of another, you shall find a harvest in your own bosom; while every sorrow which you pluck out from the thoughts and feelings of a fellow creature shall be replaced by beautiful peace and joy in the sanctuary of your soul".[81] In other words, helping others by enhancing their happiness and diminishing their misery is enlightened morality. It helps us to cleanse our own consciousness, which, in turn, acts as a catalyst for consciousness-change. The fact is, it is much easier for animals to lead more moral lives than we humans.

That is because animals cannot but live morally; for us it is huge effort. For them, there is no need to know right and wrong. For us, knowing by itself does not meet the need. Human society is far more complex than animal society, and it is through morality that we try to reconcile the inherent conflict between self and others, a tool for social order, amity and brotherhood. Society is a conglomerate of autonomous and self-centered individuals, and if they can manage the conflict in a spirit of accommodation and sharing then society will be tranquil and peaceful. For that we have to subordinate what the ancient Greeks called *Eudaimonia* or pursuit of personal happiness of an individual to the pursuit of public interest. But that is not easy because we do not possess any moral safety net, and no God, no scientific insight can protect us from the forces of immorality and evil. In fact, these forces have proven much stronger both in the world outside and the world within. They attack our will to live morally from two fronts. First, they do not allow us to choose what is right. Second, they do not let us act on our moral choice. A factor that further muddies the matter is that morality too, like much else, is contextual and sensitive to the passage of time. And the passage of time can change the dynamics and the priorities, or make room for the entry of the new. The moral context influences the moral content, and moral content must serve the common good. For long, the common good was served through individual goodness. If individuals are truthful honest, sincere, dutiful, considerate and conscientious, then *ipso facto* what is common good becomes a logical outcome. That is still true but not sufficient. The center of gravity of modern life has shifted from the personal to interpersonal and private to public, from home to the workplace. How we conduct ourselves away from home, to make a living, is now a matter of serious moral concern. In fact, a good deal of anxiety, stress, and tension is generated in our effort to reconcile our private persona and our public persona in moral terms.

In very elementary terms, the most important public moral issue, perhaps of all time, pertains to our own, as a species, moral right to tarry much longer on this planet. Fact is, we have not conducted ourselves as a responsible species. We have fallen far short of what is needed to harmonize morality and modernity. On the other hand, we have been grossly exploitative, rapacious, and predatory. Sharing the earth with other species is an important human responsibility, and we have so grievously betrayed that responsibility that our own moral right is in question. As a result, life on earth, and *earth* itself as a planet in the solar system, is at risk now. This, in fact, is the lethal fallout of the much-talked-about advent of the *Anthropocene* epoch, the recent age of man, which is believed to have begun around 1950. In such circumstances, what should be our moral duty and existential response? The morally responsible answer can only be that if we cannot bring about a fundamental course correction in our mindset and the whole way of life, then we should hasten our extinction. But that might not be necessary; course correction is possible if we ensure that the forces of good, virtue or righteousness gain and keep an upper hand in the endless war within. If that happens, the very Age of the Anthropocene—the *Kali Yuga* of Hinduism and the *Iron Age* in Greek mythology—could become a time akin to the Greek *Golden Age*. We then don't have to take recourse to desperate measures like merger with machines or try to be gods because, it would then be said, mankind lived harmoniously among the gods and interacted with them. And we will be able to live to a very old age, and when our time gets over, death will come during sleep without subjecting us to any pain. And, at last, we may even dare hope that morally contented man might not then even seek immortality, as a gesture of justice to generations to come and other sentient life awaiting elevation to become human.

Chapter 5

From Death to Immortality

Death, Be Not Proud

Many things in the contemporary world are unsettling, but none more than what we are doing with death. Nothing fascinates us more than death, nothing frightens us more, nothing so certain seems so uncertain, and nothing as near is treated as so remote as death. Central to human thought from time immemorial has been to free himself from that fear, to erase that certainty and play the game of life and death according to *his* rules, not those of nature. Eternal life, and deliverance from the cycle of death to death that scriptures say ought to be the purpose of earthly life, we now say we want it here and now, not in spirit but in flesh and blood. Man wants to conquer death without really knowing what it is. In so doing, he might be running the risk of doing himself more harm than good by, so to speak, throwing the baby with the bathwater, or worse, by 'throwing hand grenades to fight house rats'. Is death no different than repositioning molecules on the physical level, and liberating consciousness from a walking cage to one of a free nature? Is it death that holds the meaning of life we seek? Have we got it all wrong? Is death really what we hope life is? Or is death forever an unknowable absolute, a fundamental state? Can it be codified as part of some basic bedrock, a detail of an unknown whole rather than merely a random and meaningless event? The human death rate is cent percent. Yet, that hasn't stopped us from trying to postpone death or to find ways to reverse it. Even scriptures have told us that life, not death, in fact, is the fundamental condition, the initial stage and an integral part of the entire unified process of human existence. The Bible says, "But when this perishable body will have become imperishable, and this mortal will have put on immortality, then what is written will happen: 'Death is swallowed up in victory'". Death, where is your sting? Hades, where is your victory? Still as living beings, it is death that frames life. The triad of practical questions that often come to mind are: Why must we die? What happens after we die? And how come the certainty of death is so powerless to influence our daily existence? There have been many answers but none that are definitive enough.

For the first, the obvious answer is because, as Hamlet[1] tell us, "Thou know'st 'tis common; all that lives must die, Passing through nature to eternity". For the second, the answer is, 'it depends on which theological faith we follow'. And for the third, the answer is, 'it is both banal and profound'. The simple one is 'to let you live'; because if death is a factor in everything we do, we will actually do nothing. In the Indian epic Mahabharata, this subject was alluded to when the Pandava king Yudhishthira was asked by a *yaksha*, a celestial being, "What is the most surprising the most wondrous thing in the world?" Yudhishthira answered, "Man sees death all around, but behaves as if he is deathless." Everyone knows that death is the ultimate fate or truth, but everyone behaves as if that truth does not apply to his own life. In short, everyone is mortal but he thinks and behaves as if he alone is immortal. It is that paradox that frames the human condition. The truth lies in the words of the Spanish philosopher Miguel de Unamuno: "For the present let us remain keenly suspecting that the longing not to die, the hunger for personal immortality, the effort whereby we tend to persist indefinitely in our own being, which is, according to the tragic Jew, our very essence, that this is the affective basis of all knowledge and the personal inward starting-point of all human philosophy, wrought by a man and for all men".[2]

Yudhishthira's answer itself was another riddle, a paradox. But what he did not realize is that that very apparent incongruity—that we will be around when others, particularly our tormentors and enemies bite the dust—was what kept peace and order in human society. What modern science is trying to do is to make immortality not a delusion but an actuality, by technologically empowering man with the means of dodging death. To make it more personal and tempting, we are told that if we are alive in 30 years, we'll be alive in 1,000 years, which means that at least *de facto*, if not *de jure* immortality. Mankind might acquire the technical capacity to radically extend the human life span, but in a world like ours, it will not be within the reach of the vast majority. That could disrupt human society like nothing else before. Not since the time of the hunter-gatherer in human evolution is human mortality so circumscribed and circumstantial and unpredictable than at the beginning of the third Christian millennium. Everything matters; where one is born, where one grows up and goes to work; how and where one travels; indeed, the smallest detail of life has a bearing on how one might die. After the thousands of years of 'progress', the very symbols of progress have become symbols of death.

We must remember why mortality is there in the first place in nature. It is through mortality that nature renews itself. Even the natural length of a species life span is a vital part of the overall life-balance that sustains biodiversity on earth. No species has a right to its own life or death. Nature ensures a balance even between predator and prey. One species seeking to unnaturally disturb it opens a Pandora's box, or a can of worms. Apart from upsetting this delicate symmetry in nature, humanity will get divided into what Yuval Harari calls 'superhuman caste' and the wholly human sub-caste, a perfect recipe for a revolution and a dystopian horror. The space entrepreneur Elon Musk offers another horror, and fears that unless artificial intelligence is strictly regulated, we will end up with an 'immortal' digital dictator who could forever trap humanity in its grasp. It could be the most inter-generationally selfish and socially destabilizing and morally troublesome development. For it is death, rather its impartial inevitability and across-the-board ambit, that held a cap on its gross injustice, inequity, inequality, oppression, exploitation. If we truly believe it will be the other way around, that we will die but the villains in our lives could prolong almost indefinitely, then the world will witness a kind of violence and vengeance the like of which it has not seen so far. For, immortality is not impregnability; the immortal sentient beings may not die, but they can be killed, just like Tolkien's *Elves*. Although the immortality that science is seeking is of a different genre, most people, regardless of race, religion or culture, tend to believe they don't 'dissolve like salt in water' with death. They believe that a part of themselves, some indelible core, soul, consciousness or some sort of essence, will endure—through progeny, name, fame, memory, art, literature—and transcend the body's death and live forever. But that is different from what science is focusing upon: the body and brain. It is also very different from what most religions envision as immortality. For example, according to the Upanishads, 'the mortal in whose heart desire is dead becomes immortal'. The Katha Upanishad says that the mortal in whose heart the knots of ignorance are untied becomes immortal. These are the highest truths taught in the scriptures. The very two things which we are summoned to overcome—desire and ignorance—are the very two things we are hostage to. Our feverish pursuit of scientific, not spiritual, immortality throws up another huge downside. It is siphoning off vital intellectual and financial resources at the expense of more worthy and socially imperative priorities that can lift the lives of billions of people from subhuman misery.

In any case, immortality, in its literal strict sense, is impossible, pie in the sky. Even if one lives for thousand, or ten thousand, or a million years, he will still not be immortal. One day, he too will 'die'. In the Mahabharata, the great Bhishma was given the boon to choose the time of his death (*Ishtartha mruthyu*), not deathlessness. Although his mother was a goddess, River Ganga, he was nevertheless born a human, and could not wriggle out of reach of death. Even if the current limit to human life extends from 120 years to 1,000 years or more, a person can still be killed or die from disease or from an accident. We tend to think that it is simply a radical reflection of what is already happening: humans have been living longer and longer all the time incrementally, much more in recent times. But it is not that simple. Although some zealots say that there is no biological limit, new research suggests that humans can only live so long, and we are reaching the natural biological limit. For other researchers, "If a human life span was extended beyond 125 years, it would require other scientific interventions beyond improving someone's health".[3] It means that any significant extension, let alone immortality, can only happen through non-biological ways. It is then nonhuman life, not human. As we now define it to be. And the children of these 'immortals' will not be born 'immortal', unlike gods or angels; they will have to start all over again or else we will have the perverse situation of 'immortals' having to bury their own children and grandchildren. The other important question is if some humans acquire superhuman abilities—and live like the biblical Methuselah for 969 years, or like *Lazarus Long* of Robert Heinlein's science fiction novels, live up to 2,000 years—how would they behave? How would it affect their mindset and consciousness? Would they be more responsible, kind, and compassionate, or more reckless, predatory, and cruel? Would the climate crisis, for example, be abated and or get aggravated? Will inequity, indifference, intolerance and injustice and selfishness become less or more? If they cannot 'die' but get bored to death, would such humans seek out and check into 'killer clinics' to end their lives? Already, even with our current life span, some apparently healthy people are seeking help to end their lives, out of sheer fatigue or revulsion with what the human condition has come to stand for. A good way to look at it is to see what happened since 1900 to now: average life expectancy has doubled but human behavior is no better; if any, it is far worse. There is no reason to believe it will be any different if some of us live up to a thousand years. The bottom line is this: without consciousness-change that involves a radical reduction in the leverage of our mind, a *de facto* immortal man is likely to be far more mean, malicious, and malevolent. That, in turn, could provoke a more violent and vengeful reaction. As a species which prides itself to be the only one capable of reflection, reasoning, and rationality, we should carefully contemplate and cogitate on how we are trying to transit through the human condition.

In the *Brihadaranyaka* Upanishad, there is a famous mantra called the *Pavamana mantra: Om, asato ma sad gamaya; tamaso ma jyotir gamaya; mrtyor ma amritam gamaya*. It is loosely translated as, "Om, from falsehood lead me to truth; from darkness lead me to the light; from death lead me to immortality". Some scholars substitute the word 'through' for 'from' and say that we cannot get away from illusion, darkness or death. This *mantra* captures the essence of the human spiritual journey. Although they look different, many interpret that all three portions of the mantra have the same meaning, and complement each other. Death here symbolizes not only the end of a life, but also darkness, delusion, untruth, and the unreal. Immortality signifies truth, light, self-realization, and eternal life of the *Atman* or soul. The mantra is not just talking about physical death, but also the ones in our minds. Man might yet 'conquer' death, but could still lose his soul; and what earthly good would that do? The fact of the matter is that we cannot comprehend death unless we comprehend life. Death becomes a 'problem' if life is viewed as a problem, and life becomes a problem if it is viewed as inane, or as one might like to call it, an insane interlude from birth to death.

The Mystery of Mortality

We might not know what is worth living or dying for, but death has been so traumatic for so long that we know not if there was a time when, as Thomas Hardy tells in his classic poem *Before Life and After* (1909), "If something ceased, no tongues bewailed; if something winced and waned, no heart was wrung; if brightness dimmed, and dark prevailed, no sense was strung". But the 'mystery of mortality' has always fascinated and frustrated man. Deep within, we know that we too will follow, but we scarcely glance at those who have gone before. Human culture itself is ultimately an orchestrated, symbolic defense mechanism against the awareness of our inevitable mortality, which in turn acts as the emotional and intellectual response to our basic survival mechanism. The level at which human consciousness functions in most people has never allowed us to accept death with a certain measure of equanimity. The Buddha said, "Death is only the temporary end of a temporary phenomenon" For Tagore, 'death is not extinguishing a light but putting off a lamp because dawn has come'. We wish we could adopt and maintain such an attitude, but when death does strike and snatches a loved one, all our restraint goes up in smoke. Even great people and avatars are not immune. In the Ramayana, when Kumbhakarna (brother of the 'evil' Ravana and of the virtuous Vibhishana) dies on the battlefield and Vibhishana is grief-stricken, Rama consoles him and says that death is inescapable for everyone born. But when his brother Lakshmana is mortally wounded later, Rama becomes inconsolable and even says he will take his own life. In the Mahabharata, Lord Krishna teaches the Bhagavad Gita to Arjuna. One of the main messages he offers is to treat death with equanimity, as it is just another passage. But when Arjuna's son Abhimanyu is killed, Arjuna becomes distraught with grief and vows vengeance. All teachings of Krishna seem to have simply gone out of the window, as though Arjuna never heard them—that death is but another phase of life, no different than discarding of worn-out clothes; that only the body 'dies', not the soul; that we should not grieve over that which is inescapable. However much one gets prepared, we are never prepared enough when the creepy shadow of death comes close. What baffles and beguiles us is not only death's invincible inevitability—that someday we will turn ice-cold—but also the unsettling uncertainty about when and where death will lay its icy hand on our brow. There have always been masters like Swami Vivekananda and Adi Sankara, who just *knew*. Vivekananda had not only said that he would not cross forty years, but also that he 'knew the time and place' of his death. The point is that knowing made a difference to their life, not to their death. The fact is that there is not much room in death but a lot in life, and that is the difference between life and death. Then again, as Socrates said, after being sentenced to death and minutes before the hemlock took effect, "Which of these two (life and death) is better God only knows". One of the 'sacred cows' of human thought, for which there is no evidence, is that animal consciousness cannot comprehend death. Ernest Becker, in *The Denial of Death* (1973), reflects this view. "The animals don't know that death is happening and continue grazing placidly while others drop alongside them. The knowledge of death is reflective and conceptual, and animals are spared it. They live and they disappear with the same thoughtlessness: a few minutes of fear, a few seconds of anguish, and it is over. But to live a whole lifetime with the fate of death haunting one's dreams and even the most sun-filled days—that's something else".[4] The 'animal' we associate with a lower form of life, but it is also said that 'what we here feel as 'animal' in quality and nature is the basic element in which the dead live. The kingdom in which the dead live can easily be changed when it enters into us; what is higher life in yonder world can become lower when it is within us on earth'.

The Moral Purpose of Mortality

Mortality has failed its practical purpose: to give us a 'moral' meaning to life. Instead of inducing himself to look at the 'finiteness' of life as an incentive to spend 'quality time' on earth, and to make his temporary presence of permanent value, man has turned that 'perspective' to make life itself finite-less, a license for profligacy. Instead of spending the 'limited' time to prepare ourselves to 'meet our maker', we are doing our best to postpone permanently such a tryst. Emily Dickinson wrote, "Because I did not stop for death; he kindly stopped for me". Now we do not want any such 'stops'; we want *sops* to live forever. It all comes down to 'perspective' and 'practice'. 'Perspective', either as a means for harmony in life, or to make life itself everlasting, or so long that death ceases to be a factor in life. 'Practice', or *abhyasa* in Sanskrit, is needed to achieve anything in life, or even to 'die' with dignity. Plato wrote, "True philosophers are always occupied in the practice of dying". Human response to the inexorability of death has, over the ages, ranged widely, from outright denial to defiance, from 'accept and make merry' to outright combat and conquest. And we tend to look at an other's death from our perspective. Confronted by conflicts and contradictions all around, man's mind has found an ingenious way to outflank them: it is to acknowledge its inevitability, at least in the immediate future, but to indefinitely defer its applicability to his own life. In other words, death cannot be wished away; but shut the 'doors of your mind' to your own death. But, at another level of consciousness, man continues to wonder: Is this life all that there is? What happens to me when I 'die' and where will I be in the hereafter? Is death the enemy of life and who ordained it that way? The state of the mind of man is well captured by William James in his book *The Varieties of Religious Experience* (1901–1902), when he wrote that "the fact that we can die, that we can be ill at all is what perplexes us; the fact that we now for a moment live and are well is irrelevant to that perplexity".

Along with the evolution of the human brain and dramatic changes in the modes of living, human perceptions of death in life also changed. In his book *The Hour of Our Death*, Philippe Ariès emphasizes "the relationship between man's attitude towards death and his awareness of self, of his degree of existence or simply of his individuality". According to him, the concept of death as a familiar, anonymous event was replaced by suppression of death. In the very early human communities, the motif was 'death-in-life', and death was marked by a simple, public ritual largely controlled by the dying person, which continued till the Middle Ages. With increasing individualism and weakening of traditional communities, an individual life was no longer subsumed in the collective destiny of a group, and that led to a shift in the focus of redemption from group ritual to personal conscience. With the early advent of science, death came to be perceived, not as part of a continuum, but as a rupture or a break of life, something very unpleasant, a matter better put out of the mind. With industrialization acquiring a firm hold over human culture, the focus of death shifted from the 'dying individual to the death of one's significant others' and 'death became romanticized', and the 'graveyard became the focus of somber and mournful dispositions relative to death'. With 'increasing privatization and institutionalization in the twentieth century, 'death denial became the reigning orientation', which soon gave way to the endeavor of science to conquer death and make man eternal. The irony is that despite all the 'accumulated wisdom' about death, very few actions in life of very few people are influenced by this knowledge. Such a strong disconnect, it is hard to imagine, is a wholly human failing. If there is Divine sanction for this amnesia, what was the purpose? It may be so, because if man truly and wholly believes that he could die any time, he may lose all interest in life and cease to do his *karma* and *dharma*. Without death, life can be an endless entrapment and unbearable burden, no end to misery, no hope of betterment. In fact, it is the definitiveness of death that makes life worth living. There is life because there is death. It is due to death that man understands the value of life; it is its task to make man realize and enhance life. Death really is a gate, not the, "sluice through which the different elements of this world go as they move from one stage to another in the cosmic evolution of all empirical reality".[5]

Mortality has framed every aspect of human activity and creativity, and has always been a defining element in literature, poetry, play, drama, art, religion, philosophy, and science. Mortality, which some say is a gift, while many consider it a curse, is perceived in multiple ways, as the authentic existential dilemma, a part of the natural cycle of decay and renewal, a stepping stone to spiritual self-discovery, a means to find immanent meaning in life. In effect, it has amounted to be the unknowable center around which our thoughts inescapably, even morbidly, swirl. As someone succinctly put it, "The question here is, how do we live? We want to be gods, or at least angels, heroes, or saints. But we are animals. Plus we don't want to die, or even admit the possibility of death".[6] But we still die, lock, stock and barrel. There is nothing we can do about death, but everything we do has something to do about it. We cannot escape it, but we cannot also accept it. We feel so impotent, emasculated, embittered, enraged. Dylan Thomas expressed the mood memorably when he wrote, "Do not go gentle into that good night… Rage, rage against the dying of the light". Sacred texts and seers might say that 'dark is right', that is, death is integral to life, but most men, when that 'night' creeps in, are always aghast and not ready to 'go' at all.

Becoming a Jellyfish, at the Least a Turtle

The central theme of our great epics and enduring works of literature, like the *Epic of Gilgamesh* (Mesopotamia) is the mystery of mortality. King Gilgamesh attempts to learn the secret of eternal life by undertaking a long and perilous journey to meet the immortal flood hero, Utnapishtim, who tells Gilgamesh, "The life that you are seeking you will never find. When the gods created man they allotted to him death, but life they retained in their own keeping".[7] And the epic gives us some wrenching advice, which is music to modern ears: "Fill your belly; day and night make merry; let days be full of joy; love the child who holds your hand; let your wife delight in your embrace; for these alone are the concerns of man". What Gilgamesh was told was *not* possible is what is high on the wish-list of man of this millennium. We take heart from the fact that it is not 'unnatural'. For, that which exists already in nature in a lowly creature cannot be unnatural, or cannot be dismissed as an 'unreasonable' aspiration for the human, the most evolved species. Scientists have discovered that the tiny 'immortal jellyfish' has found a way to cheat death by actually reversing its ageing process. If the jellyfish is injured or sick, it returns to its polyp stage over a three-day period, transforming its cells into a younger state that will eventually grow into adulthood all over again. Another case is that of the 'the slow and steady' turtle, known to live for centuries; researches have found that their organs don't seem to break down over time. It means, literally, that we, as individuals—not as a species—want to be still walking on earth centuries from now essentially with the extant body and brain. The single most important truth that has so far stood the test of time, the substratum of all scriptures, the common thread of all human thought has been, as Osho puts it, "Death has already happened in birth; there is no way to transcend it. It is going to happen because it has already happened. It is only a question of time unfolding. You are rushing towards it each minute".[8] Rabindranath Tagore, in his classic poem *Gitanjali,* expresses it exquisitely: "Thou hast made me endless; such is Thy pleasure. This frail vessel thou emptiest again and again; and fillest ever with fresh life". Scriptures say that the only way to avoid or escape from death is to avoid or escape from birth. Science says 'not necessarily'. Advances in microbiology and genetics seem to indicate that the prospect of immortality, or at the least, of exponentially increased individual life spans, is not as far-fetched as earlier believed. If 'immortality' means inability to die; it means inability to actually be killed by anything. That is not going to happen; no organic body can be indestructible. In fact, beyond a threshold, say half a millennium, living 'forever' has no practical meaning. If the world comes to an end, can we live thereafter? If we are run over by a train, can we survive that? If a person wants to end his life, can immortality stop it? Can the body survive a bullet hit, or being run over by a bus? What about morality and the rights of the yet-to-be-born, the future generations? Will it stop the human reproductive cycle? If everyone becomes old, how would the world be? And what about other species? If they continue the cycle, will they get an upper hand over man? If no one 'dies', 'with infinite life comes an infinite list of relatives', and everyone 'alive' would have had altogether too much of themselves, condemned to an existence of boredom, déjà vu and will consider lucky in having the chance to die.[9]

From time immemorial until even a century ago, questions on issues like values, morality, God, and death have been the concerns of religion, philosophy, humanities, and sociology. They defined the parameters and determined the dynamics of the debate. Such subjects were considered beyond the purview of the other major player on the human stage, science. All that has changed in the recent past, and science is beginning to claim that it has answers to such questions, and that "meaning, values, morality and the good life must relate to facts about the well-being of conscious creatures—and, in our case, must lawfully depend upon events in the world and upon states of the human brain".[10] In this view, the key player is the human brain; which many call the most astounding, most complicated and sophisticated entity in the known universe, while some others (David Linden, *The Accidental Mind*; 2007), describe it as a 'mouse brain with extra toppings', a 'cobbled together mess', and say that its design is 'quirky, inefficient, and bizarre'. Some[11] are now calling it a 'spiritual organ'. Whether the human brain is a marvel or a mess, we cannot ignore that there is an emerging scientific sense that "human experience shows every sign of being determined by and realized in, states of the human brain".[12] It is a far cry from the pristine days of Francis Bacon who cautioned about too much admiration for the powers of the mind and as an extension of science.

There is a certain feeling that the time has come for man to assert his authenticity; that everything that man has ever sought and thus far failed to find can be discovered not in the stars or in the laps of gods but in his head, the brain, culminating in the ability of the human intellect to bridge the gap or blur the boundary between facts and values, a long sought-after goal of moral philosophers. The new-found optimism that science can help us become a 'moral being' is based on the finding that "beliefs about facts and beliefs about values seem to rise from similar processes", and that "we have a common system for judging truth and falsity in both domains".[13] Such is the height of hoopla, that it is being suggested that "morality should be considered an undeveloped branch of science".[14] And, that "human knowledge and human values can no longer be kept apart. The world of measurement and the world of meaning must eventually be reconciled".[15] In short, what we are being told is that what scriptures and saints have failed to do—make man an instinctively or intuitively a moral being—science would now be able to do by simply suitably 'fixing the brain' or by making it 'smart'. We admiringly say 'he is so smart' or 'so clever', as a contrast to 'he is stupid'. But there are other voices who tell us that, in Chesterton's words, "There is no man really clever who has not found that he is stupid". And there are some very perceptive people who say that what a man might gain through his intellect or cleverness, he might lose in his spiritual perception, and that he alone is a wise man who can conquer his own cleverness. Euripedes said, 'cleverness is not wisdom', and Rumi wrote, "Yesterday I was clever, and so I wanted to change the world; today I am wise so I am changing myself".

As for man's other aspiration, immunity from death, science is now trying to achieve, besides physical or biological immortality, another 'kind' of immortality—*digital* immortality. That is, making permanent what is being referred to as the 'online presence personality', distinct from the physical, to ensure that our digital 'footprints' outlive our physical forms. It is explained as having the means to store and restore the thousands of trillions of bytes of information represented in the pattern we call our brain. Ultimately, "software-based humans will be vastly extended beyond the severe limitations of humans as we know them today. They will live out on the Web, projecting bodies, whenever they need or want them, including virtual bodies in diverse regions of virtual reality".[16] It is suggested that it might be possible that our brains and memories could be transferred—uploaded or downloaded, as the case may be—into a synthetic medium, that is, we will become 'immortal' through a machine. Then again, we are told that hackers are developing a virus to infect human brains; that synthetic biology—deliberate creation of living organisms from elementary materials that are not themselves alive—is accelerating faster than computer technology, which could be used to control behavior and for bioterrorism. We also read reports that 'headless human clones can grow organs in ten years'. Elsewhere, one tells us that we could have amidst us 'biological robots' sooner than electronics-based robots.[17] Yet another says that a 'crawling bio-robot runs on rat heart cells', which could 'someday attack human disease'.[18] And maybe soon, mindless 'human' robots can be cloned for manual labor or sex slaves? Such prophecies are usually paraded to demonstrate what man can do to transcend biology and outsmart nature! There are some who sound a note of caution. In the words of Prof. Andrew Linzey, Director of Animal Ethics at Oxford University, "It is morally regressive to create a mutant form of life… scientific fascism". How are we supposed to put this in perspective? Should we say it is incredulous, impossible, or is it the end of the bridge between animal and *Overman*, with man being the connecting rope, that Nietzsche talked about? Zarathustra says, "Man is something that shall be overcome. What have you done to overcome man? All beings so far have created something beyond themselves; and do you want to be the ebb of this great flood, and even go back to the beasts rather than overcome man? What is the ape to man? A laughing stock or a painful embarrassment. And man shall be just that to the Overman: a laughing stock or a painful embarrassment".[19] Is the human organism that nature fashioned as a part of the living world, his brain and/or body capable of such manipulative, mechanical metamorphosis? Trouble is that is that human beings are still on the prehistoric mode—10,000 BCE model as it is subbed—designed for agriculture, with decision-making software adequate for walking, running, and digging and climbing trees. Mechanization has further eroded even that vitality. Perhaps it is useful to pause and ponder over what we think is missing in mortality. "The desire to live forever is the desire never to be ended or closed-off; the desire, in effect, to contain everything, so that there is nothing outside oneself that one will not eventually grasp".[20] Or is it that we are unaware of the sea of possibilities for us which are going to be shut off by death? Is it that there are places that we cannot reach or simply that there will be people we know who we will cease to know? There are no certain answers, and we end with the paradox that while there will always be reasons to labor to live longer, even much longer, there will always be reasons to worry why living forever would turn 'death' into what we think life is.

Immortality—Are the Gods Hitting Back At Us?

The irony is that humans want to conquer ageing, disease, and death, but at the same time, every day, they are discovering or inventing new and innovative reasons to kill each other, not reasons to live for or die for, raising the question if the propensity to kill each other itself is integral to evolution, without which we would not have survived as a species. Every human killing falls into two types: authorized and unauthorized. It is only the latter that is deemed as a crime or sin or evil. And whether it is 'authorized' or not depends on who you are, where you are and how it happens. The same action by the same person at a different time, place and circumstance can become horrendous or honorable. Leonardo da Vinci said, "We live by the death of others. We are burial places". Byron wrote, "This is the patent age of new inventions for killing bodies, and for saving souls. All propagated with best intentions", words which served as an epigram for Graham Green's classic *The Quiet American* (1955). Man has always physically eliminated another man since the time he sharpened a stone, and will continue to do so, increasingly for more reasons than he thinks he has to live for. 'Killing' satisfies many diverse urges. In Biblical terms, at least man's revolt against God in the earthly paradise was followed by the deadly combat of man against man, Cain and Abel. Although debatable, by and large human society has tended to view killing as the ultimate crime as well as punishment, and a deterrent against future unlawful killings. Individually, it can be a product of unbridled passion and anger; it can even be unintentional and circumstantial; it could be simply a matter of sheer survival—'it is either he or me'. In karmic terms, killing or getting killed is not very different from other forms of death; it is another settling of karmic debt. The killer and the killed are playing their parts. In the Bhagavad Gita, when Arjuna hesitates to kill those he revered, Krishna says that those people are already standing to be killed; that Arjuna is simply playing his part as an instrument. Man will do anything to enjoy perfect health, but he is almost hypnotically poisoning the very infrastructure of life on earth, raising the question if that is the manifest of our collective 'death-wish'. Could this be the way gods are getting back at us for seeking to undermine their monopoly on immortality? Whether it is divine wrath or human folly, the fact is that after over a million years of human evolution on earth, "the global human enterprise is on a collision course with the physical and biological limits of earth".[21]

We may like to defy death, physically, or digitally; but the grind and grandeur of life is a given, something we learn to live with. Also 'given' is our state of ignorance about the fundamentals. Socrates lamented that all his life he had sought knowledge and didn't find it, and it was said that he was called the 'wisest man' among his contemporaries because he knew that he knew nothing. We are told that the human alone, among all the creatures on earth, wants to know more than we need to know to be alive. Lest we miss the point: according to the Bible, man was thrown down from the heavens because he ate the fruit of 'The Tree of Knowledge' (called *Etz haDaat tov V'ra*, in Hebrew). It is the lust 'to know' that defines us. Indeed the very name we have given to ourselves, *Homo sapiens*, means 'wise being' or 'knowing being'. We have known a lot but the essence has been elusive and like Tennyson's *Ulysses* (1842), we too are 'made weak by time', but still we want 'to strive, to seek, to find, and not to yield', and hope that 'some work of noble note, may yet be done', while still doing what we need to do to stay alive. But unlike Ulysses we are 'not strong in will'; nor are we 'one equal temper of heroic hearts'. We are wobbly in will and our hearts too are getting weary of us. Still that 'wary' will is the most powerful force on earth, rivaling the very divine. That is the paradox—and peril. We cannot speak for other species, but as far as the human is concerned, the human consciousness, more precisely the human mind, has demonstrably fallen short in handling power, domestic or societal, personal or public, physical or psychological, economic or political, religious or spiritual. Our darkest desires, deepest flaws seem to come into full play in circumstances when we dispense power over those who have none or not in equal measure. Some say 'will to power' is intrinsic to being alive. Nietzsche wrote (*Beyond Good and Evil*) that "Anything which is a living and not a dying body, will have to be an incarnate will to power, it will strive to grow, spread, seize, become predominant—not from any morality or immorality but because it is living and because life simply is will to power. 'Exploitation'... belongs to the essence of what lives, as a basic organic function; it is a consequence of the will to power, which is after all the will to life". Without some kind or degree of 'exploitation', at least human life is almost impossible. The poet WH Auden said, "Almost all of our relationships begin and most of them continue as forms of mutual exploitation, a mental or physical barter, to be terminated when one or both parties run out of goods". One of the tragedies of human life is that although a healthy relationship is supposed to be mutually reinforcing, they have become mutually restrictive. No relationship can be exempted from this restriction including the most important, the man–God relationship. Our 'behavior' also substantially changes depending where we are positioned. We are almost different human beings at home, at work, at play. This, in turn, brings out a philosophic question about the innate nature of life. Is it irretrievably, irreversibly 'unfair', unequal, a 'hell', as Schopenhauer characterized it, to be done away with as soon as possible? Or is it 'beautiful', a divine gift, to be savored and experienced to its brim? A supplementary question is how should one 'do our time' here on earth? Some say that it is to get away as far as possible and the way is self-sacrifice and self-imposed poverty. Others say enjoy it as much as you can, live for the day, let the senses have their fill… As Scarlet O'Hara told herself when Rhett Butler walked away, which is the last sentence in *Gone With the Wind*, "after all, tomorrow is another day". The real question, though, is not if there is or there isn't an after-life, or if life is 'ugly'; or rapturous'. The question is: like anything we have on our hand, how do we use it, be it 'useful' or 'useless'.

When Death Strikes Home

Our 'differences' with death essentially are four. One, it is its awesome finality, its utter completeness; its no-holds-barred nothingness; its intrinsic irrevocability. Two, the absolute absence of any rhyme or reason, fairness or justness in the way it strikes. Three, death may be ordained but not orderly; pre-determined but not predictable; there is not a single universal principle, save its inevitability, that governs death. Four, it is one state of 'existence' about which 'experience' makes no difference. Nor does our preparedness, or who stops from whom, death or us. Emily Dickinson wrote an 'immortal' poem (*Because I Could Not Stop for Death*) about mortality: "Because I could not stop for Death; He kindly stopped for me; The carriage held but just Ourselves; And Immortality". The poem is often portrayed as the 'mortal experience from the standpoint of immortality', of the 'conflict of mortality and immortality', 'defining eternity as timelessness'. Emily envisions death as a 'kindly', not grim and cruel, carriage driver, who is lauded for his 'civility', and stops for one who could not stop for him; the only other 'passenger' inside is immortality. The drive, Emily describes, was reassuring, 'with no haste', and the passage is through life experiences, which is captured in metaphors like school, setting sun, children, grazing grain, swelling on the ground, each symbolizing a stage in life, until finally, the last is a grave.

The carriage is headed to eternity, with Death as the charioteer; the passengers, mortality and immortality. We travel through life with the twins, *mortality* and *immortality*; sometimes they may clash; sometimes they can be cuddly, but never far from each other. As Schopenhauer said, "Each day is a little life; every waking and rising a little birth; every fresh morning a little youth; every going to rest and sleep a little death".

How we perceive death affects how we live. Some say that when whatever we do comes to a screeching halt, what difference does it make to what we do or do not do? If we kill somebody, so what; anyway that person is going to die sooner or later... Others posit that the very reason to conduct your life is so that it makes some positive difference to other people's lives. Whatever we might say, we do adopt 'double-standards'. To put death in perspective and to erase the fear of death, scriptures like the Bhagavad Gita tell us that death really is no big deal, that life and death are parts of a continuum, that what we deem as death is but another passage, like from youth to old age, and that what passes through or out is the physical body, not the imperishable *Atman*. But in actuality, we mourn death and celebrate life. And when death does come too close for comfort, all wisdom and equanimity evaporates. That is true of great as well as garden-type men. Two examples illustrate the point. In the Ramayana, when the mighty Kumbhakarna is slain by Rama, and Vibhishana (Kumbhakarna's brother) wails in grief and remorse, Rama consoles Vibhishana saying that his brother died doing his dharma, that death is only for the body. But when Rama's own brother Lakshmana is mortally wounded by Indrajit (son of Ravana, and nephew of Vibhishana), Rama becomes inconsolable, and even says that suicide is preferable to going back to his kingdom Ayodhya without his brother Lakshmana! Similarly, in the Mahabharata, Krishna expounds the great Bhagavad Gita to Arjuna, on the battlefield of Kurukshetra. The essence of the Gita, according to Krishna, is that one must perform *nishkama karma* (action without attachment to the fruits thereof). Arjuna then picks up his mighty bow and kills his own very dear and revered grandfather, Bhishma. But, later, when his own son Abhimanyu gets killed in the battle, Arjuna becomes inconsolable and vows vengeance on Jayadratha, who had simply blocked the attempt of Arjuna's brothers to aid Abhimanyu, but had no hand in his actual killing. Although one could argue that a young boy is different from a centurion man, the point is that in death too we discriminate, and that when it actually strikes where it hurts most, we react differently.

But it is noteworthy that no Hindu avatars flinched from killing to fight evil. In fact, it was the preferred mode, the very aim of the avatar. The evil ones God descended to kill were actually His devotees who were cursed to become demons, and it was a favor that He did to them, to liberate them from the curse. In the epic wars of Ramayana and Mahabharata, no one was taken a prisoner or let off mortally wounded or incapacitated to wage war. No 'villain' or evil-doer repented and sought forgiveness or surrendered, or was even allowed to surrender, to bring the war to an end without further killing. In fact, 'killing' is considered 'logical', the only way to achieve the purpose of war. In the Kurukshetra war, after almost every enemy warrior is killed and Duryodhana is hiding alone in a pond, Krishna says that his killing, not surrender or capture, is necessary to end the war. Maybe our very premise, that killing is the highest evil, is wrong.

In the age of the Mahabharata, the dharma of one's inherited calling was deemed the primary, even mandatory, duty or social obligation. Krishna invoked the *Kshatriya dharma* to exhort Arjuna to pick up his bow and fight. It is interesting that the same Kshatriya dharma was cited by Yudhishthira for *not* refusing the invitation of Dhritarashtra to play the game of dice, which he knew could be calamitous. Yudhishthira maintained that a Kshatriya cannot refuse an invitation for the game of dice or for war, perhaps implying that they both lead to ruin. The moral legitimacy of upholding the narrower caste dharma over others, such as ahimsa or non-violence, and virtues like *kshama*, forgiveness, which was what Arjuna preferred, is hard to understand. This is particularly so as Krishna himself warned that a major war like the one at Kurukshetra would be a colossal catastrophe and everyone would be a loser. But Krishna was emphatic that the victory of dharma over adharma was more important than saving lives, even of the innocent and the virtuous. He also reminded Arjuna that he (Arjuna) lives in society; that society does not live in him, implying that Arjuna must subordinate his personal reluctance (to fight) to the needs of the *samaja* (society) and that required the dharma yuddha. But to fight injustice is the dharma of everyone. One cannot say that only Kshatriyas should resist evil and others should surrender. In the Kurukshetra war, even Drona—a Brahmin, and the 'guru' of both the Pandavas and the Kauravas, the two 'enemies'—went into battle; in fact, he was the commander-in-chief of the Kaurava army until he himself was killed through a ruse. Another avatar of Vishnu, Parashurama, born a Brahmin, killed all the Kshatriyas of the world not once but twenty-one times, in revenge for the killing of his father, Jamadagni. So, why did Krishna emphasize the Kshatriya's duty as the reason for Arjuna to fight? There is also the issue of reasonable proportionality; the response has to be measured, appropriate, and no more or less than what is necessary to redress the injustice.

The key concept here is *kartavya* (duty), and like other concepts such as dharma and karma, it is difficult to translate it precisely. The fact is we have so many kartavyas, or duties specific to a relationship, as a spouse, parent, family, friend, citizen, professional, social, religious, and so on. And often they are conflicting and difficult to harmonize. Ultimately, we do make a choice because without choice action is not possible. But it is often based on expediency, the one that gives us pleasure and avoids pain, or the one that is in the interests of the narrow circle of 'near and dear'. From time immemorial all great men, faced with conflicting priorities, agonized over what their kartavya was in the ever-shifting circumstances of their life. And they made hard choices, which sometimes entailed suffering of the 'innocent', but had they chosen a different course, they would have been guilty of not performing their kartavya. Epics are replete with examples. In the Ramayana, Rama had to abandon his pregnant wife Sita, usually revered as the incarnation of goddess Lakshmi and a personification of purity, at the altar of his kartavya as the king. Was he right? In the Mahabharata, Bhishma fought on the side of adharma or evil, as he felt that his kartavya was to honor his vow to serve the king of Hastinapura. Was he right? Life is far more complex and complicated now, the borders between right and wrong, and between caste, creed, and class are at once blurred and sharper, and our desire to discern our kartavya is far more agonizing. Our angst for a purpose in life, our search for meaning is a longing for our kartavya that takes us beyond the drudgery of our mundane desires, desires which are the reason for our countless births and deaths. If only we could know what it is that we must attain—for which everything else can be sacrificed—life would be both simpler and tangible. We often find that our duties and obligations to different people, entities, and institutions clash with each other, and that our cognition and faculties are inadequate to harmonize them and show the way to our kartavya. Is our kartavya confined to family and to personal relationships? Is it possible any more to be a 'good' citizen of a country and also be a global citizen? What kind of sacrifice do we have to make in contemporary life to do our kartavya that will benefit humanity? What is the *moha* (delusionary attachment) that we have to *tyaga* (give up) to do our cosmic duty? Given that our identity is defined by several relationships—member of a family, employee or employer, citizen of a country, global citizen—which responsibility should we cherish and which ones we should give up? Where does our moral culpability begin and end? When patriotism clashes with our duties as a global citizen, what is our kartavya? If our employer adulterates food or peddles poison, but we play no direct part, while he pays us well, what is our kartavya? Is a killing a murder only if we are the direct assassin, not an indirect accomplice? Does inactivity in the face of injustice tantamount to being an accomplice?

'Desirable Death' and *Anaayesaena maranam*

The shadow of death is everywhere but we pretend it is nowhere. In fact, as the English clergyman Thomas Fuller said, "The first breath is the beginning of death". And Nietzsche said that our very language is a cemetery, and if we scratch any word we'll find a dead metaphor. Although we tend to think that even thinking about death is inauspicious, scriptures have told us otherwise; in the words of the ancient Therevada Buddhist text *Visudhimagga* (The Path of Purification), our "Constant task will surely be; This recollection about death". Death is everywhere all the time, and yet we fear that even to think or talk about it is inauspicious, and brings our death nearer. It is the ultimate 'relief' from life but we view it as the 'ultimate evil'. That is why we treat it as taboo, and avoid even to utter the dreaded 'D' word. Instead, we use euphemisms and say things like 'he is no more', 'he has gone', or 'passed away'. Someone said that death has replaced sex as the great forbidden subject. As we grow older, we see more and more of 'no mores' till we ourselves become another 'no more'; and the world moves on to other 'no mores'. We want to banish it from life, on the implicit premise perhaps that that which we don't even think about cannot come to pass. The *Taittiriya* Upanishad says: "When the body falls into weakness on account of old age or disease, even as a mango-fruit, or the fruit of the holy fig-tree, is loosened from its stem, so the Spirit of man is loosened from the human body and returns by the same way to Life, wherefrom he came". In the Bhagavad Gita, Lord Krishna says, "As leaving aside his worn-out garments, a man takes other new ones, so leaving aside worn-out bodies the embodied soul goes to other new ones".

Why do we then mourn death, move heaven and earth to put it off, or postpone as long as we could, and long and wish each other to be a '*chiranjeevi*' (immortal)? If death is like changing an old car for a new one, then why do we go to such extreme lengths to maintain, repair, and rejuvenate this creaking, rickety body? We often lament and ask why do the good, the young die early, and the evil ones linger and live long. It is hard to fathom the aspects of how and why each mode of death is chosen. We cannot 'explain' why in the same accident, or deadly collision, some walk away unscathed, some are injured and some die. Or, why one falls in the garden and breaks his neck, while another falls seven floors and is saved, cushioned by the same lawn. Although no one really knows what a 'good death' means, we usually mean it to be *Anaayesaena maranam*—quick and painless. In other words, a 'bad death' is one that is protracted and painful, or violent. The Vedic prayer, *Anaayesaena maranam*; *Vinaa dhainyaena jeevanam*; *Daehi mae kripayaa shambho*; *Thvaya bhakthim achanchalam*, is a prayer to Lord Siva, requesting him to give death without trouble or pain, life without poverty, and to grant out of compassion, unwavering devotion in Him. Everyone says that those who die at a ripe age, without any preparation or pain, are blessed people. It does not mean that those who die ailing and in agony are sinners. Maybe they are burning a bulk of the bad karma that way. Each dies according to their own prarabdha karma. We must also view death in a broader setting. Everyone has a dharma or swadharma, the natural righteous duty to perform, not only to redeem his karmic dues and for the common good, but also to contribute to a cosmic cause. Not only is one obligated to perform it, but also each is given moral leeway that others are denied; but they have their own. God too has His own swadharma with limitless leeway, as it embraces the entire creation. Even death has a dharma to do. That is why in Hinduism the god of death is called *Dharmaraja*, the Lord of Dharma. But the complicating factor is that the concept of swadharma is a casualty of the passage of yugas. No one can say or know what one's swadharma is, since everyone does what anybody else does; it depends on one's capability, and what a certain relationship or work requires. Nothing, no career or job or work is barred because of one's birth or family or lineage or heritage, and that is modernity and equality in law. Without anything we can call 'swadharma', and caught between conflicting obligations and responsibilities stemming from various relationships, it becomes almost impossible to zero in on anything as one's essential, overriding duty, often at the expense of something else apparently equally important. There are no 'entitlements' on life, not even life.

All these are assumptions that stem from the primal perspective that 'living' is 'good' and death is bad. The good or the young 'die' not because they are good and young, but because simply their 'time is up'; they have expended their allotted karma, paid back their karmic debts in various ways, and must move on. The old or the bad live not because the nature and quantum of karma required them to stay on. A 'good' life may guarantee a 'good' after-life; but does not necessarily lead to a 'good death'. 'Good men', like sages Ramakrishna and Ramana, died of cancer while many 'bad' men died in their sleep. A 'good death' might amount to spending away a lot of good karma; and a 'bad' death, the spending of bad karma, which is good. But then again, neither karma enables us to break the cycle of birth and rebirth. While 'good' karma gives you a temporary time in heaven, bad karma takes you to hell, but still temporarily. Good karma binds us with golden chains, while bad karma binds us with iron chains. Depending on what and how we do, and with what intent, we earn both 'good' and 'bad' karma through almost everything we do every day. If we help another person we earn 'good' karma. If our actions hurt or harm, we attract bad karma. There is no way to either prove or disprove any of it, whether it is a 'scientific' method or spiritual effort. For, "absence of evidence is not evidence of absence", but it also does not establish that anything actually exists. Basically, and logically, it is possible to prove 'existence', and impossible to prove or disprove that something doesn't exist.

Whichever way we perceive our terrestrial existence, once born, there is little escape except to live through life, until this body-machine ceases to operate. Many people, thinkers, writers, and poets, some stricken with terminal illnesses, have written about what it is like to be sitting in death's ante-room. Ideally most of us 'want' to die and get resurrected so that we can recollect and regale how it is on the other side. "I could not see to see", Emily Dickinson mused, imagining the moment of death. Ezra Pound famously wrote, "Pull down thy vanity, it is not man; Made courage, or made order, or made grace; Pull down thy vanity, I say pull down". Faced with this 'double-ignorance'—of what life is for and death amounts to—our mind, true to its nature, comes up with a clever ruse. We don't deny death; we just pass the buck, leave it at every other person's door, not ours. Not only do we *not* know why or when or how, but, more fundamentally, *what* it amounts to. What Plato said is still true: "No one knows whether death, which people fear to be the greatest evil, may not be the greatest good". That is because we don't know the before or the after; we lack perspective. We are all born one way but die in multiple ways. We don't know where the *Darth Vader* lurks, waiting for the appointed moment to pounce. Incidentally, it is interesting that the gender of death differs in languages. While the grim reaper, as well is masculine in English, in Greek mythology, Thanatos is a man but is personified by *Persephone*, a woman. In Latin and Italian, death is feminine. Masculine or feminine, its fatal sting is the same. The messenger and the medium could be a malicious mosquito—which incidentally kills and maims more people than any other creature; an estimated half a million each year worldwide—or a murderous man, or a doomed airplane, or a simple fall in the toilet. Death could be within; in an innocuous cell or any organ. In fact as we live we die within. Sometimes the very thing that gives life can kill too. Nature, it seems, has a sense of wry, if not wicked, humor. A prime example is the most basic of all things: food. Creation itself began with food. The Taittiriya Upanishad says, "From food indeed all creatures are born, whatever creatures dwell on earth; by food, again, surely, they live; then again to the food they go at the end". Without it, we cannot live; people in millions die of deprivation of food, starvation. But the irony is that science tells us that the 'starvation syndrome' or 'calorie-reduction' is so far the only known recipe for longevity, if not immortality. For reasons that are unclear, this 'caloric restriction' regimen also postpones the onset of many degenerative diseases normally associated with ageing. A Nigerian proverb tells us, "The death that will kill a man begins as an appetite". We all say, sometime or the other, that life is transitory, and resonate George Harrison's lyric (1970), 'all things must pass; all things must pass away'. But that does not affect the choices we make. In fact, we think we are 'alive' because we don't know what being dead is, or could be. Now we can't be even certain when someone is truly and irrevocably deemed 'dead'. Scientists tell us that the concept of true death is not the same as it was. It used to be that once you died, you died. Today, we understand that the cells in your body die hours after your supposed death, and 'even after you've become a cadaver, you're still retrievable'. So, it means that we just don't know when we are really dead, may still have a chance to 'wake up to life' a century or two later to a new world. The only 'proof' we are alive is that we can walk and wink, speak and scowl, and because it hurts when we pinch. Research is also under way on another hair-raising dimension that goes beyond immortality. It is to bring back the brain-dead or near-dead to life. That truly is terrifying, attendant with scary side effects like leaving the patient in a state somewhere in between brain-dead and comatose. 'Death technology', we are being enlightened, might even allow your family to use your data to talk to you online after you die. Interacting with someone from beyond the grave may no longer be the stuff of science fiction. Scientists say that it might be possible to make realistic robot clones or androids that are 'fully conscious copies' of our dead, loved ones, or, tangentially, of anyone we fancy. Or fear. Just as 'being human' is not good enough to tell what happens after we die, similarly we cannot tell what might happen on our attempt to achieve such goals. Apart from the question who really wants to live with a simulated-dead one, the fact is that there will be many unforeseeable and unsettling consequences. Is the risk worth taking?

We think we die only once, but 'death' occurs all the time inside each of us; every minute, 300 million cells in our body 'die'. According to Dogen Zenji, the founder of Japanese Soto Zen, Shakyamuni Buddha said that in twenty-four hours "our life is born and dying, rising and falling, 6,400,099,980 times. So in one second our life is born and dies around 70,000 times".[22] In another sense too, we die inside: our sensitivity, our tenderness, our righteous reactions are smothered to death by our own behavior. Someone once said, "Death is not the greatest loss in life. The greatest loss is what dies inside us while we live". That 'death' we don't see but the one we do see everyday does nothing to empower us to be better prepared to face it when our time comes. It is amazing how we never allow death to interfere in our daily decision-making. We never ask ourselves before choosing, 'What if I am dead tomorrow or the day after?' And we never ask, What did the dead lose by dying? How should we live, what must we do, if we do not fear death and accept it as natural? And what if there is 'life after death'? Whose loss—or whose gain—is it anyway? Our small-mindedness, short-sightedness, pettiness, squabbling, bouts of irritation, and 'accursed anger', pleasure-in-other's-pain mindset, do not get dented by the certainty of death. We erect a firewall between the dynamics of our daily deeds and the fickleness of our life. In practical terms, what bothers us is not someone 'being dead', whatever it might mean; it is the physical aspect that irks us. It is our inability to relate with them through our five senses that bothers us. We can no longer feel their presence; we cannot touch or talk to them; they are no longer there when we need them; they become faint memories. One of man's 'irrational' longings is to be remembered, not to be 'forgotten' even after he is dead. It is 'irrational' because we have no clue what happens—what, if any, 'me' or 'mine' lingers after death—and still we want 'permanence' as a memory. But actually we are not content with remembrance or memory in others' minds; we want the medium of the physical body for perpetuity. Sometimes, the bereaved go to psychic 'mediums' to talk through them with their loved-dead, and once they do, or believe that they have done, they no longer grieve, or even want to talk a second time. We feel okay that they are 'okay', wherever they are.

Missing the 'Dead'

We might prefer a zombie, or a person in deep coma, as long as he is still 'alive', to a dead person. The Kathopanishad clearly states, "For the soul, there is neither birth nor death at any time. It does not come into being at any time; it is unborn, eternal and primeval. It doesn't die when the body is put to death". But that kind of implicit eternity is not what modern man seeks. And that doesn't give us an 'alibi' when someone dies. It is possible that we don't see, speak to, or even think of a person for years, and yet when they die, we say we 'miss him/her'. But do the dead 'miss us', or more likely, feel relieved? Maybe we should worry about those who are not yet 'dead', and stop being insensitive, rude, and indifferent. When a person dies, we say good things about him/her that we might have never said when he/she was alive, which they would have been happy to hear. In any case, we don't bother about them once the rituals are over. Is it hypocrisy or magnanimity or pragmatism? In any way we are safe; the dead can't appreciate or complain. That is what dying does, brings out the best and worst from us. Is it all because we do not know what 'being dead' means in relation to 'being alive'? Is it some kind of a 'survival hangover' from the early times when death was mostly sudden and unexpected, and 'being alive' itself was a cause for celebration? Or, is it that, even without our being aware, we are 'happy' there is one less to compare and compete with? It is this 'ignorance' we must dispel to come to terms with mortality. The other reason is that the very thought that we live, struggle, fight so many battles and spend so much time and energy only to lose out and 'die' is unsettling. Man has never accepted mortality; he always waged a war but against hopeless odds. 'Absolute acceptance' would have meant paralyzing life itself. Man spends all his life between seeing the reality of mortality and stubbornly unwilling to accept that reality. The *modus vivendi* he arrives at is to banish that 'reality' from his daily life; to put it away at other people's door; to reject its immediacy and blur its inevitability. Scriptures have told us to accept gracefully what life offers, and to turn that acceptance into a dedication to the divine and utility to fellow humans. Life and death are perceived not as opposites, but as two sides of human existence. Zen master Dogen Zenji says, "Within death there is life; within life there is death.... Viewed from one side, it is life; viewed from the other side, it is death. We are living in each moment and dying in each moment. Life and death are a moment of arising and a moment of decaying, and there is death within life and life within death. Both life and death are facts of the moment. Therefore, life is itself death and death is itself life. The essence of life is nothing more than the interrelation of life and death".[23] Each of us is a 'prisoner' of these two. The question is: What kind of a prisoner do we want to be? We can either turn the prison into an opportunity to do good, or fret, fume, and make others' life hell; it is a choice of disposition. Dogen Zenji continues, "To pursue life outside the present and to tremble at death outside the present is delusion. Therefore, when facing death, you should die with thoroughness... It is well to work with all your effort while you are alive. When you have to die, it is well to withdraw quickly. We must be true to ourselves here and now".[24] Buddhism holds that life itself is no-life and death itself is no-death.

We have been reading and hearing all such soaring and thought-provoking statements for ages. Like our basic 'willful blindness' about death, such descriptions about death receive the same treatment. All that makes no practical difference to our way of life or state of mind, or to our behavior. What is new is the entry of science into the fray, echoing similar thoughts. Science is now telling us that we do not have to 'accept' even that physical 'limitation'; that man now has the means to achieve, if not life forever, at least the life of a *mini-Methuselah*. Science is also now beginning to say that 'there might after all be life after death', and acknowledges that some sort of awareness or consciousness might well survive at least for a while after a person's heart and brain stop functioning. Scientists sum up and say, "Yes, there is life after death and it looks like this applies to everyone.[25] These findings are still tentative, too early to draw any credible conclusions from. But what if, what if science makes a major breakthrough to keep man alive for centuries, if not forever? And what if science develops the technology to establish beyond reasonable doubt that there is 'life after death'? Can we then remain 'human'?

Morbidity and Mortality

As for the 'dull and dreary' (in the words of Somerset Maugham) but deadly tryst we call 'death', human thought has never managed to grasp its true meaning and message. It is too overpowering to be objective; too much of a leap into the void to be rational. It is perhaps a measure of the moral distance we have travelled, that many people might want to apply 'dull and dreary' to life, not death. For them, it is life that has become a deadly battle, and death to them is the release from those very attributes. And we have not found a way to deal with two sets of apparent opposites: the certainty of death and the uncertainty of when and how; and our desire to be deathless and the almost irresistible impulse we have to nibble each other to death, if not to kill outright. On the one hand, our sacred thought tells us that death is just yet another phase of life. And, on the other hand, the best blessing we confer on each other is for a 'long life'. The highest virtue is 'saving life' and the greatest sin is killing. Death is said to be as natural as shedding old clothes for new ones, but we are forbidden from any voluntarily action to hasten that end. 'Right to life', which means to live in dignity, is deemed a human right, but not the 'right to die', that is to die with dignity. Our equation with death, always ambiguous and ambivalent, tenuous and tentative, has become even more convoluted and driven by many contradictions. In everyday terms, death has changed from the ultimate recourse and an extreme remedy for terminal situations, to be the preferred escape route in coping with the routine pressures and temptations of modern life.

Here is an intriguing irony that escapes our attention. Man is seeking, through science, eternal youth and immortality, what is being described as the "realization of the possibility of a radical extension of human life by means of cybernetic technology".[26] But, as always, nothing is so simple. We tend to think that eternal life automatically includes eternal youth, but it is not so. It is possible that we will end up as *Tithonus* (Greek mythology), a mortal who became immortal, but still grew old and frail and eventually begged for death. Alongside our search for life eternal, many are finding that life itself—theirs and of others too—is not worth all that bother. More than death, it is the wear and tear of ageing and the attendant debility, and dependence on others that has marred human life, and which is now a major problem in modern societies. Many are grappling with ageing populations, and that has had serious social side effects. Science is tackling this 'problem' by treating it as a 'disease', to halt and even to undo through technologies like stem cell therapy and organ transplants. When something is called a 'disease', like common cold or cancer, the implication is that it can be 'cured'. It is hard to differentiate between disease-related by-products and age-related debility, and the difference between 'care' and 'cure'. We are culturally conditioned to think that as we become 'old' we should expect to have degenerative diseases, and one is not 'normal' in their absence. We also mix up 'health' and 'well-being', like 'being' and 'becoming'. But there is no doubt that anything science can do to mitigate the ravages of ageing and age-centered diseases, which above all result in loss of control and dignity, is worthy of serious, and morally desirable, pursuit. It is now reported that "scientists have identified a male hormone that reverses cell ageing, potentially setting up new treatments to counter diseases caused by cells getting old and worn out".[27] But the question remains: How would we use the extra youth and energy? Studies have shown that what we call 'lifestyle changes' have a greater effect on 'morbidity' or the incidence of ill health, than on 'mortality' or incidence of death. And that itself, reducing the vulnerability to disease, is a huge plus. It is possible for a disease that is widespread (high morbidity rate) to have a low mortality rate, or vice versa. Morbidity is a cause of mortality, but we can manage morbidity more than mortality. In fact, the major preoccupation of human effort must shift from 'immortality' to reducing 'morbidity', including reducing the terrible toll that even 'intrinsic' ageing takes on human life.

But what we find is that while we search ways to eliminate not only extrinsic but also 'intrinsic ageing', a new study finds that we have with us the reverse, 'accelerated ageing'; that many young people are ageing three times faster than the usual, that their biological age is 20 years older than what their birth certificates indicate.[28] It is debatable whether or not environmental or lifestyle factors can actually inhibit and retard the development of the pathology of ageing. We cannot say that extrinsic causes have nothing to do with diseases. We cannot, day in day out and in every possible way, pollute and poison everything that goes into us and say it has nothing to do with us being more susceptible to debilitating diseases. While we have some control over our eating, we have practically none over the air we breathe; the only way to have 'clean air' all around would be perhaps to go live in the mountains. Some years ago, a study showed that air pollution kills nearly 9,500 people in London (UK) every year. It would no doubt be far higher in such densely populated urbans centers as Mumbai or Shanghai or Rio. But we accept it as a price of modern life—we can't give up our SUVs, how then can we complain? Sadly, road rage gets us worked up; not deaths due to air poisoning. We are a stunningly strange species that mocks at any neat description. On the one hand, we want eternal youth and immortality and on the other hand, we poison our bodies for the sake of money, and kill ourselves and others at the slightest irritation or provocation. Few even notice this paradox. But with all these apparent anomalies there has been a central change in the human perception and equation with death.

Generally all religions view death as a part of the continuum of life; they say that we should welcome it, but at the same time they disapprove of suicide. Even many philosophers echo this view. Socrates maintained that philosophy is essentially a lifelong 'meditation [or mindfulness of] on death' (*melete thanatou*). When asked to explain the paradox of welcoming death and shunning suicide, he said that we are the possessions of the gods, and so have no right to harm ourselves, which is also what religions say. The only religious exception is Jainism, which is older than Buddhism, and which has a scripturally sanctified and respected practice of 'suicide' called *santhara* or *sallekhana*. It is even deemed sacred as a way of detaching oneself from life and easing oneself into after-life.

The method adopted is to fast unto death voluntarily. It is considered an act of ahimsa, of non-violence, as a way of subjugating one's passions. In his daily prayer, the person wishes to be able to face death after having taken the vow of santhara. What was accepted as an ancient religious and spiritual practice attracted wider public attention in recent years, with an Indian high court declaring it as tantamount to committing suicide, which is illegal in India. It may be recalled that Gandhi used 'fast unto death' as a formidable social and political weapon. The British prosecuted him for treason, but not for trying to commit suicide. Gandhi's 'fast into death', unlike that of the Jains, was to compel others, even if it was for good, to do his bidding, which was in itself an act of violence in spirit. It was intended to remove hatred from the human mind; and he failed, following the hallowed line of avatars like Krishna and prophets like Christ and Buddha. But the broader question is: How much right does an individual have to choose when to discard his worn-out clothes (which is how the Bhagavad Gita describes death), or should he helplessly cling to those tattered clothes until they drop off at someone else's bidding?

'Practical Immortology' or 'Immoral' Immortality

We all want to find happiness in life; we all want to evade death; we all want God (or the gods, or karma) to smile on us; we all wish life were less mechanical and more magical; we all want surcease of sorrow. We *want*. We want want. And what we want most is to insure that we keep wanting. In fact, our longing for life, eternal youth, and eternity on earth is to have more time to 'want' more desires. Without 'want' we are worthless in our own mind. Gandhi said that "Man falls from the pursuit of the ideal of plain living and high thinking the moment he wants to multiply his daily wants. Man's happiness really lies in contentment". Down the ages, man has struggled to harmonize three basic 'wants': to make sense of life; to live life fully; to live forever. Plato's *Republic* quotes Socrates as saying, "I do not think that we have adequately determined the nature and number of the appetites, and until this is accomplished the enquiry will always be confused". Those 'appetites' are human wants; the 'confusion' is now about the means to get them. It is more accentuated with the transformation of the human into an avaricious animal with unquenchable appetite for consumer goods, which now far exceed the bounds of convenience and comfort. Assuming—an assumption that itself begs questioning—that 'being human' entitles us to live at a higher plateau of life than other animals, and that what we call 'basic human needs' are of a higher order than the basic needs of other animals, which primarily are confined to survival and reproduction, the question is: How should man satisfy his higher needs and how does morality impact on that endeavor? In our contemporary culture, almost every day, new 'needs' or rather 'wants' are being added, which is at the root of the economic, environmental, and ecological problems the world raises. And often we find that what we desire, what we do, and what we get are different and out of sync, and that leads to the discontent and despair. In the end, every desire, the way it arises, the way it gets fulfilled, becomes a moral statement.

The desire to live forever is a dominant drive in human beings. It takes many forms—as a desire for progeny, for fame or fortune, to leave behind something that does not let us be forgotten. While these are ways to 'indirect' immortality, science is now attempting 'direct' immortality. It is reported that "by tweaking our DNA, we could soon survive for hundreds of years", possibly up to 800 years.[29] Scientists are also trying to solve the riddle of ageing and to let us enjoy eternal youth, like angels. We cannot read Einstein's, and Hawking's 'mind of God', or the probable response of nature, but we have to choose whether we want to live forever in this world. That could be the ultimate moral choice. Or maybe the computer will make that choice for us and for nature and God, and solve the problem: turn on man and annihilate humanity! Are we really paving that way by incessantly empowering computers? We are told that computing power is now doubling every year, and that by 2020, personal computers will have the processing power of the human brain—some 20 *million billion* calculations per second. That, by 2030, it will take a whole village of human brains to match a $1,000 computer. And, finally, that by 2050, about $1,000 worth of computing will equal the processing power of *all* human brains on earth. By the close of the 22nd century, some say, 'nonbiological thinking will be trillions of trillions of times more powerful than that of its biological progenitors, although it will be still of human origin'. It is also being envisioned that brain-consciousness and chip-consciousness would merge, creating what is being called 'consciousness-singularity'. What science is grappling with is, according to Alexandra Elbakyan,[30] "How to engineer a neural implant that will integrate itself successfully within a complex network of neurons; how the neural implant can fit well within the complex, self-organizing system that is the brain; and how separate, autonomous neural networks such as brains of different people can be wired together so that they will work as a system with single, unified consciousness". Ultimately, however, the earth's technology-creating species will merge with its own computational technology, that is the brain. Through technologies such as 'zapping', brain-scientists are also said to be on the verge of precisely identifying specific regions or parts of the brain responsible for specific functions, habits, and addictions including such mundane things as 'saving' and 'spending'. Stimulating particular parts to achieve particular results and behavioral changes and getting rid of 'bad' habits and inducing 'good' habits might be possible. It is hard to imagine, much less anticipate, how and where this brain-body-machine triangle will lead us.

The other road to 'immortality' is spiritual and scriptural, the emphasis being on the 'spirit' rather than the body, not on overcoming death but on eliminating birth. The Chandogya Upanishad says, "He who knows both the transcendent and the immanent; With the immanent overcomes death; And with the transcendent reaches immortality". A distinction is made between 'overcoming' death in the immanent state of innateness, and reaching 'immortality' in the state of being beyond. Prayers in the Brihadaranyaka Upanishad sum up the spiritual goals of human life to attain which a person seeks divine guidance. According to the purifying chant, *Pavamana-Abhyaroha mantra*,[31] what we call death is itself the unreal; and what is other than death is the immortal, it is the Real. We seek divine help to go beyond the unreal to the Real, which is the same as to transcend from death to immortality. These words have special meanings with highly philosophical connotations, and great rishis and sages have internalized and expounded on them. In this light, it means that the world in which we are living, the world of appearances, the phenomenal world, is the world of death, *Mrutyuloka*, the realm of the dying, the world of unreality. The prayer is for one to be transformed or transmuted, from the confused state of consciousness that sees the unreal world as real, to the realm of Reality. That which appears to be real, and yet, is not real—that is the *Asat.* The difficulty most people have is that they cannot relate to something that is so real and tangible, the world we live in, the joy, the love, the pain, the suffering, all being called unreal. But what *asat* or unreal does not mean is that the world is unreal; it is *the way we see it,* the appearance that is unreal, because it is our senses, controlled by the mind, that filter our comprehension and conception of the world, not our real Self. Unreal is not non-existence; it is the colored and corrupted perception of existence. It is this kind of existence or non-existence that drives our lives and incubates and generates the plethora of desires.

As for the intergenerational dimension, the underlying idea of the words *mrtyor ma amritam gamaya*, is that the world of 'life' is really a world of 'death' and seeks divine mercy to take us to the world of the Immortal, beyond the cycle of birth and death. Socrates said, either intuitively or inspired by Upanishadic thought, something quite remarkable, "All men's souls are immortal, but the souls of the righteous are both immortal and divine". The Upanishads say, "When all the desires that surge in the heart are renounced, the mortal becomes immortal". Without desires there is no more birth, and without birth we cannot die, and that is immortality. The Kathopanishad elaborates, "The mortal in whose heart desire is dead becomes immortal. The mortal in whose heart the knots of ignorance are untied becomes immortal. These are the highest truths taught in the scriptures". When desire dies, when ignorance drops away, immortality is revealed, not attained. The reason is that we are inherently, and always have been, immortal and divine, but out vision is clouded and murky. The Indian mystic-guru Sri Chinmay explains: "The outer life is humanity. The inner life is immortality. The life around is reality. The life above is divinity. The life below is obscurity. When divinity descends into humanity, the soul of humanity becomes hopeful. When divinity descends into immortality, the soul of immortality becomes meaningful. When divinity enters into reality, the soul of reality becomes fruitful. When divinity enters into obscurity, the soul of obscurity becomes prayerful".

Cornered, our 'conscience', or rather what little of it still remains, tells us that we should rid ourselves of desire and ignorance, but how can we achieve such a state of consciousness, especially since we have been in the vice-like grip of these very two ogres for a very long time? Since the spiritual effort seems too Sisyphean, and we cannot attain that state, we opt for other, easier, ways. In fact, all our life, all effort—the ultimate desire—is to attain 'immortality' of some kind or the other. We want to be remembered; 'live' forever, if not in our bodies, at least in other bodies or in others' memories and minds. We want to have children for immortality; we want to acquire property for immortality; we want fame—or infamy—for immortality; our creativity—or destructiveness—is for immortality. But it is far, far from what scriptures have alluded to. It is to transit from one state of consciousness, death, to another, immortality, through the eternity of creation. The Upanishadic prayer is for assistance in realizing the truth that "I was never born, nor can ever die, as I am not the body, mind, and intellect, but the eternal, blissful consciousness that serves as the substratum of all creation". What science is trying to do is to equate the body with the Self, and present life with eternal life. That, coupled with the growing ascendancy of avarice and malice in human affairs, raises a crucial question: How will the possibility, let alone the probability of 'immoral immortality', of even tripling or quadrupling of life expectancy, affect and influence human behavior? Which of the two sides innate in the human—the *deva* or the *asura*, the god or the demon—will come to the fore and dominate our personality? Without the fear of hell or evil, will all those hidden and thus far hesitant desires burst out, and make man truly and properly the 'King of Beasts'? Or would man, freed at last from the fear of death and knowing that he has all the time in the world to do the things he wants to do, attain the goal of Self-realization, the Upanishadic goal of human life? Or could it be that, as Billy Graham said, "We cannot truly face life until we face the fact that it will be taken away from us", leaving us to wonder about what will happen if we know that 'it will not be taken away'?

The awesome act of whacking out another's life is not as fearsome or forbidding as before. Is it just another symbol of violence in the world, as foretold in Hindu scriptures (in the description of Kali Yuga), or is there some far deeper message from nature? Suicide was never confined to the terminally ill, weak-minded, mentally feeble, clinically or manically depressed people, or to those weighed down by failed marriages, crippling debts, or crushing problems. Hundreds of celebrities, stars, writers, and philosophers have at some point found no 'rationale' to continue to live. Sometimes, it is not even a sudden or impulsive decision. Virginia Woolf, who took her own life in 1941 at the age of fifty-nine, wrote way back in her dairy in 1925, chillingly and almost casually: "I do not any longer feel inclined to doff the cap to death… no leave-takings, no submission, but someone stepping out into the darkness".[32] Another case is that of the actor

Robin Williams (who committed suicide in August 2014), who brought such joy and laughter to so many millions. Some successful and sane people are simply concluding 'life, that is not for me', a kind of repudiation of one of our most embedded beliefs: survival instinct. It seems that nothing is too trivial or terrible to end a life. Benumbed as we are, trying to come to terms with this terrible truth, we hear and read about the strides being made to realize man's immortal quest for immortality. There has always been, at least for an untrained mind, a fog of ambivalence and ambiguity around mortality and immortality in both sacred and secular thought. On the one hand, scriptures tell us that it is just another phase in life akin to the passage from infancy to adolescence to youth to old age. At the same time, the most common blessing in all cultures and the one that saints bestow is 'may you live long'—no one blesses and says 'may you die soon'. Imposing death—capital punishment—is deemed the highest punishment and a deterrent. If death is not such a big deal, then why is any killing by the State or society or even individual such a horrendous thing? Has the time come when we should treat death—any death—as a 'good' thing for the individual as well as for the world? It is not mortality that is a threat to mankind, but *immortality*. Whether it is 'making' life in a lab, or seeking immortality, or destroying the biosphere or global warming, human predation is now the most destabilizing activity on earth. When God made man his regent on earth, and when nature allowed him to lord over other forms of life on earth, the deal was that man will be moral and remain mortal. Man is now reneging on that premise and promise. These are testing times not only for man but also for God and nature. Such is the baneful impact of human activity on earth that they cannot dismissively brush it aside with, as Shakespeare (Puck; *Midsummer Night's Dream*) puts it, 'Lord, what fools these mortals be!' That 'foolhardiness' coupled with hauteur has become a mortal threat and now carries cosmic consequences. No longer can morality be left confined and defined by the present parameters. Even if we set aside potential divine displeasure or the danger of crossing the line between the formidable forbearance of nature and provoking nature's vengeful fury, the fact is that unless we reach some kind of a new conceptual and operational understanding on what 'being moral' has to be in the modern age, and whether mortality is simply a personal matter or if it has social—and spiritual—implications, we will not be able to make any headway in making human society peaceable and harmonious.

We have never been sure how to face death: whether to look forward to it, like Socrates did, or just await with resignation, or even, as Dylan Thomas (1951) implored us, "Do not go gentle into that good night; Old age should burn and rave at close of day; Rage, rage against the dying of the light". Scriptures enjoin upon us to turn the inevitability of death as a spur to be good, do good and leave behind good imprints which, they tell us, will help us to go to heaven or reap the dividends in another life. In other words, to be moral and to ensure a better after-life. But the truth is that it has not worked; we behave as if we are immortal and we spend much of life in grabbing, acquiring, and accumulating goods and possessions regardless of morality or means. In short, death has not dimmed or diluted greed, aggression, and hate, and we have remained captives of anger, violence and malice. That paradox threatens to become a mortal peril with science promising bodily eternity and man sliding inexorably into evil. And that is a 'deadly mix' and how that will affect human nature is hard to predict because we have no precedents to go by. In fact, it is the 'fear of punishment—by society or God—and 'hope of reward', here or hereafter, that keeps most men 'moral'. If that is taken away, what kind of a social—and spiritual—being would man become? In fact, mortality might be the only 'comparative cosmic advantage' we have over the angels. Socrates said that death is the greatest of all human blessings. With so much pain and suffering in life, even a life span close to that of a mini-Methuselah could become intolerable. We might then long for death as we are longing for deathlessness. As Norman Cousins said, the greatest loss in life is not death but what *dies inside us* while we are alive. What dies inside is true morality. We still debate if morality—to be 'naturally' altruistic—is built-in or built-up, innate or inspired, a 'social' necessity or a divine imperative.

Immortality of the Soul

Mythical tales of immortals are found everywhere, from Greek myths and alchemists' notebooks to modern movies and futuristic science-fiction books. Ever since humans first saw 'death', our mortality has been front and center in our long list of woes, the most enduring of the challenges. In every culture, in every age, many people have attempted to cheat death. Qin Shi Huang,

Emperor of China in the 3rd century BCE, feared death and desperately sought the fabled elixir of life that would allow him to live forever. The biblical Adam and Eve lost it. Alchemists have long tried to brew magic potions for immortality. To live forever while keeping well and retaining the glow and vigor of youth is one of humanity's oldest and most elusive goals. Science is saying that it can deliver what legendary figure like Gilgamesh failed to grasp. According to the distinguished Russian scientist and philosopher Igor Vishev, it is likely that there are people alive today who will never die. He calls his line of thought 'practical immortology'. As the science of ageing advances, scientists have made tremendous progress in extending the human life span. From lowering infant mortality rates to creating effective vaccines and reducing deaths related to disease, science has helped increase the average person's life span by nearly three decades over the past century. Genetic engineering, replacement of natural organs with artificial instruments, nanotechnology, and other developing technologies could now extend our lives well beyond today's assumed limits. But immortality will not mean invincibility, or bodily impregnability. People could still die, accidentally or by their own hand, or by some disease or other. People will still kill, the body can yet be destroyed. Suicides and homicides and fatal road accidents will not vanish. Eventually, techniques of 'practical resurrection', towards which today's cloning is but a tentative first step, would be able to restore life to those who somehow lose it. Does that mean that a million years from now, man will be walking on earth with the present body? If that were so, what about mutation and evolution? What about the mind/consciousness? In an immortal society, how do you make room for new generations? Science also dangles before us, through what they call 'age disrupters or interrupters', a cure for ageing, if not the elixir of eternal youth. One line of thinking is that ageing is plastic, that it is encoded. And if something is encoded, you can crack the code. The secret to becoming immortal lies, according to scientists like Aubrey de Grey, not in some mysterious elixir of life, but in the power of regenerative medicine. His strategies for engineered negligible senescence (SENS) are based on combating what de Grey has identified as the 'seven deadly assassins' in our bodies, including our immune system. We must remember that what differentiates the immortality of the scriptures and of science is that the scriptural is indirect, implicit and of the soul or spirit, while the scientific one is direct, explicit and of the shell, but melded with a machine.[33] In the Bhagavad Gita, Lord Krishna explains: "For the soul there is neither birth nor death at any time. He has not come into being, does not come into being, and will not come into being. He is unborn, eternal, ever-existing and primeval. He is not slain when the body is slain". The body is simply an external covering of the soul. Being material, the body is by nature temporary, and must at some point decay, deteriorate, and die. The soul on the other hand is spiritual in nature. For it, there is no beginning or end. Krishna further clarifies: "One who has taken his birth is sure to die, and after death one is sure to take birth again. Therefore, in the unavoidable discharge of your duty, you should not lament". He describes death as "a man casting off worn-out garments taketh new ones, so the dweller in the body casting off worn-out bodies, entereth into others that are new".

Swami Vivekananda further amplified it and said, "Even the lowest of the low have the *Atman* (Soul) inside, which never dies and never is born, immortal, without beginning or end, the all pure, omnipotent and omnipresent *Atman!*" Not only scriptures and sages but also philosophers have envisioned the 'immortality of the soul'. One of them is Immanuel Kant (*Theory of Ethics*) who wrote, "Pure practical reason postulates the immortality of the soul, for reason in the pure and practical sense aims at the perfect good (*Summum bonum*), and this perfect good is only possible on the supposition of the soul's immortality". Another 18th-century philosopher Marquis de Condorcet wrote, "Would it be absurd now to suppose that the improvement of the human race should be regarded as capable of unlimited progress? That a time will come when death would result only from extraordinary accidents or the more and more gradual wearing out of vitality, and that, finally, the duration of the average interval between birth and wearing out has itself no specific limit whatsoever? No doubt man will not become immortal, but cannot the span constantly increase between the moment he begins to live and the time when naturally, without illness or accident, he finds life a burden?" (*Sketch for a Historical Picture of the Progress of the Human Mind*, 1822). The irony here is that on the one hand, we want to shrink or slice off or slow down ageing and attain bodily permanence, while at the same time deliberately poisoning everything that goes into our body through our sense organs—what we see, eat, drink, hear, and breathe—that makes us sick and debilitated. It is only when we can instinctively connect with others' pain that we can attain the kind of 'immortality' that is implied in the words of Norman Cousins: "If something comes to life in others because of you, then you have made an approach to immortality". In fact, man's time-worn longing for immortality belies his claim to be the only rational animal. In life, he wants everything 'new'; discards everything out of boredom, even 'partners'; he constantly wants to 'experiment'; yet, he wants to cling to this body, even when it is terrible to behold, worn-out, when it is no longer able to give the one thing man pursues all life: physical pleasure and sensory satisfaction. Why does he want to carry the boulder of such a body eternally? Is this some kind of cosmic curse on the *Homo sapiens*, his inane or insane desire to evolve into *Homo immortalis?*

While scientists and researchers are trying to curtail, if not cure, old age, and double or triple our life span, if not outright personal eternity on earth, an ever-escalating number of people are unable to absorb or accept what 'being alive' entails, and are prematurely terminating their allotted tenure on earth. For the rest, every minute they are alive is actually a sort of 'suspended animation', simply 'living' by default, or, as the 112-year-old Japanese supercentenarian, Sakari Momoi put it, "simply have not died yet". Despite the fact that "in less than a century more years were added to life expectancy than all years added across all prior millennia of evolution combined",[34] and despite the wonders of medicine and our bodily obsession, the truth still is that both an individual life span and the timing of death remains a matter of random luck and pure perchance. But every minute also, as Henry Miller[35] noted, "is a golden one for him who has the vision to recognize it as such". Whether it will be 'golden' or 'ghoulish' hinges on the state of our consciousness. The pertinent question about 'practical immortology' is, if freed from the fear of death, how will man behave? What will man do with eternal life? We are completely at a loss about what to do with ourselves in a life span of less than a century. Those who want immortality have no idea either; they just don't want to die, that is all. If the entire complex of our culture, mindset, and perception of life were to move from one based on the certainty of human mortality to one based on the prospect of human immortality, what will happen in the 'war within'? What might happen to man's quest to be a moral, spiritual being?

The practical possibility of death becoming a human choice, not an implacable inevitability, has affected the human psyche profoundly. It raises some very fundamental issues and turns everything upside down. Our evolution has not prepared us for this, nor our consciousness. How to prepare for and cope with the certainty of death at an uncertain time is the central theme of all religions. We cannot pinpoint when man first became aware of the fact that life ends in the endless darkness of death, but nothing has been the same since. In fact, it was that 'awareness' that was the beginning of religion, philosophy, and human inquisitiveness about the meaning of his being and his manifest mission on earth. The two things that make life so difficult for man are the certainty of death, and the uncertainty of the hour of death. Although all 'living' beings die, death is, in its effect and impact, a quintessentially human grief; other animals are not tormented by it as we are. When the time is up, often as a prey of another animal, they just die and are done with it. But after billions of words spoken about it, and despite John Donne's *'no man is an island'* and *'every death diminishes me'*, the fact remains that each of us wants to be a 'walled island'. What we truly detest is not death but *our* death. Some deaths we might mourn, because a bit of us too dies when someone we love dies; other deaths we do not mind at all; inwardly we might even be relieved.

The social dimension of mortality must be given far more importance than we do now. On a planet so crowded and with so many deprived of dignity and decent 'living space', the question crops up: Is immortality itself immoral? And could it be that 'hastening' a mortality is the height of morality? Is death dissolution or deliverance, simply shedding of worn-out clothes for new ones, as the Bhagavad Gita says, or is it turning totally 'naked'? Is mortality the only route to reach God? If human birth, being the highest form of life on earth (so we self-proclaim), is required for all creatures to end the cycle of birth and death, then does deathlessness of a few deprive the rights of millions? Do we have other bodies besides the physical one we live in, and is there such a thing as soul, and are we the only privileged ones? And the most troubling question: Is there any cosmic cause and divine design in the suicides and homicides in the world that are fast approaching pandemic proportions? In other words, could this be nature's response to man's pursuit of bodily permanence?

Four Paths to Immortality

To arrest the 'drift', to recover lost ground, we must get down to the basics; get to know what happens inside each of us as we get on with our myriad choices of our mundane lives. It is a telling paradox how much 'knowledge' we have of the world outside and how little of the one within. Billions of people go about their lives without any awareness of anything about their essence and inside. And it also tells a lot about the human condition, human travails, and frustrations and about why we behave the way we do, so completely beyond our own control. We do not know why we behave the way we do, simply because we do not know what makes us do what we do. It is like wondering why the car is breaking down, without opening, or being unable to open, the bonnet and peering in. Our 'behavior', our very way of thinking, our priorities are all baffling paradoxes. Had they been exhibited in any other species, we would have called them either daft or deranged or perverse. On the one hand, we are doing everything we could to hasten our collective mortality and, on the other hand, we are sedulously seeking individual immortality. The belief is that immortality might be possible if we stop programming our consciousness about mortality, and reject all our preconceived notions about death. We are also not sure what we really mean and want from 'immortal life'. Does human 'immortality' offer immunity from suicides or homicides or fatal accidents? In fact, in all probability such deaths could well be the major and infectious 'diseases' of the future. Among the three—suicides, murders, and accidents—the less noticed but increasingly more lethal is accidents. And within the rubric of 'accidents', which include industrial accidents like Bhopal and Chernobyl and Fukushima, airplane crashes, crippling injuries, and fatalities on the road are mounting. In fact, our roads and highways have become the new killing fields of the world, outranking the toll in wars and natural calamities like typhoons, volcanic eruptions, and earthquakes. Man kills himself on the roads with the aid of the very machines he has developed to 'kill' distance. Our insane fascination with speed also contributes. An estimated 1.2 million people are killed in road crashes each year, and as many as 50 million are injured, occupying 30% to 70% of orthopedic hospital beds in developing countries. And if the present trends continue, road traffic injuries are predicted to be the third-leading contributor to the global burden of disease and injury by

2020.[36] According to the Commission for Road Safety, fatalities on the road are estimated to go up to 19 million from the current level.

The core of the problem is that man chases the mirages of permanence and perfection, which are the attributes of the divine. What Bernard Shaw said about love applies to all life: perfect love is possible only via correspondence. Death is the most frequently happening 'happening' in the world. In the year 2012, an estimated 56 million such 'happenings' happened. But we behave as if it is someone else's 'happening', another person's sorrow. It has been said that 'the classical man's worst fear was inglorious death; the modern man's worst fear is just death'.[37] The paths towards that end have to be four-fold. One is to freeze the status quo: to simply go on 'living' in this body and on this earth. Two, to 'rise again and/or 'live' in different bodies with some sort of continuity like a soul, atman, spirit etc., which is the essence of religious 'immortality'. Three, to live forever through some sort of 'legacy': biological, through children and blood-ties, cultural, like art, literature, and so on. The fourth is a modification or 'improvement' over the first, in fact of all the above, which is what science is trying to do. It has convinced itself that bridging the gap between life and death is the only true measure of success; everything else is a detail. It is to make 'death' not final but temporary, restore the dead to life after a period of deep slumber through technologies like cryonics.[38] The curious question is: If someone who has been 'dead' for a century or two comes to 'life', what kind of person will he be? Will he carry and retain all his characteristics, say stammering or alcoholism, or say spouse-bashing? Or will he be a different personality? If he is 'different', how can he be the same person? And if he is the 'same', mentally, psychologically, and habitually, then what is the point? For the whole idea of immortality is to overcome the state "in which they strive to devour each other", to borrow the words of the 19th-century thinker Nikolai Fyodorov, or overcome their 'state of cannibalism'. If human consciousness remains frozen along with the body, then any such 'immortality' would be the grossest monstrosity. We want to give 'death' to death and substantially shrink old age. Woody Allen simplified how we want to deal with death: "I don't want to achieve immortality through my work; I want to achieve immortality through not dying. I don't want to live in the hearts of my countrymen; I want to live in my apartment". As of now people do die in abodes and 'apartments', and dying still means a physical process. We live and die in the 'world of mortality', live in the world of physical reality to which the laws of 'Increasing Entropy' apply, and a world which ends at the moment of death. When that 'moment' arrives, only the good we do helps. In *Engaging in Bodhisattva Behavior,* a Tibetan Buddhist scholar writes, "So, for the sake of this impermanent life, I've caused so much negative karmic force to build up... When seized by the messengers of the Lord of Death, What help are relatives? What help are friends? Only my positive karmic force will provide me a safe direction then".[39]

While seeking and searching for immortality to the species, what modern man has done is to turn 'death' itself into the ultimate weapon against another man. 'Killing', in essence, induced or enforced 'deliberate death', is fast becoming a preferred choice for dispute settlement, a fevered finale to personal frustrations and inadequacies in the human world. What we forget is that, as Bernard Rieux says, 'the order of the world is shaped by death'. For some kind of 'killing' takes place all the time, in nature, inside our own bodies. Doctors 'kill' pathogens, bacteria, and viruses to cure a disease. We terminate and exterminate 'life' in our life every day in the guise of self-preservation, but actually for supremacy. We can 'kill' without actually killing; and it does not have to be one lethal blow. We can 'kill' with a withering glance, a curt dismissal, a cutting word, even brusque body-language; each time anything makes us 'feel small', makes us say 'I wish I were dead', something does 'die' inside. We can 'kill', not necessarily by 'taking a life', but by taking away one's dignity and self-respect. And we can 'die' drip by drip, until actual 'killing', or death in any other way, becomes a breather. All 'killing' is of course not the same. Killing a mosquito is not the same as killing a man; although the mosquito might think otherwise. It might think, 'I am just acting according to my nature and I will die if I don't'. Man has no such alibi. The human is the only one responsible for unnecessary, unwarranted, and unnatural killing in nature, particularly in relation to other species. But man alone is capable of turning 'killing' into an act of mercy, like in euthanasia. Man alone also kills for profit, pleasure, and for fun and for control. Other animals more routinely kill, but often no more than needed for filling their stomachs. After his famous 'anaconda and earl' experiment, Mark Twain said, "The fact stood proven that the difference between an earl and an anaconda is that the earl is cruel and the anaconda isn't; and that the earl wantonly destroys what he has no use for, but the anaconda doesn't. This seemed to suggest that the anaconda was not descended from the earl. It also seemed to suggest that the earl was descended from the anaconda, and had lost a good deal in the transition". Indeed, there are few, if any, causes or reasons, for which man does not kill anyone who is deemed an obstacle or inconvenience, not even his own children or parents. It is the 'circumstance', the context, which determines, to a large extent, any act's moral standing. But 'circumstance' is so circumscribed, so elastic that, without right intent, it can become a cover. And in the English language, at least, ironically, as a kind of Freudian slip, 'killing' also means a 'great success'; we say 'we made a killing' when we hit the jackpot.

We are 'killers' in an other way. We bemoan how short-lived humans are but what we do is to 'kill' that precious time in worthless viewing and doing. The real danger, the terrifying prospect is that while for much of human history 'survival' was the default mode in human cognition, what neuroscience calls default mode network, 'death' seems to be fast replacing it. One of many paradoxes that dot the modern human mindset is that despite his growing self-love and selfishness, his survival instinct is faltering, like to some extent the maternal instinct. Perhaps it is the price we are paying for crossing the '*Lakshmana rekha*', or the forbidden line, in our ceaseless endeavor to become 'immortal' and to enhance our brain-led 'intelligence', more particularly by merging or integrating human and machine intelligence. What Adam Smith said about division of labor in a mechanized factory, in which most workers perform 'simple operations', applies even more to our increasing reliance on machine intelligence; that it would make workers "as stupid and ignorant as possible for a human creature to be".[40] In the case of division of labor, it is because they lose the 'habit of exertion'; in regard to excessive reliance on machines to do much of our work, it will be because much of our related faculties atrophy. If we believe that the earth is a living organism, as the Gaia hypothesis posits, and that nature has some immutable laws that govern and keep harmony in the cosmos, then it could be that in so doing, human 'intelligence' has become an intolerable threat to nature. In the natural world, 'intelligence' above that which is necessary but not necessarily sufficient for sheer survival is programmed to extinguish itself. 'Being too clever' is too much of a peril to the exquisite balance in the world. What could be more ironic that a species supposedly acquiring the know-how to cure the 'disease of death' is turning death into a default-mode of that very 'intelligence'. Our 'intelligence', the one which we prize most, the one with which we differentiate and discriminate and look down upon some and venerate some others, the one with which to conquer the stars and make man an immortal superman, is the issue, the problem and obstacle. It is this intelligence that has paved the way for the much-talked about 'Sixth Extinction', for turning the human into the most feared life-form on earth and into what Edward Wilson called, an 'environmental abnormality'. Nature's answer is what we ourselves are doing with our brain. While we are trying to enhance its power and reach, nature is 'fixing' it so that every time we face a 'problem', an unwelcome or irksome or painful situation, we turn to self-extinction as a way of solving it, if not salvation.

Pandemics of Suicide and Homicide, and the 'War'

Whatever are the contributory causes, the reality is that it is leading a growing number of people to become, in the words of Barbara Gowdy, "enraptured by the idea of *no longer existing*".[41] At a time when many also believe, as Sartre said, that 'existence precedes essence', that good living is more important than good life, such an 'entrapment' is a telling testament to how adrift, anchorless, and empty human life has come to be. In the phenomenal world, which is the world as it appears to be, mystery and misery coexist: the mystery of 'life' and the misery of living. The question that we have never been able to answer is: Are we for 'real'? Or are we an 'act'? The tension between the two has always held sway over man's mind, but some kind of delicate détente has prevailed for much of human history. However, that has virtually come apart in modern times, leading to an almost irresistible *cupio dissolvi*, a 'desire to be dissolved', a desire to go 'anywhere outside this world'. In the final reckoning, it is 'desire' that is destiny. The Brihadaranyaka Upanishad eloquently cautions: "You are what your deep, driving desire is. As your desire is, so is your will. As your will is, so is your deed. As your deed is, so is your destiny". If 'dissolution' is our collective desire, so will it be. Desire becomes, after a length of time, involuntary and indistinguishable from thought and belief. What we believe we will become, we become. It is possible that, although death is not a matter of perception but physical, we all die, because for over a million years we made up our minds that we all die, and therefore we die, actually die. That 'belief' or that 'thought' is not only mental; it is embedded in every cell in our body and at the deepest layers of our consciousness. That is what those living in the *Immortality Commune* of Gavdos, a tiny island off the coast of Greece, believed in. The causal question is: Why is the contemporary human, who thinks he has mastered nature and who now wants to master mortality itself, thus far the sole sanctuary of 'gods,' so disillusioned, distraught, discontented, and in such despair about his lot, and in such a state of restless rebellion against the present? At this pivotal and perilous point in human evolution and history, the truth of the matter is that whatever constitutes the human essence, whether we are a mere mortal body or an infinite immortal soul, modern man is battling several crippling contradictions—self-centeredness and self-destruction, narcissism and nihilism, fear of 'imminent implosion', and aspiration for a 'god-like' existence, ugly affluence, and abysmal poverty. And this battle or 'war' is taking a heavy toll on the human psyche, personality, and inner harmony.

What we witness in the world outside by way of restlessness, angst, insensitivity, intolerance, meanness, and senseless assault on nature, are the by-products of this war. Even without our being fully conscious, the silent pandemics of suicide and homicide are sweeping across the globe, and while the thresholds of restraint become lower with every passing day, the triggers are also getting more and more trivial.[42] It is contemporary, but foreseen long ago. In fact, one of the characteristics of the current Kali Yuga, as it was written in Hindu epics and scriptures, is that "people will have thoughts of murder for no justification, and they will see nothing wrong with that mindset. Family murders will also occur. People will see those who are helpless as easy targets and remove everything from them". It is hard to assess which is a greater tragedy—killing oneself or others, when one is down and driven to desperation. The stress and strain of modern life is enticing some very vulnerable people into embracing necrophilia: love for all that is violence and destruction; the desire to kill; the worship of force; attraction to death, to suicide, to sadism.[43] For far too many people these days, Edna St. Vincent Millay's *Lament*—Life must go on; I forget just why—is not good enough to keep them alive. Suicide, even homicide, is alarmingly becoming the preferred escape from suffering; the only way to terminate an intolerable situation. That is happening although all religions prohibit it and call it a great sin, and although it attracts terrible punishment. The *Garuda Purana,* the Hindu text that describes what happens after death and the soul's journey, says that those who commit suicide are stuck in the spirit world for 65,000 earth years. If, as has often been said, life and suffering are inseparable, the sufferer takes the next logical step and says, separate them through death and be rid of suffering. The fact of the matter is that, despite breakthroughs in fields like psychology, the suicidal mindset has remained impregnable. We can never typecast or stereotype a 'suicider'. We will never know, even if one survives the attempt, if they really thought through the alternatives and consequences. It doesn't matter how young or old one is. Money has emerged as a malevolent motivator and a terrible trigger, shattering many a life and family. The trail of money can be seen in many a suicide and homicide, even a crime. While the earlier adage was 'frugality is morality', the metaphors of the modern age are 'obscene opulence' and ostentatious living. Even Machiavelli said, "Of mankind we may say in general they are fickle, hypocritical, and greedy of gain".

Through greed we have created a manic world nauseous with the pursuit of material wealth. Many also bear their cross of imagined deprivation, while their fellow human beings remain paralyzed by real poverty. That 'real poverty' is taking real lives, and mutilating many more. The 'double-tragedy' is that, on the one hand, the difference between life and death in many cases is so little money and, on the other hand, so many have what it takes to 'save' those in need. And yet, what is even more tragic, those 'who have' don't do what needs to be done, not because they don't want to but because there is no social 'connectivity' that brings the 'needy' and the 'willing' together in a world which is often called a 'global village'. One of the urgent tasks in the world is to create the public policy infrastructure for spreading money evenly; to reverse the flow, which is presently from the 'poor to the rich', both from individuals and nations. Needless to say, a mountain of money, like a mound of candy attracts an army of ants, and also acts as a trigger for heartburn, envy, and hatred. Like evil, money has acquired an identity and dynamic of its own, it influences human behavior, for good or bad. The consequence is that on the 'day of judgment' or in the reckoning of Chitragupta, the Hindu celestial record keeper of the earthly doings of all human beings, one additional question that might be raised to decide our after-life fate could well be this: how we earned and utilized money while on earth.

We have never been able to come to terms with the certainty of death and the uncertainty of where, how, and when. For the fact is that 'as soon as a being comes to life, it is old enough to die'. We claim, as a mark of our superiority, that the human is the only animal that knows it must die, but that 'knowing' hasn't helped much. What 'modern man', a term usually used to separate him from the 'primitive or traditional' man, is attempting, is to convert that 'certainty' (of death) into uncertainty, and erase the 'uncertainty' (of where, how, and when) altogether. And going for the jugular, as it were, instead of waiting for the call of death, is calling it to his 'aid' as a route of escape, whenever he feels confused and cornered, helpless and hapless, restless and rebellious. This 'calling up' has come to such a pass that virtually any dispute, disappointment, and despair, even denial, is now a potential incubator of induced or enforced death. What Walt Whitman called "a voice from Death, solemn and strange, in all his sweep and power",[44] we hear all the time, at times as a silent whisper, sometimes as a helpless wail, and more often as hideous howl. We might, as the 'voice' pleads, 'bow our faces' and 'veil our eyes' but we cannot shy away from the almost daily 'dance of death', at home, at work, on the streets, on the screen, in our otherwise uneventful lives. Whitman reinforces in this poem the theme that death should not be deemed as a threat, and urges us to bear in mind the briefness and brittleness of life, and reminds us that life is time-bound, and to live it to the brim because every moment is a gift.

The paradox is that while over the past half a century, millions of lives have certainly been bettered, millions in the material sense, millions more, at the same time suffer from deep deprivation, dejection, and depression. It is not an economic or sociological problem, or of upbringing or alienation, or a problem of youthful disillusionment or disgust with a soulless society. All of them have something to do with such issues, but more fundamentally something terrible has snapped in the human consciousness and no one has a clue. We have all, in different degrees and ways, turned into a 'human bonsai': potted, trimmed, controlled, cut to size—to suit the taste and temper of human culture. Maybe, that is the way to contain the human hubris! So forbidding is 'life within a lie', that many, while still bodily breathing feel suffocated, while being mobile feel a sense of being boxed in, and feel that the only way to break out is destruction, the most direct way to which is 'death'. Many, tragically too often the makers of our future, are breaking the 'mirror of the modern man' even if they know they are the 'mirror' itself. In a twisted sense, death (rather fear of it) holds us no terror. We have both demonized and trivialized it. We 'demonize' it by believing that everything goes up in smoke at death, that it is a bottomless pit into which we are all thrown, that life is in vain because we die. Death can be a form of entertainment. Once you cast aside your humanity, it is easy to make fun of the sounds and faces people make as they die. It is not uncommon to encounter macabre music lyrics or movie dialogues and blood-and-gore that trivialize death, such as, "I shot a man in Reno just to watch him die", and "I am a false prophet, god is a superstition!"

'Induced or enforced' death' is fast becoming just another option, often escapist or opportunistic, even the preferred route, to settle scores, disputes, depression; a hole to hide, as it were, a refuge from alienation, hurt, humiliation and a way to vent hatred. A time comes in everyman's life when a certain single situation or a problem or pain overwhelms everything else, and all other experiences and aspects of life, however weighty they might be, recede into the background and we feel utterly helpless, hapless, distraught and despondent. In most cases we still cling to hope, but in many situations, when people, for reasons still mysterious, feel bereft of any hope, they come to the determination that the only way out is to end it all. Then the very prospect of being rid of that problem becomes more irresistible and alluring than anything else that we value, like religion, family, friendship, or that we obsessively pursue in life like money, sex, pleasure, and power. Sometimes, the 'problem' or the cause of disaffection is such a trifle that it blows our mind away even to believe that such a thing is possible within the human consciousness. Whatever is true for suicide equally fits well with homicide. Indeed, both are the two sides of the same coin. In one sense, man has taken away the power of life and death from the gods, and how gods react and how much of the ugly and horrific of what we see around us, can be explained away. This way only gods can know. As a self-professed 'rational' species, one would have thought that since we all meet the same mortal fate, death would be a unifier. Poet John Donne wrote "All mankind is of one author, and is one volume; when one man dies, one chapter is not torn out of the book, but translated into a better language; and every chapter must be so translated..."[45] Donne's words cannot be more apt: "... as therefore, the bell that rings to a sermon, calls not upon the preacher only, but upon the congregation; so this bell calls us all... No man is an island, entire of itself; every man is a piece of the continent, a part of the main... Any man's death diminishes me, because I am involved in mankind, and therefore never send to know for whom the bell tolls; it tolls for thee". Such is the hold of death, and the lure of life, on the human mind. Donne underlines two central themes: interconnectedness of mankind and the common destination of death. Neither of these has taken a firm foothold in the human consciousness, and human behavior is as though every man is an island unto himself, and death is what happens to others. From that mindset to that of a 'killer' is but a short leap.

Death—the Default Mode

Modern science is trying hard to comprehend the basic facts about the cognitive conditioning of a 'killer', but the fact is that the human, at least since the times of the Old Testament, has always killed himself, and others, in more ways than one. But what was once a 'last resort' is now, in a growing number of instances, an 'opening option'. While homicide was condemned, suicide was usually condoned, often viewed as an escape from evil, shame, dishonor or insufferable sufferance. What is new is the growing ordinariness and the casualness of both suicide and homicide. Many are turning towards that route as they find themselves incapable of either accepting or enduring or escaping or transcending the superficiality, sordidness, coarseness and callousness of modern-day human life, which largely revolves around the *Trimurti,* the three gods, of free will, free choice, and free markets, not only in the economic domain but also in the social and political spheres. They are no longer on the margins of human life; they are in the mainstream of normal life, and the seeds are sown deep in our own consciousness. Too many people too often feel that anything, absolutely anything, nothing excluded, is better than living through, what to them was an obscenity, 'life', and coping with what it has come to entail and demand—make a living, climb the profession ladder, manage a marriage, raise a family, repair a broken home, reform a rebellious child, handle spurned love or a jilted lover, keep the wolf at bay, keep up with the Joneses... And they ask if, after all that struggle and stress, we are anyway destined to end up being 'dead', why not advance the deadly date? In his work *The Myth of Sisyphus* (1942), Albert Camus raised the mother of all existential questions: Does the realization of the meaninglessness and absurdity of life necessarily require suicide? He himself answered: "No. It requires revolt". What he does not clarify is 'revolt' against what and how? You cannot 'revolt' against 'meaninglessness'; that itself becomes meaningless. We have not done well with revolts or with revolutions. They have always been messy and bloody and have led to greater misery than what we revolted against. Our love for orderliness, ordinariness, our longing for an unwrinkled life, and our lust for lasciviousness and luxury abhors the upheaval of what revolt entails, and devours its idealism and chasteness. Since we do not know what happens next, the questions remain unanswered. Is suicide running away from responsibilities or taking up new ones? Is it an escape or an opening, a sacrifice or sacrilege? Is the world better off with or without us? Are we helping or hindering nature if we choose to eliminate ourselves?

Morality of Murderous Weapons and 'Murderous Martyrdom'

In practical terms, what we call a 'problem' is what stands between life and death. Without life there can be no problem or a personification of a problem. It is being perceived as the easiest and the most 'efficient' way to resolve issues and solve problems. Until perhaps even a century ago 'taking life', one's own or an other's, was usually under extreme provocation or desperation, and when all other options were shut, or appeared to be shut. Taking life, one's own or of an other, always a 'probable possibility', is now alarmingly a 'possible probability'; no longer off-the-table or unthinkable for thousands of perfectly normal people. New phrases have come into play like suicide bomber, murderous martyrdom, human bomb, ethnic cleansing, collateral damage, drone deaths,[46] and new and sinister associations have sprouted; mass murder is now called a 'just war'; torture is called eliciting 'truth' or 'intensive interrogation techniques', and 'rectal rehydration as a means of behavior control' of suspected terrorists. Not only are new 'techniques' of killing and torture being invented, but some of these, like the drones or unmanned aerial vehicles, are brazenly being called, sans any shame, 'moral',[47] by those who authorize their launch. The person who makes such a description is generally considered a 'devout' Catholic who opposes the death penalty! The irony is that he truly is a 'good' Catholic and he truly believed in the morality of what he did, much like Adolf Eichmann and many others of that ilk! Such is the devilish ingenuity of the human mind. But it is but a myth that these killings are 'precise', or that drones kill only the 'terrorists'. According to one report, drones kill 28 innocent people for every 'bad guy'.[48] We are now told that new micro-aerial vehicles known as CICADAs,[49] which are actually micro-drones, are being developed by the Pentagon. These can be deployed from military aircraft at altitudes close to 50,000 feet and still fit in the palm of your hand, and they can possibly fly into a house and kill the target. The justification is that they do not entail any human casualties on the attacking or drone-launching side. Should we call that 'moral' or callous? This is a case in point that tells a lot about modern man's mindset, our endless ability to find moral explanations and ethical justifications for all the trivial and terrible things we do as a part of 'doing our job', or rendering 'public service'.

Morality and 'Gamification' of Violence and War

It is a cliché, but true to say technology is a double-edged weapon. It can do both good and bad. The 'bad' is easier to identify; it is mainly military technology, even granting that many of these have had civilian impact. It was military technology that, through the machine gun, first automated killing in the 19th century, and which now is giving us lethal autonomous robots (LARs) that can operate without human intervention. Human dignity is also at stake here. LARs are another step towards a dehumanizing trend in warfare. It is not individual bravery or even human numbers that are decisive; it is technological superiority. Some 'realists' argue that killing from a distance and engaging targets as mere objects is but a normal evolution in the advancing technology of war, which is being described as the 'gamification'[50] of violence and war. Some warn of the impending tsunami of robots that strive to look and act eerily human. Humans now can kill thousands without any human involvement, ridding us of unpleasant sensations like regret and remorse. Although we associate war weaponry with sophisticated and lethal weapons such as missiles, nuclear bombs and drones, it all began with the use of sharpened stones about two million years ago. It has steadily advanced and took a quantum leap with the fusion of indigenous technology and modern science.

With the advent of the 'atomic age' and advances in bio- and nanotechnologies, military technology has enabled man not only to cripple his own kind but potentially also Planet Earth itself. Scary, 'Star Wars' kind of weapons are being developed with large-scale diversion of skills and resources that could, if properly channeled, do immense good to the world. 'Immense good' could also accrue to the environment if we can curb our lust for war. Just to deter or defeat, or make life more difficult for the 'enemy', we don't mind or care if the environment is imperiled. Indeed, throughout history, the environment has been a silent victim of human conflict. In the 5th century BCE, the retreating Scythians poisoned water wells in an effort to slow the advancing Persian army. Roman troops razed the city of Carthage in 146 BCE, and poisoned the surrounding soil with salt to prevent its future fertilization. The American Civil War in the 19th century saw the widespread implementation of 'scorched earth' policies. During the Vietnam War, the United States implemented *Operation Ranch Hand* to devastating effect, to destroy vegetation used by the enemy for cover and sustenance, through the use of chemicals such as *Agent Orange*. Attempts were also made to deliberately modify the environment to create floods along vital supply routes utilized by the North Vietnamese forces. The existing rules under international humanitarian law, international environmental law, and international criminal law, purporting to limit deliberate environmental destruction, have largely been ineffective and inappropriate. The impact of environmental destruction has paled when measured against perceived military advantages. The United Nations International Law Commission is currently looking at this issue in an attempt to establish the relevant applicable principles.[51]

Military technology now is at the frontline of the march towards self-determining machines. Its evolution is producing an extraordinary variety of species. The *Sand Flea*, an 11-pound robot that drives like a radio-controlled car on flat terrain, can jump 30 feet into the air to overcome obstacles; it can leap through a window or onto a roof, filming all the while. It then rolls along on wheels until it needs to jump again. *RiSE*, a six-legged robo-cockroach, can climb walls. *LS3*, a dog-like robot, trots behind a human over rough terrain, carrying up to 180 kg of supplies. *SUGV*, a briefcase-sized robot, can identify a man in a crowd and follow him. There is a flying surveillance drone the weight of a wedding ring. And there is a robot that can carry 2.7 tonnes of bombs.[52]

These machines have turned mass or targeted 'killing' into a relatively low-risk or no-risk affair. While they might inflict what is euphemistically called collateral damage—that is killing of non-combatants and civilians who have nothing to do with the decision to wage the war—the side that deploys such weapons does not incur any 'human' causalities, insulating the 'war-wagers' from any domestic pressure. Their people, or public, care for only one thing; they don't want their 'sons' to be put in the harm's way.

Mrityor ma amritam gamaya: From Death to Immortality

All religions and scriptures accord centrality to matters of death. Indeed, it is death that makes them deathless. The famous *Shanti mantra* in the Brihadaranyaka Upanishad says, inter alia, *Mrityor ma amritam gamaya*—lead me from 'death to immortality'. The Isha Upanishad says: "May my life merge in the Immortal, when my body is reduced to ashes. O Mind, meditate on the eternal Brahman. Remember the deeds of the past. Remember, O Mind, remember". The Old Testament says: "The dust returns to the earth as it was, and the spirit returns to God who gave it".[53] The Bible says that God alone possesses immortality, and in Islam, Allah alone can bestow immortality. An Anglican funeral liturgy which is recited at the gravesite says "In the midst of life we are in death: of whom may we seek for succor, but of thee, O Lord, who for our sins art justly displeased?... Earth to earth, ashes to ashes, dust to dust".[54] We must not forget that gods always punished man for trying to 'become like one of them', and man was banished from Eden perhaps not for his divine disobedience, but to preempt him from seeking immortality.[55]

Death has been the final frontier, the ultimate conquest, the true challenge to human intelligence. Ever since man came face to face with is called 'mortality salience', that is, awareness of his eventual death, man's attitude towards, and relationship with death has radically changed, including his relationship with his fellow-men and nature and God. It has also affected man's moral sense. It has, on the one hand, strengthened people's connection with their in-groups and on the other hand led people to feel more inclined to punish minor moral transgressions.[56] The means have changed, as also the destination but the almost visceral revulsion of death and quest to conquer it remain. All that scriptures have told us and science tells us have made little impact. Why death is 'bad' and why we fear, dread, and loathe death is inexplicable. We do not dread similar, albeit less draconian, situations. We do not fear, indeed long for, sleep, which in many ways is similar. We do not resist, even if we do not welcome, other passages and transitions such as youth to old age. We hate pain but we detest death, although it relieves us of a lot of pain, physical or mental or psychological.

The very meaning and aim of immortality have changed; from going 'beyond the body' to retaining and augmenting the body. The means have changed from spiritual to scientific. We are now told that, in another decade and a half, we might have the option to 'keep repairing our current body or move into a new one'. As the article predicts, "[In the year 2032]... the growing of 'blank' bodies has become all the rage, and by using your own genetic material, body farmers can even recreate your own face at age 20".[57,58] In the process, the very 'logic and language' of death have profoundly changed. In death, the apparent end of what we know as life, nature confronts man with the most daunting dilemma. Despite its unpredictable imminence, few are prepared and most would say, like the hero in Philip Roth's novel *Everyman*, "O Death; thou comest when I least had thee in mind". Death might become 'optional', but it will still be the cessation of life. But the causes that culminate in death have changed, encompassing all the way from involuntary bodily decay and dissolution, to voluntary embrace of death. There is a growing convergence of suicide and homicide, some in the name of love and some in the name of religion, and some just for the 'thrill' of it. 'Killing' has come to be viewed as the ultimate test of faith and a revered rite of passage into martyrdom, and a hallowed highway to heaven. Birth, for some time has been optional, but now even death looms as a choice. While scriptures profess that death is no different from being a phase and part of life, science posits that death is the opposite and antithesis to life. We are living at a time when human power can 'fix' anything, even a broken heart, and regain anything we might lose, even youth and vaginal virginity. Now we are being reassured that even 'lost life' can be restored. While scriptures say that the way to be deathless is by overcoming desire, science says deathlessness is just another desire to be satiated, just another 'disease' to be cured. As man has entrenched himself on earth and assumed ascendancy over all other forms of life, a profound change in the place and perception of death in the context of life has taken hold. In no other aspect of life is the gap between scripture and science as wide as it is in regard to death. A centrality in human thought has long been that birth and death are inseparable in the continuum of life, of cause and effect. Man has always recognized, but not accepted, that 'centrality', and has turned either to the divine, and when it seemed impervious to his pleas, to science. If science prevails, man will then be able to make life at will and keep 'death' at bay, as if it were 'on call', another toy or ploy to play with. The idea is that if 'eternal life' becomes too drab and devoid of delight, then we can summon death to deliver us.

Man has always entertained two dreams: to live as the gods do—eternally and in bliss; and, even if he does not know what to do with a single dreary day, to 'go on living', forever and ever; to live for its own sake, not to achieve something or anything. What used to be the stuff of mythology, legends, epics, and fantasy fiction, we are being told, could be a reality soon, that man could well conquer, or cure, the 'disease of death', that mortality need not be our destiny. The ultimate test of morality is how man handles mortality. It has long been a subject of much comment and commentary. Most humans are too 'busy' to have any time to 'think' about such irksome matters. They live, as has been said, as if they will never die, and die as if they never lived. Some are so terrified that, as Henry Van Dyke said, 'they never begin to live'. Goethe said, "As long as you are not aware of the continual law of Die and Be Again, you are merely a vague guest on a dark Earth". An Italian proverb perhaps best sums up how to expend the interlude between birth and death: "When you were born, you cried and the world rejoiced. Live your life so that when you die, the world cries and you rejoice". We now have money as a new factor. With enough money, we might soon be able to buy 'immortality'. The question, according to science, is not, 'if' but 'when' man will achieve technological singularity, and be able to cheat death by merging with the machine. We read predictions like, 'If you draw the timelines, realistically by 2050 we would expect to be able to download your mind into a machine, so when you die it is not a major career problem.'[59] Another says, "The human race will achieve immortality within 25 years as a result of minds being transferred into computers, and that robot bodies capable of housing human brains could even be available by 2025". By that year, "Dying bodies could be replaced by robot vassals housing human brains. By 2035, human minds will be transferred into computers, eliminating the need for a body altogether. By 2045, artificial brains will control hologram entities".[60] Another probability, we are told is that in 30 or 40 years, we'll have microscopic machines traveling through our bodies, repairing damaged cells and organs, effectively wiping out diseases. But we are also warned that, "In a mature form, molecular nanotechnology will enable the construction of bacterium-scale self-replicating mechanical robots that can feed on dirt or other organic matter. Such replicators could eat up the biosphere or destroy it by other means such as by poisoning it, burning it, or blocking out sunlight. A person of malicious intent in possession of this technology might cause the extinction of intelligent life on Earth by releasing such nanobots into the environment".[61] The nanotechnology will also be used to back up our memories and personalities. Craig Venter says that, "We now have the ability to transmit life at the speed of light, just sending it through the computer. When we colonize Mars we could [transmit] a new organism to the colony in Mars".[62] We read about other real probabilities, such as 'teleporting',[63] the 'capability to design and create life from scratch'.

These are all exciting, or, for some, paralyzing predictions. The lay public is left wondering what to make of them, whether the awesome risks are warranted and what kind of 'humans' their grandchildren are likely to be, and what kind of 'life' they are likely to live. But we must get some clarity of what 'biological immortality' means. For example, would man survive and 'live on' despite a direct hit by a rocket or collision with a truck? Does 'immortality' mean an impregnable and indestructible body? And suppose we get bored with the 'tedium of immortality', can we give it up and become 'mortal' again? In other words, can immortality be temporary but reversible, a kind of default condition? Would it assure us of perpetual physical health and unimpaired mental agility? But then we cannot, at the most basic level, address any such issues without knowing what it means to be 'dead'. How can we choose life itself, let alone endless life, without any inkling of what the alternative is tantamount to? Since that knowledge is denied, at least, while being alive, we have no 'logical' reason to change the status quo of life coming to close at a certain but unknowable time. For a species that takes pride in its ability to make informed and 'intelligent' choices, our timeless desire to transit from a time-bound life to endless life is perhaps the most 'irrational' of all our choices.

Assuming that death is 'bad', undesirable, to be evaded in every way, the big question then is this: would physical 'immortality' or unending existence make man a better being, at peace with himself and with the world, and help him to evolve in the right direction? Or would it, in the words of Bernard Williams, mean 'endless life [that] would eventually collapse into infinite boredom'[64]—and possibly unhinge the psychic balance that makes us 'human'? Put differently, would 'endless existence', or a life span so long that 'forever' is pointless, transfer the human into a humane being or, freed from the fear of being killed, turn him into a demon? Can man be both moral and immortal? The implied assumption about immortality is that we will live as the same person with the same body. We will not be wasted by the daily dribble of death nor do we have to ruminate, in Philip Larkin's words, "Unresting death, a whole day nearer now, Making all thought impossible but how, And where and when I shall myself die".[65] We are not interested in 'anonymous' or 'indirect' immortality, which is inherent in nature. All of us are 'immortal' through remembrance, memory, progeny, writing, art, music, anything creative. Modern man is not interested in that kind of 'immortality'. He wants permanence of the physical status quo. He wants to be immortal by just being alive without an end, and even if he has no idea what to do with the present life, let alone eternal life. He is not interested in ideals or artistic excellence or questions of morality, or even of 'the Fate of the Earth'.[66] We have long convinced ourselves that, whatever death might or might not mean, however dreary and distasteful life might be, the ultimate test of our creativity is to destroy death. Tagore says, "We have come to look upon life as a conflict with death—the intruding enemy, not the neutral ending—in impotent quarrel with which we spend every stage of it".[67] Someone said, "We do not believe in immortality because we can prove it, but we try to prove it because we cannot help believing it". Whichever way, the idea of 'immortality', which the serpent in the Garden of Eden claimed was the word invented by it for 'eternal life', has long been the stuff of epics, mythology, science fiction, and science. Some argue that the continued existence of humanity far into the future is important not only for the future but also for the present, and that "we are not individualists; we are dependent for much of what we value in our lives on the survival of humanity into the future",[68] and that, "even the present value of much that makes up our lives depends on its continuation and development long after we are gone".[69] It means that if we seriously entertain any thought about 'early extinction' of the human species, that by itself has a direct and immediate bearing on our lives.

No one really knows who the first human was, who, seeing someone dead, wondered what happens hereafter, but that question has haunted mankind down the ages. The mystic and mystery of death has always transfixed the human mind, and although there has been remarkable unity about the nature of death at the esoteric core of religious faith, there has been an equally striking diversity of cultural beliefs at the exoteric level. At the behavior level, dying or killing have always had something to do with human aggression, cruelty, and barbarism, and even honor and heroism. Death, for the classical hero, was a 'masked figure, willing to struggle, face to face, one to one, for trophy or dust'.[70] In the Katha Upanishad, the young Nachiketa asked none other than the god of death, Yama, "There is this doubt about a man when he is dead. Some say that he exists; others say that he doesn't. What is it?"

Put more personally, the question is, "Will I be there, and where will I be, and what might happen to me, when it all ends down here?" There has been no direct 'satisfactory' answer to that simple question since then, not even from the god of death. We are left hanging in doubt. The result is that we meander and muddle through 'life', not knowing what to do, or not do, to insure ourselves for an uncertain and unknown future. 'Surviving death' has been viewed by men of all times and cultures and civilizations as the final frontier, the ultimate challenge to 'being human'. What has maddened man is his realization that life really is not 'living' but, in the words of Schopenhauer, at best 'delayed dying'. But what is 'profoundly problematic' is the pace of dying which varies from person to person. Or, in the words of Tolstoy, the 'dragon of death' waiting to tear us apart. Whatever the scriptures and sages might tell us, our practical experience tells us that every breath we take delays that sinister shadow hovering over us. It plays with us and ultimately triumphs, for, by being born, we already became its prey. We do not mind being played with so long as we can prolong it, in the words of Schopenhauer, "just as we blow out a soap-bubble as long and as large as possible, although with the perfect certainty that will burst". Unlike other experiences, our awareness of death is by analogy and observation of people dying. Other animals, we are told, 'know' death only when they die, and that in fact enables them to lead fuller lives, freed from the fear that the very next minute they might be dead.

The fact is that no other aspect of earthly existence is as impenetrable and impervious to human insight and imagination as the mortal triad of why, when, and how 'life' ends, and what happens thence. The question is one of 'absoluteness'. Is birth an 'absolute' beginning and 'death an 'absolute' end? Are we 'born' or 'reborn', and if it is the latter, what remains after 'death' and what is the continuum between 'birth' and 'birth', and what moves on into the new body? If the body is mortal, and the soul, as the Gita says, is birth-less, death-less, immortal, and eternal, pure, then who is the 'dweller in the body' that sheds off one body and assumes another? Is that '*jivatma*'? But it is a part of the '*paramatma*' and how can it be subject to birth, death and rebirth? Then again, how does one put it all in the context of the Upanishadic *mahavakya Aham brahmasmi* (I am God)? If the body disintegrates and gets absorbed into the *panchabhutas*—earth, water, fire, air and space—, if the Atman or soul is eternal and cannot be corrupted and sinless, if we are inherently divine, the question is who or what is 'reborn', and who pays for past sins and pays back? In other words, when we say we want to be 'immortal', whose immortality is it anyway? All this spiritualism and sophistry apart, whatever the Gita or some scripture might have meant, when modern man talks of 'immortality' he means, as brutally laid bare by the student Thrasymachos to the philosopher Philalethes: "Don't you see that my individuality, be it what it may, is my very self? To me it is the most important thing in the world. 'For God is God, and I am I'. I want to exist, I, I. That's the main thing. I don't care about existence which has to be proved to be mine before I can believe it".[71] To which Philalethes replies: "It is the cry [for immortality], not of the individual, but of existence itself. It's the intrinsic element in everything that exists". Schopenhauer adds, "The effect of this is to make the individual careful to maintain his own existence; and if this were not so, there would be no guarantee for the preservation of the species". So, it could be that our love of our body, love of life, craving for sheer existence isn't all that selfish and could be turned around for common good.

When we look around nature, we are also befuddled about the 'normal' length of life spans. No one can tell why different species have different 'normal' life spans. For example, why do turtles and parrots live so much longer, ten times than dogs, and why even within a species, is the length of life so indeterminate and whimsical? We are not even sure if without 'prolonged or perpetual youth' we want eternal life. Do we want to 'live' long or forever, as it were, as is where is, subject to decay, old age, disease? Can our body become indestructible and can we 'live' if we fall from the Eiffel Tower? Does it mean that no one or nothing can kill such a human being? William James pictures what we want, "The fact that we *can* die, that we *can* be ill at all, is what perplexes us; the fact that we now for a moment live and are well is irrelevant to that perplexity. We need a life not correlated with death, a health not liable to illness, a kind of good that will not perish, a good in fact that flies beyond the Goods of nature."[72]

Factually, it all comes down to the 'body'. Our attitude to our physical frame is riddled with paradoxes. Even scriptures are ambivalent. On the one hand, they say get rid of body-identification, and that that is the chief obstacle to spiritual growth. The great Adi Sankara wrote, "You never identify yourself with the shadow cast by your body, or with its reflection, or with the body you see in a dream or in your imagination. Therefore you should not identify yourself with this living body either".[73] On the other hand, scriptures also say it is the abode, a temple, of God, and we must tend and take care of it. How we came upon earth and how we depart has little to do with what we do. Not to be born is, beyond all estimation, best; but when a man has seen the light of day, this is next best by far, that, with utmost speed, he should go back from where he came. For when he has seen youth go by, with its easy merry-making, what hard affliction is foreign to him, what suffering does he not know? Envy, factiousness, strife, battles, and murders. Last of all falls to his lot old age, blamed, weak, unsociable, friendless, wherein dwells every misery among miseries.[74] Put differently it is: "Naked came I upon the earth, naked I go below the ground—why then do I vainly toil when I see the end naked before me?" We feed it and starve it too; we put in 'supplements', but poison it too. We are not really happy with it but we want to keep it forever. We 'worship' it, but we abuse it perhaps more than any other material thing. In fact, we don't mind a 'better body' but so long as it is 'alive' in this body. We are not happy with any back-door, indirect or implicit 'immortality' through things like procreation, pencil or pen or paint. Plato's prescription, in *Symposium*, that 'mental procreation' is the sublime way to immortality has never quenched human thirst to 'live forever'. Nor has the Hindu belief—that it is only the body that perishes but not the soul, which is deathless, immortal, and eternal—dimmed our dream of immortality. We want to freeze the physical frame, here and now, nothing else, nothing less. We don't want to live in or through others; we want to be ourselves and yet become immortal. We want 'life', even if it hurts a lot. We are prepared to tolerate any kind and amount of suffering, if only we can survive. Philosophers like Socrates might say that death is not a bad thing; indeed, it is even a good thing, but most people will skip 'good' death and choose 'bad' life. We are not too interested to, in the words of Mark Johnston, to live in the 'onward march of humanity'; we want a continuum of this very life. We do not want to 'live' either as an invisible but eternal soul, or as a corpse in a freezer. We want this body, worn out and wrinkled, feeble and frail it might be, to experience life. Our 'obsession' with immortality is but a reflection and extension of our obsession with our body. For some, man becomes a soul, *à la* Henry Wood, "after a certain event called death", but that he is the same here and now does not occur to them… man is not a body having a soul, but a 'soul having a body'.[76]

Mortality and Famous Last Words

The fact is that death precedes life, follows life; it frames life. As Somerset Maugham wryly noted, 'death is a dreary affair', and we all wish we could follow his advice 'to have nothing to do with it'. But it shadows every step we take and, as Greek philosopher Epicurus (341–270 BCE) noted, 'the unacknowledged fear of death and punishment' has become 'the primary cause of anxiety among human beings and the source of extreme and irrational desires'.[77] Ernest Becker wrote, "The irony of man's condition is that the deepest need is to be free of the anxiety of death and annihilation; but it is life itself which awakens it, and so we must shrink from being fully alive".[78] In one of Bob Dylan's songs, we encounter, "he not busy being born is busy dying".[79] Epicurus asks, "Why should I fear death? If I am, death is not. If death is, I am not. Why should I fear that which cannot exist when I do?"[80] We are told by Lord Krishna, that "Certain is death for the born; and certain is birth for the dead; therefore, over the inevitable thou should not grieve".[81] It was said that when Rabbi Simcha Bunam lay dying, his wife burst into tears. He said, "What are you crying for; my whole life was only that I might learn how to die". So often, we discover 'good' things about the dead we did not notice when they were alive. Instead of extolling them when they are dead, it would do us a lot of good to be good to them when they are still alive. Every time we go to a funeral or cremation—setting aside the comical remark about funeral attendance: 'Do go to people's funerals so that they can come to yours'—we should ask ourselves, "I knew him when he was alive; what did I do to make his life a bit easier?" The 'dead' have no need to worry what we say about them, alive or dead. They have a journey on their hands.

The scriptures describe how a soul departs from the body. The underlying idea is that death or dying is a process, not an event, and the dissolution of the physical body by burial or cremation does not mean the person is 'completely dead'. In many traditions and cultures, the ceremonies go on for different periods, the belief being that some kind of presence or energy lingers until that time. In Hindu homes, after a person is 'dead', a lamp with ghee is lit and left to burn for 24 hours, which creates a certain aura that helps the passage to after-life. Hindus believe that the soul leaves the body from one of its natural openings or exit points, some of which are considered 'good' or auspicious and others are not. The *Garuda Purana* says that the soul of a sinner leaves through his lower regions, such as the anus, and that the soul of the virtuous departs from the head, from his eyes, mouth, nostrils, or ears. For the really pious and truly religious, or for whom prescribed rituals like pouring of *tulasi* leaf water are performed, the point of exit is said to be the top of the head, called the *Brahma-randhra* or *dwara*. The dying moment, the moment when life leaves and the soul departs, has long been considered a very special time. In a certain sense, a person's whole life is but a preparation for that moment. The character of consciousness at death determines the next destination. Vedic scriptures even say that a man will be born in his next birth as that thing about which he was thinking most at the time of his death. The well-known *Jada Bharata* in the Hindu scriptures *Vishnu* Purana and Srimad Bhagavatam, recounts a story about the virtuous emperor, Bharata. When he grew old, Bharata apportioned his kingdom to his sons, and repaired to the forest, to immerse himself in austerities and religious rituals. He became a great sage. Once, when he was offering prayers to the Sun god, he saw an old pregnant deer quenching its thirst at a nearby stream. Terrified by the roar of a lion, the young deer gave birth to a little fawn and fell dead. Whereupon, Bharata took pity on the fawn, and tended it and took care of it at his *ashram*. In this process, the old sage became so intensely attached to it that, when he himself lay dying, the fate of his deer was uppermost in his thought. As a consequence, the story goes, notwithstanding all his righteous life and virtuous deeds, Bharata was born as a deer in his next life. Our first reaction is to cry foul: showing caring to another helpless creature in dire need should be rewarded, not penalized. The message of the story is that compassion and affection are noble qualities; when they turn into obsessive attachment, the spiritual decline follows. We are advised to draw a fine but clear line between affection (which ennobles) and attachment (which enslaves), and between love (which elevates) and desire (which entraps).

Many 'last words' uttered by, or attributed to, great men have become legendary. It has sometimes been said that people tend to become most honest and wise when they are about to die, since they are not 'afraid', they have nothing to lose or gain, and their soul or spirit is in ascendency at that time. Some have even said that of all the words a man utters in his entire lifetime, it is what he says on his deathbed that makes the most sense. But the phrase 'last words' itself is ambiguous. Are those the 'words' uttered seconds before a man 'dies' or the words that were last heard? And what about the 'state of mind' and lucidity? Usually by that time one becomes extremely weak and emaciated. The fact of the matter is that most people at the actual time of their death are unconscious, and hence unable to say anything or even 'think' of anything. When God was once asked what happens if a devotee suddenly dies and hence unable to think of Him, the divine reply was 'Then, I will think of My devotee'. If 'last words' mean last spoken or last heard words, they may not be true to the spirit; if the person did not know he or she was dying soon thereafter, those words might fit the description of being 'honest', 'fearless', or 'spiritual'.

Historically, one of the most intriguing last words were those of Socrates. As the effect of the hemlock was slowly rising up from his feet to his heart, the last words of Socrates (according to Plato) were: "Crito, we owe a cock to Asclepius. Do pay it. Don't forget". Those few were much scholarly, and led to spiritual speculation. Three interpretations are possible: one, they are factual; he said what he meant; two, they are hallucinatory, effect of the creeping hemlock that had reached up to his waist; three, they are profound, with a hidden meaning and message. The first, for the admirers of Socrates who are legion, seems somewhat of a let-down, unworthy of his renowned sagacity and wisdom. The second seems less uncharitable; after all, he was human and poison is poison for everyone. The third, which was offered by other philosophers like Nietzsche, who argued in the *Gay Science*, that Socrates was glad he was going, as he believed the soul was immortal, that he was about to be 'cured' of the disease of life, and so he wanted Crito to make an offering to Asclepius, the Greek god of healing, and offering a cock in sacrifice was a way of thanking him for healing Socrates with the hemlock. But other and more recent philosophers question this interpretation, particularly comparing life to a disease, that such cynicism was unbecoming of both Socrates and Plato (who was not present but recorded it). But the pragmatic question is: if that was what Socrates meant, why did he not say so, instead of leaving it, as he surely would have known if he remained lucid. Why make his last message clothed in riddles, and Socrates was always direct in the words he chose. One must also reasonably assume that Socrates was not hallucinating as he was in good health and fully coherent at that time, and the deadly hemlock, as the jailor explained, was slowly rising up from the legs and had reached up to his waist when he said those words. He was to die when it reached his heart, and so, when he said those words, both his heart and brain were 'normal'. He was not dying of any disease, nor was he mentally impaired. And so, if he was saying what he wanted to say and if there was no reason for him to make it up, it means the great man could not think of anything else to say or he did not want to say anything profound or philosophical. Buddha's last spoken words were translated as, "Be a lamp or light unto thyself", or "Work hard to gain your own salvation".

Nostradamus reportedly remarked, "Tomorrow I shall no longer be here". Voltaire, when asked by a priest to renounce Satan, said, "Now, now, my good man, this is no time for making enemies". Thomas Carlyle's last words were: "So, this is death. Well!" Salvador Dali said, "I do not believe in my death". Emily Dickinson's were: "I must go in, the fog is rising". The famous dancer Isadora Duncan apparently said, "*Adieu, mes amis. Je vais à la gloire!*" (Farewell, my friends. I go to glory!). Although some say that anyone shot directly in the chest will not be able to utter a single word, it is popularly believed that Gandhi's last words were "*Hey, Ram!*", the name of one of the avatars of Lord Vishnu. At least, that was his 'last wish'. Some great men 'know' that death is at hand, and express a wish how they want to go. Shortly before his death, Gandhi wrote, "I have expressed my wish at prayer that, should someone kill me, I should have no anger in my heart against the killer, and that I should die with *Rama Nama* on my lips". Some are able to look their killer in the eye and show no fear. Ernesto Che Guevara, the iconic Marxist Cuban revolutionary leader, moments before his death and facing his assassin, Mario Teran, a Bolivian soldier, when asked if he was thinking about his immortality, replied that he was thinking about 'the immortality of the revolution' and said, "I know you have come to kill me. Shoot coward, you are *only* going to kill a man".[82]

Death, it is said, is a great leveler. It has intrigued and inspired the greatest of our minds, and poets like Keats and Emily Dickinson and philosophers like Carl Jung and Tagore. It is not a coincidence that they all had what we call 'near death experiences'. Direct and intimate exposure to death does deepen and heighten one's sensitivity of death, almost in a mystical way. Keats, who nursed his mother and brother as they succumbed to tuberculosis, himself died of the same illness at the ridiculously young age of 25. But it was such suffering that flowered his genius and yielded masterpieces like *Ode to a Nightingale*, *Ode on Melancholy* and *Ode to Autumn*. The pivot of his poems is the thought that 'one's sense of mortality deepens one's appreciation of beauty and that life accrues value precisely to the extent that one intensely experiences its fragility and transience'.[83] And, "by embracing mortality—not just passively accepting or stoically resigning himself to it—Keats discovers that autumn has its own music".[84] Through his life-long brushes with death, Keats came to the realization that death is the 'mother of beauty' and that the music of mortality can only be heard when one not only accepts death but *embraces* it. Keats' work can be seen as an attempt "to alter the very paradigm of what constitutes the spiritual, just as Einstein would later redefine space".[85] Themes of death including her own, after death and immortality, run through much of the work of Emily Dickinson, such as "Because I could not stop for death"; "I Heard A Fly Buzz-When I Died"; "After a Great Pain, a Formal Feeling Comes"; and "I Felt A Funeral In My Brain". Her best works were written after the death of a close friend or family member. In her vision, immortality is a state of continuous birth, death, and rebirth, and as a state of existing in the hereafter, or in Heaven. Rabindranath Tagore's fascination with death, which was a constant theme in his meditations, had its roots in the suicide of his sister-in-law and the muse of his life, Kadambari Devi, when she was 25 years old (and Tagore was 23), and in the sixty-hour period when he was hovering between life and death in Shantiniketan in Bengal, India. Carl Jung too experienced another such 'brush', came 'to the edge of death', which made him realize that death is a change of consciousness, not the absolute termination of life, and that "a practical continuation of life of a sort of psychical existence beyond time and space"[86] is possible after death. He also held the view that communication and contact between the living and the dead in some special way is possible in the immediate aftermath of death.[87]

When we feel life is unfair, and that some have all the luck and enjoy good health and good fortune while we are stricken with ill-health and misfortune, it gives some deviant delight to remember that all that will be of little avail when death comes calling. Yet again no two are all equal in death too. Some deaths, and the way some die, can change or chart the course of history. Often how a 'great' man dies has much to do with his legacy of greatness. Had they died 'normally' they might have been quietly consigned to oblivion. In many instances, the way they died or were killed for a cause, we remember as much, or even more, as what they accomplished in their lives. Abraham Lincoln, JF Kennedy, Martin Luther King, and Mahatma Gandhi spring to mind. Martyrdom is integral to their greatness. It raises the question: Should one die violently to be acknowledged as a great man? Some have even yearned to be killed. Gandhi said, on the night of 29 January 1948, less than twenty hours before he was shot, "If I die of a lingering illness, nay even by as much as a boil or a pimple, it will be your duty to proclaim to the world, even at the risk of making people angry with you, that I was not the man of God that I claimed to be. If you do that it will give my spirit peace. Note down this also, that if someone were to end my life by putting a bullet through me, as someone tried to do with a bomb the other day, and I met his bullet without a groan, and breathed my last taking God's name, then alone would I have made good my claim".[88] In the end Gandhi's wish was fulfilled and he was pierced by a bullet, whether or not with Rama's name on his lips, as he wanted. One wonders, what would have happened, and how history would have treated him, if, as he once said, he had lived up to the age of 125 years. Gandhi was 78 years old when he died, and if he had lived up to 125 he would have died in 1995. He would have survived all his disciples like Nehru, Nehru's daughter and grandson, and all his children. He would have been ignored, possibly lost his charisma and imprisoned for 'anti-national' activities. Nathuram Godse, in this sense, saved Gandhi, and by killing him, fulfilled Gandhi's wish and made him forever a Mahatma! Death does strange things to mortal men.

Climbing Heaven's Hill With Mortal Skin

Contemplation on death and impermanence of life are regarded as very important in Buddhism for two reasons: it is only by recognizing how precious and how short life is that we are most likely to make it meaningful and to live it fully; and by understanding the death process and familiarizing ourselves with it, we can mitigate our fear at the time of death and ensure a good rebirth. Paramahansa Yogananda, in his essay *Where There Is Light*, described death: "The consciousness of the dying person finds itself suddenly relieved of the weight of the body, of the necessity to breathe, and of any physical pain. A sense of soaring through a tunnel of very peaceful, hazy, dim light is experienced in the physical body".[89] However 'irrational' it might appear to be, what unites most people is the wrenching terror of death, which cuts across all cultures irrespective of which religion one swears adherence to. A Hindu fears death as much as a Christian. Whether it is the Law of Karma or the accounting on the Day of Judgment, it makes little difference to the dread of death. The favorite blessing in all cultures, despite what their scriptures say about the 'naturalness' of death, is 'may you live long!' Despite belief in multiple rebirths, some possibly better than the misery of the current one, prolonging the present life is the most longed-for desire even for Hindus. Despite the angels, damsels and allures of Heaven, few Christians or Muslims want to die. As someone quipped, many want to go to heaven but none want to die, or like Yudhishthira, in the Mahabharata, all of us want to climb up heaven's hill with a mortal skin. There are still exceptions. For instance, Niccolo Machiavelli (*The Prince*, 1513), supposedly said, "I desire to go to Hell and not to Heaven. In the former I shall enjoy the company of popes, kings and princes, while in the latter are only beggars, monks and apostles".[90]

While Hinduism and Buddhism, for instance, advocate a 'desire-less' state as the transparent path to moksha or nirvana, neither religion tries to curb the strongest of all desires: the desire for eternal life. They castigate attachment as the source of sorrow, but not the most addictive attachment: to life itself.

Perhaps it is in the very nature of life itself to hold all living beings in its hypnotic thrall. Not only humans but also the lowliest of creatures, even a worm in a dung heap, cling to life, and want to prolong their miserable existence even if a better life after death is dangled before them. The human mind clings to the seeming certainty of the present package to the apparent uncertainty of the future. Reassuring statements like "Nothing changes with death, it is only a change of the state of consciousness", and *à la* Oscar Wilde, "To have no yesterday, and no tomorrow. To forget time, to forgive life, to be at peace", make no difference to our state of consciousness. What we fear most in life is 'definitiveness', because it robs us of hope; and death is nothing but definitiveness. Death has been, since time immemorial, the primary obsession and the biggest business in the world. Someone estimated that every day about 150,000 humans 'die' but when the day begins no one knows who they will be and who will see the next sunrise. Anyone could be, any one need not be, no one can tell.

We do not how the dead feel, but the living mourn the dead and presume to be sorry for them. Even for those whom we hardly know, when death strikes, we feel 'sad and sorry', though for what and for whom is not quite clear. Maybe the dead, if they could compare their 'dead lives' to ours, feel sorry for the 'living dead', which most people are. Death and dying are deemed so horrendous that even a dying person is left in a cloud of deception, in a you-are-going-to-be-okay syndrome, rather than being told that he or she is dying, which we say is all-natural and inevitable in any case. Even the talk of death is called inauspicious, harmful, and impolite. We shun death; even the thought of it is considered morbid. The body that we hugged just the other day, we fear even to touch it. The loved one becomes the feared one. The warm body becomes ice cold and decays before our very eyes. If one touches a 'dead body', the very one we hugged and loved before, we are told to take a cleansing bath. No one understands and tries to help a dying person's state of mind. No one helps him to face the fact of death or to prepare for what inevitably follows. Even doctors are afraid to tell the truth, and those that do are often called insensitive. Since we don't know what happens after death, all this doom and gloom seems downright silly. Those who know they are going to die within a certain time are the luckier ones. In the Srimad Bhagavatam, when King Parikshit is cursed to die on the seventh day of a snake bite, and is paralyzed with fear, the sage Suka tells him what a lucky man he was, to know how much time—seven full days—he has unlike others who could die any minute. It is widely believed in many cultures that the dying moments are precious and that the state of mind at that time has a bearing on the nature of after-life. Vedanta advocates limiting or restraining passions, obligations, relationships, and transactions. Such a state of mind, it says, leads one to obtain *Nitya mukti,* liberation as you are, where you are, right now, without waiting for any future event, or for death, or going to heaven, etc. According to medieval Christian belief, the last moments of life were the most critical, for demons lurked around the deathbed ready to seize the unprepared soul as it emerged with the last breath. 'The last moments of life' also, according to Hindu scriptures, determine the nature of next life. In the Bhagavad Gita, it is said that whatever state of being one remembers during the dying process, he will attain that state, being absorbed in its thought. In India, even today, people go to *Kasi* (Varanasi) to die, because it is a holy place. It may sound simple and a bit unfair that one last moment of thought or remembrance or utterance can outweigh a lifetime of work, good or bad. The fact is that when the moment of death comes, it takes something to be aware enough to say what you want to say. Most people die in unawareness but we really do not know their state of consciousness. But to come to a certain kind of awareness in that moment, you must practice such awareness for a lifetime.

Death and 'Worn-out Clothes'

But then, if death is simply shedding of 'worn-out' clothes, one could argue, why should not the wearer himself decide or choose when to discard the old clothes, instead of waiting for the clothes themselves to 'naturally' drop off? And why do we say that life is a gift of God, a precious gift, and one should not 'take life'? Why do we wish each other 'long life'? Does that mean we must keep the worn- or torn-out clothes long after they no longer give us cover or dignity? Such questions bother but few. What most people want is 'permanence' of the present through maintenance and medicine, that is, keep sewing, stitching, and mending the same garment till it becomes too torn to be tended. Dylan Thomas forcefully expresses this view: "Do not go gentle into that good night. Rage, rage against the dying of the light" (*Lament*). Miguel de Unamuno expresses a similar sense: "If it is nothingness that awaits us, let us make an injustice of it; let us fight against destiny, even though without hope of victory". Bertrand Russell comes to a different conclusion: "I should scorn to shiver with terror at the thought of annihilation. Happiness is nonetheless true happiness because it must not come to an end, nor do thought and love lose their value because they are not everlasting". We may all have mixed feelings about death in abstract but when confronted by the death of someone close to us, or contemplating our own inevitable death, we are not comforted by such words of wisdom or by what scriptures say, such as what Lord Krishna declared in the Bhagavad Gita: "Never, at any time, have I been not; neither you nor these rulers of men. And never shall we all cease to be hereafter". That kind of 'immortality' has never been good enough for the inebriated human mind. We want everything, even eternity, 'here and now', as is, where is. Nor are we lured by the possibility that, "When each of us dies, there will always exist elsewhere an infinite number of copies of ourselves, possessing all the same memories and experiences of our past lives but who will live on to the future".[91] It means that we could well live with the same 'persona' in the cosmos, besides the one we have on earth. That too is not good enough. The bottom line is the body; and it is this miserable mass of flesh, bone, and blood that we want to exist forever. We want to feel thirsty, hungry, we want to experience the 'good things of life'; we do not mind sickness and debility even bereavement if the trade-off is bodily infinity. We want the present to be eternal; today to be timeless, the moment to be momentous. That is the 'meaning' we want from 'life'. We wouldn't be enthused by any 'doubles'. We want to colonize space and go and even 'live' on other planets, but if we do find a 'double' or duplicate we will probably kill him or her! Or, as another science fiction author Larry Niven implies in his short story *All the Myriad Ways* (1971), we will probably kill ourselves and kill others once we realize that the parallel 'I' might be making other choices different from others here on earth. We want everything 'personal'; we seek everything here and now; we want our individuality on earth to be eternal. Although the body changes all through life and gives us much pain,[92] we want to 'keep' it going for all time, free from 'pain'.

Conclusion

So, then, what do we do with death? It has been like a bone in the throat. We can't spit it out, nor can we swallow it. Why do we despise death? Do we really know what we want from immortality? Is it glory or greed, a trophy in the showcase, very little to do with death itself? Heaven forbid, have we got it all wrong? Is our unquenchable longing for immortality the ignorance of life's meaning, of death's purpose, and of the state of after-death? As Milan Kundera (*Immortality*, 1990) says, "Man doesn't know how to be mortal. And when he dies, he doesn't even know how to be dead". In this light, which Achilles should we trust: alive (gods envy our mortality), or dead (rather be a paid servant on earth than the king of kings in the land of the dead)? Is our almost obsessive desire to be not floating but walking gods, completely self-defeating? Is immortality the ultimate *immorality*? If we have to measure up to our claim to be a moral, let alone a spiritual being, what must we do about our mortal fate?

First, let us have some clarity on what our mind conjures as immortality, and what science is trying to achieve, what is possible and probable, and what the likely implications and consequences are. Immortality means a state of absolute, total deathlessness; we continue to live indefinitely for millions of years, whatever happens to earth. That is simply impossible, and we should eliminate such an expectation from any serious consideration. For, even if we do achieve 'biological immortality', we can still die by other means like injury and disease, and we can get killed. We must understand that our quest for life forever makes sense only as a quest for eternal youth. This too is practically impossible. We cannot freeze our age at a certain point (whatever that might be, twenty or forty) and live ever after at that age. It means that the three things that appalled Prince Siddhartha and transformed him into the Buddha—sickness, old age, and death—will continue in some form or degree or the other. Even if we merge with a machine, that will be inescapable. Machines also age, break down and finally 'die' or get discarded. The human body, through techniques like organ-augmentation and periodic repair and renewal, can go on only up to a 'point'. The irony is that we replace a machine at the first sign of trouble, but we want the human machine to last forever. We replace models almost every year, but we want this particular 'model' of earthly existence to be permanent. For science, the bottom line is the body. It wants to keep the shell of the body as much as possible intact, and 'mechanize' every organ therein to not only overcome a disability or disease but to enhance or 'improve' its power and performance. As for the brain, the tactic here is to do what is called 'mind' uploading, uploading mental contents to computers or to the 'Cloud', as a way of preserving the 'software' even as the hard drive 'dies'. For, the Cloud too is not a metaphysical structure, but rather a complex network of servers, and is therefore not itself indestructible or infallible.

What will probably happen, even if science finds the elixir of eternal life, is that we will still fall sick and get old and die, albeit some of us will live much longer and be more fit, and be more of a machine than a man or a god. The only question is how much longer. It is generally believed (even the Bible is supposed to have said it) that the age limit for the human is 125 years. It is unlikely that the maximum will rise much higher, but more of us might cross the century mark. It also depends on who we are referring to: a wholly human superhuman or humanoid or cyborg. Indeed, the future world might well be inhabited by a conglomerate. Humanity will probably be divided into a few who will be *de facto* 'superhumans', and the rest pretty much as we are now, and that could very well turn out to be the last straw on the broken backs of the non-rich. The all-important question is what kind of consciousness such a 'being' will have. The more powerful *it* or *he* is, the more the need for a compassionate consciousness. We have to ask ourselves: Will physical immortality or inexorable death be a better catalyst for human beings to move to a higher plateau of consciousness? The answer is that immortality, which is just to 'keep this body' going on and on, is stagnation and regression. Only through new lives and new experiences and adaptation to new environments could man develop his consciousness, which 'will ultimately cause him to live in such a manner that it raises the awareness of other people around him and transform the world into a better place for every one'.

What we have to take full cognizance of is that making available the technical means of immortality or extended youth, or doubling or trebling of the human life span, will not resolve any of the problems that afflict human society. Poverty, prejudice, discrimination, inequity, bigotry, will not only exist but also get further exacerbated. The climate crisis will not get resolved; it may make the 'one-percent' more brazen with the knowledge that they could be less affected, as they already are. We will still have wars. In short, if you do not die in any other way, you won't die of death. Most deaths then will be violent deaths and escaping such a death will have a high premium; because then you can live virtually forever. But, make no mistake, death will still get you: or an iPhone will explode in your face; or the roof will collapse on your head, or a drone could hit you by mistake. Whatever science can do to prolong life or make you deathless, it cannot shield your body from harm's way, even if we become all-metal; in which case, it makes no difference anyway. What is called 'digital immortality', or mind-uploading, does not also sound so endearing. Who wants to 'live' in a machine without the pleasures of the flesh? In any case, we do 'die' and are reborn as our digital copy. And, on top of it, what we might end up with in our quest for immortality adds one more dangerous divide, and as good a reason as we can ever get to kill each other. The 'immortals' will still live in dread of death as they will not be impregnable to either disease or accident or the wrath of the left-behind and locked-out humans. We will have two more sedative triggers for suicide: extended boredom for some, and deep disaffection of much of the rest. The massive diversion of scarce resources, creative and economic, to this line of research, at the expense of far more worthy and critical priorities, will tantamount to adding fuel to the fire. Really, there will be no winners but a lot of losers in such a wounded world. What science needs to focus upon is not technologies that cure the 'disease of death', but on technologies that improve the infrastructure for a healthy and fulfilling life of the masses and, which, in turn, will automatically improve the average life span. It is important that the global community, not individual nations or corporations, take a fresh look at what science is trying to do by dangling before us the irresistible lure of never having to die, bearing in mind that without a new mindset or a new consciousness whatever emerges from the current effort could only make the world a more destructive and dangerous place. Along with the other two 'M's—morality and money—, the way we are thinking and dealing with this 'M' (mortality) has become a serious impediment to influence the flow of the war within in the right direction. And if that doesn't happen, nothing will happen for the good in the world.

The End of the Beginning

Are Humans 'Worthy' of Survival?

However much we might ruminate over our essential identity as existential beings and about our niche in the story of the cosmos—'the measure of all things'[1] (Protagoras), the best in nature or its 'serious mistake'[2] (Alan Watts), a blank slate or a noble savage or a civilized brute, a work still in progress—we surely are one of a kind, quite an awesome package of powers, passions, abilities, and weaknesses that nature fashioned, or God wrought from His own breast, or perhaps magically grew from the blundering baboon. A new study says that humans are 'just a bunch of freaks', and that there is no such thing as a right or wrong way to be human, and no such thing as normal or abnormal or optimal. In a nutshell, there is no such thing as the 'nutshell' of our nature. It only means that, not only as a species but even as individuals, we are *all* singular and customized. All species are unique, but only we humans are *individually* unique. It means that there is oneness in existence and uniqueness in all beings. And, most important, what it amounts to is that every one of us is a small but singular 'self', and every one of us can be an alchemist on a species-scale. That is what offers a glimmer in the gloom and darkness of today's world. We don't need 'species-scale' reach for 'species-scale' change. A 'critical mass' of thoughtful global citizens would do as well. To recall the words of anthropologist Margaret Mead, "indeed, it is the only thing that ever has".

We also have to reckon with two baseline factors: (1) whether any one of us is, in Norman Mailer's phrase, 'the original seed of evil', or simply a victim of one's environment; the suffocating smell of evil permeates all around us. Two, the fragrance of goodness continues to linger here and there. And, as William Saroyan reminds us, "Nothing good ever ends. If it did, there would be no people in the world—no life at all, anywhere" (*The Human Comedy*, 1943). The upshot of all this is that as humans, as JRR Tolkien puts it in *Lord of the Rings* (1954), "we have no way of judging what the ultimate effects of our deeds might be, good or bad". To which we may add, we have no way of differentiating fact from fantasy. Worse, we tell ourselves, 'it can't be that wrong if it feels this right'. As Lord Acton said, "Men thought they could make good the evil they did". Too many moral choices these days leave us insecure and groping, and expose us to what Spanish philosopher José Ortega y Gasset called 'moral hemiplegia'; the tendency to condemn moral transgressions of other people, but staying close-eyed to the same of our own. So much of our aggressiveness springs not from exuberance of strength, but from this moral ambivalence. The point of departure for any honest introspection has to be this: our own behavior boggles us most; and we all are afflicted by an epidemic of what the ancient Greeks called *akrasia*—lacking command (over oneself) or weakness of will; acting in a way contrary to one's sincerely held moral values; knowing the right thing to do but induced to do the opposite. This was the spirit of what St. Paul lamented about when he said, "For the good that I would I do not: but the evil which I would not, that I do". Why anyone will do anything that he *knows* is wrong has long been the question that has baffled many, from Greek philosophers to modern-day psychologists. But it is part of everyday life, and we all experience it in multiple ways and to different degrees. Sometimes, it is also possible that we are akratic in our behavior without being weak-willed or perversely-willed. The question is this: Is it beyond retrieval and redemption, or is there still time and hope? Some scientists say that we all have a 'moral molecule' in the human brain—the hormone *oxytocin*, dubbed the 'hug hormone'—which induces empathy for others and causes us to behave morally. Others say that the truth is more nuanced, that it fosters trust and generosity in some situations, but envy and bias in others, and that it can produce opposite effects in different people. The real answer to akrasia and to our moral impotence lies, quite simply, in the war within our consciousness, the war between good and evil.

Scriptures have long told us that every man is born with two opposing inclinations that pull him to act either in a bad way or a good way, but that, in the final analysis, it is man himself who decides how he is to act. The Katha Upanishad says that every person will always and at every stage get the option of treading the path of that which is right, righteous, and good—the spiritual path of *sreyas*, or of succumbing to the path of convenience, comfort, and pleasure—the sensual path of *preyas*. The Babylonian Talmud says, "Everything is determined by heaven, except one's fear of heaven", which means that man's choice to be either good or evil, righteous or wicked, dharmic or adharmic (in terms of Hindu scriptures), falls in the realm of free will. But then, the religious text is silent about how this 'free will' is exercized and gets actualized. Nobody is entirely good for nothing, or bad to the bone, and yet the ugly truth is that we often fail to do what we *know* is right. We have unfailingly failed to recognize that every external challenge can be reframed as an internal one, and that the circumstances that lead to our anger, avarice, stress, envy, hurt and suffering aren't the problem; the feelings themselves are, and to where they are directed. It is 'feelings' that finally matter, and one of the problems why we are so unmoved by existential threats is that "We know something is true; we don't feel that it's true. We don't live as if it's true."[3] We really are clueless about what exactly will happen beneath our feet before we appear to make a choice or decide. To our rational mind, nothing that is happening is making any sense; everything is out of joint and, to paraphrase Darwin, there is 'nothing beneficent in the details'. But then, our mind itself, which has been compared to a drunken monkey smitten by a scorpion, is our main impediment to a better man and to a stable world. It is the unchallenged sway of our mind over our consciousness that is the cradle of all that is so wrong in the world—climate collapse or moral meltdown or technological adventurism or growing militarization or escalating intolerance or economic inequality. The only way to meaningfully address any of these issues is to cage the monkey, and the only way to do that is to channel all our skills and resources to wage and win the war within. The greatest mystery, it has often been said, is man himself, and that 'human complexity is more complex than our present models of complexity'. That is true, but it is because we are looking at human complexity solely as a matter of behavior, ignoring its epicenter, the war within. We need to recognize that the way to 'win' this war is startlingly simple and straight: just do *morally* what we ordinarily do everyday, not heroically or exceptionally or extraordinarily. Not having any control over the course of this war, we live in daily dread of what we might do to others, as well as to our own selves. One of the impediments to better ourselves is that we reflexively speak as if we believe in something, but it becomes obvious from our behavior that we really don't.

Frustrated by his inability to bridge this abyss and to look inwards, and faced with serious risks to his very survival, man has concluded that the only way to get a grip on his future is either to 'redesign' himself gene-by-gene, or 'upgrade' his body, piece by piece, or even to turn 'auxiliary' systems into implants in his only body. And if nothing works, man will disappear into what is called a 'computer cloud'. But then, like the mythical emperor's new clothes, what we fail to see is that a better body or a brighter brain does not make a better man. And it raises the troubling thought: are we sacrificing the human for the sake of humanity, or is it the other way around? While human transformation has long been an overarching aspiration, the means earlier were spiritual and transcendental; now, they are technological and mechanical. And it implies a critical break away from the laws of nature. In the most elemental way, it is the drift from, and defiance and degradation of, nature. In almost everything modern man does as his way of life, that is at the epicenter of every crisis man faces today, like seemingly unstoppable 'climate collapse'. That is why it is so difficult to get ourselves to scale fast enough to meet the magnitude of this existential crisis. That is perhaps why biologist EO Wilson says that the only way to meet the challenge of climate collapse is to "dedicate fully half the surface of the earth to nature".[4] Whether it is utopian or impractical given man's acquisitive nature, it underscores the need to arrest our onslaught on Mother Nature. Few things will be done 'naturally' in the future; almost everything will be 'artificial', no matter if it is birth or death, rain or moon. Man's goal is to virtually turn the human into a blend of bionics and cybernetics, someone like the cyborg character Roger Torraway of Frederik Pohl's *Man Plus* (1976)—a near-monster, a mutant perfectly adapted to survive on Mars. We may soon run out of other options the way we are making earth 'uninhabitable'. This is typical of our willful mendacity—our give-up-nothing-but-grab-more attitude; our reflexive tendency to use and blindly discard everything. Our watchword seems to be, as the French say, *après nous, le déluge*—we could not care less about what happens after we are dead and gone, come hell or high water.

We must also, at the very outset, flag one basic issue. Everything is pretension; we really don't know who we are when we are not pretending to be someone else. And it is not always our fault. Nothing is really what it seems, because everything is immeasurably greater than it seems, and the "greatest force of all is never traceable by the eye of flesh, but is to be discerned only by the eye of spirit".[5] That is, nothing human can be error-free, nor do we have to live with stagnant acquiescence in error. It means that we are sentenced to live our lives according to an anonymous adage that "there are three sides to every story—

yours, mine, and the truth—and no one is lying". The 'truth' however is that *all* are lying but they don't know; that is because they (and all of us, for that matter) are lying not only to the world but even more fundamentally to themselves; that is what Orwell's 'double think' is about (*1984*). Science itself—which someone said is 'organized skepticism'—is not static. The message from the history of science, if it has taught us anything, is that almost all scientific theories, when first propounded, have something deficient which gets identified with the aid of new methods and scientific instruments. For instance, each advance of science has moved our understanding further from a purely materialist world to one ever closer to the metaphysical. We must also bear in mind that we are living at a time when, as Frank Furedi[6] reminds us, science has replaced God as the ultimate authority at the societal level, and medicine is replacing morals and physicians and priests as sources of authority. Existential anxiety bordering on panic is a part of everyday existence, and risk is now round the corner, in the realm of high probability, not remote possibility. To top it all, we are wholly driven by our mind; for a wholesome human life, we need both intelligence of the mind and intuition of the heart. For too long, our mind has been our nemesis and has come to control the commanding heights of our consciousness. Our whole perspective has focused on narrowing things down to a point and denaturing things. The content has overshadowed the context; we are adrift in the labyrinths and purblind to the big picture. The need of the hour is, "no matter who says what, spare your time for the places, events, ideas, people, and activities that make your heart shout loud".[7] Einstein once said, "I never came upon any of my discoveries through the process of rational thinking". It is important to bear this in mind when man is facing an unprecedented array of mostly man-made existential threats. Our benign passivity in living under the shadow of such threats to our very survival suggests the existence of what in French is called *l'appel du vide*—the call of the void—and an apocalyptic barrier where, not too long ago, our way ahead looked almost clear. It now looks very clouded and foggy. And the world, surveys show, is "sadder, angrier, and more worried than ever before recorded".[8] That is as much due to what is happening in the world outside as in the world *within*. There is an interiority to everything we do and to all that happens, and our failure to factor that in is responsible for most of our misjudgments. To that we must add another 'factor': we humans simply can never know how to judge anything truly and justly. In fact, we are better 'judges' of others than of ourselves. We instinctively assume that the world is nothing but the human world, and that our fate is a cause for cosmic concern. Is that so? Or is our story as a species almost done, save collecting the ashes and embers? Looking at the toxic footprints of humanity, it is necessary to tell ourselves that, in Admiral Adama's words, "It is not enough to survive. One has to be worthy of survival".[9] A central question we have to address before going any further is this: are all the problems that we have created, that make us doubt our 'worthiness', merely offsprings of modern civilization, or do they stem from something more basic and inherent from the core of being human *per se?* The real answer is, *none of the two*. It is our ignorance of what goes on inside us; how the balance between our virtues and our vices plays out in the war within. Whatever is the truth, even terminal patients simply don't want to 'survive'. They too have priorities besides just surviving no matter what. They have things to do before they die. We, collectively, are not very different. What about our unfulfilled desires before we become extinct? And should we give away our lives before we can spoil any further? What is it that we can sacrifice just to survive? We must remember what Byron said: "Who on earth could live were all judged justly?" For, 'being human' is living unjustly—that is the awful burden all of us have to carry. Sadly, what is naturally possible to other species is denied to the species that desperately aspires to be a moral species. At a time when man seems prepared to surrender everything at the altar of becoming an immortal inter-planetary species (a.k.a. god), this is particularly pertinent. What we also forget is that, to paraphrase Emily *Dickinson*, there is no forever if there is no 'now', and that we seem intellectually prepared to offer at the altar, the Now of everything that is human to live 'forever', regardless of where. Instead of worrying if we are 'worthy' of survival, we behave as if we have come to believe that the planet is not worthy of saving.

The fatalistic way we negate, nibble, and nullify each other, the casual cruelty we show to animals, the reckless abandon with which we abuse the planet, and the contempt we shower on nature is getting worse by the day. A time might well come, as the Book of Isaiah prophecies, when "the wolf will live with the lamb, the leopard will lie down with the goat, the calf and the lion and the yearling together… the infant will play near the cobra's den, and the young child will put its hand into the viper's nest". But such is our genius and genre that man cannot let his guard down when dealing with another man. We need peace inside for peace outside. Man has become a blend of bad and mad, blindsided and blindfolded; 'a scurrying mass of bewildered humanity crashing headlong against each other'.[10] It is worth noting in passing that, as Richard Powers (*The Overstory*, 2018) so well shows, this is in sharp contrast to how trees, with which we still share a quarter of our genes, 'live'. And the ways they help and provide for, and take care of each other, and other living things too numerous to count. Man must go for the sake of man. Like they used to say in the olden days, "the king is dead; long live the king", we have to both bury and resurrect the man. First, we have to officially announce his death. And his epitaph might well read as: 'Abundantly blessed by nature, the *Homo sapiens* has had his time, had his golden moments, mastered much but fatally failed to get a grip on his world within; in consequence, he hopelessly went awry, courted his own abolition; became someone no one missed much when no more'.

What we have to fully grasp is that even as we struggle to survive on a daily basis, the ground is shifting and the foundations are shaking. And we have nothing to hold on to, no anchor to keep us in place. We cannot massacre other species in millions and stake a claim for 'survival' simply because we are human. And we must remember, as EO Wilson puts it in proper perspective, that "If all mankind were to disappear, the world would regenerate back to the rich state of equilibrium that existed ten thousand years ago. If insects were to vanish, the environment would collapse into chaos".[11] Even more, one could argue that it is *only* humans, of the millions of life forms on earth, who have proven themselves 'unworthy' by their conduct. In Franz Kafka's classic *The Trial* (1925), the protagonist, Josef K claims he cannot be 'guilty' as he too is human like the other, to which the priest answers, "But that is how the guilty speak". We are all 'guilty' but, being human, we are incapable of accepting responsibility for it. Does that mean that nature and life in general will benefit with our early departure? Some outcomes, even the most worthy ones, should not be brought about if we have to give up everything to achieve them. But then, some skeptic with a sneer might say, 'What is there to become? We already *are!*' What Kafka called 'monstrous vermin'. And an ancient theory (of the Greek philosopher Empedocles) even says that we came from 'monstrous creatures'. Be that as it may, what we now have to ponder over is *what* there is to 'save' in saving the human species, and *why* should we be 'saved' if we are not only self-destructive but also nihilistic. In any case, 'saving life' itself has lost its sheen; it is easier to grab our attention with news about the latest software than with news about how to save lives. The French 'existential' philosopher Simone de Beauvoir (*The Ethics of Ambiguity*, 1947) pertinently posited that man, "conscious of being unable to be anything... then decides to be nothing". And from 'nothing' to nihilism is a small step. Let us not forget that the sole serious threat to our 'survival' comes from our own activity, and creativity, not from any extraterrestrial or colliding comet or crashing meteorite. Even the most benign of inventions can be turned toxic by the human mind soaked with malice. No one has ever explained why we are the only animal with malice in its mind. It is malice, not violence, that 'transformed' the human from a fairly average species of large mammals into a dreaded menace. And, in EO Wilson's words, a 'danger to ourselves and to the rest of life'. If we cannot get rid of it or at least keep it under check, nothing good can ever happen. And the only way to do that is to 'win' the war within. With malice reigning over our mind, and our mind supreme reigning over our consciousness, we cannot even trust our own inventiveness. In some cases, even the inventors have come to regret their accomplishment. For example, the Wright Brothers, pioneers of powered flight, thought they would make everyone essentially equal, and therefore remove the specter of war. Much later, Orville Wright lamented, "We dared to hope we had invented something that would bring lasting peace to the earth. But we were wrong. We underestimated man's capacity to hate and to corrupt good means for an evil end". Alfred Nobel regretted the invention of dynamite, and to atone for this 'accomplishment' and to relieve his conscience, he instituted his award for the promotion of peace. Another famous 'regret' was that of Einstein, for his contribution to the development of the atomic bomb. It is said that the guy who invented television (in 1927) became so disenchanted that he forbade his kids from watching it. Our mind empowers us to create extraordinary things and yet entices us to misuse them.

The terrible thing is, what can we possibly do if what we do for good comes back to haunt us? What the human has now become is well captured in the Latin proverb, *Lupus est homo homini, non homo, quom qualis sit non novit*: "One man to another is a wolf, not a man, when he doesn't know what sort he is". And even if we do want to end human presence on earth as penance or reparation, what more could we do? Maybe we should unleash a global nuclear Armageddon. But that will do irreparable harm to the planet, and that nullifies the purpose of our voluntary exit, to save the planet from the human predator. Our presence is so pervasive and deep that anything we do to harm ourselves endangers the earth as well. That prospect, instead of being a deterrent, seems to act as an incentive for unhinged recklessness and frenzied *hara-kiri*. Although a few of us still actually take the 'extreme step', we have long been self-destructive as a species, whether it is evolutionary or existential. By any reckoning, it has now reached an unrecoverable tipping point, and we are clueless about what we can do to arrest, much less reverse it. It is a terrible thing to say, but the best we can do is to 'accelerate', push the pedal to the metal, so to speak. Some are even asking: 'Has procreation itself become immoral?' They say that the morality of bringing new human life into the world is "the most pressing question of our time". Is all this hype and panic warranted? The answer is yes. For the stakes cannot be any higher and what needs to be done cannot be any more challenging.

Just as the proof is in the pudding, what matters to nature is how we behave, no matter if we are in essence man or machine, madman or mahatma, god or goat, devil or donkey. It is 'behavior'—how we do what we do—that impacts on the planet, now more than ever. And more than ever, our choices, however minute or mundane, do matter. Just as human behavior influences our warming planet, the climate crisis influences human behavior. It is this 'behavior', particularly our preferences and habits, in the *'ism'* in which we live, what Shoshana Zuboff[12] calls 'surveillance capitalism', that has become the chief source of commercial concern, the primary platform for 'making money'. The aim is to make us behave—through 'behavioral modification'—in a way that is advantageous to the producer or provider, often at the cost of the individual and society. Ultimately, behavior is, as Goethe said, a mirror in which everyone displays his own image. What we have been forgetting is that that 'image' is formed inside, a reflection of the state of our consciousness. Although we still do not know what consciousness truly is or isn't—some even speculate that it resides not inside us but in an as-yet-unknown space in the universe—that it is the key to human transformation and evolution has long been a part of indigenous wisdom. Exploring expanded states of consciousness is now at the cutting edge of science. If we are able to change *that* state for the better, then our behavior will become better and we will not be a threat to anyone, much less to ourselves. We can then be, in good conscience, 'worthy of survival'. What it all underscores is that for anything good to happen to man, or to the planet, a profound metamorphosis must be triggered in the deepest depths of our being. Only then can our behavior routinely, if not reflexively, put another's needs on par, or above, our own, which is the alpha and omega of the transformation we need in our day-to-day life. Otherwise, we can, with a status quo consciousness, turn even Shangri-La into Pol Pot's Kampuchea. For, as James Hilton says, "If we have not found the heaven within, we have not found the heaven without". That is the way to find the way to 'love each other' and that as, Walt Whitman says, will 'make us invincible".[13]

All these are tantalizing possibilities, but for now, heaven is still high in the sky, and we cannot even live with each other, let alone love each other. And the baseline is that we are all beast inside and outside. What is striking is that, even as an animal, we are actually the microcosm of the macrocosm of virtually the entire animal kingdom. That is because all human traits exist—to some degree—in other animals, because our pasts are intertwined, as Darwin said in his *Descent of Man* (1871). We subsume in us almost all the defining features of other animals—the sociability of a lion, the ferocity of a tiger, the aggressiveness of a wolf, the intelligence of an elephant, the meekness of a lamb, the cunning of a jackal, the nobility of a dog, the venom of a serpent, and the free spirit of a bird. In fact, our 'gold standard' for excellence is what other creatures can do better. Our ego says if they can do, why not we? If a certain jellyfish can be literally immortal, why not we? If a certain marine worm can literally sprout new heads (including brains), why not we? But, in the end, as Mephistopheles (in Goethe's *Faust*) says, we are "more bestial than the beast". That is now a greater peril than ever, with what technology is trying to do to the mind (mind control) and creating human-like machines more intelligent than man himself. Our history is animal, and destiny is divinity; the bridge between that we are trying to build is the machine. We read that research is on to conduct human–animal embryo experiments, and we really have no way to know where and what we might end up as. Half a century ago, Marshall McLuhan, who coined the famous phrases, 'the medium is the message', and 'the global village', warned that tools are merely outreaches of ourselves, reinforcing our own virtues and flaws. And now, "we have created a godlike intelligence stained with the fingerprints of our own sins".[14] The real problem is not the machine; it is the mind and its unchallenged sway over our consciousness. It is the way we want to resolve any 'problem'; destroy or eliminate whatever happens to be in the way. Instead of finding ways to optimize human labor alongside machines, we seem determined to turn ourselves into a sacrificial goat as an offering at the altar of our 'progress'.

Tomorrow's monster will be the result of an out-of-control, technology-boosted *human* mind, vastly different from Mary Shelley's monster, who was the tragic result of misapplied technology—and who, by the way, was basically good-natured, but driven to be a monster by man. What is truly terrifying is that the new-age demon will not have the visible grotesqueness of Mary's 'monster', but will be far more monstrous in his *mind*. Our mind makes mortals into monsters and then puts them away as they are its own reflections. Still, we cannot turn our back on our symbiosis with technology; what we need to do is to curb our 'techno-lust' on the one hand, and, on the other hand, develop a *mentalité* or way of thinking *not* dominated by the mind. The machine, if rightly directed, can change the nature of work from the present paradigm of doing what we need to do to survive, to what we want to do to blossom into 'higher' human beings. We want the machine to amplify and supplant the organic limits of the human body, and make up for its fragility and feebleness. Indeed, what we don't like is being 'limited' in any way in anything; we want abundance; we want unlimited life and liberty, health, and wealth, growth and glory, power, leisure, and luxury. Many believe that the unhindered pursuit of pleasure itself is a basic human right. And what we call 'work' consumes more of our life than anything else. We need to move the momentum away from having all of one's dignity and worth tied up with the particular labor we engage in, which we detest, in any case. We must understand that job satisfaction effectively translates as life happiness. At the same time, we cannot let our sense and limbs become dysfunctional through disuse, because that risks reaction from nature in ways we cannot predict. Our relationship with the machine will probably be the most important relationship in the coming age, perhaps even supplanting our current relationship with the divine. We are even prepared, indeed eager, to pay to the machine the ultimate obeisance we hesitate to offer to the divine: absolute surrender, or *saranagati* in

Vedantic philosophy. What attracts us is the lure that the notional space of the machine will be more comforting and conducive than the troubled world of human life. What in another way also is 'comforting' is that it is not going to be anytime soon, and if things do finally go wrong we would not be around to face the consequences. And that is how we are able to so shamelessly seek more and more comforts everyday. And that is perhaps why we are so glib and blasé about all the talk about mind-melding merger with the machine; thank God, we won't be around. The underlying hope is that machines will do all our bidding and we stay in command. But many fear that such hope is a naïve delusion, and that we might well end up with the machines evolving and eventually obliterating us, through hive-minded activity and skill-sharing. The helper could turn out to be the terminator. That, after all, is what we would do if we exchange places. Yet, so beguiled we are that we even look up to the machine to make us what we have long wanted: free us from our biases, prejudices, and pettiness and make us moral, if not spiritual, beings. What is likely, however, is that they will magnify and replicate the tendencies inherent in human judgment, instead of avoiding them. Some like Normal Mailer even posit that "technology was the Devil's most brilliant creation… aspires to create a mechanized world",[15] possibly as a way to enlist us in his eternal fight with God inside us. We must also not forget that the irresistible lure offered to Adam by Satan was to become a 'god'. It is now the same temptation that is at the heart of the agenda of science. We have now sanctified science as our 'God' and, in return, it now wants us to make us a 'god-machine'.

While virtually 'becoming' a machine—which some call 'disappearing into cyberspace'—is an avant-garde idea, we have long been bewildered by the realization that any of us can become anything at anytime—bestial or celestial, saint or sinner, bodhisattva or barbarian, murderer or martyr. We can, like chameleons, change the content of our conflicted character, to grease our greed, to hide our putridity, and to masquerade our malevolence. And, most maddening, we have no say in what shape our deep-seated fury and frustrations might take, or what we might do, and when. We never know what to hope for or fear, or when a dream can turn into a nightmare. We are naked without a stitch before our own vanity, venality, and depravity. In the human condition, whether it is inherently absurd, as Camus famously proclaimed, or an unending agony as biologists like Jeremy Griffith tell us, or an affliction from which we need liberation, the only constant has been what Schopenhauer called 'the terrible certainty of death'. Not knowing what death really is and yet all too aware that all living is waiting for death has played havoc with the human psyche. If the veto of destiny is death, what good is anything, any effort, any result, any difference anyone can make? How laughable all life then is? Oh, if only we learn to laugh at ourselves! If 'being mortal' is what we are born to be, why then should we be moral and miss out? Not finding any answers we have decided to, as it were, go for broke and try to make death itself optional, put an end to the *End*, as it were. We want to, as the Immortalists would say, 'look beyond the past of dying to a future of unlimited living'. *À la* Dylan Thomas, we don't want to go gentle into that good night. We always wonder: what do we miss when we die, and who will miss us and why? Being alive is itself a congenital fatal condition; the diagnosis is death; what is unknown is the trigger and the timing. Wisdom lies in making every minute an opportunity to turn, as it were, the 'candle in the wind' into a 'candle in the dark'; to use life to, in George Eliot's words, make life less difficult to others; so that when our time is up, we don't look back and see a wasteland or a graveyard. Accepting death means to be clear and candid, as Atul Gawande (*Being Mortal*, 2014) puts it, about the boundaries on our quality of life that we are unwilling to cross when pursuing medical treatment. What is paradoxical is that the more medical science and technology advances, the more it is revealing how ignorant, fallacious, and mistaken we still are in many ways about issues of health, illness, life, and death. In the midst of that 'uncertainty' we have reached a stage when to a large extent, a human doesn't have to die when death comes, notionally though not yet operationally. And we are completely ill-equipped to internalize it. And, as a result, we face a surreal situation; death is under more of our 'control' than our own creativity. And much of what we 'create' or innovate—our technical capability—has become a threat to our own existence and to planetary well-being.

Part of the problem is that we never see the world as it is, because we don't see the world *within*. Whatever happens in the external world is but a reflection and projection of what happens in the world within. What is 'happening' there is a process that we call *war* in the outside world, a war between our own innate instincts, emotions, and impulses. And this 'war' is the untold story inside us. According to biologist Jeremy Griffith, our "good and evil conflicted", psychologically upset lives are the result of the underlying battle between our original instinctive self and our newer conscious self (*Freedom*, 2016). But he also says that humans are "not just good but the heroes of the story of life on Earth!"[16] Joseph Murphy (*The Power of Your Subconscious Mind*, 2015) expresses the same idea in terms of psychology, and says, "Life events are actually the result of the workings of your conscious and subconscious minds", which in our language, is the 'war within our consciousness'. We have always struggled to know who we are, who we want to be, and how to, in the words of the poet Jericho Brown,[17] "more fully inhabit and become this person I have been being." Perhaps the best we can hope for is to *always be maybe*. That 'maybe' must be what we must be. Essentially, the warring forces are of two kinds: on one side, what the Bible calls 'Fruit of the Holy Spirit'[18]—love, joy, peace, patience, kindness, goodness, faithfulness, gentleness, self-control; and on the other side, the opposites—hatred, misery, indifference intolerance, cruelty, evil, treachery, insensitivity, and intemperance. Put in Jungian terms, it is a war between the '*persona*' (what we would like to be, and how we wish to be seen by the world), and the '*shadow*' (the unconscious mind, which is composed of repressed ideas, instincts, impulses, weaknesses, longings, perversions, and embarrassing fears). It is interesting to note that the word *persona* itself is derived from a Latin word that literally means 'mask', implying that the personality we project is nothing but a collection of masks.

We are often aghast at our own actions and appalled at what we see in the world. In human life, the foundation for anything to happen for the better is to recognize that the fountainhead of our troubles and the source of our well-being are both within us. We must also recognize that our lives are fashioned by our choices, and our choices are now to a large extent aiding the wrong side in the war within. The fact that the wrong side is winning in this war accounts for why we are so easily succumbing to polarization, tribalism, xenophobia, and sectarian thinking, and why we are unable to strike a common narrative to tackle complex problems like climate breakdown. And that has extracted a terrible toll on us: loss of self-esteem, to what we might call 'climate fatigue'. It explains the apathy of the good and ardor of the evil, bringing to mind what WB Yeats wrote a century ago: "The best lack all conviction while the worst are full of passionate intensity" (*The Second Coming*, 1919). Whether we are able to manage our mental and emotional fragility at a time of transformative turbulence, and whether enough of us can see ourselves as part of a larger '*Us*' instead of an atomized '*I*', hinges on what happens collectively in this war. In fact, much of our greed and sorrow comes from the nagging feeling of *not having enough* of anything we want—money, success, work, leisure, recognition, reward, etc. The more we have, the more it is 'not good enough'. For instance, more money, as Benjamin Franklin once said, instead of filling a vacuum, makes one. We cannot overcome that feeling so long as the mind dominates our consciousness, and the way to overcome that is to win the war within.

We must also remember that an individual is just as responsible for not refusing something as for choosing it. To induce such a perspective, we need a radical change in the way we lead our lives, particularly the way we make choices germane to the three things that dominate our mind and mood: *morality*, *money*, and *mortality*. We have to redirect our attention, intelligence, and energy to ensure that the forces of goodness prevail over the forces of evil, bearing in mind that evil too has 'evolved', and changed its colors. It is indistinguishable from our 'culture', and implicit in the infrastructure of everyday life. As Andrew Kimbrell tells us, "Evil no longer requires evil people to purvey it as it did in the past".[19] That is because evil, what Kimbrell calls 'cold evil', has transcended the individual and infiltrated all human institutions. And it also no longer requires 'proximity' or physical presence; horrific evil can be launched thousands of miles from the 'target'. We must also bear in mind that the word 'evil' is more than the sound of a malevolent incantation, much more than massacres and murders, and, in the broader setting, violence itself is much more than overt physical aggression. Let us not forget that at the most basic layer, we have a propensity for violence, and evil itself "is the refusal to see one's self in others."[20] In the most elemental sense, nature is violence, *eros* is violence, birth is violence, death is violence. Systemic violence is so subtle, stealthy, and seemingly so harmless that it escapes any attention. It is the failure to take notice of this genre of generic violence that has made scholars like Steven Pinker affirm that 'violence has declined over long stretches of time, and today we may be living in the most peaceable era in our species' existence' (*Better Angels of Our Nature*, 2011). And then, absence or decline of violence is not the existence of 'peace' on the planet, let alone in the human mind, which really is the vortex of all wars. What goes on in wars is the very worst evil and yet we accept it, even view it as the way. In the words of Stevenson's *Dr Jekyll*, "All human beings... are commingled out of good and evil". They are, as Tolstoy said, interchangeable, and have no status in isolation; they are always relative to each other. But Tolstoy also said that evil cannot be vanquished by evil (*The Kingdom of God Is Within You*, 1893). Our biology does not make us innately good or evil. It is our tendency to overuse and misuse the natural survival needs of the physical body that is harmful. Thus, eating becomes gluttony, procreation becomes promiscuity, passion becomes toxic, and compassion curdles into concupiscence, and so on. Everything is possible for everybody. Criminals have at times done good, risking getting caught or risking their lives, while great, even holy, men have mistreated many, taking immoral advantage of the helpless and hopeless, the gullible and the weak. Nobody is perfect, nor is anyone all vile. Even very flawed people can do a lot of good, and even a moral mahatma can be incredibly mean. The vast majority of us have the potential to act in either direction; the trouble is that we ourselves do not know which of the two we will do when, and why. The principal reason why we have failed to get a grip on our behavior is our belief that it all depends on external forces, ranging from the culture and context in which we are born, to the details of a particular circumstance. What we, as humans, might do when we are desperate in traumatic situations has long baffled us. The truth is that it is much more; it is deeper; it is not circumstance but *consciousness* that is the key. As Andrew Kimbrell says, our consciousness has become both 'dysfunctional' and 'destructive', and that we need to change 'the habits of perception and thinking'. As Owen Barfield[21] aptly reminds us, it is not only what we perceive, but also what we *fail* to perceive, that determines the quality of the world we live in. Whether we do good or bad in our daily life depends on what happens in the fight between good and evil in the war within. We must also recognize that extreme physical violence is not always the virulent evil; a murder can be manslaughter while our mouth, not our hand, is our most violent weapon. The reach of evil is across-the-board and its knife-like penetration goes right down to the soul. Evil is hydra-headed. Extreme poverty is evil, bigotry is evil, viewing might as right is evil, inequity is evil, injustice is evil, intolerance is evil, indifference to evil is evil, cruelty to animals is evil, and hurting and humiliating is evil. Above all, like much else about human behavior, it is the way we treat others that determines whether any action of ours is evil or immoral.

The new dimension, or cold evil, is systemic and embedded in conditions where individuals and their sweeping range of emotions play at best marginal roles, but in which we are all complicit implicitly. The paradox is that most of us consider ourselves to be, and may even actually be, good persons. But, at the same time, the institutional infrastructure of everyday life, which we are not even aware of, underpins and sustains evil. The fact is that each one of us participates in evil every single day, when we make a choice about how we want to live in the world. We must recognize that the actions we take in deciding which products to buy or which services to use or render, will also have an equal bearing. We must also alter our relationship with work; work is at the 'hinge of our holiness', where we increasingly ignore ethical principles and implications. If 'cold evil' is to be contained that must change; for, so much of life is work-related and work-sanctified. To truly prosper, we must know that the ways in which we occupy our waking hours are not based on the mere pursuit of pleasure or money or any other material goal. What is happening is that even if we try our very best to desist from doing any evil, our actions and activities, what we do to 'make a living', to make it big, to have a 'good life' and to be upwardly mobile, could all implicitly backstop evil. No human institution, national or international, is untouched by 'cold evil', the nation-state, corporation, even the family. The first two in fact have become the primary fountainheads of such evil. They no longer have to be discreet or devious, or even pay lip-service to fairness and fair play. As Sylvia Federici said about 'corporate capital', "the monsters now can move without the mask".[22] The reality is that what is good for the nation-state is not good for the globe, and what is paramount for the shareholders of a company may not always be beneficial to society. But we have to come to implicitly accept that they are exempt and above the moral laws that govern us as individuals. Somehow, we have come to believe that an 'office' is loftier than the 'office-holder' and an institution is immune to individual ethics. And that has, in effect, become acquiescence to evil. A major challenge we face now is to find ways to harmonize national interest with global imperatives and corporate profit-making with the public good.

The basic point is that wherever power comes into play, the potential for cold evil exists. Quite apart from Lord Acton's lesser-noted axiom that 'great men are almost always bad men, even when they exercise influence and not authority', as JRR Tolkien says, 'evil occurs when individuals fall to the temptation of wielding power for personal gain'. And institutions have marginalized the individual, and 'imaginary people are put before the real people who made them up'. And when we boast about man's power over nature, it is actually, as CS Lewis reminds us, "a power exercised by some men over other men with nature as its instrument" (*The Abolition of Man*, 1947). In effect, we are violating both nature and man. We must clearly realize that confronting this kind of insidious evil is not possible unless we proactively alter many things that we have taken for granted as trappings of our technological civilization, and make our daily decision-making more moral than now. More than ever, morality is not a matter of calculated choice; some of the most lacklustre choices we make have a deep moral meaning. What moral philosophers call *virtue ethics*—the moral position that the objective of our actions is to become virtuous by acting in a way that a virtuous person would act—is now ingrained in our much-maligned 'meaningless lives'. It is true that in the end, everything is situational, and there is no 'one-size-fits-all principle'. What is happening in today's world is that in our obsession with the extraordinary, we are often tempted to sacrifice wholeness; in the pursuit of super-specialization, we are forgetting that the whole is more than the sum of the parts; and in the name of seeking super-intelligence, we are corrupting intelligence itself. The only way to make sure that we do not morally err is to deliberately bring to bear in our everyday life, qualities like what Buddhists call loving-kindness, empathy, compassion, and sharing. That has long been our aim. It goes back at least to the days of 18th-century philosopher Adam Smith, who placed 'sympathy' (something closer to what we would now call 'empathy') at the epicenter of ethical life. A century later, George Eliot wrote, "If art does not enlarge men's sympathies, it does nothing morally". The good news is that recent research by organizations like the Greater Good Science Center (USA) shows that such qualities can be acquired, cultivated, and optimized, like any other desired skills, through systematic practice and training. Helen Riess, in her book *The Empathy Effect* (2018) says, that 'while empathy is a built-in biological response to suffering, we still need to work at it'. That means we don't have to simply trust our good sense and Godspeed, good instincts and good luck, to do the right thing. Like anything else, we can hone our 'positive' mental skills through application and practice and training. If these findings are further corroborated, it will mean that we can get a grip on our own erratic behavior and do the kind of things that help the forces of good in the war within. Neuroscience, it is said, allows us to see inside the human brain and better understand our minds. With this knowledge, we can begin to make daily choices of mindset and behavior that not only reshape our neural circuitry but can alter the way human beings interact with one another. Scientists say that 'our brain's neural circuitry is malleable and can be rewired through neuroplasticity'. While we have long racked our brains on how we could be better persons, we are now told that by selectively stimulating specific parts of that very brain, we can strengthen our positive qualities and suppress the unsavory ones. Man might have at last found the Holy Grail of goodness: how to 'love thy neighbor as thyself' and 'do unto others as you would have them do unto you".[23] This has long been the stuff of science-fiction and scientific pursuit: to be able to break into others' minds and, like in the movie *Inception* (2010), insert ourselves into another person's dream to change that person's behavior in real life, for an array of purposes, ranging from wrecking revenge to aborting a murder or massacre to maximizing corporate coffers. In human relationships today, regret and revenge rule the roost; remorse and redemption are rare. But then, even if all such primrose promises come true, we cannot still wish away attributes like competitiveness, aggression, smartness, and ruthlessness. For long, it has been a broadly-shared belief that we humans have savage genetic 'primal instincts' that we are born with, and therefore cannot be dispensed with. It means that a huge part of us is competitive and aggressive, and there will always therefore be bad people, wars, massacres, cruelty, and inequality, and all life will be a battle with these primal passions. And yet there are others who argue that we humans are inherently good and godly, and our primary urges and drives are for conciliation, cooperation, and compassion, and that it is civilization that put them under eclipse. The third view is that humans are born with both streaks, and the blend is particular to a person, which is why there is so much diversity in human behavior.

What has been ignored or insufficiently appreciated in discussing the dynamics of our behavior is the critical place and role of consciousness. Our outward life reflects our inner life, and our inner life reflects the state of our consciousness. As philosopher Jonathan Rowson reminds us, we need a deeper appreciation of how our inner worlds influence our outer worlds.[24] Without such an appreciation, "living an inner life and not an outer life at the same time is like living in a house that has no foundation, a house that gradually either settles or develops gaping cracks or totters until it collapses".[25] It has also been said that "the ability to imagine someone else's inner life is where compassion begins". The state of our consciousness has always been a state of war between our two opposing sets of primal passions of good and bad, competition and cooperation, conciliation and confrontation, cruelty and empathy, and so on. Our worldly disposition depends on which of the two sides of our own personality gain dominance in this dichotomous struggle. How we live and how we address the twin questions posed by Padraig O Tuama—Who are we to be with one another? How are we to be with one another?—will influence how the war within goes. And how we live is dependent on the kind of intelligence we bring to bear on everyday life, what we do to raise everyday existence out of the grind of the commonplace. For, in the end, those choices determine what we are and what kind of future looms ahead: utopian, dystopian, transhumanist, or post-apocalyptic. And at a more fundamental level, we must face up to the fact that what lets us down most is the way we have evolved to make choices and decisions. Our decision-making is now not only about human life but about what being human ought to mean, raising the question: who gets to decide whether and how to grow a 'human'? We need brand new 'decision-analysis' tools that will let us choose the way we want to. First and foremost, we must free our consciousness from the Svengali-like sway of our mind. Our mindset must not be synonymous with our mind. And it is because the mind, as someone said, is like a puzzle with too many pieces missing, and trying to make sense out of it makes no sense. We cannot change the mind and we need it; what we should do is to counter its power with our heart-power. Unless we do this, nothing else can change anything in the world or in our lives for the better. We must remember that even if we achieve a symbiotic relationship with artificial intelligence as we hope to, such 'intelligence' would still be primarily brain-based, and might even carry the same biases, propensities, and prejudices. We suffer from what is called 'cerebral mystique': everything, from creativity to drug addiction, is a matter of the brain. And yet it is the perceived limitations of our brain—dismissively called *wetware*—that are driving the rush to submerge human autonomy into automated systems. Worse, some fear that these very 'systems' like artificial intelligence (AI) could evolve into a new life form that could inherit the earth after we render it too toxic for human habitation. According to transhumanists, who advocate human transformation and enhancement through technology, "The hardware we do have is really great for... cracking open skulls on the African savannah, but not much use for the world we live in now".[26] What they seem to ignore is that AI-powered machines, like AI itself, may have a different hardware, but their software would be similar to human intelligence software, even if exponentially more efficient. What we need now is not more *efficiently* (to do things rightly), but more *effectively* (to do the righteous things). The fact is that, as Stephen Talbott tells us, "The intelligent machine gathers its menacing powers from hidden places within you and me".[27] We all know that we hide things we are aware of but don't want to see, but secretly hope others do. Being more 'efficient' it drags out the darkness that lies deep within. "We are thus confronted from the world by the active powers of our own, most mechanistic mental functioning".[28] So, what does all this add up to? All that human beings create remains unchangeably human, just as everything God creates is divine, and the fate of man-made machines can be no different. If we are a bundle of good and evil, so will they be; just as we don't know when we will do what, so will it be in their case. An 'emotionally-intelligent' machine, which science is trying to make, might well be even more unpredictable and out-of-control. Emotions both unite and divide the personal and global worlds in which we live, motivating the best and the worst of our actions. What we should focus upon is to find a way to ensure that our 'good' emotions have an upper hand on the 'dark' emotions in our consciousness. No 'emotionally-intelligent personal assistant' (EMMA) can be a surrogate for an emotionally unstable person. We can't mine the mind of god, as Einstein too wanted to; but we must mend our mind. There are no short-cuts and quick-fixes to better ourselves or to save the world. The way to do it is the way within, through consciousness-change. That is the only way to change our 'mindset', and without that nothing will ever happen for the good.

But, first things first. We must, despite our dreams or delusions of becoming an immortal interplanetary species, remember that Mother Earth is our sacred home and silent witness, and will be so for a long, long time to come. EO Wilson puts it this way: "Despite all of our pretenses and fantasies, we always have been and will remain a biological species tied to this particular biological world".[29] Now, instead of mending our ways and saving the planet, we are making plans to abandon it. Our laid-back nonchalance in the face of a dying planet could well be due to our successes in space exploration, which have made us both cocky and complacent. And it has distorted our priorities, and resources that can save the planet and enhance the lives of billions are diverted; the American space agency NASA alone has already spent an estimated 1.32 trillion dollars since its inception. Our reckless, almost religious zealotry to merge with the machine is to get prepared to emigrate and be able to live in space. It is worth mentioning, at this point, the exploits of *Mara*, the ultimate tempter, in Buddhism. It is said that when Mara asked, "Who is the witness to your seat of enlightenment", Shakyamuni, the Buddha-to-be, put his finger down to touch the ground and replied, "I call the Earth as my witness". When everything fails, it is always the earth that stands behind us. According to the Gaia hypothesis, the earth is a self-regulating, living organism; whatever we do to it, it can feel and suffer. Many ingenious cultures revere the earth as a mother. In Hinduism, it is a goddess, *Bhoodevi*. If we don't stand for what we stand on, what is our worth? None of that has stood in the way we plunder and profligate and ruthlessly ravage the planet, and many observers are saying that we are living far beyond what is called earth's *caring* capacity, not simply its carrying capacity. As a result, the burning planet itself is becoming less alive. It is because the earth cares for us, not simply carries us, that we have got away with what we have done. If science has its way and we continue to behave the way we do, we might soon have an 'immortal' man and a 'mortal' planet. We need also to step aside and pause and, as it were, in Miguel de Unamuno's phrase, 'brood in a moonless night' over what we are doing to each other, invoking the legitimacy of being human. Scientists say that 'the human rate of lethal violence is seven times higher than the average for all mammals', and that slaughter is the defining behavior of our species. The provocation for 'slaughter' is now anything any man does anyway. And science is seriously interested in making us at once more 'moral' and murderous. In one direction, research is going on to make a 'morality pill' that would correct bad behavior arising from faulty DNA. In another direction, research is going on to improve 'the methodology of efficient violence'. This comes on top of a finding that all of us "house in our large brains specialized psychological circuits that lead us to contemplate murder as a solution to specific adaptive problems".[30]

Our mind has developed a *modus vivendi* to make us see certain groups, races, and ethnicities (especially outsiders and vulnerable people perceived as being of a low status) as being less than fully human. We have now carried that 'tendency' to its twisted end, and to simplify matters, we have brought it into the mainstream: anyone who comes in the way of our will, and citizens of 'enemy' nations, are to be seen as less than human. And that offers a moral alibi to do whatever we wish to do to them, the 'nonhumans'. Although it gained steam in modern times, it has been happening over and over again throughout our soiled history, which Stephen Daedalus (*Ulysses*) described as "a nightmare from which I am trying to awake". And the 'nightmare' is the sinew that binds our 'then, now, and yet'. The nightmare is the consequence of what we are doing to each other in our minds; the nightmare is what will follow from what we doing with nature. And the continuing nightmare is what the world will be if human consciousness remains unchanged. The tragic irony is that we love our children so much that we will die for them, but we are, in reality, giving them *de facto* death by what we are unwilling to give up; by the same way, we are single-mindedly poisoning the planet and its life-supporting systems. We risk so much just to be able to live with our conveniences and gadgets and gizmos, and in effortless comfort. Our vision of utopia includes the tantalizing freedom to do what one wants, when one wants, and how one wants, all to live in the cocoon of unceasing comfort. And if in future, simulation becomes more really 'real' than the real, and if automation and a guaranteed 'basic income' will free us from all work, there is no telling what kind of 'nightmare' our craving for comfort will yield. We now even claim the 'right to be lazy', blurring the boundary between labor and leisure. What we are forgetting is the potential risk to our future, indeed to our evolution. Recent research is showing that what we use and how we adapt the body in so doing can affect physiological evolution.

A new study has found that the human body has shown an adaptation to technology used in everyday life. A recent newspaper headline says it all: 'Mobile users develop horns'.[31] The fact is that even if more terrifying findings emerge, nothing will change, and people will que up hours ahead to be the first ones to buy a new gadget. It brings to mind the lethal power of persuasion, and the vulnerability of the human mind. In 1978, in 'Jonestown' (Guyana, Africa), some nine hundred followers of the cult leader Jim Jones (*Peoples Temple*) knowingly stood in a long line to drink a poisoned soft drink. Jim Jones called it 'revolutionary suicide'. In fact, 'Jonestown' and its ill-fated inhabitants remain an apt metaphor for much of the modern world and mass of humanity. Many are 'comfortable' spending much of their time constantly dangling on the edge of the abyss to clasp the latest popular thing they see on the screen. The human mind instinctively prefers to live in a comforting daydream than in painful reality. Instinctively, we also feel that, like Plato's cave-prisoners, abandoning the captivity of ignorance is unbearable. Today's technologies like virtual reality (VR), augmented reality (AR), and mixed reality (MR), and even more those in the offing, are capable of creating such sophisticated imitations of reality that the imitations can be mistaken for reality itself; that is, they make one wonder if there is anything 'really real', or if everything is surreal. One could even argue that if imitation is more comforting and makes it easier to live, then why do we need the 'truth of the real'? This sort of twilight-living instills in us a need for superficialities that would never be satisfied, which is what today's society and mass media relentlessly endear to do. To quote the Rolling Stones: "I can't get no satisfaction, 'cause I try and I try and I try and I try, I can't get no, I can't get no." Never being satisfied, and always wanting more, we become slaves unto our senses. At least in this respect we are getting perilously close to what God said of Satan before his heavenly expulsion: "You corrupted your wisdom because of your splendor".[32] For us, it is the splendor of craving for comfort. If we continue on this slippery slope, a time might not be far when man's fate might well come to resemble that of the people of the kingdom in Gertrude Landa's tale, *The Palace of the Eagles* (1919). In that fable, the inhabitants, inured to a life of comfort and luxury, so depleted their resources that when hunger came they had nothing to eat, and had to resort to grinding pearls and rubies into finer flour. But, as they could make no bread and died, in an ironic twist, in death through their bones they became food for the eagles.

No other species can rival the pain, misery, and suffering we inflict on each other through multiple and macabre means: vengeful mass murders, regicide, matricide, patricide, infanticide... all the *cides* really. What is heart-wrenching is that it calls for so little to soften suffering; sometimes, just the offer of a comforting shoulder could do. It might well be true that, as is often said, 'pain is inevitable, suffering optional', but more than pain it is suffering (which is mainly mental) that is the killer. We seldom realize but all killing as a human being is self-killing, all *cides* are shades of suicide. The human species has always struggled with the inevitable 'ending of life'—with the choice between letting it happen and making it happen. Contrary to what Pope Francis said—"Always safeguard life, God's gift, from its beginning until its natural end"—many see that the ending is no longer a solitary, 'end-of-life' event, something that happens in its own right at the fag end of life. South African writer Karel Schoeman, who committed suicide at the age of 77 (he preferred to call it *selfbeskikking*, self-determination in Afrikaans) wrote, "You reach a point when the handle in the shower cubicle is more important than immortal prose" (*At Close of Day*, 2018). For some, physical debility could prove too limiting for a fruitful life, but in the end, suicide is mental and the mind of a 'suicider' is the ultimate sphinx. Why some, as a recent suicide note confessed, 'succumb to the situation' and others don't will always remain a riddle. A sea-change has occurred about homicide too, in the human mind. We don't really know why or how or when, but at some point in our not-too-distant past, a devilish thought crossed the human mind that at the core of every pricky problem lurked a living human body, and if one could somehow get that 'body' out of the way, the 'problem' would have no leg to stand on. For it is life that complicates matters and if there is no life there is no problem. Life itself is no longer non-negotiable.

Humanity has fallen under the spell of what Saint John of the Cross (16th century) called 'the dark night of the soul', by which he meant a state of spiritual myopia, despair, and desolation, as a prelude to profound self-realization. Tolstoy wrote in the introduction to his book *My Religion* (1885) that after he went through a sudden transformation, he realized that he was 'nailed to a life of suffering and evil by an incomprehensible power' that caused so much suffering. What is paradoxical is that, as Buddhist scholar Shantideva once said, we want to shrink suffering but love its causes (*The Way of the Bodhisattva*). What we are traumatized by is mental and psychological rootlessness, crushing emptiness, a creeping sense of hopelessness, and a gnawing hunger for belonging or a more authentic and close-knit way of life. We are so obsessed with self-satisfaction, success, and strength, that we do not realize that there is nobility in humility, virtue in vulnerability, and incandescence in the bleakness of what has come to be called the human condition. The fact that we often tend to choose the dark side makes us feel bad about ourselves. Some like Jeremy Griffith argue that since we cannot accept our badness and yet do bad, we live in a state of denial. The real reason is that we do not choose anything, neither good nor evil, darkness nor light. What we think that we have chosen is but a reflection of the state of the war within. If, for example, the forces of love, kindness, and compassion are dominant at that time, then we choose the options that are compatible to them. If, on the other hand, the opposite forces come to call the shots, then our choices would be selfish, socially injurious, and environmentally hazardous.

Our behavior is nothing but a sum of our choices. And our choices are the 'food' for one or the other side in the war. We have long been bewildered by our own behavior, and have wondered, as biologist Edward Wilson once ruminated, if we are a suicidal species. 'Being suicidal' is wider than contemplating or committing suicide. It is being self-destructive. Our driving desire to 'merge into a machine' is 'suicidal', even if we are 'reborn', as we hope, a smarter and stronger being. Another example is how we knowingly pollute and adulterate everything we put into our body. A study of fifty common ingredients, taken randomly from a cookbook, found that forty of them were the subject of articles reporting their cancer risks.[33] Even if these studies are a stretch, the fact remains we routinely cut corners of all kinds to maximize money-making, and somehow think we ourselves are immune or at 'low-risk'.

At a more basic level, we are all committing a kind of 'spiritual suicide' by leading wholly material lives, by being wholly immersed in satiating material desires, instead of cultivating spiritual sensitivity. The line between needs and wants, desire and delusion is blurring. Symbolic of this is the suicide note left behind by the American jazz-age cartoonist Ralph Barton to the effect that that even though he had every 'success' in life and few difficulties, he was "fed up with inventing devices to fill up 24 hours of the day". That was because he, like the rest of us, viewed 'success' as a purely personal pursuit of his own happiness. To give meaning to 'success', we should find someone or something 'to be successful for', 'good life' to do good to others. Every action should be to serve and give. The thrill one gets will swamp all thoughts of self-destruction. Then we will find that Barton's suicidal 'too-long-to-fill 24 hours' is not long enough to care for and help others. Throughout human history, suicide has provoked an astonishingly large array of reactions—bewilderment, condemnation, glorification, empathy, anger, moral or religious reprimand—but it is never uncontroversial. The act is the same but the motivations, the tipping points and triggers have changed. In a culture that preens itself on its ability to fulfill every human fantasy, suicide is becoming for many a 'defiant declaration of liberation', no longer a shameful act of cowardice, an escape from the 'malaise' of the human condition, not a violation of the divine dictum, and a way to deal with their own inner desolation, the 'dark night of their soul'. And for many others, it represents a secure place to go where no one can go after them, and make life miserable for them. For, suicide is never an act in isolation; it is often an act aimed at another person or society. As Aristotle, in addressing the question, 'Can a man treat himself unjustly?' says, "The just and the unjust always involve more than one person". Suicide, and in its broader sweep, self-destruction, is now a major manifest of the state of human of society. Society is the aggregate conglomerate of individuals all interdependent; when that cracks, the individual becomes self-destructive as a way to assert his resentment at society. What it means is that if we want to change our suicidal way of thinking, we need to bring about a cathartic consciousness-change. Everything is consciousness, and all differences are different states. God is supreme consciousness. Christ is called Christ consciousness; Krishna is Krishna consciousness, also described as *cosmic* consciousness. Consciousness is what both unites and separates us. It unites, as all are reflections or sparks of the same divine *Consciousness*. And yet, we have separate consciousnesses as individuals. It is what defines who we are, and all evolution is the evolution of consciousness, and all transformation is the transformation of consciousness. But there are those who say that consciousness itself is but a mistake of nature, and that all our problems began when we became 'self-conscious' and realized that life ends in death. It is in the territory of our consciousness that the *war within* takes place… it is also the trophy at stake. In that sense, the consciousness of each of us is the battlefield of *Kurukshetra*, the great war of the Indian epic Mahabharata. The only difference is that in that war, Lord Krishna was on the side of the Pandavas, the righteous side, but in 'our' war—the war within—he is more of a *sakshi*, a witness, than a charioteer. Krishna was also the *sutradhaar* (anchor, narrator) of the war, and

He was the one who goaded the reluctant Pandavas to transgress some rules of a just war to 'win' the war, giving rise to the often-asked question, "Do wrong ends justify the right results?" What we forget is that Krishna was the personification of the divine, and, as Einstein said, "Morality is of the highest importance—but for us, not for God".[34] What is implied is that we cannot comprehend, with our 'weak and transitory understanding', the dynamics of divine justice. For the considerations that come into play in divine decision-making are a billion times more varied and complex than those of the human.

Still, the question that has often been asked is: With so much going for him—made in God's image, inherent divinity, self-awareness, the capacity to separate the good from the bad—why is man so self-righteous and self-destructive? Einstein once said, "Only two things are infinite, the universe and human stupidity, and I'm not sure about the former". For it is only stupidity—the full spectacle of our stupidity, as someone described—that makes any sense of two human traits; willful blindness and wanton destruction. We are masters at turning the blind eye to the utterly oblivious things, and at scapegoating others for our faults. According to Margaret Hefferman,[35] the biggest threats and dangers we face are the ones we *don't* see, not because they are secret or invisible, but because we are willfully blind. The current climate crisis is a case in point. Ninety-seven percent of scientists say that it is real, but we remain unmoved, or feign helplessness. Actually we are not helpless; it is our refusal to confront our bedrock belief that 'abundant energy enables modern life' that makes it hopeless. We behave like observers, as if the matter at issue has no bearing on our lives, whereas it is a matter of the gravest import not only in our lives but also in the lives of our progeny. A recent study revealed the 'dramatic effect of carbon dioxide on human nutrition' and that 'everything is becoming more like junk food'.[36] What is strange is that the very parents who are worried about the effects of excessive exposure to computer/phone screens are unconcerned about climate change and its effect on their children's lives. We must remember that the climate crisis is created by human behavior, and it can only be resolved by that very behavior. It is said that even by 'changing our diets to a soil-nourishing, regenerative agriculture diet', we can reverse global warming.[37] Whether or not it is true, the fact is that no one is going to switch his diet to save the planet or make the world safe for our kids. But if that diet is aggressively marketed as a way to lose weight, many are more likely to go for it. Instead, since cutting emissions requires some lifestyle changes, which we shamelessly say is too much to ask of us, as an alternative, science is trying to develop 'carbon-sucking' technologies. It is like saying, 'You are addicted to defecating all over, therefore improve your skills of cleaning up'. Our attitude has not changed even after the latest 'news' that the boiling point might well come in our own lifetime, not in our children's lifetime. Our capacity to be oblivious of the obvious and our ability to deny and deride any amount of evidence we don't like, is truly staggering and chilling. In that sense, climate change, apocalyptic as it is likely to be in its impact, is still a symptom, not the malady. The malady is the mind itself, rather the way it works. And it is not a new insight. Hindu scriptures have described the mind as feeble, fickle, mischievous, and malicious. The Bible[38] says that the key to the 'good life' is the 'renewal of our mind'. What we need is not 'renewal' in the literary sense, but consciousness-change. Our lifestyle is self-destructive; almost everything we let into our body is self-destructive; our industrial civilization is self-destructive. And now that man has become an agent of evolution and a geological force, human destructive power has an opportunity to go beyond the species-scale. And if man becomes a multiplanetary species, the limitless outer space can become a war zone, and the temptation to test or use the next generation of weapons, with minds of their own, can be irresistible. What, so to speak, could be like blood to a shark is the new-found knowledge that the outer space contains mind-boggling quantities of mineral wealth. According to one estimate, the mineral wealth [of near-earth asteroids], if equally divided among every person on earth, would add up to more than $100 billion each.[39] Some say that 'Star Wars' or 'Shadow Wars' are already a reality, and orbiting in outer space we have what are being called 'killer satellites' and 'kidnapper satellites'. Scientists are exploring how to 'most efficiently reach and settle the 100,000 star systems that have been determined to be habitable and suitable for life'. It could lead to a situation in which 'we will create billions of settlements with unbridgeable differences; each will have weapons to annihilate, but no way to negotiate'.[40] Philosopher Philip Torres says, "In a colonized universe, the probability of annihilation of the human race could actually rise rather than fall". It means that while we wait for our turn to escape earth to survive and flourish, what might happen is the reverse. As for our other escape route—merger with a machine—, although we talk about machines having 'minds of their own', they actually will have *versions* of our own minds; for the only thing our mind is capable of doing is to project its own image. It is a fallacy to think that the intelligence in these machines will be any different from our own intelligence. Whether it is man or machine or a blend of both, it is all the same the human mind. And, mind you, the human mind is the real 'existential threat' we face; it is behind every existential 'threat' we face, be it a climate threat, a rogue technology threat, or a nuclear war threat.

Can We Win the War Within?

When we constantly talk about the world, we really don't mean a thing. We may sing 'the world is us', but we don't mean a thing. No one cares for or speaks for the world. At best, we care, beyond our own selves, for our family, community, or corporation or country; not for the world. We will do to other planets what we are doing down here: make them uninhabitable to any life. It is entirely okay to try to go 'where no man has gone before'. That is natural to the human spirit. What is wrong is the wrong we do wherever we are—exploit (resources), eradicate (other life forms), and escape. Yet in our mind there is nothing wrong: *What else is earth for?* We have to change such a state of mind if we want peace of mind and peace on earth, two of our long-sought goals. Sharing the earth with other species is an important human responsibility. For peace of mind, we need the mind to be in its proper place, and for peace on earth, we need our behavior to be benign. And for both—putting the mind in its place, and benign behavior—the arena of actual action is the war within. It is through the 'war within' that we can bring about consciousness-change, and it is through consciousness-change that we can cut the mind down to its size, which is imperative for man to be essentially a moral and spiritual being. For the most terrifying place in the cosmos is the human mind. The Upanishads say that an uncontrolled mind is our worst enemy, and a controlled mind is our best friend. And they add that impossible things like drinking the ocean dry or swallowing fire are far easier than controlling one's own mind. That is why the mind is sometimes compared to a drunken monkey bitten by a scorpion. The Preamble to the Constitution of UNESCO famously declares that "since wars begin in the minds of men, it is in the minds of men that the defences of peace must be constructed". And it is the mind that stigmatizes and dehumanizes those with whom we disagree. Seeing others as less than fully human offers us an alibi and an outlet to do things which otherwise we consider inhuman, and it is now commonplace, consequential, and contagious. In his 1651 book *Leviathan*, the English thinker Thomas Hobbes argued that humans are warlike by nature. When we believe that we are waging a war, everything turns topsy-turvy; that which we consider as evil becomes heroic and honorable, even rape. All wars save those for a social purpose are horrendous, cold-blooded mass slaughter, and yet we are enraptured by war, and without being at war, there is little that we can achieve. Yet, within each of us a war rages, a war we are not even conscious of; and the opponents are two siblings, two sides of our own self. The truth is that much of our misery, many of the festering problems and existential threats we face, stem from a simple fact: the *wrong* intelligence (mind) is in control of our consciousness; we are looking in the *wrong* direction (outer space and cyberspace); and we are not engaged in fighting the right war, the war within. We are not only being driven by the wrong intelligence, we seem determined to even augment it, through artificial general intelligence (AGI). Why we seem so obsessed to create an intelligence that surpasses human intelligence is beyond being stupid; it is suicidal. If that happens, consciousness-change in the right direction will not happen, and we will continue to lose the war within.

One of the clear signs that we are losing the war within and that the forces of goodness are in retreat is the persistent absence of *shanti*, or peace, in the world. That is because we tend to look at each other with ill will, distrust, envy, and animosity, and put selfishness before service. The place to begin is where we are, and with the people in the proximate 'acting one at a time, upon those beside them'. For, to paraphrase Dostoyevsky, it is easier to sacrifice in the cause of humanity than not be nasty to the next man. And despite our ritual chanting of *shanti, shanti, shanti* (the peace mantra of the Upanishads), the fact is, as Immanuel Kant said, "war seems to be ingrained in human nature". Fact is, we have waged war since the beginning of time; we have never really had real peace on the planet. We should not confuse absence of armed conflict as peace, and peace must serve a purpose. Either as individuals or as a society, we need an adversarial target, an enemy to fear, to fight, and to dominate. What we don't realize is that the one we view as an 'enemy' also views us the same way, and the truth is, as poet HW Longfellow reminded us, "If we could read the secret history of our enemies, we should find in each man's life sorrow and suffering enough to disarm all hostility" (*Drift-wood*, 1857). But war makes our 'longing for ignoble things' and our darkest desires come to the fore. That is why we condone, even extol, in war what we otherwise condemn or feel ashamed of. Present-day human society and culture is often accused of turning a benevolent baby into a malevolent man. The real reason, however, is that man has never been able to get to the root, the source of the conflict—the world *within*, the inner universe. It is a world that is embedded in us; and yet it is an alien land, a forbidden place, just as the strangest of strangers is our own self. The fact is that we 'live' in two worlds, within and without, internal and external. What is lacking is connection, communication, and conversation between the two. Even the war within and the wars outside have to be connected. It is not that this 'inner world' has gone unnoticed over the times. The Hindu *Yajurveda* talks about man's inner radiance. The Supreme Being, it is believed, manifests without a form (*Nirguna Brahman*) and with form (*Saguna Brahman*), and that formless eternal god is within the cave of the human heart. Gandhi said that the 'still small voice' within him is the only tyrant in his life. Similarly, unless there is an internal world, how can one internalize lofty values that many great people have spoken about? Even in our own times, the thinker and writer Charles Haanel[41] wrote, "There is a world within—a world of thought and feeling and power; of light and beauty, and although invisible, its forces are mighty". And American poet Wallace Stevens reminded us that 'the world about us would be desolate except for the world within'. Some have talked about the *evil* within or 'evil inclination', what in Judaism is called *Yetzer hara*, and some, about the *struggle* within.

Some say that at the center of human nature there is 'dark matter', and that forces of evil—intentionally behaving in ways that harm, abuse, demean, dehumanize, or destroy innocent others[42]—are as intertwined into us as DNA is. So 'intertwined' that, few of us, if any, have been able to get a hold on our own thoughts, feelings, emotions, and passions in our myriad points of contact with other humans. We have always been a bundle of beliefs, but it is behavior that has always escaped our grasp and grip. It has baffled and bewildered us; it is so unpredictable that we are terrified of what we might ourselves do if we are, for example, to find ourselves in the shoes of a 'killer'. For a species that prides itself on being a 'moral' and 'spiritual' species, such a possibility is truly soul-shattering. What makes it worse is that we cannot bring to bear another of our prized attributes, rationality, to understand why we are so vulnerable. And 'vulnerability' itself is not failure or feminine; or necessarily a handicap. It is what makes us 'human'. It is this vulnerability that offers us an opening into the meaning of our lives and breaks walls and builds bridges to other people. Vulnerability, it has been said, "is the core, the heart, the center, of meaningful human experience".[43] The true truth is that we certainly do have dark, sinister, and savage urges deep inside us, but at the same time, we do have the opposites, like kindness, empathy, supreme sacrifice, compassion, and altruism. If we are able to harbor what in German is called *schadenfreude* (the ability to derive pleasure from other's pain), we are also equally able to entertain what in Buddhism is called *mudita*—delight at the other's happiness or rejoicing in the other's joy. After all, even a serial killer or a mass murderer does not kill every day; he could be a Good Samaritan, a good neighbor, on the other days. The American serial killer of the 1970s, Ted Bundy, who confessed to killing some thirty young women and girls, once reportedly jumped into the water to rescue a three-year-old child. It doesn't mean he was far from being a fiend; it only underscores the point that, as Martin Luther King Jr once said, there could be some good in the worst of us, just as there could be some bad in the best. From the other side, we have saints, who led public lives of depravity before their hearts were converted. They wrestled with the same faults and addictions, the same sins and bad habits that make us feel so weighed down. The point is that serial killers and saints too were human like us, and a 'war within' waged within them too. We can take heart from both: from killers, that in the worst of us there is some goodness; from saints, that the best of us are also fallible. But, with effort, we can overcome all failings.

Everything in nature and creation is dichotomous and exists as *dwanda* or pairs of opposites, including our own emotions and passions, love and hate, cruelty and compassion, indifference and altruism. It is possible to show both 'opposites' towards the same person. For example, one recent finding is that "murderers are generally still in love with the people they kill".[44] And the opposites are constantly at each other's throats in our consciousness. We have long known this, but not its true dimensions and earth-shattering implications. The war within is not a skirmish or squabble or struggle; it is of a different genre altogether. It is a full-scale war that shapes and makes sense of whatever happens in the world outside. It rationalizes everything we have found irrational, makes sense of all that we find bizarre in our behavior, and lets us be not too harsh on ourselves. It gives a purpose to our lives and an agenda to mend our meandering lives, and serves as an anchor to the world that is adrift. The fact is, as Jane Austen's Fanny Price said, "We have all a better guide in ourselves, if we would attend to it, than any other person can be".[45] Scientists, biologists, and psychologists have long studied what makes some people 'snap' into rage and violence, while others, similarly situated, don't do so. At a more generic level, they have examined what biologist Jeremy Griffith called our 'good-and-evil conflicted human condition'. We find gaping holes in every theory that tries to explain alarming tendencies—natural-born violence, genetic predisposition, domestic disarray, social scapegoating, sexual delinquency—and we remain perplexed, fearful, and guilt-ridden. Even if we fully acknowledge and accept that deep within we have a diabolic disposition, whatever might be the wellspring—innate or evolutionary—, it will not still get us 'freedom', emotional or psychological. On the other hand, internalizing such a 'disposition' might make us more complacent and more blatant and glaring in our behavior and strengthen the forces of evil in the war within. For any sort of 'freedom' or any kind of transformative change, the key is consciousness. Without it, we are left with the Hobson's choice between the discomfort of becoming aware of our mental maladies and the discomfort of being drained. Some call us a species in denial; but perhaps more accurately, we are a species in deep discomfort.

In the modern world, above everything else, might is money; wealth is wielded as a weapon. While money *per se* is neither good or bad, the current reality is that, as AQ Smith points out, "It is basically immoral to be rich... people who possess great wealth in a time of poverty are directly causing that poverty".[46] Wealth has the capacity to heal people who are suffering, and by not helping them we are letting them suffer. It means that not only amassing but retaining wealth is inherently immoral. Money's sway over us is both symptomatic and sinister. It greases greed and causes much grief. In its spell, we cut corners and make morality meaningless. Indeed, as Abraham Polonsky said, "Money has no moral opinions" (*Force of Evil*, 1948). Even our odyssey for eternal life is finally coming down to a matter of how much money we can muster, to live forever or, at the least, longer than anyone else. When Aubrey de Grey, an immortality activist and pioneer, was asked what one's chances are of living to a thousand years, he replied: "I would say perhaps a little better than fifty-fifty," and then, after a pause, added, "It is very much dependent on the level of funding".[47] In reality, all these are but symptoms of a more basic and deeper affliction. It is a warped mindset, corrupted consciousness, and, above all, siding with the wrong side in an internal war that we are not even aware of. It is a war between good and evil. It is a war with ever-fluctuating fortunes that translate and trickle and shape how we behave. 'Shadow' is as important as 'persona', and without a well-developed shadow side, a person can easily become shallow. 'The shadow represents energically charged autonomous patterns of feeling and behavior and their energy cannot simply be erased by an act of will, however powerful it may be. What is needed is rechanneling or transformation'.[48] But in our attempt to disown our shadow, what we do is to project it onto another person and hate him and fight him as a proxy of our own shadow.

The war within is at once a civil war, a spiritual war, an eternal war. If we want to be in the main a moral being, if we want to mend and better our behavior, and if we want to free the world from any of its problems, then we need to ensure that the forces of light and goodness (i.e., of the 'persona') dominate over the forces of evil and darkness—of our 'shadow' self. But, paradoxically, we also have to ensure that not only the evil side, *but also the 'good' side*, does not triumph. For, evil too plays an important role in our psyche and equips us with what is necessary for self-preservation. The 'good' that evil does is as important as good itself. Although evil has penetrated and polluted everything, it is important for our wholeness. Indeed, had evil been defeated or exorcized from our psyche, we would have perhaps been extinct long ago. Had we been, in Jungian language, a 'walking persona', we would have been a sitting duck and easy meat. We must constantly strive to achieve a sort of union of the opposing forces, to maintain the 'positive' balance—that is tilted slightly towards the good side—in this war. It is similar to the principle of equilibrium in the natural world, in that any excess is opposed by the system in order to restore balance. It is imbalance that triggers both ill-health and evil. It is the dissolution of the balance of power that shatters relationships. When things get to their extreme, they turn into their opposite, which means that when good becomes too threatening, we must strengthen the very forbidden and unacceptable feelings inside that we try to fight and subdue. It is a complex conundrum. The world within, the theater of the war, is so opaque and inaccessible to our understanding, that we can never know what evil may not be necessary in order to produce good, and what good may very possibly lead to evil. It is somewhat similar to what the ancient Chinese philosophic thought *I Ching* implied. Its central premise is that *yang* lines become *yin* when they have reached their extreme, and vice versa.

Another thing to bear in mind is that *we* cannot see our behavior; others can. In the words of psychiatrist RD Laing, "The other person's behavior is an experience of mine. My behavior is an experience of the other.[49] Everything we do, even the smallest action, every day has a double-effect. It affects others and it serves as ammunition to one or the other of the two dichotomous sides—in HW Longfellow's poetic words, "instinct that enjoys, and the more noble instinct that aspires" (*Haunted Houses*, 1858)—in the war within. We do not have to fight the devil and demons to fight evil. We have to fight our own weaknesses and wickedness. We must strive to do good when evil seems easy, to thwart evil when opposing it seems foolhardy, and to resist complacency when it seems quiescent. And to be 'good' one does not have to be 'great' or a hero or martyr. In fact, too often goodness is the casualty or collateral damage of greatness. Most men believe that our quest for greatness sanitizes every moral infringement. The qualities required for greatness (ruthlessness, cold calculation, disregard for morality, callousness for consequences, steeliness) are not what are required for goodness—gentleness, empathy, compassion, kindness, non-injury, etc. The real tragedy is that most of us do measure up to be 'great' in what we accomplish, but still manifest its icky attribute. We have long struggled to live caring, empathetic, and compassionate lives, but without much success. It is partly because we just do not know how to turn it into action and, equally, because our idea of 'success' itself is skewed. Success, we now associate with power, money, fame, and professional promotion. The most dreaded 'L-word' is *loser*. There are many who commit suicide because they are not 'successful', not being able to be the 'best in the world' in their profession. We need a fresh approach to this issue. The real issue is not success or failure. The root of it is that in modern societies 'success' is sanctified and failure is fatal. They place an often unattainable premium on excellence, increasingly a trigger for suicide. That has to change, as well the purely materialistic way we view and measure success. We must let children know that it is okay to make mistakes, to stumble, and to fall and fail, so long as they learn from that. We must shift the focus from 'what' an adolescent wants to be as an adult, to 'who' he wants to be, in the first place. One of the most important conversations we should have with our children is to put 'success' in the right perspective. That is also a part of our effort to give new meaning to what ought to be viewed as an 'accomplished life', a life well lived, and to bring in the moral and spiritual dimension into everyday life.

The absence of this 'dimension' has led to a pathological impossibility to view a situation from another person's perspective. That makes it almost impossible not to be selfish or unfair, and not hurt someone else. Because, if we cannot know what a problem is from another person's prism, how can we help him out even if we wish to? Now, it seems that a huge leg-up might come from an unexpected source—technology. So far, in the main, technology, which some equate with society, is acting as a mirror and tends to magnify even the ugliest (blackest) aspects of human nature. It is dehumanizing the individual, on the one hand, and collectively empowering us to commit mass suicide, on the other hand. Experts now tell us that with coming technological advancements users of 'virtual reality' will finally be able to know what it is like to really take another person's perspective, which in turn will allow us to improve ourselves to become a more empathetic and compassionate society.[50]

While we are preoccupied with wars in the world, whether it is a war on poverty or terrorism or war on consumerism or a war of civilizations, the reality is that 'some of the greatest battles we will face will be fought within the silent chambers of our own souls'.[51] The battles that count aren't the ones for gold medals. The main challenges lie with the struggles within ourselves, the invisible, inevitable battles inside all of us. And we will either be saved or destroyed from within. While negative passions like anger, envy, hate, and malice dominate our consciousness, we try to contain them in the crucible of everyday living. We seem to be bogged down in this war for life without any escape or reprieve. Unlike other wars, this war can neither be terminated nor abolished. It is a strange war in which we have to do everything possible to help one side, the good side, but still make sure that the opposing side, the evil one, if you will, is not routed or reduced to rubble. This evil or wicked side is also indigenous and integral to our own selves. And it is there for a purpose, although we do not know exactly for what. In other words, the evil within us is evil, but it is a part of who we are. It is the dark pixie that lurks in the deep corners of consciousness and hides in those places that we train ourselves to overlook and intentionally avoid. We have to live with it, make a virtue of necessity. Horrible things happen in the world because at that proximate time, the war within would have taken a horrible turn. What takes place in the world depends on how we process that world within. We must make sure, as much as we can, that the thoughts, feelings and emotions, impulses, and instincts are of the 'right' kind—gentle, generous, altruistic, and empathetic—so that they do not make us act in a way that is harmful to others. Instead, we must make life easier and less difficult to them.

Since we are totally oblivious of this deeper dimension, we are looking to our new God, technology, for *kaivalya*, deliverance. Despite being touted as the greatest transformative force in our history, technology has had no ameliorating effect on man's basic instincts and impulses, drives, and urges. These have only become more coarse, competitive, and conspicuous, and they have turned the world into a marketplace for malice and murder. Technology has fundamentally altered human personality and also turned us into 'schizoid men', characterized by emotional apathy, secretiveness, and solitary lifestyle. Technology, it has often been said, is a double-edged sword, which can further both human welfare and human misery. Technology constantly changes, but how and why we use it will depend on the state of consciousness and the state of war within. It could give us augmented soldiers, autonomous weapons, and remotely-operated killer drones, or it could serve to combat mass poverty, climate apocalypse, and global epidemics. If the forces of good prevail, we will target technology to do good. However, the way technology is being used today, to fuel corrosive consumerism and militant militarism, it indicates that the 'evil within' us, a sinister version of a dark psionic entity, which some call the 'dark phoenix', has become dominant in the war. Consumerism has turned us into zombies, and militarism has turned us into malignant beings. The first owes its origin to our innate avarice, and the second to the malice in our mind. There is simply no way we can seriously address the climate crisis without 'doing more with less', without radically curbing consumerism. And there is simply no way we can ensure any kind of peace on earth without radically reversing the militarization of human civilization—indeed the human mindset—and halting the production of weapons of mass murder. In 2014, global military expenditure reached $1.8 trillion dollars, a massive diversion of scarce public resources which, if deployed properly, can resolve many pressing problems like mass poverty and improve the lives of those living little better than their livestock. We must also notice that many cutting-edge technologies that can do a world of good, including carbon dioxide removal have not become practical for want of funding. Militarization is a killer in another way: a new study of Prof. Neta C Crawford highlights a little-noticed fact that the United States' military is the largest institutional emitter of greenhouse gases in the world.[52] Furthermore, militaries have ceased to be the monopoly of governments. And there are countries like USA where we now have 'private governments'[53] and private armed forces. More guns are owned than the population of the country, and there are a lot of people who see no difference between a gun and a gadget, and think that the 'right to a gun' is an essence of 'freedom'. Having a weapon not only gives one lethal power, but it changes the mindset: it makes an ordinary person feel like a superman; arrogant, vengeful, and aggressive. That person then feels he can take on the world for a cause or a grievance or glory. And when death holds no terror for him, he truly becomes the god of death. The more destructive the weapon is, the more he would be tempted to put it to use as a statement of his manhood.

Technological devices like smartphones are now being deemed a basic requirement for any meaningful social life, to the extent that some even openly say they are worth more than their very life. It is ironic that man has made himself virtually invulnerable to the laws of nature, but he seems to feel he needs external aid to survive in his own civilization. Jalal ad-Din Rumi once said, "Look inside yourself and everything you need you already are". Not knowing how to 'look inside', and as a consequence unable to optimally utilize what nature has endowed him with, man has turned the machine, once regarded as a lifeless contraption, into a 'living being', a companion or a partner who can help overcome his limitations. It also helps man to resolve what Albert Camus called 'the constant confrontation between man and his own obscurity' (*The Myth of Sisyphus*, 1942). But man is doing nothing about his most basic 'limitation'—his own mind-driven consciousness. For, even if he becomes a 'silicon being', and the farthest reaches of space open up for him, it will do man no good, and possibly a lot of harm, if he remains as he is and his 'world within' does not change.

Albert Schweitzer said, "Man has lost his capacity to foresee and forestall, he will end up by destroying the world". We have, in particular, lost two critical 'capabilities': the first is the ability to function holistically, to see the whole picture, to do the 'right thing' reflexively, to be able to care for the whole of humanity, if not all life. Spanish cellist and conductor Pablo Casals aptly said that 'the capacity to care is the thing which gives life its deepest significance'. Karl Marx characterized the machine as a weapon employed by the capitalist to quell the revolt of specialized labor. What is happening is that the blend of man and machine, coupled with the sudden explosion in machine intelligence and rapid innovations in gene research and nanotechnology, have led to the dawn of the age of super-specialization and over-fragmentation. We have experts for different limbs of the body; sometimes even 'sub-limbs'; we have workers in factories functioning as 'human assembly lines', and as 'untrustworthy human robots', to borrow a phrase from Simon Head. Although we think of a machine as an external device, scientists say that in fact 'we consist of trillions of electrochemical machines that somehow coordinate their intricate activities in ways that allow our bodies and minds to function with the required reliability and precision'. The big difference is that these machines are *in situ* and integral, whereas the machine that we want to unite or merge with, is external. Through such a merger, science is seeking to create humans with vastly increased intelligence, strength, and life spans, a near embodiment of gods. What it amounts to is, in the words of EO Wilson, "We have created a Star Wars civilization, with Stone Age emotions, medieval institutions, and godlike technology".[54] Good men have long wanted to be 'men of God'; now, the material man wants to be *a god.* The key question is: is it necessary because it is possible? We have long been warned to be wary of what we want. What moral philosophers like Aristotle called the 'ethics of desire' is now more important than ever before in our pleasure-seeking, entertainment-centered society. As the *Mundaka* Upanishad says, 'He who longs for objects of desire, making much of them, is born along with those desires in places where he will realize them'. A truly desire-free man or a man unattached to material things, according to the *Brihadaranyaka* Upanishad, "being Brahman (Supreme Self) goes to Brahman" after his death. Human desires or wants were a peril to human spiritual progress. Now, they are a planetary peril, even an intergalactic threat, as man has acquired the technical capacity, without any ethical underpinning, to go 'where no man has gone before' and to get whatever he 'badly' wants. A 'want' is not necessarily bad, but we must take it to a deeper and more profound level. There is a growing chasm between 'goodness' and what we *think* is good for us. The implications of shifting our goal from union with God to merger with machine are controversial, and potentially apocalyptic. Some say that it will make us more, not less, human, make it more possible to see ourselves more candidly in the mirror. According to the World Economic Forum, "If managed wisely, [machine integration] could lead to a new age of good work, good jobs and improved quality of life for all, but if managed poorly, pose the risk of widening skills gaps, greater inequality and broader polarization".[55] Whether we manage 'wisely' or 'poorly', and with what consequences, hinges upon the state of our consciousness.

Sceptics say that such a 'merger' with a machine could give life to what has for long come to be called, in literature, as in the works of Herman Kahn (1960) the *Doomsday Machine*, a machine or mechanism that brings about the end of the world, or the end of only the human race. What has set in is a kind of *mechano*-morphism, turning all life into machines and then judging and changing life utilizing the mechanistic value of efficiency.[56] What is sad and self-defeating, as Jaron Lanier says, is that 'people degrade themselves in order to make machines seem smart all the time'.[57] Humans have a tendency to let themselves *be used* by the gadgets and machines they possess, and as a result, humans themselves lose the sense of which is more valuable or dispensable. We must bear in mind that our gluttonous greed for gadgets is an offspring of our technology-driven, materialistic, mechanized mindset. And greed of any kind remains one of the seven deadly sins. Technology itself is now a drug to which we are all addicted. However, unlike the caution we exercise when we have to take pharmaceutical drugs, we are not alarmed, and we don't think twice, about the possible terrible side effects that certain technologies could hold. Every day brings reports of discoveries and developments in science and technology, some of which appear downright impossible to believe, like the 'breaking news' that we now have the technical capability to change reality at our will. But, man, especially in the last two centuries, has time and again made the 'ultimate unthinkable' clearly possible. It is difficult to predict the limits of human intelligence and innovativeness, but prepared we must be for the most unexpected. And if something makes us shake our head in dismay and disbelief, the best we can do is to stay silent.

Arguably the most important challenge we face now is to bring about a foundational change in our mindset, a change that makes it possible to release the mindset from the grip of the mind. That will trigger a consciousness change, which, in turn, could tilt the scales in the war within positively. Contemporary ethos emphasizes competence over character and efficiency over ethics. The message is clear and unambiguous: for any beneficial change in human basic behavior, there is no other way than the way within, and one must intervene in the war and ensure the dominance of the virtuous side. And the way to do that is to imbibe the spirit of one of the central messages of the Bhagavad Gita—*nishkama karma*—which is to perform one's actions and duties diligently, without anticipation and expectation of the fruits thereof. All the evil and good that comes to us, comes from ourselves: from the *karma* we would have created in the past. In that sense, we alone harm and we alone help ourselves. And we harm ourselves if we harm others, and help ourselves by helping others. Karma needs company. Depending on how we react to each experience, we create the karma that will color our future. Our reaction, based on our experience, ignites new karma and a new cycle of creation and experience. We can allow that cycle to continue in an endless sequence. The great drag in virtuous or spiritual life is the burden of radical selfishness. Expectation is selfishness; freed from expectation, our myriad activities will become dharmic or righteous. These, in turn, will act as appropriate 'feed' and food for the fighting wolves of the 'Cherokee story' of good and evil. As it is said in that original fable, "If you feed them right, both will win… How you choose to interact with the opposing forces within you will determine your life. Starve one or the other or guide them both". How can we 'feed them right' and ensure that 'both win' is the conundrum. The fact is that both wolves have no other source of nourishment except what we provide. We feed them, even by what we ingest, and how we live, what we eat, see or hear, and by the choices we make with our thoughts, emotions, and feelings. We have a tendency to ignore the small, ordinary things of life, the trillions of things done by billions of people, and try often in vain to do extraordinary, exceptional and out-of-the-box deeds. But actually, it is the 'most ordinary' ones of our everyday life, which some call the 'miracle of the ordinary', that are the most important for spiritual life and for the war within. And it is that 'miracle', the millions of our daily doings, that can also combat the climate crisis, not any 'miraculous' discovery. If we live righteously and act in the spirit of nishkama karma, and with an attitude of gratitude, consideration, and compassion, the 'goodness in us' will be the dominant. And if we live with meanness, malice, and egocentrism, then the 'evil within' will call the shots…

But whatever we do and whichever way we do it, we must remember that *both* opposing sides will survive. The bottom line is that there is a 'within' in each of us, and that within is in a state of war. Only by going within can we aid the forces of goodness and righteousness to occupy the commanding heights of our consciousness, which is to have the upper hand in the war within. It is now clear that what once served as a moral watchdog—our pricky conscience—is either unequal or has been rendered redundant. Had it not been so, there would have been no climate crisis or the problem of intolerable economic inequity. While, generally, the climate crisis is viewed as a potential existential crisis, economic inequality is regarded purely as an economic issue. What is at risk is the bedrock idea that equality means that everyone has equal value not only under law but as a form of life. There is mounting murmur that this inequality is now so intolerable that it is bound to blow up. Some are also arguing that we must get rid of the malaise of the modern world, what Daniel Cohen called the "infinite desire for growth",[58] which, by common consent, is a major cause of the climate crisis. Stanford professor Walter Scheidel posits that throughout history, economic inequality has only been rectified by one of the 'Four Horsemen of Leveling': warfare, revolution, state collapse, and plague (*The Great Leveler*, 2017). Current economic inequality, by any reckoning, is glaring and vulgar, a sign of creeping decadence, a major source of, in Bertolt Brecht's words, injustice without outrage (*To Those Born After,* 1939). There is no outrage because what we have is secret envy; we want to be 'one of them'. And 'being one of them' means the lure of owning a Lamborghini, a yacht, a Hawaiian island or, perhaps the latest fad, possess the skeleton of an extinct species. The opposite of 'owning' is losing and the fear of losing, what Henry Miller called 'the most terrible bond of all' (*Sexus*, 1949); it makes us virtually mad and induces us to do horrible things. For example, it is this 'fear' of someone else 'owning' that is primarily responsible for turning a lover into a killer. In almost every decision we take, in every activity we undertake, money is a major, even preeminent factor, and often its influence induces us to do the wrong thing, to make the wrong choice. In the real world, money improves a person's circumstances that often constrain and confine their life. Money wipes out all human deficiencies with it; it does not matter what else we do not have. And money in multiple ways can be a saver or a killer. As Bill Gates said, "For under a dollar, there were interventions that could save lives that just weren't being delivered".[59] On the other side, millions of children die because their parents do not have, or are unable or unwilling to earmark enough money to keep them alive. Again, as Gates said, "Children died because their mothers and their fathers had no power in the market and no voice in the system". Perhaps the greatest challenge man faces now is not to seek to make the world 'money-free', but to transform money into a moral medium. For that to happen, we have to bring to bear in our daily decision-making factors like kindness, empathy, and compassion. The choice we will make will then be different and moral.

The key is the heart. Longfellow implored us to live 'with a heart for any fate' and to 'learn to labor and to wait' (*A Psalm of Life*, 1839). For it is only with the heart that one can see rightly; what is essential is invisible to the eye. Cutting-edge research indicates that it is the energy of the heart that literally links us to each other, and that every person's heart contributes to a collective field environment. We must learn to listen to our heart's calling, which some call the 'inner voice', to be able to see what the Quakers call 'inner light'. In ancient Greek and Egyptian civilizations, the heart was considered the seat of intelligence and consciousness. Research is able to reveal how, in myriad ways, the brain and the heart communicate, and, in fact, work back and forth on each other. The crying need of the desperate hour is to add more heart to our broken world, and incorporate heart intelligence and emotional energy (which we try to suppress) into our day-to-day experiences and interactions. It will also help us to 'win the war within'. When asked what the essential quality was for prayer to be valid, Prophet Muhammad replied, 'presence in the heart'. He meant the spiritual heart, and we are everywhere but absent from our own heart.

We scan all over looking for ways to boost our intelligence, but ignore our own heart intelligence. Einstein said, "We shall require a substantially new manner of thinking if humanity is to survive". That new manner of thinking can only come from a new source and that ought to be the heart, not artificial intelligence (AI). We must also clearly understand that our obsessive passion for AI and the machine is, at its core, our lack of faith in our own selves; we don't believe anymore we are good enough for our greed, or to turn 'green'. But then, as EM Forster says, "Something good enough had long since been accepted by our race" (*The Machine Stops*, 1909). Since we are not 'good enough' for our own good, we think that a machine will do better. We think we are more secure stashed away in a computer than in our own soul. Most of all, we identify ourselves as no more than a body and, as a consequence, we believe that if we can somehow hang on to our bodies everything will be fine. Actually this is science's 'Plan B' for immortality: in case we fail to achieve at bodily immortality then we will upload our thoughts and feelings and all we can of our existence into computer programs and live out our existence there.

Not only do we want to 'exist' forever at any cost and in any way, we want to do nothing in such existence. Our idea of utopia is no work and all play, although, as someone quipped, we don't know what to do with ourselves on a rainy Sunday. It means 'money for nothing' and every need, if not want, is a given. Mechanization of human life is the means. That might not actually even come about. Karl Marx was right when he wrote that 'machinery is the surest means of lengthening the working day' (*Das Kapital*, 1867). What we need to do is not to strive for a 'world without work' in the sense of what 'work' has to mean, but move its focus towards *service*. What we are gravely underestimating is the pivotal place of 'work' in the human as a social being. Work is not merely a means for distributing purchasing power. It is also among the most important sources of identity and purpose in the lives of individuals. In a world without work, we have to figure out not only what to do with ourselves but with one another. What we tend to ignore is that people are happy only when they earn their own success. It's not the money *per se*, which is merely a measure—not the source—of this earned success. Work is what we do in cooperation with others to achieve a common goal, to make or serve something for society. It is through 'work' that we fine-tune our faculties; it is through work that we can labor for the common good.

In the Bhagavad Gita, Lord Krishna says, "There is no work prescribed for Me within all the three planetary systems. Nor am I in want of anything, nor have I a need to obtain anything—and yet I am engaged in work".[60] And the ancient Greek philosopher Hesiod wrote, 'Labor is a universal virtue of Man' (*Works and Days,* 700 BCE). If an AI-inspired epidemic of automation gains speed, and machines replace men, and even if (a huge 'if') making money is NOT any more tied to work (universal basic income; or basic economic security), gaping inequalities will still remain, and, as Robert Theobald says, wealth would still be transferred to the rich, fuelling deep dissent and resentment, possibly leading to what is called 'the revolt of the rest' (*Free Men and Free Markets,* 1963).

For both consciousness-change and contextual-change, harnessing the heart intelligence is a prerequisite. And, above all, to help the forces of good and righteousness in the war within, it is consciousness that we now have to focus upon. We must understand that everything is a state and level of consciousness, from the mineral to the divine. The Buddha is a state of consciousness; so is Christ; and so is a stone or a sinner or a psychopath. Even death is a state of consciousness. What unites is consciousness, and what both unites and divides is consciousness; we are all sparks of cosmic consciousness; and yet we also have consciousness of our own. All beings in the biotic community are bits and pieces of the cosmic consciousness. The renowned Vedantist Swami Vivekananda foretold that he would not live past forty years. He explained that the reason was that his soul (which is pure consciousness) was getting bigger and bigger and that his physical body would not be able to hold it much longer. On the other hand, the default mode since long happens to be that the good guys are on the losing side. The downward spiral is supposed to have begun eons ago, with the onset of Kali Yuga, the age of darkness and evil, but it has now gathered speed. And that 'speed' has, in more recent times, become a precipitous fall. It is not that there was no evil, or evil men, in the earlier ages. They were vastly outnumbered by goodness and good men. It is the other way around now. That is the root reason for the terrible state of affairs in the world in modern times.

The paradox has always been that in human society those who care do not matter, and those who matter do not care; and the few who both care and matter do not connect. The root of the paradox runs deeper. It is that the essence of human nature, in its historical context, and what is essential for a 'humane' human community, have always been at odds. Put differently, there has always been a gap between human necessities and human narratives, needs, and wants, which in fact is the basis of what we call 'culture'. Even more bluntly, much of our life is spent 'immersed in sensual passion, on fire with sensual fever, being chewed up by our sensual thoughts'. If 'love' is the essence, then there ought to be no issue; if it is avarice, as it seems, then society becomes factitious. And 'love' is nothing if not sharing and self-sacrifice; and it is not 'love' if we love one person and ignore or hate the rest. And 'love' is not a two-way street; not even an acknowledgment need be expected. Anyone has a right to love anyone, but not the right for anything in return. But the reality is that our whole attitude to life is rooted not in sharing but in reciprocity, which is responsible for much heart-burn, anger, resentment, and violence. What we have to learn is to separate the action from the act, like giving and forgetting the gift; smiling, ignoring the insult, and loving those whom we don't like. If there is one habit we should cultivate in a divisive and polarized world, it is 'sharing'. The spirit of love as sacrifice is best voiced by Charles Dickens' character Sydney Carton, in *The Tale of Two Cities* (1859). Standing in for Charles Darnay, husband of Lucie Manette, the woman whom he secretly loves, Sydney goes to the gallows muttering, "It is a far, far better thing that I do, than I have ever done; it is a far, far better rest that I go to than I have ever known". And it is also true that, as Gabriel Garcia Marquez says, "The invincible power that has moved the world is unrequited, not happy, love" (*Memories of My Melancholy Whores,* 2005). 'Unrequited love can summon both the very best and the worst from us. When and why 'romantic rejection' or 'lovesickness' can make someone a Sydney Carton or a 'stalker-killer' is hard to tell. Modern man, buffeted by his own virtuosity and intoxicated by his own 'invincible power', has turned toxic both in his touch and his reach. He is held hostage by his hubris, and adrift in the sea of his own unbridled ambition. He is foxed by his own behavior, aghast like Oscar Wilde's Dorian Gray at the hideous image in his own mirror, perplexed over what he discovers he is capable of doing, often the reflection of his darkest depths. In our present times, so harrowing and haphazard has life become that it has ceased to be ordinarily possible to distinguish the banal from the bizarre, fiction from falsehood, normative from the 'new-normal'. And in his search for safe havens, man easily falls prey to social viruses like extremism, sectarianism, jingoism, terrorism, racism, etc. At the very hour of his smug satisfaction and temporal triumph, when he seems to be on the brink of achieving his long-sought-after aspirations, man is stricken by a paralyzing sense of both acute agita and insidious inadequacy. But that 'inadequacy' itself is due to the 'unnatural' nature of his aspirations. The reality is that the part assigned to the human in the grand cosmic play is of a mortal earthly being. But our yen for immortality and our everyday awareness that this is impossible to achieve leads to what Miguel de Unamuno described as the "tragic sense of life".[61] What modern man is attempting to do is to transform that 'tragic sense' into transhumanistic euphoria—"that we can and should eradicate ageing as a cause of death; that we can and should use technology to augment our bodies and our minds; that we can and should merge with machines, remaking ourselves, finally, in the image of our own higher ideals".[62]

The highest 'ideal' we have ever had is divinization. Now, with the help of modern technology, man, in one magical leap of faith or, as some may say, in a surge of insanity, is planning to break free from biology and alchemize *Homo sapiens* into *Homo 'Deus'.*[63] So 'free' that we can even conceive of, to borrow an OB Hardison[64] phrase, 'mind children', who are created and hatched by downloading the spiritual essence of a person into a machine. But we cannot be sure if what emerges through such a 'merger'—dubbed as the Fourth Industrial Revolution—would be a *Deus,* or a demon in human form, augment our capabilities or annihilate us. Without the corresponding consciousness-change, what Andrew Kimbrell calls '*metanoia* in consciousness', the high probability is that the latter is what the 'marriage' is more likely to yield. The *mindset* of the human, the paradigm of perception and prioritization and the dynamics of his thinking will not change. Technology will still be misdirected, and artificial general intelligence will be governed by the same mindset, even if it is a million times more 'efficient'. And it will therefore be more dysfunctional and destructive. Becoming a *Deus* does not mean we *cannot* die, or that we will become bullet-proof; it only means we will be able to escape or postpone death in our bed, or in the hospital. We may not die of cancer, but probably in a car crash, not by a heart attack, but by homicide. Death will still remain our destiny, but evil will be more effective in infecting and infiltrating the human world; and globalized institutional evil will become inter-generational evil. Some say that, although a menacing undertow of horror is so much integral to daily life, still this kind of 'life' will be the horror of horrors. That is because, although our ostensible aim is to transform ourselves into a divine being, what we are actually trying to do is to catapult from a 'machine-user' into a machine, to become a tool of the tool, an appendage to our own contraption. Some others say that it may well be so, but there is no other serious alternative for human survival; if man doesn't become a 'god' and stays earth-bound, he will soon be rendered redundant. What is not clear is what '*become*' means; how can anything become something else? The fact of the matter is that man has always thought of himself as more than a mere episode in the cosmic process, but never fathomed what his niche is. Spiritualists, on the other hand, speak in terms of what is called the 'sacramental way of life', of the soul's search for the 'Blessed Beloved', the seeker's craving for the cosmic soul. In the Bhagavad Gita, Lord Krishna says that one must perform every action sacramentally, and be free from all attachments to the results.[65] This holy longing, this sacramental yearning, is a hidden feeling with many disguises. It can also go horribly awry if we misplace or misproject it. Furthermore, scriptures like the Upanishads say that Man already *is* wholly God. The *Isha* Upanishad says, '*So ham*' (I am He). We must understand that this is not the egotist's "I am God!" proclamation, but rather the full realization of the absolute truth that God is the only Reality. What we forget is that everyone else and everything is also the same Supreme. By loving them, you are loving God, and in hating or hurting them, you are hating or hurting the divine.

Those who are pushing for man to be made into a *Deus* eagerly argue that the earth will, maybe in a century or two, become inhospitable to human life, and that man must migrate to the Moon or Mars. But he will not survive there with a purely 'lived body', in the words of Vivian Sobchack, a sentient, sensual, and sensible ensemble of materialized capacities. Perhaps, as no other human venture before, this deep driving desire of direct divinity of modern man affects his mindset and could well determine the future of our species. It may even hasten our doom. We could even speculate that such a 'desire' was seeded in our consciousness by the Divine Himself, to get rid of us as we have become too much of a risk to His other offspring. To paraphrase Peter Wessel Zapffe (*The Last Messiah*, 1933), the idea is to make us infertile and let the earth be silent after us. Although the spotlight is on the population explosion, there are reports that already at least half of the people in the world live in countries where the birth rates are at, or below, replacement. The UN projects global population to peak around 2050 at 7.7 billion, and the decline could then start; where and how it might end is hard to foresee. As the new book *Empty Planet* says, "Once that decline begins, it will never end".[67] For a variety of reasons—from selfishness to altruism—some say we must be prepared for the 'extreme step' of forsaking 'having children in the future for the future'; the purpose is not to bring kids into a place 'where you have to just survive and suffer'. It is also being seen as a 'contribution' to combating the climate crisis. It is said that each child you choose *not* to have, can save 58.6 tonnes of carbon a year. One estimate is that 'if the average number of births falls to a level of 1.3 among the women of the world, our species would disappear in 300 years'. As a kind of a warning shot and adding credence to this line of thought, a new study says that Neanderthals, our closest extinct human relative, became extinct not because of any catastrophic event but due to a 'slight decline in fertility'. Could it be that what could blow in our face might not be Paul Ehrlich's 'Population Bomb' but the opposite? We don't know which doomsday scenario will eventually unfold when our time is up, but a high probability is that it is not human numbers but exponentially excessive human behavior that could tilt the balance. And to better our behavior what we need is consciousness-change, not forsaking kids who could in fact undo the damage that we the adults have done.

To that dire 'pregnant' possibility we must add our growing a Dracula-like taste for bloodletting—what Mark Twain called 'the joy of killing; the joy of seeing killing done[68]— which is not new but now seems contagious. Unwittingly, we could be drifting into a twilight zone of 'double-danger'; one through radical reproduction-reduction, and the other by turning killing into a default mode of conflict resolution. We kill other forms of life without batting an eye, and don't even feel that it is 'killing'; and we kill future life on the plea that 'life' is really not life. And killing, or taking one's self or that of others, is almost a way to handle everyday situations and stress, whether the launching pad is a rocky marriage, spurned love, dreaded school-reopening, making money, wrecking revenge, or rash road driving. As RD Laing reminds us, "Society highly values its normal man. It educates children to lose themselves and to become absurd, and thus to be normal. Normal men have killed perhaps 100 million of their fellow normal men in the last fifty years".[69] That is because, as David Buss points out, "a deep psychology of killing has been and is an essential component of human nature".[70] We live in what Pope John Paul said, "a veritable structure of sin", and in a "culture which denies solidarity and in many cases takes the form of a veritable culture of death".[71] Yet in this very 'culture', paradoxically, we want to erase the 'certainty of death'. In this effort, we have been looking around for a 'role model' in nature. And not finding anything befitting our ego, we have come to the conclusion that the only worthy ideal could only be a god, someone similar like a Greek god and Indian *deva*. In the case of Greek gods, the difference between human and divine agencies may sometimes not even be discernible. These are celestial beings, but not the Supreme Soul or cosmic consciousness or 'the Father in Heaven' or the Creator we worship. These 'beings' have eternal youth and are immortal, which is why we want to be them. That might be the aim, but the possibility, given the fact that so often in the past what we intended to achieve has yielded something very different, we might end up as the very antithetical archetype, as the foes of the gods, the *rakshasas* or demons. That is partly because we already have many of their attributes deep inside. Even if we do acquire the knowhow to become *de facto* demigods, the high probability is that, at least for quite a time, the vast majority will be left out in the new 'gilded age'. And those 'left-outs' are unlikely to stay quiet for too long. It could germinate so much anger, resentment, division, and disparity, that it could let loose the ultimate reign of terror on earth. Suicides and homicides, already major causes of death, could become the new plague. Between the two, suicide is a better barometer of the state of shattered social health than homicide. Contrary to what it seems, suicides are not only increasing in many countries, but also more people are materially and mentally affected than in a homicide, bringing into mind the ominous words of the historian Arnold Toynbee, "Civilizations die from suicide, not by murder" (*A Study of History*, 1934–61).

Clearly there are some ominous signs that call for a radical rethink, or 'unthink the habits of thought' as some like philosopher Owen Barfield (*Saving the Appearances*, 1957) prefer to say, on our frenzied rush towards medical immortality. We can get away with 'playing-god', but with death it is another matter. In the Bhagavad Gita, Lord Krishna proclaims unequivocally, "I am immortality, and I am also death personified".[72] Man now wants to be just that:

he seeks immortality, but does not want to give up on the goodies that mortal flesh allows us to enjoy. And also, let us not forget, man wants immortality in his own body, not in heaven! The Greek hero Achilles, who, when he was alive said 'gods envy our mortality', changed his mind once he found himself in the Kingdom of the Dead. He told the visiting Odysseus, "Say not a word in death's favour; I would rather be a paid servant in a poor man's house and be above ground than a king of kings among the dead".[73] Although we talk of man becoming a god, what we are seeking is not a state of species-scale absolute deathlessness, but exponentially extended youth and life span. For man, by any other moniker, is man; born as a *sapiens*, he must die as a *sapiens*. He cannot hope to do what a creepy caterpillar could: transform itself into a beauteous butterfly. In order to be able to become a butterfly, the caterpillar completely decomposes down to its very essence, devoid of any shape or consciousness. The caterpillar literally dies, and the butterfly starts to put itself together—from scratch. But *we* don't want to turn into some kind of a soup in a cocoon or pupa for any kind of transformation like the caterpillar. We don't want to give up anything, not even the qualities we detest; we want to get a 'free-upgrade' from coach to first class and get someone (the machine) to do the heavy lifting and bring forward our whole bodily baggage. We have more chances of becoming, or being treated like, a hideous cockroach, like Kafka's Gregos Samsa (*The Metamorphosis*, 1915) than become a carefree butterfly. For, in the end, 'man and roach are more the same than we know'. Both live all life by clinging on to something or the other. Both elicit fear and repugnance. They are each as worthy of extinction as the other. Every species has certain given unique 'attributes', even immortality (like the jellyfish), and they cannot be exchanged. What has long been our undoing as an individual is the desire to selectively exchange places with another person, and as a species to acquire particular attributes of some other species. What we should aspire to do is not to be someone else, but aim to attain our own dreams that will make someone else realize their own dreams. The secret to success in life is encapsulated in the New Testament: "Let no one seek his own, but each one the other's well-being".[74] The shortest route to fullness of our life is not a straight line, but a bypass through helping others achieve what they need to achieve. Instead, we deliberately try to exclude others from our success and, even worse, at their expense. We want to be supra-human without a foundational liberation from self-centeredness. We want to *become* a 'god' not by spiritually attaining '*samadhi*'—the sublime state of oneness with God—but by *becoming a part of the machine*. God incarnated as a man, but no man ever, delusions apart, physically became a 'god' through his own body. That is possible, according to some ancient theological schools of thought, if a person has evolved through all the levels of relative existence and attained the transcendental state of perfect liberation (*moksha*), which is nothing but total union with the Supreme Consciousness. While ancient spiritual philosophies like Indian Vedanta tried to bring man and God together by saying that the best way to worship god is by service to humanity, science is saying that whatever the divine was meant to deliver, technologies could do as well, perhaps even more. The machine now is the modern-day messiah. We live at a time when, to get any serious attention to whatever we seek to do, we have to somehow smuggle in the magic prefix *science*. Everything is now science: even science of happiness, science of compassion, science of gratitude, and science of the heart. The reality is that, in the words of astrophysicist Neil deGrasse Tyson, "from climate change, to biotech, to artificial intelligence, science sits at the center of nearly all decisions that civilization confronts to assure its own survival". The scientist is also a human being, and his decisions are equally subject to the same limitations, foibles, temptations—recognition, glory, greed, and money.

It is also necessary to factor in a new reality, which is that new technologies—biotech, nanotech, cybertech, as well as artificial intelligence—empower groups of individuals to have an effect by error or by design, which could escalate very broadly, even globally. To this we must add yet another important factor. We must remember that whenever man wanted something badly, and knew that he could not get it directly, he achieved it stealthily. He wanted to fly like a bird; he invented the airplane. He wanted to run like a cheetah; he made the automobile. The means he has chosen now is mechanization and genetic manipulation to be what he wants to be. What he is forgetting is that our life is more than our physical and mental apparatus. He is, like Narcissus in Greek mythology, enthralled by his own creation, the machine. The incongruity that escapes our attention is that man is, on the one hand, telling us that individual death is not inevitable; but, on the other hand, he is doing all he can to accelerate collective death. It may appear exciting and euphoric, but some say that medical science is coming close to replicating the first deception of Satan in the Garden of Eden: 'And the serpent said unto the woman, Ye shall not surely die'.[75] Moreover, medical science has, or is trying to, rudely cut us loose from the only certainty and the crooked yet comforting thought that has held us together for maybe a million years—that not only is death certain, but everyone else, rich and poor, president and plumber, oppressor and oppressed, celebrity and common man, all have to die too. That regardless of who you are or what you did, the closure, absolute oblivion, awaits us all. In death we see justice denied by life. The transformation of death from a unifier to divider carries tectonic consequences.

What draws us to the machine, among other things, is the perceived ability to neutralize many of the things we fear about death. After all, we can keep maintaining it regularly and keep replacing or updating it part by part from time to time. Smart as we think we are, we want to piggyback on it to our own immortality, not realizing that it is like riding on the back of a tiger. By so doing, science hopes to exorcise the primordial place of the divine in human consciousness. But, as John Robinson reminds us, "the necessity for the name 'God' lies in the fact that our being has depths which naturalism, whether evolutionary, mechanistic, dialectical or humanistic, cannot or will not recognize" (*Honest to God,* 1963). The paradox is that science says there is no need for God, or that he is now dated or dead, but wants to make man a *Semi-deus* or *Deus.* But then, if God is redundant or irrelevant, how can there be demigods? For, it is God who created demigods. In the Bhagavad Gita, it is said, "In the beginning of creation, the Lord of all creatures sent forth generations of men and *devatas* or demigods".[76] These *devatas*, according to Hindu mythology, live within this material universe, in the higher planes of existence, called *swarga*, or the celestial abodes. The devatas are not God; they are souls like us. They occupy specific posts in the affairs of running the world, such as *Agni Deva* (the god of fire), *Vayu Deva* (the god of the wind), *Varuna Deva* (the god of the rains), Indra Deva (the king of the celestial gods), etc. What science is trying to do is to play God and turn man into a deva by mating with a machine. For some, it is nothing new or any need to be concerned because, according to what is called de La Mettrie's doctrine,[77] we are essentially machines ourselves and no soul and no substance separate from matter. What kind of 'being' or world will emerge from such a technological trick is hard to tell, but easy to imagine. More possibly we might move towards Aldous Huxley's *Brave New World* (1931). When Huxley wrote his dystopian book, he thought we would be safe from such a scary society for at least a few hundred years. By 1958, he realized he had been too optimistic. While we aren't entirely yet there, the march of technology continues to bring us the tools which make it ever simpler to make it possible. And why would anyone resist such a 'new world' if it gives us what we so desperately want: security, stability, progress, drugs for every need, and above all, what the Danes call *lykke* (happiness) as the only acceptable state of mind?

Science is, intentionally or inadvertently, trying to uproot the most stabilizing factor in human consciousness: what we might call 'the sensation of the sacred'. What the Japanese call *yūgen* is described by Jordan Bates as "an expansive feeling, a mystical awareness, an almost soaring reverence for existence that is summoned forth by a poignant confrontation with the ineffable details of reality."[78] Perhaps the one man who seamlessly sewed spirituality and science in our own time, Albert Einstein, once said, 'The finest emotion of which we are capable is the mystic emotion. Herein lies the germ of all art and all true science. Anyone to whom this feeling is alien, who is no longer capable of wonderment and lives in a state of fear is a dead man'. The truth is that a human, to be truly human, needs such a sensation, something that lets him stand rapt in 'secular awe' or 'spiritual reverence', the sense of something that challenges his understanding really exists, of something that is bigger and loftier than his life. An instinct for the supernal lives on in the human psyche. Reverence for the mysterious forces that backstop the world is a basic human instinct. Without that, man will himself become that which he is now trying to construct mechanically, a clumsy thinking machine. We live in a world of high-intensity anxiety and gnawing uncertainty, a kind of a twilight zone and surreal time, "which is precisely the conditions in which logic is not the appropriate framework for thinking about decision-making".[79] Physicist Lawrence Krauss even says that in science the very word 'sacred' is profane. While there are others who say that 'sacredness is no threat to the practice of science', the fact remains that the lay public is led to believe that sacredness is dated and science, and its twin, technology, can well be a substitute. One of the lopsided things that technology has done is to erase, as someone described, the disproportion between powers and satisfaction, aspiration and attaining. The human now feels that if he really wants something he can get it. And that which he can get, he doesn't respect, much less revere. We should not confuse 'sacred' only with God or religion. An atheist too can have that sense and spirit of sacredness and reverence. By undermining sacredness, science thinks it is fostering the spirit of rationality. In truth, what it is promoting and furthering is not rationality but recklessness. Even the assumption that we are 'rational' beings is now in doubt. Firstly, no one is quite clear what 'rationality' means, and then the fact is that most decisions we make are subjective and that is for good. Some, like the 'risk' guru David Ropeik say, "To be rational, we need both facts and feelings. We need to be subjective".[80] The fact is, we are not rational beings in the truest sense of the phrase; a really rational person cannot be selfish. We are simply clumsy beings; so many mistakes were made and so much misery and mayhem was caused not because we were clever, but because we were clumsy. Although at one time we were good at judging what is dangerous and what's safe, when our very survival was on the line, that instinctive capability was eroded by our overdependence on technology. Now we are so 'confused' that we actually feel smug when we should 'panic'; we feel secure while being self-destructive. We are so 'confused' that consequences carry no consequence; all that matters is contentment, convenience, and comfort. We have become a 'soft species'. Modern man looks frighteningly similar to Nietzsche's *Last Man* (*Thus Spake Zarathustra*), the antithesis of the *Ubermensch*, the Overman. While Zarathustra wants us to strive to go beyond being human, we are exhibiting the qualities of his Last Man. Like the Last Man, today's human is tired of life; he takes no risks, and wallows in comfort, mediocrity, and security. All of these, plus pacifism and peace, are what man now thinks he will find in the suffocating embrace of the machine. Even in death we seek what we desire in life—ease and comfort and security; we now have suicide pods for death in style, hip and cool new ways to end one's life.

We live in an amoral world in which victims are blamed, and where technical solutions are thought to be better than common sense, and scheming companies cynically exploit our sensory weaknesses. In today's militantly mercantile world, the fact that nothing is sacred means that everything is for sale or for exchange. If we cannot buy God, we can exchange him for an algorithm or the computer 'cloud'. And that is what is happening now. Man can do anything, get anything, and go anywhere if he could. There are no limitations, restraints or taboos. The fact is that without any sense of sacredness, awe, reverence, and respect, man is no different from any other beast. Indeed, it is worse. Other animals might not have any 'sensation of sacredness', but they have what we so sadly lack: sensation of satisfaction. As Walt Whitman wrote, "Not one is dissatisfied, not one is demented with the mania of owning things", and, "they do not lie awake in the dark and weep for their sins" (*Song of Myself; Leaves of Grass*, 1855). When its belly is full, a wild beast ceases to be a ruthless killer until it is again hungry. Not so the human beast; it is the sacred and supernatural that keep him in check, not his need; nor his morals. A huge chunk of 'supernatural' is the whole gamut of ideas, thoughts, and emotions under the rubric of 'God'. And if this is marginalized, or brought under disrepute, man will yearn for other anchors like gadgets and godmen, both of whom have much in common, and both will try to fill the divine void, and the void of loneliness within our souls. For, as Ivan Karamazov of Dostoyevsky's *Brothers Karamazov* said, "If God does not exist, everything is permitted", including the abomination of man becoming a god via the machine.

The question then arises: is there more to it than meets the eye; is man trying to erase the ontological distinction between God and his creation? Just as the ape evolved into a man, man cannot, through the same process, evolve into a god. We can acquire god-like powers but we cannot physically be a god. The irony is that we seek something that we already have. Many great thinkers have referred to the 'potencies of man's inner being' that largely remain unfathomed. The divine is within, so are divine powers. Our aims actually are more material than metaphysical. A *de facto* god is not really our goal; it is the model and means. We don't want to appear and disappear, nor, like gods, bestow boons. In fact, we want to do better than angels and gods: we want to reverse ageing, and bring the dead back to life. Humans may have to wait for a while, but scientists, through gene-editing and 'CRISPR' technology, are already trying to bring extinct species back from the dead, what is being dubbed as *de-extinction*. We want to 'look good', not be good, eat or breathe good. What we are aiming at is very different from what the ancient *rishis* of India strived towards, through intense *tapas* or deep meditation, and spiritual *sadhana*, or practice. Their goal then was not to *become* a god or a deva but to attain a state of divine consciousness. Whether or not we believe that death is a gift of God and the basis of life, it is essential to the balance between life and death. In fact, there is no such thing as 'living'; it is actually dying—what Shakespeare described as ripe and ripe, rot and rot, hour to hour (*As You Like It*)—that comes to an end as death. And, 'So it goes', as Kurt Vonnegut says in his book *Slaughterhouse-Five* (1969). Somber as it is, we must remember that 'from death comes life', and that if we tamper with death, we might put life itself at risk. Even more, by trying to become gods, we are not trying to overcome our ego or vanity, our frailties and our propensity for evil, or to raise our consciousness. Our love of our body is such that we want it to last forever. But it is through this body-consciousness, according to Henry Wood, that man has "come into servitude to sin, disease and death, and innumerable other limitations and infelicities".[81] Wood goes on to say, "The world has been mistaken in regarding man as a material being. This belief is the basic reason for his ever-present frictions and trials".[82]

God has never been separate from man, whether or not one believes in Him, or in His very reality. We always thought that the next and ultimate step can only be to become a god; what else could there be? We don't know how other animals imagine or relate with God, but *man* has effectively 'humanized' Him. He has made Him in his image. What science is doing now is to replace the theological God with a technological God, and upgrade us to a god in flesh and blood right here on earth. Few, if any, have experienced the 'theological' God, and the mystique and mystery has remained intact. Nothing man did or could do was ever able to dethrone God. But that hasn't discouraged some like Nietzsche's madman to declare '*God is dead*'.[83] Killed by us humans! If not dead, God has at least become dated, making it necessary to invent 'Tomorrow's God',[84] which, according to Donald Walsch, is 'our greatest spiritual challenge'. But today, science views this as a *technological* challenge, one that is even greater and riskier, because science is trying to fuse two objectives: inventing tomorrow's God, and creating '*Tomorrow's Man*'. It is both a total *takeover* and *makeover*. The main takeaway from the package is that man, through technology, will enjoy godly perks and wield godly powers, and the 'old' God will be primarily ceremonial. Such a 'God will be more a cyborg (there are already about 100,000 'cyborgs', people with chips inserted under their skin) than a celestial shepherd, more metal and silicon than flesh and spirit. Things are moving fast and the latest 'revelation' is that tomorrow's God would simply be an *algorithm*, residing in the lifeless metal maze of a supercomputer. It is part of a more generic idea that technology will be the brand new religion of the brave new world of the 21st century. Like in regard to Aldous Huxley's *Brave New World*, what is truly terrifying is that we too love our technological slavery. And like the citizens of that dystopian world, technology keeps us endlessly distracted and views solitude as a social malaise. We are very close to creating, like in Huxley's world, a society that pops pills to eradicate any vestige of negative feelings and escape the drudgery and doldrums of everyday living. Whichever and whatever, we must recognize that despite his declared death and datedness, God is very much 'alive' in the human consciousness, although a bit under the weather. In fact, that is what is keeping a lid over so much of misery, exploitation, oppression, inequality, and inequity in the world. If that lid is removed, even God cannot save humanity. That is so because God as an idea is larger than an entity or almighty or energy to be worshipped, and as a parachute in despair. He or It is also the source and symbol of love, justice, awe, greatness, wonder, order, truth, role model, reverence, beauty, and everything else that seems to draw humans beyond themselves. And that is unlikely to change even if science turns man into a god or angel or anoints AI or the algorithm as the New Almighty. For we need the sense of the sacred, the supernatural, and the superhuman, a sense of awe, wonder, and reverence, for us not to mutate into moral maniacs. As Pope John Paul II says, "When the sense of God is lost, there is also a tendency to lose the sense of man, of his dignity and his life; in turn, the systematic violation of the moral law, especially in the serious matter of respect for human life and its dignity, produces a kind of progressive darkening of the capacity to discern God's living and saving presence".[85] Without some kind of bedrock belief that there are forces higher and superior to him in the universe, that can make a difference to his life and after-life, man cannot be trusted to do what he is capable of. The belief in divine forces and a divine existence have always tempered human actions until 'quite recently'. But, the exceptional power placed in man's hands by scientific and technological progress is now proving to be an irresistible temptation to fulfill his darkest dreams and wildest wants. Therefore, bringing back some measure of belief in the divine, and a sense of the sacred, is not only urgent, it is also a prerequisite to consciousness-change.

The fact is that whatever is the exact mix and make-up, man is both a material and spiritual being. A 'divine void', if it ever happens, can utterly destabilize, disorient, and dehumanize us, and make us wholly material beings. Indeed, there are many thoughtful observers who are already asking *'Is God back?'* And some see signs of the foretold return of Jesus. But God never went away, in the first place. The question is, would we return to spiritual means, or would we keep our faith with technology all the way? We must understand one thing clearly: when people say *'man wants to be a god'*, what they mean is that man is ready to go to any length to eliminate his present human limitations. The Buddha summed it up well: "When young, one is subject to ageing; when healthy, subject to illness; when alive, subject to death". Man's sense of inadequacy revolves around these three—ageing, sickness, and death. Therefore, in order to make himself more adequate, his strategy is to dangerously dabble with artificial intelligence, going to the extent of allowing it to take over his own faculties. Some warn that 'AI is going to change the world more than anything in the history of mankind'. AI symbolizes our chronic inability to ensure that our creativity does not work in a way injurious to our interests. It is more than technological unemployment that is on the line; it erodes a huge chunk of 'being human'; it is more a matter of mental muscles than physical labor; it undermines our innate longing to 'earn' what we get, to be a partner, not a patsy. Artificial intelligence can do a world of good provided it is channeled properly. And for that we need decision-making that is different from what it is now. That, in turn, requires consciousness-change. We must also face a more fundamental fact: the human is chronically poor at priority-setting, particularly in a climate of scarcity. It becomes even more skewed when the 'prioritizers' are the plutocracy and the elite. That is why we spend tens of billions of dollars on space exploration and on colonizing the Moon and Mars at the expense of socially far more critical priorities like access to clean water for the billions of people who, despite breakthroughs in agriculture and farming and sanitation, are still starving or dying of dysentery. According to a new report by UNICEF and the World Health Organization, despite significant progress, 2.2 billion people around the world do not have safely managed drinking water services, and 4.2 billion people do not have safely managed sanitation services. The fact of the matter is that we are facing serious issues here on earth, and they are only getting worse. These include climate change, and more particularly the disappearance of the rainforests, the pollution of the oceans, and galloping desertification on a catastrophic scale every year. What we are losing sight of is that the world is a network of interpermeable systems. As Jedediah Purdy tells us, "What comes out of a smokestack can travel through wind, rain, groundwater, and soil, and end up in flesh".[86] Today, more than 23% of the earth's landmass has been degraded by desertification, and 1.5 billion people are affected. The other side of the dismal picture is that we read about astonishing technological breakthroughs that benefit the common man, like 'making it rain where and when we want it', or using human poop as a renewable energy source, and extracting unlimited water from the air. But they fade away for want of patronage and funding. Research on eradicating extreme poverty is grossly underfunded. What we fail to realize is that erasing abysmal poverty is a more humane way to extend the average human life span. It is the best investment one can make for a healthier and happier humanity, a better alternative to mass suicide or merging into the machine. One estimate (Jeffrey Sachs) puts the cost to end poverty at $175 billion per year for 20 years, a fraction of what we spend on high-profile projects like space exploration, silicon immortality, and artificial intelligence, even excluding military R&D.

Our ever-growing fascination of AI and biological immortality, and the disproportionate attention and resources, human and financial, expended in that direction, offers us a snapshot of human insatiability and technological hubris, and of how much we are off-course, as a self-proclaimed spiritual species, in answering the fundamental questions of human life. Hermann Hesse once wrote, "The true profession of man is to find a way to himself". What we are doing has nothing to do with finding a way to ourselves; instead we are too eager to give up on ourselves. We don't accept who we are and view our vulnerabilities as liabilities and weaknesses to be overcome. Our very vulnerability—our capacity for doubting, getting hurt, softness, tenderness, sacrifice, love, spirituality, sensitivity—is our true strength. Vulnerability, it has been said, is an act of courage because you merge with your authentic self, instead of hiding behind a façade to appease others. It is this misconception—that we must exorcise our softer side in order to be strong, smart, and successful—that has led us to the machine. The machine now is viewed as the 'city on the hill', the gold standard, our role model; it is pure, it has come to symbolize the sufficiency we miss and seek in ourselves, it never fails or lets us down. Some say that the next neo-biological civilization will be the one where we grudgingly accept that humans are the random ancestors of machines, and that as machines we can be engineered and augmented ourselves. We have come to implicitly accept that, unlike the machine, the human is simply incapable of not just clinical efficiency, but also fairness, impartiality, and justness in his interpersonal interactions. This is also an indirect backlash in the face of one of our greatest failures: our innate inability to reconcile the personal and interpersonal in any kind of trade-off. The machine will then be a way not only to overcome our cognitive and corporeal inadequacies, but also to serve as a hedge against our moral failings. The human could then become akin to the ancient Greeks (of the time of Homer's *Iliad*) who thought of themselves as 'physical vessels for the will of the gods'; it will then be the whim of the machinic-machine. Or would we become, as Freud once predicted, prosthetic gods? It is at the same time a statement of surrender and of haughtiness. Surrender, because we have thrown in the towel, as it were, conceded that we are not good enough to be who we want to be. Haughtiness, because we think that we can still get what we want not through the spiritual route, but by 'cyborgization'—that is, using technology to modify and enhance our bodies and brains and merging with our supplements, our technological appendages. The result, as philosopher Philip Torres puts it, "could be beings with completely novel cognitive architectures (or mental abilities), emotional repertoires, physical capabilities, lifespans, and so on".[87]

There are some very worried people who think that we have virtually reached the vanishing point, beyond which one will not know what is human or not human, producing in the process the erasure of the human in the inhuman. Long ago, we 'discovered' that the easiest way to treat another person horribly, even to get rid of him, is to learn to view him no longer as 'human'. Once we cross that line, whatever we do is no more a crime or sin or inhuman in our mind. This is a momentous shift, which some describe as the 'zero-point' of humanity, in human perception, and deserves our fullest attention. In the name of perfection and excellence, we cannot renounce or denigrate our own integrity and then try to find solace in someone else's bosom, hoping that that will empower us to get what we want from the world. Our quest for immortality is also a part of our unquenchable thirst for perfection. The Buddha once said that 'affection is always greater than perfection'. And reviving the living is better than reviving the dead, as Rabbi Menachem Mendel of Kotzk once said. And, it is not all technology's fault. It is human nature. If not technology, we will invent something else not to do what we can and must do. In fact, that is what we do with God too. And no wonder we want to our technology in His place. We have chosen to ignore what the 20th-century Indian spiritual teacher Swami Vivekananda exhorted us to always bear in mind: "All power is within you; you can do anything and everything. Believe in that; do not believe that you are weak". The problem is that we have never had access to what we already have within. Furthermore, we really do not know what 'adequacy' or 'perfection' mean in human terms. What some derisively dismiss as nature's mistakes in our making could be part of a grander and greater plan of life on earth. Different forms of life have different traits integral to that kind of earthly existence. Nature exquisitely balances the skills of both predator and prey so that both survive in the game of outsmarting each other. If every part, every organ, every faculty is 'fool-proof', independently of others, the sum of all these would be hideous, not pretty or perfect.

Let us remember what our central problem is, and what the only lasting solution could be. The problem is not AI or the algorithm or nanotechnology. All of them have the potential to do immense good if properly directed and channeled. Even in the worst-case scenario in which a kind of reversal of roles takes place between man and machine, the machine then will do what man does and vice versa… man still will matter. The problem is the state of our consciousness, which depends on the state of the war within. With the right kind of consciousness, even man plus machine can be a force that can transform both the human condition and the fortunes of the planet. We need a consciousness in which the 'intuitive intelligence' of the heart plays a much more assertive role than now. GK Chesterton once wryly said, "You can only find truth with logic if you have already found truth without it", which means mind-driven logic is irrelevant and superfluous to anything serious in life. We have to accept ourselves as we are, and strive to use more holistically what nature has thought fit to equip us with. Godly powers without godly-consciousness could make us not a well-meaning Frankenstein-monster, but a monster in nihilistic mode. Through her portrayal of her hideous but good-natured monster, Mary Shelley tells us that our society, past and present, focuses too much on our external characteristics.

Whoever a person may be on the inside and however great and generous he or she may be is altered by that person's physical self. It shows the superficial nature of man. Without upgrading or enhancing our consciousness, any 'upgradation' or 'augmentation' or enhancement of our body or brain could be risky. Let us not forget that it is brain-based, linear, sequential, and reductionist thinking that has destroyed the synergistic system of the earth's biosphere, with its many intertwined parts interacting in complex and unfathomable ways. Yet, once society accepts, as we now do, that humanity needs upgradation from what nature has left us with, means and morality become dispensable, wherein lies the greatest danger.

The merging of man with machine, an 'upgradation' that science is currently pursuing, really is tantamount to integrating the human mind—all of humanity in fact—with superfast, supersmart computers. In a practical sense, we already have merged ourselves with machines in our daily life. What is new is what might happen when the much-discussed technological singularity comes calling—and super-intelligent machine creations become self-aware. When they have a mind and agenda of their own, and may even be able to create copies of themselves that are more intelligent than themselves. The D-Day is said to be the year 2045, by which time, we are told, humans on an average will live up to 100 years and will change the way they live, mate, work, and play in the future. But what kind of change will that be? What will not change, but what must change, is how we will be with each other, and the intelligence that drives and determines what we will do with that long or unlimited life span, and with the body or 'shell' that we would have made for ourselves by merging with a machine.

Lest we forget, as mentioned earlier, however advanced machine-intelligence might be, it will remain essentially human brain-intelligence. There is no denying that. The means we are planning to employ, to upgrade ourselves into a far different and far more powerful being, are rooted in the same genre of cognitive power that is based on the neural network of the human brain, and that is 'mind-infected'. It means that the dynamics of our choice-making and decision-making will not change, without which nothing else will change. Decision-making in today's taxing times often involves weighing tangled nuances in increasingly complex situations and involving intricate motivations. And yet so ordinary that any of us can be a 'Sophie'[88] anytime. The moral dilemmas we confront are not very different in the 'post-modern' world than those faced by inmates of Nazi camps. What is it that we must not give up, and what can we give up to get what in return? What is the moral minimum and non-negotiable and what is the larger utilitarian good? Indeed, as Adam Kirsch reminds us, "It is possible to think of the [concentration] camps as what happens when you cross three disciplinary institutions that all societies possess—the prison, the army, and the factory".[89] There are a lot of people who feel that a 'prisoner' is more free than they are in the 'free' world; that their lives are more regimented than in an army, and that they are not very different from exploited factory-workers. It is this crushing feeling that finds utterance in so many ways. The hard moral trade-offs and choices we have to wrestle with will not change even if we are able to 'remove the brain from our heads, preserve it for eternity, clone it or send it through space' and become a 'silicon-immortal'. And our inherently inadequate brain-based 'intelligence', even if it becomes a 'digital brain', cannot better our behavior, much less turn us into a divine being or a super-suave superhero. And whatever we become and wherever it leads we will still fall short or go astray. The Upanishads categorically proclaim that by realizing his true divine identity man attains immortality. Jesus voiced the same thought when he said, "I and my Father are one".[90] But for the modern man, the body is all there is, all he cares about; and all that he wants to preserve. It is the shell that matters, not the substance.

The irony is that we don't have or carry the same body through life; our body changes constantly, from toddler to a teenager, youth to old age, and in the end, the body we want to make immortal is the one that is the weakest and least pretty of them all—aged, wrinkled, worn-out, and wasted. At the same time, scientists are also trying to combat ageing—what James Joyce (*The Dead*) described as "fade and wither dismally with age"—on the hypothesis that while we associate old age with susceptibility to several diseases, ageing itself is nothing but a 'cellular disease', and can be cured like any other. What are the implications of what biologist Aubrey de Grey calls 'undoing ageing'? We don't have to be apologetic about our efforts to lengthen the springtime of our youth and shorten the years of our fall. But it is the quality that maters, not the quantity. We should aim to have what is called 'optimal ageing'—the capacity to function across many domains: physical, functional, cognitive, emotional, social, and spiritual—to one's satisfaction and in spite of one's medical conditions.

The bottom line is that immortality *per se* will not solve any social problems, even if some of us with enough money do live exponentially much longer than any of us. Worse, it could widen social rift and unrest. For if somebody privately discovers a truly effective and expensive anti-ageing agent, it is unlikely it will be universally shared, and money may then hit a brick wall. The planet will be imperiled with greater impunity. Violent death might replace natural death and suicides might well become the path to escape from the squalid reality of the eternal bored. On top of it, it will create another issue of social friction, one more divide—*enhanced* long-living humans and *wholly human* humans. It is money again that matters and muddies. That has been the case since the ancient times. After all, as the Gospel of Matthew says, it was for just thirty pieces of silver that Judas betrayed Jesus. Everyone is now a 'Judas'; for money we will marry or murder anyone and barter our very soul. As philosopher and US civil rights leader Grace Lee Boggs says, "There are so many creative energies that are part of human history that have been lost because we've been pursuing the almighty dollar. We haven't recognized at what expense we've done that, the expense not only of the earth, not only of people of color, but of our own selves".[91] The challenge is not to shun it as evil but transform it into a moral tool.

The fact is that, even if science achieves breakthroughs in research in ageing and dying, only the wealthy can afford what it requires. The tragedy is that, while science, on the one hand, is determined to help man live as long as he wants, on the assumption that that is all he wants, simultaneously, a profound transformation is taking place in the human mind, on how death is beginning to be perceived as an opportunity to live with life. Death too has mutated; it is simply not the same as it has been known as, since the time of the first death. And death is not simply the inescapable end of life, to be awaited with fear. It is now an everyday choice, to tackle every situation, a way to overcome any impediment, a means to get anything we want. Death has often been called the ultimate liberator, the universal leveller, and impartial dispenser of final justice. More and more people are beginning to see it as the immediate liberator, instant problem-solver, and an unfailing friend-in-need. But, death has also become a new source of division and discord. Everyone doesn't die the same way. Money matters; wealth is weighty. The very rich symbolize 'capitalism's moral bankruptcy'. They can often purchase impunity for even the most loathsome of crimes. They are not only, as Scott Fitzgerald said, "different from you and me" (*The Great Gatsby*) in the way they live, but also the way they die. While the lower-class people die in the same 'old' ways—stillborn, wrinkled and withered, of malnutrition, of tuberculosis, of cancer, of heart disease, and so forth—the upper classes can choose to be either immortal, or die by choice in hip and cool new ways. Now, there's an assisted suicide pod so chic and hip that some are calling it the 'Tesla of Death'. It induces a sort of dry drowning: the device induces hypoxia, which leads to a euphoric loss of consciousness followed by a peaceful death, without the negative effects of, well, choking for breath and panicking.

If ever a time comes when death is denied its natural role in human life, then man will turn on man more than ever. He cannot simply wait him out. It is another man's certain mortality that is acting as a check against homicides. Once the hope that one day the relief in the form of death—of ours or of our tormentors—evaporates, then suicides will skyrocket. Suicide already ranks higher in many societies, including USA, than homicide. According to the World Health Organization, suicides make up 15% of all violent deaths globally, that is, five times as many each year as all the deaths in war. There is growing evidence that screen-time, time spent using various gadgets, might have some connection with the recent spurt in teenage suicides. We are all brought up on the bedrock belief that self-preservation is the strongest instinct. It doesn't seem all that strong now. The growing acceptance, if not attraction, of death as the antidote to the rude reality of living is perhaps the most telling indictment of the current techno-industrial civilization. Terrible and troubling as it is, should we read a deeper and darker message in this? It is said that when gods want to destroy anyone, they first make them mad. Is that what is happening in the world? As it is said in Genesis, "And the Lord was sorry that he had made man on the earth, and it grieved him to his heart".[92] Has God finally had it and decided to get rid of his own image on earth? We may consider ourselves special and exceptional, but nature might have its own way of judging the utility of a species, its own eugenics, and could come to conclude that the human species has forfeited its divine lineage and earthly utility, and has to be weeded out. Has the viceroy become a villain and a traitor? Have we become, once again, a chosen species—this time chosen for destruction by our own hand? Or, has self-destruction become our 'way of making amends for our scorching presence and reckless rapacity'? The horrifying magnitude of our massacre of other forms of life on earth can be gauged by the results of a survey by the World Wildlife Fund: 'Mammal, bird, fish and reptile populations have fallen on average by 60% since 1970'. Experts are warning that the annihilation of wildlife is now an emergency that threatens civilization. And we must remember, as the Fund says, "Nature is not a 'nice to have'—it is our life-support system". If wildlife disappears, so will we, at some point.

Even if such somber thoughts are unfounded or greatly exaggerated, the fact is that what we call the 'human way of life', not any particular belief system or culture or civilization or ideology, has progressively become more and more ravenous and reckless. Man constantly wants more and more of everything, whereas the crying need is 'less and less'. It is not *over-population*—no one can tell what an optimum population is—but over-consumption, primarily in the affluent societies and sections, which is our principal problem. We have become the mythical 'hungry ghosts', except that we have a mouth like that of the Hindu demon *Kabandha*[93] who was headless, and had a large mouth on his ever empty belly. Man has consistently shown that when it comes to what he thinks he wants, he will stop at nothing, respect no limits, and will not care about the consequences to the planet or other species. Some fear that the quest for the 'novel and new' might drag in sex, too, which has up to now guided natural evolution. We already have sex-robots, and some even speculate that in the future one of the ways of dying will be to 'get killed by a sex-robot'.

If there is one issue on which we need to make a seminal shift, it is our almost blind belief in the brain; the belief that it is the answer to every problem, and that it is a launching pad for our future lift-off. The brain is a marvel, no doubt, but it is still a brain. To think that all we need to do to be a 'good' person is to stimulate a specific part of the brain periodically is too simplistic. For example, it is said that the part that produces love is also the part that causes addiction. The bottom line is that the brain cannot play any other role than what a brain is supposed to. Just as a hand is a hand, and can never be a leg. What is required, therefore, is a broadening of the very basic base of intelligence. Science is trying to do that through artificial intelligence and machine-merging. But in so doing, it is overlooking the alternative intelligence that nature itself has provided: *heart intelligence*. Until modern times, heart intelligence played a vital role as a foil as well as a complement to head-intelligence. Given its present state of somnolence, our urgent challenge is to awaken it as part of consciousness-change, the need of the hour. Philosopher Owen Barfield (*Saving the Appearances*) says that human consciousness is in the process of evolving from what he calls 'participatory consciousness' to 'final consciousness'. Only then, as the *Katha* Upanishad puts it, will we be able to see that the consciousness within us is the same consciousness within all living beings. Instead, what science is attempting to do is to employ technology to scan our consciousnesses into computers, and to live inside them as software, virtually and forever. The real problem we face is not so much that interfacing with the machine is necessarily all bad; it is about relying exclusively on the present paradigm of failed human intelligence. And there are those who fear that machines might well trivialize, even destroy us, obeying some ghastly iteration of their programming or malicious code inserted by one malicious human.

The crying need of the hour is a cathartic course-correction, and one that is not confined to our intelligence. At the most elemental level, we must shift our gaze inwards, and focus on the world 'within'. And focus on the *war* within, which scriptures like the Quran and saints like Saint Paul have spoken about. We now have an urgent duty cut out for ourselves: invade our own world within to initiate corrective action, which in turn will set right what ails the world outside. It is a daunting task. It might well be that even in the future, if the direction and dedication stay intact, we might find it easier to be a 'Moon-tourist' than an immigrant to the land within. The voyage within, it has long been said, is a most important and difficult journey. When the Buddha uttered his last words—*Appo Deepo Bhava*, 'be an island unto yourself'—he probably meant, 'be your own witness', and 'seek your own truth within your own self'. We do not realize but it is through different 'ordinary' settings that we construct who we are, and who we are not. We have to turn to what we routinely and reflexively do in the annals of everyday existence, in the spectrum of human life—our work, our play, our relationships, our every movement, our every breath—into spiritual tools capable of impacting on the war within. We must learn to look at the everyday narrative as the story of our life. If, in this way, we succeed in 'spiritualizing' our lives, we can decisively influence the war within, which, in turn, will enable us to ethically cleanse our daily doings. Cleansing is what we also need within our consciousness. We have been for centuries putting in so much muck and filth into every nook and crevice of our consciousness. It is now full to the brim. But we have no tools to do the job; we have no vacuum cleaners for use inside. The only way is to engage in spiritualizing our daily doings.

We must bear in mind that our sense organs act as a two-way street. In Hinduism, they represent the pleasure principle and are considered divinities or gods in the microcosm of the body. They connect the world within and the world outside. They act as exit points for the war within to impact on our behavior, and as entry points for us to send in supplies and reinforcements to the opposing forces within us. It is left to us to decide what we send and for whom, to the good side or the evil side. If we behave thinking of the other's needs more than our own wants, with what Buddhists call *maitri* or loving-kindness, and, in Einstein's words, by 'widening our circle of compassion to embrace all living creatures', the corresponding forces in the war will become stronger. Recent research is indicating that compassion is a key component of both quality of health and quality of life. It depends on each one of us, and on the way we act and react in the context of daily life. Numbers do matter. Fortunately, we do not need every human to come on board; the minimum 'critical mass' of like-minded individuals is sufficient to create an unstoppable momentum for the triumph of the good within, as well as in the world without. But there is no way to know the threshold number of people and actions below which we lose the war, and above which we can win. Prudence tells us that each of us must believe and behave as if he or she is that very threshold.

Strangely, there has never been an in-depth analysis of this war despite the fact that the very word 'war' transfixes our attention, and we mobilize all our resources more fully in this situation than in an other. War also allows us to let loose the worst in us and satisfy our darkest urges. It can be explained by the fact that although this 'war within' is the 'mother of all wars', it is invisible, and there is no apparent cost or casualty. And the weapons of the war are our own urges, drives, and raw passions. Anything that calls for determined and sustained effort is termed a 'war' primarily to motivate and mobilize the public. Then again, there is always in every society, a constituency for wars, which drags the rest along. There is no such advocacy group for this war within. This war wages without our consent, complicity or connivance, and that is why we pay no heed to it.

But if we stay still and remain unconcerned, and ignore this war, we will continue to lose all earthly wars on social ills and evil. Perhaps the most fateful war we are waging at the moment on earth, is the war against runaway climate change, caused primarily, if not wholly, by human activity on earth. There are clear signs that, despite global efforts to contain and curb greenhouse gases and global warming, mankind is losing this war too. But there is still hope, if we can make some sacrifices in the way we live, particularly in industrialized and affluent sections across the globe. But, instead of taking serious steps to reduce our emissions, we are contemplating more risky and potentially more damaging radical remedies. Such thinking is typical of our mindset. We want to pass the buck, separate us from the problem we face and make others responsible. And it brings to the fore one important message, which in fact is applicable to the other stubborn problem we face. It is another 'inadequacy': our abject inability to do what we know needs to be done for our own good, particularly if it calls for short-term sacrifice. It is a form of self-deception that lets us lead our smug, shallow, and self-destructive lives. The only way to resolve climate change is consciousness-change. Only such a change can make us look at this problem not merely as an economic or environmental issue, but as an essentially moral crisis. It might perhaps be the most challenging test that man has ever faced, a real test of our claim to be a moral and spiritual being, our claim that we are a 'higher animal'. It is a moral issue because the impacts of climate change are greatest on the poor and disadvantaged, who contribute relatively little to the problem. It is a moral issue because it involves inter-generational equity and justice. The decisions we are making now—whether proactively or by default—will very likely impose horrific consequences on future generations, on our own progeny, who of course have no say in those decisions.

Climate change brings to the fore a central fact of modern life; indeed human life. It is that our very existence, and the way we have organized our civilized life, makes it virtually impossible to lead a moral life. Indeed this is not new. Tolstoy wrote, "My very existence, entangled with that of the State and the social existence organized by the State, exacts from me an anti-Christian activity directly contrary to the commandments of Jesus" (*My Religion*). The dilemma is not only a Christian issue but generic and general. It is that not only our moral life is in crisis—but morality itself, its intent and content, philosophy and purpose. The context of human life has so radically metamorphosed, that old norms of what constitutes a moral life need also to be revisited. Man is at once a more selfish and social being. He is more self-centered in his desires, demands, dreams, and drives, and rage and resentment arise when we are socially obligated to be more prudent than just, more pleasing than honest, truer to others than to ourselves. And in this sense of frustration and resentment, all the countless miseries of man lie in germ. In a world fundamentally and irremediably bad, irrational, and meaningless, is morality another absurdity? Emerging advances in technology are raising new issues such as the moral status of an embryo, and when we should call a fetus one of us. Under what conditions would helping someone to die become an act of compassion or callousness? If a certain technology is inaccessible to a needy person for reasons of affordability, are we all morally culpable? Can we be factually and semantically correct and morally obsolete? The simple fact is that man cannot endure for long except as a moral being. Moral he must be, but that 'moral' must also be contextual, not counter-productive. Morality, like all else, must serve a purpose, and the purpose must be to make the human a humane and harmonious being, and the world an arena in which everyone lives in the spirit of synergy. Former US President Woodrow Wilson once said, "There is only one power to put behind the liberation of mankind, and that is the power of mankind". The fact is that human liberation can never be realized unless our consciousness is liberated from the grip of the human mind. In today's world, being a 'good' man in the traditional sense is not good enough to be a moral being. He or she must act in line with the Gandhian dictum, 'be the agent of change you want to see in the world'. Morals contained in religious commandments and conveyed through classical moral stories are grossly insufficient as guideposts to face the challenges that modern society churns and throws up. Fundamentally, the focus and emphasis must move from personal piety and probity to common good and social congruity. It is not that traditional virtues and values are now obsolete. They remain relevant but not sufficient, and where there is a clash, they must yield place to what society requires for fairness and stability. A similar, indeed even more urgent updating has become imperative about the rightful place and relevance of money in human life.

We live in a warped society in which those with money have relatively few unsatisfied wants, and those with many unsatisfied needs have no money.

Wordsworth characterized our relationship with money by the words, "getting and spending, we lay waste our powers" (*The World Is Too Much With Us*, 1807). The Bible warned us that we cannot worship God and Mammon at the same time. But we have pretty much managed to do the impossible: we have *merged* both 'worships'. In fact, we seek God's help more on Mammon-matters than anything else. Perhaps a great indictment of human ingenuity is that money is man-made, yet is so essential for human life. So many people need so little to, as it were, keep their body and soul together, but human ingenuity hasn't found a way to make it accessible and available where and to whom it is needed most. On the other hand, it has become a major source of tension, stress, anxiety, and friction, and a trigger for every kind of violence and homicide. It is now becoming increasingly clear that unless we are able to comprehensively alter the way money, both private and public, is spent, used, and dispensed, we cannot bring about the right contextual-change or significantly improve or better our social life, or abort a future financial meltdown. Every time we spend money, we must ask ourselves: what else can this do? How can we give value to the world and to the community? Legal money is not necessarily moral money. No amount of money, and no way of making it, is too small or sinful to share. Money is neither evil nor good; it depends on its flow. If we open ourselves up to a greater flow of abundance, we can then choose what we are directing it towards.

What needs to be done about the third 'M'—mortality—is different. We are so much in love with the perks and trappings of the 'good life' that we want this life-affair not to end even at death. And for that, man wants physical continuity and bodily permanence on earth. For that, some are prepared to be deep-frozen for two hundred years and pay close to a million dollars to have a surgeon sever their dead head and freeze it, in the hope that cutting-edge technologies will use their DNA to grow a new body so that they can have it reattached and carry on for another hundred years. Big money is flowing into the search for immortality; already many affluent societies spend almost 50% of their healthcare money "in the final six months of life, literally throwing money at death".[94] Yet there are many observers like James Watson,[95] who question whether more life is always better and if "the desire for immortality" (or at least life-extension) "would rectify the problems it was originally intended to solve".

And then, when does a life become *not* worth living and under what criteria? It is mortality—the visceral conviction that not only 'I' but everyone else will die one day—that has kept whatever semblance of peace and order we have had. We have long derived some consolation in the thought, in the words of Shakespeare's *Juliet*, that "If all else fail, myself have power to die". The philosopher Bernard Williams, in his essay, '*The Makropulos Case*', posited that "immortality, or a state without death would be meaningless… so, in a sense, death gives the meaning to life". The other risk of immortality, as Williams puts it, is the risk of eventually altogether having too much of ourselves. Mortality is also seen as the final level playing field and the ultimate justice. If that is disturbed, even the possibility of immortality or even radical life extension, could destabilize human society like nothing before. If life extension adopts the universal divide between haves and have-nots, it will probably further widen an already growing life span gap, with the poor dying earlier and the rich dying later, resulting in the creation of a minority of ultra-wealthy immortals. What, one wonders, will they be doing with their mountains of money in comparison to what today's *uber*-rich do—buy the bones of dead species like dinosaurs! We must remember that corporate money is coming in on the expectation that there is much more to rake in. And corporations are not going to stop at anything to get their pound of flesh. That certainly means riding roughshod over morality, and on far higher priorities like funding research on providing basic needs of those over a billion at the bottom of the heap. On the other hand, if these very resources are spent elsewhere, on creating the very conditions that have lengthened the life span in the developed world—sanitation, healthcare, education, nutrition, etc.—we could turn it to increase the global average of human life span. In other words, we can achieve the very spirit of 'immortality' in a better and shared way. Another major recent development is that the concept of the 'right to life' is now being stretched to include the 'right to die', thereby opening many thus-far-forbidden doors. In some countries, grounds such as 'unreasonable obstinacy' are becoming grounds for shutting off life support to critically, not terminally, ill patients. Earlier, the decision to end one's life was wholly personal. Now it is equally, if not more, social or even moral. It is raising new ethical issues like, 'Is saving a life worth it if life itself is not worth living?' 'What is worthiness?' Some are even asking that about the highest moral issue of our time: 'Do any of us have the right to live, after all that we have done to life on the planet?' Should we actively work towards creating a society like the one in the '*Planet of the Apes*'?

A grisly time might still come when 'do-gooders', if not Good Samaritans, may even invoke the moral 'right to kill', a kind of 'just killing', if you will, much like a 'just war', at the personal level to right a slight, to eliminate an irritant. We might well have the 21st-century's Rodion Raskolnikovs (of Dostoyevsky's classic *Crime and Punishment*). In that novel, the so-called anti-hero Raskolnikov kills an old pawnbroker and her innocent but inconveniently-in-the-way sister for her money, which he wants to put to good use. The idea is that exceptional people have the license to kill anyone who opposes their genius and vision that historical progress derives from violence, and great men of the past often got fame by being 'great destroyers'. Many see that the moral dilemma that Dostoyevsky envisioned over 150 years ago is now even more topical. In fact, philosophers like Jonathan Glover say that it has already become a 'background assumption' of modern life. After all, one could argue, is not 'assisted death' also a form of killing? All these might seem dystopian nightmares, snapshots of weak or warped minds, but they do reflect what many fear in their bones. Whether it is a dystopian or a utopian nightmare, or a dream, it all depends on the state of consciousness. And for consciousness-change we need contextual-change.

For contextual-change, we have to reflect and reconstruct the roles of the 'three Ms'—morality, money, and mortality—which obsess our mind and dominate our lives. The three are intimately intertwined. To put it very simply, while morality is very sensitive to money, and money at best is condescending to morality, the way we are dealing with mortality is raising serious moral issues, and money is coming to play a big part in when and how we die and what happens afterwards. Without a complete overhaul of the three Ms, the dynamics that propel the contemporary and emergent contexts of human life will not move in the right direction. And without that, there can be no consciousness-change, and our mischievous and malicious mind will continue to call the shots in the war within. We must clearly come to grips with the central truth that without venturing within and 'winning' the war therein, we cannot elevate our consciousness, and without that there can be no spiritual growth or humane human transformation. And if we fail, the divisive, detrimental, and destructive forces in the world will become stronger every passing day.

In short, either to get a hold on ourselves, or to surmount the forces of anarchy, darkness, and evil in the world, or to resolve any of our festering ills and problems, we must find a way to go within, intercede in the war, and help the forces of good, virtue, and righteousness. Indeed, how to engage and deal with evil, as John Steinbeck said, is the only story in life, in nature, and in literature, and the driving force behind God taking on human likeness. The riddle is this: with so much going in our favor, why are we so tormented? Homer says, "There is nothing alive more agonized than man, of all that breathe and crawl across the earth".[96] We have long struggled to make sense of the duality of relationship between good and evil. Most men will, at some time in their lives, succumb to their evil inclination. The Book of Ecclesiastes, said to have been written by King Solomon, clearly tells us, "Indeed, there is no one on earth who is righteous, no one who does what is right and never sins".[97] Some say that evil, like everything else, has no legs to stand on except as a part of divine design. Others posit that evil is nothing but the absence of good, or that it is independent. Scriptures say that a truly spiritually evolved person rises above both good and evil, and, in a nasty twist, psychotic killers are claiming the same state of mind. Some hold that good and evil are the two sides of the same coin. That may well be so, but it does seem that the evil side is more firmly embedded than the good side. Robert Wright elaborates: "Human beings are a species splendid in their array of moral equipment, tragic in their propensity to misuse it, and pathetic in their constitutional ignorance of the misuse" (*The Moral Animal,* 1994). It means that, as we all know well, it is easy to do bad, but difficult to do good. For Aleksandr Solzhenitsyn, "The line dividing good and evil cuts through the heart of every human being. And who is willing to destroy a piece of his own heart?" Kahlil Gibran said, "For what is evil but good tortured by its own hunger and thirst? Verily when good is hungry it seeks food even in dark caves, and when it thirsts it drinks even of dead waters". And, as a kind of a faint flicker to those of us who often fail to do good and feel awful about it, Gibran's *Prophet* reassures, "You are good in countless ways, and you are not evil when you are not good". So, if evil is but a 'hungry' good, and we are not evil if we are not good, then why all this angst and remorse about not being good? Then again, many scriptures and wise men have told us that good and evil actually need each other, but that they are constantly at war with each other. Echoing the scriptures like the Quran, the

Bible, and the Bhagavad Gita, Eric Burdon tells us, "Inside each of us, there is the seed of both good and evil. It's a constant struggle as to which one will win. And one cannot exist without the other". It really means that statements and questions like 'why we seem to be drawn to evil more than to goodness' can be answered only in the context of the war within. And it has also been emphasized, strange as it sounds, that we should not aim at eradicating evil or vanquishing it in the constant struggle. This is one war in which we must make sure the 'enemy' is not dead but stays barely alive for our own good. At the same time, we cannot simply stay on the sidelines because when we do nothing in the struggle between good and evil, it is wickedness that prevails most often. The soil within us seems suited to the seed of evil and wickedness.

Even God in the Bible "saw that the wickedness of man was great on the earth, and that every intent of the thoughts of his heart was only evil continually".[98] Although it is generally believed that good deeds bring good things, and bad deeds beget bad, some nihilists even say that good things come from bad things. But then, what is good for one can be bad for another; what is good for a lamb, escaping from the throat of a tiger, for instance, is bad for the bigger beast. And then, we do have what Nietzsche called the 'master and slave morality', and 'the higher man and the herd'. Therefore, there is neither good nor bad in absolute terms; it is all in the mind. What we are exhorted to do by the scriptures is to rise above this duality. But to be able to do that requires spiritual *sadhana* and a higher level of consciousness. Perhaps we can get some inspiration from the way God Himself—from whom both derive their legitimacy—copes with and handles evil? He treads a fine line, doing a kind of balancing act. He accepts evil in the world but vows to protect the righteous. But when evil becomes overpowering, He intervenes in favor of the virtuous. He slew many *rakshasas* not because they were powerful and denied and defied Him, but because they threatened and made life difficult for the virtuous who are also His devotees. To establish or restore dharma or righteousness does not mean that evil or wickedness cannot exist on earth; it means it cannot be allowed to overwhelm righteousness and goodness. It is essential to note that the ambit of dharma, like Brahman in the Upanishads, is beyond narrow or rigid codification, and it is central not only to Hinduism but also to Buddhism, Jainism, and Sikhism. A celebrated aphorism in Hindu scriptures says, "*Dharmo rakshati rakshitaha*"—dharma protects those who uphold dharma. What it implies is that to safeguard this balance and ensure a tilt in favor of dharma requires constant care and watchfulness. Watchfulness not in regard to what others may or may not do, but what we ourselves do in the casual course of everyday existence as we perform our chores and duties, interact with others, serve our family, our neighborhood, our society and country, and the world. If we act in accordance with dharma in daily life, then dharma will ensure that good will remain dominant over evil in the war within. Restoration of the dharmic balance is the spirit of the famous and solemn declaration of Lord Krishna in the Bhagavad Gita that He will incarnate from age to age on earth. And this is also, in spirit, the purpose of the Second Coming of Jesus Christ.

But then, why and when, and under what conditions, does evil become so overwhelming on earth that God has no choice but to descend? It is said in the Bible that God might have not destroyed Sodom and Gomorrah had there been even ten virtuous men on earth at that time. What could possibly have been the number of virtuous humans at this time of our age? The question is, what would have been the divine primary motive: saving the good humans or destroying the insidious evil? Or, establishing the 'right balance between good and evil on earth, the numbers known only to God? In fact, 'balance' is, in Hindu *dharma shastras*, a critical difference between what is good and what is evil or bad. Good is represented, among other things, by balance, and evil is represented by imbalance. At least we can feel a little lighter about one thing. After the destruction of Sodom and Gomorrah, God vowed, "I will never again curse the ground on account of man, for the intent of man's heart is evil from his youth; and I will never again destroy every living thing, as I have done".[99] That means that even if God does destroy much, if not all of, mankind, the earth and other 'living beings' would endure. That facile and false premise robs us of the guilt that on account of us the rest of life on earth will get destroyed. That is God's choice and Man's Fate. What we have to grapple with are the more proximate empirical matters. Why do so many good-intentioned men allow themselves to be so easily seduced by the lure of evil? When we want to be good, what comes in the way? From where does evil in the world derive its strength and support, so much that God has no choice except to descend on earth and take on the vain, venal, flawed, and frail form of a human being? Many have addressed similar questions: Why does God allow evil to exist, and why does a good and merciful

God stand by silently when good people suffer? Is he indifferent or incompetent, or is He Himself evil? Our mind equates evil with terrorism, mass murders, sadistic rapes, and so on. And we, with revulsion, separate ourselves from them. And yet, as RD Laing says, "We are all murderers and prostitutes—no matter to what culture, society, class, nation, we belong, no matter how normal, moral, or mature we take ourselves to be".[100] And there are subtler forms like oppression, discrimination, bigotry, exploitation… that cause suffering. Is it God who is responsible? Don't we pride ourselves about our free will and precious powers of choice-making? And when we say that the innocent suffer, what do we mean by innocence? According to what time-frame? Both perpetrators and sufferers are humans. And no one thinks of, or thanks, God for the good things, but makes Him accountable for the bad. Some may even ask, why must good be 'good', and bad, 'bad'? The advice and guidance of the scriptures and ancient wisdom has generally been to be good in thought, word, and deed. They have exhorted us to put the well-being of others ahead of our own, and to cultivate, nurture, and practice caring, kindness, compassion, and empathy in our interpersonal interfacing.

What is universal (happiness, misery), we try to individualize; and what is internal (peace, harmony), we externalize. All our life we seek perpetual pleasure. We equate peace with absence of war and conflict. That is 'passive peace'. Proactive peace is a state of harmony: harmony between people; harmony between humanity and nature; and harmony within ourselves. Above all, in every situation, we want to extract 'profit'. We even poison ourselves for profit. Xun Kuang (Xunzi), a Chinese Confucian philosopher, said that 'a person is born with a liking for profit'. That is because we instinctively want to profit from every situation and every person. As Steinbeck says in *The Grapes of Wrath*, "Children dying of pellagra must die because a profit cannot be taken from an orange. And coroners must fill in the certificate—died of malnutrition—because the food must rot, must be forced to rot". We view the 'other' person as completely separate and different from us, and that his 'profiting' can do no good to us. Our mind tells us, 'O fool! You are not a mahatma; you are a man. The other fellow's victory can only be at your expense; so, by hook or crook, cut him down!' It is for profit that transnational corporations flood the market with harmful or addictive products. They spend billions on advertising, pollute the natural environment with toxic waste, subvert the system and sabotage laws that protect workers and consumers. Corporations can do all that because deep inside we too are like them—we want to extract profit from life. We too, given a way, would exploit others, gain and take advantage, enrich ourselves, and demean others. Instead of fighting them we want to emulate them. Today the workplace is the most exploited place. In reality, as Elizabeth Anderson argues, the modern workplace is a coercive, authoritarian regime in which workers are unfree in the republican sense due to domination by their employers.[101] It is this that makes it so difficult to practice compassion—the ability to feel others' pain in our bones. Compassion for all living beings truly is the benchmark, the true test and touchstone of morality, the surest and infallible test of a really good man. Schopenhauer wrote, "Only insofar as an action has sprung from compassion does it have moral value; and every action resulting from any other motives has none" (*On the Basis of Morality*, 1840). Further, even though the sufferer is experienced as an external being, Schopenhauer said, "I nevertheless feel it with him, feel it as my own, and not within me, but in another person". The Dalai Lama said, "If you want others to be happy, practice compassion; if *you* want to be happy practice compassion". As long as any man anywhere is constitutionally capable of deriving pleasure from anyone else's pain, and of deriving happiness from the unhappiness of others, the human race cannot lay claim to be a moral species. We cannot claim that we are all connected, parts of the same Whole, and like a snake, shed the skin of guilt and shame for what another of our species does. What comes more naturally to many a modern man is indifference, which is not too far off from callousness, which is a mark of the darkest moral deficiency. Many of us might not actually share Thomas Hardy's opinion: "Know that thy sorrow is my ecstasy, that thy love's loss is my hate's profiting!" (*Hap*, 1898), but tears do not well up reflexively when we see another shriveled and sunken person. We shrug and say to ourselves, 'It is their own doing or divine remiss; a consequence of karma or a 'natural' balance in nature'. To be capable of feeling another person's pain 'within' us, to practice compassion as a tool of happiness, of ours and of others, requires the birth of a 'new man'. To cultivate the positive of compassion, we should first get rid of the negatives of indifference to others' misfortune, and intolerance of others' opinions and convictions. The root of the malaise is that we have not been able to integrate, imbibe, and internalize the fundamental principle of creation that nothing exists independently and unconditionally, that everything is conditioned on something else other than its own self, that everything is finite and incomplete, and susceptible to decline, decay, and death. Simone de Beauvoir put it well when she reminded us that 'one's life has value so long as one attributes value to the life of others' (*The Ethics of Ambiguity*, 1947). Often, the life of others we value in proportion to its value to ourselves. Life teaches us that death, extinction, and annihilation are as much ingrained in nature as in human life, and how a particular life comes to an end has very little to do with how that life is lived or indeed deserves.

It is the illusion of nothingness as completeness—the idea of autonomous entirety, that a life is worthy regardless of its impact on the world—that is the main impediment to attaining the yearning for universal harmony, peace, and happiness. As the Vedas proclaim, *Vasudaiva kutumbakam* (The whole earth is a family); *Om, shanti, shanti, shanti* (Peace, peace, peace); *Loka samastas sukhino bhavantu* (Let everyone everywhere be happy); and *Sarvejana sukhinobhavantu* (May all people live happily). Whether it is the life of a saint or a sinner, the life of the great or the garden-type, no life can be insulated, unlike the climate, from the rest. The only question is, do we all add to others' happiness or misery? An individual will always remain frail, flawed, imperfect, unfinished, and the only way to 'grow' is to seek completeness and wholeness through others' lives, through our effort. However much we 'augment' and 'upgrade' or 'enrich' ourselves and our sense organs, we cannot be foolproof or flawless, impregnable or immaculate. We will only cease to be 'human', and what happens thence is hard to tell. The problem with historic man is that instead of striving for perfection or completeness through seeking complementarities, what he has been doing is to be 'one-up' on another man, on nature and on God. As for 'another man', the very foundation of human culture is to view the approaching person with trepidation, as a stranger, a rival, as a competitor; as someone whose life, if pursued as he wishes, is bound to collide with and diminish our own life. The watchwords in interpersonal relationships are not trust or brotherhood, but exhortations such as 'be wary', 'be vigilant lest you are taken for a ride, or someone steals a march over you', or 'lest someone leaves you behind in the struggle to become successful'. As for nature, we still debate if, as Rose Sayer says in the classic movie *The African Queen* (1951), "Nature is what we were put on earth to rise above", or whether we should be respectful and reverential to nature, and behave as a part of it, not above it. As for God, we still wonder about His existence, nature, role, and relevance, and if there is—or ought to be—any strict 'division of labor' between Him and us. And if 'playing God' is an affront to Him or easing His work on earth. Instead of transforming his world within, man wants to transcend the inherent nature of reality: to become permanent when everything in nature is impermanent and transitory.

From Akrasia to Enkrateia

The way out, paradoxically, is the way in. Every other way we have tried, but have found ourselves stymied, stranded at the skin level. If the battlefields are two, within and without, we have to fight on both the fronts. On both fronts we have to starve the forces of evil by choking the lines of supplies. We cannot fix the world outside without fixing the world inside. If we allow evil to overwhelm the good inside our consciousness, how can the good overwhelm the bad outside? It is consciousness, and the war for its commanding heights, that we should focus upon. The scriptural paradigm is still relevant. Indeed even more, but it needs to be viewed and put into practice in the setting of the war within. We have to see that what our senses let in is input of the right kind. We have to build bridges between the social and the spiritual, and between peace, prosperity, and the planet. And what it needs is the minimum 'critical mass' of committed and connected like-minded people.

Albeit still sporadic and scant, hope now rests on two counts. One, there are, in the terrible times we inhabit, in the awful midst of disarray and desperation in the world—shootings, terror attacks, wars over race and religion, riots, and ethnic and civil unrest—signs of a subtle shift towards a resurrection of faith and spiritual awakening, of global citizenship, and cosmic consciousness with or without religious affiliation. Across the world, there is a growing, albeit still muted, recognition that we are responsible for each other and accountable to future generations. As the old Irish proverb says, 'It is in the shelter of each other that the people live'. The much-lamented 'unbelief' of the millennials of the world is itself a sign of subtle transformation, from believers to seekers, a class of people the world needs most. Second, we now have the technical means to connect, to synergize disparate and isolated efforts. The very technology that gave us the toxic triad of materialism, consumerism, and militarism, can now serve as the lift-off platform and to build the critical mass for consciousness-change and contextual-change. So dark are our days in these times that the words we hear or read about, or the stories we see on the screen, are about impending doom, about post-apocalypse survivors, and dystopia. But we are told that, in Biblical Greek, the word 'apocalypse' actually means 'an uncovering'. So, it is possible that the 'apocalypse' we fear is not the end of the world but, an uncovering of our consciousness. In fact, many are already behaving as if the end is around the corner. Yet it is possible that the doom, discord, and decadence we are experiencing could be the harbingers of 'the end of a new beginning' in human history.

Technology has the potential to turn us into a global tribe; it is up to us to choose between being a 'tranquil tribe' or a 'warring' tribe. In fact, some *New Age* gurus see wisdom in extolling the internet—which David Bowie called an alien life form—as an extension of the human mind and the harbinger of a collective consciousness, portending a great leap in human spiritual development. The hope is that it would foster, in the words of Deepak Chopra, "more collective creativity, collective problem solving, collective well-being and collective intention as to what we want". Not only that, it could also help us overcome a crippling handicap in our current and past attempts: the lack of a critical mass of committed people. Yet, there are others who see it differently. For PW Singer, "The Internet is the first thing that humanity has built that humanity doesn't understand, the largest experiment in anarchy that we have ever had" (*Cybersecurity and Cyberwar*, 2014). We must also bear in mind what Carl Jung reminded us: harmless creatures can coalesce into a mass, and could emerge as a Hannibal Lecter (*The Silence of the Lambs* movie, 1991). What the 'mass' earlier lacked, it has now: the technological means to mobilize. While many warn us about the negative aspects of social media, they could also serve as a force to transcend traditional boundaries such as ethnicity, race or nationality, and geography, and instill a planetary mindset. If the content of human life gets spiritualized in its right sense, then the 'supplies' that get in through our senses can dramatically strengthen the righteous side in the war within. Similarly, if we choose to tread the Upanishadic path of *sreyas* (good), and not of *preyas* (pleasant), then we will be able to resolve climate change. Essentially it is our desire to cling to what seems 'pleasant' that induces us to not just turn a blind eye to the mounting evidence, but also to still ask if global warming is real and if human actions have any bearing on climate change…

The right contextual-change will help trigger the right consciousness-change, and elevate human consciousness to a higher level and make a deeper difference. And, in the reverse direction, it will help mitigate and dilute our 'negatives' and help confront the vices of greed, vanity, and violence. We must however remember that we can only mitigate or contain them, not erase them. These 'negative' emotions possibly served a purpose in our earliest days, when we were fighting simply to survive. Technology has turned things 180 degrees. The hunted is now the hunter. The upshot is that these destructive traits are now a more dominant part of our consciousness, as the 'positives'—like love, kindness, altruism, and compassion—have taken a back seat. They are weaker because their role in our daily context of life, in the ordinary things we do ordinarily, have become weaker in comparison with the role of our 'shadow'. Whatever you want to achieve in life—to be a global citizen, a moral being, a spiritual person, or to resolve the climate chaos, or any other pressing problem, and more fundamentally 'to win' the war within—all that you need to do is to be *righteous* in whatever you do, with a helpful, not harmful, intent towards another 'person'. You need to constantly and consciously try to put someone else on par or above yourself in any reckoning. Concretely it means putting our sense organs—what we see, touch, hear, smell, and eat—to good use, consciously and deliberately. Science now says it can help. Researchers have found that a part of our brain called the right 'temporoparietal junction' is activated when we contemplate the perspective of someone else, even when it differs from our own. All this does not mean that the world will be crowded with awakened empaths, effective altruists, and self-sacrificing Good Samaritans—but it does mean that evil, whether it is a thing in its own right or absence of something else, banal or brazen, will not be able to look straight into our eye with a smug sneer; our behavior will be more benign, and our reflexive reactions less motivated by egotism, mendacity, and malice. We will be able to deal with the triad of our obsessions—morality, money, and mortality—bearing in mind the common good of the commonwealth of mankind. We must get a firm hold on these 'three Ms', and ensure that the way we think through and take relevant decisions are for the benefit of the masses, not just for the miniscule minority of the affluent and privileged. We need to put all three in their proper place. That will decisively change the context and content of human life, which, in turn, will trigger the consciousness-change. That will reverse the waning fortunes of the forces of righteousness in the 'war within'. And that is the only way we can avert or abort the looming existential threats such as climate change, rogue artificial intelligence, nanotechnology, and suicidal man–machine-merger.

To avert what David Wallace-Wells[102] calls 'climate genocide' we need consciousness-change, and for that we need to 'win' the war within. Much of what causes us so much distress and dismay, anguish and angst, springs from the fact that we are obsessed with the wrong wars and are even unaware of the only war that counts. What is heartening is that we don't need the entire mass of mankind; a 'critical mass' of global citizens that could trigger a chain reaction would as well do. We must remember that the right way to 'win' this war is to see that both opponents win. It is not conquest; it is ensuring that the 'good wolf' consistently keeps an upper hand. If we 'win' this war this way there will be no more wars like the ones we now wage. And that means being able to view life *not* as a zero-sum game or a game of cat and mouse or a ruthless rat race. Waging and 'winning' this war is the antidote to what Philip Zimbardo called the Lucifer Effect, the tipping point in time when an ordinary, normal person first crosses the boundary between good and evil to engage in an evil action. It is this war—the way it is waged, how we feed the opposing forces, and its outcome—that will determine the balance between dharma and adharma in the world. And if we so conduct ourselves so as to sustain and strengthen dharma, then we will be doing His will on earth. And 'winning' this war could not only let us get off, in Bill McKibben's words, the "long escalator down to Hell", but also abort what is being called the ongoing 'sixth human-caused mass extinction of life on earth'. 'Winning' this war will, at last, save us from ruminating in desperation and despair, the twin questions with which we began the 'beginning' of this book: *Why can't I be good? Why do I do bad?* And then our proclivity to *akrasia* (lack of self-control or the state of acting against one's better judgment) will yield to cultivating *enkrateia* (self-control, control over one's own passions and instincts, and self-mastery). When that moment comes, the human world will come close to what Hindu scriptures so eloquently proclaim: *Vasudaiva kutumbakam*—the whole earth is one family.

References and Notes

The Beginning

1. "I do not understand my own actions because I do not do what I want to. But I do the very thing that I hate. … I can will what is right but I cannot do it. For I do not do the good that I want, but the evil I do not want is what I do." [Romans 7:15]. "Why is a person impelled to commit sinful acts, even unwillingly, as if by force, O descendent of Vrishni?" [Chapter 3, verse 36].

2. "It is not *we* who sin, but some other nature that sins within us… My sin was all the more incurable because I did not think myself a sinner." Confessions, Book V, Section 10.

3. "On bended knees I beg: when men can get all they want, the four *purusharthas*—*dharma*, wealth, pleasure, liberation—by following the path of *dharma*, why do men indulge in *adharma*? Source: *Immortal Words: an Anthology*. 1963. Bharatiya Vidya Bhavan. Bombay, India.

4. *Dharma* is a key concept in Hinduism. This Sanskrit word has multiple meanings, and there is no single-word translation for it in Western languages. Dharma signifies one's comportment in life in accordance with the Order that makes life and universe possible, and includes duties, rights, laws, conduct, virtues, the 'right way of living'. In Jainism, dharma is the body of doctrine pertaining to the purification and moral transformation of human beings. In Sikhism, it means the path of righteousness and proper religious practice. (Source: Wikipedia). What is not dharma is 'adharma'.

5. Source: Pandava Gita, 57:58.

6. 20th century American cartoonist and caricaturist.

7. Storr, A. 1999. The Essential Jung: Selected Writings. Introduced by Anthony Storr. New York, USA: Princeton University Press.

8. Cited in: Serpell, N. 2019. The Banality of Empathy. *The New York Review of Books*. USA. NYR Daily. 02 Mar 2019.

9. Wood, H. 1923. Studies in the Thought World, or Practical Mind Art.

10. Source: Lerner, M. (ed.). 2007. Tikkun Reader: Twentieth Anniversary. New York, USA: Rowman and Littlefield. p.282.

11. JK Rowling's Harvard Commencement address: *The Fringe Benefits of Failure, and the Importance of Imagination*. 5 Jun 2008, Harvard University, USA.

12. Kimbrell, A. 2000. Cold Evil: Technology and Modern Ethics. Annual E.F. Schumacher Lecture. Schumacher Center for a New Economics. Lecture delivered on 28 Oct 2000.
13. Kimbrell, A. 2000. Cold Evil: Technology and Modern Ethics. Annual E.F. Schumacher Lecture. Schumacher Center for a New Economics. Lecture delivered on 28 Oct 2000.
14. Hensell, K. 2009. The Shifting Concept of Good and Evil in Paradise Lost." Edifice Project. The University of Alabama, USA. Retrieved from <http://edificeproject.ua.edu/wp-content/uploads/2009/05/shifting-concept-of-good-and-evil.pdf>.
15. Challa, B. 2011. Man's Fate and God's Choice—An Agenda for Human Transformation. New Delhi, India: Kalpaz. p.3.
16. Plato. *The Theaetetus*. Becoming Like God.
17. Levy, D. 2007. Love and Sex with Robots: The Evolution of Human-Robot Relationships. New York, USA. Harper Perennial.
18. Source: Szczepanski, K. 2018.The Invention of Gunpowder: A History. ThoughtCo. 23 Apr 2018. Retrieved from <https://www.thoughtco.com/invention-of-gunpowder-195160>.
19. Wood, H. 1923. Studies in the Thought World, or Practical Mind Art.
20. Wood, H. 1923. Studies in the Thought World, or Practical Mind Art.
21. The 'Cloud' is a general metaphor that is used to refer to the Internet. The term typically denotes a vast global network of remote servers, each with a unique function, which are hooked together and meant to operate as a single ecosystem. The Cloud is not a physical entity. The remote servers of the Cloud are designed to either store and manage data, run applications or deliver content or services such as videos, web mail, software or social media.
22. Buss, D.M. 2005. The Murderer Next Door: Why the Mind is Designed to Kill. New York, USA: The Penguin Press.
23. Proverbs 18:21.
24. Adolf Eichmann, one of the major organizers of the Holocaust.
25. Oskar Schindler, German industrialist and a member of the Nazi Party who is credited with saving the lives of 1,200 Jews during the Holocaust.
26. Nathuram Godse, the man who assassinated Mahatma Gandhi.
27. Lanier, J. 2010. You Are Not a Gadget. New York, USA: Alfred Knopf.

28. Cameron, CD. 2017. Compassion collapse: Why We Are Numb to Numbers. *In*: Oxford Library of Psychology. The Oxford Handbook of Compassion Science (Seppala, EM, Simon-Thomas, E., Brown, SL, Worline, MC, Cameron, CD., and Doty, JR., eds.). New York, USA: Oxford University Press. pp.261–271.

29. Zimbardo, P. 2007. The Lucifer Effect: Understanding How Good People Turn Evil. New York, USA: Random House.

30. Fields, R.D. 2016. Humans Are Genetically Predisposed to Kill Each Other. Psychology Today. 02 Oct 2016. Retrieved from <https://www.psychologytoday.com/us/blog/the-new-brain/201610/humans-are-genetically-predisposed-kill-each-other>.

31. Zimbardo, P. 2007. The Lucifer Effect: Understanding How Good People Turn Evil. New York, USA: Random House

32. Kimbrell, A. 2000. Cold Evil: Technology and Modern Ethics. Annual E.F. Schumacher Lecture. Schumacher Center for a New Economics. Lecture delivered on 28 Oct 2000.

33. DeSteno, D. and Valdesolo, P. 2011. Out of Character: Surprising Truths About the Liar, Cheat, Sinner (and Saint) Lurking in All of Us. New York, USA: Crown.

34. Micu, A. 2018. The Faults in Our Personalities Are All Expressions of Our 'Dark Core'. *ZME Science Newsletter*. 28 Sept 2018. Retrieved from <https://www.zmescience.com/science/dark-personality-traits-core-825236432/>.

35. Whatever is done for love always occurs beyond god and evil.

36. Ligotti, T. 2011. The Conspiracy Against the Human Race: A Contrivance of Horror. New York, USA: Hippocampus Press.

37. Galatians 5:17.

38. Pontoppidan, H. 1905. Lucky Per. Chapter 25.

39. Laing, RD. 1964. Transcendental Experience in Relation to Religion and Psychosis. *The Psychedelic Review*.

40. Revelation 12:7–10.

41. Ephesians 6:14.

42. Srimad Bhagavatam. Canto 12, Chapter 3, Verse 25.

43. Srimad Bhagavatam. Canto 12, Chapter 2, Verses 2 and 4.

44. Source: Kirke, M. 2019. 'Rise and Grind': On the Pathology of Work. Mercatornet. 02 Feb 2019. Retrieved from <https://www.mercatornet.com/features/view/rise-and-grind-on-the-pathology-of-work/22141>.
45. Wong, D. 2018. How Mediocrity Can Quietly Destroy Us All. Blogpost in Cracked on 21 Feb 2018. Retrieved from <https://www.cracked.com/blog/how-mediocrity-can-quietly-destroy-us-all/>.
46. Hebrews 12:22–24.
47. *Manichaeism*. Wikipedia: The Free Encyclopedia. Wikimedia Foundation. Retrieved 23 Dec 2017.
48. Eliot, G. 1871. Middlemarch: A Study of Provincial Life. London, UK: William Blackwood.
49. Bhagavad Gita. Chapter 5, Verse 22.
50. Bentham, J. 1789. An Introduction to the Principles of Morals and Legislation.
51. Freud, S. 1930. Civilization and Its Discontents.
52. Adam Curtis. 2002. *The Century of the Self*. BBC Two documentary series.
53. Luke 13:32.
54. Lyrics from the 2018 song *Honey* by Swedish singer Robyn.
55. Source: Kaneda, T. and Haub, C. 2018. How Many People Have Ever Lived on Earth? Population Reference Bureau (PRB), Washington, DC, USA. Retrieved from < https://www.prb.org/howmanypeoplehaveeverlivedonearth/>.
56. Buss, D.M. 2005. The Murderer Next Door: Why the Mind is Designed to Kill. New York, USA: The Penguin Press.
57. An American military science fiction television series, and part of the *Battlestar Galactica* franchise. (This series was a re-imagining of the 1978 *Battlestar Galactica* television series).
58. *Cylon* (*Battlestar Galactica*). Wikipedia: The Free Encyclopedia. Wikimedia Foundation.
59. Title of the 2011 book by the renowned horror writer, Thomas Ligotti. *The Conspiracy Against the Human Race: A Contrivance of Horror*. Hippocampus Press.
60. O'Leary, D.B. 2007. Escaping the Progress Trap. Quebec, Canada: Geozone Communications.
61. The Papal Encyclical *Evangelium vitae* (The Gospel of Life), promulgated on 25 Mar 1995 by Pope John Paul II.

62. Talbott, S.L. 1995. The Future Does Not Compute: Transcending the Machines in Our Midst. Chapter 25. New York, USA: O'Reilly & Associates.

63. Laing, R.D. 1967. The Politics of Experience and The Bird of Paradise. London, UK: Routledge & Kegan Paul. Chapter I. Persons and Experience.

64. Talbott, S.L. 1995. The Future Does Not Compute: Transcending the Machines in Our Midst. New York, USA: O'Reilly & Associates.

65. Cole, T. 2016. Known and Strange Things: Essays. New York, USA: Random House.

66. Charlie Brooker is the creator of the British science fiction anthology television series, *Black Mirror*, which examines modern society, particularly with regard to the unanticipated consequences of new technologies.

67. Source: Hamer, A. 2017. Curiosity: When Your Beliefs Change, You Probably Don't Realize It. Curiosity: Mind and Body. 08 Dec 2017. Retrieved from <https://curiosity.com/topics/when-your-beliefs-change-you-probably-dont-realize-it-curiosity/>.

68. Russell, B. 1928. Science. In: Whither Mankind: A Panorama of Modern Civilization (Beard, C.A., ed.). London, UK: Longmans, Green & Co.

69. Source: Solly, M. 2018. Earth Lost 2.5 Billion Years' Worth of Evolutionary History in Just 130,000 Years. The Smithsonian SmartNews. 16 Oct 2018. Retrieved from <https://www.smithsonianmag.com/smart-news/earth-lost-25-billion-years-worth-evolutionary-history-just-130000-years-180970558/>.

70. Monosson, E. 2014. Unnatural Selection: How We Are Changing Life, Gene by Gene. Washington, DC, USA: Island Press.

71. Source: *Aurora Leigh*, a poem by Elizabeth Barrett Browning.

72. Morris, W. 1858. The Defence of Guenevere.

73. Source: Anderson, J. 2019. Beyond Mindfulness: The Only Metric of Success That Really Matters Is the One We Ignore. Quartz. 12 Mar 2019. Accessed at <https://qz.com/1570179/how-to-make-friends-build-a-community-and-create-the-life-you-want/>.

74. Ellul, J. 1980. The Technological System. [Translated from the French, *La technique ou l'enjeu du siècle*]. Oregon, USA: Wipf & Stock.

75. Alex Zhavoronkov is Director of the International Aging Research Portfolio, and Director of the Biogerontology Research Foundation, UK.

76. Kurzweil, R. 2005. The Singularity Is Near: When Humans Transcend Biology. New York, USA: Viking.

77. Greenfield, S. 2009. Tomorrow's People: How 21st-Century Technology Is Changing the Way We Think and Feel. London, UK: Penguin.

78. The HeartMath Institute, 14700 West Park Avenue, Boulder Creek, California 95006, USA.

79. Comment (2015) attributed to Ray Kurzweil, director of engineering at Google.

80. Subject of a new book in Korean—*Alien Visitations and the End of Humanity*—by Dr. Young-hae Chi, instructor in Korean at Oxford University's Oriental Institute.

81. Source: BigThink: The Science of Why We Can't Live Forever. Retrieved from <https://bigthink.com/videos/why-we-die-2636378903>.

82. Psalm 90:12.

83. Kundera, M. 1999. Immortality. [Translated from Czech *Nesmrtelnost* by Peter Kussi]. New York, USA: Harper Perennial Modern Classics.

84. Quote attributed to Rudyard Kipling.

85. Source: Mars One Mission: Five Britons Shortlisted for One-way Trip to Red Planet. *The Telegraph*, UK. Tuesday, 28 May 2019.

86. Romans 5:12.

87. Rabindranath Tagore. 1915. Essays. Sadhana: The Relation of the Individual to the Universe.

88. Zaki, J. 2019. The War for Kindness: Building Empathy in a Fractured World. London, UK: RandomHouse.

89. Romans 9:3.

90. Miller, G.A. 1962. Psychology: the Science of Mental Life. New York, USA: Harper & Row.

91. Kniss, M. 2013. The Heart of Consciousness: a Brief Introduction to Heart Intelligence. USA: Primal Force Media.

92. Kniss, M. 2013. The Heart of Consciousness: a Brief Introduction to Heart Intelligence. USA: Primal Force Media.

93. Weber, M. 1905. The Protestant Ethic and the Spirit of Capitalism. [*Die protestantische Ethik und der Geist des Kapitalismus*].

94. *Man a Machine* (*L'homme machine* in French) is a work of materialist philosophy by the 18th-century French physician and philosopher Julien Offray de La Mettrie, first published in 1747. Wikipedia: The Free Encyclopedia. Wikimedia Foundation.

95. Kirkpatrick Sale, author of *Rebels Against the Future: The Luddites and Their War on the Industrial Revolution: Lessons For The Computer Age*. (Perseus, 1995).

96. Wilde, O. 1891. The Fisherman and His Soul.

Chapter 1: Musings on Mankind

1. Bowles, N. 2018. A Dark Consensus About Screens and Kids Begins to Emerge in Silicon Valley. *The New York Times*, 28 October 2018.

2. Cited in: World Tranformation Movement. 2018. About the Transformed State. Retrieved from <https://www.humancondition.com/wtm-faq-how-can-everyones-lives-be-transformed/#global_print>.

3. Twain, M. 1896. The Lowest Animal.

4. *Purnam adah, purnam idam purnat purnam udachyate; purnasya purnam adaya purnam evavasisyate*: 'That is the absolute, this is the absolute; from the absolute, the absolute becomes manifest; when the absolute is added to or taken away from the absolute, the absolute remains. Om. Peace! Peace! Peace!'

5. Tegmark, M. 2017. Life 3.0: Being Human in the Age of Artificial Intelligence. Borzoi/Alfred Knopf. New York, USA.

6. Bergan, B. "Holy Grail" Microchip Might Surpass the Power of the Human Brain. Futurism.com. 27 Sept 2017. Retrieved from <https://futurism.com/holy-grail-microchip-might-surpass-the-power-of-the-human-brain/>.

7. Source: Pearce, D. 1995. The Hedonistic Imperative. <https://www.hedweb.com/hedethic/hedonist.htm>.

8. Ratner, P. 2017. This New Religion From a Silicon Valley Pioneer Worships AI as an Emerging Godhead. BigThink.com. 5 Nov 2017. <https://bigthink.com/paul-ratner/this-new-religion-from-a-silicon-valley-pioneer-worships-ai-as-an-emerging-godhead>.

9. "We can't solve problems by using the same kind of thinking we used when we created them" — Albert Einstein.

10. Already, we have artificial intelligence (AI) systems capable of creating other AI systems, ones that can communicate in their own languages, and ones that are naturally curious.

11. Stone, G. 2009. Fertility Doctor Will Let Parents Build Their Own Baby. ABC News, 3 Mar 2009. Retrieved from <http://abcnews.go.com/Health/story?id=6998135&page=1>.

12. Christian, B. 2011. Mind vs. Machine. *The Atlantic Magazine*. March 2011. Retrieved from <https://www.theatlantic.com/magazine/archive/2011/03/mind-vs-machine/308386/>. Brian Christian is the author of *The Most Human Human: What Artificial Intelligence Teaches Us About Being Alive*.

13. Sacred space. *Times of India*, Hyderabad, India. 18 Dec 2012. p.10.

14. Tenner, E. 1996. Why Things Bite Back: Technology and the Revenge of Unintended Consequences. New York, USA: Random House.

15. Cited in: Herper, M. 2013. No, This Is Not How the Human Face Might Look in 100,000 Years. Forbes: Pharma & Healthcare. 7 Jun 2013. Retrieved from < https://www.forbes.com/sites/matthewherper/2013/06/07/no-this-is-not-how-the-human-face-might-look-in-100000-years/#6daa1a02c78a>.

16. Cross, G.S. and Proctor, R.N. 2014. Packaged Pleasures: How Technology and Marketing Revolutionized Desire. Chicago, USA: The University of Chicago Press.

17. Shermer, M. 2015. The Moral Arc. USA: Henry Holt & Co. p.124.

18. Hurley, D. 2014. Smarter: the New Science of Building Brainpower. New York, USA: Viking Press. p. xvi.

19. Underlying ability to learn, the capacity to solve novel problems, and figure out things that were never explicitly taught [Hurley, D. 2014. Smarter: the New Science of Building Brainpower. New York, USA: Viking Press. p. xvi.].

20. Sharma, R. 2013. The Monk Who Sold His Ferrari. New Delhi, India: Jaico Books. p.69.

21. Hurley, D. 2014. Smarter: the New Science of Building Brainpower. New York, USA: Viking Press. p.113.

22. Youn, A. 2015. 6 Extreme Body Enhancements to Expect in the Next 10 Years. *The Huffington Post*. 25 August 2015.

23. In the Indian epic *Ramayana*, Lord Rama's younger brother Lakshmana draws the '*Lakshmana rekha*' outside their hut in the forest. Lakshmana asks Rama's wife

Sita not to cross this line for the sake of her own safety. However, the demon king Ravana, disguised as a mendicant, successfully induces Sita to cross this line, which allows him to abduct her. Such a version is not found in the original *Valmiki Ramayana*, but has gained popular currency far beyond the epic, as an idiom to symbolize a forbidden act, or a strict convention or rule, breaking which invites disastrous consequences.

24. Pietzker, M.A. 1872. Miscellaneous Poems. London, UK: Griffith and Farran.

25. Alexander, E. 2012. Proof of Heaven: A Neurosurgeon's Journey Into the Afterlife. New York, USA: Simon & Schuster. Prologue.

26. Srinivasan, B. 2013. Software is Reorganizing the World. *Wired*. Retrieved from: <http://www. wired. com/2013/11/software-is-reorganizing-the-world-and-cloud-formations-could-lead-to-physical-nations/>.

27. Srinivasan, B. 2013. Software is Reorganizing the World. *Wired*. Retrieved from: <http://www. wired. com/2013/11/software-is-reorganizing-the-world-and-cloud-formations-could-lead-to-physical-nations/>.

28. Srinivasan, B. 2013. Software is Reorganizing the World. *Wired*. Retrieved from: <http://www. wired. com/2013/11/software-is-reorganizing-the-world-and-cloud-formations-could-lead-to-physical-nations/>.

29. A pure, virtuous person.

30. Ram, U. and Ram, K.S. 2015. Identity: I Am Not Nothing, I Am No-thing! Speaking Tree. *Times of India*. Hyderabad, India. 22 October 2015. p.14.

31. Jeans, J. 1930. The Mysterious Universe.

32. Monod, J. 1971. Chance and Necessity. New York, USA: Vintage.

33. Tegmark, M. 2007. We're Not Insignificant After All. In: What Are You Optimistic About? (John Brockman, ed.). London, UK: Pocket Books; UK. p.74.

34. Homer. *The Iliad*. Book 21. Lines 460–465.

35. Kahane, G. 2013. Our Cosmic Insignificance. Wiley Periodicals. Retrieved from <http://onlinelibrary.wiley.com/doi/10.1111/nous.12030/pdf>.

36. Norberg-Hodge, H. 2000. Economics, Engagement, and Exploitation in Ladakh. Tricycle. Winter 2000. Retrieved from <http://www.tricycle.com/node/31766>.

37. Source: Created: a second skin to make wrinkles passé. *The Times of India*. Hyderabad, India. 11 May 2016. p.21.

38. Richard Maurice Bucke, author of *Cosmic Consciousness: A Study in the Evolution of the Human Mind*. Originally published in 1901.

39. The Divine Life Society. 2011. Cosmic Consciousness. Retrieved 23 May 2014, from < http://sivanandaonline.org/public_html/?cmd=displaysection&section_id=1727>.

40. Source: Petranker, J. 2000. The Present Moment. Tricycle. Winter 2000. Retrieved from < https://tricycle.org/magazine/present-moment/>.

41. The Economist. 2011. Welcome to the Anthropocene. *The Economist*. UK. 28 May 2011.

42. The Economist. 2011. Welcome to the Anthropocene. *The Economist*. UK. 28 May 2011.

43. Lynas, M. 2011. The God Species: Saving the Planet in the Age of Humans. Washington, DC, USA: National Geographic. p.5.

44. Luna, A. 2016. The Mystical Bond Between Man and Ocean is Being Destroyed. Here's How to Save It. Retrieved from < https://lonerwolf.com/man-and-ocean/>.

45. Young, G.M. 2012. Do You Want to Be Immortal? Really? The Huffington Post. Retrieved 03 Apr 2015, from <https://www.huffingtonpost.com/george-m-young/do-you-want-to-be-immortal_b_1731203.html>.

46. Lyrics from the 2010 song *Modern Man*, by the Canadian indie rock band *Arcade Fire* (*The Suburbs* album).

47. de Beauvoir, S. 1947. The Ethics of Ambiguity.

48. Cited in: Frankl, V.E. 1988. The Will to Meaning: Foundations and Applications of Logotherapy. New York, USA: Meridian. p.53.

49. Proverbs 1:10–19.

50. American actress Ms. Megan Fox, quoted in *Hyderabad Times*, India. 17 March 2012.

51. Quoted in the BBC documentary, *The Beyond Within: The Rise and Fall of LSD*. 1987.

52. *Suicide*. Wikipedia: The Free Encyclopedia. Wikimedia Foundation. Retrieved 12 Mar 2010.

53. Tavernise, S. 2016. U.S. Suicide Rate Surges to a 30-Year High. *The New York Times*. USA. 22 April 2016.

54. Thomas Merton: '*What can we gain by sailing to the moon if we are not able to cross the abyss that separates us from ourselves?*' [Author of *The Seven Storey Mountain* (1948); and, *No Man Is An Island* (1955)].

55. Matthew 5:43–44.

56. Okawa, R. 2011. The Rebirth of Buddha. New Delhi, India: Jaico. First Jaico Impression. p.49.

57. Job 14:1.

58. Friedman, R. 2014. The Best Place to Work: the Art and Science of Creating an Extraordinary Workplace. New York, USA: Perigee.

59. Wizard, M. 2011. The City of Brahman. Retrieved from <https://www.opednews.com/Diary/The-City-of-Brahman-by-M-Wizard-110505-703.html?f=The-City-of-Brahman-by-M-Wizard-110505-703.html>.

60. Easwaran, E. 1987. The Upanishads. Introduced and translated by Eknath Easwaran. California, USA: Nilgiri Press.

61. Osborne, A. (ed.). 1962. The Teachings of Ramana Maharshi. London, UK: Century Hutchinson. [Revised edition, 2014, Rider Books, London, UK. p.56].

62. *Human Mission to Mars*. Wikipedia: The Free Encyclopedia. Wikimedia Foundation. Retrieved 30 June 2014.

63. Verne, J. 1865. From the Earth to the Moon.

64. Lewis, C.S. 1943. The Abolition of Man.

65. De Jesus. 2016. Russia Claims It's Building a Nuclear Space Bomber Capable of Striking Any Country in the World. Futurism. Retrieved from <http://futurism.com/russia-claims-its-building-a-nuclear-space-bomber/>.

66. Source: *Space Colonization*. Wikipedia: The Free Encyclopedia. Wikimedia Foundation. Retrieved 26 Jan 2015. [In 2006, Stephen Hawking stated that humanity faces two options: either we colonize space within the next two hundred years and build residential units on other planets, or we will face the prospect of long-term extinction].

67. A quote of Marianne Williamson, an American spiritual teacher and author. (*A Return to Love*, 1992).

68. The words, '*Here lies one whose name was writ in water*' were chosen by the poet John Keats to be inscribed on his tombstone.

69. Ezra Bayda, author of *Beyond Happiness: the Zen Way to True Contentment* (2011).

70. Jung, C. 1962. Memories, Dreams, Reflections. Retrieved from <https://archive.org/stream/MemoriesDreamsReflectionsCarlJung/Carl%20Jung%20Quotations%20sourced%20final_djvu.txt>.

71. Retrieved from <http://www.leonardcohenforum.com/viewtopic.php?t=26378>.

72. Einstein, A. 1931. Living Philosophies. New York, USA: Simon & Schuster.

73. Osborne, A. (ed.). 1962. The Teachings of Ramana Maharshi. London, UK: Century Hutchinson. [Revised edition, 2014, Rider Books, London, UK]. p.9,10.

74. Osborne, A. (ed.). 1962. The Teachings of Ramana Maharshi. London, UK: Century Hutchinson. [Revised edition, 2014, Rider Books, London, UK.]

75. The Mahabharata. Chapters 33 through 40 of the *Udyoga Parva*.

76. Pope Francis. 2015. Encyclical Letter *Laudato Si': On Care for our Common Home*. The Vatican, Rome, Italy.

77. Clark, A. 2003. Natural-Born Cyborgs: Minds, Technologies, and the Future of Human Intelligence. New York, USA: Oxford University Press.

78. Cited in: Brockman, J. 2000. Natural Born Cyborgs? Edge.org. Retrieved from <https://www.edge.org/conversation/natural-born-cyborgs>.

79. Bromwich, D. 2015. Trapped in the Virtual Classroom; *The New York Review of Books*. USA. 9 July 2015. p.14.

80. Heidegger, M. 1954. The Question Concerning Technology.

81. Becker, E. 1973. The Denial of Death. New York, USA: Simon & Schuster.

82. *Head Transplant*. Wikipedia: The Free Encyclopedia. Wikimedia Foundation. Retrieved 17 Nov 2017.

83. 'Rosie' the maid is a humanoid robot, a fictional character in *The Jetsons* animated television series of the 1960s.

84. Robot 'Mother' Builds Babies That Can Evolve. *The Times of India*. Hyderabad, India. 17 Aug 2015. p.11.

85. Bernal, J.D. 1929. The World, the Flesh & the Devil: An Enquiry Into the Future of the Three Enemies of the Rational Soul.

86. Hoffman, D. 2007. Solving the Mind-Body Problem. In: What Are You Optimistic About? (Brockman, J., ed.). London, UK: Pocket Books. p.280.

87. Reedy, C. 2017. A New Brain-Interface Device Lets You Control Animals With Your Thoughts: We're One Step Closer to a Real-Life "Avatar". Futurism. 28 Mar 2017. Retrieved from <https://futurism.com/a-new-brain-interface-device-lets-you-control-animals-with-your-thoughts/>.

88. Source: Interview with Arne Naess. Part 8 – Gandhi. Tvergastein, Norway, June 1995. Retrieved from <http://www.natureartеducation. org/R/Interviews/Naess8. htm>.

89. Comment attributed to the business magnate Masayoshi Son, founder and current chief executive officer of SoftBank.

90. Source: 'In ten years, every home will likely own a drone'. Prediction by Parimal Kopadekar, NASA scientist. *The Times of India*. Hyderabad, India. 4 Aug 2015. p.11.

91. Source: Robert B. Silvers Annual Lecture, delivered by Joyce Carol Oates at the New York Public Library on 12 Dec 2014.

92. Santos, M. 2016. Chinese Scientists Say They Have the Ability to Clone Humans. Futurism. 9 Mar 2016. Retrieved from <http://futurism.com/human-cloning-in-sight-says-chinese-scientists/>.

93. Klam, M. 2017. Who is Rich?: A Novel. New York, USA: Random House.

94. Source: Thirteen Advanced Humanoid Robots for Sale Today. Smashing Robotics. 16 Apr 2016. Retrieved from <http://www. smashingrobotics. com/thirteen-advanced-humanoid-robots-for-sale-today/>.

95. Technological singularity: a time when the accelerating pace of smarter and smarter machines will soon outrun all human capabilities, which some say will be 2045 and others say is still long way away.

96. Source: Einstein on God. Retrieved from <http://www. 2think.org/einstein.shtml>, on 22 May 2015.

97. Source: Will Durant: We Need More Insight Than Cold Logic. *The Times of India*. Hyderabad, India. 23 Apr 2015. p.14.

98. Panikkar, R. 2010. The Rhythm of Being.

99. O'Donnell, J. 2006. Augustine: A New Biography. New York, USA: Harper Perennial.

100. Lecky, W.E.H. 1878. History of European Morals: From Augustus to Charlemagne. Volume 1. p.103.

101. Torwesten, H. 1985. Vedanta: Heart of Hinduism. New York, USA: Grove Weidenfield. p.121.

102. Besant, A. The Bhagavad- Gita. 7.27. Chennai, India: Theosophical Publishing House. p.114.

103. Quote by C. JoyBell C.

104. Ahuja, A. 2015. When a Moral Machine is Better Than a Flawed Human Being. *The Financial Times*. 13 Jan 2015. Retrieved from <https://www.ft.com/content/53e4d546-9a76-11e4-8426-00144feabdc0>.

105. Powell, C.S. 2007. Corrective Goggles for Our Conceptual Myopia. In: What Are You Optimistic About? (John Brockman, ed.). London, UK: Pocket Books; UK. p.358.

106. Chopra, D. 2014. The Future of God: A Practical Approach to Spirituality for Our Times. London, UK: Rider. p.1.

107. Pope John Paul II. 2005. Memory and Identity.

108. Pope John Paul II. 2005. Memory and Identity. p.2.

109. Whitehouse, H., François, P., Savage, P.E., Currie, T.E., Feeney, K.C,, Cioni, E., Purcell, R., Ross, R.M., Larson, J., Baines, J., ter Haar, B., Covey, A. and Turchin, P. Complex Societies Precede Moralizing Gods Throughout World History. *Nature*. 20 Mar 2019.

110. Juergensmeyer, M., Griego, D. and Soboslai, J. 2015. God in the Tumult of the Global Square: Religion in Global Civil Society. California, USA: University of California Press.

111. Dostoyevsky, F. 1880. Brothers Karamazov. A Hymn and a Secret. Part 4. Book 11, Chapter 4.

112. Jean-Paul Sartre said that all of French existentialism is to be found in Ivan Karamazov's contention that if there is no God, everything is permitted.

Chapter 2: The Two Cherokee Fighting Wolves Within—And the One We Feed

1. Besant, A. 1977. Bhagavad-Gita (2.58). Chennai, India: Theosophical Publishing House. p.39.

2. Elizabeth Cashdan, professor of anthropology at the University of Utah, USA. Cited in: Whipps, H. 2009. The Evolution of Human Aggression. LiveScience. 25

Feb 2009. Retrieved from: <https://www.livescience.com/5333-evolution-human-aggression.html>.

3. *Martin Buber*. Wikipedia: The Free Encyclopedia. Wikimedia Foundation. Retrieved 23 Mar 2016. Buber's *Ich und Du* was published in 1923, and first translated from German to English in 1937.
4. *Martin Buber*. Wikipedia: The Free Encyclopedia. Wikimedia Foundation. Retrieved 23 Mar 2016. Buber's *Ich und Du* was published in 1923, and first translated from German to English in 1937.
5. Cited in: Shallis, M. 1986. The End of Intelligence. *New Internationalist*. Issue 162. 5 Aug 1986.
6. Carr, N.G. 2008. Is Google Making Us Stupid? What the Internet Is Doing to Our Brains. *The Atlantic*. July/Aug 2008.
7. Wilson, C. 2010. Beyond the Occult. London, UK: Watkins Publishing. First South Asian Edition. p.55.
8. Wilson, C. 2010. Beyond the Occult. London, UK: Watkins Publishing. First South Asian Edition. p.73.
9. Wilson, C. 2010. Beyond the Occult. London, UK: Watkins Publishing. First South Asian Edition. p.87.
10. Kardec, A. 1857. The Spirits Book (Le Livre des Esprits).
11. Steiner, R. 1918. The Dead Are With Us. Lecture on 10 February 1918. Nuremberg, Germany.
12. Gladwell, M. 2007. Blink: the Power of Thinking Without Thinking.
13. Wilson, C. 2010. Beyond the Occult. London, UK: Watkins Publishing. First South Asian Edition. p.501.
14. Lotto, B. 2017. Deviate: the Science of Seeing Differently. London, UK: Weidenfeld & Nicolson.
15. Harari, Y.N. 2015. Homo Deus: a Brief History of Tomorrow. London, UK: Harvill Secker. p.25.
16. Peter Diamandis, founder and chairman of the X Prize Foundation.
17. Harari, Y.N. 2015. Homo Deus: a Brief History of Tomorrow. London, UK: Harvill Secker.
18. Wallach, W., and Allen, C. 2010. Moral Machines: Teaching Robots Right From Wrong. London, UK: Oxford University Press.

19. Harari, Y. 2016. Salvation by Algorithm: God, Technology and the New 21st-Century Religions. *The New Statesman*, 9 Sept 2016.

20. James D. Watson, American molecular biologist, geneticist and zoologist, is best known as one of the co-discoverers of the structure of DNA (1953), along with Francis Crick. They were awarded the 1962 Nobel Prize in Physiology or Medicine.

21. HeartMath Institute, USA. <https://www.heartmath.org/research/science-of-the-heart/coherence/>.

22. Krishnamurti. J. 1973. The Awakening of Intelligence. USA: Harper.

23. Quote by Gabriel Iqbal. Retrieved from <https://www.goodreads.com/author/quotes/10787600.Gabriel_Iqbal>. Gabriel Iqbal is author of the book *Heart Intelligence*.

24. HeartMath Institute, California, USA. Research FAQs. <https://www.heartmath.org/support/faqs/research/>.

25. HeartMath Institute. 2015. Science of the Heart: Exploring the Role of the Heart in Human Performance. Volume 2. California, USA: HeartMath Institute. < https://www.heartmath.org/research/science-of-the-heart/>.

26. Cited in the blog post *Jiddu Krishnamurti—a Radical Transformation of the Mind*, on 8 Mar 2009. Retrieved from <https://thecriticalthinker.wordpress.com/2009/03/08/krishnamurti-mind/>.

27. Pope Francis. 2015. Encyclical Letter *Laudato Si': On Care for our Common Home*. The Vatican, Rome, Italy.

28. Statement by Karen Armstrong, author of books like The Case for God,2008, and 'Three steps to a compassionate life, 2010, on being bestowed with the 2017 Princess of Asturias Award for Social Sciences; 31 May 2017.

29. Svetasvatara Upanishad. Chapter 2. Invocation to Savitr. Retrieved from <http://www.esamskriti.com/essay-chapters/Svetasvatara-Upanishad---Chap-2-Invocation-to-Savitr-(The-Sun)-and-Practice-of-Yoga-2.aspx>.

30. Source: Collected Works of Carl Jung (1936). 6:964 (Psycological Types).

31. Mark 8:36. For what shall it profit a man, if he shall gain the whole world, and lose his own soul?

32. Solzhenitsyn, A. 1973. The Gulag Archipelago. p.312.

33. Dasgupta, A. 2015. Lessons from Russalana: In Search of Transformative Thinking. New Delhi, India: Harper Collins. p.140.

34. Source: T S Eliot's 1930 essay on Baudelaire.

35. St. Macarius on the Heart. Cited in blogpost *From Under the Rubble* on 26 May 2011. Glory to God for All Things. Retrieved from <https://fatherstephen.wordpress.com/tag/solzhenitsyn/>.

36. Source: Isn't Religion to Blame for Most of History's Killings? Retrieved from <http://www.provethebible.net/T2-Objec/G-0101.htm>.

37. Source: Frankenstein (Curran, S., ed.). 2009. Mary Shelley's Introduction to the 1831 edition of Frankenstein. Romantic Circles. <https://www.rc.umd.edu/editions/frankenstein/1831v1/intro>.

38. Source: Ivereigh, A. 2015. Pope Presents Curia With List of Virtues to Counter Temptations. Mercatornet. 30 Dec 2015. Retrieved from <http://www.mercatornet.com/above/view/pope-presents-curia-with-list-of-virtues-to-counter-temptations/17391>.

39. Matthew 18:22.

40. Plato. Republic. [Translated by G.M.A. Grube; revised by C.D.C. Reeve. 1992. Indiana, USA: Hackett Publishing.].

41. Graves, C.W. 1974. Human Nature Prepares for a Momentous Leap. The Futurist. Retrieved from <http://www.clarewgraves.com/articles_content/1974_Futurist/1974_Futurist.html>.

42. Coleridge, S.T. 1798. The Rime of the Ancient Mariner.

43. Turkle, S. 2013. Alone Together: Why We Expect More From Technology and Less From Each Other. Basic Books.

44. Capra, F. 1984. The Turning Point: Science, Society, and the Rising Culture. Bantam. Reissue Edition (1 Aug 1984).

45. Harari, Y.N. 2013. Sapiens: A Brief History of Humankind. Vintage. p.74.

46. Harari, Y.N. 2013. Sapiens: A Brief History of Humankind. Vintage. p.82.

47. Kolbert, E. The Sixth Extinction: An Unnatural History. New York, USA: Henry Holt.

48. Source: How Modern Humans Have Become Weaklings Compared With Our Ancient Ancestors Who Could Outrun and Outlift today's Top Athletes. *Daily Mail Online.* 28 Apr 2014. Retrieved from <https://www.dailymail.co.uk/sciencetech/article-2614780/How-FARMERS-fitter-athletes-Human-strength-speed-peaked-7-300-years-ago-declining-rapidly.html>.

49. Source: Children Growing Weaker as Computers Replace Outdoor Activity. *The Guardian International Edition*. 21 May 2011. Retrieved from <http://www.theguardian.com/society/2011/may/21/children-weaker-computers-replace-activity>.

50. Source: How Today's Computers Weaken Our Brain. *The New Yorker*. 9 Sep 2013. Retrieved from <http://www.newyorker.com/tech/elements/how-todays-computers-weaken-our-brain>.

51. Cited in: Weisberg, J. 2016. We Are Hopelessly Hooked. Review of Nir Eyal's 2014 book, Hooked: How to Build Habit-Forming Products. *The New York Review of Books*. USA. 25 Feb 2016. p.9.

52. Simon McKeown, quoted in the post *Can the Internet Make Loved Ones 'Immortal'?* by Denyse O'Leary on 4 Nov 2015. Retrieved from <Mercatornet, http://www.mercatornet.com/connecting/view/can-the-internet-make-loved-ones-immortal/17119#sthash.Pr7rcqbO.dpu>.

53. Prof. Maciej Henneberg, quoted in 'Humans Not Smarter Than Animals, Just Different, Experts Say'. Phys.Org. University of Adelaide, Australia. 4 Dec 2013. Retrieved from < https://phys.org/news/2013-12-humans-smarter-animals-experts.html>.

54. Source: Non Physical Abuse and Violence. <http://newbuddhist.com/discussion/8634/non-physical-abuse-and-violence>.

55. Khazzoom, L. 2010. Violence Is Not a Physical Act, It is Energy, It is Intention. 10 Mar 2010. Retrieved from < http://loolwa.com/violence-is-not-a-physical-act-it-is-energy-it-is-intention/>.

56. Arendt. H. 1969. Reflections On Violence. The New York Review. USA. 27 Feb 1969.

57. Tagore, R. 2012. The Religion of Man. India: Niyogi Books. p.68.

58. von Bernhardi, F.A.J. 1911. Germany And the Next War.

59. Bobbitt, P. 2003. The Shield of Achilles: War, Peace, and the Course of History. New York, USA: Anchor.

60. Long, J.A., Mark-Kurik, E., Johanson, E., Lee, M.S.Y., Young, G.C., Zhu Min, Ahlberg, P.E., Newman, M., Jones, R., den Blaauwen, J., Choo, B., and Trinajstic, K. 2014. Copulation in Antiarch Placoderms and the Origin of Gnathostome Internal Fertilization. Nature. 19 Oct 2014. pp.196-199.

61. Eisenstein, C. 2013. The Ascent of Humanity: Civilization and the Human Sense of Self. New York, USA: North Atlantic.

62. Mutukat, J. 2015. Shrinking Sex Life and Neutering Mankind. Human First. 11 Jan 2015. Retrieved from <http://www.humanfirst.in/discussions/shrinking-sex-life-and-neutering-of-mankind/>.

63. The Daily Mail Online. 2011. No Sex Please, We're Japanese: Country Heads for Extinction As Survey Reveals Young People Shunning Marriage. [National Institute of Population and Social Security Research in Japan]. Daily Mail Online. 28 Nov 2011. Retrieved from <https://www.dailymail.co.uk/news/article-2067327/Japan-heads-extinction-survey-reveals-young-people-shunning-marriage.html>.

64. Merton, T. No Man Is An Island.

65. Source: Opiniatrety: Half- to Quarter-Baked Thoughts. Blogpost of Matt Weiner, 6 Apr 2004. Retrieved from <http://mattweiner.net/blog/archives/000180.html>.

66. Alexander, E. 2012. Proof of Heaven: A Neurosurgeon's Journey Into the Afterlife. New York, USA: Simon & Schuster.

67. Tagore, R. 2012. The Religion of Man. India: Niyogi Books. p.106

68. Source: Speech delivered by Prof. Martin Luther King Jr. at Ebenezer Baptist Church, Atlanta, Georgia USA, on 3 Mar 1968. Retrieved from <https://kinginstitute.stanford.edu/king-papers/publications/knock-midnight-inspiration-great-sermons-reverend-martin-luther-king-jr-9>.

69. Adam Smith. Moral philosopher and a pioneer of political economy. One of the key figures of the Scottish Enlightenment. Adam Smith is best known for two classic works: The Theory of Moral Sentiments (1759), and An Inquiry into the Nature and Causes of the Wealth of Nations (1776). (Source: Wikipedia: The Free Encyclopedia. Wikimedia Foundation).

70. Andersen, R. 2012. How Engineering the Human Body Could Combat Climate Change. The Atlantic. 12 Mar 2012. Retrieved from <http://www.theatlantic.com/technology/archive/2012/03/how-engineering-the-human-body-could-combat-climate-change/253981/>.

71. Bloom, P. 2013. The Baby In The Well: The Case Against Empathy. The New Yorker. USA. 20 May 2013.

72. Baier, K. 1995. The Rational and Moral Order: The Social Roots of Reason and Morality. The Paul Carus Lectures 18. Chicago, USA: Open Court. p.27.

73. Yanofsky, N.S. 2013. The Outer Limits of Reason: What Science, Mathematics, and Logic Cannot Tell Us. USA: MIT Press.

74. Russell, B. 1950. Unpopular Essays.

75. Steve Grand. Creator of Lucy, a robot baby orangutan, and author of Creation: Life and How to Make It.

76. Source: Seltzer, A. The Heart and Its Energy. Chabad.org. Retrieved from <http://www.chabad.org/kabbalah/article_cdo/aid/380377/jewish/The-Heart-and-Its-Energy.htm>.

77. A poem by Charlie Chaplin written on his 70th birthday, on 16 Apr 1959.

78. Pearsall, P. 1998. The Heart's Code: Tapping the Wisdom and Power of Our Heart Energy. New York, USA: Broadway Books.

79. Besant, A. 1916. The Coming Race. Adyar Pamphlets. Lecture delivered at the Theosophical Conference held at Chittoor on 17 March 1916. Theosophical Publishing House. Adyar, Chennai, India. Retrieved from <http://hpb.narod.ru/ComingRaceAB.html>.

80. Source: Seltzer, A. The Heart and Its Energy. Chabad.org. Retrieved from <http://www.chabad.org/kabbalah/article_cdo/aid/380377/jewish/The-Heart-and-Its-Energy.htm>.

81. Source: Seltzer, A. The Heart and Its Energy. Chabad.org. Retrieved from <http://www.chabad.org/kabbalah/article_cdo/aid/380377/jewish/The-Heart-and-Its-Energy.htm>.

82. Marinelli, R., Fuerst, B., van der Zee, H., McGinn, A., Marinelli, W. 1995. The Heart Is Not a Pump: A Refutation of the Pressure Propulsion Premise of Heart Function. Fall-Winter 1995 Issue [Vol.5, No.1] of Frontier Perspectives, the journal of the Center for Frontier Sciences at Temple University in Philadelphia, USA. Retrieved from <https://www.rsarchive.org/RelArtic/Marinelli/>.

Chapter 3: Money—*Maya*, *Mara*, and *Moksha*—All-in-One

1. Daly, M. 2017. Killing the Competition: Economic Inequality and Homicide. New York, USA: Routledge.

2. The original and more accurate Latin phrase '*canis caninam non est*' translates as 'a dog doesn't eat dog's flesh'.

3. Carlyle, T. 1831. Sartor Resartus: The Life and Opinions of Herr Teufelsdrockh.

4. Cited in: Moore, C. 2017. Moral Materialism. <http://www.plough.com/en/topics/justice/social-justice/moral-materialism>. Retrieved 12 Feb 2017.

5. Sunstein, C.R. 2015. Why Free Markets Make Fools of Us [Review of *Phishing for Phools: The Economics of Manipulation and Deception* by George A. Akerlof and Robert J.Shiller, Princeton University Press.]. The New York Review of Books, USA. 22 Oct 2015.

6. Swami Sukhabodanda. 2012. Difference Between Longing and Desire. *Times of India*, Hyderabad, India. 15 Nov 2012. p.12.

7. Corinthians 13, The Message.

8. Adorable and Hilarious Kids' Letters to God. Retrieved from <http://www.ba-bamail.com/content.aspx?emailid=17189>.

9. Ventrella, J. 2013. Immortality: Can Humans Attain Eternal Youth And NOT Destroy the Planet? <http://ventrellathing. wordpress. com/2013/11/28/immortality-can-humans-attain-eternal-youth-and-not-destroy-the-planet/>. Retrieved 29 Apr 2014.

10. Ventrella, J. 2013. Immortality: Can Humans Attain Eternal Youth And NOT Destroy the Planet? <http://ventrellathing. wordpress. com/2013/11/28/immortality-can-humans-attain-eternal-youth-and-not-destroy-the-planet/>. Retrieved 29 Apr 2014.

11. Kurzweil, R. Cited in Varma, S. 2013. By 2029 Computers Will Match Human Intelligence. *Times of India*, 13 Aug 2013. p.10.

12. Segal, D. 2013. This Man is Not a Cyborg. Yet. *The New York Times*, USA. 1 Jun 2013.

13. Oxfam. 2018. Reward Work, Not Wealth. Oxfam Briefing Paper January 2018. <https://www.oxfam.org/sites/www.oxfam.org/files/file_attachments/bp-reward-work-not-wealth-220118-summ-en.pdf>

14. Statement attributed to US Senator Mark Hanna.

15. Lawrence, D.H. 1928. Lady Chatterley's Lover.

16. Dylan, Bob. 1965. *It's Alright, Ma* (I am only bleeding).

17. The eight secondary manifestations of Lakshmi, called the 'Ashta Lakshmi' are: *Adi* (primeval) Lakshmi; *Dhana* or *aishwarya* (money or prosperity) Lakshmi; *Dhanya* (grain or agricultural produce) Lakshmi; *Gaja* (elephant or giver of animal wealth) Lakshmi; *Santana* (giver of progeny) Lakshmi; *Veera* or *dhairya* (valor or courage) Lakshmi; *Vijaya* (victorious) Lakshmi.

18. Kolakowski, L. 2001. Metaphysical Horror.

19. Maruyama, S. 2012. Approaching Crisis of Global Cooling and the Limits to Growth: Global Warming is Not Our Future. Xlibris.

20. Frankl, V.E. 1988. The Will to Meaning: Foundations and Applications of Logotherapy. New York, USA: Meridian.

21. Østman, B. 2011. Pleiotropy. 1 Aug 2011.

22. Srimad Bhagavatam. 3.33.7. Sri Caitanya Caritamrita. 11.192.

23. Goleman, D. 2007. Social Intelligence: the New Science of Human Relationships. USA: Bantam.

24. Oxfam. 2014.Working for the Few: Political Capture and Economic Inequality. 178 Oxfam Briefing Paper – Summary.

25. Rand, A. 1957. Atlas Shrugged. USA: Random House. [Francisco d'Anconia's 'money speech'].

26. Pickett, K. and Wilkinson, R. 2009. The Spirit Level: Why More Equal Societies Almost Always Do Better. London, UK: Allen Lane.

27. Pickett, K. and Wilkinson, R. 2009. The Spirit Level: Why More Equal Societies Almost Always Do Better. London, UK: Allen Lane.

28. Darshan Singh, M. 2002. Power, Money and Nexus: a Freudian Nexus. India: *The Sunday Tribune*. 26 May 2002.

29. Cited in: Chalapathi Rao, I.V. 2007. Culture Capsules: Living Through Changing Times. Hyderabad, India: Sri Yabaluri Raghavaiah Memorial Trust. p.67-68.

30. Cited in: Beck, S. 2006. Ethics of Civilization. Volume 2: India and Southeast Asia to 1800. Literature of India. Retrieved from <http://www.san.beck.org/EC12-Literature.html#4>.

31. Matthew 19:24.

32. Matthew 6:19–21,24.

33. Heffernan, M. 2011. Wilful Blindness: Why We Ignore the Obvious at Our Peril. London, UK: Simon & Schuster. p.4.

34. Kasser, T. 2002. The High Price of Materialism. USA: A Bradford Book.

35. Waldron, J. 2012. A Cheerful View of Mass Violence. Review of Steven Pinker's book *The Better Angels of our Nature: Why Violence Has Declined*. The New York Review of Books. USA. 12 Jan 2012.

36. Rand, A. 1957. Atlas Shrugged. USA: Random House. [Francisco d'Anconia's 'money speech']

37. Lyrics from the 1976 song *Money, Money, Money*, by the Swedish pop group ABBA.

38. Fitzgerald, S. 1926. The Rich Boy. [All the Sad Young Men].

39. Davies, L.A. 2013. Agenomics: Trivializing Death. Retrieved from <http://agenomics.ca/2013/09/trivializing-death/>

40. Gross, J. 2013. Six Studies on How Money Affects the Mind. TedxMarin talk by Paul Piff. Retrieved from <http://blog.ted.com/2013/12/20/6-studies-of-money-and-the-mind/>

41. Gross, J. 2013. Six Studies on How Money Affects the Mind. TedxMarin talk by Paul Piff. Retrieved from <http://blog.ted.com/2013/12/20/6-studies-of-money-and-the-mind/>

42. Miller, L. 2012. The Money-Empathy Gap. *New York*, 1 July 2012.

43. Porter, E. 2013. How Money Affects Morality. *The New York Times*, 13 June 2013.

44. Porter, E. 2013. How Money Affects Morality. *The New York Times*, 13 June 2013.

45. Source: Forget ObamaCare – Get Cryonics Insurance! Immortality is Cheaper than ObamaCare. Posted on 25 Apr 2014 at <https://medium.com/i-love-charts/forget-obamacare-get-cryonics-insurance-a236dfae087e>. Retrieved 02 April 2015.

46. *Georgism*. Wikipedia: The Free Encyclopedia. Wikimedia Foundation. Retrieved 26 Apr 2014.

47. *Georgism*. Wikipedia: The Free Encyclopedia. Wikimedia Foundation. Retrieved 26 Apr 2014.

48. *Progress and Poverty*. The Free Encyclopedia. Wikimedia Foundation. Retrieved 26 Apr 2014. [Progress and Poverty: An Inquiry into the Cause of Industrial Depressions and of Increase of Want with Increase of Wealth: The Remedy, published in 1879 by Henry George.].

49. Goodman, LE (ed.). 1972. Ibn Tufayl's Hayy Ibn Yaqzan: a Philosophical Tale Translated with Introduction and Notes. New York, USA: Twayne Publishers. p.146.

50. DiBona, C. 2007. High-resolution Images of Earth Will Thwart Global Villainy. *In*: What Are You Optimistic About? Today's Leading Thinkers on Why Things are Good and Getting Better (Brockman, J., ed.). USA: Simon & Schuster. p.244.

51. Fitzgerald, R. 2006. The Hundred-Year Lie: How Food and Medicine Are Destroying Your Health. USA: Dutton.

52. Source: Mind Disrupted: How Toxic Chemicals May Change How We Think and Who We Are. Retrieved from <www.minddisrupted.org>

53. Source: NSCDC (National Scientific Council on the Developing Child). 2010. Early Experiences Can Alter Gene Expression and Affect Long-Term Development. Working Paper 10. USA: Center on the Developing Child, Harvard University.

54. Eisenstein, C. 2007. The Ascent of Humanity: Civilization and the Human Sense of Self. Chapter II: The Origins of Separation: The Biological Origins of Self. Online version Retrieved from <https://charleseisenstein.net/books/the-ascent-of-humanity/the-biological-origins-of-self/>.

55. Proverbs 10:2; 11:18; 20:17; 21:6.

56. Seton, E.A.B. (1774–1821) was the first native-born citizen of the USA to be canonized by the Roman Catholic Church.

57. Easterly, W. 2013. The Tyranny of Experts: Economists, Dictators, and the Forgotten Rights of the Poor. New York, USA: Basic Books.

58. Cited in the blog post *Dedroidify* on 21 Dec 2008. Review of the 1972 book *An Outline of Occult Science* by Rudolf Steiner, Retrieved from <http://dedroidify.blogspot.com/2008/12/rudolf-steiner.html>.

59. Paul Josef Crutzen. 1995 Nobel Prize-winning, Dutch atmospheric chemist.

60. Lapham, L.H. 1988. Money and Class in America, Notes and Observations on Our Civil Religion. New York, USA: Weidenfeld & Nicolson. p.9.

61. Cited in: Hinduism Today. 2016. Good Money, Bad Money. Satguru Sivaya Subramuniyaswami. Retrieved from <http://www.hinduismtoday.com/modules/smartsection/item.php?itemid=4857>.

62. Source: Principles of Islamic Banking. *Nida'ul Islam*. November–December, 1995.

63. Hathaway, B. Money and the Kingdom of God. Retrieved from < http://www.reality.org.nz/articles/28/28-hathaway.php>.

64. Lapham, L.H. 1988. Money and Class in America, Notes and Observations on Our Civil Religion. New York, USA: Weidenfeld & Nicolson. p.7, p.27.

65. Lapham, L.H. 1988. Money and Class in America, Notes and Observations on Our Civil Religion. New York, USA: Weidenfeld & Nicolson. p.30.

66. Pope Francis. 2015. Laudato Si': On Care for Our Common Home. Chapter Five: Lines of Approach and Action. Para 195. Vatican City: Vatican Press. 184 pp.

67. Clark, J.R. and Lee, D.R. 2011. Markets and Morality. *Cato Journal*, Vol. 31, No. 1, Winter 2011, 1-25.

68. Arevuo, M. 2015. Free market capitalism and morality. London, UK: Institute of Economic Affairs. Retrieved from <http://www.iea.org.uk/blog/free-market-capitalism-and-morality>.

69. Marx, K. and Engels, F. 1848. Communist Manifesto. Chapter 1: Bourgeoisie and Proletarians.

70. Marx, K. and Engels, F. 1848. Communist Manifesto. Chapter 1: Bourgeoisie and Proletarians.

71. Nordhaus, W.D. 2015. The Pope & the Market. Review of the encyclical letter by Pope Francis, *Laudato Si'*: On Care for Our Common Future. *The New York Review of Books*, USA. 8 Oct 2015. p.27.

72. Lapham, L.H. 1988. Money and Class in America, Notes and Observations on Our Civil Religion. New York, USA: Weidenfeld & Nicolson. p.93.

73. Lapham, L.H. 1988. Money and Class in America, Notes and Observations on Our Civil Religion. New York, USA: Weidenfeld & Nicolson. p.224.

74. Lapham, L.H. 1988. Money and Class in America, Notes and Observations on Our Civil Religion. New York, USA: Weidenfeld & Nicolson. p.156.

75. Lapham, L.H. 1988. Money and Class in America, Notes and Observations on Our Civil Religion. New York, USA: Weidenfeld & Nicolson. p.78.

76. Lapham, L.H. 1988. Money and Class in America, Notes and Observations on Our Civil Religion. New York, USA: Weidenfeld & Nicolson. p.222.

77. Lapham, L.H. 1988. Money and Class in America, Notes and Observations on Our Civil Religion. New York, USA: Weidenfeld & Nicolson. p.219.

78. Frankl, V.E. 1988. The Will to Meaning: Foundations and Applications of Logotherapy. New York, USA: Meridian. Revised edition. p.76.

79. Sharma, G. 2015. 'Skul'duggery Files: The Curious Link Between Property Disputes and Craniotomies. *The Week*, 27 Sep 2015. Retrieved from < http://www.theweek.in/theweek/statescan/curious-link-between-property-disputes-and-craniotomies-in-haryana.html>

80. Laski, H.J. 1925. A Grammar of Politics. London, UK: George Allen & Unwin Ltd. pp.173,174.

81. Cited in: William Howard Taft Quotes. William H. Taft, 27th President of USA (1909-13). Retrieved from <http://thinkexist.com/quotes/william_howard_taft/>

82. Fromm, E. 1976. To Have or To Be?

83. Rousseau, J-J. 1754. Discourse on the Origin and Basis of Inequality Among Men. Retrieved from <https://www.marxists.org/reference/subject/economics/rousseau/inequality/ch02.htm>.

84. Steinbeck, J.E. 1939. The Grapes of Wrath.

85. Cited in: Trachtman, R. 1999. The Money Taboo: Its Effects in Everyday Life and in the Practice of Psychotherapy. *Clinical Social Work Journal.* Vol. 27, No.3.

86. Trachtman, R. 1999. The Money Taboo: Its Effects in Everyday Life and in the Practice of Psychotherapy. *Clinical Social Work Journal.* Vol. 27, No.3 (Fall, 1999).

87. Diane Barth, F. 2001. Money as a Tool for Negotiating Separateness and Connectedness in the Therapeutic Relationship. *Clinical Social Work Journal.* Vol. 29, No.1.

88. Pope Francis. 2013. Address to the New Non-Resident Ambassadors to the Holy See: Kyrgyzstan, Antigua and Barbuda, Luxembourg, and Botswana. Clementine Hall, Vatican City. 16 May 2013.

89. Pope Francis. 2013. Address to the New Non-Resident Ambassadors to the Holy See: Kyrgyzstan, Antigua and Barbuda, Luxembourg, and Botswana. Clementine Hall, Vatican City. 16 May 2013.

90. Merton, T. 1948. No Man Is An Island.

91. Aldous Huxley in *After Many a Summer Dies the Swan* (1939): "For the Truth is that we are kind for the same reason as we are cruel, in order that we may enhance the sense of our own Power".

92. Dunn, E. and Norton, M. 2014. Happy Money: the Science of Happier Spending. New York, USA: Simon & Schuster.

93. Oxfam. 2015. Extreme Carbon Inequality: Why the Paris Climate Deal Must Put the Poorest, Lowest Emitting and Most Vulnerable People First. 2 Dec 2015. <https://www.oxfam.org/sites/www.oxfam.org/files/file_attachments/mb-extreme-carbon-inequality-021215-en.pdf>.

94. George, H. 1879. Progress and Poverty: An Inquiry Into the Cause of Industrial Depressions and of Increase of Want with Increase of Wealth: The Remedy.

95. Halpern, S. 2014. How Robots & Algorithms Are Taking Over. Review of Nicholas Carr's book The Glass Cage: Automation and Us. *The New York Review of Books.* USA. 2 Apr 2014. p.28.

96. Mark 10:25.

Chapter 4: Towards a New Vocabulary of Morality

1. Kimbrell, A. 2000. Cold Evil: Technology and Modern Ethics. Annual E.F. Schumacher Lecture. Schumacher Center for a New Economics. Retrieved from <https://centerforneweconomics.org/publications/cold-evil-technology-and-modern-ethics/>.

2. Keltner, D., Marsh, J., and Smith, J.A. (eds.). 2010. The Compassionate Instinct: the Science of Human Goodness. New York, USA: W.W. Norton.

3. Matthew 7:1–5 (King James Version).

4. NSF (National Science Foundation). 2010. Methane Releases From Arctic Shelf May Be Much Larger and Faster Than Anticipated. National Science Foundation (NSF), USA. Press release 10-036. 4 Mar 2010.

5. Flannery, T. 2013. They Are Taking Over! Review of Lisa-Ann Gershwin's book Stung! On Jellyfish Blooms and the Future of the Ocean. *The New York Review of Books*. USA. 26 Sep–9 Oct 2013. p.18.

6. The tragedy *Antigone* by Sophocles.

7. Crawford Flitch, J.E (tr.). 1932. A Selections from *The Cherubinic Wanderer* (1657) by Angelus Silesius. London, UK.

8. Rawls, J. 1985. Justice as Fairness: Political Not Metaphysical. *Philosophy and Public Affairs*, Vol.14. No.3 (Summer 1985). USA: Princeton University Press. pp.223–251.

9. Bergson, H. (Arthur Mitchell, trans.). 1911. Creative Evolution. New York, USA: Henry Holt and Company.

10. Fox, D. 2011. The Limits of Intelligence. *Scientific American*. USA. July 2011.

11. Kosslyn, S.M. 2007. Human Intelligence Can Be Increased Dramatically. In: What Are You Optimistic About? Today's Leading Thinkers on Why Things are Good and Getting Better (Brockman, J., ed.). New York, USA: HarperCollins. p.285.

12. Thompson, R.L. 2003. Maya: the World as Virtual Reality. USA: Govardhan Hill Publishing.

13. Gianani, K. 2015. Now, a Gym for Your Brain. Retrieved from <http://www.mid-day.com/articles/now-a-gym-for-your-brain/16081193>, on 9 Oct 2015.

14. Kosslyn, S.M. 2007. Human Intelligence Can Be Increased Dramatically. In: What Are You Optimistic About? Today's Leading Thinkers on Why Things are Good and Getting Better (Brockman, J., ed.). New York, USA: HarperCollins. p.285.

15. Bhagavad Gita, Chapter 4, Verse 8.

16. The British Union for the Abolition of Vivisection (BUAV) estimated (2005) that 100 million vertebrates are experimented on around the world every year. Source: *Animal testing*. Wikipedia: The Free Encyclopedia. Wikimedia Foundation. Retrieved 18 Jan 2015.

17. Source: The Anarchist Library. 2004. Militarization and Civilization: Articles from "Green Anarchist". The Military Abuse of Animals. Retrieved from <https://theanarchistlibrary.org/library/various-authors-militarization-and-civilization-articles-from-green-anarchist>.

18. National Anti-Vivisection Society (NAVS), Chicago, USA. The Failure of the Animal Model. <http://www.navs.org/science/failure-of-the-animal-model> Retrieved 20 Jan 2015.

19. The Guardian. 2014. Number of Animal Experiments Continues to Rise in UK. <http://www.theguardian.com/science/2014/jul/10/animal-experiments-rise-again-uk-genetic-research>. Retrieved 20 Jan 2015.

20. Casey, M. 2015. Animal Experimentation Up 73 Percent, Study Says. CBS News. <http://www.cbsnews.com/news/peta-study-finds-animal-testing-in-federal-labs-on-the-increase/>. Retrieved 01 Mar 2015.

21. Primack, J.R. and Abrams, N.E. 2006. The View From the Center of the Universe: Discovering Our Extraordinary Place in the Cosmos. New York, USA: Riverhead Books.

22. Shakespeare, W. *As You Like It.* Act II, Scene VII.

23. Lovecraft, H.P. 1926. The Call of Cthulhu.

24. Cited in: Kakar, S. (ed.). 2014. Death and Dying. Penguin/Viking p.xiv.

25. von Goethe, J.W. 1774. The Sorrows of Young Werther.

26. Rai, T. 2015. How Could They? Aeon. 18 Jun 2015. [Tage Rai is a research associate and lecturer at the MIT Sloan School of Management in Massachusetts, USA. He is the co-author, with Alan Fiske, of *Virtuous Violence* (2014)]. Retrieved from <https://aeon.co/essays/people-resort-to-violence-because-their-moral-codes-demand-it>.

27. Montana, C. 2016. Orlando: Rethinking Morality. HuffPost. USA. 21 Jun 2016. Retrieved from <https://www.huffingtonpost.com/cate-montana/orlando-rethinking-morali_b_10562852.html>.

28. Abd-Ru-Shin [Bernhardt, O.E.]. 1926. In the Light of Truth: the Grail Message. Retrieved from <https://grailmessage.com/what-seek-ye-101/>.

29. *Lie*. Wikipedia: The Free Encyclopedia. Wikimedia Foundation. Retrieved 02 Sept 2016.

30. Paul Rusesabagina, in an interview with Michel Martin, host of the show 'Talk of the Nation' titled *'An Ordinary Man' Navigates Rwanda's Genocide*. 10 Apr 2006. National Public Radio, Washington, USA. Retrieved from <https://www.npr.org/templates/story/story.php?storyId=5334369>.

31. Dukas, H., and Hoffmann, B. 2013. Albert Einstein, The Human Side. Glimpses from His Archives. New Jersey, USA: The Princeton University Press.

32. McGinn, C. 2010. Is Just Thinking Enough? Review of John R. Searle's book: Making the Social World: The Structure of Human Civilization. *The New York Review of Books*. USA. 11 Nov 2010.

33. Lewis, CS. 1942. The Screwtape Letters.

34. The central headquarters for the Communist Party of China and the State Council (Central government) of the People's Republic of China.

35. Lars F.H. Svendsen. Norwegian philosopher. Author of *A Philosophy of Evil* (2010).

36. Oates, J.C. Haunted: Tales of the Grotesque. New York, USA: Plume.

37. *Kybalion*. Wikipedia: The Free Encyclopedia. Wikimedia Foundation. Accessed 24 April 2014. *The Kybalion: Hermetic Philosophy* is a 1908 book claiming to be the essence of the teachings of a certain *Hermes Trismegistus*, published anonymously under the pseudonym 'The Three Initiates. ' The term *Trismegistus* means 'thrice great,' and the name Hermes Trismegistus is synonymous with 'Fount of Wisdom. '

38. Besant, A. 2003. *The Bhagavad Gita: the Lord's Song*. 20th Reprint. Tamil Nadu, India: The Theosophical Publishing House. pp. 203–204.

39. Jalal ad-Din Rumi's poem "The Guest House".

40. Phrase used in a letter that Gandhi wrote to Mahadev Desai in July 1918.

41. Words of Marin Luther King Jr.

42. Doniger, W. 2009. The Hindus: The Alternative History. USA: Penguin. p.265.

43. Micu, A. 2018. The Faults in Our Personalities Are All Expressions of Our 'Dark Core'. ZME Science Newsletter. 28 Sep 2018. Retrieved from <https://www.zmescience.com/science/dark-personality-traits-core-825236432/>.

44. Micu, A. 2018. The Faults in Our Personalities Are All Expressions of Our 'Dark Core'. ZME Science Newsletter. 28 Sep 2018. Retrieved from <https://www.zmescience.com/science/dark-personality-traits-core-825236432/>.

45. Source: Pianka, E.R. Natural Selection. Retrieved from <http://www. zo.utexas.edu/courses/Thoc/Natural.Selection.html>. Eric R. Pianca is the author of *Evolutionary Ecology* (1983).

46. *Dating*. Wikipedia: The Free Encyclopedia. Wikimedia Foundation.

47. Lewis, C.S. 1943. The Abolition of Man.

48. Kinrei Bassis, cited in the blogpost Parabola: The Search for Meaning. The Buddha Calling the Buddha. Posted by Luke Storms on 10 Dec 2013.

49. Swami Vivekananda's address to the first Parliament of the World's Religions, held in Chicago, USA, in September 1893.

50. Burke, E. 1757. The Sublime and the Beautiful. [A Philosophical Enquiry into the Origin of Our Ideas of the Sublime and Beautiful].

51. Whitall, P.N. 1975. The Coming of Coriolanus. *Studies in Comparative Religion*. Vol. 9, No. 4, Autumn, 1975.

52. Source: The Tikvah Advanced Institutes. 2014. The Future of the Family. Retrieved from <http://tikvahfund.org/advanced-institutes/the-future-of-the-family/>.

53. Source: The Thiru Kural. Advancing the Family. Verse 1021. Retrieved from <http://tamilnation.co/literature/kural/kuralE8.htm>.

54. *Family values*. Wikipedia: The Free Encyclopedia. Wikimedia Foundation. Retrieved 18 July 2014.

55. Lawrence, M. 2012. King of Thorns. Book Two of The Broken Empire. New York, USA: Ace Books.

56. Camus, A. 1947. The Plague.

57. Huxley, T. 1893. Evolution and Ethics and Other Essays. p.71–72.

58. Martin Luther King Jr. 11 Dec 1964. Lecture delivered at the University of Oslo, Norway, a day after receiving the Nobel Peace Prize.

59. The Arbinger Institute. 2008. The Anatomy of Peace: Resolving the Heart of Conflict. Oakland, California, USA: Berrett-Koehler.

60. Quote attributed to Etty Hillesum (1914–1943), a Jewish woman whose letters and diaries, kept between 1941 and 1943, describe life in Amsterdam during the German Occupation during the Second World War.

61. Burke, E. 1844. A Philosophical Enquiry Into the Origin of Our Ideas of the Sublime and Beautiful. New York, USA: Harpers & Brothers.

62. Schopenhauer, A. The Essays of Arthur Schopenhauer On Human Nature.

63. Rich, N. 2015. The Super Bowl: the Horror and the Gory. *The New York Review of Books*. USA. 5 Mar 2015. p.54.

64. Rowling, JK. 2008. The Tales of Beedle the Bard.

65. Cited in: Everyday Sadists Take Pleasure In Others' Pain. Association for Psychological Science (APS). 12 Sep 2013. Retrieved from <http://www.psychologicalscience.org/index.php/news/releases/everyday-sadists-take-pleasure-in-others-pain.html>.

66. Whitehead, A.N. 1926. Religion In The Making. Lowell Lectures, 1926.

67. Speckhardt, R. 2014. Behaving Badly? Stop Using Religion as an Excuse! HuffPost. USA. 02 Apr 2014. Retrieved from <http://www.huffingtonpost.com/roy-speckhardt/behaving-badly-progressive-religion_b_5069730.html> on 13 Apr 2014.

68. Eiseley, L. 1960. The Firmament of Time. New York, USA: Atheneum.

69. *Global village* is a term coined by Marshall McLuhan, who popularized it in his books *The Gutenberg Galaxy: The Making of Typographic Man* (1962) and *Understanding Media* (1964).

70. Harris, S. 2010. Morality: 'We Can Send Religion to the Scrap Heap'. Interview with Sam Harris in the *New Scientist*, Special Report, 13 Oct 2010. Retrieved from <https://www.newscientist.com/article/mg20827822-100-morality-we-can-send-religion-to-the-scrap-heap/>.

71. Lyrics from the 2010 song *Good Man, Bad Habit* by Laura Marling.

72. Sheldrake, R. Morphic Resonance and Morphic Fields: an Introduction. Retrieved from <https://www.sheldrake.org/research/morphic-resonance/introduction>.

73. Yogananda, Paramahansa. 1997. Journey to Self-Realization: Collected Talks and Essays on Realizing God In Daily Life. Volume III. USA: Self-Realization Fellowship.

74. Romans 7:24.

75. The other two are right belief (*samyak darshana*) and right knowledge (*samyak gyana*).

76. Kierkegaard, S. 1849. The Sickness Unto Death.

77. "What draws a man to err and sin, as if against his own will?"

78. "I do not do the good I want, but the evil I do not want is what I do."

79. Mark 10:18.

80. Nietzsche, F. 1891. Thus Spoke Zarathustra: A Book for All and None.

81. Extract from Jeremy Bentham's 1830 letter, to the daughter of a friend, cited in Richard Layard's book *Happiness: Lessons from a New Science*, (Penguin, 2005).

Chapter 5: From Death to Immortality

1. *Hamlet*. Act I, Scene II, Line 73.

2. de Unamuno, M. [Crawford Flitch, J.E. (tr.)]. 1954. The Tragic Sense of Life. New York, USA: Dover.

3. Britton, B. 2016. Humans Have Reached Their Lifespan Limit, Researchers Say. *CNN Health*. 06 Oct 2016.

4. Becker, E. 1973. The Denial of Death. New York, USA: Simon & Schuster.

5. Panikkar, R. (ed., tr.). 1977. The Vedic Experience: *Mantramanjari* An Anthology of the Vedas for Modern Man and Contemporary Celebration. London, UK: Darton, Longman & Todd. p.572.

6. Source: The Denial of Death. Goodreads. Retrieved from <http://www.goodreads.com/book/show/2761.The_Denial_of_Death> on 23 Apr 2014.

7. *Epic of Gilgamesh*. Wikipedia: The Free Encyclopedia. Wikimedia Foundation. Retrieved 28 Aug 2014.

8. Source: The Speaking Tree. *Times of India*. India. 7 Aug 2011. p.4.

9. Barrow, J.D. 2005. The Infinite Book: A Short Guide to the Boundless, Timeless and Endless. London, UK: Vintage Books. p.254.

10. Harris, S. 2012. The Moral Landscape. London, UK: Black Swan. p.17.

11. Nelson, K. 2006. The Spiritual Doorway in the Brain: A Neurologist's Search for the God Experience.

12. Harris, S. 2012. The Moral Landscape. London, UK: Black Swan. p.20.

13. Harris, S. 2012. The Moral Landscape. London, UK: Black Swan. p.24.

14. Harris, S. 2012. The Moral Landscape. London, UK: Black Swan. p.15.

15. Harris, S. 2012. The Moral Landscape. London, UK: Black Swan. p.22.

16. Gray, J. 2011. On the Road to Immortality. Review of *Transcend: Nine Steps to Living Well Forever* (Ray Kurzweil and Terry Grossman); and *The Singularity is Near: When Humans Transcend Biology* (Ray Kurzweil). *The New York Review of Book*. USA. 24 Nov – 07 Dec 2011. p 48.

17. Durrant-Whyte, H. 2013. Robotics Asks a Fundamental Question: What Makes Us Intelligent? *The Times of India*. Hyderabad, India. 10 May 2013. p.16.

18. Than, K. 2012. Crawling Bio-Robot Runs on Rat Heart Cells. National Geographic Daily News. 19 Nov 2012.

19. Nietzsche, F. 1891. Thus Spoke Zarathustra. First part. Zarathustra's Prologue.

20. Barrow, J.D. 2005. The Infinite Book: A Short Guide to the Boundless, Timeless and Endless. London, UK: Vintage Books. p.256.

21. Terborgh, J. 2011. Can Our Species Escape Destruction? Review of Tim Flannery's *Here On Earth: A Natural History of the Planet*. *The New York Review of Books*. USA. 13–28 Oct 2011. p.29.

22. Roshi, M. 2001. Appreciate Your Life. Dharma Talk. *Tricycle Magazine*. Spring 2001. Retrieved from <https://tricycle.org/magazine/appreciate-your-life/>.

23. Reiho, M. (Tr.). 1958. Zen in Daily Life: Zen Teacher Dogen and the Soto Approach to Zen. Shoji (Life–Death). Layman Buddhist Society Press. Retrieved from <http://www.zenki.com/index.php?lang=en&page=Shoji>.

24. Reiho, M. (Tr.). 1958. Zen in Daily Life: Zen Teacher Dogen and the Soto Approach to Zen. Shoji (Life–Death). Layman Buddhist Society Press. Retrieved from <http://www.zenki.com/index.php?lang=en&page=Shoji>.

25. Source: German Scientists Prove There is Life After Death. World News Daily Report. Retrieved from <http://worldnewsdailyreport.com/german-scientists-prove-there-is-life-after-death/>.

26. One of the aims of the *2045 Initiative*, a nonprofit organization founded by Russian entrepreneur Dmitry Itskov in 2011.

27. Source: Scientists Think They've Found a Hormone That Reverses Cell Aging in Humans. *Futurism*. 28 July 2016. Retrieved from <http://futurism.com/scientists-think-theyve-found-a-hormone-that-reverses-cell-aging-in-humans/>.

28. Age-related Decline Has Increased in the Past Few Decades Among the Younger Generation. India Today. Delhi, India. 10 July 2015. Retrieved from <https://www.indiatoday.in/lifestyle/wellness/story/youngsters-ageing-biological-age-chronological-age-ageing-process-281746-2015-07-10>.

29. Connor, S. 2008. Who Wants to Live For Ever? A Scientific Breakthrough Could Mean Humans Live for Hundreds of Years. The Independent. UK. 23 Jan 2008.

30. Alexandra Elbakyan is a leading neurotechnology researcher who is working on the *Brain Machine Interfacing Initiative* project and actively working on ways of creating a brain implant that would expand the consciousness of the bearer.

31. The Pavamana-Abhyaroha Mantra: *Om, asato ma sad gamaya; tamaso ma jyotir gamaya; mrtyor ma amritam gamaya.*

32. Cited in the article *Inspiration And Obsession in Life and Literature* by Joyce Carol Oates, published in The New York Review of Books, 13 Aug 2015. p.80.

33. The theory goes: Man can meld with the machine, and he can survive as a cyborg with robotically enhanced features; survive, that is, until the day when he can eventually upload his consciousness onto a hard drive, enabling him to 'live' forever as bits of information stored indefinitely; immortal, in a sense, as long as he has a copy of himself in case the computer fails.

34. Carstensen, L. 2015. The New Age Of Much Older Age. Time Magazine. USA. 02 Mar 2015. p.57.

35. Henry Miller, author of *Tropic of Cancer* (1934) and *Tropic of Capricorn* (1939).

36. Worley, H. 2006. Road Traffic Accidents Increase Dramatically Worldwide. Population Reference Bureau. Retrieved from <https://www.prb.org/roadtrafficaccidentsincreasedramaticallyworldwide/>.

37. Taleb, N.N. 2010. The Bed of Procrustes: Philosophical and Practical Aphorisms.

38. Already, there are over 900 cryogenically stored bodies, including that of baseball player Ted Williams, in Scottsdale, Arizona, USA.

39. Berzin, A. (Tr.). 2005. Engaging in Bodhisattva Behavior. By Shantideva. [Translated from the Tibetan, as clarified by the Sanskrit]. Retrieved from <http://www.buddhistische-gesellschaft-berlin.de/downloads/bca.pdf>.

40. Smith, A. 1776. Inquiry Into the Nature and Causes of the Wealth of Nations.

41. Gowdy, B. 2003. The Romantic. USA: Picador. [Barbara Gowdy is author of *The White Bone*; *Falling Angels*].

42. Some typical media reports: 'Husband hangs himself because his wife refused to go out for dinner with him to celebrate her birthday'; 'Young girl kills herself for being scolded by her mother'; 'Young girl commits suicide after an argument with

her brother over a television remote control'; 'A doctor hangs himself for failing to be the best doctor in the world'.

43. Fromm, E. 1965. Credo.
44. Walt Whitman, in *A Voice from Death* (1889).
45. Cited in: Lethem, J. 2007. The Ecstasy of Influence: A Plagiarism. Harper's Magazine Archive February 2007. Retrieved from: <https://harpers.org/archive/2007/02/the-ecstasy-of-influence/>.
46. Deaths caused by drone attacks.
47. Panetta, L. 2014. Worthy Fights: A Memoir of Leadership in War and Peace. New York, USA: Penguin.
48. Rall, T. 2014. U.S. Drones Kill 28 Innocents for Every 'Bad Guy'. *The Japan Times*. 05 Dec 2014. Retrieved from <http://www.japantimes.co.jp/opinion/2014/12/05/commentary/world-commentary/u-s-drones-kill-28-innocents-for-every-bad-guy/>.
49. CICADA: Close-In Covert Autonomous Disposable Aircraft. As small as the real cicadas, insects of the order Hemiptera.
50. Gamification is the craft of deriving all the fun and addicting elements found in games, and applying them in a non-game context.
51. Freeland, S. 2015. Crimes Against the Environment: The Silent Victim of Warfare. *The Conversation*. Australia. 09 Nov 2015. Retrieved from <http://theconversation.com/crimes-against-the-environment-the-silent-victim-of-warfare-50215>.
52. The Economist. 2012. Morals and The Machine. Robot Ethics. The Economist. UK. 02 Jun 2012.
53. Ecclesiastes 12.7.
54. Book of Common Prayer. The Burial of the Dead. First Anthem.
55. Genesis 3.22.
56. *Mortality salience*. Wikipedia: The Free Encyclopedia. Wikimedia Foundation. Retrieved 15 Sept 2014.
57. Frey, T. 2012. When Death Becomes Optional. Future Speaker. Retrieved from <http://www.futuristspeaker.com/2012/03/when-death-becomes-optional/>.
58. Frey, T.J. 2011. Communicating With the Future: How Re-engineering Intentions Will Alter the Master Code of Our Future. Colorado, USA: DaVinci Institute Press.

59. Prediction of Ian Pearson, futurologist and mathematician, former head of the Futurology Unit at British Telecom.
60. Russian multimillionaire, Dmitry Itskov.
61. Bostrom, N. 2002. Existential Risks: Analyzing Human Extinction Scenarios and Related Hazards. *Journal of Evolution and Technology*, Vol. 9, No. 1. Retrieved from <http://www. nickbostrom.com/existential/risks.html>.
62. Venter, J.C. 2013. Life at the Speed of Light: From the Double Helix to the Dawn of Digital Life. New York, USA: Penguin.
63. Transfer of matter from one point to another without traversing the physical space between them.
64. Williams, B. 1973. The Makropulos Case: Reflections On the Tedium of Immortality. London, UK: Cambridge University Press.
65. Philip Larkin. *Aubade.*
66. Title of Jonathan Schell's book.
67. Tagore, R. 2012. Religion of Life. India: Niyogi Books. p.199.
68. Nagel, T. 2014. After You've Gone. Review of the book *Death and Afterlife* by Samuel Scheffler. *The New York Review of Books*. USA. 09 Jan – 09 Feb 2013. p.26.
69. Nagel, T. 2014. After You've Gone. Review of the book *Death and Afterlife* by Samuel Scheffler. *The New York Review of Books*. USA. 09 Jan – 09 Feb 2013. p.26.
70. Parabola. 2001. (Eleventh Printing). Volume 2. Issue 1. Tamarack Press. Publisher D.M. Dooling. Review by Robert Meagher of the book *The Survivor: An Anatomy of Life in the Death Camps*. Terrence Des Pres. 121
71. Schopenhauer, A. 1851. Immortality, A Dialogue. (Translated by Saunders and Kline).
72. James, W. 1902. The Varieties of Religious Experience: A Study in Human Nature. Lectures VI and VII.
73. Adi Sankara. *Vivekachudamani.*
74. Sophocles. Oedipus at Colonus.
75. Johnston, M. 2011. Surviving Death. USA: Princeton University Press.
76. Wood, H. 1923. Studies in the Thought World, or Practical Mind Art.

77. Source: Epicurus. Stanford Encyclopedia of Philosophy. Retrieved from <http://plato.stanford.edu/entries/epicurus/>.

78. Becker, E. 1973. The Denial of Death. New York, USA: Simon & Schuster.

79. Dylan, Bob. 1965. *It's Alright, Ma* (I am only bleeding). Retrieved from <http://cherieswebwanderings.blogspot.com/2006/04/he-not-busy-being-born-is-busy-dying.html>.

80. Source: <http://www.positiveatheism.org/hist/quotes/epicframe.htm> (Positive Atheism's Big List of Quotations).

81. Swami Tapasyananda, Srimad Bhagavad Gita. Sri Ramakrishna Math, Mylapore, Madras, India. Second Chapter, Verse-27.

82. Source: English Club quotes. Retrieved from <https://www.englishclub.com/ref/esl/Quotes/Last_Words/I_know_you_are_here_to_kill_me._Shoot_coward_you_are_only_going_to_kill_a_man._2720.php>, on 22 July 2014.

83. Kakar, S. (ed.). 2014. Death and Dying. New Delhi, India: Penguin/Viking. p.xvi.

84. Kakar, S. (ed.). 2014. Death and Dying. New Delhi, India: Penguin/Viking. p.xvi.

85. Kakar, S. (ed.). 2014. Death and Dying. New Delhi, India: Penguin/Viking.

86. Source: Fanning, J. 2012. Beyond Time and Space. Retrieved from <http://johnfanning.me/carl-jung-beyond-time-and-space/>.

87. Dourley, J. 2012. Jung's Near-Death Experience and Its Wider Implications. In: Death and Dying (Kakar, S., ed.). New Delhi, India: Penguin/Viking. p.117.

88. Gandhi, Manubehn Jaysukhlal. 1962. The End of An Epoch. Translated from the original in Gujarati by Gopalkrishna Gandhi. Ahmedabad, India: Navajivan Publishing.

89. Source: Understanding Death, Selections from the Writings of Paramahansa Yogananda. Retrieved from <http://www. yogananda-srf.org/writings/death.html>.

90. Source: English Club quotes. Retrieved from <http://www. englishclub. com/ref/esl/Quotes/Last_Words/I_desire_to_go_to_Hell_and_not_to_Heaven._2722.htm>, on 22 July 2014.

91. Barrow, J.D. 2005. The Infinite Book: A Short Guide to the Boundless, Timeless and Endless. London, UK: Vintage Books. p.158.

92. Brodie, R. 2011. Virus of the Mind: The New Science of the Meme. California, USA: Hay House.

The End of the Beginning

1. "*Man is the measure of all things*". Statement of Greek philosopher, Protagoras, of the 5th century BCE.

2. "*...has not nature, in bringing forth man, made a serious mistake?*" Quote of Alan Watts [1951. The Wisdom of Insecurity: A Message for An Age of Anxiety. New York, USA: Pantheon Books].

3. Rowson, J. 2019. Integrating Our Souls, Systems, and Society. Podcast *On Being With Krista Tippett* with host Krista Tippett.18 July 2019. Retrieved from < https://onbeing.org/programs/jonathan-rowson-integrating-our-souls-systems-and-society/>.

4. Wilson, E.O. 2016. Half-earth: Our Planet's Fight for Life. New York, USA: Liveright.

5. Colville, W.J. 2017. Fate Mastered, Destiny Fulfilled.

6. Furedi, F. 2018. How Fear Works: Culture of Fear in the 21st Century. London, UK: Bloomsbury.

7. Karan, P. 2019. Nature Is My Teacher: Baby Steps to Follow Mother Nature. New York, USA: Xlibris.

8. Gallup. Gallup Global Emotions 2019. Washington, D.C., USA: Gallup.

9. *William "Bill" Adama* is a fictional character portrayed by Edward James Olmos in the re-imagined *Battlestar Galactica* television series (2004) produced and aired by the SyFy cable network. Source: Wikipedia: The Free Encyclopedia. Wikimedia Foundation.

10. Hilton, J. 1933. Lost Horizon.

11. Wilson, E.O. 1992. The Diversity of Life. New York, USA: The Belknap Press.

12. Zuboff, S. 2019. The Age of Surveillance Capitalism: The Fight for a Human Future at the New Frontier of Power. New York, USA: PublicAffairs.

13. Whitman, W. 1865. Over the Carnage Rose Prophetic a Voice.

14. Source: O'Gieblyn. 2019. Good Shepherds: The Intelligence of Machines Has Exceeded Our Own to the Extent that Programmers Accept Their Decision-Making with Blind Faith. Does That Make AI Our New God? *The Believer*. 1 June 2019. Issue 125.

15. Mailer, N. 2007. On God: An Uncommon Conversation. New York, USA: Penguin Random House.

16. Griffith, J. 2017. Freedom Essay, 46.

17. Jericho Brown, author of *Please*, *The New Testament*, and *The Tradition.*

18. Galatians 5:22.

19. Kimbrell, A. 2000. Cold Evil: Technology and Modern Ethics. Annual E.F. Schumacher Lecture. Schumacher Center for a New Economics. Retrieved from <https://centerforneweconomics.org/publications/cold-evil-technology-and-modern-ethics/>.

20. Powers, R. 2018. The Overstory. New York, USA: W.W. Norton.

21. Owen Barfield, British philosopher, poet, and author, among others, of *Saving the Appearances: A Study in Idolatry* (1957).

22. Taylor, A. 2019. Silvia Federici in Conversation with Astra Taylor. *The Believer*, 1 Jun 2019. Issue 125. Retrieved from <https://believermag.com/silvia-federici-in-conversation-with-astra-taylor/>.

23. Bergland, C. 2013. The Neuroscience of Empathy: Neuroscientists Identify Specific Brain Areas Linked to Compassion. Psychology Today. 10 Oct 2013. Retrieved from <https://www.psychologytoday.com/us/blog/the-athletes-way/201310/the-neuroscience-empathy>.

24. Rowson, J. 2019. Integrating Our Souls, Systems, and Society. Podcast *On Being With Krista Tippett* with host Krista Tippett.18 July 2019. Retrieved from < https://onbeing.org/programs/jonathan-rowson-integrating-our-souls-systems-and-society/>.

25. Swedenborg, E. 1758. Heaven and its Wonders and Hell From Things Heard and Seen.

26. Tim Cannon cited in Paul Laity's post "*To Be a Machine by Mark O'Connell: Review – Solving the Problem of Death*". [Review of Mark O'Connell's book *To Be a Machine* (Granta)]. The Guardian. 23 Mar 2017.

27. Talbott, S.L. 1995. The Future Does Not Compute: Transcending the Machines in Our Midst. California, USA: O'Reilly.

28. Talbott, S.L. 1995. The Future Does Not Compute: Transcending the Machines in Our Midst. California, USA: O'Reilly.

29. Wilson, E.O. 2016. Half-Earth: Our Planet's Fight for Life. New York, USA: Liveright.

30. Buss, D.M. 2005. The Murderer Next Door: Why the Mind is Designed to Kill. New York, USA: The Penguin Press.

31. Source: Bending Forward Is Affecting Form: Mobile Users Develop Horns. *The Deccan Chronicle*, Hyderabad, India. 22 Jun 2019. p.8.

32. Ezekiel 28:13–17.

33. Schoenfeld, J.D. and Ioannidis, J.P.A. 2013. Is Everything We Eat Associated With Cancer? A Systematic Cookbook Review. The American Journal of Clinical Nutrition. Volume 97, Issue 1, pp.127–134.

34. Dukas, H., and Hoffmann, B. 1979. Albert Einstein, The Human Side. Glimpses from His Archives. New Jersey, USA: The Princeton University Press.

35. Heffernan, M. 2011. Willful Blindness: Why We Ignore the Obvious at Our Peril. New York, USA: Bloomsbury.

36. Wallace-Wells, D. 2019. The Uninhabitable Earth: Life After Warming. New York, USA: Tim Duggan.

37. Tickell, J. 2017. Kiss the Ground: How the Food You Eat Can Reverse Climate Change, Heal Your Body & Ultimately Save Our World. New York, USA: Enliven.

38. Romans 12:2.

39. Barker, J. 2019. Artificial Stupidity. Los Angeles Review of Books, USA. 28 Jun 2019.

40. Source: Why Humans Should Not Colonize Space. *Times of India*. Hyderabad, India. 11 Mar 2019. p.13.

41. Charles Haanel, American philosopher and author of *The Master Key System* (1916).

42. Zimbardo, P. 2007. The Lucifer Effect: Understanding How Good People Turn Evil. New York, USA: Random House.

43. Tippett, K, host. 2012. On Being. *Brené Brown: The Courage to Be Vulnerable*. Air date 22 Nov 2012. Retrieved from <https://onbeing.org/programs/brene-brown-the-courage-to-be-vulnerable-jan2015/>.

44. Buss, D.M. 2005. The Murderer Next Door: Why the Mind is Designed to Kill. New York, USA: The Penguin Press.

45. Austen, J. 1814. Mansfield Park. Chapter 42.

46. Smith, A.Q. 2017. It Is Basically Just Immoral to be Rich. Current Affairs. 14 Jul 2017.

47. Aubrey de Grey cited in Paul Laity's post "*To Be a Machine by Mark O'Connell: Review – Solving the Problem of Death*". [Review of Mark O'Connell's book *To Be a Machine* (Granta)]. The Guardian. 23 Mar 2017.

48. Source: Zweig, C. and Abrams, J. (eds.). 1991. Meeting the Shadow: The Hidden Power of the Dark Side of Human Nature. New York, USA: Tarcher/Putnam.
49. Laing, R.D. 1967. The Politics of Experience and The Bird of Paradise. London, UK: Routledge & Kegan Paul.
50. Source: Dennis, D. 2018. Why Practicing Empathy Matters, And How VR Can Help. Big Think. 12 Dec 2018. Retrieved from <https://bigthink.com/videos/virtual-reality-experience-empathy-compassion>.
51. Quote attributed to American religious leader, Ezra Taft Benson.
52. Source: Hendricks, S. 2019. The U.S. Military Emits More Greenhouse Gases Than Sweden and Denmark. *The Big Think*, 17 Jun 2019.
53. Source: Anderson, E. 2017. Private Government: How Employers Rule Our Lives (and Why We Don't Talk about It). New Jersey, USA. Princeton University Press.
54. Wilson, EO. 2012. The Social Conquest of Earth. New York, USA: Liveright.
55. Source: WEF (World Economic Forum). 2018. The Future of Jobs Report 2018. Centre for the New Economy and Society. Geneva, Switzerland.
56. Kimbrell, A. 2000. Cold Evil: Technology and Modern Ethics. Annual E.F. Schumacher Lecture. Schumacher Center for a New Economics. Lecture delivered on 28 Oct 2000.
57. Lanier, J. 2010. You Are Not a Gadget. New York, USA: Alfred Knopf.
58. Cohen, D. 2018. The Infinite Desire For Growth. New York, USA: Princeton University Press.
59. Bill Gates. 2007. Harvard Commencement Address.
60. The Bhagavad Gita. Chapter 3, Verse 22.
61. Title of Miguel de Unamuno's 1912 classic, *The Tragic Sense of Life*.
62. Mark O'Connell (*To Be a Machine*) cited in the post '*No Death And An Enhanced Life: Is the Future Transhuman?*' Robin McKie. *The Guardian*. 6 May 2018. Retrieved from <https://www.theguardian.com/technology/2018/may/06/no-death-and-an-enhanced-life-is-the-future-transhuman>.
63. Harari, Y.N. 2015. Homo Deus: a Brief History of Tomorrow. London, UK: Harvill Secker.
64. O.B. Hardison Jr. Author of *Disappearing Through the Skylight: Culture and Technology in the Twentieth Century* (Penguin, 1990).

65. The Bhagavad Gita. Chapter 3, Verse 9.

66. Sobchack, V. 2004. Carnal Thoughts: Embodiment and Moving Image Culture. Berkeley, USA: University of California Press.

67. Bricker, D. and Ibbitson, J. Empty Planet: The Shock of Global Population Decline. New York, USA: Crown.

68. Twain, M. 1897. Following the Equator: a Journey Around the World. American Publishing Company.

69. Laing, R.D. 1967. The Politics of Experience and The Bird of Paradise. London, UK: Routledge & Kegan Paul.

70. Buss, D.M. 2005. The Murderer Next Door: Why the Mind is Designed to Kill. New York, USA: The Penguin Press..

71. Pope John Paul II. 1995. *Evangelium Vitae* (The Gospel of Life). Encyclical. 25 March 1995. Rome, The Vatican. Retreived from <http://www.vatican.va/holy_father/john_paul_ii/encyclicals/documents/hf_jp-ii_enc_25031995_evangelium-vitae_en.html>.

72. The Bhagavad Gita. Chapter 9, Verse 19.

73. Homer. *The Odyssey*. Book XI.

74. 1 Corinthians, 10:24.

75. Genesis 3:4.

76. The Bhagavad Gita. Chapter 3, Verse 10.

77. *Man a Machine* (*L'homme machine* in French) is a work of materialist philosophy by the 18th-century French physician and philosopher Julien Offray de La Mettrie, first published in 1747. Wikipedia: The Free Encyclopedia. Wikimedia Foundation.

78. Bates, J. 2015. Should We 'Revere' the Universe? — A Reflection on Yūgen. Posted on 6 Nov 2015. Jordan Bates is the creator of the blogpost Refine The Mind, a cozy cabin for compassionate freethinkers. Retrieved from <https://www.refinethemind.com/should-we-revere-the-universe/>.

79. Henry Brighton, professor of cognitive science and artificial intelligence at Tilburg University, the Netherlands.

80. Ropeik, D. 2010. How Risky Is It Really? Why Our Fears Don't Always Match the Facts. New York, USA: McGraw-Hill.

81. Wood, H. 1923. Studies in the Thought World, or Practical Mind Art.

82. Wood, H. 1923. Studies in the Thought World, or Practical Mind Art.

83. '*Gott ist tot*'. A widely quoted statement by German philosopher Friedrich Nietzsche, which first appears in Nietzsche's 1887 collection, *The Gay Science*.

84. Walsch, N.D. 2004. Tomorrow's God: Our Greatest Spiritual Challenge. New York, USA: Atria Books.

85. Pope John Paul II. 1995. *Evangelium Vitae* (The Gospel of Life). Encyclical. 25 March 1995. Rome, The Vatican. Retrieved from <http://www.vatican.va/holy_father/john_paul_ii/encyclicals/documents/hf_jp-ii_enc_25031995_evangelium-vitae_en.html>.

86. Purdy, J. 2015. After Nature: A Politics for the Anthropocene. Cambridge, Massachusetts, USA: Harvard University Press.

87. Torres, P. 2019. Why We Should Think Twice About Colonizing Space. Blogpost in *Nautilus* of 18 Feb 2019. Retrieved from <http://nautil.us/blog/-why-we-should-think-twice-about-colonizing-space>.

88. As in William Styron's *Sophie's Choice* (1979).

89. Kirsch, A. 2015. The System: Two New Histories Show How the Nazi Concentration Camps Worked. *The New Yorker*. USA. 6 Apr 2015.

90. John 10:30.

91. Tippett, K, host. 2015. On Being. *Grace Lee Boggs: A Century in the World.* Air date 21 Mar 2012. Retrieved from <https://onbeing.org/programs/grace-lee-boggs-a-century-in-the-world/>.

92. Genesis 6:6.

93. *Kabandha*. Wikipedia: The Free Encyclopedia. Wikimedia Foundation.

94. Ostaseski, F. 2017. Dying is a Sacred Act. Posted in Spirituality and Health. 18 Aug 2017. Retrieved from <https://spiritualityhealth.com/blogs/thefiveinvitations/2017/08/18/dying-is-a-sacred-act#>.

95. Watson, J. 2009. The Harm of Premature Death, Immortality: The Transhumanist Challenge. *Ethical Perspectives* 16 (4)435–458. Retrieved from <https://philpapers.org/rec/WATTHO-7>.

96. Homer, *The Iliad*, Book 17.

97. Book of Ecclesiastes, 7:20.

98. Genesis 6:5.

99. Genesis 8:21.

100. Laing, R.D. 1967. The Politics of Experience and The Bird of Paradise. London, UK: Routledge & Kegan Paul.

101. Source: Anderson, E. 2017. Private Government: How Employers Rule Our Lives (and Why We Don't Talk about It). New York, USA: Princeton University Press.

102. Wallace-Wells, D. 2019. The Uninhabitable Earth: Life After Warming. New York, USA: Tim Duggan.

Index

B

C

I

N

T